The Collected Works
of

EDITH STEIN

Sister Teresa Benedicta of the Cross
Discalced Carmelite
1891–1942

Volume One

Edith Stein with a Young Relative (1921)

The Collected Works
of
EDITH STEIN

Sister Teresa Benedicta of the Cross
Discalced Carmelite

Volume One

LIFE IN A JEWISH FAMILY
Her Unfinished Autobiographical Account

Edited by
Dr. L. Gelber
and
Romaeus Leuven, OCD

Translation by Josephine Koeppel, OCD

ICS Publications
Washington, D.C.
1986

The original version of this work was published in German by
Archivum Carmelitanum Edith Stein under the title of (Band VII)
Aus dem Leben einer Jüdischen Familie,
Das Leben Edith Stein: Kindheit und Jugend.
Translation authorized.
© R. Bosman, Druten 1985.
English translation copyright
© Washington Province of Discalced Carmelites, Inc. 1986

Cover design by
Adrian Cooney, OCD
and
Romaine Welch, OCD

Typeset by the Carmelites of Indianapolis

Library of Congress Cataloging in Publication Data

Stein, Edith, 1891-1942
Life in a Jewish family.

(The Collected works of Edith Stein; v. 1)
Translation of: Aus dem Leben einer jüdischen Familie.
Includes bibliographical references and index.
1. Stein, Edith, 1891-1942.   2. Jews—Germany—Biography.
3. Converts from Judaism—Biography.   4. Carmelite Nuns—Germany—
Biography.   I. Gelber, Lucy.   II. Leuven, Romaeus.
III. Koeppel, Josephine.   IV. Title.   V. Series: Stein,
Edith, 1891-1942.   Works. English. 1986; v. 1.
B3332.S672E54   1986   vol. 1   193 s   84-25164
     [BX4705.S814]   [193] [B]
          ISBN 0-935216-04-9

Contents

I.C.S. Introduction vii

Preface 1

Editors' Foreword 7

LIFE IN A JEWISH FAMILY

Foreword 23

Chapter I
My Mother Remembers 27
1815-1891

Chapter II
The World as the Two Youngest Knew It 62
1891-1897

Chapter III
Cares and Dissension in the Family 80
1897-1906

Chapter IV
The Two Youngest Grow Up 115
1907-1910

Chapter V
Student Years in Breslau 185
1911-1913

Chapter VI
Diary Notes . . . Two Young Hearts 223
1913

Chapter VII
Student Years in Göttingen 239
1913-1914

Chapter VIII
Nursing Soldiers in the Lazaretto at M. Weisskirchen 318
1915

Chapter IX
Of Encounters and Decisions of Conscience 368
1915–1916

Chapter X
The *Rigorosum* in Freiburg 397
1916

Chronology 415
1916–1942

Translator's Afterword 436

Notes 469

Photo Credits 513

Index 515

Map 548

I.C.S. Introduction

Six years after her own conversion to Catholicism Edith Stein used her translation skills to make available to the German-speaking public the *Letters and Diary* written by John Henry Newman before his entry into the Catholic Church. By publishing the present volume the Institute of Carmelite Studies is pleased to reverse the linguistic flow and start providing a series of her original writings to the English-speaking world.

A strong feeling of pride mixed with deep satisfaction has led I.C.S. to begin publication of the Collected Works of Edith Stein, the nun known in our Order as Sister Teresa Benedicta of the Cross: pride, because the highly talented person who was Edith Stein has provided us all with the shining example of balance in the search for contemplation and for truth; satisfaction, because her writings address many important concerns of our times. She taught philosophy and wrote about woman's professional status in society; she was a committed layperson and commented on the important place of liturgy in Christian spirituality; she dedicated herself to God by profession of religious vows, then composed a scholarly exposition of John of the Cross's mystical teachings.

In *Life in a Jewish Family*, the book which begins our series, she draws many lessons from her own personal background and crafts them into a compelling account of how her Jewish relatives faced daily the same problems, the same pleasures as their neighbors. Her main purpose is to tell the story of her family, and in so doing, she leaves us with many a fascinating description of life in Germany at the turn of the century and up to World War I. The story of her family, intertwined with her own, presents us with customs, events, and a world quite different from ours. As in its other volumes, I.C.S. has devised a format that is faithful to the original text, yet offers several contextualizing features. One of them, the map of "Edith Stein's World," favors more accurate and deeper understanding of her narrative by English-language readers.

Other translations are already underway or in the planning stage, and Edith's essays on woman will be the second volume in our series of the Collected Works. We appreciate our collaboration with the *Archivum Carmelitanum Edith Stein* in Europe, and look forward to publication of other volumes of the German *Werke* of Edith Stein by the *Archivum* so we can include them in the Collected Works.

John Sullivan, OCD
Chairman, I.C.S.

PREFACE

[To the Unabridged German Edition]

Whoever ventures to write an autobiography does well to have arrived at deep inner maturity. For, beneath apparently placid reminiscences, an inexpressible amount of searching, turbulent life may lie concealed. Spirit and emotion require exposure to light and to peace before the hand ventures to take up the pen to describe what it was that made life worthwhile for oneself or for others.

From the perspective on this higher level, the self discerns significant connections between events which formerly appeared to be unrelated and haphazard. One observes a picture evolving with increasing clarity, and is certain at the same time, that it is not of one's own inception. The influence of many different individuals becomes apparent, in each case to a degree determined personally by each character. All one has experienced, even more, all one has suffered, is collected within a single frame, while, otherwise, life would remain overshadowed by the unsolved question: Why did it have to be so?

Looking back over her own life, Edith Stein expressed the thought: "What was not included in my plans lay in God's plan." One has to have reached the summit of the interior life to have such an insight. We, who well know the outcome of the way of sacrifice she trod, bow our heads before the Light which streams from those words.

Presaged in the earliest morning hour by steadily dawning light, the new day's sun which brightens the sky in the morning's glow, eventually rises above the horizon and sends its rays onto the earth. Just so, in this autobiography we see the dawning of

1

the figure of Edith Stein destined one day to light up the world very much like a sun.

May the perceptive reader grasp in this imagery the deeper significance of the first part of the biography: dawn's rosy glow reveals the candidly searching spirit of Edith Stein and the loving generosity of her heart. The account of the second half of her life demonstrates how faith and knowledge complete the portrait of Edith Stein.[1]

Allow me to give an illustration which will sharpen the observation made on the spiritual development of Edith Stein.

There was something clear and luminous about Edith's presence from her youth. Her disposition was open to all that was good and beautiful. However, at an early age, her reason also recognized the shadow which every terrestrial light casts.

Hers was an empathetic heart long before the problem of empathy stepped into the limelight of her philosophical investigation as the theme of her dissertation.

To discover in full clarity the more profound meaning of things and to penetrate to the very source of their being was her sincere longing. This led Edith to arrive at the fountain of all becoming and happening, and she recognized the meaning of being in the eternal Logos who is imaged individually in the soul of every person.

Edith's ascent to a conclusive repose in the Truth can be delineated only when the second half of her life story is told. The autobiography of the first half of Edith Stein's life bears the imprint of her own moving words with which she summed up her life in retrospect: "My desire for the truth was one sole prayer."

This prayer was heard in Heaven even before she herself perceived where her valiant struggle was to lead her. After all, this is the kind of prayer which the Father on high hears with particular joy even while the child's heart making the plea has not understood its meaning.

A few years before his death, Fritz Kaufmann, a friend of Edith since their young adulthood, sent me the following reflection which nobly witnesses to a religious philosophy and to human greatness:

[1]Romaeus Leuven, OCD, *Heil im Unheil*, Vol. X of *Edith Steins Werke* (Holland, 1983).

It is my sentiment and conviction that prayer constitutes a sharing of life, and that it throws open the door to life's rooms which reach far beyond the individual. I am also convinced that our praise of this incomprehensible Power which governs all things unites us to Him. After all, this is the sense of the Jewish kaddish: one praises the Almighty even at the grave of one's loved ones. Even though it is very, very difficult for me, I understand and accept that what was alive and active in them remains actively alive — not merely due to remembrances *we* grant them, but rather by grace that is given to *us* and which preserves *us* — just as it was earlier present in what was given us before it was taken away. I well know that for yourself "resurrection" and "immortality" have an even deeper and fuller resonance; but I must be content with this faint and lovely tone. After Edith Stein had become a nun, she did urge me insistently to forget all cleverness and to become like a child, so as to be able to enter the Kingdom of heaven.[1]

In this volume of Edith Stein's biography, we present — in unabridged and literal form — her own portrayal of her childhood and youth. The author deliberately wrote in a manner which would present, unmistakably, the endeavors, the tragedy, and the happiness of Jewish family life in all its intensity and charm. She means the light which illumined for her the most intimate bonds between her and her family to shine fully before our eyes as well.

The form and color of her self-portrait are determined by her deep ties with her loved ones, with her nation, with all those of whom she took note, and whom she has sketched with a masterful pen. Throughout her life, Edith Stein bears the features of the family from which she comes.

That Edith Stein was impelled to write this life story as an apologia is emphasized in her Foreword. This may seem less necessary now since the ancient and the new people of God have been brought closer together precisely by the persecution they suffered in common at the hands of the Nazis. Nevertheless, the family's story continues to make a substantial contribution toward a deeper understanding of the uniqueness of the Jewish

---

[1]This letter, dated at the University of Buffalo, N.Y., (USA), October 10, 1953, is kept in the *Archivum Carmelitanum Edith Stein.*

people. Here we find all the data of the human situation; also, we find an inclusive portrayal of the evolving strengths which culminated in an ascent to the heights. We become familiar with the foundation at home which made outstanding achievements possible and which gave the necessary inner composure that perdured in the most difficult hours of destiny. These hours were, after all, also part of God's Providence.

The luminous characteristics of Edith Stein, the woman, shine clearly through the narrative of her journey. The account of her own life story needs no further elucidation.

Before concluding, however, it is fitting to remark how closely related the illustrations are with the unspoken, deeper content of the portrayal. Photos and handwriting speak a language of their own even when they appear merely to repeat the text.

In this garden of reminiscences of her family, Edith Stein has woven a wreath of character sketches of her closest relatives, of her friends and fellow students, of her teachers and superiors, of many persons whom she met in her professional life. Diffused in the delicate fragrance and the glowing colors of this wreath, we discern the beautiful features of her own soul. The thistles and thorns she has woven into the wreath signify some of the harsh rigor of existence, the sharp contours of individuality, and the candid self-criticism so genuinely characteristic of Jewish family life. The longer we linger in the garden of Edith's remembrances of her youth, the deeper the impact made on us by her life's milieu, in which nature and grace molded the personality of the future religious.

By publishing this work, the *Archivum Carmelitanum Edith Stein* wishes to throw open this garden to all who, with us, place our trust in God's providence and in the strength of human goodness. We offer it to all who wish to sing praise of the wonderful ways of God in concert with Sister Teresa Benedicta of the Cross.

Waspik (Holland), July, 1963   P. Fr. Romaeus a S. Ter., OCD

REGARDING THE COMPLETE EDITION 1985

It is possible to present the complete edition of Edith Stein's own notes on "Life in a Jewish Family" which cover the period of her childhood and youth, only now because of the wish expressed in her [last will and] testament. She requested that it be released only after the last of her brothers or sisters had died.

This unabridged version of the original text is being released with full agreement of the family and also of the Carmel of Cologne, "Maria vom Frieden" to which community Edith Stein belonged.

Brussels, January, 1985   L. Gelber

EDITORS' FOREWORD

[*Archivum Carmelitanum*]

AUTHENTICITY OF THE EDITION

Origin

The main body of the manuscript was written in the year 1933. National Socialism seized power in January, 1933; and when, very few weeks later, Edith Stein was dismissed from her teaching position in Münster, she returned to Breslau. There, in the time span of barely six months, from about April to September, 1933, she wrote the first segment *My Mother Remembers*. The second segment *From the Family History: The Two Youngest* originated in the following year-and-a-half. It remained incomplete, since the author had to discontinue writing the memoirs in May, 1935, shortly after her first profession because of having to complete her philosophical study *Finite and Eternal Being*.

On January 7, 1939, Edith Stein decided to continue her work on the biography; it was but a few days after she had fled to Echt. Unfortunately, during the next four months, very few pages were written. The final paragraphs of these supplementary annotations were written on April 27, 1939, the first anniversary of Edmund Husserl's death. The memoirs definitively end with these notes.

We have no specific explanation for this fact; however, we can easily surmise what kept Edith Stein from continuing the work. On the one hand, living conditions were extremely unfavorable for completing the work; on the other hand, the author was commissioned to write a study on St. John of the Cross to mark the 400th Anniversary of his birth [1942].

Archival Property

1. The Principal Segment of the Manuscript without Title or Heading.

It is fragmentary in two respects:

a)The literary draft is incomplete. Edith Stein was able to write and to revise more than 1,000 pages; at least as many, on the remembrances from the years after about 1916, remained unwritten.

b) Some pages which, undoubtedly, Edith Stein did write are missing from the manuscript:

1 page was lost, in all probability, during the war; so far it has not been recovered in the reconstruction of the manuscripts kept by the *Archivum*.

33½ pages were removed from the manuscript by an unidentified hand. The presumed content of these pages as well as handwritten alterations in these particular portions of the manuscript make it appear obvious that Rosa Stein removed the pages from the manuscript without Edith's knowledge.

DESCRIPTION:

Paper: 352 double and 349 single sheets, 8½ " x 6½ " and 8½ " x 6". Some of these pages carry on the reverse side the carbon copy of the typescript of Stein's work on St. Thomas Aquinas' *Investigations of Truth*; a second quantity of sheets are of unused paper of varied quality; a third, of corrected sheets from students' notebooks (used in practice teaching of unidentified women instructors in the middle schools of Cologne, about 1928–1930).

One set of six pages (pp. 417–22) is written on the back of yellowed pages from a book of poetry printed in 1856 (Wetzlar, April and May, 1856).

Page 842a is written on the reverse of the first page of the manuscript for an article *History and Spirit of Carmel* by Sister Teresa Benedicta a Cruce, OCD, written in Cologne-on-the-Rhine.

Script: In Latin script, ink, pages predominantly written on one side only. Individual corrections in pencil in Edith Stein's handwriting. On Pages 15 and 16, correction in cursive script in Rosa Stein's handwriting.

COMPILATION OF THE MANUSCRIPT:

	Pages
Foreword (Heading on p. 1): loose sheets	I–VI
Three bundles plus loose sheets, without a wrapper, with the heading on p. 1:	
"My Mother Remembers"	1–225
loose sheets	1–52/52a
	53–111
first bundle	112–117
loose sheet	118
second bundle	119–161
N.B. In numbering this bundle, Edith Stein skipped the number 151. Accordingly, a page 151 is missing only in numeration not in content. Half of page 161 has been cut away.	
missing sheets (gap in the manuscript)	162–190
loose sheet	191
third bundle	192–219
missing sheets (gap in the manuscript)	220–224
loose sheet	225
Wrapper with the heading: "From our Family History: The Two Youngest"	
In this wrapper there are five bundles	226–381
first bundle	226–276
second bundle	277–307
third bundle	308–331
fourth bundle	332–355
fifth bundle	356–381

Pages

Wrapper without a heading. In this
  wrapper there are six bundles plus
  loose sheets   382–558

    first bundle   382–415
    loose sheets   416–422
    second bundle   423–432
    loose sheets   433–435
    third bundle   436–459
    fourth bundle   460–469
    fifth bundle   470–473
    sixth bundle   474–477
    loose sheets   478–558

      N.B. Edith Stein mistakenly numbered two
           consecutive sheets as page 506. In con-
           sequence, the manuscript contains two
           different, valid pages numbered 506.

Wrapper without heading. In this wrap-
  per there are, exclusively, loose sheets   558–628/628a
                                             629–696

      N.B. Edith Stein mistakenly repeats on the
           first sheet in this wrapper the number
           558 which was the final number in the
           preceding wrapper. Accordingly, the
           manuscript contains two different,
           valid sheets numbered as page 558.

Nineteen bundles and loose sheets without a wrapper   697–1067
    first bundle   697–718
    second bundle (first lot)   719–727
                                            727a,b,c,d
                                          728–732
    missing sheet (gap in manuscript)   733
    second bundle (second lot)   734–737

      N.B. Edith Stein mistakenly numbered three
           pages as 724, 725, and 726, a second
           time. In consequence, each of the
           numbers 724, 725, and 726, have been
           given to two different but valid pages.

	Pages
third bundle	738–753
fourth bundle	754–769
fifth bundle	770–789
sixth bundle	790–809
seventh bundle	810–828

N.B. Edith Stein mistakenly numbered two consecutive sheets as page 816. The manuscript therefore contains two different, valid sheets with the number 816.

eighth bundle	829–842
	842a,b
	843–852
ninth bundle	853–871

N.B. Edith Stein mistakenly numbered two consecutive sheets as page 868. In consequence, the manuscript contains two different, valid sheets numbered as page 868.

tenth bundle	872–891
eleventh bundle	892–911
twelfth bundle	912–931
thirteenth bundle	932–951
fourteenth bundle	952–971
loose sheets	972–975
fifteenth bundle	976–991
sixteenth bundle	992–1011
seventeenth bundle	1012–1031
eighteenth bundle	1032–1051
nineteenth bundle	1052–1067

2. Continuation of the Text with a *Preliminary Remark* at the top of the first page and the date: Echt, January 7, 1939. The manuscript terminates at Page 19; Page 14 carries the final dating: April 27, 1939.

DESCRIPTION:

Paper: 19 single sheets, $9^3/_8''$ x $9^3/_4''$.
Script: Latin script, ink, written on one side of sheets only.

3. Typescript of the Foreword and of the first 51 pages of the manuscript bearing handwritten emendations in pencil by Edith Stein. The first page of the typescript begins with the heading: *Life in a Jewish Family.*

Relating to this typescript, we discovered the following letter from Ruth Kantorowicz on the reverse of a sheet Edith Stein used to copy out excerpts from Mauser's *Wesen des Thomismus* [*Essence of Thomism*]:

September 13, 1935

Reverend Sister Benedicta,

I am so happy about this manuscript; I do thank you for letting me type it. In the contents I find many avenues of thought which I can follow easily. The battle against psychologism!

I must inquire about [the spelling of] some names: Dr. Moskiewicz, Erich Danziger, Lilli Platau, von Heister, Achenbach, Reinach, Hedwig Martius (??), Alexander Kerpré, Grethe Ortmann, Erika Gothe. The one that gives me the most pause is Frau Conrad's maiden name. I would be most grateful for advice about any mistakes. For the rest, it is all *very* legible. I'll come to the turn tomorrow for my answer. Pardon me for raising these questions, but, in this text, I am particularly anxious to avoid misspelling any surname.

This afternoon I am going to Bonn to Herr v.d. Driesch's.

Too bad that the ceremony for the renovation of vows is not a public one.

With respectful greetings, I am yours

Ruth Kantorowicz

Based on the date and contents of this letter, it appears that the main portion of the manuscript was completely composed by autumn of 1935, and that all the sheets were at hand without any omissions.

Furthermore, the contents of the letter, together with pencil notations in the manuscript, leads one to conclude that the typescript of Ruth Kantorowicz covered at least 691 pages of the manuscript.

DESCRIPTION:

Paper: 20 single sheets, 8½ " x 11 "
Script: typewritten with emendations in pencil.

First Editions

The manuscript has never been published.

Structure of the Text

The edition is based word for word on the manuscript.

The composition of the manuscript: the text has been divided by the editors in deference to the presumed intentions of the author; see the [above] subdivision: Archival Property.

On the titles in the manuscript: As may be seen from the description of the archive's property, the main title *Life in a Jewish Family* comes from the typescript. The handwritten manuscript contains the three headings: "Foreword," "My Mother Remembers," and "From our Family's Story: The Two Youngest." All other divisions of the text and the headings for these were supplied by the Editors.

COMPLEMENTING THE PORTRAYAL

Edith Stein's Curriculum-vitae (Freiburg, 1916)[1]

On October 12, 1891, I, Edith Stein, daughter of the deceased businessman Siegfried Stein and his wife, Auguste, nee Courant, was born in Breslau. I am a Prussian citizen and a Jewess. From October, 1897, until Easter, 1906, I attended the Victoria School (a municipal girls' school) in Breslau and, from Easter, 1908, until Easter, 1911, the educational institution (*Realgymnasium*) which was affiliated with it. There I passed the examination to graduate. By passing a supplementary examination in Greek at St. John's *Gymnasium* in Breslau, I earned a leaving-certificate from a humanistic *Gymnasium*, in October, 1915. From Easter, 1911, to Easter, 1913, I studied philosophy, psychology, history, and German philology at the University of Breslau, then, for a further four semesters, at the University of Göttingen. In January, 1915, at Göttingen, I passed the state boards for teaching preparatory philosophy, history, and German.

I interrupted my studies at the end of this semester to serve for some time in the Red Cross. From February until October, 1916,

---

[1] Inaugural Dissertation, *On the Problem of Empathy*, Halle, 1917, p. 133.

I substituted at the above named school [the *Realgymnasium*], in Breslau, for a secondary-school teacher who was ill. Then I moved to Freiburg-im-Breisgau to work for Professor Husserl as his assistant.

I would like to express my heartfelt thanks, at this point, to all those who stimulated and encouraged me during my student years, particularly those of my teachers and fellow students who unlocked for me the passage to phenomenological philosophy: Professor Husserl, Dr. Reinach, and the Göttingen Philosophical Society.

Erna Biberstein, née Stein. Reminiscences (New York, 1949)[1]

Edith was the youngest of us seven siblings and the one closest to me in age. We were just two years apart, and so it was a matter of course that, from our earliest childhood until we went our separate ways, we were very close, closer than any of our other brothers and sisters.

Her earliest childhood coincided with the time when our mother experienced her greatest worries due to the sudden death of our father and when her work load was so great that she was unable to spend much time with us. We two "little ones" were accustomed to get along together and to keep busy by ourselves, at least in the morning, before the older ones returned from school.

As far as I know from my Mother's stories and those of my siblings, and according to my own recollections, we were fairly well-behaved and rarely quarreled. One of my earliest memories is that Paul, my oldest brother, carried Edith around the room and sang student songs to her, or that he showed her the illustrations in a history of literature and lectured her on Schiller, Goethe, etc. She had an excellent memory and retained everything. Many of our numerous uncles and aunts would tease or try to confuse her by telling her that *Maria Stuart* was written by Goethe, or the like. This misfired with deadly certainty.

---

[1]May we be permitted, at this point, to express our enduring thanks to Dr. Erna Biberstein and her husband, Professor Hans Biberstein, for this valuable complementary article to Edith Stein's autobiography.

From her fourth or fifth year, she began to show some knowledge of literature. When I started school, she felt terribly alone. Therefore Mother decided to send her to kindergarten. That was a complete fiasco. She felt so dreadfully unhappy there and was intellectually so far ahead of the other children that they gave up on that, also. Very soon after that she began to plead to be allowed to start school that autumn, since she would be six years old on October 12. And, although she was exceptionally small and no one believed her to be six, the principal of Victoria School in Breslau was willing to grant her urgent request; we four older sisters had been attending that school before her.

So she began her schooling on her sixth birthday, October 12, 1897. Since it was not the custom at that time to start the school year in autumn, Edith attended the lowest grade for six months only. Despite that, she was one of the top students by Christmas. She was gifted as well as diligent, dependable, and possessed of great perseverance. However, she was never inordinately ambitious in a bad sense; instead she was a good comrade, ever ready to be of help.

Although she achieved excellent grades all through her years in school, and we all assumed as a matter of course that, once finished with her studies at the girls' school, Edith, like me, would take the new *Realgymnasium* at the Victoria School in order to go on to the university, she surprised us all by her decision to leave school. Since she was still tiny and delicate, my mother agreed and sent Edith, at first, to my oldest sister Else, partly to get a rest and partly to help Else who was married, lived in Hamburg, and had three small children. Edith stayed there for eight months and carried out her duties conscientiously and tirelessly even though housework did not suit her well. When my mother went to visit there after about six months, she hardly recognized Edith. She had grown a lot, had gained weight and looked radiant. At that time, however, she told my mother in confidence that she had changed her mind and wanted to return to school, so that, eventually, she could attend the university. She returned to Breslau and prepared for entrance to the *Obersekunda* with the help of a pair of tutors in Latin and mathematics; she passed the entrance examination with flying colors.

The remainder of her time at the *Gymnasium* brought us no further surprises. She was, as always, at the head of her class and at the finals, when she took her *Abitur*, she was excused from the oral examination. Aside from school, she participated fully in all our social activities; she was never a spoilsport. One could entrust to her all one's troubles and secrets; she was always ready to advise and to help and all confidences were in good hands with her. The university years (I had begun to study medicine in 1909) were for us a time of serious study but also of wonderful sociability. We had a large circle of friends of both sexes with whom we spent our free time and our vacations in an atmosphere of freedom and lack of constraint which was unusual for that time. We discussed scientific and social topics in larger groups or in the more intimate circle of our friends. Because of her unassailable logic and her wide knowledge in matters of literature and philosophy, Edith set the pace for us in these discussions. During our vacations, filled with a zest for living and adventure, we took trips to the mountains.

When, later, she went to Göttingen with one of our mutual friends, Rose Guttmann, to study history and philosophy, she again made many new friends, who were to remain close to her all her life. But our old group remained unchanged for her, and her loyalty was steadfast. After our medical State Board Examinations, my friend, who later became my husband, and I decided to visit Edith and Rose in Göttingen. We spent an unforgettable time, with delightful excursions and hours of fun in which she did her best to show us her beloved Göttingen and its attractive environs at their best. Following that visit, we took a hike through the very beautiful Harz Mountains.

That was in Spring, 1914, and shortly after my return to Breslau I started my internship; however, that was soon interrupted when World War I started. For me, my work as a doctor changed only in that I moved to a different hospital, while Edith felt obliged to interrupt her studies to go to a field hospital in Mährisch-Weisskirchen as a volunteer Red Cross aide. There, as everywhere else, she was engrossed wholeheartedly in her work and was equally popular with the wounded soldiers, her colleagues, and her superiors. There too, I visited her during my first wartime leave and spent two weeks with her.

In 1916, Edith went to Freiburg to become the private assistant of Professor Husserl, under whom she had studied in Göttingen. Two of our old friends, Rose Guttmann and Lilli Platau, and I decided to spend our 1917 summer vacation with her in the Black Forest. (In the meantime I had gone to Berlin as a medical resident.) Those days are one of the times which remain a shining memory, although we all felt depressed by the war, and the somewhat frugal diet could have affected our mood. We hiked, read together and, for the most part, had a lot of fun. The following year I returned to Breslau and had to take my vacation alone this time. Again I could think of no better plan than to visit Edith. We stayed in Freiburg, took several wonderful trips from there, read together and made plans for our future.

When in 1920, I married my college friend Hans Biberstein, Edith, of course, was present at the wedding. She composed delightful poems for all the nieces and nephews, in which she recalled the most enjoyable events of our student years and childhood. When she taught at the convent school in Speyer [1923–1931], she spent all her vacations in Breslau.

In September 1921 our first child, Susanne, was born, and Edith, who happened to be at home just then, looked after me most devotedly. However, a deep shadow overcast that otherwise happy time. Edith confided to me her decision to become a Catholic and asked me to get Mother used to the idea. I knew this was one of the most difficult tasks I had ever faced. As much as my mother had shown understanding for everything and left us children a wide range of freedom in all matters, this decision of Edith was the most severe blow for Mother, for she was a truly devout Jewess. She considered Edith's adoption of another religion an act of deep disloyalty. The rest of us were hit hard, also, but we had such great confidence in Edith's innermost conviction that we accepted her decision with a heavy heart after trying in vain to talk her out of it for our mother's sake.

After Edith became a Catholic she continued to visit home regularly. She took care of me again after the birth of our son Ernst Ludwig, and she tenderly loved both children, just as she loved all our nephews and nieces, and was loved and revered by them in return. I remember especially how often, when she was working in her study, she had one of the children with her, how she would give them a book to look at, and how happy and contented they were.

In 1933, when Edith had to give up her position as lecturer at the Catholic Academy in Münster because of her Jewish descent, she returned home once more. Again I was her confidante, to whom she first communicated her decision to enter the Carmelite Order in Cologne. The weeks that followed were very difficult for us all. My mother was truly in despair and never got over her grief. For the rest of us, too, the farewell this time cut much deeper, although Edith herself did not want to admit it, and even from the convent continued to take part in everything with steadfast love and family loyalty and with undiminished concern.

When in February 1939 I followed my husband to America with my children, she would have liked us to visit her in Echt, where she had transferred in the meantime. We had booked passage via Hamburg, and, since crossing the Dutch border was considered to be particularly troublesome, we did not want to risk it. We kept in touch by mail, and I felt fairly well reassured that, now, in the shelter of the convent she was safe from Hitler's aggression, just like my sister Rosa, who through Edith's intervention had also found refuge in Echt.

Sadly this belief proved to be unjustified. The Nazis were not deterred by the convent but deported both my sisters on August 2, 1942. Since then all trace of them has vanished.

REGISTER OF NAMES

This register lists persons' names, giving the location within the text: surname, given name, chapter, paragraph.

. . .

Names of members of the many branches of the family, on the maternal side, frequently appear in the text in incomplete form. Therefore, it is possible that our listing may be, in some difficult instances, inaccurate or incomplete.[a]

[a][REGARDING I.C.S. EDITION: as is customary in I.C.S. publications, a comprehensive index of persons, places and themes has been prepared for this volume. Dr. Gelber's reference in her register of about 250 names to possible inaccuracies led us to verify and complete or correct all names of family members before incorporating them in the I.C.S. Index, as a reciprocal service to the *Archivum*.]

ILLUSTRATIONS

The illustrations in this volume . . . complement the literary portrayal of persons and happenings and bring to light deeper aspects of the presentation. . . . [a]

L. Gelber

---

[a][REGARDING I.C.S. EDITION'S ILLUSTRATIONS: since 1965, when the abridged volume of *Aus dem Leben* was published in German, the illustrations it contained have become familiar to readers. This English volume therefore brings to *Archivum* and I.C.S. subscribers photographs as yet less well known, but integrally connected with the text. One of them, the Frontispiece, provided by the Edith Stein Center (Elysburg, Pa.), has never been published before.]

Life in a Jewish Family

Translation of
Aus dem Leben einer Jüdischen Familie

In Ten Chapters

Foreword

R ecent months have catapulted the German Jews out of the
peaceful existence they had come to take for granted.
They have been forced to reflect upon themselves, upon their
being, and their destiny. But today's events have also impelled
many others, hitherto non-partisan, to take up the Jewish question. Catholic Youth Groups, for instance, have been dealing
with it in all seriousness and with a deep sense of responsibility.
Repeatedly, in these past months, I have had to recall a discussion I had several years ago with a priest belonging to a religious
order. In that discussion I was urged to write down what I, child
of a Jewish family, had learned about the Jewish people since
such knowledge is so rarely found in outsiders. A variety of other
duties prevented me from taking up this suggestion in earnest at
that time. Last March, when our national revolution opened
the battle on Judaism in Germany, I was again reminded of it.
In one of those conversations by which one seeks to arrive at an
understanding of a sudden catastrophe that has befallen one, a
Jewish friend of mine expressed her anguish: "If only I knew
how Hitler came by his terrible hatred of the Jews."

She had her answer in the programmed writings and speeches
of the new dictators. From these sources, as though from a con-
cave mirror, a horrendous caricature looked out at us. It may be
that it was sketched in honest conviction. Possibly, the specific
traits may have been copied from living models. But does having
"Jewish blood" cause an inevitable consequence in the Jewish
people? Is Judaism represented only by, or even, only genuinely
by, powerful capitalists, insolent literati, or those restless heads
who have led the revolutionary movements of the past decades?
Persons whose reply to that question will be in the negative can be

23

found in every stratum of the German nation. These persons, having associated with Jewish families as employees, neighbors or fellow students, have found in them such goodness of heart, understanding, warm empathy, and so consistently helpful an attitude that, now, their sense of justice is outraged by the condemnation of this people to a pariah's existence.

But many others lack this kind of experience. The opportunity to attain it has been denied primarily to the young who, these days, are being reared in racial hatred from earliest childhood. To all who have been thus deprived, we who grew up in Judaism have an obligation to give our testimony.

What I shall write down on these pages is not meant to be an apologia for Judaism. To develop the "idea" of Judaism and to defend it against false interpretation, to present the content of the Jewish religion, to write the history of the Jewish people — for all this, experts are at hand. And anyone desirous of instruction along these lines will find a broad selection of literature available. I would like to give, simply, a straightforward account of my own experience of Jewish life as one testimony to be placed alongside others, already available in print or soon to be published.[1] It is intended as information for anyone wishing to pursue an unprejudiced study from original sources.

Originally, I had intended to sketch my mother's memoirs. She was always an inexhaustible source of stories. As I dared not hope she herself could write them down at her advanced age, for she is in her eighty-fourth year, I wanted to attempt having her recount them to me. I proposed to write down her own words as accurately as possible. But this, too, proved to be very difficult. There were not enough quiet hours to be found for the task. It was essential to create enough order and clarity to enable an unfamiliar reader to understand the stream of reminis-

---

[1]Cf. the memoirs of *Glückel von Hameln* published by Alfred Veilchenfeld, Jüdischer Verlag, Berlin, 1920; and the *Memoiren einer Grossmutter, Bilder aus der Kulturgeschichte Russlands*, by Pauline Wengeroff, published by Verlag Poppelaner, Berlin, 1913.

[See, also, note 1, page 469.

Notes to the text found at the bottom of the page come either from Edith Stein herself (indicated by arabic numerals "1" and/or "2"), or from the Editors of the German volume (indicated by an asterisk *). All other numbered notes supplied with the I.C.S. translation are to be found together at the back of this book.]

cences. To achieve this, I have had to ask specific questions, and often it has been impossible to ascertain tangible and positive facts. In what follows I shall begin with sketches based on these conversations with my mother. After that I will present to the best of my ability, an account of my mother's life.

Breslau, 21 September 1933   Edith Stein

Chapter I

My Mother Remembers
1815–1891

1

My mother's father, Salomon Courant, was born in the year 1815. Mother cannot remember where his family came from; it seems to her it was from the French border.[1] Later his parents[2] lived in Peiskretscham, Upper Silesia. He made and retailed soap and candles. While traveling, he came to the home of my great-grandparents in Lublinitz, Upper Silesia. He saw my grandmother who was twelve years old at the time and was attracted to her immediately. From then on he came every year. When she was seventeen, they became engaged, and the wedding took place the following year, 1842.

My great-grandfather, Joseph Burchard, came from the Province of Posen as did his wife, Ernestine, née Prager. In the first year of their marriage, they lived in Hundsfeld, Silesia. When fire destroyed their little house there, they moved to Lublinitz. For many years Great-grandfather was the cantor and led the prayers. When he had to relinquish this office, he set up a factory for the manufacture of surgical cotton.

He had a prayer-room in his own home. On the High Holy Days all the sons-in-law congregated there for prayer. He was very strict both as father and as teacher. The grandsons had to come to him to learn how to pray. He scolded much but never

---

[1]Probably a conjecture was based on the surname's being a French word. But the name may have been derived from a coin used in the area at that time, known as the "Prussian courant."

struck any of them. Nor did a child ever leave the house without
having received a present.

These great-grandparents had eleven children, four sons and
seven daughters.

Once they had passed the sixty-ninth, each birthday was celebrated as a big feast; and, if at all possible, all the children and
grandchildren participated in it.

In a song their son Emanuel composed for one such occasion,
we read:

> "Not oft' may such a father be found
> Who, thoughtfully, his children heeds.
> Though seem he harsh, still, tend'rest care
> Marks every way he fills their needs."

A grandson composed another:

> "Today we count: ten sev'ns plus eight!
> Long years have flown.
> Throughout them all God cared for you,
> And you have known
> His gracious thought was ever bent on you and yours.
> Now, at your side, through joy and pain,
> Was Grandmama,
> Your faithful shield, and to us all
> She's been so good
> She keeps us all from accidents and worried mood."

This grandson, dear to the whole family, was Jakob Radlauer,
son of the eldest daughter, Johanna. He became a highly respected businessman in Breslau and died, an old man of eighty-
five who had lost both of his sons in the World War.[3] (The elder
of these sons, Ernst Radlauer, a lawyer, was in colonial administration in East Africa when the World War broke out. In disguise, and at great risk, he successfully slipped back into Germany to save some very important papers and to enlist in the
army.)

In their old age, our great-grandparents lived in great poverty, but they still managed to spare some of what they had for those who were even poorer. Each time Great-grandmother made coffee—very expensive in those days—she put a few beans aside, collecting these for a whole week. Every Friday a poor woman received what had accumulated. Any threadbare articles in her own household or in those of her married daughters were painstakingly mended before they were given to the poor. Her small granddaughters were required to help diligently with this needlework. Grandmother would gather them around her and direct their tasks, keeping a strict watch that everything was performed meticulously. Once the girls were six years old, they sewed hems while the older ones were entrusted with the long seams. Entire trousseaus for friends were completed in this sewing class.

In their last years, the great-grandparents greatly limited their housekeeping. Their meals were brought to them by our grandparents. All his life long, Great-grandfather had loved his wife most tenderly. He would not endure her doing any heavy work. Now, in his final illness, he was plagued by an obsession that made him so suspicious of her that, eventually, she could not remain in the house. He was eighty-nine when he died.

After that, Great-grandmother lived with Adelheid Courant, her daughter and my grandmother. Already ailing when she moved in, she outlived her daughter for a good many years, nonetheless. So it was that for many years she was most lovingly cared for by her son-in-law and her granddaughters. Her mind was keenly alert until the very end. She liked to have someone read to her and would listen most attentively. (The great-granddaughters, whether they lived in town or had come on vacation, were enlisted for this duty.) She lived to be ninety-three years old. Physically, she had much to suffer; she was also very depressed over the trouble she caused. My mother always called her a "truly pious woman." She prayed with the greatest concentration and intensity both in the synagogue and at the cemetery, as well as on Friday nights when she kindled the Sabbath lights while speaking the blessing. She was accustomed to close with the words: "Lord, send us only as much as we can bear."

My grandmother Adelheid Burchard was accustomed from childhood on to do a great deal of work. She and her sister Johanna had to tend their younger brothers and sisters. And, since their father's meager income as cantor was insufficient to support their large family, they supplemented it by getting up very early to do fine hand-sewing in the first morning light.

When my grandparents married, they opened a small grocery store. Having paid for their stock of wares, they had twenty-five *Pfennige* left as "capital." Since both of them were capable and hard-working, their business soon prospered. Together they deliberated about every venture. Grandmother did all the book-keeping; Grandfather would not have undertaken anything without asking for her advice. As the business expanded, the younger Burchard brothers and sisters were brought in to work under their sister's supervision.

Almost yearly, another child was born. The first died in infancy; the other fifteen all attained adulthood and, most of these, a ripe old age. My mother was the fourth of these fifteen children.

Just as Grandmother had shown her own parents the deepest respect, giving them every loving attention, so did she reap the high esteem and love of her own children.

All the daughters were expected to work as soon as they were four years old. They helped in the store which expanded with each new year; they were taught the household arts and later took turns managing the house; and they also learned to do needlework.

The older children received their elementary education in the public schools.[4] (From the age of five my mother attended a Catholic elementary school.) Later, my grandfather started a private school for his four eldest and for the children of three other Jewish families.

My mother was taken out of school, when but twelve years old, to help in the household; however, she was given some private lessons in German and French.

All the sons attended a *Gymnasium* out of town; eventually, all of them were sent to Breslau. Five went into business; two continued their education at the university (one becoming a pharmacist, the other, a chemist).

Religious instruction was imparted to them by Jewish teachers in school. They were taught a bit of Hebrew, but it was too little to enable them later to translate on their own so as to pray with understanding. The commandments were learned, parts of the Holy Scripture were read, some Psalms were memorized (in German). My mother says that she attended these instructions with liveliest enthusiasm; and, also, that it had been impressed on them to respect every religion, never saying anything against one that was strange to them. As has already been mentioned, the boys were taught the prescribed prayers by their grandfather. With all the children who were at home, both parents gathered on Saturday afternoon for the afternoon and evening prayers and for some discussion. In my grandparents' home it was no longer customary to have the daily study of the Holy Scriptures and of the Talmud which, in previous centuries, was an obligation for every Jewish man, and which is still frequently the practice of Eastern Jews in the present. However, all the religious prescriptions were observed strictly.

(Now I will go on to recount what I remember from stories told me earlier by my mother or my brothers and sisters and what I myself experienced.)

Portraits of my grandparents are hung on the wall above the sofa in our living room. My grandmother's face, its fine, delicate features framed in a small white bonnet, is very serious and shows traces of much suffering. She died long before I was born so all I know of her is derived from stories I have heard. Still, I do believe I understand her intuitively and can sense who among her daughters and granddaughters most closely resembles her and which of her characteristics I myself may have inherited. Even today, a respectful diffidence can be detected in my mother's voice when she speaks about her. With their small needs and problems, the children would run to their father rather than to her. But when advice was needed on important matters, one went to my grandmother: not only her husband and children and brothers and sisters, but many friends as well. Ladies of the nobility often called on her, coming by carriage from their large estates in the vicinity, and they considered it an honor to have her for a friend.

My grandfather presents a cheerful, good-humored expression to the beholder. I do have some memories of my own about him; he died when I was five years old. He was a short, sprightly man. When he visited us in Breslau, he would pull a chocolate bar out of his pockets for each child. But children he met on the street, even though unrelated to him, learned that he had also brought something along for them. When beautifully decorated frosted tortes had been prepared for the large family festivities, he would pluck the candied fruits from them and pop them into our mouths. He was always full of amusing inspirations and had an inexhaustible store of jokes to tell. An exceptionally capable businessman who had worked himself up from the most modest beginnings, he raised fifteen children, yet he always had something left over for others, especially for poor relatives. He lived in his own roomy home surrounded by children and grandchildren and practiced an unlimited hospitality. He was highly respected not only in the small town where he lived but in all of Upper Silesia.

The farmers of the region who stopped in to make purchases when they came to church on Sundays and to the city's weekly market on Wednesdays placed the greatest confidence in him. Once a farmer brought some money to him for safekeeping.

Grandfather took it and said, "Wait, I will give you a receipt for it."

He brought the paper. Tne farmer looked at it carefully then gave it back to Grandfather. "Keep that safe for me, too."

Even today the memory of old Herr Courant is very much alive in those who knew him. Two years ago, a woman lecturer at the teachers college of Beuthen visited me a few times. When I mentioned this teacher's name to my mother, she felt certain the family was from Lublinitz. This proved to be the case; her father had indeed grown up there but had moved away when he was only sixteen years old. One day when I called for her to go for a walk, he came into the room in order to greet this offspring of the Courant family; after all, according to him, it had been one of the most highly regarded families in the town; and he had a clear recollection of the old gentleman.

In his final years Grandfather had trouble with his throat, and a bladder illness, and often went to Bad Salzbrunn. I remember we visited him there. I also remember his eightieth birthday; on that occasion my mother took my sister Erna and me along with her. It was one of those big feasts customary in our family as an expression of filial love and of the closeness existing in the wider family; it was the first one in which I was allowed to take a part. Grandfather died the following year. He got to be eighty-three years old and was really ill for only a few weeks.*[5]

2

His home and business were taken over by his youngest son and the two unmarried daughters, and they continued to run things in their father's style. The house remained the focal point for the many-branched and widely dispersed family.

Even as an old lady my mother would say, "I'm going home" when she was making a trip to her hometown.

And for us children it was the greatest vacation treat when we were allowed to visit our relatives in Lublinitz. After the long vacation, the principal of our school who taught us geography always inquired about the kind of travelling we had done. Smiling in irony, he would let the matter rest when we had gotten no farther than Lublinitz. But that never disturbed us. In that small town we had next to complete freedom. We had hardly any supervision; we were supposed to enjoy ourselves and have a good time. The large house gave us much more space to move around in than the cramped apartment in which we spent our childhood in Breslau. Each room and corner of that house was familiar to us, and every occasion on which we renewed our acquaintance with one was cause for a celebration. There was the large store with its enticing jars of hard candies, the ample supply of chocolates, and the drawers in which almonds and raisins could be found. Everything was open to us; but because we were so accustomed to being strictly limited at home, it required repeated persuasion before we felt comfortable enough to help ourselves to anything. Next door was the hardware store which was principally the domain of my uncle. Here, too, there were tempting objects, some of which were usually given to us as souvenirs: pocket knives, scissors, and so on. In later years we

---

*This sentence was appended to the manuscript. The handwriting makes it clear that the emendation is from the pen of Rosa Stein.

were allowed to help out on the weekly market day when the farmers poured in and there were not enough hands to take care of the trade.

How proud we were when we picked up a few crumbs of the Polish dialect in order to communicate with the farmers, or, even more, when we were trusted to work the cash register! In the evening, we sat chatting on the stairs of the store. Or we went strolling about the "Ring."[1] In front of the houses we found old acquaintances seated on benches; and, there, Saint John stood between tall trees at the Ring's center.[6] We were sometimes taken along to the synagogue on Saturdays.

Occasionally we would take a leisurely walk in the forest and stop nearby to visit the beautiful cemetery where our grandparents were buried, as were, in tiny children's graves, our brothers and sisters who had died long before we were born. A trip by carriage to relatives in another small town of Upper Silesia climaxed the joy of our vacation. But what drew us most to return to our mother's hometown was our love for her brothers and sisters.

Uncle was a bit abrupt but always kind and cheerful. His wife and the younger of our two aunts were in charge of the separate households. They rivalled one another in youthful high spirits, in teasing, and joking; we children could associate with them as with peers. By contrast, we looked up to Aunt Mika with respect; she filled the position in the family formerly held by Grandmother. She was the bookkeeper and Uncle's adviser in all business affairs and was the confidante of all her brothers and sisters, whether older ones or younger, and, later, also of her nephews and nieces.

We have a picture of her as a young woman, showing her wonderful graciousness, her maidenly purity and her deep seriousness. She was the only one in the house who had preserved the faith of her parents and who saw to it that the traditions were carried out while the Jewish identity of the others had lost its religious foundation. She stood solitary in surroundings so alien to her, and her spirit longed for release from the narrow

---

[1]"Ring" is the name given in Silesian towns to the marketplace around which the town is built.

confines of the affairs of home, business, and small-town living. She loved to read, and, together with one of her sisters, made up little plays to be performed at family feasts. The persons in these plays were portrayed with loving humor and keen insight.

When she went to Breslau or other larger cities, she loved to attend the theater. One of her brothers, who, like her, had remained unmarried, used to take her along on his summer vacation trips. As we grew up, our visits also meant a great deal to her. She liked to hear about our studies, inquired after our opinions about this or that, and did not hesitate to give advice or criticism when she thought it necessary. Incidentally, she found us a bit too serious and too somber. She loved happy and lively people, perhaps to counterbalance her own seriousness; and, in all probability, she wished us to have a life sunnier than her own.

The end of her life is inextricably bound up with the loss of their home in Upper Silesia. Lublinitz is not far from the Polish border. During the entire war, troop transports passed through it, and my aunts were very active in caring for the soldiers. During these times they spent many a night at the railway station. The German authorities entrusted my uncle with the distribution of food.

The entire family antagonized the Poles by their decisive pro-German partisanship. During the plebiscite, every effort was marshalled to achieve a favorable result (for the Germans). More than fifty descendants of the Courant family who had been born in Lublinitz returned for the voting. As many as possible were put up in the homestead itself. The rest were given quarters elsewhere, but all were provided with the very best meals at the family home each day. The sad event after so much strain and effort was the more painful: Lublinitz became Polish. (The votes for Germany outnumbered the others in town; however, since the urban and rural votes were counted together, a pro-Polish majority resulted.) My relatives could not and would not think of remaining there; they sold the family seat and left their homeland.

My uncle with wife and children moved to Oppeln in the part of Upper Silesia which remained German; the two aunts went to Berlin in order to establish a household there together with their unmarried brother. At the time there was the greatest housing shortage. In order to find a place to live, they bought a house; but then they were unable to have one of its apartments vacated for themselves. They put their furniture in storage; and, in their own house, they lived in two furnished rooms for which they paid an exorbitant rent to their own tenants. The extraordinary stress and agitation of those years, the loss of their home, the cessation of work to which they were accustomed, the lack of a well-regulated and pleasant home atmosphere, all this used up whatever reserve of strength my aunt had left. While in Breslau, during a trip to Silesia, she suffered a severe stroke. It took a long time for her to regain consciousness. The entire family dreaded the thought of her dying but the doctors said she would be better off if she did not rally from her coma. After an initial paralysis, she regained her speech and sight. Then, gradually, she lost all her faculties.

She was cared for successively in the homes of various relatives until, finally, most of her brothers and sisters agreed that it would be best to put her into a hospital. My mother vehemently opposed this decision, and her children supported her protest. We realized how much the invalid would suffer if she had to live in totally strange surroundings. Her great love for her relatives, formerly demonstrated by so many good deeds, was undiminished. Now, the only way we could show our gratitude was by assuring her the consolation of being among familiar persons whom she loved. So my mother took her and her sister Clara, with whom she had lived all her life, into our home.

She lingered on for two more years with us; and my mother had to watch as this beloved sister, ten years younger than herself, slowly lost her hold on life. Hand and foot were paralyzed; her ability to speak deteriorated; finally, there were but a few words she was able to say, and these were repeated mechanically, or, again, urgently, when they were meant to convey a meaning for which she was unable to find a fitting expression. Gradually the ability to understand disappeared as much as the ability to make herself understood. Near the end, it was almost impossible to judge how much she could still grasp. She was plagued by constant restlessness. One could not leave her unattended for she tried to get up to leave. Apparently she felt herself to be in strange surroundings and wanted to go home. But the decline of all her mental faculties could not destroy the essence of her personality. She remained kind and affectionate, touchingly grateful for every small loving attention. When she could no longer find words, she expressed her thanks with caresses which she had used most sparingly before her illness. She was sixty-seven years old when she died. I was not at home at that time; but my mother and my sister Rosa were with her in her last hours. It was one of the most painful experiences in my mother's long and sorrow-filled life.

3

As I have already said, my mother was the fourth of the fifteen Courant children. (When we were small, we memorized in rhythm, the names of these fifteen brothers and sisters, just as in our religion class we had learned the names of the twelve sons of Jacob: Bianca, Cilla, Jakob, Gustel,/ Selma, Siege, Berthold, Mälchen,/ David, Mika, Eugen, Emil,/ Alfred, Clara, Emma.) From earliest childhood on, she was accustomed to work untiringly. When but six years old, she would knit in constant competition with her sister Selma. Even today the ever-present knitting seems an integral part of her. In the absence of more pressing business or household duty, she knits away and reads at the same time. But it has always been mere recreation for her. I have already mentioned that, taking turns with her sisters, she ran the large household and was active in their store as well. By the time she was eight, she was so diligent and capable that her parents could send her to help out-of-town relatives in an emergency.

Even the hardest work was not too difficult for her, and she was so much appreciated that even her otherwise stingy uncle made her expensive gifts in gratitude, giving her, for instance, a hat fit for a lady. In mid-winter she went to the market with this uncle and served as cashier while he sold his wares. The finale of this trip was indeed characteristic: during a fit of anger, Uncle took the liberty of making some offensive remarks about her parents; this she found intolerable. So she stealthily walked off and found herself a ride home in someone's farm wagon.

On laundry day, the maids in the house rose while it was still night. When she was ten, my mother wanted to learn how to wash. Although ridiculed for doing so, she got up in the night and went to work with the others. Because of her inexperience, she rubbed her fingers raw; the irritating lye soap caused her severe pain, but she clenched her teeth and stayed put; and the next time she was again one of the party.

Whenever new employees, often male relatives, had to be taught the business, they were entrusted to my mother. In this house where there was a wealth of work and of children there was a great deal of merriment. There was teasing, laughter, and singing. Life was a round of joyous activity especially when the students, be they brothers or cousins, returned home for the vacations, or when family feasts, birthdays, and weddings were celebrated. As a child, my mother had taken some piano lessons; later there was no time anymore to continue them but even today she can play a few measures of Strauss' waltz "Wine, Women, and Song." On her seventieth birthday she waltzed with her eldest grandson, and in the following year, at my sister Erna's wedding, with the bridegroom.

My mother met my father when she was nine years old. The earliest letter he wrote her is from that time. He and his sisters kept the correspondence going. In the letters of later years there gradually appeared references which showed how much they wished for an engagement. Even after his death my father's family continued to have a great respect and attachment for my mother. She was twenty-one years old when she married Father. He was working, then, at the lumberyard of "S. Stein's Widow." This firm was owned by my grandmother, Johanna Stein née Cohn, who, as a mother, was as strict as she was tender. None of her children dared to contradict her even when she was patently in error. Because Frau Stein esteemed her highly, my mother, more than anyone else, dared to express a differing conviction at times. So it was that she championed her young brother-in-law Leo when he "disgraced" his mother by aspiring to be an actor. She took him into her own home when his mother would no longer tolerate him in hers; and, when she heard him get up during the night to recite his lines, she was so convinced that his calling was genuine that she sought to mediate between him and

Grandmother. (Later as Leo Walter Stein he became well known as a playwright of comedies and as a stage director. Because of their nationalistic content, some of his theater pieces, "The King's Ballerina," and "Liselotte von der Pfalz," were even deemed worthy of presentation on the German stage of the Third Reich.) Unlike my mother, my grandmother was not a businesswoman. She entrusted her affairs to a manager who cheated her, and she refused to let herself be convinced by anyone that he was not to be trusted. Consequently, my parents finally severed the business connection and left Gleiwitz. They went to my mother's hometown intending to go into business for themselves with her parents' aid.

The family already numbered six when they moved to Lublinitz.* My mother bore eleven children of whom four died in childhood. Among the sorrowful memories which she recounted from time to time was that of an epidemic of scarlet fever in Gleiwitz. (Such epidemics occurred frequently in Upper Silesia.) During this particular one, little Hedwig, a particularly lovable child who had already begun to be a help to her mother, succumbed to the fever. My eldest brother Paul recovered, but my mother thinks the illness changed him. He had been a very handsome, highly-talented, lively child. Afterwards he became a quiet, shy, retiring person who was never able to make the most of himself or of his gifts.

The years in Lublinitz were a constant struggle against business reverses. My proud mother surely must have been severely humiliated by constantly having to call on her parents for help. There, also, she had to lose a child she particularly loved, her little Ernst. (The other two babies who died were so very young that the pain at their loss was not as great as in the case of these two who had already been a little older.)

My parents lived in a neat little house with a large garden, the so-called "Villa"[7] owned by our grandparents. My mother delighted in raising her own vegetables and fruits, and she had good luck with them. During that time she planted a row of apple trees, but she herself did not get to harvest any of the fruit. (House and

---

*We read a pencil correction on the manuscript, probably in Rosa Stein's writing, or influenced by her: "There were already five in the family when they moved. . ."

garden were later sold to friends. As guests of this family on our vacations, we were allowed to play in the orchard and to pick as many apples as we wished.) My mother often recounts a pleasant incident that happened while she lived there. One of my cousins, about three or four years old at the time, came to visit just when the cucumbers were ripe. My mother gave her visitor several and carefully laid them into the child's apron. The little girl, tightly clasping the corners of her apron, joyfully hurried home, and from a good distance away she announced excitedly: "Auntie Gustel grows cucumbers!"

Then she spread out the apron and stood there in horrified disbelief: en route she had lost all of the cucumbers.

To this day my mother is happiest when she is able to do her own sowing and reaping and can give generously to others from the harvest. Doing so she follows faithfully the old Jewish custom that, instead of keeping for oneself the first of each kind of produce one rather gives them away. (Of course she cannot always bring herself to give them to the really poor which would be according to tradition since this conflicts with the great love she has for her blood relatives, and for her brothers and sisters in particular.)

My grandmother died during those years. My sister Rosa who had just been born had her name, Adelheid, added to the one already given her. (Among Jews it is not customary to name children after living relatives.) Three cousins, born in the following year, were also named Adelheid.

Since it was impossible to make a success of their business in Lublinitz, my parents decided to move to Breslau. Probably it was also for the sake of the children who would have had to be away from home in order to attend secondary school. My brother had already gone to the secondary school in Oppeln and Kreuzberg and had suffered a great deal because of the unsympathetic treatment he had received from the relatives with whom he was staying. Of my six older brothers and sisters, three were born in Gleiwitz and three in Lublinitz. My sister Erna was six weeks old at the time of the move to Breslau (Easter, 1890). My parents occupied a small apartment on Kohlenstrasse. This little house in which I was born was torn down long ago to be replaced by a

Edith's Family in 1895

(l.r.) back row: Arno, Else, her father — Siegfried — Elfriede, Paul
front row: Rosa, her mother — Auguste Courant, Edith, Erna.
(the photo of Herr Stein, who died in 1893, is superimposed)

Stein house—Michaelisstrasse, 38 in Breslau

Richard Courant as a student

large new one. A lot was rented in the immediate neighborhood so the lumber business could be started anew. The landlady was a quarrelsome old woman who did her best to make life miserable for my mother. Feeding the family became a real problem; the new business, burdened with debts, took a long time in getting on its feet. My mother never said a word about the difficulties she had in her marriage. She has always spoken of my father with a warm loving tone in her voice; even now, after so many decades, when she visits his grave, one can see she still grieves for him. Since his death, she has always dressed in black.

My father died of a heat stroke on one of his business trips. On a hot July day, he went to inspect a forest and had a long way to go on foot. From a distance, a postman going through that part of the countryside noticed him lying down but assumed he was simply resting and paid no more attention. Only when, several hours later, he returned by the same route and saw him still at the same spot did the man investigate and find him dead. My mother was informed, and she went to bring the body to Breslau. The place where my father died lies between Frauenwaldau and Goschütz. Close by, there is a sawmill where often the freshly felled trees were cut up into logs for us. The kindly people at this mill were a real support for my mother in those difficult days, and she never forgot them. When later she herself went to buy stands of trees in that area and had them cut, Herr Ludwig would meet her at the station with his little farm wagon; and he often accompanied her on her inspections. If a stream on the way had to be forded, he carried her across in his arms. And his good wife would serve her cool buttermilk on hot summer days or hot coffee in the bitter cold of winter. The friendship which developed thus was to last a lifetime. From the city, my mother sent clothing and groceries to the large family. In turn, when the Ludwigs came to Breslau, they brought country bread and butter, fresh farmer's cheese, and often a carp or a few tench. When their eldest daughter married, our family had to be represented at the big country wedding. They felt particularly honored when, one year, my mother entrusted my sister Erna and me to them for the entire summer vacation. We were put up in the "best room" where the clean scrubbed floor was strewn with white sand; while the others all ate out of one dish in the kitchen, we were served like ladies of the manor; and we revelled in all the unfamiliar joys of living in the country: tending cows, binding sheaves, catching live fish barehanded out of the clear stream. It was the most wonderful vacation of all our school years.

4

Our relatives came to my father's funeral and afterwards held a council on what my mother should do now with her seven children since she was without means: naturally she should sell the debt-ridden business; perhaps take a larger apartment and sublet furnished rooms. The brothers would contribute whatever was lacking. My mother remained silent the whole time, exchanging only a very expressive look with her eldest daughter who was seventeen years old at the time. Her resolution had been made. She intended to cope by herself without accepting support from anyone. At the time, of course, because the many children had taken up all her time, she did not yet understand very much about the lumber business. But she was a merchant's daughter and, by nature, possessed the special talents needed in business: her arithmetic was excellent; she had a gift for recognizing a business opportunity. When it came to knowing the right moment to act, she also had courage and decisiveness yet possessed enough foresight not to venture too far; above all else, she was supremely gifted in dealing with people. She soon familiarized herself with the technical aspects and the special calculations made in the timber trade. And, gradually, step by step, she succeeded in working her way up. Even just to provide adequate food and clothing for seven children was no simple matter. We never went hungry; but we did have to accustom ourselves to the utmost in simplicity and thrift; and this habit has never left us to this day. In the circles in which I later moved, I was often conspicuous for not keeping up appearances as was expected in my position; and, though it embarrassed me to attract attention for any reason whatever, I never succeeded in amending my habits substantially.

Supplying the bare essentials for our daily needs was not enough for my mother. To begin with, she set herself an enormous task: no one should be able to say that my deceased father's debts had gone unpaid; bit by bit, they were wiped out to the last *Pfennig*. Next, her children were all to have a good education. My brother Paul was twenty-one years old when my father died. He had gone as far as the final year in the *Gymnasium*, but there were no means for sending him to the university. Perhaps a way would have been found, after all, had he insisted upon it. But he was not one to "assert himself." As he was a passionate bookworm, he was made an apprentice in a bookstore. But he did not last there. My mother had to do what she could to get helpers in her business. I have always considered it highly characteristic of her that she neither studied bookkeeping nor ever kept her own accounts. She dealt with customers. Most of these were cabinet-makers, wheelwrights, wood-carvers, builders and contractors, or suppliers: wholesale merchants, land owners, and Polish Jews who came as sales agents. She measured and calculated the number of boards; and when a delivery wagon had to be unloaded in a hurry, she liked to climb aboard and race the workers in handing down the heavy planks.

But she had no taste for tedious office work. (I, too, have always considered this the most disagreeable occupation.) For a long time her brother-in-law and uncle, Jakob Burchard, was her bookkeeper. (He was my grandmother's brother and had married his niece Cilla.[8]) Next, my brother Paul took over the work until in turn he relinquished it to his younger brother. Paul then found himself a place in a banking concern where he remained for decades. He was exceptionally conscientious and punctual in carrying out his clerical duties without ever receiving the recognition he deserved. To compensate for the minimal satisfaction he received from his employment, he turned to books, music, and hiking in his all-too-short free hours. A few years ago he retired with a modest pension, and I have the impression that he is happier now than ever in his life. (If I must record in these pages some matters which may appear to my dear brothers and sisters as criticism of their weaknesses, they will forgive me. One cannot write about a mother's life without going into all she experienced with her children and suffered because of them. When, eventually, my turn comes, I will not come away less scorched than the others.)

My sister Else should have been a support to my mother and ought to have relieved her of running the household. But she was very talented and had decided to become a teacher (the only avenue to higher education open to girls in those days). My mother finally gave permission for her to go to the teachers college. Nonetheless, she would have to concern herself with the housekeeping and with the children until her younger sisters were old enough to take over these duties. Her management of the house was so rigorous and her thrift so extreme that all the rest came to sigh under her yoke. I was the sole exception since I was but a small child and, so, was still being called by pet names and spoiled with affection; proud of being thus singled out, I was very fond of my beautiful sister. My mother sometimes said that each of her children presented her with a specific problem. Her eldest daughter, an exceptionally beautiful and talented girl, had many and diverse interests and was constantly surrounded by admirers of both sexes.

This led her to consider herself superior to her environment and to disdain her brothers and sisters as being rather more ordinary;[1] and she was never satisfied at home. Often she spent long periods visiting out-of-town relatives, sometimes to care for someone who was ill, for as soon as anyone in the wide family circle needed assistance my mother would send one of her daughters; sometimes it was just for the sake of a change of scenery. Several times, too, she accepted a post as governess in the country. But as soon as she was away from the family, she yearned to be back even more than she had previously longed to leave. This restlessness has never left her, not even now that she has a family of her own; it even came close to wrecking her marriage. Very soon after her wedding, she began to complain about the separation from her loved ones; given her preference, she would have wished one of her brothers or sisters to stay with her always. Any distant relative, or even any stranger with but the remotest link to her home, is a most welcome guest in her house. For her,

---

[1]Here, too she made an exception in my case. When I started going to school and brought home my first award, a handsome volume of fairy tales, she proudly declared: "That's *my* sister!"

our mother represents the highest ideal; and she has fostered in her children a tender love for their grandmother and for all their relatives. All year long she saves in order to afford a trip "home." Then, when she is there, both parties suffer because it is impossible to spend the time together in harmony.

My brother Arno attended the *Realschule* in Breslau. After his exams, my mother sent him away to learn the lumber trade. When that apprenticeship was completed, he went on to get a thorough business training at an oil-manufacturing plant in Breslau. Then my mother accepted him into the business. At first he was the "junior partner," then he was manager, and finally, a few years ago, my mother transferred to him her position as head of the firm. To this very day she works side by side with him, and he could not get along without her. Both of my brothers honor her as the head of the family and ask her advice in all matters. Nonetheless, working together daily for decades caused my mother a good bit of suffering.

My brother has a temper and, when angry, loses control of himself. If this happens when there is a difference of opinion between him and my mother, she quietly leaves the room "to keep him from sinning." But his hot temper also makes it difficult for him to deal with his children so that she often has to mediate. My mother was also very concerned because, unlike her, he did not devote his entire energy to the business. Instead, he was often distracted by diverse activities in various organizations where he often accepted honorary offices. But it was by their choice of wives that my brothers caused my mother the most anxiety. My brother Paul was very young when he secretly became engaged. For years he carried on his courtship with his betrothed against my mother's will; and, finally, since he still could not get her consent to the engagement, he furtively left home. My sister Erna and I were still children at the time. We awoke one night and saw Mother weeping. We ran to her, climbed on her lap, and tried to comfort her. Only years later did we learn that was the very night on which our eldest brother was discovered to be missing; and our other brother and sisters were out looking for him. He had followed his fiancée to Berlin and wrote only after his arrival there. They were married; we celebrated the wedding as a family feast; the young couple was supported in every time of need, as a matter of course; the eldest grandchild was given the most loving attention; but a cordial relationship with her daughter-in-law never developed even though Trude, my sister-in-law, tried again and again to bring it about.

My brother Arno chose his bride with the approval of my mother and all of us. A classmate of my sister Else's at the teachers college, she had long been a friend of the family. When still very young, she had gone to America with her family, married there, but later had the marriage annulled. She earned her own living and used her savings to travel to Germany to visit my sister in Hamburg and us in Breslau. Very merry, noisy, and vivacious, she always brought a good deal of life into our quiet house. Probably she set her sights on marrying my brother long before the thought occurred to him. She was overjoyed when her wish became reality. The family, in turn, happily received her; the young couple even moved into our house which had just been bought. Indeed, for a while, an attempt was made to run a kind of joint household. But here, again, it was impossible to achieve a harmonious co-existence. What irritates my mother most about both of my sisters-in-law is that neither one has learned how to run a well-ordered home. One of them, musically talented, spends a great deal of time taking or giving music lessons. The other one loves to go shopping and visiting, and she constantly seeks new stimulation outside the house. And both are thoroughly incompatible with my mother. As kind and ready as my mother is to help anyone at all, there are some character weaknesses for which she has no patience whatever: these are, above all, dishonesty, tardiness, and an exaggerated self-esteem. Persons who love most of all to talk about themselves, and who cannot praise their own accomplishments enough, are, for her, unbearable; and she expresses her displeasure unequivocally. When, on occasion, we told her—half in jest and half in earnest —that she made a poor mother-in-law, she was very distressed. Actually, our family's strong individual cast posed a formidable obstacle to its assimilating any alien elements. The verdict: "They are altogether different from us," spoken by my mother or my sisters Frieda or Rosa, always indicated a decided line of demarcation. This put my brothers in a difficult position, and only their great goodheartedness and loyalty averted a rift. Both live very happily with their wives and in all other matters are strongly influenced by them. But my sisters-in-law know they may not touch the relationship between son and mother; the attachment to her has remained strong as ever. Throughout all the decades he has been married, my brother Paul has come to his mother's house every Friday evening to observe the beginning of the Sabbath. During the first years, my sister-in-law accompanied him. But as she never managed to be punctual and was a constant source of irritation by being an hour-or-more late, she finally stayed at home and allowed him to come by himself. The other couple first eat supper with their four children at home, then come to us afterwards. As soon as my sister-in-law Martha enters the room, no one else need be concerned with keeping the conversation going. She has a whole battery of funny stories in reserve and amuses herself by teasing all those present. It is a conversational tone she customarily used with her mother and sister, and it was not easy for her to adapt to such serious-minded persons as we are. In a wide circle of friends and acquaintances, she finds the resonance which is lacking in the family. Martha's incessant raving about America never failed to annoy my mother. She herself has always been a German patriot. She was married in 1871, and the words of her wedding song were set to the melody of *"Es braust ein Ruf wie Donnerhall."*[9] For the same reason, nowadays, she finds it incomprehensible that anyone should dare to dispute her German identity.

Along with my brother Arno, my sister Frieda has served for decades as my mother's faithful support in the business. Our eldest brother assigned nicknames to all of us when we were children. Frieda was "the Frog." She differed from the rest of us by being decidedly phlegmatic. Probably the least gifted academically, she had to struggle in school. It took a long time for something to sink in; but once it did, it stayed put. She enjoyed reciting aloud the poems she had to memorize for school. That way, I learned Schiller's and Uhland's ballads while I was still a small child, and at the age of five I could declaim "Bertran de Born" from memory. Because she was so diligent, she managed to satisfy all the school requirements and unobtrusively graduated from the *Höhere Mädchenschule*[4][‡] (we all attended the Victoria School). Then she learned housekeeping and also took a commercial course in bookkeeping. One incident during her initiation in domestic duties is indelibly etched in my memory: she was supposed to wash the kitchen floor. To do so, she seated herself on a chair in the middle of the kitchen and, brush in hand, began to scrub the floor around her. The loud laughter of her spectators quickly brought her to her feet. She was never one for heavy physical labor, not only because of her indolence, but also because she was very small and not very strong. To compensate for this, she had a real talent for setting up and managing the household. She is happy drawing up plans for decorating a home. And since we have been living in our own house, she likes, every now and then, to go in for some reorganization. Similarly, she delights in planning her own and other people's lives. She also has both skill and a liking for needlework; it is her task to keep the whole family's linens in order and to make new ones. In recent years, since the business has declined so much, she has become very adept at knitting woolen garments in order to provide for all the relatives. She is the bookkeeper for the business and also serves as cashier. She is not as generous as my mother but is useful as a moderating element in the business, warning against risky enterprises particularly when the others are on the verge of being persuaded to extend credit to unreliable clients.

She has always been an obedient daughter to my mother. Even today she is still accustomed to accept orders like a child. However, now, when she is commandeered here or there by Mother's: "Frieda, step on it!", my sister's own grown-up daughter frequently protests, calling her grandmother a "dictator." Frieda helped to raise her two youngest sisters; we attached ourselves to her with a great deal of love and, at the same time, with respect. She shared all of our schoolgirl joys and sorrows, was always most ambitious on our behalf, and was satisfied only when we got the best grades; she was always ready to help. When I wrote the final version of a composition, she would dictate to me from the rough draft, and later she typed my long papers for me. She knew just how to play with us. However, no childish misbehavior was allowed to pass uncorrected; when we were naughty, we would have to apologize to her before she would speak to us again. As attentive as she was to neatness in appearance, taking excellent care of her clothes, just so carefully intent was she on moral cleanliness. To be sure, this striving for virtue had a taint of self-righteousness about it; and she had a tendency to judge others harshly. She was the only one in the family who kept a diary. The quiet monotony of her life had one brief interruption, rich in bitter experiences, when she decided to get married.

My sisters Frieda and Rosa had little contact with persons outside the family circle. Since Frieda longed for a home of her own, she let herself be talked into an "arranged match." At the time I was still attending the *Gymnasium*. But after her suitor's first visit, I tried with all my persuasive power to talk her out of her plan. Our relatives also emphatically counseled against it. But my sister was beyond changing her decision, and even my wise mother's clear vision was clouded by wishful thinking. The bridegroom was a widower with two rather grown-up children. My sister looked forward to being a mother to them, and they were on good terms with her. Their economic situation caused a separation. Very soon after taking over the management of the household, Frieda recognized that it had an unsound basis. She was quite ready to work hard and to make do with the most modest livelihood; but she was unable to accept living off borrowed funds, as her husband and his children were wont to do; and so she lost all confidence in him. She returned to our house with her six-months-old child and had to go through embarrassing divorce proceedings before she was free again. Although, brought up as strictly as we were, we considered divorce a disgrace, my mother never gave my sister any such intimation. She took her back as a mother hen takes a strayed chick under her wings and, by being twice as loving, sought to help her over this very difficult time. Born prematurely and very frail, little Erika began to develop rapidly under her grandmother's loving care. Today she is a wholesome young girl, a head taller than any of us.

My sister Rosa is but two years and two days younger than Frieda. The two were treated like twins. We had three pairs in our family: "the boys," "the girls," and "the children"; for Else alone there was no partner. But those who were coupled together showed little similarity.

Rosa's nickname was "the Lion." It was inspired by her loud roar of rage whenever she was provoked. Of all the children, she was the most difficult to raise. Although in no way lacking talent, she was always a poor student. The most undisciplined boys in the house or in the neighborhood were her best friends. With them she tore through the streets, rang doctors' doorbells, and joined in other pranks boys usually play. She was forever having a crush on someone. Once, during her teens, she personally drew up a long list of "flames" with whom she was, just then, simultaneously infatuated: teachers, actresses, and relatives. Later, however, it was always a sole person to whom she gave monopoly of all her heart. She considered the one she admired to be perfection incarnate, the embodiment of all good. She neglected other people because of her insatiable need to give proof of her devotion to the one she loved. In reality, too, these were often persons with obvious weaknesses; far from being paragons, they were themselves very astonished to find themselves cast in such a role. When the rosy veil rent, the sobering process was all the greater, and the dethroned one had an all-the-more severe criticism . . . *[10]

showed no particular inclination for a career, it was decided that she should have a very thorough training in housekeeping, so she could later take charge of the maternal household. She was sent to be trained by the aunts in Lublinitz, there to learn every phase of the work in their well-run household. The year she spent with them was a very happy one for her, and she always recalled it with gratitude. In the merry company of the two housewives, our Aunt Clara and her sister-in-law Else, Rosa enjoyed herself as much as she had earlier playing with the youngsters on the street. But she attached herself, as well, to our more

*Here one sheet (Sheet 75) of the manuscript is missing. This gap in this particular part of the manuscript, regrettable though it be, is not difficult ot explain. Could any over-sensitive heart have withstood the temptation to keep the weaknesses of youth out of the bright light of history? What a high degree of self-denial is evinced by the fact that but a single page was removed.

reserved Aunt Mika whose suggestions to be more refined Rosa accepted with more gratitude and greater ease than she would have at home. When subsequently she took over the management of our household, our life-style changed noticeably. On the face of it, this change was possible because our financial situation had essentially improved. But it was also due to her nature. Whereas the two elder sisters had always kept house with the strictest economy, she had a need to give more generously. As a child she herself had been very fond of snacks, and as a young girl, had been overweight; later she was content to have very little herself, and no trace of her former plumpness remained. Delighted when we found everything to our taste, she liked to think up new treats with which to tempt us from time to time. Over the years the cakes she made won her a reputation among all our relatives and acquaintances.

As I was always rather pale and anemic, she made me the object of particular solicitude. When I accompanied her to the city on errands, she rarely omitted taking me to a small coffee shop where she saw to it that I had a piece of apple cake with whipped cream, or, in the summer, a dish of ice cream likewise topped with whipped cream. I never begged her for this; but, unintentionally, as we came near our usual haunt (Illgen's Coffee Shop in the *Schmiedebrücke*, where such marvelous things could be had for fifteen *Pfennige*) I would peep at the store window out of the corner of my eyes, and immediately, without saying a word, she would head for the entrance. She loved small children especially; she helped to care for many young cousins and, later, nephews and nieces, in the first weeks or years of their lives. For older children she had less understanding. She fussed too much over all slightly naughty behavior; this cooled the children's love and failed to win her the desired respect. Consequently she reaped far fewer thanks than she really deserved. Unlike my sister Frieda, she was less capable of directing others to work than of working herself. When a maid was hired to assist her, my mother was constantly irritated because Rosa delegated so little. Now, for some years, she has a woman come in only once a week: to give the entrance hall, the stairs, and the kitchen a thorough scrubbing; to clean windows as well; and even less frequently, to help with the laundry. With Mother and Frieda's support, she does everything else herself. When cooking or cleaning, she is entirely in her element; anyone else finds it difficult to do either to her satisfaction. Sewing, on the other hand, is completely out of her line; she also happily leaves to Frieda any shopping except for her kitchen needs. As we, the youngest, in the process of growing up and attending the *Gymnasium* and later the university, made many friends and had diverse stimulating experiences, she began to see her labors as menial, and felt dissatisfaction.

She regretted that she had not gotten any kind of professional training, and from time to time made plans for a new beginning. First she thought of becoming a nurse. Later she expressed the desire to buy a house in the mountains and take in friends there as summer guests. My mother never expressed outright opposition to her plans—once she even went with her to inspect a house in the *Riesengebirge*; but in the face of the numerous objections presented to her, Rosa would eventually back out and stay at her post. For a while they tried having her alternate with Frieda in the business, but the impracticality of this arrangement soon became apparent. So, finally, she resigned herself to the lot of housekeeper and from that time on merely sought some congenial sideline. She served for a good number of years in a volunteer position with the municipal government taking care of orphans. A number of children whom the city had placed in foster homes were assigned to her. From time to time she had to visit them to determine whether they were getting the proper attention. She also took care of any necessary paper work for them. It was a difficult and embarrassing position, but Rosa made the best of it. She gave the children presents at Christmas; if they found it hard to keep up in school, she had them come to her so she could supervise their homework. She was ousted from this position a few years ago by the political upheaval. But, even without any official post, she has never been without protégés who benefit from her kindness. In recent years, at the public institute for adult education, she has enjoyed taking evening courses in literature and the history of art and has worked with real enthusiasm in these classes. Gradually, too, she has formed a circle

of persons who gather socially; and these regard her highly.
More than all else, her religious development has opened for her
a world which enables her to do without all external satisfaction
and find quiet contentment in her situation. I shall have more
to say about that later.

5

Whereas the elder brothers and sisters had followed one another rather closely, we two youngest ones "came along later."
There is a difference of six years between Rosa and Erna; the two
of us are only a year and eight months apart. We grew up during the time when our family was beginning to prosper. While
we were children, our housing, nutrition, and clothing were still
characterized by the greatest simplicity, yet we never had a feeling of being poor. Aware as we were that our mother worked
hard from morning until night, it was obvious to us then that we
should not express any extravagant desires. My mother herself
saw to it that we never lacked what other children had. For a
while, three of us were attending the same school, and so tuition
charges for the third one could have been waived; but my
mother would not avail herself of that dispensation. It would
have seemed to her a form of "public assistance," and she would
have none of that. Even today she considers it a lack of self-
esteem when people are content to live "on welfare." We were
never allowed to miss a school excursion and had to contribute
to every collection. On the other hand, thrift was compulsory
when it came to text books. To our dismay, we received brand
new ones only when this was unavoidable, otherwise we had to
borrow them from older cousins. My mother would not tolerate
our speaking about teachers in the disrespectful manner customary to students. Our singing and penmanship lessons — and
arithmetic and science as well, during our elementary grades —
were given by an elderly public school teacher who was born to
be anything but an educator. As a youth, he must have been
handsome, but he became obese later. He was very good-natured
yet hot-tempered. During lessons there was a deluge of demerits
and other penalties; but as soon as the bell rang for recess, all

was rescinded. He forever carried a snuff box and a bag of hard candies in his pocket and would pull them out and help himself from one and then the other. We feared nothing so much as to be given as a reward something out of that paper bag. When we attempted at home to recount "old Freier's" latest antic, my mother would interrupt with the correction: "Herr Professor Dr. Freier."

She scarcely ever went to the school to discuss matters with the teachers. But on one occasion she was determined to register a complaint against a teacher. The woman who gave drawing lessons accused my sister Erna of, first, using a ruler without permission and, then, of lying when she denied having used one. The child, who had no talent at all for drawing, happened by good fortune to draw a straight line which earned her being suspected, given a demerit, and reported to the principal. My mother refused to allow her child to be branded a liar. Teachers and parents of my classmates, who had never met my mother, would inquire about her, assuring us we could be proud of her. This always embarrassed me. That she was as she was seemed so matter-of-course for us. Summer and winter she rose very early in the morning to go to the lumberyard. For years both the apartment and the business locale were rented; and she had a great deal to suffer from mean landlords. The apartment in Kohlenstrasse in which I was born left me with but a single recollection, the earliest memory I have, in fact. (I must have been two at the time for we moved from there soon after my father's death.) I can see myself standing before a big white door, drumming on it with clenched fists and screaming because my elder sister was on the other side, and I wanted to go to her. Nor do I recall more about our next home in Schiesswerderstrasse where, also, we had our first business site. On the other hand, I remember the apartment at Jägerstrasse 5 very clearly. That is where I celebrated my third birthday, and we lived there for many years. During that time our lumberyard was on Rosenstrasse; it adjoined the yard of our apartment building. To provide a shortcut for my mother, the apartment's landlord, Herr Böse, had a small gate set in the wall. That was all right until Herr Böse started to fight with the woman who owned the lumberyard.

Frau Olschowka was a passionate Polish woman (Viktor, her husband, belonged to this scene as a bit player only). To symbolize that all communication between the hostile neighbors had ceased, the small gate had to be walled up. The victim of this stratagem was my mother: she now had to walk around the entire block from Jägerstrasse to Rosenstrasse which ran parallel with it. But soon, Herr Böse was happily inspired to spite his enemy; he set up ladders on both sides of the wall, and on these my mother then clambered back and forth several times a day.

A little later, the inventive landlord had an even better inspiration. He had a gap made in the wall — after all, he averred, no one could dictate to him how high it had to be — and then a low stepladder sufficed. But my mother, then about fifty years old, found it all a nuisance especially in winter when the steps were icy. We could look over into the lumberyard from the windows of our apartment. In our pre-school years, Erna and I were often alone in the apartment for hours. We were strictly enjoined never to open the door to strangers. Were we in any doubt, we could call out to Mother from the window. We were very conscientious and would have done something we had been forbidden to do more readily in Mother's presence than in her absence. Sometimes my brother Arno was at home in the mornings. Then he would make a hot cereal for Mother's mid-morning snack. On days when the weather was fine, we were allowed to play in the lumberyard. It was a paradise for children, and when we had no school we were all there as were the many playmates from the apartment house, and friends from school, and relatives as well. There was room for everyone. My mother's dictum was: "Obey immediately and don't disturb anyone! Provided you do that, you can do whatever else you please."

Making a see-saw was the simplest pastime: a plank was balanced on a saw-horse; on either end, a child sat astride the board to bound into the air in turn. We would do this for hours without tiring of it. Playing hide-and-seek was also superb. There were many stacks of wood both high and low. Whatever might be damaged by weathering was kept in sheds. Some of these sheds were several stories high and had stairways; as the interior was dimly lit, one could withdraw into some secret corner to dream or to tell stories. We were also allowed to gather some of the wood to build ourselves houses. Sometimes we were called on to help unload wagons or to pile rim sections and spokes into neatly stacked towers. Mother always welcomed any child who knew how to keep busy. Mischief-makers on the other hand were summarily sent away. She would not tolerate tale-bearing. When one went to her to complain about another child, she would cut in abruptly with: "I don't want to hear any tales!"

Then, frequently, she would recall how one of her teachers had handled such situations. He had given both children a slap: the one for being naughty; the other, for telling tales.

One of my mother's favorites and one of our most faithful playmates at the lumberyard was her nephew, Ernst Courant. He was but a few weeks younger than I, still he was often entrusted to my supervision. During school vacations, he preferred to come to us rather than go away on trips. He could spend hours in playing with us or by himself. When we had been well-behaved, we sometimes were given a few *Pfennige* and were allowed to go next door to the bakery to get some *"Dreierkuchen"* (three-penny cookies). Handling the unplaned wood often caused us to run a splinter into a finger; then we would hurry to one of the laborers and have him remove it with his pocketknife.

My mother's relationship with her employees was patriarchal in every way. At Christmastime they received gifts: money, food, and clothing for their children. However, to preclude their using it for drink, the money was not given them in cash. Saving accounts were opened for them, and the gifts were deposited regularly. For many years we had a very capable young worker whom my mother liked very much. As he had been employed by other timber merchants, he was known to most of the customers who all called him by his first name, Hermann. He was completely alone in the world, having no one to look after him. He, too, used to drink more than he should and often went around practically in rags. My mother took great pains to make him more respectable. He was a very handsome lad, apparently as healthy as he was strong but in reality he had a lung ailment. Eventually he had to go to a sanitarium. He had refused for a long time to accept his illness as factual, and to the end, he hoped that soon he would be able to return to work. My mother visited him every Sunday, bringing him the best and most nourishing foods she could find. When he died, she grieved deeply.

Another man, a coworker of Hermann's, stayed with us for many years. Meissner was very surly and resented being told anything. But he was a good worker, and my mother would have sworn to his honesty. So she kept him despite his disposition, and she was also very concerned about his welfare and that of his numerous children. Through a business associate of hers in Poland, she regularly obtained a special remedy for Meissner's asthma. His first wife often helped with the housework in our home. She was very clean and neat; she cared well for her children but was not entirely honest. One day a flatiron was missing at home. My mother had no doubt at all about where it had gone and cleverly arranged to get it back. She told the husband that his wife had borrowed the iron; he was to remind her, please, to return it. Soon afterwards it was back in its place. For the children, it was a real disaster when they lost this mother. The man married a second time soon afterwards; his second wife abused the children, and he had no idea how to protect them from her. One little girl, whose life was no longer safe near her stepmother, stayed with us for several days until she was taken to live in a children's shelter. After his second marriage, the man was impossible at work. Throughout the years, he had always taken as much firewood as he needed for home-use, considering it no more than his due; and my mother had always acquiesced. But, now, when she learned that, secretly, before and after business hours he was selling wood from her supplies and keeping the money, she was forced to dismiss him.

On the other hand, another of his coworkers for many years, a man named Seidel, stayed with us until his death. He came from the mountains of Silesia; a gaunt, tall man, he also had weak lungs. He was quiet, diligent and reliable; only, at intervals, when his wife nagged him to demand a raise, would he first drink enough to get up some courage and then he would gruffly demand his work-book (to indicate that he was quitting);[11] since it was immediately obvious what he was after, a happy solution was quickly reached. When we bought our own apartment house, he and his family moved into the attic apartment; and he became the caretaker. His wife was a capable housekeeper who tenderly mothered her two children, and she was determined to make every effort to "better" their status; toward the rest of the world she energetically asserted herself and, when doing so, made use of a caustic and nimble tongue. Her husband moved about the house like some benevolent spirit endeavoring to keep everything in good order. To insure awaking no one (least of all his wife!), he would carry his shoes when he went downstairs very early in the morning to get the fire started. During the day he continued to work at the lumberyard as usual. He died in our house. His wife called us to assist as his death approached. My brother Arno and I went with her (during the war both of us had served in the Red Cross[12]). I was the one to close his eyes.

The lumberyard was my mother's domain. Before the eight-hour day became a law, the business was open as long as daylight lasted. She would come home only for a brief lunch break at noon, and continues this practice even today. As long as the lumberyard was on Rosenstrasse, a small wooden shed served as the "office." When the business was moved to Elbingstrasse, still on a rented lot, a somewhat larger, portable, wooden structure was bought. Finally Mother could afford the risk of buying herself a large lumberyard which was offered to her. There, a solid brick storage shed with an adjoining office was built. But Mother spent most of the day in the open. She went around with the customers to show them the desired wares, then measured out their selection and billed them for it; she was present and lent a hand when the wagons were unloaded and new shipments were stacked up. Again, when a pushcart loaded with boards left the yard, drawn by one of the laborers, or in earlier years, by a large dog, she helped to push it until it had passed through the gate. She was able to indulge herself by setting aside part of the roomy property she now owned to raise vegetables and fruit. Even today, she delights in watching the produce grow day by day and in picking her own strawberries, beans, peas, and tomatoes. Being constantly in the fresh outdoors certainly has helped her to remain hale and hearty at her advanced age. Even on bitterly cold winter days she would come home with hands so warm that with them she could take the chill from mine. This always symbolized for me that all life and warmth in our home came from her. But she was thoroughly fatigued when she came home in the evenings. The first thing, her shoes had to come off her aching feet. For the evening meal she preferred to take only tea with bread and butter. And if there was nothing urgent to do, she went to bed very early. Upon retiring, she used to say with deep satisfaction: "My bed is the most wonderful place in the world."

As she herself has such a need for rest, she was always appalled at having to waken anyone else. She often said: "It's mortally sinful to disturb a person who's asleep!"

That still affects me at this time. When I lift my head from the pillow early in the morning, she is wont to motion me back: "Wait, wait, there is still plenty of time."

When she went to bed at night, she liked to have someone read to her. My eldest brother was very happy to oblige her in this and was so zealous about it that from time to time he would ask: "Are you listening?" Then, hastily, my mother would rouse herself to say, "Yes, yes," whereupon she promptly went back to sleep. She had very vivid dreams and often spoke aloud in her sleep; sometimes she did so in a way that made it possible to follow an entire dialogue. I slept with my mother until I was six; consequently, I heard many of the stories through which she slept, something which, of course, had not been intended. That was while we were still in Jägerstrasse. The apartment there had three large rooms and a "closet." My sister Else occupied the parlor. She had a desk there and often worked late into the night; at times my mother would put out her lamp. "The boys" had the second room. "The girls" had to make do with the window-less closet which had no air or light except as much as came from my mother's bedroom. If I remember correctly, at first they had Erna with them, besides. Later both she and I were bedded down with Mother. The huge dining table was also in this same room.

At times the parlor was rented out to a student. One of these was a lawyer who come from a good Catholic family. It was almost inevitable that he should fall in love with my beautiful sister, Else. They progressed as far as an engagement; this however was dissolved, probably because both families, for religious reasons, opposed an intermarriage. Later the room was rented to a jovial medical student whose mother brought him to us because she had known my parents in Upper Silesia and wanted her son to have a good home. My sister often had to help him with his studies; in appreciation, he would do some of her chores around the house, for example, getting me dressed. I remember that he used to say to me: "Why, Edith! You are like a cow's tail— you grow down instead of up!"

I was as miffed by the expression he used as by the derogatory reference to my small stature.

One of our evening occupations was to close the accounts. The day's income had to be determined and entered in the receipt book. Often rolls of coins were involved, and these had to be opened and counted. I liked playing with them. One particular customer habitually paid his bill with such rolls of coins. His were my favorites; and I often begged: "Do give me a *Pukade*." (That is what we called this customer.)

As a matter of fact, we learned to know both the customers and the business procedures in this way. Most of the people my mother dealt with were craftsmen. She knew each one's family history. She found it out, usually, when they wanted goods on credit or when they could not redeem the notes they had given. My mother repeatedly followed her kind heart in these cases; sometimes she even gave the "bad customers" some additional cash when they were in need. She was often cheated; and the business was plagued with heavy losses. Despite that, it prospered.

My mother always attributed this fact to being blessed by Heaven.

On one occasion later, after I had lost my childhood's faith, she said to me, giving what she likewise considered a proof of God's existence: "After all, I can't imagine that I owe everything I've achieved to my own ability." This, of course, was correct.

But her natural talents had played a large role in her success.

One day a woman who had for a long time been my mother's friend visited us and exclaimed: "I must tell you at once what I just overheard in the streetcar. A few men were talking about the lumber trade here in Breslau, and one of them said: 'Do you know who is the most capable merchant in the whole trade in town? Frau Stein!'"

Chapter II

The World as the Two Youngest Knew It
1891–1897

1

Our mother, our brothers and sisters, our many relatives, and the lumberyard — these made up all the world in which we two youngest members of the family grew up. For my sister Erna and me life together resembled that of twins. She is the elder by a year and eight months; as a small child I once inquired how come she was at some times one year and at other times two years older than me. But we were dissimilar twins in appearance as well as in character. Always tall and sturdy for her age, Erna wore two long, heavy, brown braids, and had large dark eyes; her complexion was as white and her cheeks as rosy as Snow-White's. I was small and frail, and despite all the care given me, always pale; I wore my blond hair (which only later darkened) usually loose or merely tied with a ribbon. When comparing our looks, one always judged Erna to be much the elder. Admittedly, when I began to talk, astonishment was expressed at the "tot's" cockiness. In my brother's "zoo," Erna was the "crow" and I, the "pussycat." I do not know whether I owe his choice of my nickname to the fact that my big brothers liked to play with me as with a kitten; or, to the color of my eyes; or, to the agility with which, in all the tussles with the elder children, I managed to stay on my feet, avoiding being pinned

down. In any case, being called a crow indicated that Erna was
easily aroused and that her expressions of anger compared with
Rosa's as a crow's shrill cries contrast with a lion's roar. Erna's
were but light and swiftly passing storms.

Otherwise she was a good and easily tractable child. The
older sisters used to say she was as transparent as clear water
while they called me a book sealed with seven seals. As children,
for the most part, we were inseparable; we walked to school together; took our vacations together; we dressed alike (I usually
got my new summer dresses on Erna's birthday in February and
new winter clothes on mine in October). As long as our reading
matter was being carefully supervised and selected by our elder
sisters, we also read the same books. Now and then, Erna objected that, after all, she was older and I ought to have to wait to
get at the same material. But the objections were made on the
spur of the moment. Usually, she was quite content with our
twin-existence. Our friends, too, were mutual, at least to the extent that the friends of one would also invite the other. As was
normal, Erna went to school when she was six; she carried out
her duties without especially exerting herself, always being a
very good but not exceptional student. Ambition was totally
foreign to her; apart from school, she showed no particular
scholarly interests. Reading, in general, played a large role in
our family, but her preference was for light, entertaining books.
She had no appetite for heartier fare.

During her final year at the *Höhere Mädchenschule* she expressed a desire to go on subsequently to the *Mädchen-Real-
gymnasium*,[13] established a few years earlier as a continuation
of the lower institution. Her wish was granted immediately. So
far, she had made no decision on any definite course of study. I
really had an impression that her desire was not then associated
with any particular profession. Rather, she was just eager to
continue living in surroundings which she loved and to which
she was accustomed. Probably a girl friend's decision contributed to hers as well. However, in our family's estimation it went
without saying that, instead of being a luxury, attending the
Gymnasium denoted preparation for a serious professional education. Since she had both a liking and a talent for modern lan-

guages, she was at first inclined to study philology. When I was but six years old, I had already declared, at the time my sister Else took her examination for teaching, that I, too, wanted to be a teacher. Consequently, our relatives liked to picture how, later, we should practice our professions together. But that changed. When she graduated, our uncle David, my mother's brother, invited Erna to come to his house for a holiday; and he asked me to come along as her companion. That vacation in the pharmacist's big home in Chemnitz was wonderful. My aunt, the only child of very wealthy parents, was used to running a large household, to dressing with excellent taste, and to having a good time. Having no daughters of her own, she was particularly delighted at the opportunity to transform these young nieces into elegant ladies at least for the duration of their visit with her. Their friends vied with one another to entertain us: boat rides and automobile trips alternated with visits to the theater and invitations to evening parties. But our good uncle was intent on a more serious matter. His point of view was that the only sensible decision for us to make was to study medicine. He hoped to prevail on both of us to choose the medical profession; and in his mind's eye, he already saw us, each with a different specialty, working hand in hand in a joint private clinic. As I was not to go to the university for another two years, he confined his efforts for the moment to persuading my sister during confidential conversations.

Each evening, once we were alone in the bedroom we shared, I would say: "Don't let yourself be influenced. Do what you, yourself, consider right!" And she assured me she would remain steadfast.

However, my vacation ended before hers, and she stayed on for several weeks after my departure. Shortly before her return home, she wrote to my mother expressing her wish to study medicine; and could she please have Mother's permission to do so? As she was determined that our choice, with regard to this matter in particular, be entirely free, Mother readily acquiesced. I do not believe that Erna ever regretted her decision. She finished the strenuous program of studies, under varying trying physical difficulties at times; and she became thoroughly familiar with her profession. Later, when I assisted her occasionally during her office hours, I was quietly happy to note with what calm assurance she conducted her practice. (She in no way displayed this calm and assurance to the same degree in her personal life. That demonstrated to me for the first time in my experience the effectiveness of a thorough educational foundation.)

When, two years later than my sister, I passed my final exams, I was again cordially invited to Chemnitz. I accepted with joyful thanks but immediately added that my profession had already been chosen and that the matter was no longer open for discussion. Uncle capitulated in the face of this declaration. He refrained from making even the slightest attempt to change my decision. Several months later he remarked to my sister that, possibly in his old age, he might have to doff his hat to me but for the present it was beyond him how one could choose a profession solely according to one's personal talent and inclination.

By narrating these events, I have anticipated too much of my story but these facts about us seemed particularly significant to me. During our childhood, school played an important role. I almost believe I felt more at home there than in our house. Our school was located on the Ritterplatz; the building was formerly a Schaffgotsch Palace, now scarcely conforming to the standards of modern school hygiene but replete with romantic corners and nooks. The beautiful cloister of the Ursulines was across from it; during our "long recess" at ten o'clock we were allowed to go walking in its esplanade under the tall, ancient trees. Our dour principal (dubbed "Rex" in school jargon) and the teachers were acquainted with our elder sisters, and, because of her registering us, with our mother. All the stories we heard from our elder sisters had familiarized and involved us with the school even before we entered ourselves. But ultimately our classmates were the ones with whom we shared the joys and sorrows of school as their significance was no longer within the grasp of the grownups: the suspense before the weekly tests; the anxiety of waiting for the grades; and then the main events of the school year — trimester reports and promotion. At the close of the term, the classes were all assembled in the large auditorium. After Devotions to mark the closing, the principal read out the list of those promoted. Beginning with the lowest grade, he listed everyone in the order of rank in class, making it possible, immediately, to tell whether one had advanced or regressed. Finally, the best students in each class were called forward to receive an award from the principal. For me it was always most embarrassing to have to thread my way through the tightly packed rows of girls all the way up to the podium where the entire faculty was seated; one was the center of attention for all those present in the hall while the principal spoke a few friendly words.

I cared less about the award than about the actual rank in class, pleased though I was about getting each new book. However, my sisters, cousins, and friends greeted me with joyous pride when I was allowed to slip back into the crowd. Showing my report at home also occasioned mixed feelings for me. Mother and my brothers and sisters greeted our good marks with lively joy and rewarded us with gifts; but I did not like to have so much fuss made about them nor to have all the relatives and acquaintances told of them.

Our homework was finished in minimum time. During the summer we spent our free hours in the lumberyard; in winter, we played in the house. Companionship was never lacking: friends from school; children of the tenants; above all others, our many cousins. Like Mother, one of her sisters had five daughters and two sons (except that the sons were the youngest in that family). When they moved from Lublinitz to Breslau, the youngest of the daughters, who was but several months my senior, was put in my class. Noticeably different in temperament and inclination, we were nevertheless good comrades. She delighted with touching kindheartedness in my achievements at school. With black frizzy hair and large black eyes, she was a little imp, and was always eager for an argument. When challenged, I would merely state I had no wish to argue and calmly stuck to my point. On one occasion, I remember her becoming very upset and demanding, "Oh, for once, let me be right!"

But these little scenes never disturbed our mutual attachment. When there was a crowd of us (for instance, when the family was celebrating a birthday and the children had their refreshments at a table in a separate room), we liked to play either "school" or party games. When it came to redeeming forfeits, the ultimate consisted of "three questions on your honor and conscience." First, whoever had to answer them was obliged to leave the room while the others, with burning zeal, determined on the questions to be asked. When recalled, you returned with a pounding heart; after all, you knew the truth would have to be told "on your honor and your conscience," and you were just as certain you would be quizzed "with no holds barred." Favorite questions were: which of one's brothers or sisters one loved most; or, which adult one wanted most to emulate. A desire to delve into the secrets of the human heart lay at the root of this childhood game; it might be very difficult to answer some of the questions, but, at the same time, this descent into one's own depths made a remarkable impression on us. At dusk we liked to tell one another horror stories. At times I was successful as well in awakening in the others enthusiasm for putting on theatrical performances. I made up the plot on the spur of the moment; occasionally, I even wrote a script for such a "drama."

For many years, two cousins were our daily companions; and we were almost as inseparable from them as from one another. These boys were twins, sent from their home in Upper Silesia to attend the *Gymnasium* in Breslau. Our seniors by a few years, they were in their twelfth year at the time of their arrival. They were so identical that they were constantly mistaken for one another; but we were so adept at telling them apart that we found it inconceivable that others could get them mixed up. In temperament, however, they were very dissimilar. The more lively and quick-witted one attached himself to my sister Erna; the more serious and clumsy one, to me. By my teasing, against which he was defenseless, I often tormented him, giving him little indication of how much I liked him. They lived very near to us, staying with mutual relatives in whose house we also felt at home. When they joined us, usually early in the afternoon, they were met by our inquiry: had they already done their homework? We always finished ours after lunch; I could not have enjoyed anything had I been burdened by these small obligations. The boys, naturally, were less particular. They were very musical, and we spent a lot of time at the piano. With immense patience, they talked us into four-handed playing; even I was pressured into attempting Beethoven's symphonies despite the fact that I never achieved even a minimum of dexterity. As I grew older, we often went to concerts or to the theater together. When, at sixteen, I began to attend the *Gymnasium*, this friendship of long years' standing dissolved for no apparent reason.

Fundamentally, the two events may in some manner have been interrelated. At that very time, both of the nineteen-year-old twins awakened to a desire "to enjoy life," and this, in ways we could in no way be expected to tolerate. The "double standard," which my sister and I passionately rejected, was accepted rather generally in Jewish bourgeois circles. As a result of these differing viewpoints, the close ties we used to have with our relatives had essentially weakened. For appearance sake, we kept up the social contacts and sincerely participated in all the happy and sorrowful events within the family; however, we were reputed to have an exaggerated and naive idealism while we were repelled by much about the others which appeared to us to be frivolous. This also had an effect on my mother. More and more, notwithstanding the sincere love she had for her brothers and sisters and her need to see them often and to discuss with them the present as well as the past, she came to feel completely comfortable only in her own home.

We had little inclination for domestic chores and thoroughly disliked being ordered to dust or to dry the dishes. The more demands our studies made on us, the more we were excused from such tasks; this was hardly to our advantage since it resulted in a one-sided upbringing which, later, I often deplored.

2

Among the most important events of life at home, aside from the family feasts, were the major Jewish High Holy Days: particularly *Pesah* (the Passover holiday) which coincides approximately with Easter; also, the holy day of the New Year and the Day of Atonement (in September or October depending on the correspondence of the Jewish to the Gregorian calendar). Most Christians are unaware that the "Feast of Unleavened Bread," in remembrance of the Exodus of the children of Israel from Egypt, continues to be celebrated today in the identical manner in which it was celebrated by our Lord with his disciples when he instituted the Blessed Sacrament and took leave of his followers. Of course, a Passover lamb is no longer slaughtered since the destruction of the Temple in Jerusalem; but the head of the house, reciting the prescribed prayers, still distributes the unleavened bread and the bitter herbs which are a reminder of the suffering connected with the exile. He blesses the wine and reads the account of the deliverance of the People from Egypt. With the indomitable consistency that marks the Jewish spirit, the observances of the feast are extensive: for an entire week no leavened bread, nor any other leavened food, is eaten or even tolerated in the house. Naturally then, a large family requires a plentiful supply of unleavened bread (matzo). The large bakeries prepare it according to the precise guidelines and under "rabbinical supervision." A good while before the feast, we received it in great rolls of brown or grey paper; but touching it was not permitted before the first "Seder night" (named after the prescribed order of the ritual for the meal). On the day of preparation for the holiday, the entire house is turned topsy-turvy. All leaven has to be removed; even the last crumbs of bread are swept up to be burned. This is not yet enough. All dishes and cooking utensils are carried to the attic or to the cellar, and in their place special dishes which had been stored away all year are taken out and now thoroughly cleaned. (During my childhood, everything was done as prescribed; later, our liberal-minded elder brothers and sisters talked my mother out of some of it.) On the days of preparation, housewives have a great deal of work to get done and are very happy when evening comes and the holiday itself begins. (Jewish holy days begin on the eve when the first star appears in the sky.)

Naturally, we children always welcomed such an interruption of the everyday routine, greeting the pots and bowls we had not seen for a year, and looking forward to the delectable food customarily served at these times. However, despite that, the week would begin to drag; and it was another cause for festivity when the bread and butter which had been banned for so many days once again appeared on the table. But we also joyfully anticipated the Seder nights with the ceremonial sequence of foods and the many prayers. My participation was a special one: the ritual for the Seder evening includes a number of questions assigned to the youngest child, who asks why everything on this night is so different from all other nights. The head of the house replies, explaining the meaning of each of the observances. Later, when I had become "enlightened," I welcomed the presence of nephews or nieces who could take over this role from me. As things were, the celebrations lacked some of the solemnity due them since only my mother and the younger children participated with devotion. The brothers whose task it was, as substitute for their deceased father, to recite the prayers, did so with little respect. When the elder one was absent and the younger had to represent the head of the house, he made clear his opinion that it was not to be taken seriously.

Of even greater importance than *Pesah* were the New Year's holiday and the Day of Atonement. A two day celebration marks New Year's. On the eve, again, there is a festive meal. The mother of the family bakes the "Hallah," a fine white bread, as she does on every Sabbath; according to ritual prescriptions, this is ordinarily a braided loaf; but for New Year's it is baked into a round loaf. Principally, this bread is eaten with the meat. When it is cut at the beginning of the meal, each member of the household receives a portion; the distribution is made in exact order according to age. Before anyone tastes of it, the blessing is pronounced: "Blessed art Thou, Lord God, Ruler of the Universe, who bring forth bread from the earth." Honey and the first grapes of the harvest were also served on this evening. My mother never ate any grapes before New Year's Day. To accompany the afternoon coffee,[14] a large supply of exceptionally fine cakes were prepared. Fewer prayers are prescribed for the New Year's Day celebration than for the Seder evening; that is, for its celebration in the home. In the synagogue, there is a solemn prayer service, first for each eve, then for the days as well. Judaism has a well developed liturgy: fixed prayer times for each day and, for the High Holy Days, a liturgical service that fills a major part of the day. (From this Jewish liturgy, composed as it is of the recitation of psalms and readings from the Scriptures, the liturgy of the Church has evolved.) My mother does not usually go to synagogue for the evening services but stays at home, reciting the prescribed prayers from her prayer book; but first, at the designated time, she lights the candles in the tall silver candelabra to mark the beginning of the feast. This too, she performs with deep devotion, reciting the prescribed prayers.

But the next morning she goes to the synagogue (on foot, since no vehicles are used on holy days, for one may not do any kind of work, nor may one benefit from the labor of others); and she returns, ordinarily, only in time for the noon meal. When we were children, we did not accompany her but usually went at noon to call for her at the synagogue. We then wore our very best dresses and shoes, and congregated in the courtyard with many other children, similarly attired in festive clothing, who were meeting their parents. We did not go to school on high holy days. On such feasts, my greatest joy was to have unlimited time to read an enjoyable book; we were careful to provide ourselves with reading material ahead of time.

The highest of all the Jewish festivals is the Day of Atonement, the day on which the High Priest used to enter the Holy of Holies to offer the sacrifice of atonement for himself and for the people; afterwards, the "scapegoat" upon whose head, symbolically, the sins of all the people had been laid was driven out into the desert. All of this ritual has come to an end. But even at present the day is observed with prayer and fasting, and whoever preserves but a trace of Judaism goes to the "Temple" on this day. Although I did not in any way scorn the delicacies served on the other holidays, I was especially attracted to the ritual of this particular holy day when one refrained from taking any food or drink for twenty-four hours or more, and I loved it more than any of the others. On the eve, one had to partake of the evening meal while it was still daylight for the service in the synagogue would begin as soon as the first star appeared in the sky. Not only did my mother attend on this evening but she was accompanied by our elder sisters; even my brothers considered it a duty to be present. The beautiful ancient melodies used on this evening even attract those of other beliefs.

On the following morning, although Mother rose a little later than usual (even today she is accustomed to rise at five-thirty), she still was ahead of everyone else. Then she would go from bed to bed to bid each of us a fond farewell since she would stay in the synagogue the entire day. We remained in bed just as long as possible. (On this occasion reading in bed was permitted.) My sister Frieda never did get up at all on that day for, had she done so, she would have been unable to keep the fast. We little ones went to the memorial service at the synagogue; my mother insisted upon this so that we would commemorate our father during the service. Day and night at home, two large, thick white candles burned in memory of our deceased loved ones. In the evening, usually, one of my brothers went to bring Mother home. It was always a joy to have the whole family together again and to see that all had survived the day well. Boys are obliged to the fast once they have completed their thirteenth year; girls, after completing the twelfth year.[1] I would have wished to observe the rule conscientiously, but in my twelfth year I was considered too frail and was allowed to fast only until midday. From my thirteenth year, however, I observed it fully, always; and none of us dispensed ourselves from this fast even when we no longer shared our mother's faith nor continued observing any of the ritual prescriptions when away from home.

For me the day had an additional significance: I was born on the Day of Atonement, and my mother always considered it my real birthday, although celebrations and gifts were always forthcoming on October 12. (She herself celebrated her birthday, according to the Jewish calendar, on the Feast of Tabernacles; but she no longer insisted on this custom for her children.) She laid great stress on my being born on the Day of Atonement, and I believe this contributed more than anything else to her youngest's being especially dear to her. And since our destinies are intertwined in such a unique way, it is probably appropriate that in this portrait of my mother I say more about my own development than about that of my brothers or sisters.

[1]The law reckons with the early maturing of Oriental peoples.

3

When I was born on October 12, 1891, my parents had been in Breslau a year and a half. My father died in July of 1893. I have already told[15] how my mother held me in her arms as he bade her farewell when he set out on the journey from which he was not to return alive, and that, when he had already turned to leave, I called him back once more. So, for her, I was the final legacy from my father. I slept beside her, and when, weary after a day at work, she would return home, her first steps led her to me. Indeed, if I were ill, she would hardly take time to remove her coat but would sit down on the edge of my bed and have her simple evening meal brought to her there.

Her mere presence dispelled all of my pains and aches. When I was seven years old, I was allowed to go with Erna to Lublinitz for the Christmas vacation. On Christmas Eve I was seized with severe pain and was unable to swallow any of the fine Christmas carp. The doctor diagnosed an infection, and so I had to spend the entire vacation as a patient. As my mother could not neglect her business, she sent my sister Else to nurse me. But the following Sunday, she herself arrived suddenly, without giving any previous notice. As I had been rather lonesome in the big attic bedroom, my devoted aunts had brought me downstairs, bedding me down on a sofa in the cozy dining room. When my mother suddenly appeared in the doorway, I jumped up, clasped my arms around her neck, and stayed on her lap until she had to return home that evening.

Despite this intimate bond, my mother was not my confidante — no more so than anyone else. I went through sudden transitions, incomprehensible to the observer. During my early years, I was mercurially lively, always in motion, spilling over with pranks, impertinent and precocious, and, at the same time, intractably stubborn and angry if anything went against my will. My eldest sister, whom I loved very much, tested her newly-acquired child-training methods on me in vain. Her last resort was to lock me in a dark room. When this danger loomed, I would lie on the floor, stiff with resistance; and it took superhuman effort for my frail sister to lift me and carry me off. In my dark prison, in no way resigned to my fate, instead, screaming at the top of my lungs, I hammered on the door with both fists until my mother would finally declare we were exceeding the limit of tolerance to be expected of the other tenants; she then set me free.

Such was the behavior which my relatives usually observed in my case. Within me, however, there was a hidden world. Whatever I saw or heard throughout my days was pondered over there. The sight of a drunkard could haunt and plague me for days and nights on end. Later, I was often grateful that as far as my brothers were concerned there was never any danger of their being intoxicated, nor had I ever to see any near relative in such a disgusting condition. I could never understand how one could possibly laugh at such a state; and in my student years, without ever joining any organization or taking any form of pledge, I began to abstain from even a drop of alcohol to avoid being personally responsible for losing even the smallest particle of my freedom of spirit and my human dignity. Should anyone speak of a murder in my presence, I would lie awake for hours that night, and, in the dark, horror would press in upon me from every corner. Indeed, even a somewhat coarse expression which, in irritation, my mother once used in my presence, pained me so deeply that I could never forget this minor incident, an argument with my eldest brother.

I never mentioned a word to anyone of these things which caused me so much hidden suffering. It never occurred to me that one could speak about such matters. Only infrequently did I give my family any inkling of what was happening: for no apparent reason I sometimes developed a fever and in delirium spoke of the things which were oppressing me inwardly. My family often recounted one such instance. When I was about five years old, my sister Frieda was reading *Maria Stuart*[16] in school and was then allowed to go to see the stage play with my mother. Before they went, there was a great deal of talk about it; and, as usual, I picked up far more than was intended for me. While the two were at the theater, my feverish fantasies began and I cried out, over and over, in great excitement, "Oh, *do* cut off Elizabeth's head!"

I recall what a sequel there was to this incident. The following year, when I went to school and had arrived at barely managing to read words in print, I searched out the proper volume of Schiller's works in our bookcase at home, took it to the kitchen and asked my mother whether I might read to her out of *Maria Stuart*.

Very solemnly she said: "Go ahead, read."

How far I got at the time, I cannot remember. But it is easy to surmise that such sudden outbursts alarmed my relatives. They called it "nerves" and tried, as much as possible, to shield me from overexcitement.

The first great transformation took place in me when I was about seven years old. I would not be able to ascribe it to any external cause. I cannot explain it otherwise than that reason assumed command within me. I recall very well how, from that time on, I was convinced that my mother and my sister Frieda had a better knowledge of what was good for me than I had; and because of this confidence, I readily obeyed them. The old stubborness seemed to disappear; and, in the years that followed, I was a docile child. When I did permit myself some naughtiness or an impudent answer, I quickly sought forgiveness although the effort to bring myself to do so cost me a great deal; but, afterwards, I was very happy to have peace restored. Angry outbursts became all but nonexistent; early in life I arrived at such a degree of self-mastery that I could preserve my equanimity almost without a struggle. I do not know how that happened; I do believe what cured me was the distaste and shame I experienced at the angry outbursts of others and the acute realization I had that the price of such self-indulgence was the loss of one's dignity.

Gradually my inner world grew lighter and clearer. Whatever was heard, seen, read, or experienced offered my active fantasy material for the most intrepid constructions. One important event which preoccupied me for a long time was the eightieth birthday of a great-aunt. About a hundred persons belonging to the widespread family were invited to the celebration. The old lady herself (Frau Ernestine Radlauer whom I have mentioned earlier)[17] had kept the happy disposition of her youth and her multitalented children and grandchildren were expert at preparing splendid festivities. This time, among a wealth of attrac-

tions, the program provided for a dance popular when Grandmother was young. Dressed in the costumes of that period, eight
pairs of children were to perform. A Frenchwoman, then choreographer at the municipal "*Stadttheater*," rehearsed it with us.
My sister and I were one of the couples; we were then nine and
seven years old. As we were among the youngest and had never
had any dancing lessons before, we were not entrusted with too
much and had been positioned behind the others. But during the
very first rehearsal, Madame Prochere moved us up to the front
row. She was enthusiastic about the adroitness with which I
grasped and then executed her ideas. She kept asking me whether
I did not want to join her ballet group. I deemed the question un-
worthy of a serious reply, but it flattered my vanity. Erna was
somewhat less supple, but that did not matter since she was "the
gentleman." She wore brown velvet tails and light blue knee
breeches; I, a dress made of bright flowered material, and my
hair was pinned up in curls and adorned with roses. We had
been told we would also be made up. I protested very much
against cosmetics and was delighted when the excitement of the
festive evening made us all glow so much that the addition of
any artificial rosiness was unnecessary. The applause was very
generous. Awarded recognition as "best ballerinas," a cousin
and I were escorted to the venerable "Birthday Child" to receive
her special thanks. Then my Uncle David lifted me high over-
head and stood me on a window sill so all the people in the hall
could get a good look at the diminutive creature. That evening I
imitated all the dance steps used by the grown-ups and was eventually asked to join them. In the following weeks, my brother
Arno, an excellent dancer, completed my dancing instructions
at home. He was twenty-two at the time and was so tall that he
had to bend over quite a bit in order to dance with me. This,
however, bothered neither of the partners. On the night of that
highly successful birthday party, as we left for home, a beautiful
and much admired cousin of mine gave me the snowdrops she
had worn in her belt that evening. I carried them away most
happily. The next morning my big sisters thought it well to let
me know that all the adults at the party had noted with surprise
the coquettish expression I had while I was dancing.

I replied: "How ridiculous!" After all, the "cavalier" with whom I played the coquette had been my sister Erna! That the seven-year-old had not only understood the reproof but had rejected it shows well enough how matters stood in that small head.

In my dreams I always foresaw a brilliant future for myself. I dreamed about happiness and fame for I was convinced that I was destined for something great and that I did not belong at all in the narrow, bourgeois circumstances into which I had been born. About these dreams I said as little as I had about the fears which had plagued me earlier. However, that I was given to daydreaming was apparent; and when anyone noticed that I was oblivious to what was going on, they would startle me out of my reverie. With such a prolific fantasy, it was a good thing that I got to go to school early so that my lively spirit received solid nourishment.

When Erna was six years old and started off to school, I was very unhappy because I could not go along. As I now lacked companionship at home, I was registered for kindergarten. This I considered to be far beneath my dignity. A regular battle ensued each morning to get me there. I was disagreeable to the other children and refused to play with them. My elder brothers and sisters alternately had the unpleasant task of taking me there. One day it was my eldest brother's turn. As we left the house, I noticed it was raining lightly. I declared at once that I could not walk on the wet ground, that I wanted to turn back; or he would have to carry me. Immediately, my kindhearted brother Paul took me up in his arms and carried me the whole way to school. At noon my mother declared that a girl my size ought to be ashamed at having to be carried. Had I, at least, thanked him? If not, then I was to make up for it at once. To bring myself to do so occasioned another bitter struggle for me. After all, my brother was accustomed to doing anything I wanted without requiring either a please or a thank you. While I clutched his hair, he could carry me around a room on his shoulders by the hour, tirelessly singing student or folk songs to me. To amuse us both, he used to show me all the pictures in his bulky history of literature and asked me who or what was being represented; in his zeal he would cover the captions although at the time I was still unable to read.

As my sixth birthday approached, I resolved to make an end of the despised attendance at the kindergarten. I declared that, absolutely, once that day had come, I wanted to go to the "big school" and requested that this be my one and only birthday gift; in any case, if I could not have that, I would accept no other gifts. It happened that in that particular year, classes after the fall vacation were resumed on the twelfth of October. Actually, it was not all that simple to get what I wanted; the school year had begun at Easter. Besides, I was still unable to read or write, even though I could recite long ballads and played "Author-Quartet" with my sisters and brothers because I knew by heart what was printed on the playing cards.

My eldest sister went to the principal of the *Viktoriaschule* and begged him to take me on probation; she was willing to guarantee that I could keep up with the work. As she herself had been an outstanding student and had only recently passed her teacher's examination, I was accepted on the basis of her recommendation. On the first day of school, the overawing principal asked me whether I had already received my birthday presents, and the first grade teacher brought me a bag of chocolates. At first it was very difficult, without having had any practice, to begin writing with pen and ink and to read whole words. But by the following Easter, I was promoted with the others; and from that time on I always maintained my place among the best students.

I have already recounted some of the joys and sorrows of life in school. As a pupil I was overly zealous. I was apt to skip right to the front of the teacher's desk with index finger raised in order to "get my turn." German and history were my favorite subjects. At the beginning of each new school year, I greedily devoured the new textbooks for literature and history. The first thing in the morning, I would begin to read while my mother fixed my hair. I loved to write compositions; they enabled me to include some of the thoughts which occupied my mind. Nor was I bashful at all about handing the compositions in to the teachers. On the other hand, I thoroughly disliked having them read at home, and, even more, showing them to visiting friends who had to be given an account of my achievements. In fact, when not in school, I became so quiet and taciturn that the whole family noticed it. This was probably due to my being so cocooned in my interior world. Perhaps it was also because of the condescending way most adults deal with children. When I began to talk about matters which in their estimation were beyond me, they just laughed and exchanged comments about my curious precocity. Consequently, I preferred to keep quiet. I was taken seriously in school. Perhaps I said some things in class which most of my fellow students did not understand. But I was unaware of that, nor did the teachers give any indication of having noticed other than by giving me good marks.

Chapter III

Cares and Dissension in the Family
1897–1906

1

(Here 28 sheets are missing from the manuscript.)*

. . . preferred to have for himself,[18] not wanting to share with his many relatives. But when she was away at one of the spas and Uncle was alone at home, he invited all his brothers and sisters along with all their children. I can still see him standing on the steps leading down into the garden. Our evening meal was served out on the lawn. Eyes sparkling with delight, he encouraged us to savour it. When we visited him for the last time, he was no longer living in this beautiful home. He had been forced to let it go and take, instead, a rented apartment. On the occasion of that visit, he was especially kind and tenderhearted, setting us on his knees, and asking in great detail how things were going in school. I was ten years old at the time. I believe it was not long thereafter that we suddenly got news of his death. My mother went there immediately, even though she had to leave work during business hours. There was terrible excitement in the entire

---

*A bundle of twenty-eight sheets (Pages 162–190 of manuscript) is missing here. The last page of the preceding bundle shows unmistakably that on its lower half a new paragraph was begun. That portion of page 161 was cut off and removed from the manuscript as well.

80

family. We children were not meant to learn any of the details; but gradually it leaked out that he had shot himself. Business worries were to blame. His own business affairs were run impeccably; however, in their crises, he had helped his brothers, one in Rumania and one in Breslau, and became embroiled in their financial collapse. When all likelihood of meeting his obligations to his creditors seemed gone, he was unable to face the threatened disgrace. Later it was said that most likely his affairs could have been put in order. If I remember correctly, his was the first funeral I attended. Awaiting it, we sat with Mother among the mourners in the anteroom of the funeral chapel. Distant relatives and friends came up to us to express their sympathy by a handclasp; with a glance at us, my mother said, ". . . their second father." Then the doors to the chapel were opened and everyone streamed in. Sombre music greeted us. The room was decorated; up front, the coffin, entirely covered by flowers, was set between green trees. The rabbi began the eulogy. I have heard many such talks. They gave a resume of the life of the deceased, recalling all the good things he had done, thereby rousing the sorrow of the bereaved all the more; there was nothing consoling about them. To be sure, there was a prayer pronounced in solemn tones: "And when the body returns to dust, the spirit returns to God who gave it." However, nothing of faith in a personal life after death, nor any belief in a future reunion with those who had died, lay behind these words. Many years later, when for the first time I attended a Catholic funeral, the contrast made a deep impression upon me. The one then being buried was a very well-known scholar. But no longer was mention made of his achievements or of the reputation he had won in the world. Called by his baptismal name alone, the humble soul, in all its poverty, was commended to divine mercy. But how consoling and calming were the words of the liturgy which accompanied the deceased into eternity!

It was always a dreadful moment when the pallbearers took up the coffin at the end of the service and carried it away. Two by two, the mourners followed, crossing the vast cemetery to the open grave. Then came another horrible moment when the coffin was lowered and one heard the dull thud as it struck the bottom. On the other hand, when my turn came to throw in my three shovelsful of earth, I felt consoled. It was so like a final greeting. To close the service, more prayers were offered in the funeral chapel.

One year later, almost to the day, we experienced a very similar shock. My father's youngest brother,[19] who had taken over my grandparents' business in Gleiwitz, put an end to his life because of business difficulties. As he seldom visited us, we barely knew him; but the event in itself and its parallels to the one a year earlier had a dreadful impact. I sensed that suicide was dreadful, totally different from the horror of death as such. My mother, with her indestructibly vigorous hold on life, used to say in such cases that a person could make that kind of resolve and carry it out only in a moment of insanity; anyone with a healthy mental balance could never do such a thing. When in later years I pondered how such behavior was possible, while reflecting at the same time on the rather frequent occurrence of suicide among Jews, I found an alternative explanation. The economic war against the Jews, which has ruined so many at a single blow in the year just past, has again caused an alarming number of suicides. I believe that the inability to face and to accept the collapse of one's worldly existence with reasonable calm is closely linked to the lack of any prospect of life in eternity. The personal immortality of the soul is not considered an article of faith; all of one's effort is concentrated on what is temporal. Even the piety of the pious is directed toward the sanctification of *this* life. A Jew is able to endure severe hardship and untiring labor coupled with extreme privations for years on end as long as he sees a goal ahead. Deprive him of this goal and you destroy his vigor; life then appears meaningless, and so he can readily decide to throw it away. The true believer, of course, is deterred from such a course by his submission to the will of God.

Six children survived this uncle from Gleiwitz. The sad news recalled the two eldest daughters — twins — from a vacation trip. Thoroughly spoiled, they had, up to this time, never learned to do any serious type of work. Now they were sent to take a course in a trade school in Breslau; it was to enable them to find jobs in business as soon as possible. Separated from one another, they were lodged with their maternal aunts. Like their father, formerly they had visited us seldom. Now they came often on a Sunday and unburdened their hearts to my mother. Once, when they admitted to her, tearfully, with what little love they were treated by their relatives, my mother said, quite simply: "Come to us."

They could not believe they had heard correctly, but it was clearly evident how tempting they found the proposal. It was as joyfully welcomed by their aunts (one of the two ladies was childless, the other had an only daughter). The move was accomplished without delay. At the time we were not living in a house of our own. Still the two were given a spacious room; we simply squeezed together a bit more. Always, we could accommodate as many guests as we wished to have in our home. I cannot recall how long these two cousins stayed with us. In time, both of them married; they have always remained gratefully attached to my mother.

Because the family circle was so extensive and the ties uniting its members were so close, problems and fears inevitably had to be shared time and again, here or there. Our elder sisters took turns accompanying an ailing aunt to a spa, or giving moral support to another who was faced with a serious operation, or nursing a third after childbirth. Should such a phone call for help come from Berlin, or anywhere else, my mother, without long deliberation, would dispatch one or other of her daughters with a simple: "Get ready to go."

Such illnesses, however, were nothing compared to one common worry which caused tension in the entire family for years. Among the fourteen brothers and sisters of my mother's family, there was a "black sheep," her brother Sigmund who was several years younger than she. He was a most amiable person who, like my grandfather, took delight in giving presents to others; and so he invariably brought something for each child when he came to visit us. He also had many of the traits of a good businessman, particularly an exceptional facility in arithmetic. But he lacked the strict integrity so characteristic of his parents and brothers and sisters; and he was an easy prey for bad influence. He and his wife, no less, were inclined to extravagance. So they constantly lived beyond their means; and the relatives had to intervene, time and time again, to set them back on their feet. At first, they and their three sons lived in Glatz; then, for a number

of years, they were in Breslau. Their youngest son was that beloved nephew of my mother's who was most happy when he was
staying with us. All three boys keenly felt their mother's total inability to relate to them. When her incessant carping reached a
level beyond endurance, the middle one simply picked her up in
his arms, and carried her into another room where he would lock
her up. Once when he was visiting us, he put his arms around my
mother and said, "Why can't our mother be like you?"

The eldest suffered most at her hands because he was so totally different from other children. Although but a few years
older than we, he no longer took part in our games. From his
earliest childhood, he perplexed adults by his tireless questioning to which, frequently, they knew no answers. Later, he was
happiest when engrossed in his books; he was interested in any
and all branches of learning; but, above all, he was an excellent
mathematician.

The tragic end of Uncle Jakob[20] was related to the collapse of
the business in Breslau. In consequence of his death, such unpleasant arguments arose over business matters that the rest of
the brothers and sisters determined to have no more to do with
Sigmund and his wife. My mother suffered greatly under these
circumstances. It was terribly hard for her to know there was a
shadow on her father's name and to watch the dissension among
her brothers. However, if she did not meet her brother Sigmund
again for many years, she was all the more ready to take a heartfelt interest in his children and to be willing always to assist
them. In her lifetime, she had the happiness of seeing them all
grow up to be good and competent persons who by their own
determination made up for what their parents had failed to provide in their upbringing. Ernst, my mother's favorite, went to
Berlin with his father and mother and stayed with them the
longest. I have already mentioned that he was killed in the
World War [I]. Fritz, the second son, was sent to Rome soon
after being employed by the firm in which he had completed his
business training; and he still holds that position today. Richard,
the eldest, stayed in Breslau and earned enough by tutoring in
mathematics to put himself through the *Gymnasium* and the

University. While still in the *Unter-prima*,[21] he was already preparing others in the higher classes for their *Abitur*. When it was explained to him that this was not permissible, he left the *Gymnasium* and passed his examinations as a non-matriculated student. Then he began higher studies in mathematics and, after several semesters, went to Göttingen as assistant to David Hilbert. He joined the faculty there and later was granted the chair of Felix Klein, the second leading Göttingen mathematician. (The "purging" of the University of "non-Aryans" has deprived him, too, of his position. He is making preparations now to move to America.) As long as he was still in Breslau, he visited us often. For a time he came to dinner once a week. We looked forward to his coming because he had the most surprising flashes of wit. But in the same dry, humorous tone he would hold most serious consultations with my mother to determine how best he could help his parents and keep his father from being involved in unwise business ventures. He saw the situation keenly and clearly, but he kept in steady contact with his parents, allowing nothing to divert his filial love. In such conversations we were often at a loss whether to laugh at the comic, often dramatically exaggerated, expressions he used, or to weep over the content of his remarks.

To these serious worries there were added lesser conflicts in the family, which, nevertheless, caused my mother much anxiety. The Courant brothers are greatly attached to one another; but because of their touchiness and their obstinacy, they would often clash and then it could happen that for years they would not speak to one another and even avoided getting together. The sisters, much more peace-loving, suffered a great deal under the circumstances and always attempted to mediate; this, however, was not a simple matter. When two such "mule-heads" were successfully reconciled, they were happier about it than anyone else. Then they would shower one another with every possible attention; indeed, failing to learn from past experience, they would dare to resume such a close relationship that ere long, given their peculiarities, a new clash could hardly be avoided.

2

Every now and then upsetting events in the immediate family were added to the large and small concerns affecting more distant relatives. I have already mentioned how intensely my mother opposed the betrothal and marriage of my brother Paul. His wedding was the first in which I ever took part. Naturally, the joy we children experienced on this occasion was so great that we forgot all about our mother's grief over it. And how proud I was when, at the age of ten, I became an aunt for the first time! My mother also took her first grandson completely to her heart. But she was constantly upset over the inadequate care little Gerhard received from his mother. Every visit to my sister-in-law's "nonchalant" household cost her a tremendous amount of self-control. The happy young mother had never before seen a newborn child. She was bitterly disappointed that her little boy did not come into the world with long, blond curls. My mother was almost beside herself at her daughter-in-law's repeated assurances that her inexperience did not matter, that "maternal instinct" would compensate for it. As it turned out, her "instinct" did nothing to hinder this strong and healthy infant from deteriorating into a pitiable condition. When that happened, my mother took the little fellow into our home; and the solicitous care given him by his grandmother and aunts would soon undo all the damage. This procedure was to recur frequently. Everytime my mother found the child sick and lacking proper care, she would wrap him in a big blanket, call a cab, and take him home with her. Gerhard was nursed through all his childhood ailments at our house. Naturally his *"Grossmama"* to whom, in any case, every child was attracted, was his all; she meant far more to him than his parents.

It is understandable that this made his mother jealous. We seldom saw the second child, Harald. When only two years old, he died of a neglected case of scarlet fever. After that, Gerhard remained an only child. During his earliest years, he either stayed with us for weeks at a time, or he would visit us daily. At first, the maid carried him. By this time, he actually did have long, lovely, golden-blond curls and huge dark eyes; he was now the beautiful little boy who fulfilled all his mother's dreams. When he was carried onto the streetcar in his little white cape and hood, the comment was: "Here comes the Christchild."

He could walk and talk before he was a year old. In his second year he had already begun to go by himself to make small purchases in the neighborhood stores; indeed, it happened that he would slip undetected through the front door, thus escaping from the small courtyard in which he was playing alone, to go to the store in the adjoining house, where he would buy a bag of cherries, saying: "Grandmother will pay for them."

By the time he was three years old, he would come to our house by himself via streetcar. He was taken from his home to the nearest trolley stop; and someone met him at our end. All the conductors knew him. Sometimes he scared them by not getting off at the stop in front of our house. When they called his attention to it, he dismissed them with a careless wave of the hand. Then, at the next stop, he would make a very dignified exit and set out on his way to the lumberyard. For him also, this was a child's paradise. Naturally, with his funny tricks, this charming child was an inexhaustible source of joy for his grandmother and for all of us. But as he grew older, his mother did all she could to bind him closer to herself while weaning him from us. As soon as he began to go to school, she did his homework with him; and, as the years passed, that took up more and more time. The brilliant talent of his early years seemed to have faded away; despite all the effort, he remained a mediocre student. When, occasionally, I spent some time with him, I readily saw the reason for this. He was incredibly absent-minded, always having a thousand things in his head; nor could he concentrate for more than five minutes. On the other hand, he was thoroughly attentive when busy with games of his own creation. Now, if he were to visit us, he would collect all the chairs in the house, joining them together to play train. Usually, by the time he had made all his preparations, his visiting time was over and he had to go home. Later, his pet project was installing electrical wiring; but this, too, he never completed. When he turned the whole house topsy-turvy and, if at all possible, got all of his aunts involved in helping him to do so, he naturally became less

welcome as a guest. His aunt Rosa gave him the longest lectures
since as housekeeper she suffered most under the circumstances. But he did not allow that to hinder him at all. When,
upon passing his examinations, he began to study engineering,
his aunts had little confidence that anything would come of it.
In truth, the preparations for the experiments he had to conduct for his studies always took an unbelievably long time. Nonetheless, eventually, he attained his goal. One evening he asked
his parents to meet him at his grandmother's. He arrived in tail-
coat and top hat and announced that he had passed his doctoral
examination. That, once again, was a day on which everyone
was pleased with him. On other days, his grandmother worried
a good bit about her former darling. The older he got the more
his mother's idiosyncracies came to the fore in him. The admiration surrounding him at home made him vain and selfish. His
parents had to arrange everything according to his wishes; he
himself paid no regard to others. This greatly annoyed his
father who, nevertheless, was unable to change anything. Gerhard was successful in his profession; for the first few years he
was an assistant in the technical engineering school in Breslau.
Then he was employed by the A.E.G.[22] in Berlin and given the
chance to do research work in its institutes. He, too, was deprived of this job and of the prospect of a career in the academic
world by the tide of anti-Semitism.

3

While the marriage of my mother's eldest son brought her so
much grief, the notice of her eldest daughter's engagement was
exceptionally good news. After all, Else had always been a real
problem child for her. Having passed her teacher's examination, she was employed by various families as governess. Sometimes this was in Breslau when she merely had to supervise homework each afternoon; a few times it was in some small town in
the province where she had full charge of the instruction and
upbringing of the children. She put her heart and soul into being a governess, had a strong influence on her charges, and was
much loved by them. But she never lasted long in any job. Some-

times she resigned her position because the lady of the house became jealous at having to share her home with such a young and beautiful girl. The relationship with the children was often an enduring one; my sister tends to be a faithful friend and has maintained many a lifelong contact with a teacher or a school companion.

Ever since her graduation, she had been seeking employment in the school system. For a Jewess in Prussia, this was next to impossible; and, therefore, she followed a girl friend's suggestion to try in Hamburg.[23] As it turned out, she succeeded in being accepted at a private school there. It was not to be for long. In Hamburg she met a relative, a cousin of our mother's, who had been practicing as a dermatologist there for several years. One day in September of 1903, we received notification of her engagement. I can distinctly remember the particular circumstances. It was a beautiful Sunday, and the entire family had been invited to a customer's large orchard not only to enjoy the ripe plums, but to take home as many more as we were able and willing to pick. Gerhard performed marvels on this occasion. In his white lace dress he sat on the grass under a huge tree, held an immense apple in both little hands and became absorbed in enjoying it. The apple was finished; several plums followed it, then another apple, and so on. When, upon our arrival back home, he demanded some more of the fruit we had brought back, his father finally decided enough was enough and refused to give him any more. Aggrieved, the little fellow came to me, complaining, *"Edi, der gibbt nischt."* [Edi, he won't give me any.]

As a small child he spoke with a very decided Silesian intonation although no one else did so, except that his mother slipped into the dialect of her native Ohlau when she was a little careless.

On the very occasion I mentioned, in the middle of the merriment attending the fruit-gathering, the special delivery letter arrived from Hamburg. In it, Max Gordon briefly informed his cousin Gustel that he had become engaged to her daughter Else. Later, my sister told us that he had placed the completed letter before her and asked her consent to mail it as it was. That was how the engagement came to be; its duration was no less extraordinary. It lasted a mere two months. Else kept on teaching until October and then came home for a very short time only. In her absence we had worked on her trousseau with feverish activity and immense pleasure. Catalogs were studied, and many things were bought ready-made; but even more were sewn at home. A seamstress came to the house, and in her capable hands linen, damask, and Swiss-embroidery were transformed into marvelous creations. My sister Frieda helped most diligently. We were allowed to help, also, when we were not in school. At times, even some of our cousins joined in. When that happened, we all sat in a large circle sewing and embroidering while one of us read something humorous aloud. Finally everything was completed; and the whole splendid array disappeared into crates and went off to Hamburg. We were disappointed that, as it was to take place in Hamburg, we could not attend the wedding. Our new brother-in-law never travelled anywhere except, at times, to his mother in Berlin for a two-day holiday. He was unwilling to cancel any office hours or to hire a substitute, as he was at swords' points with his colleagues. My mother had to make some allowances which were not at all to her liking. Most painful of all was the fact that the engaged couple refused to consider a religious ceremony. Both were utter nonbelievers. My mother made a great sacrifice when, despite this, she went along to the wedding with . . .* brother-in-law, which likewise intimidated people as soon as a difference of opinion arose.

He had fashioned for himself a whole range of views which contrasted sharply with those held in his milieu; and they were also the source of ever increasing difficulties concerned with his livelihood. Repeatedly he had confrontations and lengthy legal altercations with the Leipzig Medical Association whose concept of "professional ethics" he found unacceptable. As a young doctor, he had established his practice in Hamburg by regularly advertising his office hours in the newspapers. Because of his specialties (dermatology and venereology) and because that port city had a constant influx of foreigners, this had proved to be profitable. The medical society perceived this businesslike approach as

---

*Here four sheets of the manuscript are missing: Page 219 is the final page of the preceding bundle; pages 220-224 are missing; page 225 is a loose sheet. The next bundle begins with page 226.

"unfair competition" and as a violation of professional ethics. My brother-in-law could not see why a capable and conscientious physician should not inform his suffering fellow humans by simple and practical means where they could find help. He considered the zeal for professional ethics manifested by his colleagues to be a mask for professional jealousy; and he calmly accepted his expulsion from the medical society and the social isolation consequent to that expulsion. In several hearings he defended himself with great acumen and with the honest indignation of a good conscience. Anyone introducing this theme into conversation naturally touched a sensitive spot.

Max was very amiable and not easily ruffled when it came to other matters. But, on this one point, he could become very caustic, indeed he would brook no contradiction to his views. The changes in medical practice during this past decade involved him in new difficulties. He was always antagonistic to health insurance because he felt that the large volume of patients treated by doctors under health plans made conscientious treatment impossible. He persisted in this view even when the expansion of these insurance groups caused a continued drastic reduction in the number of private patients so that his income steadily declined more and more. In conclusion, although the introduction of salvarsan in the treatment of syphilis was generally greeted with great acclaim, he could not bring himself to place any confidence in this treatment; and he kept to his older, proven methods. These circumstances all contributed to the fact that his practice dwindled to a minimum and increased the risk of a confrontation whenever he was in the company of anyone holding an opposing view. Naturally, his wife, too, was involved in all of these difficulties. She loved and admired her husband and, in his absence, defended his views as passionately as though life or death depended on them. However, she herself was not deterred by all this from contradicting him at every possible opportunity; so, despite their mutual affection, there was no peace in their home. What was intolerable for my brother-in-law, to begin with, was that my sister could find nothing in Hamburg to satisfy her, that she constantly complained about her loneliness, that she longed "for home" and pined for her relatives. On one occasion, when, in the very first year of their marriage, he found her depressed and asked the reason for it, she said she missed the "children" so much. This statement disconcerted him; the birth of their first child was still a few months in the offing. So she explained that "the children" were her youngest sisters. Immediately, he was more than ready to have her invite us for the summer vacation. This trip to Hamburg was a great event for us.

Never before had we gone so far away; besides, we had not even met our brother-in-law as yet. We had every reason to be charmed by him. He received us with brotherly affection and plied us with attentions. Of course, only our sister went with us to all the tourist attractions of Hamburg as he did not have time for that; but on Sunday he went out with us. When he took us to the Alster Pavilion, where we could choose any cake or tortes we wished to have with our coffee, we were a more appreciative audience than our sister as we sat there among an elegant and international crowd of tourists, enjoying the view of the Inner Alster with its many steamships and sailboats. We also appreciated having a supper of hitherto unknown delicacies set before us in the attractive *Ratskeller*. We thoroughly enjoyed our brother-in-law's pranks; he scarcely ever spoke in a serious vein and, instead, inexhaustibly produced quips for every variety of situation. Usually it took the form of an amusing anecdote which, when occasion demanded, could be delivered in a very dry tone. We also listened with the greatest pleasure when he played the piano and sang for us by the hour. He had never had much instruction; but, being very musical, through constant practice he became an accomplished pianist. Besides, he was a born comedian; a brother of his actually followed that profession. Accordingly, my brother-in-law was in no way at fault when, despite the many pleasures it offered, Hamburg lost its attraction for us over the years and we failed to satisfy our sister's desire to spend all our free time with her. At fault were the unpleasant circumstances just described, which gradually mounted in their household.

With the advent of their children, the difficulties increased. The telegram informing us of the birth of their first small daughter arrived on what was, again, a memorable day. It was the twenty-seventh of September, 1904, and my mother and all her employees were busy moving the huge lumber supply to her recently acquired property. When my sister Erna delivered the good news from the apartment to the lumberyard, Mother turned to the owner of the wagon being used to transport the wood. She said to him: "I have to go on a trip. I entrust everything to you and rely on you to see that all will be done properly."

He was one of those business associates who revered her as if she were his mother. He accepted the assignment with pride and joy.

She went home, prepared for the trip, and set off on the very same day. My sister Frieda had already gone to Hamburg to nurse Else in her confinement. After the delivery, the obstetrician who took care of my sister teased her for having continually cried out: "Send a telegram! Send a telegram!" He was delighted to meet this mother whose presence had been demanded with such vehemence.

We were all allowed a vote in the choice of a name. The aunts were all in agreement: the little one was to be called Ilse. To this, her paternal grandmother's name, Mathilde, was added as was that of the friend at whose invitation my sister had gone to Hamburg: Felicitas. Tiny Ilse Mathilde Felicitas was a frail child. But then, her mother was also frail. Teaching until shortly before her wedding had exhausted her strength; she suffered constantly from headaches and had a very difficult pregnancy. When we were in Hamburg a few months before the baby's birth, no one mentioned the expected event to us. After all, we were still children; at home such things were not discussed with us although our friends had long since "enlightened" us. Ever after, my sister commended me for having been so solicitous about her in those weeks, helping her up and down the stairs, etc., even though, officially, I was "uninformed." Upon returning home from this vacation, we were initiated into the secret after all, because the "grown-ups" could not bear to send off the baby's entrancing layette without showing it to us.

My sister was determined to breast-feed her children and this for as long a time as possible—so long, in fact, that only a new pregnancy would compel her to stop. They all developed well;

Ilse remained frail but was really healthy; the others were sturdy youngsters from birth. The eldest was most attached to her mother and shy toward strangers. Her grandmother was baffled by the fact that, when she was visiting, the child did not want to come to her; other children had always been drawn to her. Later this reticence disappeared. The children all shared fully their mother's passionate love for her relatives and demanded, time and time again, to be allowed to visit in Breslau.

Prior to that time, my mother had hardly traveled anywhere; only "going home," i.e., to Lublinitz, regularly to see her brothers and sisters and to visit the graves of her parents, as well as the tiny ones of the children she had left behind there. Ordinarily that trip required only a Sunday. On rarer occasions she paid a short visit to her relatives in Berlin. Her youngest sister Emma was married there. After the death of their parents, Emma's brothers and sisters had looked after her as though she were a child; and there was something childlike about her all her life long. On one visit my mother arrived at Emma's house unexpectedly. When her young brother-in-law opened the door he was so happy to see her that he picked her up bodily to carry her in to his little wife. That whole family, parents and three children, often spent their vacation with us.

Naturally, for my sister Else there was no greater joy than a visit from her mother. In the first years, Mother spent a week with her at Christmastime. That was a long, long time for her and for us. Even though ordinarily she was away from home during the whole day, the house seemed to be dead and empty while she was in Hamburg; and we did not know what to do with ourselves. She was just as uncomfortable. As a rule she was never ill, but the climate of Hamburg to which she was unaccustomed gave her rheumatic pains. Besides, she found it very difficult to spend such a long time in any household that was not kosher. She normally had a very good appetite and ate heartily; there, however, everything was distasteful to her. The most painful aspect for her, though, was that she felt bound to disapprove of her eldest daughter's methods of housekeeping as well as of Else's accustomed manner of treating her husband and children. These maternal remonstrances, given unsparingly, were totally ineffective since Else refused to consider herself in any way at fault. The pleasure of being together was spoiled for them both by these constant arguments. It was almost worse when Else visited us in Breslau for there she ran into a closed phalanx.

When her second child was born, I was living with my sister. I had left school at Easter in 1906 and, at Else's request, had gone to keep her company and to help her; while doing so, I was to learn how to run a household and how to care for children. My return ticket, good for six weeks, was used by someone else and I stayed on. At home, as the spoiled youngest in the happy circle of family and relatives, my life had been far more pleasant and comfortable. Despite that, I never expressed a desire to go home. Knowing how deeply I would hurt my sister by such a request, I dared not make it. She was fifteen years my senior and had lovingly cared for me when I was a small child. Even now, she assured me, she loved me as dearly as she did her own children. Little Ilse was still alone when I arrived there; she was a year-and-a-half old. My principal task was to take care of her. Although usually extremely shy, she got used to me very quickly and stayed with me as happily as with her mother. Generally speaking, children have always been attracted and attached to me even when I paid them no attention. At first my brother-in-law told my sister (not in my presence, but she often repeated it to me later) that it was beyond him how she could entrust her child to a girl who was such a dreamer. She would reply, emphatically: "*That* girl is *my* sister!"

Actually Else was justified in trusting me. When during the summer, our future sister-in-law, Martha, came on a visit from America, they would sometimes "go shopping"[24] together for an entire morning, leaving me with both children and all the housework. Despite all the usual interruptions, my brother-in-law, who arrived punctually on the minute, would find his dinner ready and the babies cared for. The second child was born on the fifth of June. He was a sturdy little fellow. As his sister had received three names, he was to have no fewer. His father demanded equality. The aunts could not reach unanimity this time. The majority were for Werner, a small minority for Ulrich. The second place was reserved for my father's name. So he became Werner Siegfried Ulrich. A licensed maternity nurse was engaged for a short stay. After that, I cared for mother and child; true, before long, my sister was up and about and resumed her duties. Still she was in need of some care and assistance.

The little boy was truly a sunny child, beaming with contentment and amiable toward everyone. The following year, when he came to visit in Breslau for the first time, he charmed everyone and became the favorite there. Of course, as I had known him from his very first days, he was most attached to me. Once the American guest had introduced us to photography, we took a lot of pictures with a small camera I received as a gift at the time. My sister carefully mounted all the pictures in an album. When the children began to talk, she also wrote down their bright sayings. I almost believe that the days I spent with her were the happiest ones of my sister's marriage. During that time she had the company for which she always yearned. Together we did all of the work, and together we shared the joy in the children and the worry about them. Often, of an evening, when the children were asleep and it was not yet time for my brother-in-law to come home, we would read something together. And, when, rarely, a trustworthy girl was available, we went to the theater or to a concert. Even though I was still so young, Else discussed everything with me. Usually I listened quietly and did not readily contradict her. When it happened that I felt duty-bound to express a differing opinion, it was done so calmly that no excited argument ever arose. Because my sister was contented, things were easier for my brother-in-law as well. I liked him very much and was always glad to have him come home after his office hours at noon and in the evening. I had even taken to studying the stock quotations since, usually, his first question was: "Edith, how are the Lombards doing?" (Max, that is to say, had begun to do some speculating on the stock market, cautiously and after many calculations, so as to have a second iron in the fire when and if his practice should at any time fail to support the family.)

And so I stayed in Hamburg for ten months. My mother did not clamor for my return although she certainly missed her youngest very much. Indeed she was most happy when she had all her seven children with her. She probably had the same reason for not recalling me as I had for staying: the fear of hurting my sister. My other sisters and brothers could not understand my long absence; to them it seemed to show a lack of affection. In the end a peremptory summons came after all. The serious illness of little Harald, our eldest brother's second child, occasioned it. Of course, my efforts to help were of no more avail than those of the others; but whenever a serious blow threatened the family, we closed ranks in order to meet it together. Only two other times did I go to Hamburg for longer periods (i.e., for the summer vacation). Later, my visits became shorter and less frequent. However, the bond between us was not weakened on that account; my sister wrote often and in great detail. Besides, if at all possible, she came home to us at least once a year; and, as long as the children were small, she brought all of them along.

My sister Rosa was the maternity nurse when the third child was born. But Erna and I got to know Anni Martha Erika while she was still an infant as we spent our vacation there soon after her birth. My brother-in-law was a very affectionate father. When he came home at noon he would pick up the youngest at the moment, and, singing, he would carry it around in his arms; when the little one was old enough to eat at table, it was seated beside him in the high chair so he could feed it. But as they grew older, he no longer knew how to treat them. The children naturally suffered because of the increasing tensions between father and mother. The eldest, without their realizing it, was most influenced by her mother and took sides with her against her father. The youngest was most capable of taking care of herself. She had inherited the characteristic sociability of the paternal side of her family and was always cheerful and enterprising; and even as a child, she spent most of her time outside her home with her friends. The little boy had the hardest time. Of all the things my mother deplored in Hamburg, the treatment this child received caused her the most intense anxiety. My sister, who had brought up so many children and who prided herself on her ability to understand them, was never able to establish any rapport with her only son. He, who as a baby had always been so amiable and sunny, began to declare by the time he was only four or five years old that he did not want to grow up; and he became increasingly naughty and embittered. He was a little teaser; when his sisters complained, his mother scolded him endlessly; and the reports of his bad behavior earned him stern reproofs when his father came home after work. Anni as a child had a habit of complaining frequently, wailing loudly: "Werner is teasing me!"

Once she was the only one to visit us in Breslau with her mother, as it was during the school term and the older ones had to stay in Hamburg. Anni was playing all alone in the garden, yet suddenly she screamed: "Werner!"

Someone went to the window and called out to her, "Why, Werner is not even here!"

Promptly she replied: "But he always teases me!"

His grandmother and aunts heartily pitied the poor little boy who, most likely, was reproved even after that kind of a complaint. The older he grew, the more he rebelled against his mother. He flew into veritable tantrums and spoke to her in a disrespectful and contemptuous way. In Breslau he was a completely transformed person: happy to be in surroundings where he knew himself to be loved; friendly to all; despite being a real mischiefmaker who liked to tease everyone, grateful for the smallest gift and for every kind word; always ready to help, and from his earliest years capable of making himself useful in the business. He liked to visit all the relatives; and they were all very fond of him. He was most attached to his grandmother. Actually, during the last few days of his visit, he would never leave her side. From her he meekly accepted the longest exhortations. She had never had as much to say to any of us. But she wished to take advantage of the vacations to teach Werner better behavior at home. He apparently had very good intentions but little hope of improvement. Tearfully he would confide to us how he was treated at home. And we knew that he was only stating facts. Since they no longer kept a maid, he slept in the maid's room and had to take care of it himself. He would have liked to make it more attractive, but he was not given the means to do so. His clothing was equally neglected. As long as the children were small, we had given them attractive new clothing on every birthday. But these "good" clothes were always kept for an occasion, and they could not be worn. Later it was more difficult to give clothing when one had no opportunity to try them on for size. Werner could not bring any of his friends to the house because his mother would not have it. Therefore he got used to playing on the street. Later he joined an athletic club, and the respect he there enjoyed compensated him somewhat for the suffering at home.

During the years in which the children grew up, things finally peaked to a crisis. The three children's arrival so soon after one another and her protracted nursing of them had sapped the mother's strength. She was incapable of handling the housekeeping chores but refused the assistance of a maid. As a result, she was always under excessive strain and grew more and more nervous. On the other hand, my brother-in-law, already suffering because of the difficulties in his professional life, found no relaxation at home. So it came about that once more we received a special delivery letter from Hamburg; this time, however, the news it conveyed was devastating. My brother-in-law briefly informed my mother that he had left his home. He demanded that she come to take her daughter home; until she did so, he refused to return to his house. According to my calculation, this must have been during the Easter vacation of 1914. At the time, I was a student in Göttingen but was at home in Breslau for the university vacation. Deeply depressed, we sat together around the table after our lunch, taking counsel together. My courageous mother did not feel up to this situation. Since I saw how she hated the very idea of the trip, I said: "If it's all right with you, I'll go there."

At once, relieved and obviously surprised, she told me: "If you want to do that, I would be most grateful."

But then she looked at me, and, as I, too, must have been pale with excitement, she immediately added: "No, it is too difficult for you as well."

I assured her that indeed I would manage, and so I was allowed to set out on the trip. At that time, our sister-in-law Martha and her first-born, little Wolfgang, were staying with my sister. Martha could be a cheerful companion; but, faced with such a situation, she was pretty helpless. As the two of them had wanted to spare my mother worry, they had called in Uncle Emil from Berlin, hoping he could persuade Max to return; but having had no luck, Uncle had returned home without having accomplished anything. I was received with joy and gratitude. We telephoned Max to let him know about my arrival, and I arranged to meet him in the city. He was very polite and friendly to me; but it was evident at once how upset he was. I had to listen to everything he had to say: all the bitterness that had accumulated in him over the years; not merely complaints about my sister but also reproaches about my mother because right after the couple became engaged, she had written to Max assuring him he would find Else an obedient wife. Our good mother! In the happiness of those days she had probably assumed that all she had ever wished and hoped for had become a reality; and she had therefore promised too much. Max insistently demanded that I take Else back to Breslau. We should have her treated by a gynecologist or a nerve specialist and see to it that she regain her health. Thereafter, on condition that she promised to behave in a way entirely different from heretofore, she would be allowed to return.

I saw clearly that he would in no way budge from his demands; and I had to do my utmost to get Else to go back home with me. This was no small matter. She was determined not to surrender her rights and duties as homemaker, wife, and mother. Most unbearable for her was the thought of the physical separation from her husband, and, despite the deep dissension and the daily irritation, she was firmly convinced that he, too, could not do without her. She was upset to an almost abnormal degree, and this was evident from her incessant talking. There was no respite from it even at night. I had to stay with her constantly; and she told me in greatest detail about her marital life; she would interrupt herself from time to time when it suddenly occurred to her that she was speaking to an inexperienced young girl; then she would ask my forgiveness for speaking about things which were probably very embarrassing for me to hear. After a great deal of effort, she declared herself ready to go back with me provided Max returned to their home before she left and only on condition that Martha would stay there to care for the household and for the two older children; Anni, who was not yet going to school, would be coming with us. Else did not want her husband to have one of his own sisters substitute for her; as she did not get along too well with her sisters-in-law, she was afraid they might have an unfavorable influence on her husband and children.

Martha agreed to everything on condition that we obtain her husband's agreement to this extension of her vacation. Because Arno was such a good-hearted fellow, that was not difficult to do. (Eventually, though, he refused to be parted from his wife and child for the whole of Else's lengthy banishment. After a few weeks he went to Hamburg and fetched them both home, and so one of the Gordon sisters took over the regime of the house after all. On that occasion the two brothers-in-law had a rather violent altercation because Max again censured my mother; and Arno, the hothead, got very excited over that. Once such an outburst was over, it was forgotten by Arno, and there remained not the slightest trace of resentment in him; but my brother-in-law harbored every insult for years, unable to forget.)

I had to apprise Max of the conditions, and he agreed to them. About the time we expected him at the house, I kept the children busy in the nursery where I distracted them by telling them stories. Else opened the door for her husband as usual. Throughout the years, she had made a habit of waving goodbye to him from a balcony when he went to his practice and of watching for his return from that same balcony so she could open the door for him promptly. Their meeting was long and intimate. I surmise that it consisted mostly of passionately tender caresses and that very little was said by either of them. Finally, the father came to greet his children. The following morning we set out for home. My brother-in-law accompanied us to the station. Before the train pulled out, he reached in at the window, to take my hand, thanking me for my help. At first, my sister was also very grateful. Later, she used to say, that while recognizing my very good intentions, she could not thank me; I had given her poor advice, and she should on no account have left the house.

En route, the lively and amusing Anni kept us so occupied there was no room for sadness. The time in Breslau was difficult for all of us. My mother wanted as much as possible to carry out her son-in-law's wishes. Else had to consult a physician and go away to recuperate. For a few weeks, she went to the *Riesengebirge*[25] and then to Lublinitz; after all, she had spent her childhood there and had kept up a close relationship with our aunts. Finally she received permission to return to her home. No such conflict ever occurred again even though Else certainly had not changed much. She had become somewhat cautious and was more careful about the way she talked. And, with advancing age, both of them had become somewhat calmer. Added to this was the fact that, as the daughters grew up, they were a support for their mother and were completely in her confidence. Besides, the dwindling of his practice compelled my brother-in-law to exercise the utmost moderation in everything. Now he had reason to thank his wife for her ability to make do with next to nothing and for her having put some savings aside in earlier days. Their pressing financial need and my sister's continued poor health constantly worried my mother, but the worst crisis in Hamburg had been weathered.

4

A few years earlier, my sister Frieda's brief marital tragedy had run its course; and, not long after Frieda, Arno had married. My mother had definitely approved of his decision to marry. She liked Martha well enough as long as she came to our house merely as a friend. Martha's cheerful disposition and her faithful attachment to our entire family made all of us very fond of her. But once we all lived together on a more intimate basis, many difficulties resulted from the great differences in our temperaments. The spacious house into which we moved shortly after Frieda's wedding was designed for two families; it was divided vertically, and had two staircases. Arno and Martha came to live with us in this house. For a while, we all used the larger section and rented the smaller one to tenants. Later, the young couple set up housekeeping in the smaller one; and my mother, her four daughters, and the one small granddaughter, Erika, lived in the larger unit. Nothing came of the hope that my sister-in-law might be a real help in the business. The manner of doing business she had learned in America was so foreign to our traditions that my mother would have preferred to dispense with her services altogether. Finally, her help was limited to her going on errands for which no one else could find time. She was always glad to oblige as "shopping" was one of her favorite occupations. One constant stumbling block for my mother was her having to witness every day such a disorganized household under her own roof. The difficulties increased, of course, as the family grew larger. Martha wanted many children; they were to be sturdy, healthy, and good-looking. She herself was well-built and a glowing picture of health.

Her hopes were long in awaiting fulfillment. She was therefore all the happier about her first pregnancy. She kept assuring us there would be "twins." During the delivery, we were all in the dining room; and she kept up a conversation with us through the half-open door to her room. When, at last, little Wolfgang was handed to her, she kept asking for the second child. My mother, and the experienced gynecologist, as well, declared they had never seen the like of it. Wolfgang was the kind of child she had longed for, as were Numbers three and four, Helmut and Lotte; all were big and sturdy, blond and blue-eyed, chubby and rosy-cheeked. However, it was apparent even in her first year that Eva, who came second, was not entirely normal. She learned to talk very late and never quite correctly, and she was also somewhat retarded. That this child was not treated properly since her parents lacked understanding and that they failed to teach the other children to make the necessary allowances for their sister caused my mother a new and nagging worry. She, herself, had far more sympathy for Eva than for the three healthy children. At times she would have the child stay with us for a while so as to teach her, most patiently, not only how to talk and how to eat properly but many other things besides. Little Erika was my mother's chief support in this endeavor, for since Erika grew up with these cousins of hers as with brothers and sisters, she lovingly cared for the unhappy little creature. My sister-in-law Martha's method for bringing up her children consisted principally in giving them plenty to eat and providing them with enough sleep and fresh air. She was proud of the fact that such treatment enabled them to thrive beautifully. Should they become ill, their mother was not only sad and worried but indignant as well, as though some injustice had been done her. She admitted in all frankness that she knew nothing about caring for the sick; and she was relieved when we came to the rescue.

Having trained as a nurse, I was the first to make myself available if I chanced to be home at such a time. In February, 1920, all of the children had the grippe at the same time; one night the temperature of all three rose above 40° centigrade [104° F.]. Helmut, four years old at the time, was the hardest hit; he had a pneumonia which dragged on with recurring attacks for nearly three months. When the others had recovered, he was isolated from them and put up in a large room adjoining my study. When he was alone, he would call out to me: "Aunt Edith, come on in. Bring your homework (my philosophical thesis was "homework"!) and do it here. My mother always leaves children lie all alone when they're sick."

At that I would gather all my papers together and make an attempt to do my writing at my brother's desk, next door. Should the small patient then call me to his bedside, continually, I would say to him: "Helmut, if you keep calling me like this, I won't be able to work!"

"Well, you don't have to!" was his prompt response. And that was so convincing that I went to play with him. As a result he became very attached to me.

When, some time after his recovery, my sister Erna became engaged, he came over to our house one Sunday afternoon while we were all seated around the diningroom table having coffee and cake. He walked over to me and whispered into my ear: "Will you be my bride?"

I accepted his proposal immediately, took him on my lap, and gave him some of my cake, saying that bride and groom had to share everything. He liked that very much; but, suddenly, he became alarmed: "I just ate some cake at home and didn't give you any."

Almost immediately, though, he calmed himself, saying: "But at that time you weren't my bride yet."

From that day on he brought me all the little projects he finished in kindergarten. I had to save them carefully for, from time to time, he would pull out the chest in which I collected them to check on how many he had given me so far. Once he stood in front of the long row of my books on philosophy and counted them. "After a while," I said, "you will have to read all of those so we can talk about them." A brief pause, then, "Yes," he replied, very decisively, "when I grow up, I'll read them all."

For years, he clung to this fantasy of our engagement. Occasionally, though, he did have misgivings about it; something seemed not to tally properly. Once he asked me: "Aunt Edith, when I grow up, will you still be grown-up?"

Finally, his elders' teasing made it clear to him that his expectations of marriage were in vain. But that happened in my absence; and when I came to visit again, he confided to his father that he would very much like to keep on with the engagement.

I remember one particular day of his serious illness very vividly. The crisis had come. Pale and unconscious, the child lay in his little bed; sometimes in his fever he would say a few words; his pulse was scarcely discernible. Erna and I sat beside him. She was already a qualified physician but had seen few cases like this. She had given up all hope, and large tears coursed down her cheeks. I was calmer and much more confident. During the war, while caring for my typhoid patients, I had seen many a case of pneumonia and had often experienced how, after a very severe collapse which closely resembled an agony preceding death, the patient would recover. At one point, my sister-in-law came in and, bending over the bed, said, weeping with indignation: "How terrible to have to lose such a beautiful child!"

Then she left again. In dismay, we looked at one another. What a very strange, almost inconceivable, sentiment these words reflected! A little while later the pediatrician arrived, accompanied by a lung specialist. They completed their examination, and the internist ordered that a tub of hot water be brought. The motionless little boy was lowered into the tub and held there; in a short while he began to kick vigorously, thoroughly splashing the gentlemen. When the little fellow, now rosy-cheeked and wide-eyed, was put back into his small bed, he was given a cup of very strong coffee to stimulate his heart. When he noticed the pungent aroma of the drink, he cried out in surprise: "But that's not children's coffee! That's people-coffee!"

Then he demanded that we darken the room and leave him alone. "When little children are supposed to sleep, then big people ought to go away."

We breathed a sigh of relief. The violent illness was vanquished at last.

Later, should any of the children say they were not well, my sister-in-law would simply come over and say to me: "Wolfgang (or Helmut) sends his love and wants to tell you he's sick."

Helmut had another bout with pneumonia when he was seven years old. It happened to be during my summer vacation. This time, once the doctor had made the diagnosis, I immediately took over complete care of him. I made one chest compress after the other and told him stories to keep him quiet. I had exhausted my entire supply of myths and fairy tales and finally resorted to Bible stories. When I was telling him about the fall of man and the expulsion from Paradise he said, reproachfully, "How can you tell me something so terrible?"

But, otherwise, he never tired of listening. If his mother brought him something to eat, he would accept it graciously but add immediately, "You can go now, I don't need two people."

Sometimes I had to deny him something he had demanded, and then, in a sulk, he would disappear under the covers. I sat quietly at my work and took no more notice of him. After a few minutes, he would pop out with a beaming smile, and peace was restored. When my brother came home at noon, he would take over from me so I could have my dinner; he did the same in the evening. At seven o'clock, the small patient was tucked in for the night. Then he would dismiss me readily, only taking care to remind me pointedly to be there at seven in the morning. One Sunday, I heard Martha, in the next room, complaining bitterly that she could no longer stand being tied down, that she just had to get away for some fresh air. My brother was very embarrassed because, as he told himself, I could surely hear everything. When he came into the nursery, I convinced him that they should feel completely free to go somewhere, and that I would gladly stay with the little boy. So the entire family went to their garden in the suburbs, and we were alone in the house. Both of us were completely happy to have it so. A few hours later the others returned much refreshed; Martha assured me she was an entirely new person again. Two weeks later the doctor came again and was very surprised to find not the slightest trace of an inflammation left. Now I could resign my nursing duties, and my sister-in-law happily exclaimed (to Helmut): "Muzchen, if you get anything like this again, we'll call Aunt Edith right away. Mama's no good with things like this."

Any time the children were sick, my mother would look in on them several times a day. But at each visit she would notice something which would annoy her. If she made any kind of remark about it, an unpleasant argument followed. Therefore, as much as possible, she avoided going to her daughter-in-law's home. The height of disorder in that home was reached when Martha's mother and sister brought the children for a visit from America.

My sister-in-law spoke constantly about these relatives, always with the warmest love, praising their beauty and their intelligence, their wit and clever ideas. As far back as their school days, she had regaled my sister Else with glowing accounts of her beautiful Mama; and she was not content until she had brought the two of them together. When that finally happened, Else had quite a shock; upon close scrutiny, one could detect in Frau Kaminski traces of former beauty in the finely drawn features, but by now she was really very disfigured by an eye disease and a skin rash. Moreover, when she came later on a visit from America, her attire made her conspicuous even from a distance; she went in for vivid colors, immense hats, and equally immense shoes. Mother and daughter had lived together in America. Since Martha's return to Germany, they frequently exchanged long letters, telling one another in great detail all the small events of daily life; and they continued in their correspondence the banter so characteristic in their conversational tone. For months, the visit of these relatives was joyously anticipated. Indeed, Martha made a point of looking forward to any coming

event as long and as thoroughly as possible as one would then be
certain in any case of the pleasure of anticipation. My mother,
on the other hand, always cautioned against premature jubila-
tion; she disliked making plans a long time in advance, and
always spoke of future events with the added phrase: "with the
help of God," or "God willing." The American guests brought
along huge trunks and baskets out of which a motley array of
contents overflowed: dresses; hats; shoes in all colors, shapes
and sizes; sweets and toys; magazines and books. All of this was
either for their own use or for distribution as gifts. It was frequently difficult to find people who could use them. It was also
impossible to find closet or drawer space to accommodate this
assortment of gaudy splendor. But then they did not even expect that. They were quite accustomed to live out of a suitcase,
and what was extricated therefrom could stay on the floor. In
America they probably had servants who continually cleaned
up after them. Here, at best, in this household with four small
children, there was but one maid; ordinarily, though, there was
only a cleaning woman who worked by the hour. When, then,
two adults and two children were added to the household, even
a semblance of order went by the board. My sister-in-law had
become accustomed to doing the housework, simplifying everything as much as possible in order to make time for other things.
Her mother was upset to see her doing chores which, in America, were assigned to husbands or to servants. This resulted in
constant friction between mother-in-law and son-in-law as well
as between mother and daughter. After her last visit, the old
lady left in such an ill-temper that we really pitied her. With all
her idiosyncracies, she was a very kind woman who dearly loved
her children and grandchildren; most gracious toward all whom
she met, she was vivacious, had wide interests, was witty and
very entertaining. She gave no indication of the many burdens
life had inflicted on her.

    Besides the deficiencies in her housekeeping and child-rearing,
there was something else which disappointed my mother about
her daughter-in-law. As long as she had been no more than a
guest at our house, Martha had showered us all with affectionate attentions (which were undoubtedly sincere), and she was

overjoyed upon being accepted into the family. I still remember how she embraced my mother, laughing and crying simultaneously, when Mother greeted her as her son's bride. My sister Else, who always looked down upon her younger brother to some extent, even insisted that Martha cared less about him than about the family. No one would have imputed to her a desire of insuring her own advantage at the expense of others. But over the years, my mother had a growing impression that her son was being influenced along these lines. As far as he was concerned, selfish motives were totally foreign to his nature. He was a very good brother to us and had formerly loved giving us expensive presents occasionally; for instance, when Erna began to study medicine he gave her an excellent microscope. Also, for a long while, he had regularly set aside some of his income for Gerhard, his eldest nephew, of whom he was particularly fond. After all, he said, as a bachelor he had no need to save for himself. Until he married, my mother was sole owner of the business; Arno and Frieda were both employees with power of attorney. My sister-in-law had a small private income which was invested in our business as operating capital; although it was a welcome aid as cash on hand, its size in comparison to the value of the large piece of property and the inventory of the well-stocked lumberyard was insignificant. Still, to her, its investment warranted a claim to co-ownership; and, as the family grew, she added to this an appeal that the children's future be secured. My mother suffered a great deal because of these arguments. She had invested all her energy on behalf of her children and anything we possessed, we owed to her. She had hardly any wants or needs for herself; indeed, her daughters had to see to it that her wardrobe was adequately maintained. We usually made birthday gifts of the clothes she needed, for, otherwise, she firmly objected to our purchasing new things. Even in these cases, she would protest that we had gone to unnecessary expense. Should we suggest that, after years of wear, she discard something or at least wear it only around the house, she would, with quite comical indignation, defend her "good, new dress." So it was that we were all content to live confidently dependent on our mother's providence, and we never gave a thought to tak-

ing precautions for ourselves; among us brothers and sisters as
well there was no keeping of accounts. Because we never even
permitted ourselves to think of a time when Mother would no
longer be with us, it could not even have occurred to us to demand anything like property settlements for the future. According to Jewish sensibility, it is a sign of heartlessness to regard
the death of a beloved one as an inevitable future event, to keep
it soberly in view, to discuss it, and to make provisions for it.
Such measures are left to the "goyim"[26] to whom one ascribed as
characteristic the lack of tender feelings and of compassion. Consequently, the introduction of such topics and considerations in
our family occasioned a great deal of pain for my mother. But
once made suspicious that her daughter-in-law was selfishly intent on her own advantage, Mother saw herself obliged, in turn,
to insure her own daughters against any future infringement of
their rights. She began to consult us to find a solution; and once
we were all agreed upon a course of action, I was to present our
proposition to Arno on behalf of my mother and sisters and in
Mother's presence. She thought out this plan because they were
all afraid of his temper and none trusted herself to have sufficient self-control to remain calm and objective in the face of his
angry outbursts.

It was a most distressing moment when Arno was called into
this family council. He was very quiet as I made my speech and
replied in but a few words which contained neither a clear yes
nor no. He was deeply hurt that he should have been dealt with
so formally and that the authority to confront him should have
been delegated to his youngest sister. He invoked the assistance
of another mediator: someone in whom both he and my mother
had complete confidence, her brother Eugen from Berlin. I
have already mentioned that this younger brother was very attached to her and that he often assisted her in business matters.
He was an exceptionally good businessman. The manufactur-
ing firm he had personally established exported machine parts
over a wide area, especially to England and Russia, and he managed the affairs of this large enterprise with great acumen. Until
he could count on his own sons to provide him with competent
assistance, he often called upon my brother to help him with the

more important bookkeeping matters; as a result, the two of them had the greatest confidence in one another. According to the first settlement we made, my mother remained proprietor and Arno was taken on as a partner with a share in the profits. When she was about seventy years old, her brothers and sisters as well as her children began to urge her to retire and to entrust the business entirely to her son. She would not hear of it, and I always supported her resistance as it was clear to me that her activity in the business was an inseparable part of her life. Ten years later it never even occurred to anyone anymore to suggest retirement. Yet at this advanced age she did undertake another extensive reorganization: she registered Arno as owner of the business and assured for herself and for Frieda only a share in the profits. But in the trio's distribution of duties there was no change at all. However, from that time on my mother called her son the "Boss." To outsiders, he was now the responsible policy-making head of the firm who concluded contracts. Among the businessmen of the city he occupied the respected position which was the prerogative of the head of such an old and respected firm. He now played the role in society which a mature man required to satisfy his self-esteem. Of course, initiates knew that he was reaping what my mother had sown, that which she had preserved and protected by a lifetime of labor.

5

Decades earlier the housekeeping had been turned over to my sister Rosa. If my mother often suffered under the violent temper of the "Boss" while at work, then her return home was frequently a matter of jumping from the frying pan into the fire. This particular brother and sister were very much alike in temperament; but neither wanted to admit that fact. Each was shocked at the other's faults, never aware of how consistently both were guilty of the same kind of behavior. Rosa's naturally quick temper had probably become excessively prone to explode because she felt so dissatisfied. Every effort on the part of well-meaning relatives to help her make "a good match" had been rejected indignantly. After Frieda's unhappy marriage, no one dared to introduce that topic anymore. Although she was quite independent in running the household, she never really felt herself to be mistress of the house. Mother and sisters all had particular preferences which she had to take into account, though this often happened only after she had made strong and very vocal objections. She suspected the others disparaged her work, and so she yearned to be doing something else. However, while she expressed her feelings vocally when faced by the family's opposition, she lacked sufficient initiative and energy to implement her plans for a career. My mother who longed for peace and quiet at home suffered a great deal because of this daily tension. Anything she or Frieda suggested, any opinion they voiced, immediately met with violent opposition in most instances. Both of them gave generous help with the household chores, taking time for this in the early morning hours, as well as in the lunch break and in the evening after working hours. Besides that, they had converted an area of the lumberyard into a garden which they tended, sowing, planting, and harvesting; indeed, if they had any time left over, they prepared the vegetables and fruit so that, when they were picked up, they were ready to cook. But all of their services were rewarded with sharp criticism.

My mother often had to submit to being rebuked like some incompetent servant, as though she herself had never run a household. After all, she had cooked in her own parents' home for the huge family and for numerous guests to everyone's satisfaction. And her children were never happier than when Mother herself cared for them. Naturally, after our father's death she had to relinquish the housekeeping to others; and now she was unaccustomed to some of its details. But on Sundays, she delighted in taking over all the housework herself because she was so happy to see all of us sisters go out together for a morning's excursion; then, in leisurely fashion, she prepared everything for our return and, with evident pleasure, lovingly served us her own home-cooked food. During my years as a student when I secretly dreamed of an ideal home, it was always one in which my mother lived with only Erna and me and in which she cared for us both. The daily domestic disturbances were exhausting enough for everyone; but more profound disagreements were added to them. My mother wanted to keep the family together as much as possible; all of us should share both joys and sorrows. Most of all, those who were paired off because of their closeness in age should not be separated. Where Erna and I were concerned, this was no problem. As it was, during our student years, we reinforced the bonds between us anyway so that we were even closer than we had been in childhood. We objected only when, simply because they had so few acquaintances of their own, our much older sisters were expected to join the group when we got together with our friends. More serious difficulties arose between Frieda and Rosa. These two were vastly dissimilar in character and had very little in common to add to the bond of blood by way of shared intellectual interests. Moreover Rosa's unsatisfied need for independence now manifested itself by her demand for something of her very own. She began to object to "always being paired off with Frieda." She refused to keep on dressing alike; she wanted a room of her own which she could arrange to her own taste; she also wanted to have a social life of her own. These were valid, reasonable requests. I was provided with all these things as a matter of course without ever having said a word about any of them, yet in her case they aroused opposition because she demanded them so bluntly. Moreover, as it had been my mother's special concern since Frieda's divorce to spare her further grief, Rosa's craving for independence, primarily directed against this sister, pained my mother extremely. Added to this was the not totally unfounded suspicion that in friendly discussions with acquaintances outside the family circle Rosa complained about her mother and sister and about the conflict at home. Not infrequently it happened that women who had originally been my friends would look after Rosa in my absence, establishing very close ties with her. If, occasionally, I learned from them what impression they had gained of our home life from Rosa's stories, then, despite my appreciation of Rosa's daily sacrifices, I had to set some of the accounts straight.

Naturally she wanted to tell no more than the truth; but she mentioned only her own suffering; and it never occurred to her to mention what the others were putting up with. These friends were enchanted by the goodness of her heart, her delicate attentiveness. In their company she was so genuinely meek and kind that they could not imagine her being so totally different in her behavior within the family circle.

My mother used to wish that Rosa would expend on her next of kin a small portion of the kindness she lavished on her friends. But even the relations with her friends suffered because of her reserve and a certain narrowness and inflexibility of judgment. My mother came to dread contradiction and brusque rejection so much that finally she appeared afraid to express her preferences in her own home. In later years, she would come to me with any urgent requests she might have so that I could mention them to Rosa. "You have to tell her that. Were I to do so, she would only be contradictory."

That is to say that as I grew older I came to have more and more influence on my sister without having made any effort to do so. I will mention only one example: as the Silver Wedding anniversary of our eldest brother was approaching, my mother wanted very much to celebrate it in our house because we had the most attractive rooms for such celebrations. By comparison, the rented apartment in which the celebrants now lived was small and crowded with all kinds of household goods and so, was entirely unsuitable for such a festivity. Mother well knew how much trouble and work Rosa would take upon herself if the party were to be held at our house. Even more than that, she hated the thought of having to deal with her daughter-in-law whose personality she found particularly difficult. But she considered it a duty of love and justice toward her eldest son. I could well empathize with her, and I also knew how to get it across to my sister. The objections were written all over her face, but she did not express them and agreed to everything without further ado. The proposal was made (by Rosa) and accepted with the greatest gratitude (by the couple). I was unable to attend the celebration myself because of a professional obligation elsewhere. According to all accounts, all went well and peacefully. How it came about that my sister, so much older than myself, allowed herself to be led by me so willingly, and how her path eventually joined my own, I must recount later in the proper context.[27]

Chapter IV

The Two Youngest Grow Up
1907-1910

1

When I reflect about the seven of us, brothers and sisters, then I must say that Erna was, by nature, the most favorably endowed of us all: pretty, open, and communicative, with deep purity and kindness of heart, exceedingly modest and unaware of her superior qualities, very talented, skilled and adaptable. So she seemed just made to be happy and to make others happy. Naturally, she also had her faults; and these were not overlooked in the bosom of the family: flaring up readily, being altogether too impressionable, and possessing a certain passivity. But these were faults of a nature easily tolerated and forgiven. Granted, her mother came to experience deep distress associated with this child, but it was not due to a difficult temper or lack of docility; rather, life would impose a heavy burden on this daughter, in which all who loved her were to be involved.

I told above about the childhood and youth we shared and about Erna's choice of a career. Even our first long separation, when I spent those ten months in Hamburg, was shortened when Erna came to spend the summer vacation there. Upon my return home, we again shared a room. And when, the following year, I passed the entrance examination for the *Gymnasium*,

115

she said: "Thank God. Now I won't have to go to school alone anymore."

For the following year, then, just as we had during our childhood, we made our pilgrimage together each morning on the bridge over the Oder to the *Ritterplatz*. On our way, she liked to recite her lessons for me; I also had to help her prepare for her *Abitur*. Attempting to break the monotony of drumming things into her memory, I would think up all manner of exercises for my "candidate." For instance, when the question had to do with English or French history, I required her to give the answer in the English or French language. She moaned a bit about my heaping on more difficulties; but, when I assured her that this would provide a most useful preparation for the examination in modern languages, she acquiesced after some minor objections. She had a very stiff examination to face. Not until the following year was our girls' school authorized to administer the tests to its own graduates. Until then everyone was referred to one of the boys' schools for examinations administered in almost all the subjects by teachers who were total strangers. Naturally, the entire family shared in the ordeal of these examinations. During the orals, I spent nearly the entire day in the school's waiting rooms where I could get a report as soon as possible after each subject, and where, also, during the breaks, I was able to offer encouragement and comfort to my sister and to her companions in affliction. By evening, Mother and nearly all of our brothers and sisters had arrived to escort the victor on her triumphant way home from the battlefield. I have already told about accompanying her on her post-graduation trip. I had to go with her when she enrolled and on her other early visits to the university. During my Pentecost vacation, I had to sit in on one lecture in each of her courses to get acquainted with the professors and the whole system. To keep her company while she studied, she even took me along to the collection of bones and ligaments kept in the Department of Anatomy. But all this lasted only during the first weeks of the semester; before long, she had other companionship. The comely young lady attracted the attention of her fellow students. The most venturesome among them introduced himself and a few of his closest acquaintances. Two of them would accompany her regularly from one class to another. Soon they arranged a tennis date; on the tennis court I met the one who was soon to supplant me at my sister's side, however not in such a way as to result in a real separation for us. This was totally unnecessary since the two of us, Hans Biberstein and I, hit it off at once. Immediately, as he took his place opposite me on the tennis court, I liked him very much. The white tennis outfit admirably set off his tanned face and his shining black hair, both of which were singularly contrasted by sparkling light eyes. He was slim, short, and muscular; and he, himself, bounced from one end of the court to the other as lightly as a rubber ball. He played with great intensity and could be driven to the brink of despair whenever, with stoic calm, I let a ball go by which, in my estimation, was beyond reach. As one's opponent, he was an implacable enemy as long as the match lasted. But when it was over, he would step up to the net and with an ingenuous look extend a friendly hand in conciliation. In our conversations on the way home, we soon discovered numerous common interests. He was as enthusiastic about history as I was and would have liked to make it his major, except that he judged the field had slim prospects financially. He followed all political events with enthusiasm and was a passionate patriot. Before my *Abitur* he often came to review history with me. I was aware, however, that he was not paying all that much attention to my discourses on the "chain-questions" of which our director was so fond. Once, sometime later, Hans admitted to my sister that she would have had some cause to be jealous of me at that particular time. I remained undisturbed by his distraction and accomplished the quota I had set for myself. As soon as it was finished, however, I felt we had both earned a reward. Usually then we would seat Erna at the piano, and dance while she played. One could not have wished for a better partner than Hans; I used to say that when one danced with him one forgave him every last fault. The two of us fully appreciated dancing for its own sake. My sister cared for it less than we; and only with my brother-in-law did she dance well and with pleasure.

During the first months of our acquaintance, we saw one another only away from home. I recall very well the evening on which we introduced our new friend to Mother. From the window she watched us return from playing tennis. And the introduction was made from street to window. At a ball the following winter, the two mothers became acquainted also. After that, the families invited one another frequently and went on outings together. Frau Biberstein was a widow and lived alone with her son. Like us, he had lost his father very early. Knowing mother and son, one gained an accurate image of that father not only from their reminiscences but also from their own personalities. In Laurahütte near Katowice, he had been a teacher not only for Jewish children but also in a public school. He must have been a real gentleman, very kind, as well as quiet and studious. Should a poor farm boy among the Polish pupils in his class desire to become a priest, he would gladly and without any remuneration prepare him for his studies. Decades later, it could happen that Frau Biberstein was joyously greeted on the street in Breslau by a Catholic priest who would then introduce himself to her as one of her husband's former students. His other pupils also remembered him with lifelong gratitude. From his father, Hans inherited a talent for teaching as well as the questing nature of a researcher.

From his mother, Hans inherited his lively temperament and natural sociability: he is an accomplished raconteur; and his fund of amusing and surprising inspirations is endless. When it came to telling stories or verses in the Upper Silesian dialect (at times these were his own compositions), or Jewish jokes, one could listen to him for hours and would end up laughing helplessly. No wonder then that he immediately became the center of attraction in every group he joined; that invitations poured in; that mothers and daughters alike considered him "a real catch." True, he was not possessed of a fortune; but, no doubt about it, he would be a success. Frau Biberstein was her husband's second wife. A son and daughter had been born of the first marriage. After the father's death, she had remained with the children for a few more years in Laurahütte, supplementing her small pension by fees earned in teaching needlecraft. When Hans was ten, she moved to Breslau. The elder son, Fritz, studied medicine, and, eventually, settled as a dermatologist in

Gleiwitz. As he soon had a good practice and, besides, had married a wealthy woman, he was able to give his mother and brother a regular subsidy. Then, Frau Biberstein no longer needed to work for a living. Fritz is a quiet, modest person, obviously very much like his father. His stepmother always insisted she loved him as much as she did her own son; likewise, the relationship between the brothers was the best imaginable; in fact, for as long as possible, Hans was kept in ignorance about their not having the same mother. On the other hand, one had the impression that Frau Biberstein had little regard for her stepdaughter, Rudolfine; at any rate, she never had much to say in her favor. One gathered from her own accounts that she had made life difficult for the child from the very beginning; and we surmised that, as life at home made the young girl so miserable, she consented to marry a man whom, otherwise, she would hardly have accepted. Hideous to begin with, he was horribly deformed and there was little in his personality to offset his physical handicaps. Nevertheless, the marriage seemed a good one. Rudolfine was kindhearted, devoted, and trusting, yet apparently had none of the intellectual gifts her brothers possessed; and she was incapable of bringing up her three daughters properly. On the whole, the Biberstein and Böhm families had as cordial an association as was customary for relatives. They visited each other, exchanged gifts, and helped one another in difficult situations. What made us reluctant to believe that all was as harmonious as appearances implied was the freedom with which son and mother not only criticized their relatives, but the way they also made fun of their weaknesses in front of us and of more distant acquaintances. But, taking this outspokenness as a true indication of their attitude would have been a mistake since it had become so habitual with them to amuse themselves at the expense of others that hardly anyone among their relatives and acquaintances was safe from their sharp tongues. In the long run, under these circumstances, relations with them were liable to become strained. Besides, both were excessively sensitive and suspected that an intent to offend lurked behind the most harmless remark made to them; they were likely to take offense instantaneously and obviously. My good mother, who always freely spoke her mind and who could never get accustomed to weighing her words scrupulously, unwittingly conjured up a storm on countless occasions. The Bibersteins, mother and son, were passionately devoted to each other. For Frau Biberstein the sun rose and set on her Hans and she spoiled him thoroughly. Despite the fact that their circumstances were modest, he was brought up to demand the best in food and clothing. His superior qualities were constantly sung in his presence, and woe betide the one who failed to join in the chorus! Since everything revolved about him, he had become inconsiderate of others on the domestic scene without being aware of this himself. On the other hand, his filial love was demonstrated in most moving ways. His mother had a heart ailment and had to be prepared at all times for a heart attack. Besides Hans, there was no one to provide nursing care, since, ordinarily, their sole domestic help was a very young maid who was far from dependable; so he slept in the same room as his mother. As he feared she would overwork whenever she started some ambitious needlework project, he would help her with it himself; his fine, skilled hands were as adept here as they were preparing specimens for anatomy classes and, later, in his medical practice. He even obeyed when maternal solicitude escalated into loving tyranny. So, when we first met him, we were amazed to learn that he was not allowed to go rowing with us. It had been forbidden him, once and for all, as too dangerous. For decades he spent every summer vacation accompanying his mother at the same resort. Out of gratitude for all she had done for him, he had made a resolution never to be parted from her, always to live with her, and to care for her in her old age.

For this reason, he had resolved not to marry, or if he did, then only a wealthy woman whose means would enable him to make the evening of his mother's life as pleasant as could be. These youthful plans for the future were seriously imperiled when he became acquainted with my sister. He often recounted for us how that had happened. He had come to the university with the prejudice that all girl students were ugly, older than himself, and wore glasses. When he went to be enrolled (at the

(l.r.) women in back row: Frau Platau, Frau Dorothea Biberstein, Frau Auguste Stein
middle row: Rose Guttmann, Paul Berg, Erna Stein, Hede Guttmann, Elfriede Stein Tworoger
front row: Edith, Lilli Platau (holding Erika Tworoger, Frieda's daughter), Rosa Stein

(l.r.) back row: Sophie Mark, Frau Guttmann, Edith
middle row: Erna Stein, Rose Guttmann, Lilli Platau

Registrar's where each student had to give the required information in person), Erna was in line ahead of him. He saw at once that she was pretty and that she wore no glasses. He could also peer over her shoulder and read her birthdate as she wrote it, and doing so, ascertained she was two months younger than himself. A few days later, a fellow student of his, Weiss by name, introduced them. Everyone at the university soon grew accustomed to seeing them together constantly.

Together they went from one lecture to the next; they sat side by side in the lecture hall, studied together, and took all the examinations together. A classmate facetiously called them "Erna-cum-Biber"-Stein. It was commonly believed that they were engaged. But they addressed one another as "*Sie*";[28] and as far as our family was concerned Hans was no more than a friend. However, before long, both of them acknowledged the attraction to be mutual. True, numerous young ladies continued to set their caps for this very desirable young man, and this gratified him; but he never again gave any of them serious consideration. And my good sister never even looked at another man. Of course, she became acquainted with other men in her classes, and was friendly toward them; but none could flatter himself that he had any prospects where she was concerned. I learned the truth about their real relationship only much later. They often discussed their situation with one another quite frankly since they were together constantly and daily. Hans painted her a detailed picture of all the obligations he had toward his mother and finally they concluded they would never marry. If I remember correctly, they kept this conviction for years. This unusual circumstance naturally created severe psychic stress for Erna. To top it off, frequent quarrels were occasioned by this pampered only son's extreme sensitivity. Her burden could well have proved unbearably painful had she not had some intimate friends who shared it with her. In the class between ours, which would graduate one year after Erna and a year before me, there were two inseparable friends, Lilli Platau and Rose Guttmann. Between classes, I had often talked to the two on the school grounds; we had shown one another our compositions and for a time had even taken private literature courses together. Only when Lilli began to study medicine, and so shared the same lectures and lab courses, did Erna get to know them better. Soon Erna and Lilli formed close ties. Rose was taking mathematics and natural sciences; and when I came to the university, we found ourselves attending philosophy and psychology lectures together. Soon we, too, were bosom friends; and the two pairs then fused to form an indivisible four-leaf clover. As he was inseparable from Erna, Hans was grafted on like some fifth leaf. But in no way was it a matter of our tolerating him merely for her sake, rather each one of us had a bond with him, not only of sincere friendship but of mutual intellectual interests as well. However, we were not at all as compliant to him as were his mother and Erna. Instead, we were determined to do battle when we considered him in the wrong; frequently this resulted in a hot dispute which, however, always ended in honest and solemn reconciliation. Since, during the semester, our assignments took us to separate locations, we arranged to spend one evening each week together. Whenever possible we got together outdoors in summer. I can still remember the deep contentment and joy with which, in complete candor and sincerity, while gathered for an evening meal, after the day's burdens, under a blossoming apple tree in one of the gardens outside the city limits, we discussed the questions or concerns which moved us at the time. In winter, we took turns holding these gatherings in our homes, and there we studied some of our subjects together. For instance, the medical students insisted that the philosophers had an obligation to contribute toward making their friends' cultural development more comprehensive. Lilli, in particular, an exceptionally lively girl with a nimble mind and wide-ranging interests, forever feared she ran the risk of getting into a rut through concentrating on the study of her specialty. Without a moment's hesitation, and as could have been expected, we plunged into Kant's *Critique of Pure Reason*. I no longer recall how far into it we got. With death-defying fervor, during one semester, we plowed through all of Meumann's *Experimental Psychology*, although the bulky tome with its multitudinous reports on experiments bored us tremendously and often seemed highly ridiculous.

At that time we were all passionately moved by the women's rights movement. Hans was a rara avis among the male students: he spoke up for equal rights for women as radically as any of us. We often discussed the issue of a double career. Erna and our two girl friends had many misgivings, wondering whether one ought not give up a career for the sake of marriage. I was alone in maintaining, always, that I would not sacrifice my profession on any account. If one could have predicted the future for us then! The other three married but, nevertheless, continued in their careers. I alone did not marry, but I alone have assumed an obligation for which, joyfully, I would willingly sacrifice any other career.

2

Besides gathering in this intimate little group, we also met one another in a larger social circle. The Guttmann and Platau families had already been seeing a good deal of one another, and now they became acquainted with our families as well. Frau Platau was a widow and also had a son, one year younger than Lilli. Her husband died even before the second child's birth; like our mother, she had no choice but to take steps to provide for her children herself. It was much more difficult in her case since neither her nature nor her inclination took such a direction.In her home, she set up a shop for machine embroidery where she employed a good number of girls. But, always she was most happy to leave the workroom and return to her simple yet comfortable living quarters.

Both her children, but especially the talented and spirited Lilli, constituted her pride and joy. Certainly she loved her Hans just as much; but he was quiet and unassuming, and his bright and self-confident sister often put him in the shade. However, this was totally unintentional; and dissimilar though they were, they were deeply devoted to one another. Frankly speaking, Lilli was homely; but one soon forgot that when speaking to her because of her vivacity and charm. Her mother, on the other hand, was a beautiful woman with noble features and large, soulful eyes; she retained her exceptionally gracious manner to a ripe old age. She took a lively interest in all of our studies and concerns; all the same, though herself experiencing a real need for intellectual stimulation, she was much calmer and more delicate than her daughter. I was very much attracted to this fine, kindly woman; and she, too, had a warm affection for me which has lasted all her life. The Plataus lived very near the university, and Lilli offered me the use of her small study for those hours when I had no class. Many a time I sat there at her desk between lectures. Frau Platau came in only to greet me briefly and to bring me some refreshment; then she would leave me undisturbed. Especially enjoyable were the evenings when Erna and I were the only ones to have been invited to this hospitable home. To begin with, we talked most companionably over tea; the affectionate homemaker generously provided all manner of delicacies. Then Frau Platau and Erna would play four-handed piano; Lilli and I withdrew to her small adjoining room. I had to make myself comfortable on her chaise longue; she sat beside me, and we exchanged our most intimate thoughts.

In the well-ordered, harmonious household of the Plataus, we were completely at home; we felt less so with the Guttmann family. Here, both parents were alive. The father was a tall, stately man, a bit brusque, and taciturn. His small, bustling, effervescent wife set the tone in that house. The three children, Rose, Hede, and Karl, the spoiled "baby," were all deeply attached to her, showing her devoted love and admiration. While our mother and Frau Platau did everything for us as a matter of course, without demanding any services from us in return, here, on the contrary, the mother was pampered by her daughters. They called her "Kitten" and took over from her as many household chores as possible; both were capable and skillful, and so, much more was demanded of them than of us.

Since their father was unable to earn enough from his accounts to support them all, both girls began working at an early age to supplement the family's income, Rose by tutoring in mathematics, and Hede by giving music lessons. Always overworked and often plagued by illness, Hede, even as a young girl, suffered in particular from severe attacks of asthma. Slim and well-proportioned, Rose was gifted with excellent taste in dress.

Her most beautiful adornment however was her hair: two long, glossy black braids worn with simplicity wound around her head. Strictly speaking, her face was not beautiful; it was rather spoiled by staring brown eyes. Despite that, she was very attractive. Lilli's lively and warmhearted way of reaching out to every person with unaffected cordiality was foreign to Rose. With strangers she was reticent and almost thrust them away; therefore, in our family no one besides Erna and me could warm up to her; and even Erna, after her initially cordial advances, withdrew from an intimate relationship while continuing in pleasant but more impersonal relations with her. Using her exceptional gift of empathy, Rose would captivate persons whom she valued. As she was a consummate listener, one was drawn to confide in her. In intellectual matters her grasp of another's thoughts was rapid and facile; and she could then participate in a discussion on the topic with remarkable fluency. Most persons failed to notice that what she said seldom was based on her own mental resources. Her intellectual talent was usually overrated, and possibly she may have deceived herself about it; still, I am convinced that deep down she was aware of the reality, and that, despite the self-confidence she outwardly displayed, she was insecure at heart. All this enabled me to indentify the trait which eventually alienated Erna and Hans from her: a certain dissembling. She never advocated personal convictions with any consistency, but, rather, would adapt her views to those of her audience, and so came to express wholly contradictory views. Nor could one rely upon her factual statements. My mother was particularly repelled by her habit of constantly speaking about her achievements and her success. This she did in a quiet, knowledgeable way as though touching but casually on these matters. Nevertheless, her intent to brag was obvious. Her talent as a teacher was indisputable and entirely beyond the ordinary as was her strong influence on her students. When Hans Biberstein and Rose met, they were strongly attracted to one another. Although by nature Erna was not at all inclined to be jealous, she was unable to remain calm throughout this situation. On the other hand, it was precisely this attraction to the same man which drew the two girls together. Rose's lack of dependability proved to be an insurmountable disillusionment for Hans and Erna. While Lilli and I also recognized the weakness and were pained by it, we did not withdraw from her.

Upon my arrival at the university, I, too, came to experience Rose's magic spell. At first hers was the dominant role in our friendship but that soon changed. Because of the precision with which I constructed my views and vindicated them against any and all, and also later, probably because of my capability for independent study, I gained a strong influence over her. Once, after the others had given up on her, the two of us had a very thorough discussion. Responding to her complaints, I told her outspokenly that I found the reproaches made against her to be completely fair. Nor did I conceal how I had explained her weakness to myself. However, I added, I would never consider withdrawing my friendship because of a person's weaknesses. She gratefully accepted all I had to say without taking offense, and from then on, she was even more attached to me. I believe her way of relating to me differed radically from every other relationship she had. That, rather than enhanced by artificial illumination, I saw her in plain daylight surely pained her but, on the other hand, it gave her a measure of peace and security she found nowhere else. She never referred to this in our talks, nor do I know whether she ever clarified it in her own mind. She felt impelled simply to write me from time to time to say how much she loved me, adding, often, that it was an "unrequited love." Under the circumstances, that was probably true since it was impossible for the feelings to be mutual. However, I remained, always, her true and affectionate friend.

Music played a prominent role in our gatherings with the Guttmanns. Hede was being trained as a pianist and music teacher; she also had a good voice and was a born actress. We never tired of the songs she sang to the accompaniment of her lute. But though these talents often put her in the limelight of our group, she still felt excluded in some way. In appearance, she was even less attractive than her sister. Besides, just as was the case with our elder sisters, she felt herself unequal to us "academicians." After all, we were always up to our necks in studies and just could not cut out the "shop talk." A special bond of friendship developed between Hede and Hans Platau. A young businessman, he usually contented himself unobtrusively listening to our conversations. My mother, who predicted even at that early stage of their friendship that Hede would never let go of him again, thoroughly disapproved of the attachment. Because he was so quiet and so serious, she liked Hans very much. She was sorry to think that such a handsome young man should get a wife not only so unattractive but so ailing as well.

A whole succession of persons other than members of our own immediate families augmented our social circle. As we were all taking different courses and the number of semesters we were taking did not coincide, each of us had additional personal acquaintances whom we gradually introduced to the others. Lilli acquired two outsiders as faithful satellites, the medical students Skupin and Jakobi. They were most welcome in our crowd; Hans Biberstein, in particular, befriended them. On the other hand, all of us decidedly rejected a third friend of Lilli's who later joined the circle. Paul Berg came from the province of Posen. He was raised as a strictly orthodox Jew and knew far more about Judaism than anyone in our group. The Guttmanns,' Bibersteins,' and Plataus' style of living was even more liberal than our own; none of them kept a kosher home anymore. We could not complain that Paul Berg offended us by his views for he scarcely ever referred to them. Nor had he even the slightest trace of that unpleasant intonation common to the uneducated Eastern Jews which irritated the German "assimilated Jews" even more than it did the "Aryans." Rather, he spoke a very pure and cultivated German. Actually, the only objection we could have to him was that he was exaggeratedly polite and obsequious, and that his soft, cloyingly sweet manner was completely at odds with our unaffected, even rather audacious, collegiate manners. His presence always provoked me to shock him by particularly unrestrained expressions; and Hans Biberstein continually baited him with biting sarcasm. Apparently his intentions toward Lilli were really serious, so he was impervious to it all. However, we were indignant at the thought of him at her side as he was as far from being her peer intellectually as could be imagined. We did not know what to make of Lilli. Her defense of him in the face of our attacks was pretty weak; still she persisted in maintaining the friendship so that, whether we would or not, we had to get used to him. On one occasion when our foursome plus our sister Rosa went to the *Riesengebirge* for winter sports during the Christmas vacation, he joined the party as our sole male companion; and he eagerly constituted himself our "chambermaid." When, soaked by all the snow, we arrived at a shelter, he helped us off and on with sweaters; he replaced missing buttons, and if anyone of us was exhausted by the climbing, he readily pulled the sled. We accepted all this with laughing good humor. Then when, in the evening, we congregated around the huge round table in the comfortable *"Landhaus Martha"* in Oberschreiberhau and got hot-headed while discussing our world-views, he participated with obvious enthusiasm. We were aware how grateful he was to be accepted in such a highbrow group, and this made us all soften toward him. Thereafter, I tended to speak up in his defense when in his absence he became the target of the customary ridicule.

We all welcomed with delight a young mathematician Rose introduced to us. His name was Willy Strietzel. (That enfant terrible Karl Guttmann said that combining Willy's and Rose's names gave one *Rosinenstrietzel* — raisin bread.) Willy was from a lower middle class family, his father being a cabinetmaker. Nominally a Protestant, he really was a nonbeliever. He was short, wore his blond hair in a crew cut, had somewhat of a snub nose and spoke with the strong Silesian dialect which was not at all customary in our "better" circles. The difference in background and of station was immediately obvious, but neither side found this at all disturbing. His exceptional talent as a mathematician assured him the respect of his fellow students. He was bright and alert, full of good humor, as happy as a child; in our circle he was perfectly at ease, even with my mother. The high point of all our social gatherings was New Year's Eve which for years was celebrated by the four families all gathered together. The party took the form of a "Picknick,"[29] that is, everyone contributed something to the refreshments and to the entertainment. This joint celebration of New Year's had already become a custom for the Guttmanns and the Plataus before we became acquainted with them; when we were added to the group, the parties were held at our house because our rooms were the largest. Frau Guttmann had a knack for planning these affairs. She was good at making up doggerel verse, could paint posters, and was quick at getting up short skits. Hans Biberstein and I contributed to the parties by writing special songs and a witty program[30] styled like a newsletter. On these occasions, then, everyone could expect to be taken to task thoroughly as in song and jest the events of the foregoing year passed before us in review.

From earliest childhood on, the climax of our summer fun was the family's excursion into the country. My mother would rent a huge wagon for the occasion, and then early some Sunday we would set out for the woods. Provisions were taken along so we could have a full meal at noon when we arrived at the camp site in the forest. We carefully made room for a number of guests as well as for the immediate family. Formerly these guests had been only our cousins, now our friends and their relatives were invited. In the evening everyone returned to our house; when all traces of the day's dust had been banished, we all had a simple evening meal. Loath though my mother was to have any guest leave the house before she had served some refreshments, at the same time she disliked "making a fuss;" all should feel themselves at home and be spared the embarrassing impression that everything was being turned topsy-turvy on their account. The unbidden guests were also undemanding, being more than content with tea or milk, bread, butter, and fruit. Most enthusiastically welcomed was the hearty rye bread which my mother herself still baked according to Upper Silesian custom.

In the summer vacations of 1911 and of 1912, while we were still studying at the University of Breslau, our clover-leaf foursome went to the Silesian mountains for several weeks. On the first occasion we chose Gross-Aupa as our headquarters. This is a straggling village on the Bohemian side of the *Riesengebirge*. As it lay a great distance from the railway, one had to take the post-bus from Johannesbad. Except for us, if I remember correctly, there were no summer guests; we were the whole show. At night when we, singing our student songs at the top of our lungs, strolled along the street in the moonlight, all the inhabitants took note. Once we were even invited by the town elders to come to sing for them at the local inn where they regularly got together. Without a moment's hesitation, we complied. Our innocent fun was a novel treat for the simple, honest folk in this quiet corner of the world.

On this trip, too, we were not alone. Frau Guttmann and her unmarried sister, who suffered from hyperthyroidism, were with us. For a very small sum, we had rented several rooms in a baker's house. The two ladies cooked their own meals. The rest of us took our noon meal at the inn and provided our own simple breakfast and supper. For part of the time, my mother sent Frieda to join us. She had but recently been separated from her husband; still quite depressed over the experience, she was in need of some diversion and recreation. We had other guests, besides, who visited for brief or longer intervals. A school companion of Lilli and Rose was entrusted to us by her concerned parents because they hoped our companionship would be good for her. She was a lovely, quiet girl who had just begun at that time to manifest early symptoms of strange behavior: the first indications of a *dementia praecox* which became acute soon thereafter. On the other hand, Lotte Baerthold from Sagan was a merry companion. She had attended the *Gymnasium* with Erna. During those years, she had boarded in Breslau and had come nearly every day to our house to study with Erna. In return, my sister had to spend part of her vacation as a guest in her home. Her father had a textile factory in Sagan. He was an enthusiastic politician, a genuine old-time liberal; for a long time he was a city councilman. The mother was a kind, lovely woman who had preserved all the charm of her youth. An only daughter, Lotte had two brothers, one older, one younger. She was given an excellent education, had the impeccable manners especially cultivated in good Protestant families, but had remained, for all that, very natural and simple in her ways, lively and happy. Now, with unrestrained joy, she became one of our group; this friendship, too, was a lifelong one. As her parents often had to do business in Breslau, we eventually became acquainted with them as well; and, later, during the long train ride en route home to Breslau, I often spent the long layover in Sagan in their comfortable, hospitable home. After her *Abitur*, Lotte decided to study modern languages. She studied in Berlin for one semester; for the second, she went to Paris. While on the way there, a fellow traveler, a young engineer, came to her assistance. He looked her up in Paris and often met her thereafter. To ask her parents for her hand in marriage, he followed her when she returned home at the end of the semester. So the wedding was imminent that summer of 1911; and she joined us in Gross-Aupa for some relaxation after the rather exhausting preparations. Other acquaintances, on vacation elsewhere in the mountains, looked us up occasionally to spend a day or only a few hours with us. A medical student, a cheerful young girl who wanted to visit us, merely asked someone on the street for directions to the house "where all the young ladies are living" and was immediately directed to the right place. The Aupa, a narrow stream, flowed beside our little house. By stepping out the back door you reached the water directly. There was a grass-covered slope on the opposite bank. When we wanted to stretch out there, we had to balance our way across on some flat stones in the stream. Usually this was our first exercise of the morning. Often, Frau Guttmann accompanied our maneuver with little cries of alarm for her pillows or blankets which we were carrying across.

We also made it a point of honor to climb to the top of the steep slope once a day. Our guests, too, had to fulfill this requirement. In order to lie down comfortably, we each had our special vacation hairdo. I wore mine coiled like snail shells over my ears. The other three did not now wrap their long, heavy braids in Gretchen style round their heads but rather looped them back and forth above their foreheads so as to leave the nape of the neck free. We had provided ourselves with an adequate supply of books for the vacation; so, lying outside, each of us would get engrossed in her own. I remember that Rose had brought along Nietzsche's *Zarathustra*. Sometimes she would interrupt her reading to call on me for help.

"Chick, you're so smart; can you tell me what this means?"

They called me "Chick" because I was the youngest member of the clover-leaf. Besides, I looked so young that Frau Guttmann used to say that when we returned to Breslau again they were going to enroll me in school. I had just finished my first semester [at the university] and had brought along Spinoza's *Ethics* to read during that vacation. I was never found without the small book. If we went into the woods, I carried it in the pocket of my rainproof cape; and while the others lolled around under the trees, I would search out a deer lookout, climb up to it, and then become absorbed, alternately, in deductions about the sole substance, and then in the view of sky, mountains, and woods.

On one occasion, Hans Biberstein was allowed to come on a visit from Bad Reinerz. His mother had given him a few days off to make an extended excursion. He came for us and, together, we visited the mountain town Adersbach-Weckelsdorf. By the following year, he was taken so much into consideration that we chose to vacation in a place in the vicinity of Reinerz: Grunwald on the *Hohen Mense*, the village with the highest altitude in all of Prussia. Erna and I were acquainted with it from our childhood, for we had been there on one excursion with our sister Else and our sister-in-law Trude. It had been my first glimpse of any mountains. Erna and I preserved dismal memories of that sojourn; several times the two venturesome ladies had left us children to fend for ourselves for the entire, long day, providing us with very limited rations. As we were staying in the teacher's home, no mishap occurred; but, eventually, the two of us grew very tired of looking for blueberries and of eating bread spread with honey, which got drier and drier from one meal to the next. To us, those days had seemed to stretch out interminably.

However, on this present visit we put up in the inn. There was one other guest, Burgomaster Westram of Ratibor. He was an elderly gentleman to whom, however, the company of four young women students on vacation was most welcome. For years thereafter he kept up a correspondence with us and later did us a great favor. Before going to Grunwald, however, we had spent a few days in Altheide where we met our sister Else who had come there for some relaxation with one of our aunts from Breslau, and who was now ready to go home. Cause for much greater excitement was our success in talking our Mother into coming along. With this exception, Mother never visited any spa; in fact, in all her life she never travelled any great distance from home.

The adverse conditions prevalent then had robbed her of a honeymoon (she was married in 1871); at the time, my father promised her they would make it up someday; but then the children began to arrive one after another, and, inevitably, the honeymoon was postponed. When she talked about it, she would suggest the prospect of someday making that omitted wedding trip with us; and now we were taking her at her word. So she came along [to Altheide]. She was very satisfied; we were in a house very near the woods, and she had always thoroughly appreciated the beauties of nature. But after three days, we could no longer detain her; and she returned home. We then proceeded to Reinerz where the four of us packed ourselves and our luggage into a wagon for the ascent to our destination on the heights. Rosa joined us up there for a while on this occasion. It was a rainy summer, with a heavy downpour nearly every day. But as soon as the weather brightened up a bit, we were outside, looking for berries or mushrooms, or climbing even higher. Hans often visited us. In turn, we frequently went down to Reinerz. As Frau Biberstein was fond of bilberries, we always took along a huge pitcherful for her. It especially amused us, thus burdened, to trudge along the promenade side by side with the distinguished patrons of the fashionable spa. Once again, the highpoint of the entire vacation was an excursion lasting several days. Hans worked out the program; and as he was intent on setting new hiking records, he planned that we should make about 40 kilometers [about 25 miles] a day. First, we took the train to Wölfelsgrund in order to climb the *Glatzer Schneeberg*; and from there we would go on into the *Altvatergebirge*,[31] new terrain for all of us.

Rose Guttmann, who had some trouble with her heart at the time, dared not risk such a trip; she spent those days in Gräfenberg and was to rejoin us at the border station, Mittelwalde.

Our sister Rosa replaced her in our quartet. Unfortunately, a touchy situation developed at the very start of the excursion. I had sprained my foot on the ascent of the *Schneeberg*, and hiking was now very painful for me. Going uphill was somewhat easier, so, whenever we had climbing to do, I was especially careful to make up whatever time had been lost on my account at each descent. Every step downhill was agonizing; and whereas, ordinarily, I revelled in dashing downhill at top speed, now, gingerly, I had to put down one foot before the other. Hans was exasperated. The excursion which he had so joyfully anticipated was totally ruined for him. When, at intervals, I walked a stretch at top speed, he did not look on that as a manifestation of my good will, rather, he said: "See what she can do if she really wants to!"

He hurried ahead in his usual stride, and Erna went with him, although she was miserable doing so. The poor thing had the worst of it. She had to put up with the disgruntled outbursts of her pampered friend and, on top of that, had to endure the reproaches of my companions who were indignant at the behavior of these two budding medicos and who, despite all my protests, insisted on roundly berating the couple. Of course, the situation worsened with each succeeding day. On the final one, to get to the railway station, we had to go down a rather steep and stony ravine, a descent that took several hours, and Lilli put her arm firmly around me and practically carried me rather than letting me walk.

The hike took us through the most marvelous mountain scenery, and, once the couple consistently running ahead was out of sight, the three of us, peacefully trudging along behind them, forgot all about the discord and enjoyed ourselves. We also had some amusing intermezzos which, in later years, provided us with material for many a party song or comic program. Before beginning that hike through the *Altvatergebirge* early in the morning, we planned to lodge overnight in Ramsau. When we reached it very late at night, Ramsau's railway platform lay in total darkness. With the help of a flashlight, we found our way to the exit and to the distant guesthouse. It was already filled to near capacity. Hans was given a pigeonhole-sized room in the courtyard. A larger one was to accommodate the four of us girls. After a late meal in the dining room, we were directed to our lodgings. To get to our room we had to pass through another one in which two men and a woman were in the process of undressing. We had a fellow-feeling for the poor lady; we considered ourselves lucky at least not to have been expected to put up our sulking cavalier in our room as well. After all, it did contain a fifth bed! We moved the empty bed against the door connecting our room with the one we had passed through, since the door could not be locked. After the exertion, excitement and adventures of that long day, we were anticipating a little sleep at last; but Lilli experienced some very unwelcome aftereffects of the unaccustomed fare. She was even more upset by the thought of spoiling our night's rest than by the nausea and pain. We were all relieved when dawn released us from our prison. Again we went up and down hill, from morning until evening. But this time we arrived before nightfall at a truly restful place, the lovely Karlsbrunn.

Here the tourist bureau had assigned us some clean, attractive rooms in a charming little house. After getting thoroughly cleaned up, it was heavenly to rest there. I have already mentioned the difficulties we had the next day on the final stage of the hike. At its conclusion, when we reached that railway station, we found that the Imperial Austrian Railroad worried little about timetables. The scheduled train was not running; we had to wait for hours to take another one which made it impossible to meet Rose in Mittelwalde at the appointed time. By railtelegram we informed her of the delay. When, actually on the last train of the day, we finally reached Mittelwalde late that evening there was no sign of Rose. We set out for the nearest hotel. Not one room was available. True, they had to admit that most of the rooms might still hold an empty bed; but, as it was so late, could they really be expected to wake the sleepers by bringing additional occupants to the room? Although my foot had just about reached the limit of its serviceability, we had to go elsewhere. The second inn was somewhat less elegant than the first, but by this time we were beyond caring anymore. However, their reply was very similar to the former one. The third inn lay at the very outskirts of the village and was not in the least attractive. Still, we had no choice left. I went at once into the dining room and announced we would remain seated there all night if they had no more beds. Thereupon they admitted that, in fact, they could put one room at our disposal; but this time it actually had to accommodate all of us together. The room held two beds and a sofa. Not only did we retire fully clothed but we wrapped our cloaks tightly about us as well, as we had well-founded doubts about the cleanliness of the bedding. Two apiece, the ladies took over the beds. Hans may have had better luck with the sofa, still it was obvious that he did not sleep. He kept snapping on his flashlight at very short intervals to look at his watch. In between, the tower clock could be heard striking. When morning came, we performed our *toilette* one after another at the tiny washstand.

Then we retraced the way we had come through the darkness the evening before. Just as we arrived at the fashionable hotel, Rose stepped out, looking thoroughly refreshed. She had been given, all to herself, a room which held four beds; and she had retired to it only very shortly before we had knocked at the inn's door to no avail. Until then she had been waiting for us at the station, reading while eating one sandwich after another. Finally the clerks had said no train would be coming anymore, and they had shown her the way to the hotel. We had enough humor left to laugh at this quirk of fate. Actually, meeting Rose and exchanging accounts of our experiences served to relieve the tension in the atmosphere. Nevertheless, when our sister Rosa left us to return to Breslau, the farewell she received from Hans was still pretty frosty. Obviously, offering her his hand caused him great self-conquest. He was more mollified where I was concerned. Evidently, though he never mentioned it, he had convinced himself by then that the injury had not been make-believe; besides I had not joined the others in making reproaches. I was far too depressed to do so, merely at realizing that I was innocently-guilty of spoiling the fun. We had to return to Reinerz; there was no other way to Grunwald.

Frau Biberstein received us in the lobby. From one glance at her darling's face she could tell how irritated he was. That finished us as far as she was concerned. Erna alone was invited to her room for a farewell. The rest of us were dismissed there and then. So we made use of the resort's facilities to rid ourselves of the dust of highway and train. Then the four of us were together again in a closed coach for the ride up to Grunwald. Though we all breathed easier just to be among ourselves again, we scarcely spoke en route. Erna sat there, meekly, under the impression that we were all blaming her. When we arrived at the inn's dining room, she knelt at once to remove the heavy walking shoe from my badly swollen foot. After the noon meal I was put to bed; and the two medicos bandaged my foot expertly and propped it up. Then while Rose and Lilli took a walk, Erna sat on the edge of my bed and read aloud some of Goethe's letters. The other two returned a bit later, refreshed and in excellent spirits. Rose fetched the big bar of Lindt-Chocolate she had brought from Gräfenberg for us. The clover-leaf fell upon it, and with this treat a complete reconciliation was effected without the need of a single word about what had happened. How peace with Hans was restored on this occasion, I can no longer recall. In any case, before long, the friendship was back on a good footing. All of us were ever ready and quick to make peace. But such incidents gave us pause for reflection and concern about the fate in store for Erna.

During our vacations in the mountains, we would get two rooms, each with two beds. Erna and Lilli shared one room, Rose and I, the other. In Grunwald, our friend, the Burgomaster, had the room between our two, so he could overhear that, on one side, medical textbooks were being studied jointly, while to the other side of him, discussion went on over the basic questions of mathematics and theoretical physics. But sometimes we mixed the combination of roommates, thus providing ourselves with every opportunity for a thorough mutual discussion with each one in the quartet; the quiet evening hours were most suitable for this, and, often, we exchanged ideas long into the night. I do not remember in detail what we found to talk about in these frequent and lengthy conversations. In any case we never ran out of subject matter; nor could anything give us greater joy than sharing such confidences. Usually, they concerned the affairs of our clover-leaf itself, and of the persons close to us, or of our plans for the future, the configuration of our own lives, and the ideals which we wanted to promote through our own life's efforts.

3

The winter of 1912-1913 provided one more tobogganing excursion to Schreiberhau. But the clover-leaf separated in the summer semester of 1913 since Rose and I left Breslau. Probably, the situation can be understood best if, before continuing the account of Erna's further destiny, I go back somewhat to recount my own development up to this time. I have already told about my losing the faith I had as a child, and how, about that same time, I became "an independent person", withdrawing from all guidance by my mother and brothers or sisters. When fourteen-and-a-half years old, I had finished the nine grades of the *Höhere Mädchenschule*.[4] That was at Easter of 1906. Just at that very time, the *Selecta*, an elective year which only very few girls had ever attended, was now changed into a new tenth grade; and certain privileges were attached to attending it. The principal was very upset when he received the letter apprising him of my departure from school, and he put before me all the logical arguments for continuing another year. But I was not to be swayed.

Two years earlier, just as decidedly, I had declined to transfer to the *Gymnasium*. At that time, the school system had switched from a four-year sequence of *Realgymnasium* courses following upon the ninth grade to a six year *Realgymnasium* curriculum following the seventh grade. Ours was the class caught in midstream. We could no longer enroll in a four-year program and had no alternative but to lose a year's time if we took the six-year-curriculum. That may well have influenced me to leave school. But I believe that in both instances a healthy instinct was the decisive factor. It told me I had been sitting on a school-bench long enough and needed a change. Precisely in that seventh grade I had begun to do less well in school. My grades remained among the highest, still at times I failed to come up to expectations. In part, this could have been because various questions began to preoccupy my mind, ideological ones especially, about which there was little discussion in school. But, probably, the explanation can be found primarily in the physical development beginning for me at that time. In no way would my mother oppose my categorical decision.

"I won't coerce you," she said, "I allowed you to start school when you wanted to go. By the same token, you may now leave if that is what you want."

So I quit school and, a few weeks later, traveled to Hamburg for that lengthy sojourn there which I recounted earlier.

Shortly before I left school, a second link was torn from the circle of my mother's brothers and sisters by death. Her second oldest sister, Cilla Burchard, died of cancer after a long, painful illness; and an extensive operation had merely postponed the end. We, too, experienced all the stages of her illness because we had especially close ties to the Burchard family. Uncle was my mother's faithful friend; he helped her in business matters as much as he was able. In his youth, Mother had trained him in her parents' business. Even now, he was not an independent businessman and so felt all the more esteem and admiration for his niece, who had become his sister-in-law (I mentioned earlier that he was our grandmother's brother). For a while he was my mother's bookkeeper. When that was no longer necessary, he still came pretty regularly, at least once a day, to see whether he could run any business errands for her. My mother had a grateful affection for him and used to side with him since so little respect was shown him in his own house. Aunt Cilla had an austere and taciturn nature. She was very openhanded and as a housewife loved to be lavish in every way. Her pride was injured in that her husband was unable to earn enough for her needs, that her parents had to help out occasionally, and that her beloved daughters had to start early in life to work for a living. Fritz, the only son, was studying medicine. For the time being, he could not be expected to help. It was the normal thing, generally, in those day, for sisters to work very hard in order to enable their brothers to study. Martha, the elder of the daughters, was but slightly older than my sister Else and was her best friend. As long

as Else was at home, Martha came to our house each evening
without fail; and we all regarded her as a sister. She had passed
the examination for teachers but then took a job as a clerk in the
county insurance bureau in Breslau where she was a very conscientious employee until she was pensioned after many decades.
She was as quiet and taciturn as her mother; both daughters had
also inherited their mother's openhandedness and unbounded
hospitality. Not being as harsh and curt as our aunt, Martha
was rather friendly and forthcoming in her associations. My
mother could not understand how persons so charming and helpful toward all their friends could fail to have a single kind word
left over for their own good father. Once, when she privately
chided Martha about this, she was brushed off with a harsh remark that made it obvious Martha considered her father guilty
of some dishonesty. None of us could imagine what it might
possibly be. My mother was convinced that, through misinter-
pretation, my aunt had formed some completely mistaken conclusions which were then communicated to her daughters. Adelheid, the youngest, called Heidel, was the one most pampered
by her mother. In contrast to her very quiet brother and sister,
she was overly talkative and loud, her entire manner being somewhat uninhibited. But at her jobs in the business world she
proved efficient and conscientious; she was very capable, too, at
household duties when, during her mother's illness and after
her death, she was called upon to assume these tasks. Before we
began school, Erna and I often spent our mornings in their
house. When my mother wanted to be certain we would be well
taken care of, she could always send us there. Our aunt allowed
us to do whatever we wished. Only when we were at a loss for
something to do would she provide some occupation. Thus it
was that, there, for the first time a stocking was put into my
hands for darning. My aunt showed me what had to be done
and then left me to myself. I was then perhaps five years old. I
sat on a high stool, displaying great zeal and a suitably serious
mien, and became totally engrossed in the exceedingly difficult
business. I was very put out when my big cousin (he was about
twenty years older than I) came up to me and pretended he
would snatch the work away from me. I sprang quickly from the

stool, only to be chased around the table a few times before my aunt came to my rescue with a few energetic words. Fritz loved to tease me. He was as taciturn as his mother, and his dry humor was also like hers except that his had not yet been curbed by constant worries. Later we seldom saw him. After he passed the state boards, he first made several voyages as a ship's doctor, arousing our deepest interest when he reappeared wearing a deep suntan and a blue mariner's cap. Next, he settled in a small town in Thüringen; we were told that, following his arrival there, a herald carrying a small bell went through the streets proclaiming that a new doctor had come to the town. Later, he lived in Berlin, and from there he came several times a year to spend a few days visiting his relatives. We saw one another briefly on these occasions and exchanged a few words. He faithfully remembered his observations concerning me in my childhood; and I always had the feeling that his affection for me was much like his mother's. At the time, I was definitely her favorite. This she demonstrated unmistakably even if at times rather brusquely. When she did her household shopping in the morning, we sometimes met her; and nearly always this meant that I received some kind of gift from her. Usually it took the form of a consolation prize for me on my way to the despised kindergarten. On one occasion, as I was again being dragged thither, she bought me a big bag of yellow gage plums. I was nearly staggered by such wealth. But I was not to be bribed by such material means. My antipathy to that place of humiliation never decreased. Aunt Cilla was my staunch support when I demanded so energetically to go to the "big" school. She used to remind me later that I owed her the year I had won, and she was proud of my scholastic achievements. However, she expressed her estimation in a term that I found most unpleasant: her favorite name for me was "go-getter." Of course I knew it was meant to be affectionate teasing. But, for all that, it held a concealed thorn for me.

From my earliest childhood, the entire relationship had characterized me principally by two qualities: I was accused (justly so) of ambition; and I was called, with emphasis, "smart" Edith. Both of these designations hurt me very much. The second, because I thought it had an implication that I was conceited about my cleverness; also, I thought they found me *only* clever, and I knew, after all, from my earliest years that it was much more important to be good than to be clever. When my cousin Leni Pick joined my class, Aunt Cilla promised her a reward of one mark if she ever outshone me scholastically. However both of them were convinced from the start that it was an unattainable reward.

The Burchards had kept open house from the time they had set up housekeeping. Formerly, all of my mother's brothers and cousins who were either attending school or the university or were employed in Breslau would get together at the Burchards' home every Sunday. Also the twins, Hans and Franz, our inseparable companions, later boarded there. My aunt took excellent care of them; she prepared each one's favorite foods but also, occasionally, took them in hand most energetically. If they failed to do a good job of washing themselves during their teens, they were held under the water spigot and vigorously scrubbed. Birthday parties at this house were especially popular. In no other nursery were cake and whipped cream dispensed so lavishly; nowhere else could we play as undisturbed as here. Only one unpleasant interruption was imposed: one had to put in an appearance at the table where the grown-ups were gathered to shake hands with everyone and to pass inspection before all the older aunts and cousins. The one whom I dreaded seeing most and who never missed these festive occasions was my cousin's fellow student, a physician of excellent character and well-rounded education; he had a rather eccentric and high-flown manner of thought and speech. I would predict to the other children in the group what comments he would make about me for he invariably used the same expressions upon seeing me: that I had the head of a Christ and the eyes of a Madonna; had no sculptor as yet been found to choose me for his model, lured to do so by my alabaster complexion? I could scarcely control myself when I had to endure such comments. As soon as we left the room, shuddering with disgust, I would vent my anger in nasty remarks. For example, I would point out that alabaster was alabaster totally independent of me. Once I had grown up, my arrival led this perennial guest to make comments of a different nature which, however, were just as embarrassing for me; he would propose his philosophical problems to me, and I considered the occasion of a party and the company of my relatives a most inappropriate setting for that.

Because of her uncommunicative bent, my aunt concealed the symptoms of her illness as long as possible. By the time the pain became unbearable, all hope of saving her was gone. I recall my last visit to her. She lay in bed, so weak that she was unable to sit up; and she could speak only very faintly. I had no expectation at all of being allowed to go to her room. However, Heidel sent me in at once and gave me, as well, a small plate of some refreshment which I was to feed to the invalid by spoon. I was very uneasy about this, thinking how hard it must be for such a proud and independent person to allow herself to be fed by a child. But she was already accustomed to it and accepted it calmly. Then she asked me how things were going at school. She inquired especially about an embarrassing experience of mine which someone had mentioned to her: I had received my one and only demerit of all my scholastic days.

At the time, Principal Roehl, who was strict and whom we dreaded, gave us our geography lessons. It was the subject I liked least. Despite that, it had already become customary for me to review for the entire class the whole of our assigned work, using the map, and this I did before our lessons, early in the morning. Eventually the principal caught on, it seems, but apparently had no objections; in any case, once when one of the others gave an incorrect answer, he calmly inquired of me whether I had failed to coach them correctly. Then, one morning, my cousin Leni and her friend Johanna were very late arriving at school. My recital was over and the bell for morning devotions had already rung. In their dread of being called upon, the two had begged me to stay with them at the back of the auditorium near the door, there to prepare them for class during the devotions. I was very uncomfortable about the situation but, as genuine student ethics would have it, comradeship comes before all else. So we stuck our heads together, and I whispered my lecture. Unfortunately a teacher had come in after us, and she watched us. She could not hear what was being said. However, she considered it a hair-raising crime for anyone to be talking and paying no attention during devotions.

At their close, she pounced on us as soon as we came out the door and gave us a good dressing down. As she gave no lessons to our class, she felt it her responsibility to tell the principal about the matter. He gave us a second reprimanding sermon and entered a demerit against us in our class record. I no longer know whether the other two miscreants also got the demerit or whether, having done most of the talking, I was the only one. In any case, they asked permission to speak, then employed all their eloquence in an effort to prove they alone were to blame for the whole affair and I should not be penalized for it. It was all in vain. The demerit stayed on my record. But the faculty must not have considered it too serious a crime for my next report gave my grade for deportment as: "Very good, except on one occasion." ("Very good" was, for us, the equivalent of a 1.)[4:]

This was the episode about which my terminally-ill aunt wanted to hear. She smiled in scorn at the behavior of the principal and said: "The fool!"

After that visit, I never saw her again, not even after her death. I had never seen a corpse, and my mother wished to spare me that experience now. But I went to the funeral, and later I was among the relatives who gathered once more in the bereaved's home. We were always a bit alienated and repelled by the fact that on such occasions one gathered around a table for coffee and cake and talked as one did at festivals even though the mood was, generally, solemn and somewhat depressed.

After it was all over, the apartment was closed up. The twins were put up with some other relatives; they had boarded there before their parents moved from Upper Silesia to Breslau. Martha and Heidel came to us until they were able to move into a new apartment. A room across from our place was rented for Uncle. He also took his meals with us. Martha was numbed by her grief. She could neither weep nor speak. We all vied with one another in an attempt to make her stay with us comfortable. Frieda, especially, was untiring in her loving attentions until that numbness wore off. Later the sisters, together, proffered the same bountiful hospitality that had been customary while their mother was alive. Their father lived with them until his final illness. My mother was very angry with them for putting him into a hospital when his condition became hopeless. He died during the first year of the war [W.W. I]. Despite the fact that the great difference in their personalities made it hard for them to get along with one another, Martha and Heidel stayed together. Their sisterly loyalty and attachment were stronger than all conflicts.

I have recounted these memories here because they are interwoven with the impressions of my final days in school. In general the pictures of my last years in the *Mädchenschule* are very dim and form a mere backdrop for the later ones of my *Gymnasium* and university period. Leaving school was anything but difficult for me. To begin with, I was fed up with learning. I did not feel close to any of my teachers. I have always had a horror of teen-age crushes; I had never had one myself and had ridiculed those of others. For three years, we had one teacher whom I liked very much. He was quite young when he came to us; it was his first appointment to a permanent staff. His manner was open and natural and he had a knack of getting along with children; that was a rarity in those days. Because of that, he was soon transferred as principal to Königsberg. I was thirteen at the time. At my suggestion, the class presented him with Böcklin's "*Toteninsel*"[32] as a farewell gift. He pasted a piece of paper on the back of the picture and insisted that we each autograph it. In return he presented each of us with an autographed photo of himself. Some years later, he returned to Breslau as district school superintendent. I had to present myself to him when my teaching assignment began. He recognized me at once, saying, "Goodness, you were in my fourth grade!"

Nor did I have close ties to any of my classmates. In the lower grades, I had associated almost daily with one child who lived but a few doors away from our house. Still, we became acquainted only at school. She entered one semester after me, having had private tutoring before that. Her mother, who brought her to school and called for her, noticed that I went the same way and, addressing me on the street on one of those earliest days, invited me most urgently to visit Mariechen. Later again, it was usually the parents who got me to come to their house, for they hoped that I would exert a good influence on their child. Our class was large, and the children had mixed backgrounds; Mariechen was not particular about the companions she chose. Her father, Dr. Grünberg, was a very busy general practitioner whom, later, we called to our house sometimes when Dr. Kamm, our good old family doctor and my mother's cousin, was either sick or away on a trip. Dr. Grünberg was both lively and friendly; the few small dueling scars on his round pleasant face were reminders of a fraternity affiliation in his student years. Mariechen's mother was a vivacious young Polish woman from whose harsh diction one could still deduce her origin. One grandmother also lived with them, and there was a baby sister whose first birthday I helped to celebrate—later she would be one of my pupils in the *Gymnasium*. In addition, they had a cook and a chambermaid, both of whom were very attached to the family. Their apartment was large; the nursery held many beautiful toys and books which were a tremendous magnet for me. Mariechen and I got along well enough together, though we never formed close ties. My family liked to see her because she was cheerful and friendly. In school, however, she showed some characteristics which I found repugnant. She did not always tell the truth, and she managed to prompt her classmates with false information, perhaps the worst sin possible according to student ethics. When our class was divided because of its excessive size, we found ourselves in different sections and, a year later, she transferred to the *Gymnasium*. From that time on, we were in touch less frequently; and eventually all contact ceased when we moved into an apartment some distance away.

I was friendly enough with some others to exchange invitations to our birthday parties, but otherwise we seldom met outside of class. In the higher grades, a childhood playmate joined our class after having gone earlier to a different school. Her mother, like mine, came from Lublinitz; that was the reason we had become acquainted earlier. Kaethe was Erna's age; her older sister Emma was a friend of Frieda's; her brother Emil was friendly with our brother Arno. Frau Kleemann was a tall, stately woman with an impressive bearing. (That she came from a family little respected in Lublinitz and that she had been employed in my grandparents' home as a seamstress were circumstances, however, which my mother never forgot.) By dint of diligence and energy, Herr Kleemann, once a journeyman mechanic, had worked his way up to become the wealthy owner of a factory. Nevertheless, he continued to work indefatigably; we seldom got to see him, and, even when he was present, he hardly spoke a word. For several years Kaethe sat next to me in class, and we understood one another well. During recess or en route to and from school, we often discussed questions which were ignored in school; a serious search for truth had begun for her as for me. Despite all that, we too parted ways after we left school. This probably resulted because our families had preserved no social contact even before that. The Kleemanns had moved to the south side of the city [Breslau], where, as in Berlin's West End, the newly wealthy Jews gathered; for my mother this was another example of typical behavior of the newly affluent. Because of our business, we were tied to the unfashionable north side. Moreover, Emma had married a rabbi in Hamburg (they went to America later). Emil had gone to be a pharmacist in Berlin. After we had left school, several years passed before 1909 when Kaethe and I met again at a Schiller Memorial Celebration.[33] She had but recently become engaged. We greeted one another with genuine joy, and she cordially urged me to visit her again and, if possible, to bring Erna along. Not long thereafter, we did go one evening and had a very good time. Her fiancé, a young doctor, was not there. Frau Kleemann was especially happy that Arno came to take us home because he reminded her of the former days even more than we "youngsters" did. He was urged to have a cup of tea and to stay for a while. A return visit was promised which was to bring Frau Kleemann, too, to see my mother again. But nothing came of it. More than twenty years would pass before we met again.

Leaving home was no more difficult for me than bidding farewell to school and friends had been. Of course, the visit in Hamburg was expected to last but a few weeks. Before my departure, my cousin Franz said it was to be regretted that I had not bought a round-trip ticket. Had I done so, one could have been assured I would return in six weeks; and one could have put up with that. But now it was all up in the air. I merely laughed at his comment, and none of those present knew how justified his fear was. At first, he frequently wrote to me. Since I answered only once or twice, he eventually stopped writing. It never occurred to me that he could perceive my not replying as indifference on my part. When I stepped from the train late at night upon my return to Breslau after an absence of ten months, he was the first to meet me; but I simply took that for granted. My existence in Hamburg, now that I look back on it, seems to me to have been like that of a chrysalis in its cocoon. I was restricted to a very tight circle and lived in a world of my own even more exclusively than I had at home. I read as much as the housework would permit me. I heard and also read much that was not good for me. Because of my brother-in-law's specialization, some of the books that found their way into his house were hardly intended for a fifteen-year-old girl. Besides, Max and Else were totally without belief; religion had no place whatsoever in their home.

Deliberately and consciously, I gave up praying here. I took no thought of my future although I continued to live with the conviction that I was destined for something great. My cousin Leni, who had quit school when I did, now started private lessons in preparation for entrance into a higher class in the *Gymnasium*. In council, the family had decided she was to become a pharmacist. Before leaving Breslau, I had learned about this from our mutual cousin, Richard Courant. Leni's mother had asked him to tutor Leni in the required mathematics. He did not want to refuse his aunt's request but was just as loath to waste his time on what might be a hopeless project.

"How dumb is she, anyway?" he asked me.

I said that far from being dumb she was rather a good average; but that I also doubted that she had the perseverance needed to work so strenuously for any length of time, especially since the idea did not stem from her but had rather been imposed on her from outside.

"Now if you were to want it, I would, of course, do it without hesitation," he remarked.

No, I did not want it — to prepare myself for the *Gymnasium*. If I remember correctly, he did not take on the project and, in his stead, Hans Horowitz was entrusted with it. A lawyer, he was less experienced in teaching than Richard; but he had graduated with high marks and so, surely, was familiar enough with mathematics and Latin to prepare her for the *Sekunda*.[4‡] As long as help was available within the family, one did not seek it from strangers. Leni took the entrance examinations in autumn and failed. Her sadness was evident in a letter she sent to me in Hamburg soon thereafter to congratulate me on my birthday. Expressing my heartfelt sympathy, I replied that she should not bemoan this mishap since something better might well follow upon it; that, after all, I had not undertaken anything at all so far and still I was convinced that eventually I would develop into something worthwhile.

Though at a great distance from me, my mother provided that I should not be too lonesome. She got my eldest brother to spend his vacation in Hamburg and gave him strict orders to take me along on all his sight-seeing trips and excursions; Else was to give me time off to go. A two-day trip to Helgoland[34] was the best of all. Before that I had never gone beyond Cuxhaven. I had made several trips on the Elbe. This time our boat was so shrouded in mist that one saw nothing whatever of the beautiful shores. Every few minutes the frightful foghorns could be heard signalling the passing of some ship; that was essential for only as they went close by could one see their ghostly outlines. Suddenly the mist parted, and the port of Cuxhaven lay before us with its many steamers, masts and sails bathed in bright sunlight. Then the wide expanse of the ocean was before us transparently clear and green. And, finally, out of those green waves one saw rise the steep red cliffs of the small island. There was the famous "*Lästerbrücke*" ["Bridge of Calumny"], the pier from which bored vacationers critically scrutinized both the docking boats and the newcomers. We passed quickly through the lowland which offered its big hotels; the highland with its fishermen's huts and the huge white lighthouse pleased me much more. We had a room for the night at a boarding house up there. In the evening, once more, we went out to walk to the isolated lighthouse. Not far from it, someone had tied a sheep to a post. It bleated pitiably as we came near, and in its light green, watery-clear eyes there was expressed such an abyss of mortal fear and total incomprehension that I could never forget it. From the windows of my room one could see the ocean; and at night the sound of the waves penetrated as far as my room. All this was so exciting that I could hardly sleep.

During that interval, as compared to earlier and later times in my life, it seems to me I was a bit apathetic intellectually. My physical development on the other hand was rapid and robust. The slim child blossomed to almost womanly fullness; and, since the blond hair of childhood darkened noticeably, I was scarcely recognized upon my return to Breslau. Formerly I had reminded our relatives of my cousin Martha Courant; now I was mistaken for her.

As I mentioned earlier, our little nephew Harald's serious illness occasioned my being called home. I arrived there on a bitterly cold evening at the beginning of March. Only my brother Arno and ever-faithful Cousin Franz awaited me at the station. My mother rarely relinquished the right to meet us personally. As, probably, she and my sisters were all exhausted by the excitement of the past few days and the frequent visits to the sickroom, they allowed the bad weather to keep them at home. Despite the mournful atmosphere, I was received with great joy. Smiling, my sister Frieda declared: "We said, 'If this does not bring her home, she is not our sister.'"

This reception embarrassed me so greatly that I withdrew into myself to some extent.

Little Harald died a few days after my return. Now I was actually without any real employment. I helped out in the house and took over completely for a week while Rosa went on a hike in the mountains. Otherwise, I had a lot of free time. I used it principally for reading, preferably drama: Grillparzer, Hebbel, Ibsen, and, above all, Shakespeare became my daily bread.[35] I was much more at home in this colorful world of the great passions and deeds than in the everyday life around me. But the day I produced Schopenhauer's *The World as Will and Idea*,[36] my elder sisters protested energetically. They feared for my mental health; and I had to return the two volumes to the library unread.

Upon my return from Hamburg, the twins, Hans and Franz, resumed visiting us almost daily; in my absence they had appeared less frequently and had, instead, made friends with my cousins Heidel and Grete Pick, the elder sisters of my classmate Leni. Now they usually came after the evening meal as they were busy at their jobs during the day. One was a lawyer; the other was employed in a bank. Once again there was plenty of music and some sport for we played tennis and went rowing. I was no longer the wholly innocent child. I was delighted when, without having to use words, I could achieve what I wanted with but a single glance.

Erna was now in the *Unterprima* and had to work hard. Every time an essay was assigned, she came home moaning about it. Then, having had her tell me the topic, I would inquire about the teacher's directions and then discuss with her how to tackle the project. For every proverb or quotation, several illustrative examples out of my beloved books would immediately occur to me. Then I would encourage her to make a start; and when the offspring of her labor was born, it was presented for my approval. Sometimes all had gone well except that there was no introduction. In that case I would write the introduction. One time the entire essay failed to suit me; I sat down at once and wrote an entirely different one. Erna found this one an improvement over her own; after some hesitation she decided to turn in mine. The strict Professor Olbrich was also pleased with it. Actually, my sister really did not need this kind of help; she was capable of writing very good essays, but she disliked making the required effort and she found no enjoyment in writing as I did. Once she had Goethe's poem "On Mieding's Death" as an assignment. The introduction I wrote referred to the "humorous" portrayal of the Weimar theatrical situation as described in the opening stanza.[37]

"Humorous?" Erna looked at me with misgiving. Nothing had been mentioned about such an aspect, in school; and no doubt it seemed to her questionable that an elegy should begin humorously.

I stuck to my opinion, "Just read it! It's so obvious!"

She calmed down and used the introduction. The professor had no objection to make.

At that time the thought did occur to me at times: actually it would be much smarter to go to the *Gymnasium* myself than merely share in her study on occasion. But I gave it no serious consideration; it seemed to me that several years earlier I had irretrievably missed the connection. The whole family, in its immediate as well as wider circles, awaited with interest my decision about the future. My brothers and sisters even made all kinds of suggestions. Since I had enjoyed drawing when I was a child and had done a lot of it, they inquired whether I would not like to go to art school. I declined for I was certain I did not have the talent necessary for that. Once, my brother Arno took me to a photographer acquaintance of his to check out the requirements for being trained in his studio. I listened to all that was said and then allowed the matter to rest. I could not act unless I had an inner compulsion to do so. My decisions arose out of a depth that was unknown even to myself. Once a matter was bathed in the full light of consciousness and had acquired a definite form in my thoughts, I was no longer to be deterred by anything; indeed I found it an intriguing kind of sport to overcome hindrances which were apparently insurmountable.

My mother had remained silent during all this time; that was added protection for me against burdensome importuning by the others. Toward the end of the summer, though, Mother asked me about it one morning while combing my hair — she liked doing that although I had long since learned to fix it myself. Was it really so: there was nothing at all I would like to do? I said I regretted my decision to forego the *Gymnasium*. That, she suggested, need not cause regret. After all, other people started attending there when they were already thirty; certainly then, for me, not quite sixteen, it would hardly be too late.

A few days later, my cousin Richard came to see her at her office. Having studied in Zürich during the summer, he now came to let her know he was home again. My mother at once asked his advice on my behalf. He declared it would be possible to prepare me for acceptance into the *Obersekunda*[4] by the following July; it was now September. He himself would take charge of the mathematics lessons. For Latin, he brought us an acquaintance of his who was nearing the end of his studies in classical languages and who had an excellent reputation as a tutor. A slim young man wearing a pince-nez, Herr Dr. Marek was interviewed. His manners were very correct. My mother asked him whether he could undertake to prepare me for the *Obersekunda* by the following summer. He explained that for the moment he could not guarantee to do so since, after all, success did not depend on him entirely. I understood the veiled hint; he would have to learn first how much aptitude his pupil possessed. This cautious approach appealed to me and awakened my confidence in him. An entirely different kind of life now began for me. Daily I had one hour of Latin and one hour of mathematics and was given so much homework that it kept me busy the whole day. In these subjects I had to make up three years of work missed by not attending classes in the *Realgymnasium*.[38] However, since the material to be learned had to be covered in a shorter period of time, the courses I was now given were more difficult than those corresponding three years of classes in school would have been. The Latin curriculum comprised the entire grammar as well as the early literature, Caesar and Ovid. For the other subjects, what I had learned in the *Höhere Mädchenschule* sufficed, and I needed only to refresh my knowledge in those disciplines. This I was to do without tutoring; I postponed it until the time immediately before the entrance examination. I wanted the venture, which seemed so highly daring to me, to be kept a secret from the larger circle of relatives. I disliked being the subject of discussion at any time. In the present situation, I also had a feeling that talking too much about the matter beforehand could endanger the outcome. My mother was of the same opinion. My brothers and sisters were good enough to keep it quiet—until December. Then my sister Frieda, annoyed because I would not skip my lessons on her birthday, blurted out the whole thing to an uncle of ours. He had come to congratulate Frieda and happened to run into my mathematics tutor in our parlor. Sorry to say, that teacher was no longer my cousin Richard. During the few lessons I had from him, I really learned for the first time to appreciate him fully. Then, on the advice of his friends, he went to

Göttingen as that would be decidedly advantageous for his later career. Someone to replace him had to be found. Dr. Marek had an acquaintance whom he could recommend.

Herr Dr. Grossmann was an older student, already in his thirties. He had begun his studies late after having worked at a trade. His self-assurance was apparent from the beginning and he did not impress me as very reliable. Later, some annoying habits he had got on my nerves so much that every lesson became a bit of torture. Tearing at his fingernails, he paced the room during the lesson. Also, he liked to poke fun in a manner I considered to be in poor taste, for example, he altered the figure he had drawn to show me the Pythagorean theorem into the caricature of a man and said that this was "old Pythagoras"; and he often tried to start personal conversations. Of course such attempts on his part failed, for I simply said we had no time to chatter; we would otherwise not cover the subject matter. He replied with some irritation: what more did I want? Were I not so extraordinarily gifted, we should never have achieved as much as we already had. But then, having no other choice, he would restrict himself to the lesson material. He often insisted: absolutely, I had to take up mathematics; I had the talent for it; that, as it was useful outside of school, it had much better prospects than any other subject. What else was I thinking of? Curtly, I answered that, for instance, medicine might be considered. He was completely dumbfounded; apparently he had been thinking only of academic subjects. That brought the discussion to an end, which was all I had wished to achieve with that remark. His inability to be on time was another distressing fault. Sometimes he came an hour late; sometimes he did not come at all. We had been brought up to be strictly punctual; it was a family tradition of the Courants. I found his unreliability atrocious.

"But, please, do come punctually next time!" I would say every time we shook hands at the end of a lesson.

He would promise earnestly but failed to improve. I would have been glad to be rid of this unsatisfactory teacher, but I told myself that another change would mean the loss of more time and decided to put up with the evil for the sake of my goal. On the other hand, I was totally satisfied with Herr Dr. Marek. We hardly spoke a word to one another apart from the lesson, proceeding without pause, quietly and surely. After a few weeks of work, he told me that were I to continue at the same rate I would be able to enter the *Obersekunda* early, at Easter. After all, adjusting to the class at the beginning of the school year would be more comfortable than jumping in later at midyear. Of course, I was elated by this prospect. Objections by the mathematics teacher were ignored. He was prodded more vigorously than before; and, sighing, he had to accommodate himself to the zeal of his indefatigable pupil. After my mother had initially spoken to the two men, I made all further arrangements with them myself. As was customary when speaking formally to young ladies, they addressed me as *"Gnädiges Fräulein,"*[39] and they treated me with great respect. I also was the one who handed them their fee each month. That always embarrassed me a little since I had a feeling that accepting money was in some way demeaning. I tried to mitigate this somewhat by providing myself as much as possible with gold coins for this purpose. To me they seemed to possess greater dignity than silver, not to mention paper. Without doubt, such inhibitions were totally foreign to the two gentlemen. They depended on this income; Herr Grossmann in particular was customarily in straits toward the end of the month and at times even had to ask for an advance.

This half-year of intense work I have always remembered as the first completely happy time of my life. That may be attributable to the opportunity given me a first time here: to have my mental powers fully engaged in a task for which they were eminently suited. When I sat alone at the desk in the room given me for my work, at the time I had no study of my own, I was totally oblivious of all the world outside. Each time I found the solution to a problem in mathematics I would whistle a few measures as a song of triumph. I never seriously considered making mathematics my major. For me, rather, it was a sport, a healthy form of mental exercise. But it was not what I had been born for. Latin was something else again; far more enjoyable even than studying modern languages, this grammar with its strict rules fascinated me. It was as though I were learning my mother tongue.

That it was the language of the Church and that later I should pray in this language never even occurred to me at the time.

During this period the family saw me practically only at meal-times and after supper. I was not permitted to study in the evening. As children we had become accustomed to going to bed promptly at eight o'clock. Later the time was adjusted to nine o'clock. Even in the higher grades of the *Gymnasium*, I kept to this habit for it was most important to me that I be fresh and eager for work bright and early.

In the first months when I was working so secretly, I kept from mentioning it even to my faithful knight Franz. Once he found a paper with some writing on it on my desk. I snatched it away before he could read it. Obviously distressed, he asked whether I had a secret. After a brief inner struggle I handed him the slip of paper. It bore some Latin numerals.

"You intend to go to the *Gymnasium?*"

"Yes."

He pondered that seriously but made no objections. I asked him not to mention it to any of the others; then our conversation was over. I do not know what went on within him at that moment. It could well be that he told himself he had lost me. He was more serious and brooding than his twin brother. This was precisely what had always attracted me to him. But he was much slower at learning; and after a long bout with diphtheria, which greatly weakened his constitution, he had even had to repeat one grade. After a difficult battle with himself, he had decided to leave the *Gymnasium* at the point of being ready for the *Prima* and had taken, instead, an apprenticeship in a bank. He had been bitterly disappointed in me at that time because I failed to realize how hard a decision it had been for him; I had been, after all, still very much of a child while he was going through the crises of adolescence. He knew I would be in my element, studying. But, he might well be telling himself now, it signalled the parting of our ways. I mentioned earlier that shortly after my acceptance to the *Gymnasium*, the twins stopped their daily visits to our house and that we then seldom saw one another. Both of them remained unmarried. We never talked about the reasons for which our friendship had evaporated. Hans once wrote to me from the front that it was a shame that after the splendid years of childhood we had spent together we should have become so estranged.

After I had been preparing for some time, my mother went with me for an interview with the redoubtable principal Herr Roehl. After all, I had to register for the entrance examination and to ask for advice about preparing for it. He seemed determined to do all he could to discourage me. According to him, the goal was nearly unattainable. He made a point of warning me that I needed to be fully prepared in all the other subjects as well, not merely in Latin and mathematics. He also advised me to base my study on the textbooks currently in use. In order to obtain these, I called on the companion of my childhood days, Marie Grünberg, who was attending the *Obersekunda*.

"Your old friend is here again," her mother told her with heartfelt joy.

In frankly uncomplimentary terms, her father expressed what he thought of the principal's absurd pomposity. The Grünbergs were rather more inclined to urge me to apply for the next higher grade so that I should again be Mariechen's classmate. This, however, did seem to me to be unattainable. As it was, I resigned myself to entering a class of students younger than myself because of the break I had made in my education. However, I have never regretted that such had been my decision. Those two years free of the pressures of attending school had made me so well physically that I was now a match for any strenuous task.

I left the Grünbergs with all the required books and information, and loaded with good wishes. I now began to review French, English, and history. Soon, a companion I found was helping me with my task. One of Erna's classmates told her that a young girl from Upper Silesia was boarding with her parents and that she, too, was preparing for the *Obersekunda*; she would be delighted to join me for some studies. Thereafter Trudi Mervins often came to our house. She was a charming little person, lovely to look at, cheerful, and amiable. But her knowledge was so minimal that I held out little hope for her. I had some trepidation even about myself as the time of the examination approached. I had no experience of such an examination and imagined one had to know everything included in the curriculum of the three lower grades. Only later, when I myself had to give such examinations, I learned that an examiner is happy at getting any kind of answer from one's victim. I was enraged when my brothers and sisters spoke as though I could not possibly fail.

Frieda once reported to me, "Your brother has a very high opinion of you. He said the teachers would have to be crazy if they were to fail you. After all, no one could be better prepared."

Indignantly, I retorted, "He has no idea how much it involves!"

At another time she asked me what I intended doing should I actually fail. Not that she herself thought such a thing could happen, but just in case! Frieda was our treasurer. The large amount in gold pieces I had already gotten from her for my tutoring outraged her economical mind, and she was not at all in favor of prolonging such expensive private tutoring. Her preference would have been to have it stop as soon as Richard Courant left. (This cousin had taught me free of charge.) Now her opinion was that I ought to give up the whole undertaking should I not be accepted at Easter. What I had learned would be useful to me in any case. For instance, I could get an afternoon job supervising children's homework as Leni Pick had done. To my mind the very notion of restricting myself to such narrow horizons was appalling. But I made no comment. I simply ignored the whole interrogation. There would be time enough for that after the examination was over.

When the semester closed at the beginning of March, Dr. Marek bade me good-bye. He wanted to spend his vacation at home in Upper Silesia. We had covered the curriculum; in the remaining few weeks I should review it on my own

Greatly frightened, I asked, "Are you really not going to be back before the examination?"

No, he had no intention of returning. After all there was no need to do so. Was I afraid? Yes, of course, I was afraid. He was amazed.

"Of what? Few persons are as accurate or proficient in grammar as you are; you can translate and are familiar with reading verse." Herr Marek had never once flattered me. So this assurance really set my mind at rest.

With the end of April came the dreaded day. Besides Trudi Mervins and myself, there was a third candidate for admission to the *Obersekunda*. While waiting in an empty classroom for the examination to begin, we introduced ourselves. The stranger assured us that she knew a great deal but that most likely she would be asked questions which were too simple and then she would be in trouble. We were given written examinations in Latin, mathematics, French, and English. It took several hours. Erna waited for the examiners as they left the room and asked about the outcome. Naturally, they could not say much; but they let it be noticed that things were going well. About noon, my mother also joined us in the auditorium to await the announcement of the results of the examinations. The principal read out the names of those accepted for the various classes, beginning with the lowest. I was the only one who had passed for acceptance to the *Obersekunda*. It was suggested that Trudi Mervins go to the *Obertertia*. She did attempt it; during the first weeks she would slip over to join me during the recesses, clinging to my arm. But she was unable to adjust and returned home to her parents. I do not know what became of her.

4

So I became a student again. Upon entering the school building the day classes were to begin, I met my former principal on the stairs. His greeting was as friendly as it had been ten years earlier when I had come there for the first time. I asked him where the *Obersekunda* classroom was located, and he showed me the way himself.

If I remember correctly, I was the first one in the room. Gradually others arrived. A big girl with reddish hair came in, threw a schoolbag on one of the desks and said, with a sigh, "Life is troublesome and time-consuming." That gave me a taste of authentic school jargon.

I recognized a few of my new classmates because, formerly, they had also attended the *Viktoriaschule*. One of them was Julia

Heimann who sat next to me. She was reputed to be the richest
girl in town and was probably being sent to the *Gymnasium* by
her parents because it was the best educational facility available. Many other provisions were being made for her education;
she had a "Miss"[40] who, accompanied by a fine black dog, called
for her after school each day; besides this, she received private
lessons in conversational French and Italian. She was not very
gifted, but as she worked assiduously, she was always among the
better students in the class. By nature she was inclined to be
mischievous and might not have been a well-behaved child had
she not had such a careful upbringing. She was dressed with
great simplicity, in excellent taste, and her clothing was of fine
quality. She seldom wore any kind of jewelry and told us once
that her parents had forbidden their relatives to give her such
presents. Her grandmother must have been exempt from this re-
striction for I remember a gold and turquoise necklace which she
had brought for Julia from Egypt. I was particularly impressed
to learn that Julia tucked her alarm clock under her pillow for
the night to keep it from disturbing the Miss who slept in the
same room.

Among the students of the class, there were seven other Jewish
girls besides Julia and myself, but none of us received a strictly-
orthodox upbringing. From the *Obersekunda* on, the school
provided no more instruction in religion as there was no examination in that subject. (This was later changed.) Nor, for that
matter, did I notice anything like deep piety in any of the other
girls in the class. In the higher grades, the Protestant religious
instructions were given by a gentleman who obviously set out to
win his students' adulation; and, without doubt, for some of
them he was truly a menace.

Only a single classmate was a Catholic; and she had to repeat
the *Obersekunda* because of difficulties with Latin, so after that
first year we were in separate classes. As long as the school on the
Ritterplatz was being used, we had gone back and forth together, both of us going home at noon. If ever I had to miss
school, I would get the assignments I had missed from her. She
was a quiet, intelligent, and even-tempered girl; and I liked her
very much. We never discussed religious topics. After my grad-

uation, we lost sight of one another. Much later, through a mutual acquaintance, we had news about each other once more. That is how I learned that she entered rather late the Benedictines at St. Gabriel (Steiermark, Austria). From there, within this past year, she has reestablished contact with me.[41]

When I resumed my studies, my first class was in Latin Literature taught by Professor Olbrich. As a teacher, he was thoroughly erudite and widely knowledgeable; we prized his instruction highly. But most of the girls were in fear of him because he demanded so much from us and reprimanded in an abrupt, acerbic manner. We also began to notice that he never looked at us directly and was quite obviously uncomfortable when, as we did with the other teachers, we gathered around his desk after class in order to discuss something with him or to examine something he had brought to show us. So we called him a misogynist and got the impression that he considered himself actually too good to be teaching in a girls' school.

The class was new to him; he taught only on the upper levels. He had not been my examiner and was apparently loath to trust the verdict of his colleague. In any case, I was the first one he called on to read some verses. They were from the beginning of Ovid's autobiography: *"Ille ego qui fuerim, tenerorum lusor amorum. . . . "* I was familiar with the passage and accustomed to the meter of the verse; so I read a longer piece smoothly but giving a clearly stressed rhythm.

"You can read," the strict one commented.

At first I was not certain whether practices prevailing here regarding prompting and copying were similar to those in the *Mädchenschule.* During the first test, though, a friendly poke in the ribs from my neighbor Julia put me wise. Thereafter I knew my duty and always placed my notebooks in such a position that my neighbor could comfortably peep into them.

Our first reports were distributed in the fall. Officially, the assignment of seats according to our standing in class had been discontinued, but our teacher, Professor Olbrich, gave out the reports strictly by rank. Mine lay on top. Before he handed it over, he made me a little speech in front to the whole class: I was, obviously because of my talent, by far the best. This, however, should not now lead me to stop making an effort. These well-meant words delivered, however, in his usual harsh manner, irritated me so much that at first they completely ruined my joy at having a good report. On the doorstep at home, I met Erna who eagerly grabbed the report book.[42] She could not reconcile the good marks with my unpleasant mood.

Nearly in tears, I told her what had happened and said, "What a conceited goose he must take me to be that he should say such things to me."

At home, of course, there was much rejoicing over my success; that sweetened the bitter pill for me.

The class I had joined was in a deplorable state. There had been a frequent turnover in Latin teachers; and the last one had indeed been a comical figure who had no more than a wobbly foothold in all of the many subjects he taught. Therefore Professor Olbrich found much that he could fault, and he often criticized the entire class severely. After I had been there for some time, he was inclined to set me before the class as a model. This always embarrassed me greatly. On one occasion he remarked one would have to have a pretty strong character to achieve anything in such surroundings. He mentioned no names, but immediately after class I was sarcastically greeted as the "strong character" by the other students. Another time he commented to one of the other grades, "In the class below yours we have, first of all, Fräulein Stein, then there's a big gap, after which come the others."

Of course, an account of this remark spread immediately throughout the school and then, to a large degree, in town. I resented it especially as it might well have disturbed the good relations I had with my classmates. But actually it did no real harm. We were a small number; only fifteen made it to graduation. This little flock banded together in warm comradeship, and I do believe they trusted me. Prior to every Latin class, I had to review the assignment for them. For this I usually sat on one of the tables in the center of the room with the others clustering around me on tables and chairs. Some brought me their German or French compositions to read before they made the final draft. Upon my arrival as a stranger in the class, we addressed one another formally as "*Sie*"; but before long we were all using the more familiar "*Du*."[43] During a lengthy rest stop on the first school excursion, one of my classmates asked me to walk alone with her for a bit, and in this tête-à-tête offered me her friendship. She told me in detail with whom she had been associating outside of school but that no one among them was fully satisfactory. Being approached so formally rather amused me, but I agreed without further ado to visit her soon thereafter. First I was introduced to her mother, then, having found favor in her sight, I also met her father and little sister. After that, we often visited one another. The following summer nothing would do but that I spend several weeks with the entire family in the *Riesengebirge*. Lene Koppel was younger than I and still very childlike. After Hans Biberstein got to know her at our house, he presented me with a prophecy: someday I would marry a man who would be decidedly my inferior. (Lene later married his cousin, Dr. Martin Biberstein, and relations, now, between the two families are very cordial.)

I did not allow Hans' teasing to mislead me. This young friend of mine was open, trusting, and had a deep affection for me. She was diligent and markedly talented, especially in mathematical subjects; when we worked together reviewing for a test in mathematics or physics, we both gained from it. Through her I was admitted to the literary circle of Fräulein Freyhan to which Rose Guttmann and Lilli Platau belonged. Less frequently, I also met with Lene's friends in our own class, Hanna Tworoger and Lotte Henschel. Hanna was one of the eldest in the class and had manifold interests. That gave us many mutual contacts. But there was something eccentric, restless, and scatterbrained about her manner which repelled me. It seemed to me that she spread herself too thin and therefore achieved very little in school; actually, she had to drop out of the orals at the *Abitur* while all the rest passed. Lotte was a dear, amusing companion, more gifted artistically than academically. She, too, left school to go to the Academy of Arts in Munich. That was at the end of my first year in the *Gymnasium*. Years later when we met again, she begged me insistently for instruction in philosophy and, for a while, came to me regularly for "lessons."

Another girl joined the class several months after I did. Grete Bergius, whose looks earned her the nickname "the elephant chick," was tall, robust, plump, an appearance matched by her boisterous, childlike merriment. However, all of that concealed a pure and noble soul. Full of youthful enthusiasm, she was riding a pair of hobbyhorses at this particular time: Schiller and chemistry. Her father owned a chemical plant near Breslau; after both parents died, her brother took it over. So, for her also, chemistry was without question the only course of study. At her insistent plea, I sometimes visited her on a Sunday afternoon. She lived all alone with an aunt who seemed to devote herself entirely to this child and who was delighted that some companionship for her had been found. The quiet and neat atmosphere there suited me completely. Grete liked to play chess, and to please her I brushed up my knowledge of it; as a child I had sometimes played it with my cousins.

I formed a fine comradeship with my desk partner, Julia. During Professor Scholz's history classes (I've described him above as a comical figure),[44] we relieved our boredom by searching out of single words in our ancient history textbook the letters of the Greek alphabet and so practicing it together. When, later, we sat farther apart in class, we wrote one another brief letters using the Greek alphabet; modelling ours on the exchange of letters between Schiller and Körner, we signed the letters "Julius" and "Raphael." Julia's close friends were Toni Hamburger and Hedi Kopf. Hedi was the youngest in the class, and, like Julia, came from a wealthy home. She gave the impression of being a very sheltered child. Although among the most gifted of us, especially in mathematics, she was so modest about it all that, despite her achievements, she never gained a reputation for being a "brilliant" student. Her fine, quiet manner attracted me greatly; indeed, of all my classmates, I believe I liked her most. Despite that, we did not meet outside of school. I was not the type to invite anyone to visit me first, and she probably had a similar habit of holding back. I did spend many of the recess periods with her and her friends.

The question arose among us students once (naturally not in class but rather among ourselves) which of us might be willing to get married. Hanna and I examined the pros and cons very critically. When the question was put to Hedi, she simply said, "Yes, if anyone can be found who will have me!"

That reply pleased me far more than my own strongly feminist attitude at the time. Toni Hamburger associated with the wealthiest girls although she herself came from modest circumstances. Her elder brothers and sisters had contributed much to enliven her intellectually; and probably for that reason she found herself attracted to me. She invited me to visit her, and so sometimes I spent several hours with her. The family was interested in art, and I got to see there, and also at the Koppels, many things that were lacking in my home; in comparison with literature and music, the visual arts roused little interest in our family. Toni had diligently struggled to accomplish something worthwhile in school. While mathematical subjects were easy for her, languages gave her great difficulty, so great indeed at times that she even thought of withdrawing before *Abitur*. At that period, I was taken into her confidence also; and my advice was sought, though of the entire class only her two closest friends were to know anything about the matter. We worked hard to help her through that crisis. She passed the examination easily and became a skilled chemist. Shortly after the war broke out [W.W. I], we met again at a training course for nurses. At the close of the special course, we both worked as volunteers for several weeks in different departments of the *Allerheiligenhospital* [All Saints Hospital]. While there, we resumed the old comradely relationship; but, after that we never saw one another again.

Except for Professor Scholz, who taught us German and history in the *Obersekunda*, our teachers were excellent. Our homeroom teacher in the *Unterprima*, the mathematician Professor Sumpf, was an original type who had a peculiar way of expressing himself. If anyone who was supposed to solve or prove a problem on the board became confused, he would comment: "Possibly you've been pressed through the dunce-sieve today?" or "Are you wearing woolen stockings today?"

Nor did he call us, as was prescribed for the two *Primas*, as "Fräulein X";[45] he simply used our surnames, or should he be in an especially gracious mood, he would call all of us "Lotte."

Since all this was done in a dry, good-humored way, we were inclined to accept it with matching good humor. Besides, we valued his excellent instruction highly. When we learned about acrostics in literature, I immediately made up one about him:

Small's the man you see,
Unsurpassed: our dear;
Merrily strolls he,
Pilgrim without fear.
Firmly fits his cap o'er both his ears.

In mathematics I always received "Good" [a"2"⁴⁺] as my grade; but I was now more convinced than ever that I did not have the specific aptitude for mathematics which some of my classmates had. I also felt that my achievements in some of the other subjects influenced the Professor somewhat to give me that grade. On only one occasion, though surely unintentionally, he did hurt me deeply. It happened during the return trip from one of our excursions. We were playing "Forfeits." I was sent into the next compartment on the train while the others discussed me; each one was to name either a good or bad characteristic of mine; one of them read me the list of opinions they had contributed whereupon I had to admit which one pleased me most, which chagrined me most, and, finally, I had to guess who had made the respective comments. There was only *one* accusation which pained me: someone had said I was given to gloating over the misfortune of others; and this someone was our homeroom teacher. I could hardly imagine a more detestable fault, and that anyone should consider me capable of such an attitude pained me so much that I burst into tears. To see me cry was most unusual. My classmates tried in every way possible to console me. They assured me that surely it had not been meant that seriously; that possibly I had given him that impression because frequently I laughed at some of the dumb answers given in class; that, after all, the teachers did not know us well and so could hardly have an accurate opinion about us. Hedi Kopf had at first nodded her head in agreement with the Professor's opinion; that had made me particularly unhappy. Then when she saw how much I had taken the reproach to heart, she very shyly watched me out of the corner of her eye. The good homeroom teacher said nothing at all. Probably, he had taken the whole thing as a harmless joke and was dumbfounded at its outcome.

Professor Lengert, who taught us modern languages, had paid a price of tireless effort to obtain a thorough familiarity with his specialty. He had frank admiration for anyone who achieved that with greater ease than he. One could learn a great deal from him, and all my life I have been grateful to him for the knowledge of languages I gained during his classes. But the lessons were very boring. Most of the students dozed or occupied themselves with other things. I had two methods for keeping awake. One required taking a very active part in the class. When I looked at the teacher rather pointedly, this usually induced him to call upon me either to read or to translate. But that was not something one could repeat several times during a lesson as others had to have a turn, also. When something was being recounted which interested me, I would interject questions or supplementary remarks. At times the professor would turn to me with questions so that the lesson turned into a dialogue. For instance, he had found out that I read the newspapers regularly; and he called on me when current events came into the discussion. If all this failed, and boredom threatened, I too pulled some other work out of the desk. Herr Lengert, of course, was aware of it and often attempted to catch me being inattentive. But whenever he suddenly called upon me, I always knew which point he had been making and could give the appropriate answer. Then he would shake his head, smiling, and I continued to get a "1" for attention. One spiteful classmate insisted that he kept looking at me in order to read from my expression my opinion about the work the others were doing. Another classmate called out to me on another occasion when I volunteered a comment during class: "Don't be so forward!"

At that the professor nodded in agreement, even though he did so with a kindly smile. This seemed to me to be sheer ingratitude. I considered myself his only reliable support. "Just you wait!" I thought. "You'll see what happens when I'm not 'forward.'"

During the next lesson, I sat at my place without looking up at all. Whenever I was called on, I answered quietly but made no unsolicited contribution. When the bell rang for recess, the good Lengert (we called him "*Lämmchen*" [Little Lamb]) came up to me and asked what was the matter with me: had a poor test paper been returned to me or had anything happened to me? I replied curtly that nothing was wrong with me, and the others laughed. He left the classroom deep in thought; and I stayed behind, secretly ashamed of myself. After that I behaved as usual, and both parties were content.

Herr Roehl, the principal, taught us history in the *Prima*. We no longer feared him as we had as children. He had mellowed with the years. Moreover, we were now clever enough to know how to handle him. If we wanted to avoid getting too heavy an assignment, we would interrupt his lecture with a question about social democracy. We knew that would keep this archconservative man talking until the bell rang. And thus we managed to keep the afternoon free for other work. The entire history course was thoroughly conservative-Prussian. Brandenburg, Prussia, the new German Reich:[46] that was the brilliant development offered to us. The Great Elector, Frederick the Great, and Wilhelm I were the three titans.[47] But, he would add, it was still too soon to tell whether Wilhelm II[48] might not put all of the others in the shade! I was already very critical of this biased presentation. My brother Arno was a zealous liberal in politics; at home we read only liberal papers. That served to counterbalance the official patriotic chauvinism. I found most rankling the "*Sedanfeier*" (Sedan Day Celebration)[49] observed every September 2nd. Weather permitting, the entire school, except for the youngest students, would go up the Oder River on a large steamer to Schaffgotschgarten. There in the open, a stirring patriotic speech would be delivered (the teachers were sentenced to orate by turns); we sang patriotic songs; and several of us had to recite poems. To my joy, I was never called upon to do so; that type of emotional expression was foreign to me. It was painful enough for me to have to listen to such declamations. I had a deep antipathy to the mere idea of continuing to celebrate the victory over the French after so many years. I was not a pacifist, but such an attitude toward a vanquished foe seemed to me most unchivalrous. In my next to final year in school, I once more attended this celebration in the auditorium; and, as usual, the poem "*Nun lasset die Glocken von Turm zu Turm* [Let now the bells from tower to tower]" was recited. When I heard the line "*Er warf den Drachen vom goldenen Stuhl mit Donnerkrachen hinab zum Pfuhl* [Mid thunderclaps, he cast the dragon off the golden throne into the great abyss]," the thought came to me: 'Obviously that's a reference to Napoleon III. What stupidity!' And I was so disgusted by the whole business that then and there I made a solemn resolution never again to take part in such an affair. When September 2 came around the following year, I was in a quandary: to be absent from a holiday observance was no more permissible than to miss a class. Obviously, to state the true reason was so totally out of the question that it never even occurred to me to do that. Nor did I want to give a false one; my mother would certainly never have consented to that. A saving inspiration came to me. My sister had once made a two-day excursion with her class. At the time, that was most extraordinary; and I had always intended to achieve a similar feat for our class. Now I proposed to my classmates that there was no other opportunity left before graduation. If the principal were to give us Sedan Day and the one following it off, then we would be able to get as far as the *Schneekoppe*.[50] Enthusiasm for such a trip naturally spread through the class like wild fire. Our teachers referred us to the principal but gave us small hope of success. With several other brave souls I went to his office to present our case to him in most persuasive words. He finally agreed that if we found a teacher willing to accompany us and if, en route, we would commemorate Sedan Day, he would grant the permission. We already had someone in mind to accompany us: our friendly, youthful physical education teacher who was easily persuaded. But, naturally, she refused to give the Sedan address; that was my responsibility. I composed an address in verse which substantially differed from the usual speeches. Then, on the way, I discovered someone had brought along a *Bi-ba-bo*, a fad at the time in toys for older children. (It was made by attaching doll's clothes to a celluloid Chinaman's head. Two fingers held up the head, two more were stuck in the sleeves and so one made the little man gesticulate.) I borrowed him and had him deliver the address. Therewith our duty was fulfilled. We actually succeeded in reaching the *Koppe* before dark. The summit was taken by our storming the serpentine trail, and we stayed overnight at the top. We spent a pleasant evening entertained by a play, by song, and dance; the next day, we had a fine return trip. The whole school was in suspense for a report about our unusual undertaking, and all marvelled at our boldness.

In the *Unter-* as well as *Ober-Prima* classes,[4‡] Professor Olbrich taught us German as well as Latin. We were all enthused about that. He really made a wealth of knowledge available to receptive young souls. In Schiller's philosophical poems, I found a world-view that suited me. Our regular curriculum closed with the Classic poets. But as a generous supplement, we were given an overview of the dramatic poetry of the nineteenth century. Grillparzer, Hebbel, Otto Ludwig:[51] these, after all, were intimate friends of mine. I listened with intense concentration; all due respect to our "Great O" notwithstanding, I could not resist interjecting a remark sometimes. Once, when he intended to speak about Hebbel's *"Rubin"* [Ruby] and began by giving the summary, I cried out in amazement: "But that's not from *"Rubin,"* that's his *"Diamant!"* [Diamond] Inadvertently, he actually had made that little slip.

After a presentation of "Agnes Bernauer,"[52] I put up my hand for permission to speak in order to present my divergent view. During recess that morning Olbrich came to me to resume the discussion. That was something extraordinary. He hardly ever carried on a private conversation with us. Perhaps he did not always enjoy having such a critical listener. If so, he never alluded to it.

Essays, for many the biggest cross, were still a joy for me. Olbrich always began to correct our papers as soon as he had received a few notebooks. In the old school building we were able to observe him during recess from a window opposite his desk. When, according to our calculations, he might have finished, one of us stationed herself in the vicinity of the teachers' lounge.

Suddenly the door would open slightly and out came a hand holding the note books. They were distributed in all haste and opened to the accompaniment of pounding hearts. If I found a huge "1,"[53] I would jump for joy. One of my classmates said to me once: "I'm glad you can still be so happy about it; I keep thinking you ought to be used to it by now."

But that never happened. I myself could never evaluate what I had written, and the mark always seemed like an oracular decree to me.

Moreover, since they were subject to taxation in order to raise money for our graduation party, good marks got to be an expensive proposition for us in the final two years. Poor work was not taxed; however, five *pfennige* had to be paid if you got a "3"; ten, for a "2"; twenty, for a "1." But on a composition a "1" cost fifty *pfennige*. If I reported on my work at home, my mother gladly reimbursed me for such expenses. Despite that, I seldom mentioned them; often, the family heard about my achievements in school only in roundabout ways. Then my mother was offended. Naturally, I had no intention of begrudging her pleasure. I was very intent however in avoiding the embarrassment of being the pride of the family.

My years in the *Gymnasium* were happy ones. Adjusting to the *Obersekunda* had been rather strenuous but the two *Primas* were child's play. If we had no composition to write, I was usually finished with all of my homework by four o'clock and had the rest of the afternoon free for my favorite activities. What I read then of belles lettres provided me with treasure to last the rest of my life. It became very useful, too, when I myself had to teach literature. Even more than reading, I enjoyed going to the theater. During those years, every time the presentation of a classical drama was announced, it was as though I had been tendered a personal invitation. An anticipated evening at the theater was like a brilliant star which gradually drew nearer. I counted the intervening days and hours. It was a great delight just to sit in the theater and wait for the heavy iron curtain to be raised slowly; the call bell finally sounded; and the new unknown world was revealed. Then I became totally immersed in the happenings on the stage, and the humdrum of everyday disappeared. I loved the classical operas as much as I did the great tragedies. The first I heard was *The Magic Flute*. We bought the piano score and soon knew it by heart. So, too, with *Fidelio* which always remained my favorite.[54] I also heard Wagner and during a performance found it impossible wholly to evade its magic. Still I repudiated this music, with the sole exception of *Die Meistersinger*. I had a predilection for Bach. This world of purity and strict regularity attracted me most intimately. Later when I came to know Gregorian chant, I felt completely at home for the first time; and then I understood what had moved me so much in Bach.

As *Abitur* approached, all of us had to face seriously the choice of a career. For statistical purposes, in fact, we were required, while still in school, to indicate our chosen field of further study. I had very little reflecting to do anymore. I had given thought to this matter for the first time even before I was accepted for the *Gymnasium*. Once, after our relatives had learned I was preparing myself, my cousin Franz asked me in the presence of a large group of them what I intended to study. I bade him to guess. He enumerated all the subjects. Finally he said, "I know! History of literature."

I nodded, "Literature and philosophy."

During this conversation my sister Frieda's face grew longer and longer. I seemed to give no thought at all to the practical side of life! I read her dismay on her face and was privately amused by it. True, I was not in the least concerned about my daily bread. But I understood well enough that I had to be considerate of my family. Weighing the merits of the subjects which interested me, I felt they could all be useful in a teaching career. Thereafter, when anyone asked me what I planned to study, I would name those subjects in which I hoped I would be taking the state boards: German, history and Latin. Though keeping philosophy on my program, I no longer mentioned it since at the time I did not yet know it was a possible subject for these examinations.

My cousin Richard Courant came from Göttingen to visit us once. Probably someone had already spoken to him about my impractical ideas. He, too, had at one time been advised to give up his mathematics by our uncles who promised to pay his tuition were he to become a doctor or a lawyer; they had no intention of contributing anything were he to choose a profession that offered no prospects of profit.

"How do you really explain your decision to study philosophy?" he asked me.

"Well, how did you come to study mathematics?" I countered with a smile.

He had no doubt about my meaning, but was not yet satisfied. "Have you ever done any work in this subject?"

"No, not really, so far. But I do want to. Of course, I've read a little of Haeckel.[55] But that doesn't deserve to be called philosophy."

Perhaps this opinion of mine earned his confidence in my philosophical capabilities. He asked no further questions.

No one interfered with my choice of profession. My mother's protecting hand shielded it. Of course, occasionally, she did say she would be pleased were I to study law. I could readily turn that down since at the time women were not yet admitted to bar examinations. Neither of us even thought of the social professions. Moreover, law had been merely a modest suggestion from my mother. She wanted me to have full freedom of choice.

"No one has a right to tell you what to do. After all, no one's making us a contribution toward it. Do whatever you think is right for you."

So, without a care, I was able to pursue my goal.

The class which immediately preceded ours in taking the *Abitur* had been the first one ever permitted to do so in our own school.[56] At that time, no one could be exempted from the oral examinations since, simultaneously, they constituted a test of the institution. Our class had taken active participation in that event. Before the students tackled the written examinations, all who were to take the test were treated to a torte which our class contributed. (From that time on, this treat was a tradition.) Then, during their orals, we repeatedly had returned to the school to find out how each one had fared, and in the evening we had presented each of them with a small bouquet of violets. Now, our turn had come. We were to move to another room for our written examinations. But first we danced a farewell jig in our homeroom. The torte supplied by the *Unterprima* made its fortifying appearance. Just as we were on the point of giving it our full attention, we were disturbed by a teacher with whom we had always been rather at swords' points. She had not taught any of our courses but whenever she supervised a recess in our corridor, she dutifully tried to get us out of our room while we always had something urgent to do there. Now, quickly lifting the torte, I advanced on her, asking her most graciously, "May we offer you a piece?"

She drew back in alarm, left the room, and was not to be seen again.

The composition in German came first. Usually I had required an hour less than was provided for a class composition. This time I was unable to finish writing the final draft. Actually, this was no tragedy for we had to hand in our first draft with the final work, and mine looked neat enough to be a final draft. Despite that, I was inconsolable that afternoon. Professor Olbrich, too, was a bit concerned the following day. Repeatedly, during the Latin examination, he came up to me to inquire whether I would get finished. But this time I was in command of the situation. I was sure of the translation even while the text was being dictated, and writing it down went quickly. So nothing could upset me now. Everything else went smoothly as well. In our year, now, one could be exempted from the orals. The teachers were not allowed to divulge to us anything about the results of the written exams but by their behavior they made it rather unequivocally clear. The weeks thereafter were entirely devoted to preparation for the orals; and, naturally, those who would not be required to take them were not called upon in class. I was aware of being practically ignored during all the classroom practices, but I still felt somewhat uncertain. In any case, there was no use cramming; that would have been a waste of time. In an emergency I would have enough time on the day of the examination to review the material should I have to take a test. During the year, I had made all kinds of preparations for the oral examinations. For instance, I had a notebook in which

all the Odes of Horace which we had studied were translated
and interpreted. I had worked out a series of themes in history as
well as some in the French and English languages. I now doled
out all these treasures to the needy ones in our class. Pleading
hands stretched out for them, and the gifts were received with
heartfelt thanks. I was given the coveted task of writing the *Bier-
drama* [beer-skit] during this time. I did not keep a copy of it
but I can still remember the plot. The heroine was a graduate
who had just completed her examinations. All the studying has
completely confused her spirit, and her mother takes her to a
magician who is to expel the evil spirits. He conjures them up
and they appear, one after the other: Cicero, Horace, Frau von
Stein, Gretchen, Klärchen, etc. Finally, the patient awakens as
from a bad dream; she feels well but has not a shred of knowledge left. Then she finds a paper which dispels every one of her
cares:

> Though there's no knowledge in my head
> I fear no one; nothing I dread
> This paper states in clearest type
> For the university I'm ripe.

In addition to that, a committee was appointed to prepare for
the farewell celebration. On it, besides myself, were most of the
girls from the well-to-do families who knew what arrangements
needed to be made for farewell parties. The funds from our tax-
collection were far from enough for our enterprising plans. Out
of consideration for our classmates of lesser means, we ruled out
making any further general assessments. Those who were wealthy
volunteered additional contributions: one would provide the
flowers; another would supply platters of cold cuts; others, the
beverages, cakes, and tortes. This way everything turned out
elegantly and attractively. Only the *Bierdrama* and the comic
program had a collegiate touch. We sent out the invitations
even before the oral examinations took place. The teachers took
this amiss, considering it unpardonably frivolous; they disciplined us by delivering lengthy lectures. But then they all came

just the same, even our former principal who at that time was already in very poor health.

The morning of the examinations, March 3, 1911, arrived. We had to wait in one of the conference rooms on the ground floor until we were summoned to one of the examination rooms. As everyone, including myself, proceeded there in the prescribed manner, Professor Sumpf, smiling genially, asked me in the corridor: "Well, are you *very* scared?"

That sounded most reassuring.

Gathered, awaiting us, were the examiners who comprised the Board: our teachers; a member of the district school administration; and the deputy Burgomaster, representing the city. First came a solemn address. Then the names of those exempt from the orals were announced; there were five of us. We were allowed to withdraw at once. Back in our waiting room we embraced one another; that was totally contrary to our custom as ordinarily we gave no demonstration of affection in school. But we waited for the others who were being given the schedule of their exams. Those with later appointments were permitted to go home for the interval. Julia Heimann had about two hours to wait. She asked to go home with me as it would have taken her an hour just to get to their house, whereas I lived only a few minutes away since our classes had been moved into the new school in Blücher Street. At home, I found awaiting me a torte on which chocolate letters spelled out the congratulations of the family. I could devote very little time to receiving the delighted greetings of my family as I had to look after my guest. Julia had several favors to ask. I should review some history with her. Besides that, she confessed, she had been waiting ever so long for an opportunity to fix my hair the way she would like to see it. Compliantly, I fetched comb and brush and seated myself before the mirror; while she set to work on my head, I delivered the lecture she had requested on the Thirty Years' War.[57] Previous to this occasion, Julia had never visited me. Nothing in our house escaped her notice; and I almost got the impression she had come not merely to save time but, as well, finally to see what kind of home I lived in. She frankly expressed her surprise at finding such a fine home in so modest a neighborhood. She was impressed by the wide oak stairway and the huge living room to which I took her. She also relished the "second breakfast" when one of my sisters brought two cups of chocolate and some baked goods up to us. While I was occupied with Julia, my mother relayed the good news to her brothers and sisters by phone. The uncle in Chemnitz[58] had requested a report by telephone. I was repeatedly called away to accept congratulations in person. When finally Julia's time had come, I went back to school with her; after all, I had to check up on the others who were taking tests. Obviously the visit to our house had made a big impression; in any case, Toni Hamburger, years later, recalled in great detail what she had been told about it.

5

The morning following examination-day, I stayed in bed a little longer than usual. The mail was brought to me; there were already some letters of congratulation including one from Uncle David inviting me to come to Chemnitz. I read it, and then lay there thinking it over. There was not a shred of evidence of the great happiness which I had expected to experience after examination. Rather, I felt a great inner emptiness. A beloved and familiar way of life was gone forever. What lay ahead? I weighed all of my good uncle's unspoken reproaches on the subject of my choice of profession. Had I really made the right decision?

We are in the world to serve humanity.... This is best accomplished when doing that for which one has the requisite talents.... Therefore...?

The conclusion seemed to me to be indisputable.

I shook off all doubt and that very day sent to Chemnitz the letter I have already mentioned,[59] making my position definitely clear.

The class' farewell party went well except for one unfortunate small incident. The program at table included a song composed by one of the most inept students in our class. It had been made up on our Sedan excursion and was being repeated on this occasion. It was a description of a school-day from the first bell to the last; one stanza treated of all our sideline activities during

English or French class. When the meal was over, good Professor Lengert had disappeared. No one noticed his leaving. When he was missed, everyone was upset.

"Why didn't you seat me next to him?" I asked reproachfully. "I definitely wouldn't have allowed him to leave."

They had given me our former religion teacher as table partner. We had not had any classes with him for a long time; but whenever he met us in school, he always inquired about our progress. So we had invited him, and he had come. If I recall correctly, we had also had his meal brought in from a kosher restaurant. After the celebration, Principal Roehl reproved us because of the tactless song. The class "elder," Elizabeth Spohr (who was already a teacher before she joined our class), and I were commissioned to seek out the injured party at his home and effect a reconciliation. Professor Lengert received us in his usual friendly manner. He said quite frankly that he had no objection to our having sung that song among ourselves. But in the presence of the principal, it had been embarrassing for him. The poor man! Such worries were still very far from us. When I begged him once more not to hold it against our class, he laid his hand on his heart and said, "But, *Gnädiges Fräulein*, you know me!"

The beer-skit had given me great concern because even at dress-rehearsal time the actresses had not full command of their parts. But, naturally, all went well by the time of the performance. I was not one of the actors but, rather, the director and prompter. At its conclusion, the author was called for and, at center stage, "Horace" crowned me with his wreath. Professor Olbrich assured me that at no farewell party had he ever seen a play as well ordered. This I considered a rather dubious compliment.

The comic program was read aloud. Among other items, it gave terse epigrams about each of us. As they were unable to guess to whom the verses applied, the teachers demanded that each of us rise after the one coined especially for her. Mine went as follows:

> Let woman equal be with man,
> So loud this suffragette avers,
> In days to come we surely can
> See that a Cab'net Post is hers.

All were amazed to see me stand up after that was read. Now they could clearly see for themselves how very little they had known about us fundamentally.

While we sat together talking, we asked the teachers to write some souvenir messages on the back of the programs. As usual, my surname enticed them to make a play on words. The principal, of whom we had once been in such awe, wrote the cordial phrase: "Strike the stone [Stein] and treasures will gush forth."

However, the brief quotation from Ibsen which Professor Olbrich gave me pleased me most:

"Strike blow on blow
'Til time ends here below!"[60]

We were no longer required to attend school after the examinations were over. The class dispersed and we never again congregated in one group. There was not even a formal presentation of the diplomas in the auditorium. They were mailed to our homes later. I was already in Berlin when mine arrived, and my family sent me a copy of it. My mother was so proud of it that she even showed it to her business friends. Years later I learned from a mutual acquaintance that one of them had made a copy of it for himself and showed it around in his own circle of friends.

As I have mentioned, my "mulus"[61] trip started with a visit to Berlin. My mother's favorite brother, Eugen Courant, was to celebrate his fiftieth birthday on March 19. I went there in advance; Mother, accompanied by her other daughters, followed in time for the celebration. I then prolonged my stay a while longer since my uncle was taking a trip to Italy with his wife; he wished me, along with one of his sons, to take care of their house. Since the family traits were most noticeable in him, this cousin, Fritz Courant, was, of the three brothers, our favorite. (Incidentally, their mother was also related to us; she was a cousin of ours on our paternal side. As a rule, she was not too amiable toward guests but she had taken me to her heart from my childhood on.) To "chaperone" us, we had to have an elderly cousin stay with us; she was not in the house during the day because of her job in a business concern. I made fun of this supervision but, at the same time, I was indignant at heart for, proud of my virtue, I found the notion that we needed surveillance absurd. But I got along well with this elderly cousin. Cousin Fritz, who had to substitute for his father in the office and the factory, was unable to concern himself about me during the day. Nor did I have any household duties. But filling in my time was no problem. We had many relatives in Berlin, and the only danger we ran in that respect was of offending one or other of them by failing to spend enough time with them. If one had only a few days there, it was impossible to get around to see all of them and then there were always some "offended ones." This difficulty eventually spoiled our visits to Berlin. This time, however, I was there for three weeks and was invited by every one of them in turn—sometimes for lunch, sometimes for supper, or, perhaps, to go to the theater. However, these performances to which I was taken were not to my taste. They took me to the latest operettas and the light satirical comedies for which Berlin was famous, all of a sort I would never have chosen had the decision been mine. My cousin called for me like a good fellow wherever I happened to be, and we would then usually end the evening in some café. Among the Berlin relatives, I was fondest of my cousins Adelheid and Martha Courant, both of whom were a few years older than I. They had grown up in Rumania where for many years their father had made his home as a lumber merchant. Their mother came from Galicia;[62] in her youth she had been a very beautiful woman, but her temperament and her idiosyncracies were hardly the type appreciated in the Courant family; the daughters suffered as a result. My uncle attached great importance to giving them a German upbringing. He enrolled them in a convent school and eventually sent them to Germany for a year during which they attended the *Viktoriaschule* with me. All the relatives were enchanted by them.

They were very small and, for their height, rather plump, but exceedingly pretty and amiable. We liked best to see them in their Rumanian folk costume; its rich embroidery was their own handiwork. But they could be induced to wear it only seldom and even then only for a few hours at some celebration. Adelheid formed a special attachment to me; although she was several grades ahead of me in school, we regularly spent the long recess together. While I was getting ready for the *Gymnasium*, they came once again from Rumania for a few weeks as our guests. Later the entire family moved to Berlin. Two sons had been born later: Sigurd and Helmut, handsome and very talented boys. Sigurd was now fifteen years old; he often sought my assistance with some problem in mathematics which he found difficult, and his facile comprehension always delighted me. Until then I had hardly known the father of the family, my Uncle Berthold, as obviously his visits to Germany from Rumania had been few. He was an extraordinarily able businessman, amiable and good-humored in his personal relationships, and somewhat reminiscent of our grandfather. But he had played a disastrous role in that business crisis which had resulted in his eldest brother Jakob's death.[63] I had been too young at that time to have been initiated in all the details; but they had left me vaguely uneasy with him. By now things had improved greatly for him again financially. The family lived in a large, elegant apartment in the West End of Berlin; and the house was run with a lavish hand. But the daughters were brought up to be unassuming and were capable housekeepers, skilled at any task. Unfortunately, the next time I visited Berlin, I was drawn into one of those family feuds about which I have already spoken.[64] There was at the time a rather unpleasant business conflict between the brothers Berthold and Eugen Courant.

Uncle Eugen was so indignant about the injustice (whether real or imagined) that had been done him that he forbade me to visit the "B.C.'s." I was merely passing through Berlin and had very little time. My aunt considered Uncle's demand excessive and got him to reconsider. But I was aware that he would see it as a vote of confidence if I were to side with him. I thought of his love for my mother and the kindness he had shown her, and I wanted to do him a favor now. When Martha Courant telephoned to greet me and asked when I would be coming to them, I told her I could not. Thereupon her father phoned himself, demanding to know the reason. He offered to set before me all the evidence so I could form my own opinion.

"For you are well educated and know the meaning of: "*Audiatur et altera pars!*"[65]

But I did not take him up on the offer. I told him I held no opinion in the matter but as things stood between my mother and Uncle Eugen, I felt it my duty to support him. The whole situation was very embarrassing for me and later I regretted my behavior. Uncle Berthold was angry for many years thereafter, not only with me but with my mother, also. Because a very long time passed before I went to Berlin again, I never saw him or my dear cousins again. I had sent him word once, long after the incident, that I was truly sorry about the whole affair and thereupon received greetings from him as a sign of our reconciliation.

When the travelers returned from Italy, I went on to Chemnitz. I felt completely at home in that beautiful, well-kept home and in the entire circle of their acquaintances because of my previous visit there. This time my cousin Erich was also at home. He was a year younger than I and had just begun the *Oberprima*. Now my successful *Abitur* was held up to him as a pattern; this was not at all to his liking. Once, thoroughly vexed because he had verified that I had read Part II of "Faust," he declared: "People like you only have so much time to read because you're too lazy to take part in any sports!"

Otherwise, we got along fine together. One afternoon when I returned from somewhere with my aunt, he and another young man were practicing some dance steps to the music of a record-player. As soon as Erich saw me, he asked me whether I could dance. My aunt scolded him for his audacity; but I was both happy and ready to show how accomplished I was.

Thanks to Hans Biberstein, I knew all the latest steps. Erich had to admit he was outclassed and remarked in sincere admiration: "A girl, who's made her *Abitur* and been excused from the orals, who has read "Faust," and who can waltz round to the left, should be featured at the Hansa-Theater (the theater with the largest variety shows in Chemnitz)!"

He himself graduated with excellent marks but did not go to the university. As a young businessman, he emigrated to America. Decades have passed since I saw him. His elder brother Walter had always given his parents cause to worry. The somewhat spendthrift ways of the mother had, in his case, developed to an almost pathological improvidence. It took a lot of trouble to get him through the *Untersekunda*. Then he was apprenticed to a respectable business firm as far away from home and from his old influences as possible. But neither there nor in a subsequent job did he last long, for soon he was deep in debt and mixed up in all kinds of shady deals. His father sent him to America, but before long he turned up again. When the war [W.W. I] started, he was dispatched to the front at once. A daredevil soldier, he was almost immediately home again with an Iron Cross and a serious injury to his jaw. Then the old way of life began again. My uncle finally had no alternative but to cut off all contact with him and to forbid him entry into his parental home. I know from personal experience that Walter once telephoned to Berlin to inquire about his parents' well-being and to ask whether he might come to the house. He was brusquely rebuffed. He finally married a Christian girl with a lower middle-class background. He lived in the crowded worker's apartment which belonged to his father-in-law, a respectable cabinet-maker. Walter's parents were not happy with his mésalliance and continued to ignore him and his family. But it was a good marriage, and the young wife was inconsolable when he died after a very short illness. She was left with two small children. His parents went to the funeral. On the way to the grave, his daughter-in-law clung to Uncle's arm. When the rabbi had said the final prayers and the whole group of mourners turned to leave, the young woman knelt down at the grave and, in her grief, prayed the Lord's Prayer aloud. Naturally, that was something totally unheard of in a Jewish cemetery but, instead of being offended by it, all were deeply moved.

While I was in Chemnitz, my uncle made arrangements to sell his pharmacy. He was ill at the time, apparently unable to tolerate that industrial city's polluted air.[66] Probably his wife's influence had much to do with the decision for she was eager to move to Berlin. One prospective buyer, though very interested in both the pharmacy, which was in an excellent location close to the market place, and in the big house, repeatedly rejected the high price. My uncle was imperturbable.

"His hesitation will be expensive for him," he would say. "Every time he inquires anew, I raise the price ten thousand marks."

Uncle was adamant. By the time his colleague finally decided to buy, he had to pay thirty thousand marks more than was originally asked. My uncle telephoned to my home in Breslau to announce the good news. I took advantage of his call to inquire whether any of the courses I had been considering had been announced at the university.[67] I had commissioned Erna to keep an eye on the bulletin board. I learned that some lectures had been announced for the very next day, April 27 [1911]. Although that was my good uncle's birthday, I prepared for my departure without delay. My aunt found it totally incomprehensible, but Uncle merely smiled and let me go.

Chapter V

Student Years in Breslau
1911-1913

1

The next day I stood before the famous "Black Board." A whole row of bulletin boards lined the narrow hall of our beloved old Breslau University. Their black surface was covered with small slips of white paper on which the lecturers announced the theme, time, place, and opening date of their lectures. One had to read them very carefully as there were some deviations from the information given in the printed general listing of lectures. Here I pieced together my schedule.[68] It was a good thing that many of the courses I took under consideration were timed simultaneously so, perforce, I had to be selective. Otherwise, I probably would have ended up with some forty to fifty hours a week. Plenty remained, as it was: Indo-Germanic; German grammar, both old- and modern; history of German Drama; Prussian history at the time of Frederick the Great; English constitutional history; and a beginners' course in Greek. (I had always been deeply dissatisfied that our girls' *Gymnasium* was not humanistic, and I now wished to bridge some of the resultant lacunae. Besides, history students would require some knowledge of Greek when taking their examinations.) In addition to the courses already listed were the ones I looked forward to most: a four-hour-per-week course, Introduction in Psychology, by William Stern;[69] and a one-hour-per-week course, dealing with natural philosophy, by Richard Hönigswald.[70] Both

185

men admitted me to their seminars for the first semester. The first lecture I attended was the one in my psychology course. This might have been a portent since the four semesters I studied in Breslau found me occupied principally with psychology. Stern's presentation was elementary and easily understood; I sat there as though attending a pleasant social gathering and was somewhat disappointed. Hönigswald's class was then all the more demanding. His penetrating insight and his rigorous thought process fascinated me. Avowedly, his was the critical philosophy of Kant; indeed, he is today one of the few who have remained loyal to this approach. One had to be familiar with the conceptual thinking apparatus of Kantianism to follow his presentation. The young persons in his seminar were enticed into engaging in dialectical skirmishes against such finely-honed weapons. Anyone who tried to introduce the fruit of an idea which had not ripened on Hönigswald's acre was reduced to silence by his superior dialectic and biting irony, but, at heart, was rarely vanquished. Once, an older student who was most independent in his thought told me, "There are things which one dares not even think during Hönigswald's seminar. Yet outside of class, I cannot ignore them."

Nevertheless, he afforded us excellent training in logical thinking; and at the time that sufficed to make me happy. Moreover, Hönigswald's lectures on the history of philosophy which I later attended were excellent. He gave clear, incisive explications of the concepts of systematic thought. While I valued Hönigswald on the one hand, on the other I rejected, as pretension, his colleague Eugen Kühnemann's excessively sentimental ardor and his invariable, all-encompassing enthusiasm, although he was prominent and lionized at that time. Incidentally, outside of Breslau people were always amazed to hear that Kühnemann's professorship was in philosophy. He was well known for his works on Schiller and Herder so the uninitiated thought him to be an historian of literature.

Stern and Hönigswald were barred from advancement in their academic careers because of their Jewish descent. The position in psychology in Breslau rated an associate professorship yet Hönigswald was no more than *Privatdozent*[71] and continued as such for several more years. Subsequently he succeeded in getting the appointment in psychology when Stern took a position in Hamburg. Only much later, a professorship in philosophy was given to Hönigswald in Munich. Apparently he found all this extremely painful.

The "academic freedom"[72] accorded me at the time of entrance was a two-edged sword. In those days, there were no core requirements such as were prescribed, for instance, for the medical students who followed an established plan for each semester. Our only limitations were that we would have to meet the requirements for the state board examination for teachers of higher education. Checking over these requirements, we could discern what might ultimately be expected of us. As early as my first semester, I bought a copy of these requirements, urged to do so by a fellow student who from the start had zeroed in on the state boards as her goal. That was far from being my way. After all, I would be taking the state boards merely "for the sake of my family." My primary interest was acquiring knowledge. But I recognized the common sense of taking the essentials into consideration when planning my schedule for the various semesters. But, of course, the subjects nearest my heart could not be allowed to suffer on this account. So I was pleased to discover "Introduction to Philosophy" listed among the subjects covered by the examination. Naturally, I immediately chose this subject, thus acquiring a moral cover for my pet study. For the time being, I kept all the other subjects I had chosen already. But, after a few semesters, I had to admit that taking four major subjects was spreading myself too thin. (For the examination a minimum ratio of one to two was required, i.e., one subject for the upper level to two for those on the lower levels.) Similarly, I noted that it was impossible to separate the classic languages, so, Latin without Greek would be only a token subject, whereupon, not without regret, I decided to sacrifice Latin for the sake of philosophy.

Once during this time of deliberation, I presented all the pros and cons to my mother. "My dear child," she said, "unfortunately, I can't advise you. Do whatever you consider right; you are the best judge of what you should do."

I actually knew no one else whom I could consult. And so,

confidently, I mapped out my own course. Many people spend several semesters at a university before they know clearly what they should be studying. Many change their major when they find that judgments they made at earlier stages of their education with regard to their talents or their preferences were incorrect. This is especially true of mathematics where sheer effort avails nothing if one lacks a specific ability for it. Some are discouraged by such uncertainty and may never reach their goal. Naturally, those fare best who, coming from a family of scholars, have received the right kind of direction from their father. For all that, only at the end of one's course of study is one likely to arrive at the realization: at last I know how to go about it.

My freedom certainly caused me no tribulation at the time. I was satisfied with my crowded daily schedule and swam in delight as a fish does in clear water and warm sunshine. Only many years later did I realize what unfortunate consequences the lack of knowledgeable direction produced in my case as well.

Early in those first weeks, I got to know the goal-oriented student whom I have already mentioned. She had not made the *Abitur* but had passed merely a teacher's examination. She did have two years of teaching experience. This so-called "fourth way" of entering the university was rejected by the feminist movement as a Trojan horse: such teaching was insufficient preparation for serious study, so it threatened to result in an unfavorable impression of the ability to be expected from women students at the university. Most of the women who were teachers failed to recognize their being at all deficient and they welcomed with delight the reduced requirements for admission. Those most astute, however, did not avail themselves of the dispensation and made up their *Abitur* or, at least, sought the knowledge they lacked. Kaethe Scholz was an unusually capable and gifted person. I knew her by sight since she had done her two years of practice teaching in the lower grades of the *Viktoriaschule*. That sufficed as a connection. Soon we agreed on various mutual work projects, and, engrossed in lively conversation, we would wander about together in the halls of the university during the intervals between lectures. We were not the only such constant "pair." It is an altogether common experience for students to form such firm bonds; and after but a few months at the university one got to know the combinations. Kaethe Scholz's family were country people and Protestant. She was tall, slim, and blond; her bright eyes radiated her lively, joyous, effervescent temperament. Even though her main objectives from the start were to succeed with the state boards and to have a teaching career, she was as enthusiastic as I about studying. Besides that, she was thoroughly practical. She conducted several circles in which she introduced society women to questions in philosophy and history. As this provided more income than ordinary private tutoring would have, she earned her tuition in this manner. Then, too, she liked doing it; and it was an excellent method of applying, and thereby impressing on her own mind, what she had learned in her courses. Her parents lived in rural Brockau; she commuted by train each morning and spent the day in Breslau. In her free hours, she liked to join me in working on some assignment. Soon she was thoroughly at home in our house. Gratefully and without affectation, she would accept refreshment when this was offered to us. At the university, too, she often shared my mid-morning snack with real appetite. Avidly, we studied Greek together. Three hours a week were allotted for the beginners' course; not more than one summer semester was given to the study of the entire grammar, naturally, in very general terms. In winter, a one-hour advanced course introduced the readings: Xenophon's *Anabasis* and a little of Homer. Of course, this instruction served only as an incentive to do further work on one's own. Most of the participants, the lawyers, theologians, and historians, could not commit themselves to do that; and so, after a few hours in the course, they stayed away. Their only interest was in obtaining a certificate of attendance which they could produce later. But the two of us worked painstakingly to memorize the many verb forms, and we persevered. But, of course, since we were students, we were unwilling to divert too much time from our serious study for such learning by rote. So, to my lasting regret, I never won as thorough and sure a command of Greek as I had of Latin. We also began to study Old High German together. Tatian's[73] harmonies of the Gospels, and, and a little later, Ulfilas'[74] translation of the Bible provided my first acquaintance with the Gospel (except for fragments I had learned from devotions at school). In our Gothic reader, the original Greek text was given below the Gothic text. But at that time it had no religious impact on me. Nor did I ever notice Kaethe Scholz finding in the Scriptures anything of a sacred meaning. Our differences of religion and of family background never ruffled our friendship. Had they ever occupied our minds, we would have discussed questions about religion as frankly as those about anything else. We sometimes became a bit upset during our political discussions. I was at that time very definitely under liberal influences. The Silesian rural population was Prussian-conservative in the majority because of pressure from the large landowners. Kaethe's brother was just then beginning his military career as an officer. That milieu then still influenced her somewhat even though she had widespread contacts with other circles. Subsequently, she had several changes of persuasion. That time also signified for me the beginning of a change in my relation to the state. My study of history contributed to the process. Both the elderly Privy Councillor Kaufmann, a venerable old man whose hair was a beautiful snow-white, and whose blue eyes retained the gleam of youth, and the rather young Professor Ziekursch, who was short but erect in bearing as well as smart looking, were national-liberal politicians. They took delighted pride in the new Reich in which we were all raised, but theirs was not a blind idolization of the royal house, nor were they myopically Prussian. The generous elucidation they gave of the correlations in world history awakened my old love for history again so much so that in those first semesters I was recurringly irresolute about making it my major. My love for history was no mere romantic absorption in the past. Closely associated with it was a passionate participation in current political events as history in the making. Both of these interests probably sprang from an extraordinarily strong social conscience, a feeling for the solidarity not only of all mankind but also of smaller social entities. As thoroughly as I was repelled by Darwinistic nationalism,[75] so completely convinced was I of the significance and of the necessity, both natural and historical, of individual states and variously constituted peoples and nations.

For this reason I was never influenced by socialistic concepts or other international efforts of that type. Simultaneously, freeing myself more and more from the liberal ideas with which I had grown up, I now came to hold a positive, nearly conservative, view of the state though this was never tainted by the particular stamp of Prussian conservatism. Added to purely theoretical considerations was a personal motive of deep gratitude to the state which had granted me academic citizenship with its free access to the wisdom of mankind.

I regarded all the small benefits to which our student's pass entitled us, such as reduced prices for theater and concert tickets and the like, as the loving providence of the state for its favored children. This stirred in me a desire to discharge my debt of gratitude to the people and the state, later, by making a professional contribution of my own. I was indignant over the indifference with which most of the university students regarded current problems. Some of them were intent only on their own amusement during the early semesters while others were anxious only to get enough knowledge to meet the requirements of the examinations in order to feather their nests. My deep conviction of social responsibility also made me decidedly favor women's suffrage. At that time, this was still far from being an integral part of the women's rights movement. The Prussian Society for Women's Right to Vote, which I joined with my women friends because it advocated full political equality for women, was made up mostly of socialists.

2

If, indeed, the majority of the students led a pretty apathetic existence (with furious contempt I called them "The Idiots" and refused even to glance at them in the lecture halls), I was, nevertheless, not alone with my ideals and soon discovered like-minded companions. I have already spoken about our most intimate circle of friends, my sister Erna, Hans Biberstein, Rose Guttmann, and Lilli Platau. I attended the philosophy and psychology lectures with Rose and was introduced by her to a group of young people to whom, in all likelihood, I am indebted for the most valuable results gained as a student in Breslau. The members of this "Pedagogical Group," as they called themselves, were mostly men and women from Stern's seminar. These potential teachers found the university's failure to provide anything which could be considered a preparation for a future teaching career an intolerable deficiency. Admittedly, theoretical courses on education were given; and in the state boards one had to show some knowledge gained from them. But these courses failed to provide any vital connection with the burning questions in education or with educational practices. Later, this very deficiency led to a reform of teacher training methods and to the founding of the teachers colleges. In this manner, these young people proved instrumental in helping themselves.

Stern graciously put the psychology conference room at our disposal as a meeting place. At that time it was located on the second floor of the former prison at *Schmiedebrücke 35*. (During our years at the university, the conferences in psychology and those in philosophy were relocated on the first floor, and thereupon those more attractive and more dignified rooms were made available to us.) We met there from eight to ten o'clock one evening a week. At ten the building was locked. Had our discussion not ended by then, we moved on to a cafe, or sometimes in summer to hear the nightingales in Scheitniger Park, a beautiful, old, English garden in the eastern part of the city. On these evenings, we had lectures and discussions on pedagogical matters. Our preference was to have principals or teachers from the various types of schools speak to us out of their experience. Frequently, too, lecturers from the university would address us; we were allowed to invite Stern once each semester. Should no one be available, one of us would report on some book or question personally interesting to us at the time. Questions on Friedrich W. Foerster, Kerschensteiner, Gaudig, and Wyneken[76] often engaged us in lively discussion. We all belonged to the *Bundes für Schulreform* [Leagues for School Reform] and attended these meetings as a group. But even then I was aware that during the meetings there was still a great deal of confusion and of shooting beyond the mark.

Every semester we made several field trips. Accompanied by

knowledgeable guides we visited schools for special education, for the deaf and the blind; welfare institutions; homes for the mentally deficient, and for neglected children. The home for children on the *Warteberg*, which we often visited, made the deepest impression on us. A former castle, it was situated in a beautiful area near Obernigk and had a spacious garden.[77] Children from broken homes were cared for in the light and cheerful rooms. When we first visited the home, the youngest were two-year-old twins. Clean, well fed, and well content, they lay in their twin-size carriage in the garden. The older children could be entrusted with the care and supervision of the small ones. Deaconesses belonging to Mother Eva's (the Countess Tiele-Winckler's) Motherhouse in Miechowitz, Upper Silesia, had charge of the house. Sister Friede, the slight, unassuming, and friendly headmistress, led us through all the rooms and explained everything to us. The children were grouped into "families" where older and younger ones, boys and girls, all belonged together as in a natural family. These families were given the names of flowers, and their quarters were decorated accordingly with hedge-roses, cornflowers, etc; and the little girls wore hair ribbons of the appropriate color.

In one of the workrooms, Sister Friede showed us a sewing machine. "We were desperately in need of one," she told us with natural simplicity, "so we prayed for one, and before long it came as a gift."

Those to whom she said this were probably all free-thinkers, but not one of us smiled in derision. Respectfully, we deferred to such childlike faith. Sister Friede, without any means at all, went to Warsaw during the war [W.W. I], and opened a children's home to alleviate the terrible plight of the children there.

Having finished our tour of house and garden, we were taken to a delightfully cool dining room and treated to coffee, bread, and butter, and huge bowls of strawberries from their own garden. To bid us farewell, the Sisters sang a hymn.

Hugo Hermsen, a North German born in a small town in Braunschweig, was founder and inspiration of our pedagogical group. He had nearly completed his studies at the time I began mine. About twenty-seven years old, he was short but powerfully built, healthy, a trained athlete. Having once seen him, one was not likely to forget that head: suntanned, handsome, noble features; and grey, rather deep-set eyes, aglow with ardent zeal. His soft, slightly husky voice had the timbre of one who spoke from the depths of the heart. On one occasion, he took Rose and me along to a meeting of the *Wandervögel.*[78] He read the youngsters fairy tales in his native low German (*plattdeutsch*). I particularly recall the story of the *"Machandelboom"* [Grimm's "The Juniper"], and I believe that today, more than twenty years later, I can still hear him singing the verse inserted in that tale:

> My little sister Marlene
> My bones does gather;
> In silken cloth they lie.
> Kiwitt, Kiwitt,
> What a fine bird am I!

Hermsen could not abide the modern methods of mass education. His ideal was the tutorial system of the eighteenth century. He sought to carry it out in practice as well. When I met him he was in charge of a youthful Count Rothschild, who was taking his first semester in law. They shared an apartment, and Hermsen took him along everywhere; he attended our group meetings also. Later, Hermsen went to the estate of Count Yorck von Wartenburg; there he was to educate an invalid youth, but soon every last one of the numerous children in the family was deeply attached to him.[79] After he had completed his doctorate and passed the state boards in Breslau, he was engaged to educate the Prince of Wied.[80] From there he went to the war and did not return.

Hermsen had relinquished leadership of the group to a successor by the time I was admitted to it. But he still dominated it. Instinctively, we all looked to him and awaited his opinion when he was present. When he was unable to attend, everything seemed flat. I believe that since my childhood no one had influenced me as much as he. We met only at our group's meetings and hardly ever spoke to one another in private. I have a vivid remembrance of the few conversations we did have. The first was in a cafe after a meeting at which Professor Stern had lectured. We were seated in a large group, Hermsen beside me, Stern across from us. At the group's previous meeting, I had addressed them for the first time: on co-education. Youthfully idealistic and lacking experience, I had spoken positively on the question, totally unaware of the real difficulties. Stern was interested in the subject but had been unable to attend that meeting. So he asked for a report on what I had said. Alternating, Hermsen and I replied to his questions. After a while, the professor had to attend to others who naturally also awaited a few words from him. Thereupon my neighbor quietly began a private conversation with me. It concerned a misunderstanding between him and a mutual acquaintance of ours; he hoped I might have an opportunity to effect a reconciliation. We were soon so deep in conversation that we became totally oblivious to our surroundings and woke as from a dream when everyone began to leave.

One other time, we sat together on the return trip from the *Warteberg*. The train's clatter made general conversation impossible. Hermsen quietly recounted some of his experiences in the House of Yorck and told me of his plans for the future.

Shortly before we both departed from Breslau, I for Göttingen, he for Neuwied,[81] the two of us and Rose Guttmann were invited to a farewell celebration at the home of a teacher who was studying at that time in Breslau. She liked Hermsen very much, having worked with him frequently. After the party, he walked me home. He had always left that to others after our group meetings as he lived at a distance from our house. Once we had arrived at my home he said: "Well, I wish you the good fortune of finding in Göttingen people who will satisfy your taste. Here you seem to have become far too critical."

The words stunned me. I was no longer accustomed to any form of censure. At home hardly anyone dared to criticize me; my friends showed me only affection and admiration. So I had been living in the naive conviction that I was perfect. This is frequently the case with persons without any faith who live an exalted ethical idealism. Because one is enthused about what is good, one believes oneself to be good. I had always considered it my privilege to make remarks about everything I found negative, inexorably pointing out other persons' weaknesses, mistakes, or faults of which I became aware, often using a ridiculing or sarcastic tone of voice. There were persons who found me "enchantingly malicious." So these words of farewell from a man whom I esteemed and loved caused me acute distress. I was not angry with him for saying them. Nor did I shrug them off as an undeserved reproach. They were for me a first alert to which I gave much reflection.

We met once more when we were both on vacation back home in Breslau. At that time Hermsen promised to visit me in Göttingen on his way home from Neuwied. At the beginning of August, 1914, soon after the war broke out, I received a card forwarded to Breslau from Göttingen; on it he announced his plans for the visit. Whether that trip was ever made or whether the war's events cancelled plans for him as for me, I do not know. I had no further personal messages from him. Only later did I get news from Rose that he had been declared "missing" in the war, and with it an account of his last days in the Carpathian winter until all trace of him was lost. In the fall of 1916, when I went to Freiburg-im-Breisgau, I happened to notice Hermsen's picture in a photographer's display window on Kaiserstrasse. He was wearing the attractive uniform of the German Alpine-Hunters Regiment which had been training in the Black Forest for mountain warfare. The photographer still had the plate; and so I was able to comfort the deceased man's old friends by sending them prints.

After Hermsen, the most influential member in the pedagogical group was Hermann Popp. Already over thirty years old, he had taught for several years in the *Volksschule*[4‡] before making his *Abitur* and entering the university. Long and lean, his appearance evoked the thought of Don Quixote, the Knight of the Soulful Countenance. One could count on his taking the floor in every discussion and preventing others from taking their turn for a good while thereafter. By then he had already firmly established principles which led him to approach every question he encountered with self-assurance. He presented his views with profound sentiment and emphasis, in ringing tones, and often in a humorously exaggerated manner. One found it difficult to remain totally serious even when he was most in earnest. We all esteemed him as a man of character and integrity, of independent and penetrating thought. He got his doctorate under Stern (on the Problem of Association), but he had emancipated himself entirely from the guidance of this "master." In general, our relation to our teacher was most independent. Stern represented a distinct type of Jewish personality. In his early forties at the time, he was of average height though he seemed shorter because he walked with a slight stoop. His pale features were framed by a brown beard; his eyes were kind and alert; his expression and the tone of his voice were exceedingly mild and friendly. Once when he appeared at a masked ball dressed in an oriental costume, he looked like *Nathan the Wise.*[82] He had always assured us that at heart he was a philosopher (for which reason he vehemently opposed the separation of the faculties for philosophy and psychology) and that his big philosophical work *"Person und Sache"* [Person and Thing] meant more to him than any of his other achievements. Despite that, he had gone deeper and deeper into experimental psychology and owed his fame to his psychological writings which were translated into all the languages of the civilized world. His works on "Child Speech" and "Psychology of Early Childhood" were based on exact observations he made of his own children and on the careful diaries kept by his intelligent and charming wife who was his most faithful collaborator. He was extensively occupied at that time with methods for testing the intelligence;[83] all this was in preparation for his work in occupational aptitude tests for which he later gained acceptance in Hamburg. We had strong misgivings about all these things, as well as about his general principle of "the golden mean." His malicious colleague Hönigswald once expressed an opinion about Stern's suggestion that "school psychologists" should be appointed: "The school psychologist will then become the most powerful person in the state. He will tell every man what he is to become; and if he particularly favors someone, he will destine that one to become a school psychologist!"

Stern's most eager students most severely opposed him in his own field. At his seminar, while seated to the right and left of him at the U-shaped table, we would frequently respond in unison with a very decided and resounding "No!"

He never held this against us but was consistently even-tempered, kind, and friendly; however, he held unerringly to his own point. Popp, that radical thinker, was naturally dissatisfied with so cautious a middle path. He went his own ways. I was thoroughly initiated into his problems for, from the time I was admitted to the group, he had preempted the role of my escort on the way home. Though he would never relinquish it to anyone else, several others usually joined us. Ordinarily, though, he had far from finished his discourse by the time we had arrived at our house. Then I would have to walk back and forth with him in front of the gate to our small garden and listen until he finished his lecture. Sometimes my brother would come home while it was going on; I introduced the two to one another at the garden gate.

My mother disapproved of these conversations at the front door at such a late hour. She felt she had to object and said it was all too reminiscent of my sister Else, who had often lingered outside in just this way when coming home at night. Indignantly, I begged to differ: I was not to be compared with Else. I well knew that in her case it was a matter of "admirers"; and there was not a trace of that in my situation. It is hardly likely that my mother suspected anything of the kind. But naturally, the people in the neighborhood who might observe our nocturnal promenading had no way of knowing that we were discussing problems in psychology or of the theory of cognition. In those days, it never occurred to us to take such things into consideration. We used to insist at every opportunity that we were indifferent to what "one" said, or to what "people" might think. This was one of the few times when I retorted in so brusque and ill-mannered a way to my mother; I bitterly repented of it later.

In the summer of 1912, Dr. Popp was preparing for his state boards. When the heat in his study became so oppressive that his head refused to work any longer, he would move next to the hot stove in the kitchen. Then, after a short while, when he returned to his desk, he would find the relative coolness so comfortable that his brain was reactivated. When he had the state boards behind him and was about to go to teach in a rural school, he sent me a postcard inviting me to join him for a farewell walk. He could have written the most intimate secrets on his postcards since I was the only one who could decipher his hieroglyphics. It was the first and last of such meetings. He wanted one final consummate conversation before disappearing into the land of the Philistines.

Association with persons so much older, more mature, and far more advanced intellectually than she was, presented this little student with a great deal of stimulation and an opportunity for advancement; but it also constituted a danger for her. When these companions spoke to me about their doctoral works or their preparation for the state boards, my talent for ready comprehension and my extraordinary facility in inserting myself into the other's thought process enabled me to follow almost instantaneously and, at times, I even made a critical or stimulating comment. This gave the impression that I was their equal, and it also deceived me. I chose courses and seminars for the advanced and skipped many a fundamental phase which I really should have covered.

Alfred Mann led the pedagogical group during those semesters. Like the others my senior by a few years, he was still noticeably younger and less mature than Hermsen and Popp. In the discussions, he modestly deferred to them. However, some of the comments he made during private conversations gave indication of his definitely democratic leanings (the group, as such, was totally apolitical), of his incisive criticism, and of his coarse humor. He was tall and too heavy for his age; his round, handsome face was pale; a nervous tic—a rapidly recurring twitch of the head—was disturbing. Besides that, he was very distracted and forgetful, and he made a silly habit of exploiting this absent-mindedness. Often he would telephone me before eight in the morning to enumerate the things I was to remind him of in the course of that day. Since my memory was still excellent at that time, he could then relax. During that period, one scarcely noticed about him any of that increasing self-assurance and the strident, inconsiderate manner which Mann displayed so disagreeably in his public life when after the Revolution[84] he became director of the Breslau Institute for Adult Education.

Georg Moskiewicz (called "Mos" by his friends) was a frequent guest of the pedagogical group as well as of Stern's seminar. Having at that time already earned an M.D. and a Ph. D., he was about thirty-three years old when I began my studies. Rose Guttmann saw to it that we became more closely acquainted. Mos was the son of a wealthy Jewish businessman. Out of consideration for his father, he had chosen to study for a practical profession, medicine; but, later, he received permission to transfer to the study of philosophy and psychology. He had been taught by Ebbinghaus[85] and was to have been habilitated[86] under him; but his teacher died before this was accomplished. Now he was continuing work on his dissertation in psychology without knowing who would accept it. Mos had, like many eastern Jews, reddish hair and light eyes. To see his pale, nervous features and his somewhat shy and restless expression was to know that something troubled his spirit. I was to learn only later what tragedy lay hidden in his life. At that time, I was indeed flattered that this man, who had such a many faceted education, should also want me as collaborator. First of all, he asked me to serve as a guinea pig for his project. It involved "Experimental Interrogation" according to the then much-discussed "Würzburg Method" (Külpe, Bühler, Messer, etc.).[87] We met regularly in the psychology seminar rooms, but we spent more time discussing the methods than in actual research. I gradually noticed that, except for a collection of research reports, very little of a thesis was at hand. I saw that his own doubts about the validity of the method hindered him all along, and finally made it impossible for him to do any further work. At the same time, he was severely depressed by the fact that his family was expecting his habilitation; that they had faith in an academic career for him; and that, confident of such an eventual career, his elderly father was still supporting Mos at a time when other men had long since established themselves in careers, won honors, and founded families of their own.

The pedagogical group was not the only academic society to which I belonged. During those first semesters, our entire clover-leaf[88] belonged to the Women's Student Union. Our weekly meeting was predominantly a social evening spent together. We had, as well, a small apartment near the university which we could use during the day. Soon after we gathered at our evening meetings, a delivery boy from a nearby coffee shop would come to take our orders which he then fetched. Thereupon, sitting in small groups, we enjoyed our coffee, hot chocolate, or tea, with torte, and engaged in relaxed conversation, consulted each other about our studies, or discussed, in general, some question that vitally interested all of us. The preparations for a big costume ball this Student Union gave at the end of my second semester led to a childish conflict between all of our circle and the woman presiding at that time. As we had already invited our teachers and our fellow students to the celebration, we had no alternative but to attend the ball. Afterwards, though, we unanimously tendered our resignation from the Union. However, we allowed neither the preceding difficulties nor the anticipation of the unpleasant aftermath to spoil the evening's fun for us. Else Hess, a classmate of Erna's, whose charm equalled her keen intellect, composed the invitations in spirited verse. She also gave a welcoming speech in verse. Presentations and dancing alternated until morning. Dr. Popp had appeared in an old-Germanic costume. Indefatigable, he led out my sister or me for dance after dance. At about six in the morning, he accompanied us home. My sisters walked on ahead. We followed, deep in philosophical discussion. What had attracted us most of all was, of course, to see our professors in costume and to dance with them. At the time Turkey and Italy were in conflict: Stern came as a Turk; his wife, as an Italian. Kühnemann came in Grecian garb and had a wreath on his head. He introduced himself as "Speusippos." Mischievously, I remarked, "He *says* Speusippos but he *means Plato*."[89]

I wore a Dutch costume and was told over and over that it was most becoming. Else Hess assured me with the sophisticated air of an experienced socialite that I "was a hit." That did not please me at all. I was still enthusiastic about dancing at that time; but I preferred the improvisations we could make at home to these formal affairs. Erna and I seldom attended balls. When we did, upon arriving home after such an evening, we would remark to one another, in relief, before getting into bed: "Thank God, we don't live for that alone!"

If I am not mistaken, it was a member of this student Union, a young woman taking classic philology, who introduced me to the "Academic Branch of the Humboldt-Society for Adult Education."[90] Students who belonged to this society voluntarily taught workers' classes. These courses differed essentially from those given later in the adult education academies. Classes now comprised only elementary subjects such as German and arithmetic. The people attending them wanted to brush up their school knowledge for practical purposes; for instance, they might want to qualify for a promotion from a lower to an intermediate position with the postal service. One evening a week during the first semester, I taught a course in spelling with an older student as my teaching partner. In the second semester I taught it alone. For the winter of 1912, a senior student announced a beginner's course in English. This was a departure from the ordinary and was by way of an experiment. So many participants registered for it that three parallel courses were to be provided; the teacher who had inaugurated them asked me to take one of the three. I had made this gentleman's acquaintance in a somewhat unusual manner; his name was Artur Wilhelm Wolf. He came up to speak to me after a lecture one day, and wanted to know why I had not returned his greeting when we had met on the street. Truthfully, I replied that I had been unaware of his greeting and that I had no recollection of even having seen him before. (I had an excellent memory for persons and, once I had taken note of someone, I could recognize them again years later. And, as yet, I had not ever heard of "mortification of the eyes,"[91] and so I was accustomed to looking keenly and thoroughly at persons who interested me. But the mass of students I considered a negligible quantity. Walking along corridors, I paid no attention at all to the students, and whenever possible, I sat in the first row in class so I could follow the lecturers without distraction. It never occurred to me that I could be observed from the lectern. I assumed the professors were so absorbed by their subject that they were oblivious of all else. Only later, through friendly association with the lecturers and finally through personal experience as well, did I learn what a lecture hall was like from the lecturer's vantage point.) To have been thus totally unnoticed, naturally, was more offending to a self-assured young man than to be "snubbed." He called my attention to our having been introduced to each other at one of the Academic Humboldt Society meetings; therefore, he claimed the right to greet me. I apologized, and thereafter was careful to be a bit more observant on the street; and, when I met him, I would politely return his greeting. So, now, just as pleasantly, I acquiesced to his request to teach one of the classes. Just before they were to begin, Eduard Metis, then chairman of the Academic Branch, informed me that both Herr Wolf and his friend who was to give the third parallel course were of doubtful moral character; they took advantage of their position to form relationships with some of their female students. I was indignant at such flagrant abuse of a social institution. After some thought, a happy solution occurred to me: I asked Herr Wolf to assign the "ladies" to me; he and Herr Fellmann should share the "gentlemen." The suggestion was such a natural one that it was unnecessary for me to give a reason for my request; it took the ominous Don Juan so much by surprise that he could only agree at the time. But when we met for the opening of class in the *Realschule*[4‡] on *Nikolaistadtgraben* (the courses were held there) he told me a few minutes before we were to begin that, having reconsidered the matter, the two men thought mixed classes would be preferable. I was thoroughly alarmed but had enough presence of mind to suggest we ought at least to offer the alternative, permitting the students to choose for themselves. This was again so obvious that he could find no reason to object.

So the three of us entered the large room where all the eager students awaited us. Herr Wolf greeted them, explained the necessity for dividing the group into three classes, and introduced Herr Fellman and myself. He then asked whether the ladies would like to have a class to themselves; if so, they were to join me. With the exception of a single young woman, they all raised their hands; jubilant victor in the fray, I left with my flock about me. But I still grieved a bit over the lost lamb and would have liked to bring it along; but naturally, I could not use coercion. Soon thereafter I learned that this girl had taken courses from Herr Wolf for several semesters in the past. The others followed me into our designated classroom. In words bubbling with joy and gratitude, they expressed their relief at being res-

cued from taking the course with the others; they would have
felt so awkward in the presence of the young men. Most of them
were no-longer-young business employees. Naturally, they had
no notion of what had gone on behind the scenes nor of my motives. But it meant I had won their hearts at the very outset.
They studied diligently, although, naturally, with varying success; and they developed a deep attachment to me. To express
their appreciation when I bade them farewell at the end of the
winter semester, they presented me with a huge bouquet of roses
and with a valuable book on the history of art; and they continued writing to me when I went to Göttingen.

As it happened, during my first semester that summer of 1911,
several extraordinary activities were added to the regular ones.
The one hundredth Jubilee of our "Silesian Friedrich-Wilhelm
University" was being celebrated just then. The University had
been founded by Friedrich Wilhelm III[92] in 1811, at the time of
the French occupation. It was not so much a new foundation
but rather a merger of the Protestant University of Frankfurt-
an-der-Oder, founded during the Reformation, with the Jesuit
College of Breslau, the *Leopoldiner* established by Emperor
Leopold[93] at the end of the seventeenth century. To the latter
we owed the handsome old building, thick-walled with deep window niches, and the sumptuous baroque ornamentation of both
the "Aula Leopoldina" and the concert hall. How festive were
the official celebrations! For the Emperor's birthday, or the in-
stallation of a new president of the university, and on similar occasions, the festivities provided not only the glorious colors of
the paintings on walls and ceiling plus the rich stucco decoration
in these rooms but also a colorful display of the students in "*Wichs*"
[fraternity dress uniform], with their officers holding the fraternity's banners and positioning themselves in the window niches;
finally, the entire faculty entered in procession. The Beadle
bearing his heavy mace was followed by the President, the Deans,
and the lecturers, all in cap and gown, in the colors of their faculty, many wearing, in addition, a wide colored sash across the
breast, symbol of an honorary doctorate (usually from an American university)!

The old gray building on the Oder (painted yellow a few years ago "in the style of the times") had quickly become home to me. During free periods, I liked to study in an empty lecture room; there I would seat myself on one of the wide window sills which filled the deep recesses in the wall. Looking down from such a lofty perch at the river and the busy University Bridge, I could imagine myself to be maiden in her castle. I was just as much at home in the nearby similarly venerable former hostel for theology students where now our philosophy and psychology seminars were held; so too, in the University Library, a former Augustinian Chapterhouse on Sandstrasse. Next to the latter was the *Sandkirche*, a heavy, early-Gothic building; it is the Cathedral parish church. Directly behind it, the small *Dombrücke*[94] takes one to the *Dominsel*. This is a quiet, secluded world of its own. The wide, straight Domstrasse leads from the small bridge to the main portal of the cathedral, past the *Kreuzkirche* with its high, slender Gothic steeple. On both sides are ranged the low but elegantly simple homes of the Canons, and close by, the palace of the Prince Archbishop. I was fond of taking that route across the *Dominsel*. There, in a world of silence and peace, I felt transplanted into long-gone centuries. But I did not go inside the beautiful churches, especially not while services were going on. After all, I had no business there and would have considered it bad manners to disturb others during their devotions. On one occasion only, during a free period, I visited St. Matthias' Church with Julia Heimann. It adjoined the university to which it had formerly belonged; a small doorway, now walled up, still attests to that earlier connection.

I truly considered the university my "alma mater" and so delighted in taking part in her jubilee celebration. Naturally, we attended the major festivity in the Aula, the great hall; but we had some misgivings about joining in the student festival. For this occasion, a huge tent had been erected on the royal castle's parade-ground since no hall would have been large enough to house the many "old boys" who had returned to take part in the celebration. The Women's Student Unions held many a consultation; we had received reports from the Berlin University that at the jubilee celebration there the previous year some incidents had been deplorable. For that reason we initially declined to attend. Thereupon we received a second invitation from "His Magnificence," the president of the university: he would be deeply saddened were the women students to absent themselves from the event; he would have some of the professors' wives assigned to our tables to prevent unpleasant incidents. So we agreed to attend, after all, but, considering it ridiculous, we declined his offer to provide "mothering." We decided we would stay until the actual merriment, the "*Fidelitas*," would begin, and then withdraw quietly at that point. This worked very well. Naturally, the attention of all the "old boys" [the alumni] who roamed about the large tent in search of old acquaintances was drawn to the table at which the girls, all in white dresses, were seated; after all, there had been nothing like that "in their time." A charming play written by two of the alumni, Dr. Hermann Hamburger, an editor, and Dr. Tarnowski, a lawyer, was presented for the festivities. The playwrights (both were Jews) were well known in Breslau for their liveliness and wit.

When the performances and the speeches were over, we disappeared—not one discordant note had been sounded to mar our joy.

Besides the numerous college-related activities, my schedule included an additional fringe occupation: private tutoring. Although the majority of the students supplemented their income in this way, I would much rather have given my time exclusively to studies. After all, my mother was paying for my board and tuition; and the family's financial situation being what it was, this did not impose a sacrifice on anyone at home. Therefore, to me, it seemed most desirable not to break up my time unnecessarily. Still, I was being asked repeatedly to give remedial lessons or to tutor someone in preparation for a higher class at the *Gymnasium*. It was impossible to refuse all those who asked this of me; so it came about that almost always I had a few pupils. This had begun even while I, myself, was still attending the *Gymnasium*. One day, the janitor had come to our classroom during a drawing lesson to announce that Fräulein Stein was to go to the principal. This was so unusual that the whole class was in a dither. While going down the three flights of stairs, I mentally reviewed the past few weeks; nothing occurred to me which could have earned me a reproof. So I entered the office unperturbed.

The principal was not alone; the stranger with him was the troubled father of one of the girls in the *Untertertia*.[41] She had done so poorly that there was scarcely a chance of her being promoted. The principal suggested, as a final resort, that her homework be supervised; and he now asked me to accept that task. I was not attracted by the suggestion, but both gentlemen urged me so strongly that I finally agreed. Before long, I was convinced that it was a useless effort; the child had neither talent nor inclination for studying and was tormenting herself to no avail. I explained to the principal that it embarrassed me to accept payment for a task which augured no success. He talked me into continuing until Easter. The father, he said, was aware that there was no hope; still he wanted to have the satisfaction of knowing he had tried every conceivable means of helping his daughter. So, at Easter, I was quit of this first pupil of mine. But, before long, I had another one.

In the *Untertertia*, there was a fascinating Polish youngster, fifteen years old. She had blond curls, blue eyes, and an exceptionally lively temperament. One usually saw her, during recess, surrounded by older girls who admired her; they were also amused by her funny way of speaking German. I never joined them. One day, on the schoolgrounds, she suddenly took my arm and drew me away from my classmates. She said that, as her grades were miserable, she was to spend the Pentecost vacation in Breslau diligently reviewing her classwork. Her landlady, an elderly friend of the principal's family, would be writing to me but, even before that, she, herself, wanted to talk to me to beg me to study with her. During the brief vacation at Pentecost, I went to her lodgings every morning. It was impossible to have her come to me as she was not allowed to go out alone. Lena had a good bit of talent and, now, with my help, learned eagerly. She expressed great admiration for my knowledge and, during the short vacation, developed a deep attachment to me. To get me to go to the opera with her, on one occasion, she resorted to wheedling; after all, she was not permitted to go unaccompanied and she wanted, so much, to go. *Carmen* was to be presented.

"I would like to be Carmen," she said to me, her eyes ablaze, "to make all men love me!"

Completely taken aback, I took a good look at this little person. Well developed for her age, she could have passed for an eighteen-year-old. To me, all of a sudden, in contrast to this child I seemed like an inexperienced girl compared to a sophisticated woman. The date of our evening-at-the-opera arrived. When I presented myself at her boarding house that morning, she met me with sad news. Her father had become seriously ill, and she was to go home at once. She asked me to use the tickets for my sister and myself. Aware, then, that my sympathy for her had robbed me of any enjoyment at the prospect of the theater, she urged me to go even so. Then, in tears, she embraced and kissed me. Erna and I did attend the opera, but my thoughts were with the poor child who was just then making such a sorrowful journey. Lena came back wearing mourning. When she had arrived at home, her father was no longer alive.

The same boarding house, Scheel's, provided me with several more pupils. Upon my arrival from Chemnitz[95] to begin my own studies, I already found one request for lessons. I handed over to my mother the stipend I was paid for tutoring. She was proud to accept her youngest's first earnings. These sums were not treated like ordinary income at all, that is, they could not be spent. At Christmastime, 1911, I wanted to use some of these savings to go on a winter excursion to the *Riesengebirge* with Erna. Mother readily consented and even had Rosa go with us. But she managed to pay all of our expenses out of her own pocket, and my treasure remained untouched. Of course, it had not been tucked away in a sock. All cash was put into the business and was "credited" to us. We all had an individual account in the business. Our Grandmother Stein had left a few thousand marks to each of us. When, under my mother's management, the business blossomed and some land was acquired, she raised each of our accounts to 10,000 M.[96] During the years I studied elsewhere, and later, when doing research without compensation, I met my expenses out of this fund. An account had been opened for me, first, at the Göttingen branch of the *Dresdener Bank*, and, later, in Freiburg; my withdrawals were charged to our firm. Once when I asked my sister Frieda whether I had not used up all my means, she told me that actually would have been the case had not my mother at the end of each fiscal year brought the depleted sum back to the original figure. During the war, a larger amount accumulated in the bank for the very first time. Since our firm had more supplies of foreign lumber than others had, the turnover was large; and the incoming sums could not be returned to inventory as nothing could cross the borders. War loans and inflation ate up these riches.

3

When I look back on all my activities during my first semesters, I ask myself where I found the time I needed for study. But, actually, studying filled my days. As much as was possible, I scheduled my tutoring hours for early morning or for the time just before the evening meal. All other events I attended took place in the evening. So I had the entire day free and made good use of it. Kaethe Scholz was my usual partner in study for the first semesters. Later, when she had gone to Paris, Eduard Metis replaced her. I became acquainted with him at the infrequent meetings of the Academic Humboldt Society at which he presided. At these meetings, I paid as little attention to him as to the others present. Only business matters, distribution of the courses, etc., were discussed during these meetings; and I was glad when they were over. At the close of the summer semester of 1912, a *Sommerfest* was held for all those who had taken courses and for their families. I did not care for this type of popular amusement; but we owed it to our students to participate. I went along outdoors to the country that afternoon and tried to make the best of the situation. I joined in the games the children played on the lawn more than in anything else. When it got dark, the mothers and children left; those who remained prepared for dancing.

This was my cue to depart. When I noticed Herr Metis intended to leave, I suggested to him that we walk back to town. People were crowding the railway station; and I did not relish the prospect of sitting in a packed compartment on the train. He was happy to oblige. So the two of us walked through the warm and moonlit summer night. I do not recall what we talked about. For me, the silence on that lonely path through the fields

was most pleasant. And both of us took a childlike delight in
watching in the distance a train, the lights of which alone were
visible as the train glided its way through the night like some
glowing snake. When we reached the trolley-line's terminal, we
took a streetcar as I still had a long way to go, even from there.
En route, my companion remarked that the way home had been
the best part of the whole day's affair.

I had no objection to make to that remark for I always preferred quiet to large gatherings of people. For me, that walk
home remained a happy memory; it had not seemed anything
out of the ordinary. Soon thereafter, we went on vacation to
Grunwald. One day, sometime after we had returned, I received a short letter from Herr Metis. In it he requested me to
drop in at the Germanistics seminar room should I happen to be
at the university on a certain day; he had something to tell me,
and he would meet me there. I presumed it concerned the preparatory courses for the *Abitur*, so, in passing, I stopped in at
the Germanistics seminar which otherwise I seldom visited.
Whatever work-related news Herr Metis had for me was insignificant. When he had finished with that, he asked me whether
I would ride to the Scheitniger Park with him. I noticed that he
had needed to pull himself together to make the request and
now felt he had been pretty bold. This amused me. Why make
such a big thing of taking a walk together during vacation? Giving no indication of my reaction, however, I readily accepted
his invitation. On that occasion, I really got to know this fine
young man for the first time. He was an only child whose over-
protective, affectionate mother had, so far, anxiously kept from
him all feminine companionship. Apparently she even considered a girl student dangerous and hearing of our walk that night
had probably frightened her considerably. It had actually made
a deep impression on this sensitive, upright, young man; he had
remembered it constantly all those weeks. Becoming aware of
this, I realized I would have to proceed with caution now. Not
long thereafter, Metis suggested, again by letter, that together
we attend a meeting of the town council during which questions
pertaining to the theater were to be discussed. This time I did
not accept his invitation. Taking the opportunity in my letter to

decline it, I made my "position" clear: I was accustomed to have a friendly relationship with my fellow students; I was willing to establish one with him; but he would have to relinquish any other expectations. This suggestion was accepted and, surprisingly, even though from then on we met almost daily in the university and often studied together, my new friend succeeded in suppressing whatever budding attraction he had felt; nor was there ever any need for me to be on the defensive. We began the study of Gothic German together under full steam even before the vacation ended. We planned to seek admission to an advanced level of the Germanistic seminar when the winter semester began; for this we had to give proof of a thorough knowledge of the Gothic German at the entrance examinations. We read the entire gospel text of Ulfilas;[97] to get practice in translating into the Gothic, we prepared texts for one another. We had no class in common except for German. He was taking modern languages in addition; his doctoral work was chosen from German literature (Gutzkow's dramas[98]). Once the semester had begun, he suggested we go for a walk together once a week. During those walks, we would give one another an account of the lectures we had attended. He was usually embarrassed; all he could give me were bits of dry data on philology, whereas I was able to give interesting lectures in philosophy and history. I always had much more material to share than we had time for. Even in those days, he prophesied that I should succeed brilliantly in passing the examinations. Herr Popp had made the same prediction, but his was based less on my knowledge than on his psychological analysis that I had the kind of temperament suited for taking exams.

Even in those days Eduard Metis was somewhat of a journalist as well as a student. He had solid connections with the *Breslauer Zeitung*, the old liberal newspaper read in almost all Jewish families. The Sunday edition regularly carried a literary supplement in which book reviews signed E. M. frequently appeared. Naturally, now that I knew the author, I read them with double interest. Indeed, my opinion about these first literary attempts of his was always of great importance to him. Once I found in his comments on a volume of novellas a frivolous treatment of

some erotic material. That upset me a great deal. I had formed
this friendship with complete confidence that I was dealing with
a truly chaste person. Could I have been mistaken? If so, the
friendship would have to end. I had no intention of associating
with persons who were not completely beyond reproach in this
aspect. Erna had once exchanged views on questions of this kind
with Hans Biberstein; and, after that, we were both glad to
know we could trust him completely. So, now, I decided to get
to the bottom of this matter. The following day, when we met
during our free period, the poor fellow had to listen to a proper
sermon. He heard me out quietly, in all probability even more
distressed than I was. When I had finished, he explained that it
had been extremely embarrassing for him to have to comment
on such matters at all, and, therefore, he had decided to do it
with dispatch. To get it over with, he had chosen the somewhat
frivolous tone so common in journalism. He had been totally
unprepared for such a reaction. His sincerity was beyond doubt.
So there was an immediate reconciliation. Finally, he said, "Oh,
if only my mother could have heard this conversation!"

He had a delicacy of feeling that might almost be termed
maidenly. He was tall and slim; his face, rather thin, was usually slightly flushed; outwardly he gave no indication of being
ill, but he suffered a great deal from migraines and many days
was unable to work at all. Since I was always in excellent health
during my university years, I always pitied him for being less
robust.

Metis had one attribute which set him apart from all my other
companions: he was an orthodox and observant Jew. We spoke
little about it: I let him have his own way; and he made no attempt to influence me. If he came to study with me at our house,
he would accept only some fruit. Once when I offered him some
pastry, he said with a smile, "What I can't define, I consider forbidden."

One day, when out walking with him, I had an errand in one
of the houses we passed. In the doorway I suddenly handed him
my briefcase to hold while I went in. Too late, it occurred to me
that it was Saturday and one ought not to carry anything on the
Sabbath. I found him dutifully awaiting me in the doorway. I

apologized for thoughtlessly causing him to do something forbidden.

"I haven't done anything forbidden," he replied quietly.
"Only on the street is one not to carry anything; it's allowed in
the house."

For that reason, he had remained in the entrance-hall, taking
care not to put even one foot into the street. This was an example of the talmudic sophistry which I found so repugnant. But I
made no comment.

When later in Göttingen I began to occupy myself with religious questions, I asked him once by letter about his idea of
God: whether he believed in a personal God. His reply was suc-
cinct: God is spirit; nothing more could be said on the subject.
To me, it seemed I had been handed a stone instead of bread.

In Göttingen I received a regular weekly letter from him.
During vacations, we studied German literature together; I, in
preparation for my state boards; he, for his doctorate. The first
time, he failed to make it and had to give it a second try. This
depressed him a great deal. I attended his public graduation
ceremony. On that occasion, I met his parents. Both of them,
his mother despite her earlier fears about my influence on him,
greeted me in a most friendly fashion. When, later I graduated
"summa cum laude," his written comment was, "What was inevitable, has come to pass."

He was unfit for military service in the war. In the meantime
he, too, had passed the state boards and had begun to teach. In
Freiburg I received the shocking news that he had died of pneumonia.

My relatives sent me the death notice and told me what a sad
picture the parents had made at the grave of their only child.
Naturally I wrote to them and, later, often wondered whether I
ought to visit his mother. But I was concerned that recent developments in my life would probably be beyond her comprehension; and this hindered me from going. I do not know how he
himself would have reacted to these developments. A degree of
estrangement had already resulted from my steering into the
waters of pure research. In Breslau, I had been the one to introduce him to the pedagogical group; and it pained him that

the one who had brought educational problems to his attention should herself now set out on such a different path.

4

If my studies came to no harm from my common student activities, and the social life with my friends, something else did suffer because of them: I had scarcely any time left for my family. My relatives hardly saw me except at mealtime, and sometimes not even then. When I did come to table, my thoughts were usually still on my work; and I had little to say. My mother used to maintain that one could put whatever one wished on my plate for all the notice I took. She was even glad about that since, at least, it enabled her to make certain I was eating decent meals. When, in later years, my lack of appetite worried her, she would recall this time with deep longing. It was much more difficult for me to make conversation about my studies than for Erna. In the clinic, she had experiences which everyone could understand and be interested in. But my philosophical problems could not be brought to the family table. Once, my mother happened to come to my room just as I was occupied with Plato. She took the book from my hand to see, for once, what could engross me so completely. In utter puzzlement, she said: "Why, that's something you've known for a long time."

If I am not mistaken, it was "Parmenides"; and she had happened upon a few passages about the-one-and-the-many, which, for the uninitiated, sound like self-evident platitudes.

Not infrequently my mother caught no glimpse of me for a day or two at a time. Early in the morning she went off to work; often that was before I would come down for breakfast. Her lunch hour was from noon until one o'clock; I was sometimes at lectures until one, and then afterwards I ate alone. And should anything keep me busy at the university until seven on an evening when I had arranged to attend some event downtown at eight, it was not worthwhile going home. I spent the intervening hour in the philosophy seminar rooms or in the Women's Student Union apartment. There I would eat the sandwiches I had brought along. By the time I came home, everyone was already asleep; awaiting me on the dining room table, along with the day's mail, was a snack, prepared by devoted hands.

I was unlike Erna in another respect: I did not bring my friends to meet my family as she did. As a matter of fact, I never invited anyone to our house unless some work we were doing together made it a necessity. And were anyone coming for that purpose, I felt it would be an imposition to expect him, while making the acquaintance of such a large family, to waste time by getting involved in general conversation. I made introductions only if we happened to meet anyone in the foyer or on the stairs. To my great shame I must admit that such encounters always embarrassed me very much. Yes, I was absurd enough to be ashamed of my dear mother's work clothes and her rough, toil-worn hands, should she happen to come home from the lumberyard at that precise time. Undeterred by my reticence, though, any girl friends who came to my home saw to it themselves that they met my family. Every last one of them quickly recognized my mother's unusual qualities and came to regard her with love and respect.

My participation at birthday parties and other family feasts was never curtailed; and it remained my responsibility to provide the necessary occasional poetry. For the most part, I was totally unaware of the extent to which I had withdrawn from my family and of the pain this caused. I lived only for my studies and the aspirations they had awakened in me. I perceived them as my duty and felt in no way guilty of any injustice.

This constant exertion of all my powers gave me an exhilarating feeling of living a very full life, and I saw myself as a richly endowed and highly privileged creature. On one occasion, our old principal, wishing to refer a pupil to me for tutoring, asked me to call on him. Naturally, he got around to inquiring how I was doing. When I replied with an enthusiastic: "Oh, *I'm* doing *very* well!" his large, round, and somewhat protruding eyes opened even wider than usual.

"Well, one seldom hears that!" was his surprised comment.

One experience I had soon thereafter stands out in remarkably sharp contrast to this general euphoria of mine. At that time I slept in the same room as my sister Erna, and continued to do so until her marriage. There was as yet no electricity in our house, and we were using gas lamps. The lamp in our room was equipped with a dimmer; we had a habit of leaving the burner on at its lowest setting at night, so that we could quickly turn up the light at any time. One morning our sister Frieda opened the door to our room and screamed in terror. She immediately perceived a strong odor of gas. Both of us lay in our beds, deathly white and apparently in a heavy stupor. The flame had gone out, and the gas was escaping. Frieda opened the window at once, turned off the jet, and wakened us. I returned to consciousness out of a state of sweet, dreamless rest, and what flashed through my mind upon coming to and grasping the situation was the thought: "What a shame! Why couldn't they leave me in this deep peace forever?" I myself was shocked to discover that I "clung to life" so little.

Even in my conscious daily life, I recall a time when the sun seemed to disappear. It was probably the summer of 1912 when I read the controversial novel, *Helmut Harringa*.[99] Portraying student life, it portrayed in frighteningly vivid color the deplorable conditions in the fraternities with their senseless drinking requirements and the consequent moral aberrations. I was filled with such aversion that it took weeks before I recovered from it. I had lost all confidence in the persons with whom I associated daily; I went about as one unbearably burdened; and I was beyond finding enjoyment in anything at all. What cured me of this depression is highly significant. That year a great Bach Festival was given in Breslau.[100] Bach was my favorite, so naturally I had a ticket for each of the performances: an organ concert; chamber music; and a gala evening of orchestral and vocal music. I no longer recall which oratorio was being presented that evening. I only know that Luther's defiant hymn "A Mighty Fortress" was included. I had always liked singing it in our school devotions. When, in stirring battle cry, the verse was sung:

> "And though this world with devils filled
> Should threaten to undo us
> We will not fear,
> . . . truth will triumph through us"

my pessimistic outlook vanished completely. True, the world might be evil; but if the small group of friends in whom I had

confidence and I strove with all our might, we should certainly
have done with all "devils."

5

I had studied at the University of Breslau for four semesters.
Participating in the life of my "alma mater" more, probably, than
most students, I may have seemed so deeply rooted there that I
would not leave her voluntarily. But on this occasion, as often
later in life, I was able to sever the seemingly strongest ties with
minimal effort and fly away like a bird escaped from a snare. I
had always intended to spend some time at another university. I
had made definite plans while still attending the *Gymnasium*.
For my first semester I would go with Erna to Heidelberg, the
magic of whose student life was presented so attractively in the
old student songs. This plan was scotched because during my first
semester Erna was taking her premedical exams and could not
leave Breslau. The following summer she said she was too close
to taking the state boards to go away from home. Probably the
stronger magnet for her was Hans Biberstein; the year before my
Abitur, he had studied in Freiburg-im-Breisgau and now could
not leave home again so soon. I realized then that I could not tie
myself to my sister. Nor did I want to wait until I, too, would be
held back by my own approaching exams. During the fourth semester, I got the impression that Breslau had no more to offer me
and that I needed new challenges. Objectively, this was not at all
correct. Plenty of unused opportunities were left, and here I would
have been able to add a great deal to my knowledge. But I longed
to go elsewhere. The poesy of student songs, though, no longer
played a role in my choice of a university. Something totally different made that choice unequivocal. In Stern's seminar, in the
summer of 1912 and the winter of 1912–13, we had studied the
problems of the psychology of thought, particularly associated
with the work of the "Würzburg School" (Külpe, Bühler, Messer,
etc.).[101] In the essays I studied in preparation for these reviews, I
kept coming across references to Edmund Husserl's *Logische
Untersuchungen*. One day Dr. Moskiewicz found me thus occupied in the psychology seminar.

"Leave all that stuff aside," he said, "and just read this; after all, it's where all the others got their ideas."

He handed me a thick book: the second Volume of Husserl's *Logische Untersuchungen*. I would have pounced on it at once but could not; my semester assignments would not permit it. But I determined to devote my next vacation to it. Mos knew Husserl personally; having studied with him for one semester in Göttingen, he always yearned to return there. "In Göttingen that's all you do: philosophize, day and night, at meals, in the street, everywhere. All you talk about is 'phenomena.'"

One day, an illustrated journal carried a picture of a woman student from Göttingen who had won a prize for a philosophical thesis. She was Husserl's highly talented student, Hedwig Martius. Mos knew her, also, and knew that she had just married an older student of Husserl's, Hans Theodor Conrad.[102]

Arriving home late on another evening, I found a letter on the table; it was from Göttingen. My cousin Richard Courant had recently become privatdocent[103] there in mathematics; he had just married his school friend, Nelli Neumann from Breslau. Nelli wrote to thank my mother for our wedding present. The letter also gave details about the young couple's life; here, Nelli remarked: "Richard has brought many friends to our marriage, but few of them are women. Wouldn't you like to send Erna and Edith here to study? That would balance things out a bit."

That put paid to all arguments. The following day, I informed my astonished family that I would be going to Göttingen for the following summer semester. Unaware as they were of all that had led up to this, it was as though lightning had struck out of the blue. My mother said, "If you need to go there to study, I certainly won't bar your way."

But she was very sad — much sadder than a short absence for a summer's semester warranted. Once, in my presence, she said to little Erika: "She doesn't like it here with us anymore."

The child was greatly attached to me. She loved to be in my room while I was working. I would put her down on the carpet and give her a book that had many illustrations. Then she would be silent, keep busy, and never disturb me. One could let her have the very best books; she never damaged one. Nor did she demand any other entertainment but remained quiet and contented until someone came to get her.

As a first step toward carrying out my plans, I sent a postcard to my cousin; he was to get me information about the lectures to be given by Göttingen's philosophers in the coming semester. Soon afterwards, he sent me the galley proof of the new schedule of lectures. Meanwhile, I took advantage of the Christmas vacation to study *Logische Untersuchungen*. Since the book was out of print at the time, I had to use the philosophy seminar's copy and so spent my days there. Professor Hönigswald was often there, too; and he finally asked me what I was studying so eagerly throughout my vacation. To my reply he commented, "Well! Nothing less than Husserl!"

Now my heart expanded. Beaming, I told him, "I'm going to Göttingen in the summer. Oh, if only I were advanced enough to do this kind of work myself!"

He was taken aback. That winter, for the first time, he was lecturing on the psychology of thought. He was then beginning to come to grips with phenomenology; later, this developed into sharp opposition. However, at that time, his rejection of it was not yet all that definite. But it was not to his liking that one of his students should go over to the other camp with flying colors. No such thought ever occurred to me. Despite my great admiration for Hönigswald's acumen it never entered my mind that he would dare to place himself on a level with Husserl since I was convinced even at that time that Husserl was *the* philosopher of our age. From then on, whenever the talk in Hönigswald's seminar turned to phenomenology, I was called on as the "expert."

For a New Year's Eve celebration, Lilli Platau, Rose, and Hede Guttmann presented some humorous verses. For each one present, they composed a verse to the tune of a popular song: *Ist das nicht um Kopf zu stehen?* [Wouldn't that make you stand on your head?] They performed behind a screen above which only their heads could be seen. Each time the chorus was sung, their heads would disappear and up came their feet. (Actually, they had pulled stockings over their arms and shoes on their hands.) The verse composed for me declaimed:

Many a maiden dreams of "busserl" [kisses]
Edith, though, of naught but Husserl.
In Göttingen she soon will see
Husserl as real as real can be.

But I was also given something to read in a more serious vein. In our family newsletter for New Year's Eve, there was a fairy tale about a small blue stone. Its tender symbolism clearly showed me how deeply my relatives and close friends felt the deprivation of my companionship which was caused by my absorption in scholarship. Lilli had written the tale.

Gradually all the preparations necessary for my departure had been made. Once I was assured of the summer in Göttingen for myself, a new thought occurred to me. After all, Göttingen was not only a paradise for philosophers but for mathematicians as well. So I proposed to Rose that she should go with me. Though sorely tempted, she had some reservations whether she could afford it. She was accustomed to earn her tuition through tutoring, and there would be no question of that at a strange university; there she would need all of her time for study if she were to accept the opportunities offered her. That was exactly what I wanted for Rose. Her constant overworking at such an early age worried me. I would give much to remove her from such busyness for a few months at least. One day I was alone with my mother and asked her, teasingly: "Mama, are you a rich woman?"

In similar vein, she replied, "Yes, my child, what would you like?"

With that I ventured the request that she give Rose the tuition for one semester in Göttingen. She was immediately ready to do so. When I told my friend about it, she decided to go with me; what was more, upon consulting her family, she found she could finance it herself and need not call on my mother's generosity. Our decision also made Georg Moskiewicz decide to go through with his plan to return to Göttingen. We warmly welcomed his decision as he was already acquainted there and therefore could introduce us into the circle of the phenomenologists.

I never imagined going away for more than one semester. Although the tuition at a small university at that time was very reasonable, one had more expenses than when studying at home.

The thrift we were accustomed to practice since childhood precluded any notion of taking advantage of such additional expenditure for any length of time. That made me feel my mother's sadness at the thought of our coming separation was exaggerated. Deep in my heart, though, I had an intimation (a feeling she most likely shared) that ours was a far more incisive parting. And as though determined to thwart the realization of this subconscious presentiment, I now took a step which should compel me to return: I asked Professor Stern to give me an assigned subject for a doctoral dissertation in psychology. I chose him in preference to the other philosophers since my experience with him so far led me to believe he would allow me more of a free hand than the others. But there I was mistaken. He had always accepted our criticism of his methods in a friendly way during his seminars, never taking offense. But he held to his ideas so rigidly that he could not be budged from them in the least; he also sought to have his students' research corroborate his own. This became very clear to me during our conversation. He received me cordially as ever and readily acquiesced to my request even though I was still exceptionally young. But what he suggested was inconceivable: to write a sequel to the paper I had presented that winter on the development of the thought process in children. In fact, he wanted it based on just such experimental interrogation as had plagued the unfortunate Mos for years. Stern suggested that, as I intended going to Göttingen via Berlin and Hamburg, I should visit the "Institute for Applied Psychology" in Berlin. There Stern's collaborator, Dr. Otto Lipmann, could show me the collection of pictorial material; and I was to see whether any of it were applicable to my work. Paying that visit to Klein-Glieneke was the only step I ever took toward a dissertation in psychology.

Moskiewicz was a friend of Dr. Lipmann, so he arranged an appointment for an afternoon there for the three of us, himself, Rose, and me. Our host and his charming little wife received us with warm hospitality. We were invited for afternoon coffee and then to supper; we were introduced to their attractive children; we were shown the whole house; and we were taken for a pleasant stroll along the Havelsee on which the town was located. In an interval between these activities, we were also taken to the bright basement rooms where the "Institute" was housed. The collected pictures, stored in a chest of drawers, held very little attraction for me; and the astute Dr. Lipmann confirmed my impression that they would be of little use.

I took away with me the memory of a delightful afternoon and a conviction that the project would come to nothing. It had been a mistake from the start even to think of getting a doctorate in psychology. All my study of psychology had persuaded me that this science was still in its infancy; it still lacked clear basic concepts; furthermore, there was no one who could establish such an essential foundation. On the other hand, what I had learned about phenomenology, so far, fascinated me tremendously because it consisted precisely of such a labor of clarification and because, here, one forged one's own mental tools for the task at hand. At first, recollection of my topic for a thesis in psychology caused me slight qualms of conscience in Göttingen; but I soon shrugged off these.

Chapter VI

Diary Notes . . . Two Young Hearts
-1913-

1

Before I proceed with the account of this new and decisive period in my own life, I must continue the story of my sister Erna. During my first semester, the summer of 1911, she took her premedical exam, the *Physikum*. The numerous candidates were grouped by fours. Erna and Hans Biberstein, of course, were in one group and studied together in preparation for the exam. Because their diligence and their knowledge intimidated others, they had difficulty finding two more companions. Since the tests were given publicly, nothing could deter me from attending. Because of my psychology course, I was even able to prompt them a bit in physiology; I was indeed proud of that. Erna passed with a "1" average; but Hans—the gifted, diligent, and so ambitious Hans—had one failure in zoology and had to repeat the examination in that subject sometime later. Now, it was possible to pass the premedical even despite several failures; these occurred frequently and people usually accepted them good-naturedly. Hans, however, was bitterly vexed and could not get over it for the longest while; and it may be that our mother was even more irritated than he by the "disgrace."

Poor Erna would happily have exchanged places with him, and her shining "1" was no longer a source of joy for her. Fortunately the state boards results were much better. In these they both earned a "1" in every subject. Not long thereafter, even before they had completed their theses, they were able to take the orals for their doctorate. Both had been doing serological research — Erna with white mice, Hans with rabbits — at the Clinic for Internal Medicine under the supervision of a very capable young assistant, Dr. Felix Rosenthal, the son of an orthodox rabbi. The series of experiments had been completed; compiling the results was considered nonessential and could be postponed until after the orals.

By early summer of 1914, all their examinations were over. These had exacted a toll from the candidates, and now they certainly deserved some relaxation. After their joint labors, the pair wanted very much to take a trip together. But permitting the couple to go off into the world all by themselves was altogether contrary to custom. As it was, our mothers had often seemed to themselves, and to us, like a pair of mother hens who had hatched ducklings and who were then horrified to see their offspring swim away. On this occasion, the couple's request met with a flat denial. I was moved to intervene, partly out of genuine love for my sister and my friend, partly for the fun of putting one over on "people." I invited the two of them to visit me in Göttingen, and the family council granted approval. I no longer know whether the idea originated with me or with Hans. In any case, the two of them showed up in Göttingen, one day. Erna could stay with me. Hans was hospitably put up by an acquaintance from Breslau. This good-natured soul, Erich Danziger, as well as Toni Meyer, an older girl friend of mine, also from Breslau and also studying in Göttingen for the summer, helped me to make my guests comfortable during their visit. After all, they came about mid-semester; I had a great deal of work to do and could spend relatively little time with them. But I had drawn up an all-inclusive program for them to make sure they would see: the beautiful Weser and Leine Mountains; Kassel and its magnificent picture galleries; the fascinating old Hannoverisch-Münden, and Hildesheim. Hans had to go back somewhat earlier than Erna. With her, Danziger and I made a final hike of several days' duration through the Harz Mountains. I almost feel those particular days were the most peaceful and happy ones for Erna. The hours we all spent together in Göttingen had also been cloudlessly happy. As I learned later, during excursions Erna made with Hans alone, conflicts between them had frequently marred their enjoyment of the beauty of nature and of the old cultural sites.

A few weeks after their visit, war broke out [W.W.I]. Hans immediately reported for active service. He was accepted at once as *Feldunterarzt* [Assistant Army Surgeon]. All those who had currently passed the examinations were forthwith licensed without, as usual, having to serve a year of internship. His first assignment was to a medical transport train, and in this way he got to visit Breslau rather frequently, or at least he was near enough for his mother and Erna to visit him. Only much later was he assigned to the troops at the front and was promoted to *Feldarzt* [Army Surgeon, Junior Grade]; finally he was given the rank of *Feldoberarzt* [Army Surgeon, Senior Grade]. Achieving officer's rank with this appointment, he felt every inch an officer.

Shortly after the war began, Erna had been stopped on the street by the Chief of the Gynecology Department of the University, the elderly Privy Councillor Küttner, who asked her whether she would come to be his assistant. Of course, she agreed immediately. It was an opportunity to get training which would never have been available to her in peacetime. The competition for such positions was usually so great that one was considered lucky to be accepted as a volunteer and to be allowed to work without any remuneration. Now the elderly gentleman was gathering together his women students since most of the men on his staff had to go to the front. I happened to be visiting Erna and her companions in the clinic when, in uniform, the Chief Resident came to the Doctors' Mess to bid them farewell. He told them: "Make yourselves at home, ladies. You are now the masters of the clinic!"

Even though Lilli had not taken her state boards as yet, she was also among these "ersatz"-assistants. She and Erna shared two rooms in the clinic. Theirs was a difficult and responsible position. Often called into the home of the poor for difficult deliveries, they now had to perform under most adverse conditions procedures which formerly they had merely observed or in some cases merely read about. There was no fee for this "poly-clinic" care since the poor were considered "practice material" for the young doctors to get experience. These calls (so many of them came during the night) often caused much anxiety; but others brought much joy. And, because of them, one matured, becoming self-confident and assured in carrying out one's pro-fession. There was a congenial, comradely atmosphere in the doctors' lounge. Of course, on occasion, there were also some nasty human experiences. Erna had much to tell us when she came home or when we visited her at the hospital.

Besides this practical professional activity, she finished her doctoral work at this time; and, for Hans, she assembled from books and journals the literature that enabled him to complete his and to submit it. In his stead, she also took on the care of his mother. When Frau Biberstein was ill, if at all possible, Erna had to look in on her daily. Otherwise, to help her pass the time, Frau Biberstein was frequently invited to come to our house or to the hospital. Thus Erna assumed all the obligations of a be-trothed and of a daughter-in-law without being allowed to call herself either.

After being at the Gynecological Hospital for probably a year and a half, Erna was offered a position in the Municipal Home for Infants. After lengthy deliberation and consultation, she ac-cepted it since such a thorough training in that branch would be an ideal preparation for her later practice as a gynecologist. After that, we considered it essential for her to get some expe-rience in internal medicine. Therefore, in October, 1916, she became an assistant in the department of internal medicine of the Rudolf Virchow Hospital in Berlin. This was the first time she left home for any extended period. At the same time, I was leaving for Freiburg-im-Breisgau. I travelled via Berlin and escorted Erna, together with our Uncle Emil Courant who had found the position for her, to her new home before I continued on my way. En route to Breslau for the Easter vacation in 1917, I stopped over with her for a day and a night. The Virchow Hos-pital is a small town in itself. There are straight, regular rows of pavilions along the avenues. One of these neat small buildings housed Erna's ward as well as her two-room lodgings. She let me have her bed for the night and slept on the sofa in her living room. We kept the door between the two rooms open and spent a good part of the night talking together. Aware that her mind was burdened with much that she needed to talk about, I inquired about her relationship with Hans Biberstein. Sometime earlier, Lilli had revealed Erna's hesitation to broach the subject to me since she felt I had little understanding for such matters. This impression, probably shared by the whole family, was thoroughly mistaken. Though totally dedicated to my work, I still cherished in my own heart the dream of a great love and of a happy marriage. Though I had no inkling of Catholic doctrines on faith and morals, I fully espoused the Catholic ideal of matrimony. It happened, at times, that I found among my associates a young man whom I liked very much and whom I could imagine as a future life-partner. But hardly anyone was aware of this, and so I might well appear to most persons as distinctly cool and unapproachable. Hans Biberstein had also attracted me a great deal; but I knew from the start that he was not for me as I saw clearly how things stood with him and Erna.

It pained me to think she had taken her girl friends into her confidence but not me; still, I could see how that had happened and knew it would relieve her tremendously now to talk freely to me. I therefore asked frankly: "Are you two actually thinking of marrying?"

She was almost in tears as she replied, "Why, it's almost impossible to think of it anymore!"

The war was already three years old, and there seemed to be no end in sight. Upon Hans' return, he would have to begin his practical training from scratch and would not be able to open a practice for years. Besides, he had always wanted to finish his habilitation;[104] and Erna was reluctant to have him sacrifice a career in research for her sake. I had a prompt solution for all these problems — short of ending the war. "You set up your practice as soon as you can. Then, as a start, the two of you can live on your income."

Erna could not imagine Hans agreeing to that.

"But he has no alternative. How much longer should the two of you wait?"

In the summer of 1917, Erna, Rose, and Lilli came to see me

in Freiburg; and we spent several weeks together in the Black
Forest. On *Herzogenhorn's* solitary height, we shared as carefree,
simple, and as harmonious a life as we had known formerly in
the mountains of Silesia. When the question arose whether Erna
should return to the Gynecological Hospital in Breslau after her
first year in Berlin, I urged her to do so even though much unpleasantness awaited her. It seemed to me the shortest road
toward completion of her training as a gynecologist. Rose and
Lilli wanted to spend the following summer vacation in seeing
something new. However, Erna did not join them as she preferred to visit me again. This time we stayed in Freiburg; in my
free time, I acquainted her with the beautiful surroundings.
She was facing another decision and wanted my advice: she intended to open her practice within a few months. Our mother
was all for having her at home and wanted to fix up two adjoining rooms on the ground floor as waiting and consultation rooms.
But other people urged Erna to take an apartment in the southern section of the city because that was where the wealthy Jewish
families lived. Her chances for developing a lucrative practice
would be far better there than with us in the northeast where
one dealt mostly with workers, or, at best, with low or middle-
class civil servants; in any case, her patients here would be covered by the national health insurance. Erna, however, felt no attraction to the rich and pampered ladies of the southern sector.

"I don't believe I'd know how to deal with that kind of person.
After all, I'm not out to amass riches. If I can only earn enough
for us to live on!"

I agreed thoroughly. There were practical considerations
besides. At that time, one could not afford the cost of furnishing
an apartment; and, at home, Erna could count on her sisters'
help whereas elsewhere she would have to hire strangers. So we
settled for a modest beginning at Michaelisstrasse 38.

A few months later the great collapse took place; the war ended;
revolution followed.[105] To reassure my mother, I went home at
that time. Not that the political situation scared her; it could
not; but she would have been very anxious had I been far away
during all that turmoil. Erna gave up her position at the Gynecological Hospital at about the same time to begin preparations

for opening her office. So we happened to return simultaneously to our parental home and again shared the bedroom in the attic. As I have already mentioned, she was given the two rooms on the ground floor to turn into an office. Rejoicing at my return home, my mother gave me the large "parlor" on the first floor to use as a study.

A very long time passed before Hans came home from the front. For him, the war had retained its romantic glow to the very end; and he was unprepared for the collapse. When his Captain, Professor Lehnel, a lawyer from Göttingen, fell in battle, Hans had the body exhumed every time they changed posts; and so, on the long retreat, he really brought the body all the way back to the homeland.

"Just what the ancient Goths did with their dead king," was his own comment.

When the revolution erupted, Hans and the new Captain saw to it that their troops did not disperse but, rather, returned home in an orderly march. Revolver in hand, they rode beside the marchers "to keep the pack in line." The revolvers were not needed. Disciplinary firmness sufficed.

Hans expected to find two large political parties in Germany: one, republican; the other, monarchist. He intended to support the Kaiser enthusiastically; for him, it was unbelievable that no one dared to show allegiance to the monarchy. When, finally, he returned to Breslau at the end of December, he discovered that both his fiancée and his mother belonged to the "German Democratic Party." The elections left him with no alternative but to choose it as well, for, as a Jew, he could expect no sympathy any further to the political right.

Though such deep shadows fell upon the reunion, the joy of being together again after so many years of separation prevailed. One day, at last, Hans, dressed in solemn black, presented himself to my mother to make a formal request for Erna's hand. Both families joined in a sincerely joyful celebration of the engagement in "my" parlor. But soon the couple had to part once more. Hans had to begin training for his medical specialty. Like his brother Fritz, he wanted to become a dermatologist; and, therefore, he began by spending a year with the bacteriologist

Professor Morgenroth in Berlin. In those post-war days, Berlin had its Bolshevist unrest, its strikes, its barbed wire, and its barricades in the streets. Hans could not have found more unsuitable surroundings. He buried himself in his work; he, who by nature was so sociable, now had no desire to go anywhere. Naturally, he was homesick and usually dispirited. Twice that year (1919), I went to Berlin for several days on business. He seemed to revive during those days. Early in the morning before going on duty, he met me at the railway station to take me to my relatives. Since Uncle David Courant lived in Berlin, I always stayed there on stopovers. Hans, too, was always welcome in that hospitable home. We spent as much time together as our schedules permitted. He even attended the theater with me, something he rarely did otherwise. He greatly appreciated these visits; but they increased his silent exasperation with the fact that during the entire year Erna never came to Berlin. He regarded it as a sign of indifference; and, long after they were married, the memory still rankled in him. Surely, Erna's eagerness to be together was as great as his, but she had to attend to her budding practice; just as surely, the family would have objected to a trip to Berlin "for no special reason." Because she was, by nature, so easily swayed, this would have sufficed to make her renounce her own unexpressed desire. Hans accurately assessed the family's influence on her; and, so, an antipathy began which was to increase steadily.

Erna had announced in the newspapers that her office would open on the 1st of February. A shingle was attached to the house and to the fence of the front garden. For emergencies at night a doorbell which would ring in our bedroom was installed as well. It roused me for the first time during the night from January 31 to February 1st. I had to waken Erna. Dazed with sleep, she jumped up.

"You have to go to the window," I said.

That really woke her up. There was actually a man down there wanting her to come to his wife. He took her to a worker's home in an extremely murky district. Several hours later she returned, her mission successfully accomplished. The practice flourished in an amazingly short time. The entire family took a lively interest in it and was so eager to be exactly informed about every single case that Erna, shaking her head, had to ward them off by reminding them of the well known professional obligation to secrecy. During that winter one of our older cousins was stricken by a serious abdominal illness. She was operated on by a "famous" gynecologist (my mother and Hans were indignant about that). Erna was requested merely to observe during the operation. Then, when the patient's condition worsened and became hopeless, she repeatedly asked for Erna. On one occasion, Erna was called to see her in the hospital late at night; that bitterly cold winter night she could find no transportation other than an open sleigh for her return home. As a result, she contracted a severe bronchitis which would not leave her for a long time. That, along with the strain of working a whole year without a break, plus the excitement of those days, brought her to a state of complete exhaustion; she looked terrible and lost weight. The cousin died in November. In January of 1920, Hans returned to Breslau with the intention of staying home permanently. He began his work at the University Hospital: at first, as a volunteer; later, as a salaried assistant; finally, he advanced to Chief Resident. He had joyfully anticipated his homecoming; when it came, he found both his mother and his fiancée ailing. He considered this misfortune almost a personal affront; he was indignant about it, like a spoiled child. He demanded that Erna take her temperature daily; as a matter of fact, it was usual for her to have a slightly elevated temperature by evening. Now he was convinced her lungs were affected. My mother was beside herself. She knew no greater spectre than "consumption"; and, for her, it seemed impossible that anyone in our healthy family could be thus afflicted. This daily temperature-taking seemed to her to be at the root of the evil: she believed Hans only meant to torment everyone by his dark forebodings. This was not entirely accurate, of course, though his irritation with the family played a big role along with his anxiety. Erna had not been allowed to come to visit him, but for the sake of this relative, who had considered her not good enough as a physician, she had been made to risk her health. Finally, in mid-winter we sent her to the *Riesengebirge* for several weeks. There she quickly recovered and was able to resume her practice before long.

Once Erna had left on her trip, I had a talk with my brother-in-law. I begged him to promise that during this time of recuperation he would leave Erna in peace, undisturbed by any kind of complaint or reproach. Should he or his mother feel in any way offended by any one in the family, an occurence which, as we had learned by experience, repeated itself with regularity, he was to let me know about it; I would take the greatest care to remedy the situation. After some hesitation, he agreed.

2

At the time I was not living at home. When our cousin Selma Schlesinger[106] died, I was in Hamburg but I returned to Breslau soon thereafter. Her mother, Aunt Bianca, my mother's eldest sister, had lived alone with her during the past years. The eldest daughter was married and lived in Budapest; the second one directed a children's home in Berlin. The only son, pride of the whole family, had a large medical practice in Berlin. Aunt Bianca was seventy-five years old at the time. She had an incurable eye disease and was in generally poor health besides. Despite this, having no assistance other than that of a very young maid, she took care of her own small household. Her principal occupation was to make a home for that youngest daughter who, until she became ill, held a very responsible position in an office. Naturally, the loss of this beloved child affected Aunt Bianca deeply; and thereafter, it was impossible to leave her alone. The family council decided that one of her nieces should sleep in her home. At first it was Grete Pick, then Martha Burchard. But both of them had jobs which took them away from the house during the day; and they found it a real burden not to return to their own homes at night. On my first visit there after I returned to Breslau, I saw through the situation and told my mother as we left the house that, since the others appeared to stay with her only under duress, I would be very willing to move in with my aunt. My mother was delighted by this suggestion; and it was also welcomed by all the others concerned. On New Year's Day I assumed my new position. My aunt greeted me, surprised and much moved. "Have you really come to stay with me? I couldn't believe it."

Actually, in this house, I was more of a stranger than with any other relative. A most unusual reason had caused all contact between our two families to be curtailed for years. In her youth, our eldest cousin, Jenny, had been engaged to Max Gordon, now my brother-in-law. He had broken off the relationship because of being pressured to marry before he could support a wife. Many years later when he became engaged to my sister Else, the entire Schlesinger family considered it a severe affront; and none of them entered our house anymore, even though my mother was totally innocent of having had anything to do with the engagement. One has to understand our aunt's anxiety over the fact that all three daughters, well along in years by then, were still unmarried. When finally she succeeded in finding her eldest daughter a husband, a widower with three daughters, she was reconciled to my mother immediately.

None of the household chores fell to me. On the contrary, it was good for my aunt to have someone to care for again. Her sewing table stood on a small raised platform by the window to give her a view of the street. This spot I was now to have for my work. When I was writing there, and she had nothing to do in the kitchen, she would sit at the other window, knitting a stocking, watching me with evident respect. She sincerely appreciated each quarter of an hour or so which I spent in chatting with her, as well as the times I read aloud to her, since her poor eyesight prevented her from reading.

3

Whenever Hans had anything on his mind during those weeks, he would call for me at her house; and I would accompany him to the hospital. Other times, we would arrange to meet at the hospital to go to Michaelisstrasse 38 for a visit. Now I had personal experience of the kind of discussions Erna was constantly drawn into; only I was much less affected by them. I will give an example I still recall. Hans and his mother wanted to spend an evening with us. Frau Biberstein came from her home; Hans from the hospital. He usually arrived long after our regular suppertime had passed. Since my mother craved her hot tea when she came home from the office, and, in any case, did not like to have her meal very late, we did not wait for him. When he arrived, he ate by himself. That evening, Rosa fixed a steak for him instead of our simple evening meal, convinced as she was that after the long hours on duty he needed something substantial. It never occurred to her, however, to serve one to his mother as well. I do not recall whether, that evening, she had eaten at home or shared our supper. In any case, she was served the late evening refreshment we ordinarily had when guests were there, tea, pastry, and fruit. But omitting the steak was a grievous offense; its absence was taken to indicate a lack of respect, a show of indifference. I maintained a serious attitude while listening to this reproof. Then, stating emphatically that Rosa had not had the slightest intention of offending in any way, I promised to see to it that she apologized. And, indeed, I then discussed the situation with Rosa privately, persuading her, in order to restore peace, to make this sacrifice since one had to take persons as one found them. I moved her to write a note of apology for the unintentional offense she had given. This sufficed to placate Mother Biberstein; and peace was restored until the next occasion arose.

These conversations with Hans served only to strengthen the long-established friendship between us. I remember how once in one of our talks he said to me most affectionately: "You know very well that after Erna, I place the greatest confidence in you — it's almost unlimited!"

We never again had a falling-out such as we sometimes had during our student years. This was because I had completely changed my attitude towards others as well as toward myself. Being right and getting the better of my opponent under any circumstances were no longer essentials for me. Also, though I still had as keen an eye for the human weaknesses of others, I no longer made it an instrument for striking them at their most vulnerable point, but, rather, for protecting them. Even my tendency to correct others did not affect my new attitude. I had learned that one seldom reformed persons by "telling them the truth". That could benefit them only if they themselves had an

earnest desire to improve, and if they accorded one the right to
be critical. Therefore, in these conversations with my brother-
in-law, my prime concern again was to get to know him and his
mother better since their ways differed so much from ours. This
enabled me later to support Erna on many an occasion.

Preparations for the wedding began in the course of 1920.
Linens for both of them were sewn in the Good Shepherd Convent. Out of fine wood that my mother had put aside for this
purpose, she had their furniture manufactured by some of her
customers. Hans wanted everything to be as elegant and modern
as possible; and he was not easily satisfied.

Finding a suitable apartment was the most difficult proposition. It was the time when the housing shortage was at its peak.
During the war years, all construction had ceased throughout
Germany. In addition, refugees from Poznan and Upper Silesia
had crowded into Breslau. Cards issued by the Housing Office
regulated the assignment of lodgings. Erna and Hans had Number 23,000 (the exact figure was slightly higher, but I do not
recall it). Obviously that would get them nowhere. We had no
alternative but to fix up the attic of our house for them. Before
this was possible, we had to evict an undesirable tenant by insti-
tuting a long court procedure. Every attempt to get her to move
out amicably had failed.

I stayed in Breslau all of that year. To be sure, I was on tenterhooks the whole time. I was passing through a personal crisis
which was totally concealed from my relatives, one I was unable
to resolve in our house. Still, I would not have wished to leave
before Erna's lot had been decided. Her engagement had been a
protracted torment. By the time she came down from our attic-
room in the morning, I was usually already at work at my desk.
At that time she would come in to tell me what had transpired
the evening before. The engaged couple were together daily,
either in our home or at the Bibersteins'. Frequently her first
words were, "I don't know what to do; I'm desperate!"

Then I had her sit down on the chair beside my desk diagonally
across from me (my friend Trude Kuznitsky always called it my
"consultation chair"), and I would have Erna tell me everything,
giving her whatever advice I could. My guiding principle was

always: give in, in all that is not unjust. Relieved by our talk, she would go to breakfast and then start her office hours. Usually, what had happened was something similar to the occurrence I described above. But, in reality, a far more serious matter lay behind the whole situation. When, contrary to the resolution he had made as a youth, Hans decided to marry, he insisted he could not separate from his mother. So Erna agreed to let his mother move in with them. But the entire family attempted to dissuade her from keeping house together with her mother-in-law; and she herself dreaded it. Having quickly taken his lovely and amiable fiancée to their hearts, Hans' relatives, as well, urged my mother in private not to permit such a thing since Erna would have much to suffer. Often enough, my mother said in the presence of Frau Biberstein that she herself had resolved never to move in with one of her children. Actually, the impossibility of finding a suitable apartment solved the problem. In our attic, it was out of the question to provide room for his mother as well. Besides, she was supposed to keep up her home in the southern part of the city in case, eventually, Hans might want to establish his practice there. Thus the touchy problem never needed to be explicitly discussed by those most concerned. But Mother Biberstein and Hans sensed that what bitterly disappointed them gave a lot of satisfaction to my relatives and that Erna herself was relieved. In this fashion, as I have already mentioned, an antipathy resulted, especially toward my mother. The two of them became quite blind to her fine human qualities and treated her with such a lack of respect as she had hardly ever experienced. It is understandable that she was hurt by this and that she was unable to accept her son-in-law cordially. But more than with her own pain, my mother's heart was heavy with the knowledge of her child's suffering which probably would have to be lifelong. This worry was so great, at times, that as a solution she considered ending the engagement, even though as a genuine Jewish mother she earnestly wished nothing more than to see her daughters well married. Whenever Erna was "desperate," this same thought would fleetingly occur also to her. But I never entertained it, firmly convinced as I was that the two were meant for one another and that Erna's life, particularly, would be destroyed if they did not marry. I also hoped for a great improvement once they were actually married since many a misunderstanding would disappear spontaneously in the growing intimacy of their life together.

The marriage was celebrated at the beginning of December. Two days were necessary since even our large rooms could not accommodate the number of guests. On the day of the civil marriage ceremony all of our cousins as well as our closest friends Lilli and Rose with their fiancés were invited for the evening. Only the bridal couple's brothers and sisters with their children, as well as their parents' brothers and sisters were invited to the religious wedding ceremony and the wedding meal which followed. (That is to say that all our relatives and acquaintances attended the wedding ceremony but, as soon as it was over, all but the immediate family withdrew.) Our family was so extensive that accommodating this "intimate circle" still meant seating more than fifty persons.

At that time my health was very poor, probably as a result of the spiritual conflicts I then endured in complete secrecy and without any human support. On the morning of the civil marriage ceremony, while the last heavy pieces of furniture were being carried up the stairs, I lay on a chaise longue in one of our bedrooms in so much pain that the slightest sound made me cringe. When Erna came up one time, she said she could not stand it any more, and gave me a small dose of morphine. By evening, I was fine again. At first I did not join in the dancing. But when it had grown late and I was standing near the grand piano beside Hans, they suddenly began to play an old, well known, lively number.

"Isn't that a fast-step?" I asked. That was a dance which had become popular during our student years, and I had learned it from Hans.

"Yes," he said. "Would you care to dance? I did not dare ask you earlier since you hadn't been feeling well."

We began and did not stop until the whole exuberant number was over. As Hans was about to lead me to a seat, the music for a slow waltz began.

"Well," he said, "now we have to show people we also know how to dance elegantly"; and we finished the entire waltz.

I have never again really danced since then. Years later, I did comply a few times when my pupils earnestly begged me to do so at carnival time.

The religious wedding ceremony took place in our home. With my brother Arno's help, I prepared the large "parlor" for it. At a Jewish wedding, the bride waits, seated in a place set apart, while the groom and the rabbi and the other men (there must be at least ten) pray in another room. Then the rabbi pronounces a blessing over the bride, whereupon the groom leads her in solemn procession to the "bridal canopy" for the actual marriage. We put Erna's seat against a column between two windows where my desk usually stood. Above it hung a painting of St. Francis by Cimabue.[107]

"Maybe we should take that down," said Arno, who felt that in all probability the saint was not exactly an appropriate witness for a Jewish wedding.

"Don't disturb it," I replied. "No one will even notice it."

And there it stayed. Erna was an exceptionally beautiful bride. As if she were some oriental princess, she sat on the ceremonially decorated seat between banks of green plants. I looked at St. Francis above her head and found great consolation in his presence.

After the wedding, the newlyweds went to the *Riesengebirge*. From there, Erna wrote me a letter brimming over with happiness. She said that, knowing I would share her joy, she had to let me know what a lovely time they were having. That set my mind at rest; and I now felt free to take care of myself.

Chapter VII

Student Years in Göttingen
1913-1914

2/

A long, long way lay behind me when I returned to Göttingen once more in March, 1921, nearing the most important decision of my life; it was a way I began to travel that April day of the year 1913 when I had come there for the first time.

1

Dear Göttingen! I do believe only someone who studied there between 1905 and 1914, the short flowering time of the Göttingen School of Phenomenology, can appreciate all that the name evokes in us.

I was twenty-one years old and looked forward full of expectation to all that lay ahead. During the vacation, I had made another visit to Hamburg. No lectures were scheduled before the end of April [1913], but the semester officially began on the fifteenth. From that day the administrative offices of the university were open for business; and if I were to get my registration and all the other peripheral affairs out of the way, I could then plunge right into my work the very moment life in the lecture halls began. Therefore, I left Hamburg on April 17. My brother-in-law Max worried a bit about letting me set out alone for such unfamiliar surroundings. He asked whether I could at least spend the first night with the Courants instead of in the student quar-

ters where they had made arrangements for Rose and me. I said
no to that. I merely informed them of my arrival time; and, even
though he had a sore foot at that time, Richard met me at the
railway station. It was already evening; he showed me to my new
home in the dark. Rose was to come from Berlin some days
later. I was delighted when the door was opened by a young
woman whose face was both pretty and friendly. Later, she admitted her own pleased surprise at my appearance. She had
never had any woman students in her home before and thought
they would all be old and ugly. Nearly every household in Göttingen rented rooms to students. On principle, many landladies
refused women boarders. Some had moral prejudices. Others
feared their kitchens would be in demand too frequently for
washing, ironing, or cooking; or their rooms might be damaged
by the use of small alcohol stoves. When one was looking for
lodgings, it was very embarrassing to have a grouchy face appear
at a crack in the door only to mumble a few words of rejection.
So we had been lucky indeed.

The house was on Lange Geismarstrasse, a narrow street typical of small towns, which led up from the center of town to St.
Alban's Churchyard. The house was No. 2, next door to the
Kirchhof: in Göttingen, that was what they called the squares
where the churches were located. The *Albani Kirchhof* lies at
the boundary of the old town. Extending farther out from there
are charming streets on which the professors' residences and the
more elegant boarding-houses are to be found. St. Alban's is the
oldest of the churches, and it has a completely smooth facade
and a massive tower. The bell still pealed the Angelus three
times daily, thereby revealing its Catholic past. I heard the bell
ringing; I did not know its significance. On the very day after
my arrival, I began my orientation walks. From childhood on I
had loved to make discoveries. When Erna and I were sent out
for walks on our own in Breslau or in Hamburg, I used to say,
"Today, we'll go somewhere we have never been before."

Now I could get the mastery over the whole town and its near
and far environs as well. There was plenty to see. One had only
to walk down Lange Geismarstrasse and turn right at the corner
to be directly at the *Marktplatz*. There was the beautiful Gothic

Rathaus, the town hall; red geraniums bloomed at its windows, a cheerful contrast to the old gray stone. In front of it stood Schaper's charming Fountain of the Goose Girl. In one of the side streets not far from there was Göttingen's most beautiful old house called the *Mütze* [The Cap], an old-German tavern with framework gables and bull's-eye glass for windows. The town's main street, Weenderstrasse, leads directly north from the *Marktplatz*; there, people take their customary afternoon stroll, their "Bummel" to the Weender Gate. On the right side, approximately in Göttingen's center, rises its landmark, the tall steeple of St. James' Church. This and the two less stately towers of St. John's Church are recognized as the town's distinctive skyline when seen from a distance. On the opposite side of the street is the famous pastry shop, *Kron und Lanz*, where the best tortes are made, and where, to the extent their purses will allow, professors and students take their afternoon coffee and read their newspapers. On the right side, the last house at the Weender Gate is the *Auditorienhaus,* the lecture hall, central point of all life at the university. It is not a massive building and cannot compare with our ancient *Leopoldina* in Breslau nor with the splendid modern edifices in Jena or Munich. It is a simple, sober house with simple, sober study rooms. Set back somewhat from the street, it is sheltered by green park areas where, in the few free minutes between classes, the students stroll and smoke their cigarettes. The nearby seminar building, around the corner to the right on the Nikolausbergerweg, is more modern and more elegant. It was still new at the time. Most of the seminar rooms were located there; and, as I found to be the case nearly everywhere, the Philosophy Seminar room was just below the roof. The Institute for Psychology was in an entirely separate building. Located near St. John's Church, a little to the west of the *Marktplatz*, it was an old house with well-worn steps and narrow rooms. Even the very fact of the physical separation of the buildings symbolized that in Göttingen philosophy and psychology had nothing in common. The Nikolausbergerweg winds its way from the Weender Gate to the east, out of town and up the mountain. When one has left the last houses behind, one can see the charming village of Nikolausberg on the summit. The initiate knew that the landlady of the inn had a knack for baking excellent waffles. If one made advance reservations for supper and climbed up there after the wear and tear of the day, one was served a steaming dish of them. But this I learned only much later. To the left of Nikolausberg rose a bare hill crowned with three windswept trees which always reminded me of the three crosses on Golgotha.

All of this I saw in my first days. But on my initial walk, I did not go up there but, rather, turned off to one side into a large meadow. That made me acquainted with the characteristic soil of the *Leineberge* (called in the Göttingen dialect *Laaneberge*); to return from a walk without having lumps of clay stuck to one's shoes would be unusual indeed. The town's streets also have an unusual type of asphalt paving that was softened alternately by the sun and by the rain; more often by the latter since it rains so much there. Göttingen had about thirty-thousand inhabitants at that time. There were no street cars. Before the war there was continual discussion about getting some; afterwards, it was obviously out of the question. The university and the students were the heart of the town's life: *that* made it what it was, a "university town," unlike Breslau, a town that had a university among other things.

The commemorative plaques found on nearly every one of the older houses had a special attraction for me: they told of famous persons who had formerly lived there. So, along every step of the way, one is reminded of the past: the Brothers Grimm, the physicists Gauss and Weber, and the others who did not belong to "Göttingen's Seven,"[108] who once lived or worked here are constantly brought to the attention of successive generations. The town's ancient ramparts are also preserved, planted with mighty, towering linden trees. Their scent steals into the lecture halls in the summer. (The *Auditorienhaus* is beside the rampart.) When, inside, I heard Heine mentioned, I thought that he, too, had at one time been seated on these benches, and that, probably, when he wrote of the "walls of Salamanca," he had the Göttingen fortifications in his mind's eye. I liked to go for a walk over the rampart. From there, one could so easily see the old houses of the inner city on one side and, on the other, the villas and gardens farther out of town. At one point on the bank there was a small, ancient, bark-covered house where Bismarck had lived as a student.

Rose arrived a few days after I did, and we then arranged our living quarters. We shared two rooms: both of us slept in the one; the larger one we turned into a common living room and study. Our landlady brought us hot milk and fresh rolls early in the morning; then we made our own cocoa. For lunch, we usually met at a vegetarian restaurant run by a south-German woman and her three charming daughters. It was very well patronized. The English and American students usually sat at one long table formed by pushing several small ones together. Their boisterous, harmless joviality dominated the room. Whoever got home first after classes prepared our evening meal of tea and sandwiches. Whoever came in late, found the table set. I do not recall a single argument or any disagreement between us in that summer we spent together. As much as her schedule allowed, Rose took part in my philosophy classes; I worked at her mathematics a bit, too. Our schedules differed greatly, however. Traditionally, there were no lectures in Göttingen on Wednesday or Saturday afternoons because the students and even the professors and their daughters went to the dance at Maria Sprung. Only the philosophers Nelson and Husserl failed to make allowance for this custom. Husserl held his seminar on Wednesday afternoon. But, on Saturday afternoon, we too were free. However, we did not go to Maria Sprung; rather, weather permitting, we went out into the country. First, though, we wrote letters: our weekly one home, and, then, by turns, to the friends, male and female, we had left behind. On Sundays when the weather was good, we were usually outdoors all day. Sometimes we were out from Saturday noon until Sunday evening.

After all, we intended to use this summer to get to know the countryside of central Germany. Göttingen was an excellent starting point for doing so. To the southeast, the town hugs a hill; the Bismarck Tower is on its crest. Beautiful parks stretch upward from the town limits. They extend all the way to the Göttingen Forest through which one can walk for a whole day without reaching its end, and usually, too, without meeting anyone at all. Göttingen townsfolk do not take long hikes. However, if we waited until afternoon on Sundays, we would see them setting out in droves. But their destination was only one of the two large coffeehouses, Rohns or Kehrs, located at an appropriate distance from one another about halfway up that long, long hill. The townspeople were easily distinguished from the students since they wore hats while the students, men and women, went bareheaded. Besides, the local folk all carried big boxes of cake. If they intended going farther than Kehrs, they rode in carriages. That custom of bringing cake along from town had a consequence: there was none to be found in the inns; they served only coarse country bread and Göttingen sausage. For lengthier excursions, we took our provisions along in rucksacks; and in the woods we made our meal of a loaf of pumpernickel, a jar of butter, some cold cuts, fruit, and chocolate. All this pleased us more than a dinner at the inn.

Hills and woods surround Göttingen on the other sides as well. The ample beech forests were aglow in red and gold when one arrived in the autumn for the winter semester. Old ruined castles, perched on the heights, peer into the valley. I was particularly fond of the "Gleichen," two hill-tops directly side by side, both crowned with ruins. On the saddle between the two peaks stood a simple inn; there one could find a Chronicle of the Counts of Gleichen who once lived up there. When we looked down into the valley from that height, I had such a feeling of being in the heart of Germany: a lovely landscape on the slopes, carefully husbanded fields, neat villages, and an encircling wreath of green forests. It seemed as though the very next moment one might expect a wedding procession to emerge from the woods on the opposite hill, just as Ludwig Richter depicted in one of his paintings.[109]

On our longer excursions, we got to know Kassel, the Weserland, Goslar, and the Hartz Mountains. At Pentecost, we spent several days on a hike through Thuringia. We climbed from Eisenach to the Wartburg; went along the *Drachenschlucht* [The Dragon's Ravine] to *Hohe Sonne* [High Sun]; later, on the *Rennpfad* to the *Inselsberg*. We took a train for some stretches in order to cover more territory in the few days we had. Of course,

Weimar was also on our program; and the finale was to be a tour of the free school-community of Wickersdorf. We had beautiful weather for the first two days. On the third, if I remember correctly, it began to rain towards evening. We had been underway since morning and wanted to reach Ilmenau before dark. It was to be our last destination before Weimar. The rain came down heavier and heavier; the road stretched farther and farther; our feet were totally unwilling to go on; and there was no town in sight. Rose became silent and morose from fatigue; I struggled to preserve a cheerful mood. It must have been eight o'clock before we finally reached a long-drawn-out village. It seemed to be a resort, for tourist homes dotted the street. But, no matter where we knocked, no lodging was to be found. At each house I got up the courage to ask anew, but it was always in vain. It probably took us half an hour going through that entire village before we found, at its very end, an inn that accepted us. The tourist accomodations were in a separate building opposite the inn itself. While our beds were being prepared, we went to the dining room. A nourishing hot supper revived our spirits. We asked the friendly inn-keeper where we actually were. The little village was called Manebach. Manebach: that sounded as long drawn out as the endless rain and the endless road. Our good humor was restored enough for us to laugh heartily at that. As soon as our room was ready, we slipped out of our soaking wet clothes and into the warm beds. Now a new battle plan had to be drawn up. We took out Richard's handsome military map, a leftover from a maneuver in Thuringia. Until this evening it had served us excellently. Where was Manebach? Right! There it was. We were but one train stop from Ilmenau. But we could not make up the time lost during the day, so we decided to skip Ilmenau and the *Kickelhahn* and ride to Weimar next morning. We had also taken out the train schedule to check on the earliest departure time.

In Weimar, we visited the stately Goethe House on the *Frauenplan*, his charming summerhouse on the *Stern*, and the Schiller House with its pathetically wretched room where he died. That afternoon we went out to Tiefurt. It was Sunday, so streams of people were out strolling. We were still aching all over from the previous day's long march and felt we were moving at a snail's pace; despite that, we soon left all of Weimar's citizens behind. In Tiefurt's beautiful park we had to sit on a bench to indulge an activity that was far from poetic: we had to count our cash. Before the trip I had gone to the bank to get enough funds for my needs. Rose had spared herself that bother and had failed to provide enough. Now we discovered that our common fund did not suffice for Wickersdorf. We had to cancel our arrangements there by telegram. Now we had enough left over to get us to Jena that evening, and from there the next day, we went directly to Göttingen. I was glad of the chance to see Jena and preferred it to Weimar. Quietly, one could visit all the memorable places; everything here was less obtrusive, and one did not constantly bump into groups of overawed girls from some boarding-school.

When we went to the Courants to give back the military map, of course, we had to give an account of our walking tour. We would have liked to omit all references to the humiliating conclusion, but Richard asked at once about the visit to Wickersdorf. He had a positive gift for asking questions about subjects one would rather not have mentioned.

This tour was one Rose and I made by ourselves. As a rule, we were accompanied by Dr. Erich Danziger,[110] assistant in the Chemistry Institute. He was from Breslau; there, Rose had met him in her chemistry classes. He was short, homely, and a bit awkward; but Rose said he had the most skilled hands in the entire Institute and his help was always enlisted whenever something required particularly delicate handling. He seemed to be under a constant strain, probably as a result of very sad family circumstances; his mother was, and had been for years, in a mental hospital. He and his only sister had grown up virtually as orphans. Having hardly any other associations, he attached himself now exclusively to the two of us. He was a good-hearted and faithful fellow. (It seemed to me he had taken a hidden fancy to Rose but had too little self-assurance to believe that such a spirited and elegant young woman might ever consider him.) But he was always a bit depressed because the philosophical world in which we lived was beyond him.

Georg Moskiewicz arrived some time after us. He was a good deal older than we; that May we joined in a celebration of his thirty-fifth birthday. He did not live in student lodgings, having, instead, two spacious, well-furnished rooms in the quiet *Kirchweg* near the hospital. This was befitting his dignity as a doctor of both medicine and philosophy as well as a prospective privat-docent. For him, too, we were a link with humanity. He seldom joined us on excursions, as such undertakings required one to make a decision and that was no slight task for him. But when he did come, he enjoyed himself thoroughly; more, he was as exuberant as a little boy. In his case, his deep attraction to Rose was obvious. But with so uncertain a future, how could he dare to tie her to himself? Cordial friendship and a common interest in philosophy were his bonds with me.

So, finally, in this roundabout way, I come to the essential topic — the one which had led me to Göttingen: phenomenology and the phenomenologists. In Breslau, Mos had instructed me, "When one gets to Göttingen, the first place to go is to Reinach; he arranges all the rest."

Adolf Reinach was privatdocent in philosophy. He and his friends,[111] Hans Theodor Conrad and Moritz Geiger, and a few others, had originally been students of Theodor Lipps[112] in Munich. When the *Logische Untersuchungen* appeared, they had insisted that Lipps discuss the work with them in his seminar. After Husserl was called to Göttingen, they had come there together in 1905 to be initiated into the secrets of this new science by the master himself. So the "Göttingen School" was founded. Reinach was the first of the group to be habilitated in Göttingen and was now Husserl's right hand; primarily, he was the link between him and the students since he had a gift for dealing with people whereas Husserl was rather helpless along those lines. By this time, Reinach was about thirty-three years old.

I followed Moskiewicz's good advice to the letter. I set out for Steinsgraben 28, I believe, on the very day after my arrival. That street extends to the end of the town. The house in which the Reinachs lived was the very last one. Beyond it stretched a wide grain-field beside which a narrow footpath led up to the Kaiser Wilhelm Park, then on to the Bismarck Tower and the Göttingen Forest. When I asked for Dr. Reinach, the blond maid admitted me to his study and, accepting my card, went to call him. The fine, large room in which I waited had two high windows, sombre wallpaper, and brown oak furniture. Both walls to the left of the door were covered with bookshelves reaching nearly to the ceiling. On the right side, a large sliding door with colored glass panes led to the next room. The large corner between this door and one of the windows was filled by an immense desk; and, opposite the desk chair there were easy chairs ready for visitors. The corner between the two walls of books was arranged to form a cozy nook: a table, an upholstered sofa, and several arm chairs. Opposite the desk chair, a large reproduction of Michaelangelo's "Creation of Man" graced the wall. It was the most comfortable and the most tastefully arranged study I have ever seen. Reinach had been married six months earlier. With loving care, his wife had planned the furnishing of the entire large apartment; and everything was built according to her instructions. Of course, I believe that on that first visit I was hardly aware of most of these details. For, after but a few minutes of waiting, I heard an exclamation of pleased surprise coming from the end of the long passage. Then someone came hurrying, the door opened, and Reinach stood before me. He was barely average in height, not heavy, but broad-shouldered. He had a beardless chin, a short dark moustache, and a broad high forehead. Through the glass of his framed pince-nez, shrewd and exceedingly kind brown eyes peered at you. He greeted me most cordially, pressed me to take the nearest chair, and sat down opposite me at his desk.

"Dr. Moskiewicz wrote to me about you. Have you ever occupied yourself with phenomenology at all?" (When he spoke, one clearly heard the tone of his Mainz dialect.)

I responded briefly. At once, he was ready to accept me for his "Exercises for the Advanced," but he was as yet unable to give me details about day and hour as he had to complete arrangements with his students. He promised to make an appointment for me with Husserl.

"Would you like to meet someone from the Philosophical Society? I could introduce you to the ladies."

I suggested that he need not trouble himself; Dr. Moskiewicz would see to my getting acquainted.

"Right! Then you will soon know everyone."

Göttingen Philosophical Society

(l.r.) Johannes Hering, (?) Schröder, Alfons Reinach, Hans Lipps, Theodore Conrad (eyes only), Max Scheler, Alexander Koyré, Siegfried Hamburger, Hedwig Martius (wife of Theodore Conrad), Rudolf Clemens, Gustav Hübner, Alfred von Sybel

Edmund Husserl, ''The Master''

After this first meeting, I was very happy and filled with deep gratitude. It seemed to me no one had ever received me with such genuine goodness of heart. That close relatives, or friends one had known for years, should be affectionate in their attitude was self-evident to me. But this was something entirely different. It was like a first glimpse into a completely new world. A few days later, I received a postcard with the kindly phrased information that the class would be given from six to eight on Monday evenings. Unfortunately, I had already enrolled at that time for something I was loath to cancel: Max Lehmann's history seminar. So, most reluctantly, I had to decline the Reinach class.

To begin with, I did not call at Husserl's apartment to introduce myself. On the bulletin board, he had announced a preliminary discussion to be held in the philosophy seminar room. All newcomers were to present themselves for acceptance on that occasion. Here then, for the first time, I *did* see: "Husserl, as real as he can be."[113] Neither striking nor overwhelming, his external appearance was rather of an elegant professorial type. His height was average; his bearing, dignified; his head, handsome and impressive. His speech at once betrayed his Austrian birth: he came from Moravia and had studied in Vienna. His serene amiability also had something of old Vienna about it. He had just completed his fifty-fourth year.

After the general discussion, he called the new students to come up to him one by one. When I mentioned my name, he said, "Dr. Reinach has spoken to me about you. How much of my work have you read?"

"The *Logische Untersuchungen*." (The first volume of *Logische Untersuchungen*,[114] published in 1900, was epoch-making because in it Husserl radically criticized the then-prevailing psychologism and all relativism. The second volume appeared the following year. It far surpassed its predecessor in significance as well as in bulk. Here for the first time Husserl treated problems in logic with the method which he later developed systematically into the "phenomenological method" and which he expanded to cover the entire area of philosophy.)

"All of *Logische Untersuchungen?*" he asked me.

"Volume Two — all of it."

"All of Volume Two? Why, that's a heroic achievement!" he said, smiling. With that, I was accepted.

Shortly before the semester began, Husserl's new work, *Ideas,*[115] appeared. It was to be discussed in the seminar. Besides that, Husserl announced that he would make it a rule to be at home one afternoon a week so that we might come to discuss our questions and concerns with him. Of course, I bought the book at once (that is, the first volume of *Yearbook for Philosophy and Phenomenological Research* in which it was the lead article; this yearbook was thereafter to publish the collected works of the phenomenologists). On the occasion of his earliest "at home," I found I was the first guest to arrive at Husserl's home and presented my concerns. Soon others arrived. All of us had the same question on our minds. The *Logische Untersuchungen* had caused a sensation primarily because it appeared to be a radical departure from critical idealism which had a Kantian and neo-Kantian stamp. It was considered a "new scholasticism" because it turned attention away from the "subject" and toward "things" themselves. Perception again appeared as reception, deriving its laws from objects not, as criticism has it, from determination which imposes its laws on the objects. All the young phenomenologists were confirmed realists. However, the *Ideas* included some expressions which sounded very much as though their Master wished to return to idealism. Nor could his oral interpretation dispel our misgivings. It was the beginning of that development which led Husserl to see, more and more, in what he called "transcendental Idealism" (which is not to be confused with the transcendental idealism of the Kantian schools) the actual nucleus of his philosophy and to devote all his energies to its establishment. This was a path on which, to his sorrow as well as their own, his earlier Göttingen students could not follow him.

Husserl had a home of his own on *Hohen Weg*, also at the edge of town where the road leads up to Rohns. (Rohns played an important role in his philosophical discussions; it served often as an example when Husserl spoke about the perception of objects.) The house was built to his wife's specifications to provide for the family's needs. The Master's study was upstairs; it had a small balcony where he went to "meditate." The most important piece of furniture was an old leather sofa. He had gotten it in Halle after he received a grant while lecturing there. Usually, I had to sit at one end of the sofa. Even later, in Freiburg, we carried on our discussions on idealism back and forth from one end of that sofa to the other. Among themselves, his students called him, simply, "the Master." He was aware of it and did not like it at all. When we talked about his wife among ourselves, we used her poetic first name, Malvine. She was short and thin; her gleaming-black hair was smoothly parted; her brown eyes looked at the world with lively interest, with curiosity, and always, with some degree of surprise. Her voice was somewhat sharp and hard, and always sounded aggressive but it also held a trace of kindly humor which served to mellow it. One was always a bit apprehensive in her presence: What might happen? Most often she made embarrassing remarks. People whom she did not like were treated very badly. But she also had very outspoken sympathies. Personally, my only experience of her was always of a sincere friendliness. I have no idea how I came to deserve that. In later years it might have been attributed to the valuable service I was able to give her husband. But she was that way toward me even while I was still a very minor and insignificant student. When I was with her husband, she used to pop in midway through my visit to say she wanted to say hello. (The best discussions were suddenly interrupted in this manner.) She regularly attended Husserl's lectures and admitted to me later (though we had long been aware of it) that she made a habit of counting the students. She had no inner bond with philosophy. She considered it the misfortune of her life since Husserl had to live in Halle for twelve years as a privatdocent before he got a professorship. And even then, what he received was not a full professorship in Göttingen, but, instead, a special position created for him by the far-seeing and energetic but rather authoritarian Minister of Culture Althoff. Husserl's position on the faculty was a most embarrassing one. These experiences determined Frau Malvine to keep her three children away from philosophy. Elli, the eldest, was my age. She studied art history. Very much like her mother in looks, she had something much softer and more tender in her manner. Gerhart became a lawyer; but he would not permit himself to be deprived of philosophy in later years. At the time, Wolfgang was still attending the *Gymnasium*; he had an extraordinary linguistic talent and intended to study languages. The youngest was his mother's favorite. One got an insight into her heart when, later, she spoke about him after his untimely death; he was killed in Flanders when but a seventeen-year-old volunteer. She told me once that she had never had a worry about Wolfgang's future. She had always known that, no matter where he might be or whatever his occupation, he would make those around him happy.

Both Husserls were Jewish by birth but had become Protestants early on. The children were raised as Protestants. I cannot vouch for the truth of it, but the story goes that Gerhart, as a six-year-old attending the same school as Franz Hilbert, the only child of the great mathematician, asked his little comrade what he was (that is, of which religious denomination). Franz did not know.

"If you really don't know, then you are certainly a Jew."

The conclusion was incorrect but characteristic. Later, Gerhart used to speak quite openly of his Jewish descent.

That summer Husserl lectured on "Nature and Spirit," investigating the foundations of natural science and the humanities. This subject was also to be treated in the second part of *Ideas* which had not yet been published. The Master had outlined it at the same time as the first part, but preparation of the final draft for publication was postponed to allow for completion of a new edition of the *Logische Untersuchungen*. This was urgently needed as the work, out of print for many years, was in constant demand.

Soon after Moskiewicz arrived in Göttingen, the Philosophical Society held its first meeting of the semester. It was the more intimate circle of Husserl's actual students who gathered one evening a week to discuss particular questions. Rose and I were totally unaware of our audacity in joining this select group immediately. Since Mos simply took it for granted that we would go along, we felt the same way. As a rule, several semesters might pass before one learned about this institution and then, after being introduced, one first listened in respectful silence for several months before daring to open one's mouth. But I was impudent enough to join in the discussion at once. As Moskiewicz was much older than the rest, he was made chairman for that semester. Nonetheless, probably, he felt less knowledgeable on the subject than anyone else in the group. Merely watching him at the meetings made one aware of how unhappy he was in his position. He presided at the table, but at each meeting he lost control of the discussion in a very short time. Our meetings were held in Herr von Heister's home. This was a young landowner who took delight in living in Göttingen, attending philosophical lectures, and associating personally with the philosophers. He liked us to meet at his house and was in no way disturbed when his own remarks in the discussion were usually ignored as irrelevant. His delicate, blond wife was far more popular with all of us. She was a daughter of Achenbach, the Düsseldorff artist. Numerous paintings by her father graced the house. When we arrived, often enough during a typical Göttingen rainstorm, with coats and rubbers, their butler was politely silent while he helped us remove them. But it was readily obvious that he was secretly shaking his head over these peculiar guests. And when, later, in their magnificent dining room, he poured us a drink, tea or wine according to our preference, he was obliged to witness much that was unusual. I will never forget how, during one intense discussion, Hans Lipps[116] knocked the ash of his cigarette into the silver sugarbowl until our laughter startled him.

None of the founders[117] of the Philosophical Society were present at meetings at that time. Reinach stopped attending after his becoming a lecturer and his marriage. Conrad and Hedwig Martius were living alternately in Munich and in Bergzabern (in the Palatinate) since their marriage. Dietrich von Hildebrand had gone to Munich; Alexander Koyré, to Paris. As Johannes Hering wanted to take the state boards the following summer, he had withdrawn to his hometown, Strassburg, to study without being disturbed. However a few people were still there who had worked with these coryphaei for several semesters and who now passed their tradition on to us newcomers. Rudolf Clemens was one who had a leading role. He was a philologist. His dark blond beard, his neckties, his soft voice, and his eyes, which were both soulful and mischievous, all were reminiscent of the time of the Romantics. His tone was friendly, but it was a friendliness which failed to inspire me with unqualified confidence in him. Fritz Frankfurter[118] was from Breslau and studied mathematics. His brown eyes had a look of childlike candor, trust, and kindliness. The pure delight most of us experienced in philosophizing was most charmingly apparent in him. Once, while telling me something Husserl taught in his course on Kant, which I had not yet attended, Fritz interrupted himself suddenly, "But, no! What comes next is too marvelous to be divulged ahead of time. You have to hear that for yourself."

Hans Lipps made a deeper impression on me than did anyone else. Twenty-three years old at the time, he looked much younger. Very tall, slim, but powerfully built, he had a handsome, expressive face, lively as a child's. His gaze was serious; still his large, round eyes were as inquisitive as a child's. Usually he would state his opinion in brief but very definite terms. When asked to give more detailed clarification, he would assert there was no more to be said as the matter was self-explanatory. That had to satisfy us. We were all convinced that his insights were true and deep even though we were incapable of confirming them ourselves. When he had difficulty in expressing himself in words, his eyes and his lively, spontaneous facial expressions spoke all the more persuasively. That summer, however, he was unable to keep up regular attendance on these evenings since he was preparing simultaneously for his preliminary exams in medicine and, with a thesis on plant physiology, for his doctorate in philosophy. Studying medicine and natural science was his way of filling in the hours during which one could not philosophize. He had already completed a good number of other projects. He had begun with interior decorating, and then arts and crafts; but he had been left unsatisfied by them. However, even in later years, he liked to have a project to work on and had a markedly creative bent to his nature. During his compulsory year of military service as a dragoon in the Life Guard Regiment in Dresden, he became acquainted with the *Logische Untersuchungen* and, with that, a new life began for him. So he had come to Göttingen. He was the only one in the society who often got together with poor Mos and who liked him. The others secretly made fun of Georg's insecurity and of his eternally-unsolved questions.

Philosophy was the virtual life-element for those mentioned so far, although they studied additional subjects. But there were a few others for whom the reverse was the case: their priority was their own particular field which was to be substantially enriched by phenomenology. Among these were the Germanists, Friedrich Neumann and Günther Müller, both of whom later received a professorship in their specialty in a relatively short time.

Two ladies had also belonged to the Philosophical Society for several semesters: Grete Ortmann and Erika Gothe. They were considerably older than I; both had taught school for some time before deciding to go to the university. Both came from the Mecklenburg region; Fräulein Gothe from Schwerin. Fräulein Ortmann was from a country estate; she was a tiny, delicate bit of a person but had such a ponderous tread that she usually splattered her coat, way up, with mud from Göttingen's streets. Just as ponderous were the decidedly emphatic statements which she delivered with the ring of solemn pronouncements but which, to me, seemed quite trivial. However, she did not speak often but rather listened in the seminars as well as in the Philosophical Society with an expression of ardent devotion in her big blue eyes. For her, that struck me as quite peculiar. In contrast, Erika Gothe's attitude of respectful silence attracted me very much. Fräulein Ortmann immediately and clearly demonstrated that I was not her type. In a confidential moment, later, she herself told me that Reinach once called her to task for her unfriendly attitude to Fräulein Stein "who is, after all, so nice."

The reason she had given him was: "She simply joins in every discussion. And that even though they're such difficult matters!"

Besides, at the very first meeting, Mos had asked me to take the minutes and, without much reflection, I willingly acquiesced. No one else seemed to take offense at my activity. They were friendly toward me and really took my remarks in the discussions seriously. However, in consequence of Fräulein Ortmann's attitude, it was impossible for me for the time being to have social contacts with the Society as a whole. She and Erika Gothe seemed to be inseparable, and it would have been up to the ladies to draw me more closely into the group. However, that summer I was far from feeling deprived as my acquaintances from Breslau amply supplied all the social relationships I needed. Furthermore, I could not even have had an inkling that I was being excluded since I learned only much later about all the other events outside the Philosophical Society and the university.

A few other members had been inducted by the Society besides Rose and myself. Betty Heymann, a Jewish girl from Hamburg, was small and had a slight malformation; her fine, fragile features were somewhat distorted by oversized teeth, but her beautiful eyes were unusually intelligent and bright. A student of Georg Simmel, [119] under whose guidance she also intended to get her degree, she intended at first to stay for one semester only to get acquainted with Husserl as well. Fritz Kaufmann[120] also had a philosophical background in which he took a certain pride. He had been with Natorp[121] in Marburg; and he had imbibed so much neo-Kantianism that he had difficulty getting accustomed to phenomenological methods. He was the eldest son in an apparently very wealthy family with a business in Leipzig. Since his two younger brothers could succeed their father, he was free to devote himself entirely to philosophy and could aim directly at a university career. Probably, he was the only one of us all who was not compelled to consider an income-producing career when choosing his field of study. In our circle where, usually, so little attention was paid to externals, his elegant clothes were very conspicuous. We were all secretly delighted one day when his neighbor in the seminar, an American, vigorously shook the ink out of his fountain pen, causing obvious apprehension in Kaufmann because of his light gray suit. He spoke a faultless High German free of the slightest trace of the accent common to Saxony while Lipps' first word gave him away as a Saxon, to his deep chagrin. (He absolutely refused to be considered one, insisting that he was a Prussian, having inherited Prussian citizenship from his father.)

The day Husserl interviewed us, Rose and I chose the afternoon for our first visit to the Bismarck Tower. As we eagerly picked violets on the way, Kaufmann caught up with us. Recognizing us from the morning's meeting, he greeted us and remarked in a friendly tone: "There are plenty of violets here."

So began our first conversation. I was astounded when he took the opportunity to tell me that, at his first visit to Reinach, the latter had nearly "thrown him out" and had decidedly refused to accept him in his classes. Until now it had never even occurred to me that the kindness with which I had been received might be considered a personal distinction. I found the explanation later when I attended Reinach's exercises. All his kindness and friendliness notwithstanding, Reinach rejected arrogance whenever he met it. And Kaufmann may well have seemed cocksure when he introduced himself. By this manner and his somewhat affected speech, he impaired nearly every one of his relationships. But I noticed almost immediately that these were merely superficial traits. I presumed to tease him mercilessly at times, totally ignoring his show of dignity. Then he would look at me, astounded as though something most unusual had happened; but it seemed to do him good; he gradually thawed out and it got to a point where his tone became quite unpretentious and sincere.

In Husserl's seminar, there were persons, as well, who studied directly under him but who did not belong to the Philosophical Society. One evening shortly after the semester began, I was at Courants'. Richard said to me, "If you're in Husserl's seminar, you've surely gotten to know Bell."[122]

A Canadian, he said. Though I had noticed a few Americans and Englishmen, I had no idea which one he meant.

"He's the nicest student in Göttingen. You're sure to discover him."

Soon thereafter, I noticed a bareheaded student in a sports coat standing on the ramp leading up to the auditorium. He appeared to be on the lookout for someone; and there was something winning about his unconstrained and unaffected bearing.

"That's Bell," I thought.

And it was. He seldom associated with the other phenomenologists. The Americans and the British in Göttingen formed their own colonies and were pretty clannish. Besides, Bell had a circle of friends whose specialties were in various subjects. My cousin was one of these. From him, I also learned of Bell's past. Initially, he was an engineer, but during voyages in the Arctic

Ocean, his home was Halifax, he had begun philosophizing on his own. Then he had gone to study first in England and subsequently, in Germany. He himself told me on a later occasion that a book review by Moritz Schlick[123] had drawn his attention to the *Logische Untersuchungen* and led him to Göttingen. By this time, he had been there three years and was now working for his doctorate under Husserl with a thesis on the American philosopher Royce. Although already thirty-one years old, Bell looked much younger.

That summer the Philosophical Society chose the second major work in the current *Yearbook* as the subject matter for our discussions. It was Max Scheler's[124] *Formalism in Ethics and Non-formal Ethics of Values* which has probably affected the entire intellectual world of recent decades even more than Husserl's *Ideas*. The young phenomenologists were greatly influenced by Scheler; some, like Hildebrand and Clemens, depended more on him than on Husserl.

At the time, Scheler's personal affairs were in a very bad way. His first wife, whom he had divorced, had implicated him in a scandalous suit in Munich. In consequence of incriminating disclosures during the process, the university withdrew his faculty status. So his career as an educator had come to an end; as it had been his only steady source of income, he now depended on his writings for a livelihood. With his second wife (Märit Furtwängler), he was living in a modest furnished room in Berlin; often, he travelled [giving lectures].

For several weeks of each semester, the Philosophical Society invited him to Göttingen to give lectures. He was not permitted to hold lectures at the university; nor were we permitted to announce them on the bulletin board. We could only call attention to them by word of mouth. We had to meet in the social rooms of some hotel or café. At the end of this semester Scheler came once again. At first, the lectures were scheduled for several nights a week; but, as he did not know how to allocate his time properly, there was so much material left to be crammed in that, finally, we had to meet daily. After the formal presentation was over, he would stay on for hours in the café with a smaller group. I participated in these follow-up sessions only once or twice.

Eager though I was to snatch at as much pertinent stimulation as I possibly could, an element was present here which repelled me: the tone used when Husserl was mentioned. Of course, Scheler was also one who keenly opposed reverting to idealism; and his comments were almost condescending; thereupon some of the young men allowed themselves a note of irony which infuriated me since it smacked of disrespect and ingratitude. Relations between Husserl and Scheler were not entirely placid. Scheler availed himself of every opportunity to insist he was not one of Husserl's disciples but that, instead, he had discovered the phenomenological method for himself. Although he had never been in any of Husserl's classes, Husserl was convinced of Scheler's dependency. They had known one another for years. When Husserl was still a privatdocent in Halle, Scheler lived nearby in Jena; they often met for a lively exchange of ideas. Everyone who is acquainted with Scheler, or who has merely given his writings a careful reading, knows how apt he was to pick up suggestions from others. Ideas slipped into his mind and grew there while he himself was totally unaware of his having been influenced. He could say with a good conscience that all was his own property. Added to this competition for priority was Husserl's serious concern regarding his students. He took great pains to educate us to rigorous objectivity and thoroughness, to a "radical intellectual honesty." In contrast, Scheler's practice of scattering about ingenious suggestions without pursuing them systematically had something dazzling and seductive about it. Moreover, he chose topics of vital personal importance to his young listeners, who, consequently, were easily affected by them. Husserl, on the other hand, addressed sober, abstract matters. However, at that time in Göttingen, despite such tensions, their association was still mutually friendly.

One's first impression of Scheler was fascination. In no other person have I ever encountered the "phenomenon of genius" as clearly. The light of a more exalted world shone from his large blue eyes. His features were handsome and noble; still, life had left some devastating traces in his face. Betty Heymann said he reminded her of the picture of Dorian Gray: that mysterious portrait on which the dissolute life of the original painted its distorting lines, while the person preserved the handsome features of his youth. Scheler spoke with great insistence, indeed with dramatic liveliness. Words he was particularly fond of (for example, *"pure Washeit"* [pure whatness]) were spoken with devotion and tenderness. When expressing disagreement with presumed opponents, he used a contemptuous tone. At that particular time he was treating the questions which were the theme of his recently published book *Phenomenology and Theory of the Feelings of Sympathy*. These had special significance for me as I was just then beginning to occupy myself with the problem of "empathy."

In real life situations, Scheler was as helpless as a child. On one occasion I saw him in the checkroom of a café standing in bewilderment before a row of hats; he did not know which was his.

"At the moment, you're missing your wife, aren't you!" I asked with a smile.

He nodded in agreement. At such times it was impossible to be angry with him, not even when he did things one would condemn in other persons. Even the victims of his aberrations tended to come to his defense.

His influence in those years affected me, as it did many others, far beyond the sphere of philosophy. I do not know in which year Scheler returned to the Catholic Church. It could not have been long before I met him. In any case, he was quite full of Catholic ideas at the time and employed all the brilliance of his spirit and his eloquence to plead them. This was my first encounter with this hitherto totally unknown world. It did not lead me as yet to the Faith. But it did open for me a region of "phenomena" which I could then no longer bypass blindly. With good reason we were repeatedly enjoined to observe all things without prejudice, to discard all possible "blinders". The barriers of rationalistic prejudices with which I had unwittingly grown up fell, and the world of faith unfolded before me. Persons with whom I associated daily, whom I esteemed and admired, lived in it. At the least, they deserved my giving it some serious reflection. For the time being, I did not embark on a systematic investigation of the questions of faith; I was far too busy with other matters. I was content to accept without resistance the stimuli coming from my surroundings, and so, almost without noticing it, became gradually transformed.

When describing my first days in Göttingen, I left out a detail regarding my contacts with my relatives. My cousin, Richard Courant, twenty-five years old at the time, recently had become a privatdocent and had also been married. His wife, Nelli Neumann of Breslau, was a bit older than he. Together with him, she had studied mathematics; she got her degree in that subject and had also taken the state board examination. Councillor Neumann had hesitated for a long time before entrusting his only child to a young man who had not yet established himself. Father Neumann was an exceptionally kind and noble person. Even in appearance, he was genteel and winning; tall, slender, light blond and blue eyed, he had not at all the semblance typical of a Jew from the Province of Posen (which he was) but rather that of a German aristocrat. Since Nelli's mother died when the child was but two years old, he had perforce to be father and mother to her. He surrounded her with the tenderest love, shared in all her joys and sorrows, and worked with her as with a comrade. The happiness of their life together was disturbed only by the presence of his mother-in-law. After his wife died, he had kept her mother in his home although he and the child were plagued by her moods. The grandmother died only shortly after Nelli's wedding. I spoke earlier about my cousin's sad and difficult early years.[125] He had made something of himself by his own sheer effort, and we all had the greatest admiration for his extraordinary talents and his character. His wife's wealth enabled him for the first time to have a secure existence and to know a youthful, carefree enjoyment of life.

Like Anne Reinach, Nelli took care to have their attractive and comfortable furnishings custom-built. The little house in Schillerstrasse, in which they occupied two floors, lay at the southern end of town; gardens and meadows spread out beyond them. This lovely home offered informal hospitality at all times. Richard loved to bring home unannounced guests. He had a large circle of friends, lecturers as well as older students. He also liked to bring one or other of his own students along if he had something to discuss with them. Nelli herself had encouraged me to come to Göttingen, and she received me most cordially. I was frequently invited to meals; the bath was put at my disposal; in fact, Nelli delighted in sharing the good things she had with others. She was cheerful and talkative but, for all that, a person who went to the root of matters. She was especially interested in ethical questions and undertook nothing without first thoroughly weighing the pros and cons. She still went to some of the lectures; once a week we attended the same course, and then went home together. At such times she would inquire in detail about all my affairs, following the course of my studies with great interest, happy that, evidently, here was one person following the path destined for her from birth. She was little suited to be a housewife. Her education had prepared her for anything but that. When, a few months after her wedding, she came to Breslau for her grandmother's funeral, she gave a humorous account of some of the misfortunes she had had with her efforts as a tyro housekeeper and explained: "The further removed things are from mathematics, the more complicated they are; and *nothing* is as far removed from mathematics as housekeeping!"

With her, Richard used the teasing tone which in general was customarily his. He was bound to me by our close relationship; though reluctant to admit it, he was very attached to the family and always asked me about each of its members. He was glad, too, to be able to discuss his concern about his parents with me, just as, formerly in Breslau, he had sought advice from my mother. He, too, showed a lively interest in my scholarly career.

Having come to Göttingen for the sake of philosophy, I wanted to devote most of my time to it. Other subjects, however, were not to be neglected. As I had intended to stay there that one summer only, I also wanted to take the opportunity to acquaint myself with other Germanists and historians than those I had known in Breslau. A course on "Börne, Heine and Young Germany"[126] given by Richard Weissenfels was more recreation than work. The severe and dreaded Edward Schröder I also enjoyed as a "phenomenon," without the least anxiety. A huge, powerfully built man, he wore a wide beard, parted in the middle and tinged with gray. He took pride in possessing "a well-formed language," that of his native Hesse. I thought it even more fitting to have him speak Middle High German or even Old High German; I was delighted whenever he read us a sample text during his course. Like his brother-in-law Roethe in Berlin, he was an opponent of academic study for women and had, heretofore, never admitted women to his seminars. However, I was one of those to witness his "conversion." At the beginning of that particular semester when distributing the keys to his seminar room to the members of the class (for this we had to come forward and, by a handclasp, pledge that we would not take home any book from the seminar library), he declared publicly that henceforth he would admit women to the higher level of his seminar, adding that they had earned it by their diligence and their excellent achievements. Besides all this, he was a man with deep feelings; once in a lecture when he spoke of a deceased colleague, his eyes filled with tears.

Apart from the phenomenologists, I also had Leonard Nelson for philosophy. Still young, barely past thirty, he was already famous throughout Germany, or perhaps more aptly expressed, infamous, because of his book on the "so-called problem of knowledge." In it, with penetrating insight, he "slew" one after another of the most significant representatives of the modern theory-of-knowledge by his demonstration of formal contradictions. In his course (I was taking his "Critique of Practical Reason") he was no less scathing. He had two schematic drawings to illustrate the typical contradictions; in practically every class they were drawn on the board for some new opponent and so came to be known by his students as the "guillotine." The only one to survive the slaughter was the Kantian scholar, Fries, after whom Nelson[127] named his own philosophy. Nelson's ethic culminated in a derivative of a somewhat modified categorical imperative. All told, the entire presentation was a faultless deduction drawn from several postulated theses. One could hardly evade drawing the same conclusions he did; but throughout the course I had the impression that there were errors in the assumptions. The danger lay in the fact that he unwaveringly carried out in practice whatever he theoretically deduced in his ethics; and he demanded that his students do the same. He was surrounded by a circle of young persons (principally those in the youth movement) who acknowledged his leadership and who shaped their lives according to his guidelines. Richard Courant, who had himself been for a time very much under his influence, used to say: "The recruits go to Nelson's course the way the regulars go for their morning pint."

Nelson was, by nature, a genuine leader; his strength of character, his unbending will, the silent passion of his moral idealism gave him power over others. There was little that was attractive about his appearance. He was big and broad-shouldered; he had a heavy gait; heavy lids covered light blue eyes; there was heaviness, too, in his speech along with a weariness despite the decisiveness and emphasis with which he expressed everything. His face was ugly but still attractive; his best feature was his thick, wavy, blond hair. His manner of speech was very sober and dry; the principal range of his ideas he sketched on the board; his handwriting and the schematic drawings disclosed his artistic talent.

He considered very few persons worthy of associating with him if they did not subscribe unconditionally to his philosophy and his life-style. To this small number belonged Rosa Heine, a Russian Jewish girl who had been studying psychology in Göttingen for years. I had become acquainted with her at the Psychology Institute, and as I was walking with her one day, we met Nelson on the street. She greeted him, introduced me, and stated that we should have a talk. With that she departed, leaving us to continue on our way alone. Nelson knew me by sight as I was attending his course; and he asked me to comment on it, for he knew I was one of Husserl's students; and it was seldom that anyone from that camp strayed into his. He himself was not too familiar with Husserl's writings and declared that to learn to understand such difficult terminology was too time-consuming. I asked whether he had not at one time had a discussion with Reinach; that surely would have been much easier. The answer was laconic: "Reinach is clearer, but, correspondingly, less deep."

With that our conversation ended, as we had arrived at his destination, the publishing firm of Vandenhoeck and Rupprecht. It was years before I had such personal contact with him again.

At the Psychological Institute I was taking "The Psychophysics of Visual Perception" taught by Georg Elias Müller,[128] a veteran of the old method which proceeded solely according to the natural sciences. This method had a precision which attracted me; it seemed more reliable than the one I had learned under Stern. I enjoyed it, but only in the way I did theoretical physics or mathematics; they were disciplines in which I was glad to have instruction but which, for me, held no challenge for personal work. Müller was a rabid opponent of phenomenology since for him nothing existed but empirical science. On the other hand, because Husserl saw value in our learning the methods of the positive sciences, he recommended that we study under Müller. David Katz,[129] who taught as privatdocent in the institute along with Müller, had in his student years done some work in phenomenology; that he benefitted from the study was evident in his lectures. I got to know him personally through Moskiewicz and Rosa Heine, whom Katz later married. The atmosphere of the institute was most peculiar. Müller had a bevy of students desirous of getting their degree under him although that was no simple matter. Often it was months before one accumulated all the experimental procedures and the necessary equipment. No one apprised the others of the kind of work he was doing. In the various laboratories of the old building on Paulinerstrasse, they toiled mysteriously at their machines. For a time I served as the subject of a Danish psychologist's experiments. I sat in a darkened room before a tachistoscope where, each time for but a moment, I was shown a series of differing green, luminous shapes upon which I had to report later, telling what I had seen. I concluded from this that the experiment had something to do with the recognition of the shapes, but I was given no more detailed explanation. We phenomenologists laughed at this business of secrecy and rejoiced in the freedom with which we exchanged ideas; we had no fear that one of us might pilfer the results of another's project.

Aside from philosophy, the work I did under Max Lehmann proved most important to me in Göttingen. While still in Breslau, I had studied the whole of his monumental work on Baron vom Stein;[130] and I was happy now to become personally acquainted with Lehmann. I attended his main course on the "Age of Absolutism and Enlightenment" and his one-hour lectures on Bismarck as well. I was delighted with his broader European outlook, a legacy from his great teacher Ranke.[131] I was proud that through him Ranke should have become my "scholastic grandfather." Of course, I could not agree with all of Lehmann's concepts. As an old Hannoverian, he was strongly anti-Prussian in his opinions; English liberalism was his ideal. This was obvious especially in his course on Bismarck. Since partiality always incited me to do justice to the opposite side, I became more conscious here than I had been at home of the virtues of the Prussian character; and I was confirmed in my own Prussian allegiance.

I have already mentioned that I had to forego Reinach's exercises in order to attend the Lehmann seminar which was scheduled for the same hours. Of course, I nearly regretted doing so when I realized how much work was being demanded by these studies. I had not intended to give so much of my time in Göttingen to the study of history. Our task for the whole semester was to compare the current Constitution of Germany with the constitution that had been drafted in 1849. The books most pertinent to the study of this question were collected for our use in a small room next to the large study hall. I spent many an hour there. The most unpleasant surprise, however, was that every newcomer had to prepare a term paper. Assignments for them were handed out during the very first session and in such a way, in fact, that two students, a man and a woman if at all possible, should work on the same theme. The due date was also determined at once. In the second half of the semester, these theses were discussed in the seminar. During the defense of their theses, the two victims were required to occupy the seats directly across from Lehmann at a huge U-shaped table. This enabled him to get to know us thoroughly. His vision was very weak, and he could not see us if we were seated farther away from him. At the beginning of each semester, he had a sketch of the classroom made to show the name of the occupant of each of the desks. Thereafter he recognized us by this order of seating, and we were no longer allowed to change places. My theme was: Reali-

zation of the Party Programs of the Draft Constitution of 1849.
My partner and I had our turn at the very end of the semester.
We had not known one another before then; but as we were now
groaning under the same burden, he accompanied me home
several times so that we could discuss some of our mutual problems on the way. He was an intelligent and diligent person; I
had great confidence in his work. Our task was exacting. One
had to become thoroughly familiar with the line-up of the parties in the Frankfurt National Assembly. It was necessary to find
copies of the programs. These were not readily available, even
though the majority had been printed in a handy collection.
Finally, after a long search in the Heidelberg Library, I found
only one of these programs in an old bound volume of newspapers dated 1848. Thereupon began the job of comparing.
The pressure of this work had its effect on me to some degree
throughout the entire semester. Finally the session arrived at
which Lehmann would have us under fire. He usually did this in
a very friendly fashion. In our case, too, he declared himself
well satisfied with the course the discussion had taken. All the
same, there was one tragi-comical difficulty. He had been unable to decipher my work completely since the ink I had used
was too light for his weak eyes. An older colleague (a student
teacher) gave me the good advice to look up Lehmann to ask
him whether I might resubmit the thesis in typed form. So I set
out on my way to the Bürgerstrasse where he had his own home,
an old house surrounded by a garden. I was directed to the upper story. Even the entrance to his study was covered to the ceiling with book shelves. Lehmann received me very kindly. No, it
would not be necessary to have the work copied. As it was, he
had been thoroughly informed by the discussion and was well
satisfied. The ladies, after all! What would become of his seminar were it not for the ladies who worked so diligently and so
capably! This seemed to me, now, a bit exaggerated; and I felt
obliged to defend my male colleagues: there were also men, surely,
who achieved something. He was somewhat taken aback by my
rejoinder, but agreed. "Oh, yes, a few, probably. Your partner,
for instance, did a fine job."

Then, in the next breath, he handed me a real surprise. Leh-

mann informed me that the paper had been so well done that he
would be pleased to accept it as a submission for the state boards.
I could make a few minor additions to complete the work. This
was not an unusual distinction: Lehmann had a habit of allowing well prepared term papers to be submitted as theses for the
examinations. But I was unaware of this since, until then, I had
not been concerned at all about the examination process in Göttingen. For one thing, the state boards, in my estimation, had
been something awaiting me in the distant future. I had every
intention of getting my doctorate first. Besides, I had come to
Göttingen for no more than that summer, and I counted on taking the state boards in Breslau. Granted, the closer we came to
the end of the semester, the more intolerable I found the
thought of having to go away and not returning. The months
gone by were not just an episode, after all, but rather the beginning of a new phase of my life. And now, Lehmann was proffer-
ing succor from a quarter where I had least expected it. Surely,
one could not allow a completed state board thesis to go to
waste. This would make sense to my relatives as well.

I believe that my plan was already finalized on my way home
from that appointment with Lehmann which was to have such
important consequences. Before I did anything else, I would
have to put my relationship with Professor Stern in order. He
received a report of this semester's developments: I had done
nothing whatsoever on my assignment in psychology but had,
on the contrary, immersed myself entirely in phenomenology;
now it was my most earnest desire to continue working with Husserl. He replied most graciously: if such was my desire, then one
could only advise that I get my doctorate under Husserl. Nor
was there any opposition from my relatives. Now to take the biggest step: I went to Husserl to request a doctoral theme.

"You mean you are ready for that?" he asked in surprise.

He was accustomed to having people study under him for
years before they dared to attempt an independent thesis. However, he did not turn me down. He merely pointed out to me all
the difficulties involved. His requirements for a doctoral dissertation were extremely high, he assured me; he estimated one
would require three years to complete it. Had I any intention of

taking the state board examination, he would advise me, urgently, to do that first since otherwise I would have to neglect my other subjects too much and he himself considered it of prime importance that one do a thoroughly capable job in a specialized subject. It did not suffice to take philosophy alone since a solid foundation required thorough familiarity with the methods of the other disciplines. Of course, this upset all the plans I had made and left me a bit heavy-hearted; still I was not about to be intimidated by any of this and was, rather, intent on accepting all the conditions. Thereupon the Master became a bit more cooperative. He would have no objection if I wished to choose my theme now and were to begin work on it. Then, if my preparation for the state boards proceeded satisfactorily, he would give me an assignment for that examination which could subsequently be developed into a doctoral dissertation.

Now the question needed to be settled: what did I want to work on? I had no difficulty on this. In his course on nature and spirit, Husserl had said that an objective outer world could only be experienced intersubjectively, i.e., through a plurality of perceiving individuals who relate in a mutual exchange of information. Accordingly, an experience of other individuals is a prerequisite. To the experience, an application of the work of Theodor Lipps, Husserl gave the name *Einfühlung* [Empathy]. What it consists of, however, he nowhere detailed. Here was a lacuna to be filled; therefore, I wished to examine what empathy might be. The Master found this suggestion not bad at all. However, almost immediately, I was given another bitter pill to swallow: he required that, as format for the dissertation, I use that of an analytical dialogue with Theodor Lipps. He liked to have his students clarify, in their assignments, the relation of phenomenology to the other significant directions current in philosophy. This was not *his* forte. He was too occupied with his own thoughts to take time for comparative study of others. And whenever he demanded that of us, he found us as unwilling. He used to say, with a smile: "I educate my students to be systematic philosophers and then I'm surprised that they dislike any tasks that have to do with the history of philosophy."

At first he was inexorable. Though it went against the grain, I had to make a thorough study of the long list of works by Theodor Lipps.

This was another interview, then, which had important consequences. Entirely new plans had to be made. But of these, too, I made short shrift. If I had to take the state board examination before the doctorate, then I would get it off my back as soon as possible. By this time I had completed five semesters. That did not suffice for me to apply for examination; the required minimum was six semesters. And that was because I started in an earlier period when less material had to be mastered. Now, most persons take eight to ten semesters. There could be no talk of that for me. My resolution was made: the outline of the work on empathy would have to be completed in the coming winter, and I would have to be well enough prepared for the orals that by the end of the semester I could report for the test.

This then was the result of my first summer in Göttingen. At the beginning of August, I went home for the vacation. I no longer remember whether I made this trip in Rose's company. It was her final departure from Göttingen. We gave up our apartment as it would be too expensive for me alone. I wanted to find some new quarters for myself for that autumn.

2

So, the beginning of August found me going home for the long vacation. The summer of 1913 brought a major event for Breslau: the centenary of the wars of independence. That accounted for the surprise some had felt at my decision to spend precisely that semester elsewhere. I had already missed a few of the festivities, principally the play Gerhart Hauptmann[132] had written for the event. It was presented in the new *Jahrhunderthalle* [Centennial Hall] which also had been built expressly for this occasion. This dome-shaped structure of concrete and iron was, at that time, the largest of its kind in the world. I had read the play in Göttingen and considered the plot development ingenious. By a bold stroke, the playwright showed the memorable events: Prussia's eminence, its fall and rise, Napoleon's brilliant ascent, and his defeat. All this was presented in a puppet show; but as this might appear when viewed from above. The supreme authorities, however, took offense at such a presentation. Berlin had an ancient tradition that no Hohenzollern could be portrayed on a stage. To have them appear, then, as puppets seemed to be a flagrant case of lese majesty. The German Crown Prince withdrew his patronage from the centenary celebration; to appease him and the Kaiser, the management of the festival called off all further presentations of the puppet play.

The Kaiser's visit took place while I was in Breslau. He stayed, as usual, only a very short time. (Years earlier a woman had made an attempt on his life in our city, and that may have accounted for his wariness.) When the Kaiser inspected the festival grounds and hall, the designer, Municipal Architect Berg, was on hand, expecting to be introduced and hoping for a friendly word of commendation. But he was ignored and heard harsh words: the city council would have done better had they turned over to the university the huge sum spent on the construction. The infuriated architect became a Social Democrat. What was more, the Kaiser had no time for a concert in the *Jahrhunderthalle* in which ten-thousand public school children sang folk songs. When, a short time earlier, the King of Saxony had heard them, he had addressed some friendly words to the little artists. I considered the Kaiser's behavior incredibly foolish. I thought how with a few kind remarks he could have won the hearts of so many children and made faithful subjects of them for life. But he lacked the gift of recognizing such opportunities.

Beside the choral events in the festival hall, I heard many other beautiful presentations, as, for example, a big Bach concert on the massive built-in organ.[133] Naturally, I also went to see the Centenary Exposition. The Exhibition Halls, likewise newly-erected, the historical gardens, and the other beautiful plantings around the festival hall were preserved as permanent attractions of the city.

At home I was received with heartfelt love. My plans for the future roused no opposition at all. Nor did I have the impression any longer that my studying elsewhere was painful for my mother. When I told about my two theses, Erna was filled with admiration by these independent achievements. By comparison, her own doctoral thesis seemed like child's play to her since all the questions had been formulated for her, and she needed only to carry out the experiments. In my familiar circle of friends, my academic progress roused considerable attention; but I was as much "one of them" as ever. Stern continued to include me in the most intimate circle of his students, and he had me join in preparing an important pedagogic conference and a psychological exhibition held in conjunction with it. The main attraction was a debate between Wyneken, who, with rabid decisiveness, presented his ideal that children be reared in free school communities and Stern who declared himself, more mildly but for all that as firmly, in favor of child-rearing by the family. This time I was totally on his side. Wyneken's gloomy appearance and the fanatical glint in his eyes were as distasteful to me as were his theories; confidence in his method of education was made entirely impossible when one observed the resulting blind obedience shown him by the Wickersdorf pupils whom he had brought along.

I was back in Göttingen by the latter half of October, some days before the lectures were to start. The room I rented in Schillerstrasse was but a block away from the Courants. Restorations had been made all along the street. The room was both modern and tastefully decorated; the ceiling was white, the wallpaper a light gray with a narrow gold molding. The proprietors were of the upper middle class; Frau Mussmann, though neither young nor pretty, was very pleasant. She provided me with the milk I customarily had for breakfast and the tea for my evening meal. After I was there a few months, she also took to bringing me a portion of their noon meal; this, at a minimal expense, provided me with a far better nourishment than I would have gotten at the inns. My room was outside their apartment and had its own entrance from the staircase; it was on the ground floor; so a person on the street could tap on my window with a cane. Richard often attracted my attention that way if, on his way home from a concert, he noticed a light in my room. I was very lonely that winter. As long as Rose had lived with me, neither of us had felt as much as a twinge of homesickness. I missed her greatly now. I avoided going along the Lange Geismarstrasse since the sight of our former lodging was too painful. For the same reason, I could never bring myself to visit our former landlord and his wife. The faithful Danziger continued to pick me up for walks on Sundays. But I could not spare as much time for them as formerly since I was completely engrossed in my big project. Besides, I must admit the good fellow bored me somewhat.

Moskiewicz had also returned; I preferred his company by far, although associating with him became steadily more of a drain. He usually asked me to keep Sunday afternoon free for him; but I came to expect the arrival during the morning of a delivery boy on a bicycle who brought a message cancelling the arrangement. Sometimes a second one would follow to revoke the cancellation. I did not hold this against Mos, for I recognized what lay behind it. Phenomenology was his "unrequited love." She had made him sick of his work in psychology, and in no way could he pick that up again; yet, in phenomenology he had never gone beyond a beginner's difficulties; and he was incapable of achieving anything independently. He believed I was now further advanced than he and that he should avail himself of every occasion when we were together to have me help him get ahead. At the same time, he dreaded such conversations because they discouraged him anew. When he talked about other matters, he was happy; but he seldom permitted himself this luxury. He had returned to Göttingen principally because Reinach had promised him he could come for a private session once a week. These afternoons were invested with the greatest expectations: they were to bring the solution to all his doubts. Consequently, I was horrified when once toward the end of the semester Reinach confessed to me that these conversations were an intolerable burden for him. That, knowing I was well acquainted with Moskiewicz, he would like my opinion on the matter. He himself considered him a hopeless case.

"He ought to keep at his psychology; he'll never make it as a phenomenologist. Couldn't one tell him that?"

I begged him earnestly not to do so. With my understanding of Moskiewicz's nervous state, I feared he would be unable to cope with such a shock. At once, Reinach promised he would say nothing and would patiently endure listening to a constant repetition of the same doubts and misgivings. For my part, I undertook to work unobtrusively to get Mos not to prolong his stay in Göttingen beyond this winter. As it happened, he went to Frankfurt-am-Main the following summer to get the stimulation for further progress from significant psychologists there (Wertheimer, Gelb, Köhler). [134]

For me the winter brought even more advancement in philosophy than had the summer. Husserl was giving his big course on Kant. Above all, my class schedule this time permitted me to attend Reinach's lectures, "Introduction to Philosophy," as well as his "Exercises for the Advanced." In the summer I had audited his class as a guest when occasionally I happened to have the hour free. It was pure joy to listen to him. True, he had a manuscript before him; but he seemed scarcely ever to glance at it. He spoke in a lively and cheerful tone, light, free, and elegant; and everything was transparently clear and convincing. One had the impression that the whole thing was effortless for him. When, later, I was allowed to see some of these manuscripts, I noticed to my great amazement that they were literally written out word for word from beginning to end. It was his custom to conclude his final lecture with the phrase: "Finished, thank God!" All these brilliant achievements were the result of unspeakable care and trouble.

Reinach conducted the "Exercises" at his own home. Since Husserl's class ended directly before them, it meant a run up to the *Steinsgraben* which took about twenty minutes. The hours spent in that beautiful study were the happiest of all my time in Göttingen. We were probably unanimous in the opinion that, when it came to method, we learned more here than anywhere else. Reinach discussed with us the questions which were occupying him in his own research at the time. That winter it was the problem of motion. It was, then, not a matter of lecturing and learning but rather of mutual searching similar to what we had done in the Philosophical Circle, except that now a reliable guide was present. We all had a deep respect for our young instructor; here no one lightly chanced a hasty word. I would hardly have dared open my mouth unasked. Once Reinach tossed out a question and asked for my thoughts on the matter. I had been reflecting intensely and now timidly proffered my view in a few words. He looked at me in a most friendly way and said, "That's the way I had thought it out also."

I could not have imagined a greater mark of distinction.

But these evenings were likewise excruciating for him. By the time the two hours were up, he found the word "motion" unbearable. Some of the objections made to him in our circle finally compelled him to give up his original hypothesis altogether. After Easter he made a completely new start. This clean break I was able later to discern also in his manuscript draft.

Aside from philosophy, I now restricted attending lectures to a minimum so as to have as much time as possible to study at home. Systematically I went about preparing for the oral tests in history, German literature, and the history of philosophy; this called for a tremendous amount of memorizing. Another factor came on the scene now. A few years before, the Göttingen Philosophical Faculty had been divided in two: one branch for mathematics and the natural sciences; the other, for philosophy and history. The philosophers had to decide to which of the two branches they would belong. Despite his own background in mathematics and to the chagrin of the mathematicians who had been instrumental in getting him called to Göttingen, he [Husserl[135]] chose the other branch as it was his impartial conviction that, intrinsically, philosophy's greater affinity lay with the humanities.

Now, an *Abitur* [passing the comprehensive examinations] from a humanistic *Gymnasium* was a requisite for a doctorate in the philological branch. Like myself, Hedwig Martius had attended a *Realgymnasium*;[4‡] so, with the award-winning thesis she had completed under Husserl, she went to Munich to get her doctorate there as they had no such requirement. But I determined at once that I would make up the examination in Greek which I lacked. However, to avoid being overloaded with work, I wanted to postpone taking it until after the state board examinations. Therefore, I was greatly distressed when Frau Husserl told me one day that the Greek exam had to be taken six semes-

ters before one got the doctorate. I went at once to the Dean of
the Philology Branch to inquire about the regulations; at that
time, the archaeologist Körte held the position. He looked at it
this way: there was actually such a requirement, and he had no
way of knowing what a future Dean's preference in the matter
might be; however, as far as he was concerned, he would always
favor granting a dispensation from the requirement. But for
safety's sake, I might go to the philologist Hermann Schultz who
taught the beginners' course in Greek here in Göttingen to have
him certify my knowledge of Greek at the present time. So I
spent a few weeks refreshing the knowledge of Greek I had gained
in the first semesters in Breslau and then betook myself to Dr.
Schultz. He was still a young privatdocent and lived with his
mother who was known by the unusual title of *Frau Abt* [The
Abbot's Wife]. At the time of its secularization,[136] the former
Benedictine Abbey in Bursfeld-an-der-Weser had been ceded
to the University of Göttingen. The Protestant theologians took
turns being administrator, and the one currently in charge was
considered the "Abbot." Hermann Schultz received me kindly.
When I outlined my problem, he arranged for me to come for a
brief test the following day. He had me translate Thucydides. I
had never read any of his work, but what I produced was considered wholly satisfactory. The examiner said he was gratified to
know that a beginner's course could enable one to achieve that
much. Obviously, his own teaching had given him an impression that he was struggling pretty much in vain. I was awarded a
certificate which, I hoped, would help me later to reach my
goal.

But my experience with the rest of my studies was bleak. I had
hoped one thorough review would be sufficient. But after a few
weeks I was dismayed to notice how much of it had once more
eluded my memory. At this rate how could one possibly have all
this matter at hand when it was needed? But this trouble was a
breeze compared to the grief I knew in my efforts in philosophy.
This had become by far the highest mountain peak to be con-
quered that winter. I devoted the greater part of every day to it.
My days were long indeed. I rose early, around six, and worked
almost without interruption until midnight. Since I usually ate

alone, I could continue reflecting even during mealtimes. And, when I went to bed, I kept paper and pencil ready on my night-table so as to jot down thoughts at once if they came to me during the night. I often jumped up because something had occurred to me in a dream that seemed a particularly clever insight. But when, fully awake, I wanted to give it expression, there was nothing left for me to grasp. On my way to the university, too, I kept on brooding over my problem of empathy. Often I spent a great part of the day in the philosophical seminar room, studying the works of Theodor Lipps. Sometimes I did not even break for lunch but took along some pastry which I consumed in a brief pause during my labors. When, at the scheduled times, I went from my philosophical work to the other subjects, I always felt as though my brain had to revolve a full 180°. I read book after book, taking copious notes; and the more material I gathered, the more awhirl was my head. What Husserl, judging by his brief indications, thought of as "empathy" and what Lipps designated as such apparently had little in common. For Lipps it was the concept point-blank at the center of his philosophy; it ruled his aesthetics, ethics, and social philosophy; and it also played a role in his theory of knowledge, logic, and metaphysics. As diverse as these disciplines were, just as variegated were the concepts which scintillated before me; and I plagued myself in an attempt to get a firm grip on something uniform and solid so as to understand, from that vantage point, all the variations and develop them further. For the first time, I encountered here what was to be, repeatedly, my experience in every subsequent work: books were of no use to me at all until I had clarified the matter in question by my own effort. This excruciating struggle to attain clarity was waged unceasingly inside me, depriving me of rest day and night. At that time I lost the art of sleeping, and it took many years before restful nights were granted to me again.

Little by little I worked myself into a state of veritable despair. For the first time in my life I was confronted by something I could not conquer by sheer will-power. Subconsciously, my mother's maxims: "What one wants to do, one can do," and "As one strives, so will God help" had become firmly entrenched in me. I had often boasted that my skull was harder than the thickest of walls, and now I was beating my forehead raw, yet the impregnable wall would not give in the least. All this brought me to a point where life itself seemed unbearable. I often told myself that the whole business made no sense at all. Even if I failed to get a doctorate, I surely had enough for the state boards; and, though being a great philosopher might be beyond me, in all likelihood being a useful teacher was still a possibility. But reasoning was of no avail. I could no longer cross the street without wishing I would be run over by some vehicle. And when we went on an excursion, I hoped I would fall off a cliff and not return alive.

Probably no one suspected how things stood with me. In the Philosophical Society and in Reinach's seminar, I was happy during our common effort; but I dreaded the thought that these hours, which gave me such a sense of security, would end since I would then have to resume my solitary battle. Husserl required me to give him an account of the progress on my work several times during the semester. This was to be done at his place in the evening. But these conversations brought me no relief. After I had spoken but a few words, he would feel impelled to say something; and then he might go on talking for so long that he would be too tired to pick up our discussion once more. I left, able to tell myself I had learned something; but all of it was of little use in my own work. Normally, his lectures that summer had the same effect on me.

Hans Lipps had heard about my theme from Mos, through whom he sent word that he was very interested and would like to have me tell him a bit about it. After Husserl's class one day, Lipps asked me to come with him. He conducted me to his lodgings by the most direct route: that meant going at a trot through the Botanical Institute which was opposite the seminar building, then across the Botanical Garden to the *Untere Karspüle*. Inside the Institute, he whispered to me: "Should we meet anyone, we'll have to tell them we're visiting Fräulein Ortmann since we're not really allowed to go through here."

The *Untere Karspüle* was a narrow, winding lane. Here Lipps had quarters in a tiny house owned by Frau Maass, a cabinetmaker's wife whose manners were anything but charming. Certainly, he was afraid of her. Hering, too, had lived there; if I remember correctly, so did several of the other older phenome-nologists. We climbed very steep, narrow stairs and arrived at the "study," a tiny room with sparse and dilapidated furniture. Lipps' head nearly hit the ceiling; and when he stood in the middle of the room and spread out his arms, his hands almost touched the walls. A small door led into the bedroom which was even smaller. I had to take a seat in a corner of the sofa. Lipps donned a white doctor's coat; stuffed his pipe; seated himself at his small, yellow, collapsible desk; and looked at me with expec-tation in his big, round eyes. Now there was no escaping. I had to give an exact account of what I conceived empathy to be. He seemed not too satisfied and had objections to make. But when I told him Reinach had agreed with me, he exclaimed animat-edly: "Then cross out everything I've said. I've got the greatest respect for Reinach."

I had talked to Reinach when the summer semester ended, before daring to suggest the theme to Husserl; and he had en-couraged me to go ahead. However, I was shattered by this dis-cussion with Lipps. In comparison with him, I considered my-self a newcomer to phenomenology; and the impression that I had presumed to embark on something far beyond my ability was intensified.

Occasionally in those days, I met Lipps and one of his acquaint-ances at lunch. At that time I had no regular dining arrange-ment and rather went, if at all, to the first available place that offered a meal. If the two noticed me, I had to join them at their table; that provided a brief time of relaxation for me. On one occasion Lipps apologized for being unable to accompany me to Schillerstrasse afterwards. He had to hurry home and get to sleep. He was making an experiment: sleeping as many hours as possible; then studying for the rest of the day with as intense concentration as he could muster. By this time he had attained to sleeping for fourteen hours, but he had hopes of gradually reaching twenty-one hours. That winter he was chairman of the Philosophical Society; toward the semester's end, he had to make the preparations for Scheler's guest lectures; and he greatly ap-preciated that I, too, recommended these to my acquaintances. But he would not be returning in the summer as he intended to join Hering in Strassburg. I was distressed to hear that. I was sure I would feel even more forlorn if every prospect of catching a glimpse of his tall figure or of his navy-blue jacket were gone.

Shortly before Christmas, the entire student circle was invited to Reinach's for supper. Before that, I had not visited Frau Dr. Reinach as had the women who had been his students longer than I. I knew her by sight because of her regular attendance at her husband's lectures. She was tall and very slender; her movements were somehow graceful as those of a doe. Her unfeigned Suabian dialect charmed us most of all. Once, as I was going to visit Reinach, she was walking ahead of me on the way up to *Steinsgraben*. At the door of their home she turned around, greeted me kindly and said, "You're surely coming to see my husband."

Then she took me in with her; she herself went to announce my arrival to him. Only years later did she tell me something I had not even noticed at the time: Reinach had been standing at the window on the floor above, watching her approach. She had called up to him, softly: "*Adole*, (the affectionate form for Adolf), *Büble, Herzle!*" ["Adole, Laddie, Sweetheart!"]

He had made frantic motions to her to desist as he saw me coming behind her; then, when she came upstairs, he had reproached her, asking how she could humiliate him so in the presence of one of his students.

On the evening I mentioned, we were received in the parlor, which, though elegantly furnished with silver-gray upholstered arm chairs, was less cozy than the other rooms. For the meal, we were called into Reinach's study, probably because it was roomier and more homelike than the dining room. Places had been set at small tables on each of which there was a tiny tree trimmed with candles; their warm glow was not spoiled by any electric lighting. Entranced like children on Christmas Eve, we paused at the sight. Since there were but three ladies among the guests, Frau Reinach decided that one should be seated at each of the tables; the gentlemen could then sit wherever they chose. She herself elected to be at the largest table since the hostess was naturally the main attraction. The group at that table was the most merry one. Once I caught a snatch of the conversation.

They were talking about *Kampf um Rom* [*The Struggle for Rome*],[137] probably about the eagerness with which, formerly, people had devoured its four volumes. Then Frau Reinach's voice sounded all through the room: "*Den hab'i nie kriegt!*" ["That's one struggle I never had!"]

I had chosen the smallest of the tables at which only three places had been set. My cavaliers were a rich American named Awkford, who also sat next to me in Lehmann's course, and Dr. Mense, whom I knew from the Philosophical Society. He was a rather sullen and restive person, and we lost track of him after that.

Every one of these social gatherings was a ray of light for me in those days. I anticipated them with delight and, afterwards, happily basked in their remembrance. They also furnished me with subject matter for my weekly letter home since, of course, I did not want to write about my worries and suffering.

During the Christmas vacation, I met my mother in Hamburg. We were both delighted to see one another again. For all that, our sojourn there was a very unhappy one. We both noticed what a stormy mood prevailed in the house. My brother-in-law, who had usually been such a genial host, was constantly irritable. It was impossible to carry on a friendly conversation at mealtimes. This was, after all, only a few months prior to that crisis in their marriage which I have already described. I said absolutely nothing to my good mother about my own difficulties. Had she had any inkling of them, she would have wanted to take me straight home.

The only person to know of my dissatisfaction with the progress of my work, but who never dreamed of the inner torment it was causing me, was Moskiewicz. Of course, the poor fellow could give me no help himself; but a few weeks before the semester ended, he exclaimed: "Say, why don't you go to see Reinach sometime?"

And he reasoned with me until he had persuaded me to follow his advice. The following Friday instead of leaving after the "Exercises," I asked Reinach whether I might have a minute with him privately. He agreed most cordially, asking only that I wait a bit since some other people present had some personal concerns to discuss. He withdrew into another room with one of them. Soon thereafter he came to get me. Now I informed him I would like to tell him about my work.

"But it's all still so unclear," I added, dejectedly.

"Well, one certainly ought to be able to clarify anything that's not clear."

That sounded so sincere and so cheerfully encouraging that I already felt somewhat consoled. My coming for a thorough discussion was arranged. I cannot remember whether that was to be the very next morning. When, with a heavy heart, I did present myself, I was urged to take the most comfortable armchair opposite his desk, whereupon I reported on the mass of material I had collected and on the plan I had in mind to reduce this chaos to order. Reinach's opinion was that, actually, I had made good progress. He encouraged me emphatically to begin drafting the text. Three weeks remained of that semester. At its close, I should return to report on what I had produced. That was an ambitious resolution, but I set out immediately to carry it out. Nothing I had accomplished so far had ever exacted such a heavy toll in mental effort. I believe that without personally having done such creative philosophical work a person cannot possibly imagine what it demanded of me. Moreover, I cannot recall that I experienced at that time any of the deep joy which later habitually accompanied my work once I had surmounted the painful, preliminary difficulties. I had not yet reached that plateau of clarity on which the mind, having gained an insight, can rest, and from which, with the perception of new, unfolding paths, one proceeds confidently. I still seemed to be groping my way through a dense fog. What I wrote down seemed so peculiar even to me that, had anyone else declared it all to be nonsense, I readily would have believed him. I was saved from *one* pitfall: I had no difficulty finding words. The thoughts easily and surely formed themselves into phrases within me, and then they appeared in such firm and definite terms on the paper that they never revealed to a reader even so much as a trace of the labor pains which had accompanied this intellectual birth. Every hour I could free for this work was spent at my small desk. By the end of the three weeks, I had filled about thirty large folio sheets.

Now I returned to Reinach. It was morning. The breakfast dishes had not yet been cleared away in his study. I had brought along my manuscript and intended to ask Reinach, as a favor, to keep it and look it over at his convenience. To my amazement he asked me to wait; he would read it at once. To pass the time, he gave me Hegel's *Phenomenology of the Spirit* which happened to be on his desk. I opened the book and made an effort to read, but it was impossible for me to pay attention to it. There was such excitement just in sitting there in the presence of my judge as he attempted to formulate the sentence he would pronounce on my work. He read eagerly, sometimes nodding in agreement; and from time to time he made an assenting sound as well. He finished in an amazingly short time.

"Very good, Fräulein Stein," he said.

Could that be possible? Yes; he really had no objections to make. His only urgent suggestion was that I not interrupt the work. Could I not possibly stay in Göttingen until I had finished it? Surely I would not be as undisturbed at home. He knew all too well how it was when he went to Mainz. Then one had to visit all one's aunts. Immediately I decided to follow his advice. He, himself, was about to go to visit his parents in Mainz, but only for about a week. When I had finished, I could bring him the second part of my thesis.

Vacation began, and Göttingen was deserted. I was the only one to stay behind; in my small room, I sat at my desk. Having no lectures to attend anymore, I could now write almost uninterruptedly. I finished in one week. It was about eight in the evening; a fine rain had begun to fall. But I could not bear to stay in my room. I had to get out to learn when Reinach was expected back. Just as I reached the *Steinsgraben* a taxi turned in from the Friedländerweg and drove up the street. It stopped in front of Reinach's house — a few moments later the lights in his study went on. That told me enough; I swung around and went home. It is impossible to express how much joy and gratitude I felt; even today, more than twenty years later, I can still draw some of that deep sigh of relief.

The following morning I was at hand with my manuscript and rang the doorbell. Reinach himself answered it. He was alone at home; his wife was in Stuttgart to help his sister who was making her *Abitur* there. Pauline [his sister] was older than he; she had decided to begin her studies so late that memorizing was very difficult for her. Her first attempt at taking the examination had ended in failure; the second try, then, was all the more nerve-racking. I had been at the house but a little while when the doorbell rang again, and Reinach had to answer it once more. When he returned, he recited in the tone of a youngster repeating a lesson: "The butcher! No, we don't need anything."

That had been Auguste's [the housekeeper's] firm injunction before leaving for market.

This time I was less fearful than I had been at the first session. Reinach was well satisfied. I asked him whether the work was good enough to qualify for the state boards. By all means! Husserl was certain to be well pleased with it; he seldom got such papers. I should now set out on my vacation without the slightest care. We bade one another a delighted farewell until April.

After these two visits with Reinach, I was like one reborn. All discontent with life had disappeared. I felt as though I had been rescued from distress by a good angel. By one magic word, he seemed to have transformed the monstrous offspring of my poor brain into a clear and well-organized whole. I was completely confident that his verdict was reliable. Reassured, I laid the work aside so as to devote all my efforts now to my preparation for the oral examination. Even though I had completed only six semesters, I still had an advantage in that all the time one would ordinarily expend on writing the two major theses was now at my disposal. After all, applying for the examination did not mean I was expected to have both of them already completed.

One had to submit an application for the state board examination to the county school authority, attaching: a curriculum vitae; an exact description of the course of one's studies; a transcript of the required lectures and exercises taken; and certification that one was no longer registered at the university. Then the board of examiners was appointed; those chosen thereupon selected the topics; and one was given three months to prepare the thesis for each. Not until they had all been submitted was a date set for the oral examination. One was not permitted to express any preference of persons to be appointed to the commission. To insure the choice of those one desired to have, the trick was to list the sequence of one's studies and one's areas of specialization in such a way that the only persons competent enough to be considered qualified as examiners were one's own teachers. The trick succeeded for me: Husserl was designated for philosophy, Weissenfels for German philology and German literature.[138] Incidentally, I had missed the deadline for registration. I was totally unaware that there was such a deadline and that a notice to that effect had been put up at the university. The secretary of the Board of Examiners, a teacher in the Göttingen humanistic *Gymnasium*, pointed this out to me in any but gracious terms. He condescended to accept the papers, nonetheless. I do not know anymore when I received the reply from Hannover. In all probability only after vacation was over. Lehmann had formulated his topic exactly as I had treated it in his seminar;[139] here I needed but to supplement a bit on literature; this I could easily postpone until just before it was due, that was in November. Husserl, however, gave me an unpleasant surprise. His memory had failed him, no doubt, and he phrased his topic in such a way that not only Theodor Lipps, but all the other literature on empathy had to be taken into consideration although Lipps was given priority.[140] In all probability I could leave the actual arrangement and its entire development as it was, but I would have to study the massive amounts of additional literature and incorporate them.

3

I remember in connection with that particular vacation that Erna's practical examination had begun when I arrived at home. For their state boards, the medical students had to prove their skill in all clinical subjects; and this dragged on for months. Erna was not at the station to meet me the evening I arrived; she had gone to bed, expecting to be called out to the Women's Hospital for a delivery during the night. But they immediately took me to see her. The entire family was completely involved in her examination process; by contrast, mine took a back seat, and I was glad that in my case, everything would happen in peace and quiet far away from home.

I also remember that during that vacation Metis and I worked together a great deal since he, too, was preparing for his examinations. And, finally, it was during this time that I made, as mentioned earlier, that trip to Hamburg to bring Else to Breslau. Consequently, I experienced all the stress caused by her presence and by the suspense about future developments.

Shortly before I returned to Göttingen, Rose Guttmann invited me over one evening to get acquainted with a lady who also intended to go to Göttingen that summer. Rose herself had met Toni Meyer through Moskiewicz, and she had already studied some phenomenology with her during the past winter. The Meyer and Moskiewicz families were friends. Toni and Georg had known one another for a long time; they were about the same age, in their thirty-sixth year at that time. Later, after becoming better acquainted in Göttingen, I often went to the Meyers in whose congenial household I was always received with warm cordiality. Toni lived alone with her mother, an exceptionally intelligent elderly lady. Upon her husband's death she had taken over management of his thriving business in military uniforms, showing great acumen. Her son had long since become owner and manager of the business, but she still shared in the profits. Deliveries to the army during the War [with France] of 1870–71 had brought them a considerable fortune. Now, too, everything in their home gave indications of their great wealth; however, it was not at all ostentatious. When I dined with them, I enjoyed the beautiful table setting, the fine porcelain, and the linens. The old lady still turned out the most exquisite needlework. Her small sewing table stood on a raised platform at one of the large windows of the cozy combination dining-living room. As she was lame in one foot, she seldom went out. Still, with the aid of her cane, she moved about confidently and declined assistance from others. Stimulating conversation delighted her. Her son, his wife, and their five children often visited her, as did a number of women friends to each of whom a separate day had been assigned. Her household ran without a hitch; the two maids were instructed and supervised down to the least detail; but, in return, they were also treated with kindness and generosity.

Diagonally across the room from Frau Meyer's work table, an oil painting, a portrait of Toni as a child, hung on the wall. The little girl's head was unusually lovely; she looked delicate yet vivacious. But at the time I got to know her, there was, apparently, little left of this childhood beauty except for the rich, wavy chestnut-brown hair. She wore it simply parted, with the long braids pinned up so they covered the whole back of her head. Her eyelids appeared heavy, at times her facial expression showed great fatigue; occasionally it changed suddenly and surprisingly. She was of medium height; her body was strong and well-proportioned, but her step was so heavy and dragging that it seemed as though her feet were tied together. Her clothes were always in the best taste and of the finest material, yet simple and inconspicuous. She could be very lively and joyous, even exuberant, but after she had worked intensively for an hour or had taken part in stimulating conversation, she had to lie down for a few minutes; then she could go on again. Years earlier she had tried to run a kindergarten, but the strain had proved too much for her. Her studies in psychology led her to Stern; soon she was very much at home with his family and used Frau Stern's diaries to put together the book *From a Nursery*. Now Moskiewicz had pointed her toward phenomenology; and with a great deal of fortitude she had decided to study it at the source. Fortitude was required because she had no *Abitur*; and so she could only audit the lectures with the personal permission of the lecturer. She obtained such permission from Husserl and from Reinach; and now I was to give her "lessons" which should enable her to surmount a beginner's difficulties. I read *Logische Untersuchungen* with her. These lessons made her very happy. I also had to agree to accept a fee. She insisted I do so; after all, Rose had accepted one. She herself decided on the amount; it was so much that I was embarrassed all the more.

I had kept my room in the Schillerstrasse. Toni took a roomier and more elegant apartment on the Feuerschanzengraben, not far from me. My way of life dismayed her: the long hours of work, the little sleep, the indifference about my meals, and the lack of recreation. The lady with whom she lived recommended an excellent private dining place to her on the Friedländerweg, and she begged me to join her for meals there. As I was in no way self-willed over matters that seemed trivial to me, I agreed without hesitation. Usually she picked me up and walked home with me again afterwards. Before long, she also asked leave to come to get me for a stroll in the evening. Sometime thereafter, on one of these quiet evening walks, she told me that despite her happiness at our growing friendship, she felt it incumbent on her to tell me something which might well induce me to break off my association with her. That at times she had been mentally ill; her fatigue plus other disturbing symptoms, for instance the neuralgia in her head and arm and the difficulty she had in walking, were all part of it. The illness had also made any regular course of study and the taking of examinations impossible for her. I was able to reassure her by telling her I had known about it for a long, long time (a business acquaintance of my mother's who had close relations with the Meyer family had mentioned it). I told Toni that this fact could in no way frighten me away. My reassurance obviously lightened her heart. Now, at last, she could enjoy our friendship without reservations. It seemed to her, to begin with, a great boon that a young, healthy, and well-endowed person should treat her as an equal. Over and above that, she had already felt a deep attraction for me and an esteem which made her look up to me though I was so much younger. Probably this was so because her mental condition had made her far more sensitive about people's weaknesses; and, for that reason, too, she was uninhibited when expressing her opinion. This summer in Göttingen was probably the happiest of her life. Never before and never afterwards was she so productive or so free of the attacks of depression, which otherwise afflicted her at greater or lesser intervals. She attended lectures and exercises under Husserl and Reinach, went with me to the Philosophical Society's meetings, came along on my Sunday walks with Danziger who was ready immediately to make every allowance she might need; and all this made her happy as a child.

On one occasion, we met my sister Else in Hildesheim. Getting to know the wonderful old town was a treat for all of us. What was more, Else and I had an opportunity for the thorough discussion she had always longed for. We could talk without being disturbed since Toni knew how to keep the rather awkward Danziger busy. However, she did not neglect the chance to walk alone with Else at times, so as to get acquainted with her and to show Else sincere sympathy.

It was during this summer that Erna and Hans Biberstein visited me, as I recounted earlier. As I said,[141] Toni and Erich Danziger helped me take care of and entertain my guests. Hans was quartered with Danziger. My good landlady, Frau Mussmann, was able to make a room available for Erna. We four usually had our evening meal together in my room; sometimes all of us were invited to Toni's. Most often, my guests were away somewhere at noon; otherwise, if I remember correctly, we patronized the pleasant vegetarian restaurant. Our regular dining place did not suit us during those days since everyone ate at one long table there; and it was therefore impossible to hold private conversations.

Toni surrounded me with loving care, for instance, very early on, she found a florist in our neighborhood and, thereafter, provided fresh flowers for my room; this care and her warm concern for all my affairs certainly contributed toward making that a very sunny summer for me again. Of course, this was also due to my being rid of the burden that had weighed me down all during the previous winter. Over and above amplifying the thesis since the topic had been expanded [by Husserl], there was still a great deal of work to complete for the oral examinations. But all this was child's play compared to what I had already accomplished. The chore of simply memorizing the factual material for the exam was made substantially easier because I found companions to share the task.

For the study of history, a teacher who had returned to study in Lehmann's seminar joined me: Käthe Scharf, a Silesian "compatriot" from Hirschberg. She had a happy disposition and was intent on making the examination as pleasant for herself as possible. As she wanted to prepare herself for it in a leisurely fashion, she delayed registering for it. She had informed herself in detail regarding all the stipulations of the examination about which I had never bothered. So, from her I learned the following: when giving the examination Lehmann restricted himself precisely to the matter covered in his lectures; one had to inform him which two of his long lectures and which one of the shorter ones constituted one's "specialty"; if one took the examination in history and had not come from a humanistic *Gymnasium*, it was necessary to demonstrate one's command of Greek; Lehmann made a habit of confronting his students with the first part of Xenophon's *Anabasis*. (I still remembered that section by heart, having studied it in the beginner's course I took in Breslau.)

As our special field we chose the "Age of Absolutism," the revolutionary period, as well as the Revolution of 1848-49, all of which we had prepared for the state boards. Together we reviewed our lecture notes which we had painstakingly transcribed. We had the cited source material and the most important works dealing with these historical periods brought by the cartload from the library to the reading room. It was impossible to read everything through; but, at least, we wanted to look at all of it and to have had it in our hands. I took home as much as possible and read it in the evenings, or at such times when any more strenuous work was beyond me. I read a great deal of Ranke at the time, particularly enjoying his *History of Nations,* also Voltaire, Rousseau, Montesquieu, and many others as well. It was, on the whole, a very colorful tapestry truly putting us in touch with history's vitality. We had fun quizzing one another. We did that while walking over the hills of Göttingen when the day happened to be a nice one. During this time, also, I was initiated in the technique of cramming for exams. The really important facts in our notebooks were underlined in red, a much smaller selection in red and blue, the *most* select in red, blue and green. With such a device one could review an unbelievable amount of material on the final days before an examination and be able to have at one's fingertips all the facts one needed.

If we were to spend the evening working together, we began it by mutual arrangement with an invitation for supper. When we ate at Käthe Scharf's, it was particularly cozy. That was because her mother was there to keep house for her. This good woman had accompanied her daughter to the university, leaving her husband alone at home in preference to sending Käthe to a strange town by herself. This seemed most peculiar to me, and I always felt sorry for the father. But, apparently, both parents had agreed to take this measure to protect their offspring against the dangers lurking in student life.

As study companion for the history of philosophy and in German philology, I had Lotte Winkler whom I had come to know in the Psychology Institute. In this case, our working together resulted in more than a mere pleasant comradeship. Certainly Lotte Winkler liked to enjoy herself also; but she had sincere, deep, scholarly interests. Also, she was experiencing some personal difficulties at the time; and these she discussed with me. She was a Protestant and was engaged to a Jewish lawyer whose father was decidedly opposed to the marriage. After the wedding, we continued to correspond for some time.

During this summer Pauline Reinach came to Göttingen to begin her studies. She then attended her brother's classes, accompanied by her sister-in-law. Actually, I got to know her personally only when we were all invited as usual to mark the close of the semester at Husserl's. At social gatherings, Pauline was lively, witty, and quick at repartee. But a private conversation with her alone gave one insight into a deep, quiet, and truly contemplative soul.[142] Her head reminded one of Gothic wood sculpture. Her hands were as fragile and as expressive as those of a Pre-Raphaelite saint. Her approach to her studies was correspondingly characteristic. She had chosen classical languages and could immerse herself completely in an author who pleased her; systematic study for practical purposes was foreign to her.

Her brother Ado used to say about her, teasingly: "Little Pauline—a world in herself!"

And Hein, the youngest of the three Reinach siblings, once called out to her when he saw her sitting somewhere looking off into space, "Pauline, at least hold a book in your hand!"

After being with her at several of the family gatherings, one automatically began to call her by her first name. It seemed totally unnatural to address her as "Fräulein Reinach."

There were some other newcomers to Göttingen that summer. Reinach mentioned them to me immediately on my first visit to him at the start of the semester: a Russian professor who wished to study phenomenology at its source; retired General von Gründell; and a younger man, Herr von Baligaud. Of course, the general, a short, white-haired man, was admitted only to the beginner's course. His bearing was very modest; all the same, his questions came out in a firm, military tone of voice. Herr von Baligaud was serious about his studies; therefore, he participated in everything that was available, including the Philosophical Society. When, occasionally, he reverted to a manner either too self-assured or too forward, Reinach very decidedly put him in his place. The fruits of such training were evident by the summer's end.

Hering also came for a few weeks this semester in order to take his state boards. He passed the examination; and the night we went to Husserl's we celebrated his success and that of Fräulein Ortmann as well. Her happiness made her treat me more pleasantly than heretofore. One needed only a short while with Hering to establish a good rapport with him. He accepted everyone with a childlike openness that was accompanied by a profound and gentle kindness. All the same, he was full of mischief and constantly had the most astounding inspirations so that his presence banished all the bad spirits of melancholy, ill humor, and unpleasantness. His narrow face, blond pointed beard, and his thin voice were reminiscent of the "valiant little tailor" [Grimm's Fairy Tales].

Husserl was very fond of him and had the highest regard for his philosophical talent. Hering had used a work on Lotze as his thesis for the state boards. His treatise — on being, essence, and idea — which later appeared in the *Yearbook* was taken from that thesis.

I also became better acquainted with Bell that winter since he, too, was working for his doctorate under Husserl. That created a bond between us "fellow sufferers." He disliked most of all being called upon by the Master to give an account of his progress. Bell averred this was best done while the two of them took a walk. Climbing the slope to Rohns made Husserl short of breath, and one could then get a word in.

Bell handed in the first draft of his work at the end of the winter. The Master took it along to read while travelling to Vienna for his mother's eightieth birthday. (Reinach wrote a charming letter of congratulations for that occasion on our behalf; each of us signed it individually.)

Bell told me then that if either no change at all or a great deal of change were required in his thesis, he would make a trip home before doing any further work. He had not visited his Canadian home or seen his father for five years. But, as it turned out, neither of the alternatives occurred. Instead, a number of minor changes were required; and, therefore, he determined to stay there for the summer.

When the summer began, he told me his father intended to come to Germany for a health cure at Bad Nauheim. He would meet him at the port of Antwerp; and, since his father knew no German, he would stay with him in Nauheim most of the time. Still later I learned, in one of the brief conversations we used to have before class, that his father had booked a passage on the "Empress of India"[143] but a heart attack hindered him from making the trip. Now that ship had sunk; what had been most unwelcome hindrance had saved his life. But soon an entirely different impediment prevented the reunion of father and son.

4

Our placid student life was blown to bits by the Serbian assassination of royalty.[144] July was dominated by the question: Will war break out in Europe? Everything seemed to indicate that a terrible storm was brewing. But we found it inconceivable that it would really come to that. No one growing up during or since the war can possibly imagine the security in which we assumed ourselves to be living before 1914. Our life was built on an indestructible foundation of peace, stability of ownership of property, and on the permanence of circumstances to which we were accustomed. When one finally noticed that the storm was inevitably approaching, one attempted to get a clear idea of what was likely to happen. One thing was certain. It would differ totally from all previous wars. The destruction would be so terrible that it could not possibly last long. It would all be over in a few months.

On our way home from Reinach's course at seven in the evening, Toni and I stopped at the newsstand in the Judenstrasse for a copy of *B.Z. am Mittag* ["Berlin News at Noon"] which arrived about that time via train from Berlin. Sometimes we got there before it did. Then, chatting away, we would walk up and down in front of the kiosk until the paper was delivered. Others did the same, of course. We met Reinach, his wife, and his sister on one such occasion. We had just bought some cherries at a fruit vendor's and were eating them to pass the time. As I went by them, I held out the paper bag to Reinach and the two ladies; and they helped themselves. A short while later, Frau Reinach came after us to offer us some of their own supply which she had gotten in the meantime. But her husband let her know that Fräulein Stein's cherries were much better than hers.

When I entered Reinach's study for the final session of his seminar, the room was empty. A very large atlas was spread out on his desk. Kaufmann arrived soon after I did. He also noticed the open map.

"Reinach, too, is studying the atlas," he said.

That evening saw no more philosophizing. Only the coming events were talked of.

"Must you go, also, Doctor?" Kaufmann asked.

"It's not that I *must*; rather, I'm permitted to go," Reinach replied.

His statement pleased me very much. It expressed so well my own feelings.

The excitement increased from day to day. I had already formed a habit then, which later I practiced quite consciously in such times of crisis; calmly, I went about my ordinary duties but deep inside I was prepared to call a halt to them at any moment. It went against the grain for me to increase the common agitation by running around or by useless chatter. In Homer I had always read with satisfaction how Hector directed his wife to return to her work in the house after he bade a final farewell to her and to his little son.

So, at four o'clock on the afternoon of July 30, I was seated at my small desk, immersed in Schopenhauer's *The World as Will and Idea*. I intended to go to a lecture at five o'clock. Then came a knock at my door, and Fräulein Scharf and her friend, Fräulein Merk, who was also from Silesia, came in. They told me I could save myself the trouble of going. A notice was posted on the bulletin board that a state of war had been declared and all lectures were suspended. Both of them would be returning home that evening.

A second knock sounded while we were still speaking. It was Nelli Courant. Richard had gotten his mobilization alert. Once the command to mobilize was given, he would have to leave within a very few days for his post as deputy officer in the reserve battalion in Thüringen. She was not to stay on alone in Göttingen but was to go to her father's in Breslau to await the end of the war. Since Richard was convinced that very soon after mobilization the railroads would be closed to private traffic, she was to leave that same evening. Did I want to go along? I reflected for a moment. Göttingen was in the heart of Germany and there was little likelihood it would get to see any of the enemy except possibly as prisoners of war. Breslau, on the contrary, was but a few hours' distance from the Russian border and was the most important fortification in the east. That it might soon be besieged by Russian troops was distinctly possible. My decision was made. I slammed shut *The World as Will and Idea*. (Oddly enough, I never took up that particular book again.) It was now about five o'clock; our train was to leave at eight. I still had a great deal to do before then. So I said that if I managed to finish everything, I would be at Courants' by half-past seven to ride to the station with them. With that, we parted. I believe my first errand was to go to Toni Meyer. I could not leave her behind alone. Naturally, she could not possibly make her decision as quickly as I had. Since time would not allow me to wait while she made up her mind, I told her to meet us at Courants' should she decide to come along. She went to some other Silesian friends (Professor Lichtwitz and his wife) to get more advice. I went on my way: to the bank to get some money, to our customary lunch room to pay my monthly bill, then to Reinach. I asked him to certify that I had taken his course and seminar. He did so but told me I need not go for any other certificates since, later, no one would ask for them. He wanted to know what my plans were. I would go to the Red Cross. So far, he had never been in the service but, of course, he would now volunteer; and if they were unwilling to take him, then General von Gründell, now recalled to active duty, would have to use influence to get him in. He made a note of my address; after all, we would want to keep in touch to exchange news about our situation. For the first time I saw clearly that his friendliness toward me had not been merely an expression of his ordinary geniality but was rather a heartfelt personal liking.

Now I rushed back to my rooms, packed what was essential for the immediate future, stowed everything else away in a hamper which my landlady was to keep in storage. Hurriedly, I settled my account with her also and said goodbye. I had precisely enough time left to walk over to the Courants. The car was already there, and Toni was on the spot. But we had a long wait for Nelli. Richard was to accompany us for part of the way, but they were bidding one another farewell in his study. That took time.

I was full of sympathy for them both. Actually it was amazing that Nelli should leave before her husband had to go. Had I been in her place, I definitely would not have done so. Probably concern for her father was behind it. But, then, she was always different from other people.

As was to be expected, the station and the train were crowded with travelers. Unable to go to Eichenberg where we usually made connections with the main Kassel-Breslau line, we had to go to Kassel instead. Richard accompanied us that far. In Kassel there was even greater commotion and confusion. One could not even ascertain whether the train we boarded was actually going to Breslau. As the officials themselves were not sure, they finally disappeared to evade further questioning. A guard was stationed at every railway bridge we crossed. This was a small foretaste of the war. Otherwise, the farther east we went, the more calm and orderly things became. I made a similar observation, later, when the revolution started. At one point we had to make a lengthy stop since something on the engine had to be repaired. It was now the day after our departure. From all the compartments, travelers scrambled down to stretch out alongside the tracks in the bright July sunshine. This presented a picture filled with peace and joy which moved one deeply when the thought occurred that we were traveling into the war. The faithful Danziger found his way to us somewhere en route. We arrived in Breslau late on the afternoon of July 31. My main concern was Nelli. I wanted to hand her over to her father before I myself went home. I believe I asked Danziger to telephone my people in the meantime to tell them I had arrived and would soon be there. In his joy, Judge Neumann first embraced his daughter and then me. I did not delay long; I had arranged for the taxi to wait out front and so I took off at once.

My mother was waiting at the window. She came out on the street to meet me; she was there when I opened the door of the taxi to alight.

"You've never been so obedient!" she said, beaming happily.

I could not claim the compliment; her summons to come home as quickly as possible must have arrived in Göttingen after my departure.

The entire family was assembled. Even the Bibersteins were there. To my amazement, current events had far less portent for them than for me.

"Don't be afraid," said my mother.

"I'm not afraid," I replied. "But it is entirely possible that the Russians will cross the border in a few days."

"Then we'll take a broomstick and beat them back."

It was almost more than I could bear to sit at the tea table listening as Frau Biberstein told her little tales of commonplace happenings. I was distinctly relieved when my mother sent me to bed to catch up on the sleep I had lost through traveling all night. But, of course, sleep was out of the question. Though feverishly tense, I faced the future with great clarity and determination.

'I have no private life anymore,' I told myself, 'All my energy must be devoted to this great happening. Only when the war is over, if I'm alive then, will I be permitted to think of my private affairs once more.'

The next day was the Sunday on which [we learned that] war was declared.[145] Rose came to welcome me home. From her I learned that a nursing course for women students was being organized. I registered for it at once and soon went daily to *Aller-*

heiligenhospital [All Saints Hospital]. I heard lectures on surgery and communicable diseases in wartime; I learned to apply bandages and to give injections. My former classmate Toni Hamburger was taking the same course so we vied with each other to make our training as thorough as possible. Our nurses' training manual was not explicit enough for me. At home, I studied Erna's atlas of anatomy and her voluminous medical textbooks. I also visited her and Lilli often at the Gynecological Hospital to practice bandaging. They were glad to see me so interested in their specialty.

During the course, we had to make known whether we would be available to the Red Cross and whether that would be only for the defense district of Breslau, or anywhere within the country, or without any qualification.

Of course, I placed myself unconditionally at their disposal. Indeed, all I wanted was to go as soon and as faraway as possible, preferably to a field hospital at the front. But things just did not move all that fast. There was an oversupply of helpers. We passed the aides' examination after four weeks of training. But there was no recruitment. To improve my skills, I was permitted to continue working at *Allerheiligenhospital*. For several weeks I was an aide in the tuberculosis ward, then in a ward of the surgical department where the patients were for the most part children who had been run over. Finally, I helped in the surgical polyclinic. Everywhere I found plenty to do. One never felt like a fifth wheel. *Allerheiligenhospital* is a huge municipal hospital. It employed comparatively few fully trained registered nurses; most of the work was done by nurses' aides, girls without previous training hired primarily for domestic duties. Gradually they learned and carried out the practical chores of caring for the sick under the direction of the nurse, or of the staff nurse in charge of their particular ward. I got the impression that the sick were not used to getting loving attention and that volunteer helpers therefore could find endless opportunities to show their own compassion and love of neighbor in these places of suffering. Granted, it would be a thorny task and might well mean a battle first of all just to be admitted. However, just then, nobody gave us a hard time since we were there to complete our training, and that would take no more than a few weeks.

My volunteer activity was terminated because in October I came down with a bad case of bronchitis which I had caught at work. By the time I had recovered, the winter semester was about to begin. Back in August, I had not thought that returning to Göttingen for the winter could be possible. But as there was no prospect of being called up for service at any military hospital, I had used my lunch breaks while serving at *Allerheiligenhospital* to review and put the final touches to my preparations for the state boards. The papers were to be submitted in November. And now I decided that as evidently the army had no use for me at present, it would be most prudent to go to Göttingen and get the examination over with while waiting. My attitude had in no way changed. I would have welcomed a call away from my books any day. The examination seemed to me ridiculously trivial compared to current events which kept us on tenterhooks in those months. In Breslau I had gathered a good number of wartime impressions. True, the Russians had not come. While they had actually crossed the border in Upper Silesia during the very first days of August, they had been repulsed very quickly. However, to compensate, war psychosis had invented some most amazing horror stories. The rumor that the Russians had poisoned our drinking water actually led to some very irksome official regulations. We were no longer supplied with water from the municipal waterworks. As in ancient times, one had to fetch one's water from the pumps on the street corners. To save water, bathing was to be limited to the barest minimum; and one should not wear white clothing or white shoes.

Meanwhile, with jubilant cries of victory, we followed the progress of our army into France; we used colored pins to mark the route on our big maps and awaited the day when "we" would march into Paris. It was like a brilliant replay of the campaign of 1870, thoroughly familiar to us from our school books and to our parents through personal experience. The massive defeat at the first battle of the Marne was totally incomprehensible.

One of my first depressing experiences during those war days was the sight of a long string of horses being led through the streets. They had been requisitioned for military use. I was put in mind of an enormously large suction pump that was sapping all the strength of the land. Just as oppressive was the sight I had a few months later of the port of Hamburg, completely defunct, a forest of cold chimneys and sail-less masts.

My brothers were not at the front. At every medical examination, Paul was declared unfit for service. Arno's assignment in the medical corps was such that he was not away constantly but only had to accompany transport trains. But many of my cousins and practically all of my Göttingen classmates were in active service. An entire regiment of volunteers from Göttingen was engaged in the thick of the battle in Flanders. Many students had joined the army in Göttingen while others had returned to their homes to register and so be enlisted in the local regiments of their hometown. Reinach got his artillery training in Mainz. Moskiewicz had volunteered as a physician. Incapable of serving at the front, he was assigned as Senior Physician in the Municipal Institute for the Insane to replace a colleague who was called to active service.

The first announcement of a casualty arrived as early as August: Rober Staiger, the privatdocent for the history of art in Göttingen. He had also conducted the student orchestra which eagerly performed the finest of classical music. For years, he had been secretly engaged to Elisabeth Klein, daughter of the mathematician Felix Klein.[146] The father was opposed to the marriage and forbade the suitor entrance to his home. Because of his imposing personality, Felix Klein played a dominant role in Göttingen. No one dared to contradict him. Elisabeth (whom her family and close friends called "Putti") had inherited some of her father's mathematical talent. She had continued her studies and passed the state board examination; but, subsequently, instead of teaching, she had taken up the study of music in Leipzig. Putti was as significant a pace-setter among the progeny of Göttingen's professors as her father was among the "big wigs," although her position was not due to any arrogance but rather to her gracious, spirited, and kind ways. She and her fiancé were friends of the Reinachs and often met there. Before Staiger left for active service, they had a war wedding performed. Now, only a few weeks later, he had been killed.

Nelli Courant brought me this news item together with another one she had found in the *Schlesischen Zeitung* ["The Silesian News"]. This conservative newspaper carried a reference criticizing the "unpatriotic attitude" of some professors at Göttingen. It was reported that these professors had visited an Englishman to administer the oral examination for his doctorate while he was in custody because of some anti-German statements he had made. The "anti-German Englishman" was our friend Bell; the "unpatriotic" professor, our old Master, Husserl, and his two colleagues who examined Bell in his minor subjects. Their names were all reported. Convinced at once that some facts must have been misrepresented, I wanted to get clarification. I wrote to Bell to tell him of the "shocking fiction" we had read, and I asked him to let me know what had really happened. His reply was stamped by the police department of Göttingen and came from prison. Bell, as a Canadian, had at first remained at liberty. (Citizens of British colonies were not interned until the beginning of 1915.) One day an acquaintaince of his (a German) while passing Bell's lodging had called up to him at the window. This, though so typical a practice in Göttingen, was a highly imprudent one in this case, considering the feelings of the people in those early months of the war.

He [the German] had asked, "What do you think of the Japanese declaration of war?"

Just as unthinkingly, Bell answered from the open window, "For us, it's obviously an advantage."

A woman passing by at that moment heard him and, greatly agitated, went at once to report him. In that report his comment was grossly exaggerated so that it appeared to have been an anti-German proclamation. Bell was taken into protective custody but was allowed to live at home. As he was not permitted to leave the house, he was unable to present himself at the university on the day that had been set for the examinations. So his benevolent and sympathetic teachers had decided to give him the examination at his apartment.

By doing so they aroused violent protest from their nationalist colleagues. A faculty meeting was called and the examination was declared invalid, as was the acceptance of the thesis he had submitted, even though that had been done before the war began.

Upon my return to Göttingen, Husserl told me Bell was now incarcerated in the university's "lock-up." He himself had visited Bell there; and I could probably do so, too, but one had to get a permit from the chief of police. Of course, I at once determined to get such permission for myself. Besides my natural sympathy for the prisoner, there was probably a romantic aura to the idea of "visiting the lock-up." I had never before seen this particular place. It was located in the upper story of the Auditorium which, so far, I had entered only on important festive occasions or when paying my course fees at the beginning of each semester. The university's administrative offices were in this building. The chief of police gave me the permission without demur. I was given a paper which stated I would be allowed to visit in the prison the following Sunday morning between half-past eleven and noon. Armed with this certificate I presented myself to the caretaker of the Auditorium that Sunday. His friendly wife conducted me upstairs, unlocked the door, and then — to my great astonishment — locked it again once I was inside. So, for half an hour, I was a fellow prisoner. Bell greeted me joyfully. The gesture with which he invited me to have a seat transformed the rough wooden chair into a wicker armchair. I was to look around the room first and see that it was not too bad a place to live in. He was right; it was light and spacious. On one wall was depicted *Die Mütze* ["The Cap"], the famous Göttingen inn, the most attractive of the town's ancient houses. The artistic painting had originated with one of the room's former occupants. On the other walls were more drawings by less skilled hands. There was little furniture; but he had all the necessities: an iron bedstead with a rough woolen blanket, two wooden chairs, and a solid wooden table piled with books.

The prisoner was thoroughly content with his lot and harbored no bitterness against the persons responsible for his arrest. Objections had been made to keeping him any longer under arrest in his own lodgings, and it was proposed that he be moved to the local jail. However, Göttingen's jail was not designed for a protracted term. It served only, occasionally, to confine a drunk overnight, or for some similar situation. A lengthier prison sentence had to be served in Hannover. Because of this predicament, the Rector of the University, the mathematician Runge, had intervened. He declared he could make suitable quarters available, the above-mentioned "lock up!" Professor Runge was a kind and noble person, a patriot but not a nationalist. (He had put all of the ready cash he had into war bonds, reasoning that were Germany to go under we would no longer need any private means.) However, he intervened for Bell not only because he felt that justice demanded it but for personal reasons as well. Bell was a close friend of both his sons, Wilhelm and Bernhard. Bell's relationship with them was probably more that of a leader as he was a good bit older than either of the others. The two brothers had joined the Göttingen Volunteer Regiment; and seventeen-year-old Bernhard died in Flanders. His parents received his letters; among them were those Bell had written to him while he was in the service. For the first time, these letters showed the parents how affectionately Bell had been concerned for his young friend so they now reciprocated by considering him a son of theirs.

After that visit to the lock-up I heard no more about Bell for a few months. Suddenly one day in January, I met him on the street. He was taking a walk with Runge; Erika Gothe was with me. He crossed the street to join us and recounted his latest experiences. He had not been allowed to stay long in the friendly lock-up. His "friends," the philologists, considered that, having been expelled from the university, he had no right to stay there. He was then transferred to the city jail in Hannover. But there, too, he remained no more than two weeks. Professor Runge had put in a petition and obtained permission to receive him into his own home. He pledged himself as surety, and in his company Bell was even allowed to go out. However, this happy solution did not last long either. A few weeks later the internment of all British colonials was ordered. Bell was taken to the large concentration camp in Ruhleben[147] where he had to remain until the war ended.

5

I had returned to Göttingen in the second half of October. Nelli had put her apartment and all its furnishings at my disposal. Since she herself could get no pleasure from it, I was to enjoy it. So I had my things moved on Schillerstrasse: from Number Thirty-two to Number Forty-two. It was a small, rather new, two-story house. The Pabsts, the couple who owned the house, lived on the ground floor. The Courants had rented the two upper stories. Now this was my domain. On the lower floor was a dining room, the parlor, Nelli's study and the kitchen. Of these, I used only the kitchen. I spent all my time in the upper story: Richard's study and the adjoining bedroom. Both had very large windows with southern exposure, giving an open view of gardens and fields toward the *Falsche* ["false"] *Gleichen,* a pair of hills which looked very much like the "genuine" Gleichen.[148] Now in winter, the windows also provided one with a view of both sunrise and sunset. The huge oak desk by the window was positioned to enable one to enjoy the view while at work. To the right of the desk, against the wall, there was a chaise longue above which hung Rembrandt's "Man with the Golden Helmet." The other walls were covered with books. These were not all on mathematics; in fact, there were a good many I could use. In the corner where the two walls of books met, there was a small round table. I used that for my evening meals.

Obviously, I had to have someone to keep the rooms clean; besides, I also had to have someone to take care of the central heating since the Pabsts had shut off their radiators and were using stoves. For these chores Nelli had recommended her cleaning lady, Frau Hartung, in whom she placed full confidence. I sent the lady a postcard requesting her to come, whereupon she appeared for an interview: stately, tall, and so very broad that beside her I faded to nothing. She seated herself on the chaise longue and declared that since it was Frau Doctor's wish, she would have to accept the job, of course. But she was not familiar with the heating system. That afternoon she brought her husband so he could teach her how to operate the boiler. The Pabst couple were present for the consultation as well. I felt very important, indeed, down there in the cellar since all this gathering was for the sole purpose of providing me with proper heat. From then on Frau Hartung arrived before dawn each morning. Sounds in my radiator upstairs let me know when she lit the fire; it was my signal to rise. Then she moved to the kitchen to make my coffee; she brought along milk and rolls. While I breakfasted, she put the study in order so that I could get at the desk immediately afterwards. For a while longer I heard her move about in the bedroom next door. Then she took her leave, and I was alone for the rest of the day.

Often the bell downstairs would ring on business which concerned the Courants. When I did not know what to do, I called Breslau for directions. Otherwise I handled matters as seemed best to me. Nelli was very grateful for everything; and her father declared that as long as I was in Göttingen, she needed no agent there. She often asked that I send her some of her things; even more frequently, I believe, Richard requested something. I always filled such requests as quickly as possible; and one day, Richard wrote that, as he received everything far more promptly from me than from Breslau, he would in future turn to me for anything he needed. The things he requested were sometimes astounding; and to find them, pack them, and get them off cost me a lot of time and trouble. But I was glad to be able to do something for him. Pauline Reinach was amazed that Nelli consented to being supplanted like that. But I was convinced she felt only gratitude at my saving her the trouble. She was so very clumsy and made such a fuss about everything that these things would have taken her even more time than they took me.

The shortest way into town from Schillerstrasse was across the *Albanikirchhof* and along the *Feuerteich*. One day not long after my arrival, as I was on my way home and had reached the pond, I noticed a lady walking ahead of me, whose green coat was familiar to me. She had just turned into the Hainholzweg which went in the direction opposite the one I would have to take. Then she turned around and upon seeing me, stopped to wait for me. It was Erika Gothe. Of those in the closer Husserl circle, we two alone had returned to Göttingen. So, obviously, we should now join forces. She was just on the way to Frau Gronerweg's on the Hainholzweg for her noon meal. That day I had already eaten, but from then on I was to go there with her. Pauline Reinach was at Gronerweg's for room and board. The apartment on the *Steinsgraben* was closed; Frau Reinach was in Stuttgart with her mother. Soon I felt as much at home in the house on Hainholzweg as in Schillerstrasse. I went there only at noon. At suppertime I took care of myself. Regularly once a week I received a small package from home. When my mother braided the *challah*, the Sabbath bread, in the prescribed manner on Friday mornings, she always made a small one for me (one each, also, for the children and grandchildren in Hamburg) and at noon, freshly baked, they were taken to the post office. To supplement mine, a goose liver or a piece of the Sunday roast was tucked in as well.

Frau Gronerweg was an elderly woman, somewhat dispirited and embittered because times had formerly been so good for her but were now so difficult. Her husband was still alive, but he had a stroke several years earlier; now he could move only with great difficulty, could hardly speak, and was no longer of sound mind. He ate at the table with everyone else, and this was quite an imposition on any guests who were strangers. We found the sight of the old gentleman easier to take than the moodiness of the embittered lady who, obviously constantly irritated by his helplessness, labored to disguise her exasperation by her impeccable manners. Besides Pauline, there was one other regular boarder, Liane Weigelt. I knew her slightly from Husserl's seminar and the Philosophical Society. But there she had been only seen, not heard. The philosopher, Heinrich Maier, had given her a subject for a thesis in philosophy; but it was evident that philosophy was not her line. She was more talented in her other subject, the history of art. Fundamentally, though, she was no scholar. She had a knack for making a home comfortable; that was discernible in her student's lodgings in the romantic garden cottage on Gronerweg's property. She was also good at pampering others and letting herself be pampered. Unfortunately, she had neither parents nor brothers or sisters and was actually all alone in the world. So she must have had greater expectations of the friendships she formed than the other party would have; and, consequently, she was frequently disappointed.

Pauline Reinach showed a loving concern for her. Pauline's study was, on the whole, the main focal point for all of us. After the noon meal, we usually congregated there for a little while: Erika, Liane, and I. Sometimes we were even joined by the officer who was in charge of the Fort; he also had lunch with us daily. As a Captain of the National Guard, his duty was training recruits in Göttingen; and while there, he lodged with Frau Gronerweg. He was an older married man; nevertheless, he felt very much at home in our company. We always had so much to discuss in those days: the events of the war, the news from the front, as well as our studies. How happy we were when a military postcard, or even better, a letter, arrived from Reinach! He was stationed in the vicinity of Verdun. In one letter he once sent each of us a snowdrop. He had picked them himself, and they were still fresh when they arrived. Erika and I had gotten the military addresses of our fellow students, and we began sending them food packages. Letters in response came from Hering, Lipps, and Kaufmann. That autumn also brought the first casualties from our circle: Fritz Frankfurter and Rudolf Clemens. Frankfurter's mother lived in Breslau; when the war began, her daughter, Magda Frei, went to live with her. Magda was a medical doctor married to a doctor in Göttingen who was also in the service. After the war the Freis moved to Breslau and made it their permanent residence. Toni Meyer was a friend of both Frau Frankfurter and Frau Dr. Frei; and she urged me to visit them when I went back to Breslau. For years, the two were inconsolable over the loss of their only son and brother. My visit meant a great deal to them and so did the contact they established through me with the circle in which their Fritz had been so happy. They gave me his war diary to read and his entire literary legacy to review. Most of all, they would have wanted to see his works published posthumously; but that I was unable to accomplish.

Erika's brother, Hans Gothe, was also at the front. He and a younger brother Georg were the children of her father's second wife; she and her sister Lene were from his first marriage. The father had long since died, but his second wife was truly a mother to Erika; and the bond with her brothers was also a very close one. I never got to see Frau Gothe or her house in Schwerin; but, through Erika's stories, both had become very familiar to me. Frau Gothe was a very devout Protestant; and the warmth radiating from her goodness reached us.

Despite the oppressive anxiety caused by the war, this winter may well have been the happiest time of all my Göttingen student years. The friendship with Pauline and Erika had more depth and beauty than my former student friendships. For the first time, I was not the one to lead or to be sought after; but rather I saw in the others something better and higher than myself.

I also resumed my studies [for the oral examinations] with the same two companions. When Fräulein Scharf and I now met in my comfortable study of an evening, we diligently knitted stockings and other warm items for the boys in gray. The needlework instructions I had as a child had not taught me much of the art, and I had long ago forgotten what little I had picked up from them. Now I learned it anew from my dextrous companion, and our needles clicked busily while we discussed and memorized our history lessons.

Certain evenings were set aside for studying philosophy with Erika. To make a final review, she gave me three pages on which Hering had outlined the history of philosophy. He himself and Frankfurter had already used it for their state boards; and we had now inherited it. The final entry on it noted the beginning of phenomenology; next to this was written the comment: "End of all other philosophy."

Pauline had arranged a work session between Liane and myself, and she herself sometimes read Homer with me. If two of Frau Gronerweg's boarders had an invitation for their evening meal elsewhere, I invited the third to come to my place so she would not have to dine alone with the old lady. I was then more generous when I shopped for food than I would have been ordinarily, and I would dress up the small round table as beautifully as I could. Anything required to do that was sure to be in the house; and Nelli was glad when I used her belongings. The chest in the bedroom was crammed full of lovely linens; and if I hankered for a pretty fruit bowl or a silver cake basket, I had but to go down to the dining room and reach into the huge buffet; no matter what I needed, it could be found there.

Husserl's seminar had very few students that winter. At first
the philologist, Günther Müller, was the only old acquaintance
present. Then, during the semester, Roman Ingarden,[149] a
Pole, returned. He had been in the Polish Legion but had to
leave it because of a heart defect. Formerly he had associated
chiefly with his compatriots. Now alone, he was happy when he
could talk for a while with us. Two newcomers had shown up.
One of them, Helmut Plessner, was setting out purposefully on
an academic career with philosophy as his major.[150] I also met
him at times outside the university setting. Substituting for Frau
Dr. Reinach and for Nelli Courant, I had taken over the office
of Vocational Counselor for the women students. This position
had been established by the *Frauenbildung-Frauenstudium
Verein* [Society for Women's Education-Women's Studies]. The
job put me in contact with the society's president, Frau Steinberg. When Herr Plessner's parents gave him an introduction to
Judge and Frau Steinberg, the friendly couple were delighted;
and thereafter, they would invite the two of us for lunch or for
supper. They paid close attention as the two philosophers carried on a rather unintelligible conversation while enjoying the
roast goose. Later I found myself smiling as I thought of those
invitations. My recollection, with probable justification, led me
to suspect the jurist's kindly wife had hoped her hospitality
would result in a match between the young couple. But that was
far and away the last thought either of us had. As Herr Plessner
accompanied me from their fine old townhouse in the heart of
town to the Schillerstrasse, he would outline his "system" for
me, attempting to explain on which points he took exception to
Husserl; but he still lacked the gift of making himself understood.

A few weeks before Christmas, we prepared our Christmas
packages for the servicemen. The gifts had been chosen most
lovingly, the finest treats available collected from various bakeries. In each large package we put numerous small ones, individually wrapped in pretty paper and tied with colorful silk ribbons. Reinach was to receive all those that had the gold ribbons;
Kaufmann, the violet ones; Hans Gothe, who belonged to the
youth movement, was to have those tied in peasant banding

sporting colorful flowers on a black background. The outer wrapping gave us the greatest difficulty: everything had to be sewn up in burlap. We were stretched out on the floor in Pauline's room, until past midnight, to accomplish this requirement in the most expert fashion. Then on my way home alone through the dark cemetery, I met an officer also walking among the graves, probably en route to the nearby barracks. Nonplussed at meeting me, he said as he passed me, "Well! Have you got courage!"

Back home, I read the *Frankfurter Zeitung* ["The Frankfurt News"] which at that time I studied thoroughly each day, and I glanced at my books for a while. Only then did I allow myself some rest that night.

I had submitted my theses that November and had asked for the earliest date possible for the oral examination. It was scheduled for the fourteenth and fifteenth of January. Only my closest friends in Göttingen were told about it; my letters home contained no mention of it. As few people as possible should get excited over it. I intended to stay in Göttingen over Christmas. Of course, all the others went home; and Liane, who had no home, was going to visit friends. One evening, before their departure, I heard numerous footsteps coming up my stairway; Pauline, Erika, and Liane brought me a beautifully trimmed little Christmas tree. This was to console me for having to spend Christmas Eve all by myself. It was the first, decorated, small tree which I had ever received. I was happy and grateful to light the candles. Being alone was hardly depressing for me. After all I was in no way accustomed to celebrate Christmas; and so there was nothing for me to miss.

Before the examinations I had to call on the examiners. I was least acquainted with Weissenfels, the historian of literature. Since Eduard Schröder, his impressive colleague, was a Captain at the front, Weissenfels now was in charge of the advanced philology department and was its Acting Director. He had been glad to accept me when the semester began and did not require me to submit a paper for admission. He assured me that as he remembered me well from his exercises on *Faust* of the previous semester, he knew how really capable I was. This time his exercises were on Heinrich von Kleist.[151] I attended them for the first few weeks. But as I found them boring and useless, I told him that he would surely understand that so near to examination time I needed to study at home. Would he please excuse me? Shortly before I visited him, someone had told me that if one wanted to take the examination in German for the upper level and had not submitted a state board project in this subject, one was then required to write a final paper. I asked Weissenfels whether this was so; I had called on him at his Villa directly beside Husserl's on the Hohen Weg. Yes, he said, but there was nothing to be afraid of, one only had to write a short essay within three hours. I suggested one could hardly write anything worthwhile in three hours. But nothing great was expected, came the reply. It was rather a matter of demonstrating literary style. This, it occurred to me, might be achieved in an even easier way. I proposed to him that he read one of my two long theses. He found this suggestion very practical and acquiesced at once. He inquired about my themes. I told him what they were and recommended the one on history since the one in philosophy was less accessible to a non-phenomenologist. But he declared himself to be interested in precisely that theme and promised to ask Husserl for my paper. So the oral examination was simplified as much as possible.

At that time there was, besides the examination in one's specialty, another added for "general culture" which comprised philosophy, German, and religion. Since philosophy and German were my subjects, they were eliminated in my case. Nor was religion required, as Jews were not examined in that subject. Therefore, I was spared having to prove I had "general culture." I needed only to be examined in my special areas; but, of course, since I wanted all the examinations to qualify me for advanced study, each of them had to take a full hour.

I chose Lessing as my special topic in German. I had put in a lot of good work on all of his books and on the course Weissenfels had given on Lessing. Granted, I had not personally attended the latter, but had the loan of a transcript of it; and my sister Frieda had typed me a copy during vacation. I also had to state which of the Middle High German epics I had read. I enumerated an impressive selection including *Meier Helmbrecht* by Wernher der Gartenaere[152] which I knew well, having studied it in a course in Breslau. It had also helped me gain acceptance for the seminar in Göttingen.

My visit with Max Lehmann was especially delightful. The old man was having a particularly difficult time in Göttingen just then. As an old-time liberal and an enthusiastic anglophile, he was deeply pained by the war with England. The horrid habit of using "God punish England!" as a greeting had taken hold in certain circles at that time. It upset him afresh whenever he heard it used. He was just about the only one with such convictions among the faculty, and his colleagues ostracized him. He openly discussed all this with me. His sole consolation was his seminar. Life would hardly be bearable were it not for those beautiful Monday evenings. He was just as outspoken in his criticism of the German government's attitude.

"However, we won't be discussing these topics on Friday," he said when I took my leave.

"Oh, but these would be far more congenial for me than the others," I answered with a smile.

He had made notations on my calling card about my special subjects. During the examination he held that card in his hand to keep himself on track. I had become aware that I was supposed to have a special topic for Greek and Roman history only because Lehmann inquired about it. But I was not to be daunted and quickly named the Punic and Persian wars since I remembered these crucial battles most clearly from my school days. As we had read Livy for years, the Punic wars were especially familiar to me. To refresh my knowledge and to get a broad overview, I diligently read Mommsen's Roman history in the days which followed.

The morning of the first day of my exams I confided to Frau Hartung how anxious I was. She plunked all her ponderous self down on the chaise longue once again and gave me a pep talk. Because of the work she did, she knew just about everyone on the faculty; she was regularly employed by Frau Weissenfels.

"Weissenfels won't let you flunk," she assured me categorically. "And with Husserl you can't go wrong; that's for sure."

The examination in German was to begin at five o'clock on

Thursday afternoon, January 14. I went to Gronerwegs' for lunch. The table conversation with all those people got on my nerves so much that my companions decided that on the following day Erika would cook for me at my place. She cheerfully agreed she would make all the necessary purchases and then get busy in the shining, attractive kitchen.

The examination was held in the humanistic *Gymnasium* with its principal, Herr Miller, as the formidable chairman of the examination commission. On that first day, I did not get to see him at all. I was taking my tests all alone; at the same time, in other classrooms, other candidates would be taking turns in their specialty. Together we waited in a common room assigned for that purpose. Weissenfels himself came to get me at five o'clock. Another member of the examining commission should have been present as proctor. As no one came, he proceeded on his own. He took out a small book: the Middle High German text. What would it be? *Meier Helmbrecht.* I had to take myself in hand not to betray my joy.

I read and translated fluently and was able to answer all his questions regarding grammar as well. Now we began to take a stroll through German literature. I was to indicate the later development of the Middle High German epics. That gave me an opportunity to talk about the books of folk literature. Then we arrived at the *Faust* theme and the various ways it had been handled. As I was about to say something about Lessing's *Faust* fragment, Weissenfels interrupted.

"I know you gave Lessing as your special topic, but I would rather ask you a few questions about Romanticism."

"Please do," I replied with calm resignation.

By the time I had answered these additional questions, the hour was up. My friendly examiner wished me good luck and said he was glad I had made such a fine beginning in the examination.

The one in philosophy was set from eleven to twelve on Friday morning. This time Chairman Miller was to be Proctor. I knew this made Husserl very uncomfortable; since he feared an accusation might be made that he was too lenient with his students, he was very exacting in his examination. For a full hour he asked questions on the history of philosophy. I had read a great deal of Plato, but now, of all things, he chose *Timaeus* which I had only heard in presentations. I did not dare say so for fear of embarrassing my good Master in the presence of the strict chairman. So I began rather boldly to construct the thought process of the dialogue by using the questions he put to me as my point of departure. I did likewise when I was asked for particulars about the varying point of view David Hume expressed on mathematics in his *Essay* and in his *Treatise*. The *Essay* I had not read at all, the *Treatise* only partially, but undaunted, I proceeded to make a comparison. I even enjoyed these feats of mental acrobatics; but they demanded tremendous effort; and I was glad when Husserl finally switched to logic. To conclude, he asked a few harmless questions about the history of pedagogy. I had been made to hold the fort an hour-and-a-quarter.

As I walked along the narrow path through the meadow from the *Albanikirchhof* to Schillerstrasse, I saw Erika leaning out of the kitchen window—half of her over the sill, both arms waving at me. Lunch was ready, an admirable success; the little table was beautifully set for the two of us. While we fortified ourselves at it, I had to give a faithful replay of the battle from beginning to end.

I was pretty well exhausted but as yet had no time to give in to tiredness since the last act, the history examination, was to begin at five that afternoon. This time Weissenfels was to be proctor. As he was a bit late, Lehmann took the Greek text to begin with. As usual, it was the opening of the *Anabasis*, which I knew by heart. As Weissenfels entered, the examiner greeted him with the words: "The lady is well informed in Greek."

"The lady is well informed in general," came the genial, laughing response. Then we continued.

A short question about the Persian wars. Then I got somewhat of a surprise.

"What do you consider to have been Hannibal's greatest feat?" I had never even thought about that. I did not know that it was a favorite question of his; nor was I aware that Lehmann expected the reply would be, "Crossing the Alps."

I reflected for a moment. Then, "That he moved the theater of war to Italy," I answered with great conviction.

Now it was Lehmann's turn to be surprised. From my response he perceived I had not taken the precaution of procuring a collection of former test questions with the respective answers so as to memorize them but was, instead, artlessly reflecting and expressing my own opinion. So he accepted my reply; but by interpolating a small question, he led me back to the crossing of the Alps. I knew all about that from reading Livy. The old story was but a prologue. We now turned to Lehmann's own special areas from which I had selected mine. Again I was in for a surprise opening.

"What about the accusation of militarism levelled against Prussia?"

I thought, "How neat! He has remembered that when I visited him I remarked that it would be more pleasant to discuss politics than to be examined."

But the question itself was a touchy one. It sounded like a summons to criticize the existing situation, and I did not like that. So I began my reply with some diplomacy.

"That depends upon what one understands by militarism."

Weissenfels laughed out loud. Lehmann, however, quietly gave me his definition: keeping a standing army during peacetime constitutes militarism. Given this premise, I could now unhesitatingly say that in this sense Prussia could be accused of militarism. I was asked to give the reasons why hitherto, in England, there had been so much opposition to militarism. Now we were in smooth waters, and we proceeded stroke upon stroke until it was six o'clock.

Pauline Reinach was waiting for me outside. She first took me to the *Kron und Lanz* ["The Crown and Lance"] for coffee and cake to revive me after winning the battle. Landau, a mathematician, and Katz, a psychologist, [153] were seated at a neighboring table. Katz came to our table after a few minutes. He said that Professor Landau had just told him he had seen me in the *Gymnasium* a few minutes earlier, so I must have been taking examinations. Now he wanted to congratulate me at once. I was delighted, of course. That evening I was to eat at Gronerwegs'. En route there, most likely from the small post office in the Wendenstrasse, I sent the good news to Breslau by telegram. Pauline had to entertain me for a while in her room since Erika and Liane had not finished their preparations in the dining room. When we were finally called to table, I found at my place numerous, small, burning tapers mounted on one of those round, painted, wooden frames used for birthday cakes. It was encircled by small bunches of violets. Frau Gronerweg had provided a festive meal. Erika sat opposite me, and her dark eyes sparkled for love and joy.

The next day I went to Hamburg. Just at that time my sister Rosa was staying with Else for a few weeks, and both were glad I had come to share my joy with them. The congratulations from Breslau reached me here as well. My mother's letter contained that phrase I mentioned earlier: she would be even happier were I to be mindful of the One to whom I owed this success. But for me it had not come to that yet.

In Göttingen I had learned to respect questions of faith and persons who had faith. With some of my women friends, I even went to one of the Protestant churches at times. (The sermons there, habitually mixing politics with religion, naturally could not lead me to a knowledge of pure faith; and they often turned me off.) I had not yet found a way back to God.

I intended to make my visit [in Hamburg] a brief one. I had arrived on Saturday; and on Wednesday afternoon, I was back on hand, punctually, for Husserl's seminar. He had always considered regular attendance at his exercises important; and now, he insisted on this even more so since so few of his older students remained. I had not seen him since the examination. After class I went to his office to ask him when I might come to see him for more particulars about my thesis.

The Master, ordinarily so friendly, was noticeably bad tempered on this occasion. I had committed the faux pas of not going to see him immediately after the examination. Now he explained to me that he had meant to say a great deal about my thesis at that time but by now he had forgotten it. Certainly, it would not suffice for a doctoral dissertation. (Such an idea had never even entered my mind.)

Since I had done so well in history and literature, perhaps I should now reflect whether I would not rather get my doctorate in either of those subjects.

He could not have hurt me more deeply.

"Herr Professor," I told him with high indignation, "I have no intention of finding some convenient project with which to get a doctorate. I want to prove to myself whether I am capable of an independent achievement in philosophy."

That evidently brought him to his senses. His anger disappeared immediately. His tone of voice changed entirely.

"First of all, Fräulein Stein, you need to get some relaxation. You look completely exhausted."

Not to be mollified so easily, I took my leave.

The following day, he waited for me at the door of the classroom after his lecture; he wanted to tell me that his wife, along with her best regards wished to extend an invitation for coffee the following Sunday afternoon. After all, my passing the examination had to be celebrated in some fashion. The other Fräuleins—Gothe, Reinach, and Weigelt—were also being invited. If I would like to bring anyone else, I need only let her know.

Before Sunday came, I also paid my farewell visits to Lehmann and Weissenfels. Both again assured me of their satisfaction with me. Weissenfels let slip to me that the chairman of the commission had opposed the distinction "with highest honors" on grounds that having been excused from the examination in general culture, I had had an easy time of it. The examiners, however, wanted to insist that I receive a "1."

On Sunday, Husserl laughingly assured me: "It's a fact: as a result of both written and oral examinations the report included the notation: "Passed with Highest Honors."

Chapter VIII

Nursing Soldiers
in the Lazaretto
at Mährisch-Weisskirchen
-1915-

1

Shortly after the [state board] examination, I wrote to the Red Cross in Breslau asking whether I could now enter the nursing service. As no reply came, I chose to stay in Göttingen for what remained of the semester, to attend the rest of the lectures, and to devote whatever time was left over to my work on the doctorate. I began again to brush up my Greek as I intended to take the *Graecum* [an examination in that subject] as soon as possible. But I shipped all my belongings home before I left this time, as I considered it uncertain whether I would be returning.

Soon after I was back in Breslau, I registered at the district board of education for that supplementary examination in Greek; I wanted to take it in the autumn. I had been home for several weeks when I received a telephone call; a lady from the Red Cross wished to speak to me. She told me there was still no opening for nurses in Germany, but there was a great demand for them in Austria. Were I willing to go there, I should be ready to report to Mährisch-Weisskirchen[154] at the beginning of April. My mind was made up immediately.

318

Rose Guttmann had already heard about the lazaretto[155] in Weisskirchen since a student from Breslau had been nursing there for several months. This student, Grete Bauer, happened to be home on leave just then. I looked her up to get more details. Mährisch-Weisskirchen was halfway along the train route from Oderberg to Vienna and could be reached from our place by express train in five to six hours. It had a huge military academy which had been transformed into a lazaretto: four thousand beds for those under the military command of the Carpathian front. The little student, a lively, spontaneous young person was very happy to serve there; she was due to return even before my departure date and was glad to go back.

I had heavy opposition to face from my mother. I did not even tell her it was a lazaretto [i.e., for those with contagious diseases]. She was well aware that no suggestion of hers that my life would be endangered could ever induce me to change my plans. So as an ultimate deterrent, she told me all the soldiers arrived from the front with clothes overrun by lice and that I could not possibly escape infestation. Naturally that was a scourge I dreaded—but if the people in the trenches all had to suffer from it why should I be better off than they? (A note: the delousing in Weisskirchen was organized so well that I was spared this ordeal. Occasionally I did find some of the little creatures on people's linens, indeed on washed pieces just taken out of closets.)

When this tactic failed, my mother declared with all the energy she could muster: "You will not go with my permission."

My reply was every bit as determined. "Then I must go without your permission."

My sisters were downright shocked at my harsh retort. My mother was totally unaccustomed to such opposition. True, Arno or Rosa may often have used harsher language with her. But that happened only in the heat of anger while they were beside themselves and was soon forgotten again. Now, however, granite was striking granite. My mother said no more and was very silent and depressed for several days, a mood which always affected the entire household. But when subsequently I began making my preparations, she, as a matter of course, undertook to provide the complete nurse's outfit called for. Frieda, who was the most knowledgeable about such things, had to make all the purchases and do all the sewing required.

Before I started my wartime service, I had to visit the district board of education to withdraw my registration for the *Graecum*, or, rather, to tell them I would have to postpone the date indefinitely. Privy Councillor [*Geheimrat*] Thalheim,[156] the chief administrative officer of the humanistic *Gymnasiums,* was a formidable gentleman, serious as well as strict. When he heard the reason for the postponement he showed his dissatisfaction but said nothing at first. However, as I was on my way out he called me back.

"Have your parents agreed to this?"

"My father died long ago. My mother does not like it at all."

He became quite agitated at that. (He himself had a daughter my own age. I knew her from school.)

"Of course she does not like it! As things are, I have no right to express an opinion. But since you no longer have a father, I do feel obliged to warn you. Do you know what goes on in a lazaretto?"

I did *not* know; but if, as he indicated, one was in moral danger and the nurses had a bad reputation, then that was indeed dreadfully sad; but then I found it even more essential that persons with a serious attitude should go to work there. And so I thanked the Councillor sincerely, for certainly he had manifested a great deal of goodness since he was so concerned about me; but I would permit nothing to divert me from my course.

Shortly before my departure, I met Susanne Mugdan at Nelli Courant's. She was a friend of Richard's; during his years as a student, her mother had accepted and cared for him as for a son though she had two sons and two daughters of her own. Bertha, the elder daughter, had later married Richard's friend, Julius Stenzel, a philologist in ancient languages. Julius and Albrecht, Suse's twin brother, were now at the front. She herself was serious and brooding, a very fragile and deeply sensitive person. After passing the teacher's examination, Suse had taught for some time. But, not entirely satisfied with that, she has returned for her *Abitur* and was now studying chemistry at the engineering school in Breslau. When she heard what I intended to do, she saw it as an admonition to make herself available also. Not many weeks after I left, she followed me to Weisskirchen.

Before my departure, Erna had me come to the Gynecological Hospital where she gave me the inoculations against typhoid and cholera. Many people had a bad reaction to them, becoming really ill and feverish; but I had no trouble at all.

The lazarettos in Bohemia and Moravia were for the most part staffed by German nurses. The Professional Organization of German Nurses had undertaken to set them up, and the Silesian Red Cross supplied them with aides. A lady in Breslau, Fräulein Gertrud Stein, was in charge of these arrangements. She came to see me off at the station as I left on the seventh of April, 1915, at six o'clock in the morning. She introduced me to my two co-workers from Saxony who were to travel to Weisskirchen with me. She handed us our insignia: the enamel brooch of the aides, a black bow with a red cross on a white field in its center. My two companions from Saxony were young girls, one from a good middle-class family, the other of more modest circumstances. If I remember correctly, both lived at home and had no profession. Naturally we were all excited about practicing our new duties. We reached our destination by noon. We hired a coach at the station to take us to the lazaretto, which was located a good distance outside of town. Mährisch-Weisskirchen was a neat little town. The stone *Lauben,* arcades at the marketplace, were familiar to me from the old towns of Silesia and Bohemia. Under the arches, tables pushed out from the stores behind them displayed the wares for sale. Our coach halted at the door of a long drawn out building. Three large houses immediately adjoining one another lined the county road. It took about ten minutes to walk along the entire frontage. In peacetime it had been an academy for the cavalry, with a residence for its officers, and a high school for the cadets. At the back, two riding academies were attached, one was large, and the other small. In addition, new barracks to serve as a lazaretto had been built. (I do not remember exactly how many, whether ten or twenty.) Each of these barracks housed two wards of fifty beds apiece.

First of all, we were taken to the dining hall to have a hearty dinner. Most of the nurses had already eaten. Only a few strag-

glers had stayed behind. They asked whether we had brought
any mail along for them. Fräulein Stein had indeed entrusted
some letters to us. We laid them on the grand piano, and the re-
cipients picked out their own. This forwarding of letters through
nurses traveling back and forth was a standing arrangement
since, sent by ordinary channels, much mail got lost or delayed
for weeks. Of course, this manner of evading the censorship
which existed between the allied countries was strictly forbidden. But apparently no one paid any heed to this prohibition.

If I remember correctly, after dinner we were shown to our
sleeping quarters. An aide who happened to be in the corridor
was asked to take me along. In a large dormitory, she showed
me an unassigned bed. I could make myself at home there. Other
than that, in the few minutes she could spare me, she told me I
would probably catch the flu, that almost everyone got it in the
beginning.

The notion of getting sick in these surroundings was far from
appealing. More congenial was the impression we received
when Matron[157] finally found time to greet us. She summoned
us to her office. This was a light, large room. With its solid desk
and floral decorations, it had a peacetime look about it. Sister
Margarete[158] was a small but sturdy little person, a little more
than thirty years old. The face peering out from under the white
cap was kind and friendly; her manner, simple and natural,
undemanding, but firm and determined. Before the war she
had been a community nurse in a rural district in Silesia. Like
most of the nurses here, she belonged to the Professional Organization. With a minimum of helpers, she had set up this lazaretto
under most difficult circumstances. Before she had even had
the bare essentials on hand, the first transport of cholera patients
had arrived. Now she had a flock of a hundred and fifty nurses
and aides to supervise; and she labored also under difficult
working relationships with a Czech Director, with the doctors,
and the military command. The people in the area could not be
counted on for any support. Almost exclusively, they were Czech
and anti-German. If we spoke German when asking anyone directions on the street we got no answer. Because German nurses
were attached to it, the lazaretto seldom received any donations

from the local inhabitants. We had to depend on whatever was sent us from home. While we cared for their wounded, the Weiss-kirchen girls sat, all dolled up, in the resort park listening to a concert.

Sister Margarete took a moment to reflect where she should employ the new aides. She assigned me to the typhoid ward. By telephone she announced to the large Riding Academy that I had arrived. I no longer remember who took me there. Leaving by the back door we passed by the small Riding Academy to reach the large one. It was a one-story building, actually nothing other than very roomy barracks. Just inside the front entrance, the first room on the left was a small one for the use of the physician on night duty; next to it was a room for the nurses. To the right of the entrance were found the bathroom and a small ward for any patients whose contagious disease required isolation from the others. Two doors opposite the entrance led to the two front wards. Beyond them were two more. For each ward there was a small office for the Chief Resident and one for the Ward Sister, as well as a small tea-kitchen. Each of the two front wards accommodated sixty seriously-ill typhoid patients. Each of the rear wards housed fifty-eight. Recuperating patients were transferred to the barracks.

Each ward had its own doctor, two registered nurses, and two aides; besides that, two maids (local girls), and an orderly handled the domestic chores.

Councillor Boral was Chief of the entire typhoid station, and Sister Anna was the Ward Sister. I was taken to the first ward, where I was to be one of the aides, and was introduced to the nurses.

Warmhearted and talkative Sister Loni, a small, plump woman from the Rhineland, had a markedly red face and somewhat blurred features. Sister Emma, tall and slim, though usually restrained, was at times given to passionate outbursts. The Sisters greeted me cordially. I was given a white medical gown which was to cover both my nursing uniform and its white, bibbed apron. We removed the gown whenever we left the typhoid station, minimizing the chance of carrying bacilli to other areas. Also, a basin filled with a disinfectant solution was kept in each ward; one dipped one's hands into this every time one had touched a patient. Altogether, disinfectants were in liberal use everywhere. Soiled laundry was at once put into large tubs containing a Lysol solution.

It was a matter of pride that outbreaks of new infection very seldom occurred in the lazaretto. The saying went that if Matron herself were ever to become infected, she would die not from the typhoid but from the disgrace. Typhoid bacilli are not transmitted by the breath but only through the excretions of the patients. Contact with these, of course, cannot be avoided while caring for patients. But if one is careful about washing immediately, one is safe; infection, therefore, is a sign of lack of cleanliness.

Steffi, the second aide, was a little Polish girl, fragile, blond, and melancholy. There were several Polish women in the lazaretto who were either refugees from the Galizian war sector or "soldiers" from the Polish Legion. In the neighboring ward, for instance, there was a tiny female corporal. Having been wounded, she was subsequently assigned to serve in the lazaretto although she had not been trained to do nursing. Steffi also lacked any prior training. I had the advantage in that respect. Even so, our courses had lasted but a month after which I had put in about six weeks of practical work; nevertheless, that was all six months ago. I had never yet seen a typhoid patient; I had only textbook knowledge about the causes, symptoms, and the course of the illness. So, of course, to begin with, I had to learn all about the work and I probably made some mistakes, too. I remember only one of these; in passing, I noticed one patient whose teeth were chattering from a chill. I fixed a hot-water bottle at once and put it at his feet. Even the patient laughed at that—he happened to be lying in cold packs.

Soon after my arrival, Sister Loni gave me a tour of the entire ward, showing me all the equipment, and informing me about the patients. She called my attention particularly to the patient most seriously ill at the time. He was a young Italian businessman from Trieste. They called him by his first name only. As that name refuses to come to my mind now, I shall call him Mario. His was an unusually severe case of the illness. His mouth was constantly filled with a mucus which was frequently blood-stained. Sister Loni told me I was to cleanse his mouth with a small cloth whenever I passed by his bed. A look from him always expressed his gratitude for this small service of love. Talking was totally impossible for him; he had completely lost his voice. On every round he was given a thorough examination. The doctor would then discuss his case with the nurses at the bedside as though Mario were unable to understand a word. But, by his large, brilliant eyes, I noticed he clearly understood and eagerly awaited each word. Usually he lay there very quietly, following us, however, with his eyes. The other febrile patients were nearly all in a slight stupor, noticing nothing of all that was going on about them. One tended them as one would little children, and was then amazed when, weeks later, they recovered awareness and behaved like real people. The typhoid was receding for many, but they were suffering from side effects. Pneumonia and pleurisy were frequent complications and claimed more victims than the typhoid itself. Because of the Carpathian winter, some also had frost-bitten feet which had to be treated.

While we were on that first tour through the ward, the doctor arrived for his rounds and was introduced to me. Still quite young, he was short and squat, light-blond and rosy-complexioned. After a few friendly words, he declared: "Traveling will have made Sister tired. Let us eliminate her for today."

In the meantime a case of spotted typhus had been discovered in one of the other wards. This was considered a very serious matter. The disease was usually fatal, and the risk of infection high; it was next to impossible to guard against it since the carrier had not yet been discovered. An order came from Matron that the nurses of the typhoid station were to associate as little as possible with the others. All were to be quartered in the large Riding Academy. So I had to move my baggage again from the large dormitory where I had left it but a few hours earlier. I had a hard time finding my way through the endless expanse of buildings. But I was quite content that I would be spared sleeping there, that I need not pass through long halls and then up and down a series of stairs to reach my station early each morning. In the Riding Academy, I shared a bedroom with three others: our Sister Emma, Sister Sophie from Ward III, and her aide, Marga. These two were bosom friends even though Marga was only eighteen years old and her superior probably some ten years older. The environment here seemed to me to be a dangerous one for the youngster. Sister Sophie, like most of those from the *B.O.*, [*Berufliche Organization*: Professional Organization of Nurses] was very capable and careful where her work was concerned. But her head and heart were filled with love's anguish—over the Staff Resident, as was to be expected; and all the conversations in our room were on this subject. I shut my ears to it as much as I could; in my free time, which had to be spent in that room, I sat on my bed as though it were a separate room. There I read and wrote my letters; and I accomplished whatever else needed to be done.

Despite the quarantine of our station, we ate in the general mess hall. There, probably that first evening, I saw Grete Bauer, the student from Breslau. It was a real blessing for me just to be able to say a few words to her. She introduced me to her friend, Sister Alwine, a registered nurse belonging to the *B.O.* Though a good bit older than we, she was still youthful and of a lively temperament. Blond curls peeped out from under her little cap and her big, blue eyes glowed with the joy of living. Nonetheless, one noticed immediately that she was an intelligent and highly capable person.

A few days after my arrival, the station hummed with talk about a "celebration" to be held in the large Riding Academy. The doctor from Ward II was being transferred to another lazaretto, and he had invited all his colleagues and the nurses of the typhoid station for a farewell party in the small doctors' staff lounge. He was a young Polish nobleman, but I have forgotten his name. I had noticed him only in passing and had never spoken a word with him.

Dr. Pick, our resident doctor, said to me when he made his rounds, "Sister Edith, you're coming tomorrow evening, too, aren't you?"

"I have no intention of going. After all, I don't even know the gentleman."

"So what? You'll get to know him there."

Nurses' Free Time Activities at the Lazaretto
(Edith seated on left and Greta Bauer standing on right)

I had very little desire to go; after all, we were not here to have a good time. But I asked Sister Loni for advice. She was the eldest in the ward and my superior. At the same time she took pride in her good, middle-class background, and in her impeccable morals. She advised me to go. It would cause some resentment were I to exclude myself on the very first occasion. Actually, she herself would not be coming; but when they had celebrated the arrival of the one thousandth typhoid patient a short time before, she had attended; on that occasion even the medical director had been present. Celebrating typhoid patient one thousand! My hair nearly stood on end. But I decided to follow her advice.

When we entered the small doctors' lounge the next evening, I grew a bit uneasy. A long table had been set up. On it, several tortes, some bowls of fruit, and a whole battery of liquor bottles had been arranged. My place was about in the center opposite Dr. Pick. When the refreshments were passed around I took a piece of torte and some grapes. As I never drank alcohol, I would not let them pour me a drink. At first, the new nurse seemed to attract a great deal of attention. So far I had never said anything to anyone about my "civilian profession." But perhaps Matron had mentioned something about it in the presence of one of the doctors, and word of it had gotten to the officers' mess. In any case, the gentlemen now inquired what I had studied.

"Philosophy."

That might mean anything. For the Austrians, "Philosophy" included a whole range: languages, history, etc. Anyone specializing in the subject would have used the term "exact philosophy."

Oh, well, then: "Exact philosophy."

They professed great amazement. But the taste for "cultured entertainment" soon faded. The more often the liquor glasses were emptied, the freer the tone became. Finally I sat there in silence, watching wide-eyed all that was going on around me. One doctor held one of the nurses, who wanted no more to drink, by the head and poured liquor into her. I became more and more uneasy. What all might follow? Suddenly I heard that behind me someone was speaking softly to me.

I turned around in surprise. Back of my chair stood the Polish nobleman whose guests we were. We had been introduced to one another early in the evening, but thereafter I had taken no more notice of him. He was very upset.

"Sister, what must you be thinking of me?"

I was greatly disconcerted. How could I reply?

"I won't form any opinion on the basis of this one evening," I said, reassuringly.

Apparently, the two of us were the only sober ones in the room. Most likely, he had been observing me and could read my feelings on my face. He was obviously pained to see me in such a situation. I thought of the kindly Councillor Thalheim; was there then, generally, open season regarding the nurses?

There was no escape. Nor could my titled protector get me out of the predicament. Soon thereafter someone suggested going for a walk in the garden which was shrouded in night. It seemed to me I would be safer staying with the crowd than remaining alone in the Riding Academy. After all, I could not go to the room I shared with others and lock myself in while they were still out. In the garden everyone got in line. Sister Elsbeth, a pretty brunette, took me by the arm and drew me along with her. This was something I could be thankful for since it put me in a relatively safe place, at least, and I had someone to lead me. Before that evening, I had found no time to go walking in the garden and would have been helplessly lost in the dark. Suddenly they were going through a door. It was the "Faust House." The attractive villa where the doctors lived was so named because Margareta von Skoda, the aide, was also lodged there. (Skoda was the Austrian "Krupp.")[159] Before I knew what was happening, we were all inside the room of the doctor who was on night duty. He was in bed and awoke with a start when everyone crashed in. He seemed by no means displeased by the joke. Also, he soon noticed the new face and asked who I might be. I was shoved to the front to be introduced. I curtsied like a school child. I deemed it best to make a lark out of the whole business and disappeared behind the others again. There the Polish nobleman reappeared at my side.

"Come," he said, "I will lead you back."

We went downstairs and returned to the Riding Academy in silence. The others were not far behind. At the entrance I thanked my companion and took leave of him. Now, for a quick dash into our bedroom! But there another unpleasant surprise awaited me. Dr. von Malsburg (an older, married man) had gotten in and had created "havoc in the bedroom." He had piled all the chairs on top of one another and spread a black cover over them. Now, he declared, he would take our pictures. And Sister Elsbeth and the doctor on her ward, Dr. Aldor, had also withdrawn to our room. There was no alternative but to wait patiently for the party to break up. When, finally, the unwelcome guests had all left the room, it was still quite a while before Sister Sophie and Marga returned. Only then could I lock the door and go to bed in peace.

Nothing had happened to me, nor had anyone said even so much as one improper word to me. But still trembling from revulsion, I was indignant that such behavior could go on under the very roof that harbored such critically ill persons. It had been out of the question to seek refuge in one of the wards. We were not to enter them when we were off duty.

The following day all the nurses who had been at the party (only the professional nurses, not the aides) were called to Matron's office. They probably received a severe reprimand. I was worried what Sister Margarete might think of me. After all, she had spoken to me only for those few minutes on my first day. Aware that Grete Bauer often got to see her, I begged Grete to tell her how embarrassing my involvement in the situation had been for me.

I received a very kind reply: Matron wanted me to know she heartily regretted my getting such an unpleasant impression so soon after my arrival.

2

A few weeks later the Polish nobleman, now at his new assignment, came to pay us one more visit. He arrived just as I was accompanying Dr. Pick on his rounds. Across one of the beds, he inquired, "And has Sister settled in by now?"

Dr. Pick answered for me. With a laugh, he said, "Sister Edith likes being with us. Only that one evening did not please her."

That was true. I had come to like working on the typhoid station very much. It was an illness about which doctors could do very little, but a great deal depended on careful nursing attention. We were proud of the fact that so few cases proved fatal. But often wresting a victim out of death's clutches meant a tough battle. Especially when accompanied by pneumonia, a severe infection often affected the heart so drastically that it threatened to give up. The first few times I witnessed such a collapse I thought for certain the end had come. The patient appeared exactly like someone on the point of death. But I soon learned one must not give up hope even then; after an injection of camphor, the heart would begin to function again. When the danger was particularly great, we had to give an injection every hour. Since such a great strain often left the heart damaged, we had to watch the patient very carefully after the fever ebbed to prevent him from getting up and walking around too soon. One had to watch even more carefully to keep them from stealing a piece of hard bread from their neighbor. That was necessary since as long as the fever lasted, they were not permitted any solid food. Even a single bite of roughage could pierce the severely inflamed lining of the intestines, get into the abdominal cavity and cause peritonitis.

For weeks, the kitchen sent them "Formula II," i.e., mainly thin oatmeal. This, of course, was not very tempting. The beverage we were allowed to give was more acceptable: red wine diluted with a little sugar-water. Every morning the kitchen maids brought a huge kettle of it to the ward. When those patients who were most seriously ill refused all other food, we helped them over the most critical days by spoon-feeding them egg mixed with cognac. When even this was rejected, we resorted to intravenous feeding.

Following the total loss of appetite, those people who were naturally strong and robust would experience a raging, ravenous hunger once the fever had abated. "Formula III" was not yet very tempting: mashed potatoes, or "kukuruz" (corn meal mush). The most popular was "Formula IV," a normal though not coarse dinner with a good piece of veal.

Most were unenthusiastic about graduating to "Formula V". This meant getting the rough rations served to the healthy troops: nourishing and generous, but a bit monotonous. The German soldiers particularly missed potatoes and vegetables. They quickly had more than their fill of sweet desserts. Once people had improved so much that, without hesitation, one could give them as much of whatever they wanted, it was a joy to see how quickly they recovered. Then, of course, we soon had to discharge them either to one of the barracks or directly to a transport station. From there, a few days later, they left for the *Kader* (cadre, replacement battalion).

I got along well with the nurses. They carried out their duties capably and diligently, although one had the impression that in this they were motivated more by ambition than by a love for humanity. Apparently they liked me. After all, I cheerfully accepted any kind of duty entrusted to me and was always happy to substitute for the others when they had plans for something. We had a permanent arrangement that the four of us took turns having some free time between the midday meal and afternoon coffee, an interval during which, ordinarily, there was not very much work. Time off was not important to me since I had come to work, after all, not to go out walking or to sleep. But, on general principles, Sister Loni insisted that I, too, get time off for recreation. Gradually I recognized as well how necessary it was. One had to write letters; one's belongings had to be kept in order; little errands in town had to be seen to, etc. But whenever I was aware that Steffi had a headache, and that was often, I would get permission to send her to bed, and then I would take over her duty. She never said much, but she appreciated that someone took such a friendly interest in her. After all, she was a homeless refugee. Frequently during the great German advance in Galicia[160] when, beaming, I came to the ward bearing news of some victory, she would say to me in her rather harshly accented German: "Oh, Sister Edith, you always bring such good news!"

On one occasion I was even able to tell her that her hometown of Tarnów had been rescued from the Russians. The soldiers' response to my joyful news bulletins was far more sober. They shook their heads in disbelief. They had experienced the setbacks and the continual retreat and found it inconceivable that the situation had been reversed. I was quite indignant about that.

It was also good to work with Dr. Pick. He had come from the hospital of the University of Prague; his specialty was internal medicine, and he wanted our ward to be run with as impeccable efficiency as his own hospital. He was delighted to find me so interested in medicine and liked to instruct me by lecturing at a bedside, just as his Chief may have done during the great rounds at the university hospital. From him I learned many practical things as well.

One discovery he enjoyed very much was that he could talk Latin to me as he might have to a colleague. Naturally it was the barbaric kind of Latin produced when the medical men murdered the language.

Dr. Pick used a rather genial teasing manner with Sister Loni, but he valued her because she was thoroughly conscientious. The relationship between him and Sister Emma was usually stormy. She had taken a strong liking to him; and that made her prone to be extremely sensitive and jealous. The two nurses got along tolerably well. On the other hand, there was a stupid kind of rivalry between wards. Sometimes it became necessary to borrow an instrument or some medication from one of the other wards. Should that happen to us, Dr. Pick (who never gave commands but, rather, always asked politely) would send me: "Sister Edith, I would be very grateful to you if you would go get it yourself."

He made a habit of sending me because I hardly ever returned empty-handed. That amazed the nurses; and they, too, took to sending me. I noticed almost at once why they were less successful on such occasions than I. They either demanded whatever they needed in a provoking tone of voice, or they secretly took it and then kept it as a kind of booty gained for their ward. Of course, anyone acting like that soon came to be considered a troublesome intruder and was turned away. Observing good manners, I would ask politely for whatever was needed, promising to bring back the borrowed article after its use. Therefore, I hardly ever encountered a refusal.

Most of all, though, I liked dealing with the patients even if this presented many a difficulty. There were in our lazaretto representatives of all the nations in the Austro-Hungarian empire: Germans, Czechs, Slovaks, Slovenes, Poles, Ruthenians, Hungarians, Rumanians, and Italians. Frequently there were gypsies, too. In addition, there might, at times, be a Russian or a Turk. To facilitate communication between the doctors and patients, a small manual, in nine languages, gave the most essential questions and answers in daily use. I made myself thoroughly familiar with them.

Once when I was on my way to the small tea-kitchen, I overheard Dr. Pick say to Sister Emma at a bedside a good distance away, "Watch, I'll bet she knows."

Then he called to me across the entire ward: "Sister Edith, how do you say 'to sweat' in Hungarian?"

Without making a pause, I called out the word he wanted.

With those few fragments plus sign language one managed to get along. The difficulties, no doubt, would have been much greater had these people felt a need for conversation. However, most of them were in such a condition that this never became a problem. Their total helplessness and the need for complete care made me particularly happy at my work.

One soon learned to distinguish the differences between nationalities. At the time not a single one of the patients was from the German Reich. Later I had a few. When we discovered one of our compatriots in a transport, we German nurses were jubilant. But once we had had him for a few days, we usually became very subdued. These countrymen of ours were demanding and critical; they could upset the entire ward if anything did not suit them.

Those from the "barbaric nations" were humble and grateful. I pitied them so, these poor Slovaks and Ruthenians, dragged out of their quiet villages and sent into battle. What did they know about the history of the German Reich and of the Hapsburg monarchy? Now they lay there suffering without knowing what for.

The Hungarians, so famed for their valor on the battlefield and so charmingly gallant toward us, made the most woebegone patients. If one of the newly arrived wailed aloud the first time his bandages were changed in the operating room one called to him: *"Nem sabot, Magyar!"* ("That's not allowed, Magyar!")

Then the moaning would stop for a few moments. One had not been mistaken about the nationality.

We found the Czechs, hated for what was called their "betrayal" of the German cause, to be the most patient when sick and also the most ready to help others.

Once I had to move an unconscious patient who was very corpulent onto another bed so I could clean up the one he was in. I usually moved people to another bed all by myself if they were conscious and not too heavy. That could be done rather easily if one went about it correctly. But in this instance I could not manage. As there was no nurse around, I asked a young German from Bohemia to help me. Well on the way to recovery, he strolled idly about the ward. Always friendly as a child, he was very attached to me.

"Sister," he now said, intensely embarrassed, "I'd like to do you the favor but I just can't. It makes me sick."

Then a Czech came to my aid voluntarily. He was far from being as steady on his feet as the other one.

"I don't find it easy, either," he said, "but a sick person has to be helped."

One of the Slovaks, a wealthy farmer in private life, had a huge abscess on his leg. He was so afraid of the lancing that, despite the severe pain, he refused to allow the abscess to be opened. This infuriated the doctor so much that he wanted no more to do with the leg. So, one day, during the dinner hour I went to reason with the patient. With my few poor phrases of Czech and with sign language, I kept at it until I had persuaded him to agree to the incision. Before the round began I readied at the bedside everything that would be needed. The nurses merely shrugged their shoulders; they were convinced that Dr. Pick would have nothing to do with him. When he came and asked as usual whether anything particular had to be taken care of, I calmly replied that one incision was needed. He went to work without comment and good Wessely was freed of his misery. (The names "Wessely" and "Sumtery," Happy and Gloomy, occurred frequently.)

Sometimes a military chaplain in uniform came to the ward
and went down the rows. I must say that his appearance awakened very little confidence. Nor did I ever notice that he stayed
for any length of time with any of the patients. Never, in my
experience, was Holy Communion brought to any of the sick,
nor were any of them given the Last Anointing. Unfortunately,
I was so totally ignorant in this regard that it never occurred to
me either to inquire about it or to make arrangements for it.

From time to time, the First Lieutenant in charge of the Military Command also visited us. He was always extremely polite,
and he reminded the people that they had to be as obedient to
the nurses as they were to him. This was more essential with
regard to the orderlies than to the patients. The orderlies were
supposed to help us. In the beginning I had been horrified to see
that soldiers were expected to perform the most menial and
dirtiest tasks. They did not openly refuse to serve. But the Poles
and Czechs among them had a way of showing passive resistance:
they acted as though they did not understand orders given in
German. If one wanted to have the ward swept, one had to take
one of these fellows by the shoulder and put a broom in his hand.
Then, most likely, he took his own good time to do the job. But
once one's back was turned, one knew, inevitably, the broom
would soon be back in its corner. We should have reported the
laggards to the First Lieutenant. But the Austrians inflicted
such disgusting penalties, tying them up or even beating them.
One was unwilling to cause such suffering.

With all the nurses, I associated in a friendly and comradely
way; but I maintained an appropriate distance from them. This
seemed advisable to me after the "celebration" that evening and
after noticing some other things, besides. As a result I felt pretty
much alone. Grete Bauer's presence was consoling: after all, she
came from the same circles as I did; and she shared my motivation for coming here. The very first Sunday morning there, I believe, I went for a short walk with her and Sister Alwine for the
first time.

"To St. Anthony," Alwine proposed as our destination.

His place was on the slope of a hill, a little below the summit.
Seated at his feet, we could look out, far and wide, over the lovely

landscape, the Beczwa, a pretty little mountain stream, snaked its way through Weisskirchen. Ranges of hills were strung along both banks—these are the foothills of the Beskids. One could see the ancient ruin of Castle Helfenstein atop one of the long ranges off in the distance. We found ourselves in an extremely fertile stretch of land, the "Moravian Hanna," a veritable garden spot. Even at a considerable altitude there were rich fields of wheat; deep gorges formed pockets of valleys in which meadows held a wealth of flowers such as I have scarcely ever found elsewhere. Often, we went there early in the morning before we had to go on duty, to pick flowers with which to decorate the wards. The nurses vied with one another in making the wards as pleasant and as attractive as possible.

Grete Bauer and Alwine shared a room in the high school building with two other nurses. Their clover-leaf was very closely knit and would have nothing to do with the other nurses' activities. They were devotedly attached to Matron: she called them her "small community." Sometimes I was invited to join them in the evening off-duty hours. Sister Klara, already middle-aged, was a capable nurse, big, angular, and ugly, with a deep voice and a masculine bearing, but also with a kind heart and a lively humor. Her aide, Lotte Neumeister, a tall, blond girl, daughter of a Breslau doctor, was attached to her with jealous devotion. Sometimes Sister Margarete also joined us on such evenings, but most often her duties as Matron deprived her of these short recreations. Sister Klara's taste ran to observing fraternity-type customs. She even had fraternity hats and rapiers available. The "stuff" was strong coffee, brewed in their room. Cigarettes were available; pastry was provided to go with the coffee. The pastries were bought at the small bakery on the market square during the midday free time. As the Austrians have a decided sweet-tooth, excellent choices were provided. In the bakery one usually met some of the officers in their elegant, becoming uniforms. Standing about, they would drink several small glasses of liqueur, consuming sweet tarts with it; this was an amazing sight for one imbued with German notions of "heroism." I, too, soon became accustomed to strong coffee and cigarettes. Apparently, one's nerves craved some kind of stimulation when one left the wards.

After I had been on the typhoid station two weeks, I was assigned to night duty. We took turns at it in our ward. For two
weeks one went to the ward only at night, from seven o'clock until seven in the morning; then one had the whole day to rest. At
nine o'clock in the morning the noon meal was available to those
who had been on night duty. They were expected to sleep until
about six in the evening, to take their evening meal at six-thirty,
and then report to their ward. To take along for the night, they
were given: a small pot of coffee, two thick slices of buttered
bread, and an egg. They had a special dormitory into which I
now moved. If you were fortunate enough to have good friends
who would make themselves responsible for your main meal,
you could have it at noon as usual, delivered to your bedside.
Then you need not be on the spot at nine in the morning and so
you could stay outside somewhat longer. Indeed, you had an
even greater need of light, air, and sun, than of sleep.

As I made my way to the Riding Academy on my first evening
with my small coffee pot, I met Dr. Pick with one of his colleagues.
He wished me luck for the night and said to the other man, "She's
here two weeks and already is taking responsibility for sixty typhoid patients."

But more than that awaited me. Matron called me and asked
whether I could give injections. I had learned how to, even though
I had seldom given any. So she asked me to pay some attention
also to Ward II, as the Polish girl (the little Corporal!) on night
duty there knew nothing about injections. I should also keep an
eye on Ward III because there was only an attendant there. Finally, she put me in charge of the isolation room as well; a patient
from our ward had been transferred there when it was discovered
he had diphtheria. A gypsy, he had caused us a great deal of
anxiety by his refusal of nourishment of any kind. He was dreadfully emaciated, and his brown face had turned ashen. The
diphtheria finished him. However, he was not to die during my
night duty. Instead, the little Polish girl came for me, on that
very first night, terrified because one of her patients was dying.
The poor fellow could not even make himself understood in his
agony. He was German, and she knew no German. I sent her
rushing for the doctor on night duty and meanwhile prepared

an injection. The doctor came quickly, but there was nothing he could do to help. He could only await the end and certify the death.

That was the first time I ever saw anyone die. The second instance of death came in our own ward. When I reported for work a few days after assuming night duty, the nurses greeted me with the news that a dying man had been admitted and that they had saved him for me to have that night. I was instructed to give him hourly injections of camphor. By this means I preserved the little spark of life until the next morning, and did the same for several more nights. He was a big, husky man. Since his arrival, he lay there totally inert and unconscious the whole time. None of us had ever seen him open an eye or heard him speak a single word. That final night I had also given him injections several times. In between, from my station I listened to his breathing. Suddenly it stopped. I hurried to his bedside. There was no heartbeat.

Now I had to follow the procedure for such cases: collect the few personal articles he had on him in order to turn them in to the military command (most of their belongings were taken from them when they were admitted and kept for them until their discharge). I had to call the doctor and have him fill out a death certificate for me; with the certificate I was to go to the guard at the door to arrange for the men who would take the deceased away on a stretcher; finally I had to dispose of all the bedding.

As I collected his few belongings, a small piece of paper slipped out of the man's notebook and fell in front of me. His wife had given it to him to take along; on it was a prayer for the preservation of his life. Only when I saw that did I fully realize what this death meant, humanly speaking. But I dared not let myself brood over that. I pulled myself together and went to call the doctor.

I had to go into his room to awaken him. The bed was behind a screen. There he threw on some clothes before coming out. It was Dr. Andersmann, a young Pole from the surgical ward. He looked at me and then said, sympathetically, "Sister, do sit down. You look so pale and exhausted."

He immediately wrote the information I gave him on the certificate, and only then went with me to certify the death. Thereafter I was alone again to carry out the rest of my duties. It was eerie to have the men remove the dead man this way during the night. I only hoped none of the patients would take notice; it would surely make a dreadful impression. The next morning I was relieved to confirm that actually none of them had seen any of it. Even those in neighboring beds were astounded when they saw the empty one.

Whenever I entered the ward at night, the first thing I did was to make a tour of it. In the tea-kitchen I usually found a gathering of those Hungarians well on the way to recovery. They gave me a friendly greeting and laughed when I said, "Evidently the Hungarian Club is having another meeting!" The magnet that drew them all together there was the huge kettle of red-wine punch.

The "German Club" held *its* sessions at the bedside of that German-Bohemian who at that time was not yet ambulatory. They recounted anecdotes from the front and complained about the political situation.

"After the war I'm going to register in Germany," said the young fellow. His home was not far from the Bavarian border.

I went along the rows and satisfied myself about the condition of the critically ill. When bedtime came for the patients, and nothing particular had to be done, I sat at the small prescription desk and wrote letters or read. I had brought only two books to Weisskirchen: Husserl's *Ideen* and Homer.

Close behind me in the first row lay a Czech, a middle-aged man, small and frail. His feet had been so badly frozen that some of his toes turned black as coal and had to be amputated. He hardly ever slept and kept his pipe in his mouth throughout most of the night. I said nothing to prevent that even though patients were forbidden to smoke in bed. I could not deprive him of that consolation.

Mario, too, usually lay there sleepless, his gleaming eyes wide open. Once he crooked a finger at me and using signs gave me to understand that he would very much like to dictate a letter to me. Probably he had noticed me writing sometimes. I went for paper and pen and knelt beside his bed. Then he formed the words with his lips; he could not even whisper. I watched his mouth with intense concentration, read each word there, wrote it down, and then for verification showed him each phrase as I finished it. That way we managed to get a pretty good Italian letter off to his sisters. Surely, it was the first news his family at home received since he had become ill. Not long thereafter, during a round, Dr. Pick told him that his sisters had written.

The long hours of care we had given Mario were richly rewarded. After many weeks, the stubborn illness retreated; and he regained his voice, a good, strong voice at that. He ate with a good appetite, and was finally able to get up. When his convalescence had advanced sufficiently, he was transferred to one of the barracks along with his friend, another young businessman from Trieste. The latter's illness had been a light case from the very beginning. A medical corpsman, he was a very friendly and kindly man; he was glad to make himself useful by expertly rolling freshly washed muslin bandages and by performing other little services for us. The two young fellows often came from their barracks to visit us. They were noticeably stronger, and the romantic Mario later turned out to be a real rascal.

A severely delirious patient gave me a hard time for several nights. Semi-conscious already at the time he was admitted, he seemed to be a good-hearted person but he was plagued by frightening images. Whenever I came to him, he would cling to my white coat and cry: "Sister, help me, help me!" One night he kept trying to run away. I had no alternative but to tie him up. I stretched a sheet tightly across the bed and tied the four corners to the bed posts. Only the restless patient's head now showed, otherwise he was restrained. When, however, he had worked at it for a while, he was a strong man, the knots loosened; and I had to do it all over again.

The doctor, a peaceable country physician who probably had never seen a case of typhoid before, came to see what was going on in the ward and surprised me in the act. He was horrified that I should be alone in the ward especially with a patient so difficult to handle. When he saw me cleaning up the bed, he exclaimed in alarm: "Sister, you'll get infected!"

Smiling, I pointed to our basin of disinfectant.

To give the patient and me some rest, he finally gave him an injection of morphine. However, the result was not the one desired. The man lay there peacefully enough, but he began to sing out loud and in doing so awakened all the others for me. The next morning they said it had been very pleasant to see Sister sitting at the bedside while lullabies were being sung.

At first I found eating in the ward loathsome. But, as taking some nourishment during the night kept one more alert, I got used to it.

Another duty prescribed toward morning grew increasingly difficult for me: the night nurse had to take each patient's temperature and pulse. (This was done three times daily, and, even more frequently with critical cases.) I had to get them all taken before the patients had breakfast. The kitchen maids brought them coffee about half-past six; and breakfast was to be over before the day nurses came on duty since they had to get busy making the beds then so that everything would be in complete order by the time the rounds began. I hated having to wake the poor fellows out of their morning sleep. I would touch them as lightly as possible; however, when the cold thermometer was slipped into an armpit most of them woke up. Of course, many a one dozed off again, letting the thermometer slip out. In that case one had to begin all over; often enough one found, besides, the thermometer had broken.

I particularly liked night duty because one dealt only with the patients, not with other nurses or the rest of the personnel. On one of the surgical wards to which I was later assigned, there was an aide, a Viennese sculptress, who accepted only night duty so as to serve the wounded without being hindered by unpleasant clashes with others. I stuck to the established practice and was satisfied with my two weeks.

In the morning, of course, it was a relief to leave the sickroom atmosphere made stuffy by sixty patients. The ward's bathroom was always my first stop. That morning bath, I felt, rid me of at least some of the bacilli. Leaving the Riding Academy then, I rushed through breakfast in the big mess hall and hurried outside. A companion could usually be found willing to go for a walk, be that short or long.

Upon awaking from my daytime sleep in the night-nurses' quarters one day, I found letters and packages from home on my bed. Suse Mugdan had arrived and, careful not to awaken me, had silently laid them there.

How happy I was to greet her! We had spoken to one another only on that one occasion in Breslau; and as both of us were reserved, we would otherwise hardly have deepened our acquaintance quickly. Here, however, we soon became close friends. What a blessing it was to have under the same roof a person of such purity of heart, with such a flawless disposition, such tender and deep feeling! She, too, found my presence a great support. Alone, she probably would have had even greater difficulty finding her way around than I. Suse was one of those persons for whom everything went wrong. Richard Courant who knew her well and liked her said that inevitably every conceivable difficulty would develop in every single situation for Suse. This law applied now. Since she had long delayed beginning her studies and had put in but a few semesters so far, it was a great sacrifice to interrupt them now. Her relatives did not approve at all of the interruption. She made it purely out of a sense of patriotic duty and naturally expected to be given the opportunity to contribute to the full extent of her resources. Instead, she was assigned to serve under Sister Susi in a ward in the high school where there were very few patients. To distinguish between them, the new aide was called "Sister Susanne." She was put in charge of the officers' room which was without an occupant at the time. When one finally arrived, he was a pharmacist suffering from gonorrhea. At first then, Suse conscientiously tended the room's furniture and flowers, and, subsequently, the young man with the embarrassing illness. (He needed no actual nursing care. One had only to bring his meals, and to entertain and cheer him up a bit.) Suse was unhappy that she had no challenge at her post. The situation changed later when large transports of wounded arrived.

Suse was deeply concerned for her dearly beloved twin brother Albrecht who was at the front. And there was another burden which constantly weighed upon her. By descent, the Mugdans were Jewish; but Frau Mugdan had had all her children baptized as Protestants after her husband died. She did so out of a peculiar mistaken maternal solicitude to insure for them a more prosperous future. Later I came to know her, a kind and benevolent woman, not at all intent on gaining her own advantage. Her mother's preventive measure was never a source of gratitude for Suse. Her genuine, straightforward soul rebelled against changing one's religion except from an inner conviction. Since growing up, she had often toyed with the question of revoking the step. But how could she return to Judaism about which she knew so little? Besides, having been educated as a Protestant in school, even though not a convinced believer, she had still retained a certain Christian imprint and had come to love much that was associated with Christianity. In the lazaretto, of course, anti-Semitic remarks were to be heard at times. On such occasions Suse forthrightly envied me the ability to come forward with a simple acknowledgment that I was Jewish. (By the way, this used to astound people since no one took me to be Jewish.) When she herself remained silent after such remarks, she felt like a coward. Yet if she had wanted to say anything, she would have had to give such a complicated explanation that it would have appeared odd and would not have been understood.

We had warm, frank discussions on all these matters. But for as long as we were in Weisskirchen, we never used the familiar *Du* for one another, keeping instead, to the customary and more formal *Sie*.[161] The easy familiarity with which the other nurses bandied the *Du* back and forth, when no inner bond really existed between them, made us keep the *Sie* as an outward sign of mutual respect. This happened quite spontaneously; we never discussed it at all.

When I had been in Weisskirchen a while, Grete Bauer became ill and had to go home for treatment. The "small community" asked me to replace her so that no disturbing element might be assigned to their room. I complied joyfully; after all, I had always felt most uncomfortable in the nurses' room in the large Riding Academy. Daily association with my new roommates resulted in my coming to regard Sister Alwine as my closest friend.

On the typhoid ward, in the meantime, the number of serious cases lessened steadily. Twice more we had to let death claim a victim. One of these was a little waiter, a frail, tubercular man. He died during the day while Dr. Pick and all of us nurses were at his bedside. From there another patient summoned me to come over to him.

"Sister, suppose that were me now!" he cried out in alarm.

I spoke to him encouragingly though I knew his chances of recovery were very slim. A twenty-year old bricklayer, he had a very serious case of pleurisy. He had lost all of his appetite long since and rejected almost all of the invalid's diet served him. When I asked him once whether anything at all would appeal to him, he expressed a wish for an orange. Thank God, some were available at the canteen. Just at that time I also received a gift-package with some Lindt Chocolates. He accepted these when I offered them and enjoyed them too. From that time on I fed him oranges and chocolate. Probably this had given him confidence in me. For previously, he had been sullen and silent; this was not surprising in his serious condition. Several days after the other man died, we noticed *his* end, too, was drawing near. When, during the night, I heard a commotion on the ward, I wanted very much to go over to support the poor fellow. But we were not to do that. Someone else was on night duty. He asked them to call Dr. Pick. Although he was not on duty at the time, the young doctor complied at once. The next morning, still deeply affected, he told me what had happened.

"Oh, Sister Edith, if only you could have seen that."

He showed me how the young man had held his head in both hands. The patient was crying bitterly, "Just so I don't die! Just so I don't die."

When he told me an autopsy had been made to determine the cause of death, Dr Pick exclaimed again: "If you had seen that!"

The chest cavity had been full of thick pleuristic crusts which pressed on the organs. No wonder his stomach could tolerate no more!

Our doctor was also assigned to a different lazaretto after a time. He bade us all a warm farewell and sent us beautiful flowers for the ward. Before leaving, he handed over his little realm to his friend, Dr. Flusser, who, previously in charge of only Ward III, would now also have Ward I.

"I want to call your attention to our ward log, particularly. The book is in faultless order; Sister Edith has been keeping it." He had begun it himself, but had often forgotten to make entries. Therefore he had warmly welcomed my undertaking to keep the patients' charts.

Until then Dr. Flusser was known to me only by sight and from hearsay; I had not gathered a favorable impression; but when we worked together, I found no cause for complaint. He was good to the patients and was never to be faulted in his dealings with us.

3

In the meantime, the typhoid station was gradually emptying out. The old patients were discharged upon recovery, and scarcely any new ones were admitted. In itself this was, of course, gratifying. I ascribed it to the effectiveness of the preventive vaccination program. While that had obviously been neglected in Austria at the beginning, it now seemed to be systematically practiced. Before any soldier was released from the wards for transport elsewhere, he received supplementary vaccination against typhoid, cholera, and smallpox. After I had assisted Dr. Flusser with these for a while, he was glad to let me give some on my own.

As a consequence of the gradual depopulation of our ward, I found myself no longer busy with work, and I became dissatisfied. I had spent three months on the typhoid ward. Strictly speaking, I was now entitled to a fifteen-day furlough. They urged me not to begrudge myself some relaxation. But in my estimation I had not done enough to justify it. In any case, I had arranged to have my notes for the doctoral dissertation sent to me. Probably my brother Arno brought them along when he came to visit me at Pentecost. He arrived in his medical corps uniform and brought a whole lot of gift parcels for our people from the Red Cross in Breslau. Matron put the lazaretto's wagon and horses at my disposal for an outing to the *Helfenstein* on Pentecost Sunday. I had Monday off, too, to accompany Arno as far as Olmütz and had time to see that beautiful city with him.

So it came about that I had a thick sheaf of manuscript at

hand and sometimes I peeped at a page. Besides that, I read my Homer for many an hour. But I had not come here to do this. I decided to ask Matron for a change of assignment.

We invited her to spend an evening with the "small community." Then I had an opportunity to present my request to her without fear of being interrupted. She had an immediate solution.

"Go join Sister Anni in the small operating room. After all, she is constantly moaning about having too much work!"

Such instructions were carried out immediately.

The very next day I bade farewell to the typhoid ward. Probably the nurses were a bit surprised that I should find a few good days with them unendurable. I went from one bed to the next to shake hands with each of my charges. Some of them were sad. I came to one young Czech, lanky as a sapling, who had not been there long. He had a very high fever when he arrived and since then had uttered hardly a word, nor had he given any sign of interest. We had noticed, though, his intense hunger and his determined efforts to get hold of some foods which he was not allowed to have. I scarely expected he would understand what I was doing and was therefore amazed when he said: "Systra briz? Ao nie dobre!" ("Sister is leaving? That's not good!")

The small operating room was located in what had been the cadets' Riding Academy. That led to our being call the *Kavaller-isten* ["Cavalry-ettes"].

Sister Anni, a tiny platinum-blond person, was nimble, lively, kind, and talkative. Her small domain comprised: the surgery with its three operating tables, its instrument cabinet, and instrument table; the adjoining sterilizing room; and a small, dark ante-room leading to the corridor.

When he had nothing to do, squatting there in a dim corner, Max, our orderly, guarded the entrance as if he were a snarling dog. He differed from his comrades in that he was adept and speedy, and he made himself useful in many ways. He turned out the best swabs; using tiny sticks and a bit of cotton, he fabricated perfect applicators for iodine. If we were very busy and called out pleasantly to him: "Max, please, quickly, bring this or that! You're good at that!" he flew hither and yon and outdid himself.

But before and after such magnificent feats, he liked to fortify himself with generous helpings of alcohol; and when there was none to be had anymore in the canteen, he started on our supplies. We had to lock up our store of 70 percent pure alcohol very carefully if we did not want it to diminish in a mysterious manner.

Every morning the seriously wounded from the neighboring surgical ward had their bandages changed in our room. Decisions regarding those to be operated on were made during the round. At the designated time, we then had to have everything in readiness: sterile bandages, instruments, etc. Usually Sister Anni handed the instruments to the surgeon; I loosened bandages, held the patient immobile when this was required, and finally put on the covering bandage so the doctors need not touch anything unsterile.

The Chief of the ward, a Czech surgeon, an older gentleman, was both very skilled and conscientious, so I had a very high regard for him. "Pan Primarius,"[162] however, was extremely taciturn; and there was no risk of our being spoiled by friendliness from him. I was ill at ease with the two Czech assistants. The elder of them apparently understood little about surgery and less about asepsis; and, obviously, the younger one found me a thorn in the side. If at all possible, he would not have me assist him but called, instead, our Bohemian ward maid who hung on his every glance and flew into action at a mere sign from him. One midday I met him in the garden. Contrary to all expectations, he greeted me in a friendly fashion and inquired what kind of book I was reading. I handed it to him; it was Husserl's *Ideen*. Amazed he exclaimed: "Oh, you are in philosophy?"

That broke the ice. Evidently he had been uncomfortable at having, as he supposed, a medical colleague. What he did not know was that this philosopher could also keep a sharp eye on the surgeon's fingers. On one occasion I recognized a patient who was being laid on the operating table. He had been there only a few days before. Then it had been a straighforward case of a clean wound in the leg. Now a huge abscess on that same leg required lancing. Surely there was something suspicious about that! Later, when I was alone, I checked the log of operations in which were recorded the names of the patients and all the procedures. I had not been mistaken. Such discoveries upset me very much. How infuriating that people brought there to be healed should instead go away carrying the seeds of new suffering! Yet there was nothing one could do about it. Of course, it was impossible to prove the abscess had been caused by a lack of cleanliness on the part of the surgeon. All we could do was to provide personally for every possible measure of proper asepsis.

Dr. Scharf, a friendly Austrian, was the sole German doctor in service there. He was very competent. I was delighted whenever I was allowed to assist him. He, too, liked to have a brief chat with me when all the work had been finished. He had quickly discovered what my civilian profession was. I no longer made a secret of it. I had discovered by experience in the typhoid ward that it was a kind of protective wall for me. I was safe from unwelcome importunities right from the start whenever one doctor introduced me to another as "Sister Edith, philosopher by profession."

Dr. Scharf wanted to know why I had interrupted my academic studies to come here. (They all seemed to wonder about that.) I explained to him that all my fellow students were in the service and I could not see why I should be better off than they. That seemed to impress him. However, he could not generate any enthusiasm over my suggestion that he sign up to serve at the front where he would then be able to find me a job in a field hospital as well. Nevertheless, our brief encounters came to mean a great deal to me. I began to look forward to our daily contact and was saddened when it failed to occur.

To my regret there was soon a slackening of work in the small operating room as well. This came about with good reason. One day, during the time I had been on the typhoid ward, a big fire broke out in the small Riding Academy next door. Indeed we feared the flames would soon spread to our side and that we would have to evacuate our patients. But the wind veered in the opposite direction. Fortunately the small Riding Academy had been the discharging area. The people in that building had all recuperated and could get to safety on their own so there was no fatality to bewail. But a mere shell of the building remained.

When the fire was finally extinguished, the tall mirrors, in which the cavalry-cadets had once checked their posture on horseback, were shattered; the roof and the interior walls had collapsed; the floors were piled with debris and rubble. In addition, the adjoining wing of the Cadet Academy had also been damaged. And that was the surgical ward which formed a unit with our operating room. We had fewer patients coming to us for their daily change of bandages since several rooms had been vacated as a result of the fire.

One morning Sister Alwine met me in the hall; she called out to me in passing that a transport of a thousand wounded was expected. As she was in charge of the baths, she was always the first to hear about such an influx. All new admissions were taken to the baths immediately upon arrival. From there they came directly to the surgery for bandaging. I jumped for joy at the thought of our getting something to do.

Sister Anni and I got our sterilizer going at once and prepared for a siege. The first of the wounded arrived at ten in the morning; from then on we worked through steadily, except for a late and very brief lunch break, until ten o'clock at night if I recall correctly. In addition to the doctors who worked with us daily, others came from the barracks to give a hand. These were doctors not at all used to doing surgery.

Sister Anni was to assist with the bandaging. I was entrusted with the instrument table; I had to hand every one of the doctors what was needed. It was no small task to keep the right things in readiness for so many of them. I dared not wait until something was requested but had to look around continually to see what kind of wounds were being treated so as to prepare what would be required for each.

One young woman doctor who was totally green at surgery stationed herself very close to me so I could give her the necessary directions. During my weeks in the operating room, I had learned a good bit about the elementary methods of surgery in wartime. Max, the orderly, and Helene, the ward maid, assisted me. When my supplies of swabs, applicators, iodine, peroxide, and so on, threatened to run out, I directed a plea to them, whereupon they dashed to replenish my store. Evidently the urgency of our tasks made us doubly capable; and I felt so good in this highly demanding situation that I have always remembered that particular day as the best of all those spent at the lazaretto. During one short pause, the doctors lit cigarettes and chatted a bit. I overheard one of the strangers ask who the tireless nurse at the instrument table might be. Dr. Scharf replied with alacrity telling the other man all he knew about me; it made me smile inwardly to hear how faithfully he repeated almost verbatim the answers I had given to his questions.

That day the lazaretto changed its character; from then on the great majority of patients were treated for wounds rather than for contagious diseases. Most of the barracks were filled with those with minor injuries. The worst cases came to the First Surgical Ward in the officers' building. There, too, was located the large operating room, where their bandages were changed daily or as frequently as was required.

On days when we had little to do, Sister Anni and I, as if we were hired help, we said, went to assist in the large operating room. There was always plenty to do. Many doctors were performing operations or bandaging, and they greeted us with pleasure whenever we came. Once when I was helping Dr. Andersmann apply a bandage, I was called to the phone. Matron was calling. Ears perked up in the ward. "Super-Margarete? What's the matter?"

Apparently, one always expected a "bawling out" when a summons came from Matron. But I remained unruffled. After all, I knew I had no reproach to fear from her. She asked me to go to the First Surgical Ward to join Sister Margarete (Matron's namesake, not to be confused with her!) and help out there for several hours. That occasioned my first acquaintance with the ward on which later I would serve my final assignment at the lazaretto. But meanwhile I had some other experiences.

Not long after that huge transport, we were notified of another one. They were no longer coming from the Carpathians but rather from the region around Warsaw. It was the time of the great advance into Poland.[163] The notice arrived very early in the morning before we had gotten up. Alwine had to dress hurriedly and get the key for the baths from Matron. At Alwine's request, I went upstairs with her and asked permission to help her with the baths. We had to waken Sister Margarete from her sleep. She rubbed her eyes and was still slightly dazed when she nodded her yes.

There were two large bathrooms available, one with several tubs, the other with showers. Immediately upon arrival, the new patients had to strip off all their clothing. This was taken away to be deloused. The ambulatory ones were sent to the hot showers to clean themselves thoroughly. Those unable to help themselves we had to put into the tubs and bathe them as though they were small children. Anyone so seriously wounded that he could not be bathed was washed while on the stretcher. Lively banter and mischief punctuated these ablutions. It is hardly imaginable what a blessing these baths were for persons who had been without an opportunity to give themselves a thorough washing for months; indeed, for many of them, it was the first, perhaps, for as much as a whole year. We were as happy as they that we could do them some good without thereby giving them pain. The next stop for them was the operating room, and for the majority this meant a great deal of pain. The soldiers who had come from Poland had been en route for ten days and many were still wearing their first bandage; that had been applied immediately after they were wounded. Just removing it caused torture. And what a sight the wounds were! But while bathing, they were happy as children. I sponged off a very young mountaineer from Westphalia while he lay on the stretcher. Both thighs were heavily swathed in bandages. His blue eyes, very much like a child's, beamed on me, sparkling with joy.

On the evening of that day, Matron called me over to her in the mess hall.

"Sister Edith, first thing tomorrow morning go to Barracks Six to Sister Marie Luise. You are a calm person; I think it will work out."

In other words, a new assignment and, apparently, not an easy one! I did not know Sister Marie Luise, but I received condolences from our small community. It appeared that she was such a nervous person that no aide could stand her; all of them had walked off after a few days there. Of course, I determined to do my utmost not to disappoint Matron.

Barracks Six was pretty far away from the main buildings. It was completely filled with those with minor injuries from the last two transports (two wards held fifty persons each); these did not need to go to the operating room but could be cared for in the barracks' own small surgery. The few more serious cases were cared for in their beds. Sister Marie Luise received me most pleasantly. She was a small, frail being; one saw how nervous she was just by looking at her face. Not at all up to handling the work she had, and happy about getting help, she had obviously resolved to do her best to keep herself under control so as not to drive me away as she had my predecessors. I noticed at once that she was the product of "good upbringing." Soon thereafter I heard she was a *Johanniterin* [trained at St. John's].[164] From my stint in the hospital in Breslau, I knew that without exception "St. John girls" were from good families. By the same token it was said that they were snobs who looked down disdainfully on those trained in other nursing traditions.

I was to take charge of one of the wards; but I was also to assist with the bandaging in the other ward which was directly under Sister Marie Luise's supervision. Since I had come from the operating room, she had greater confidence in my skill than in her own. She completely relinquished the assistance with bandaging to me. When I entered her ward for the first time, I immediately noticed a pair of bright blue eyes beaming at me from one of the beds. It was that young mountaineer I had cared for in the bath. He had recognized me as soon as I came through the door and was glad to see me again. His was the most difficult case for bandaging; shrapnel had inflicted very deep flesh wounds in both thighs. But as his bones were uninjured, he was still classified as a minor casualty and, therefore, was not assigned a bed near the operating room. Slipping my arms under him, I had to raise him off the bed to enable the doctor to remove and then replace the bandages more easily. During this procedure, the patient always screamed; and this infuriated the doctor. The latter was Polish and came daily from the hospital in the neighboring town to help us out. The barracks, though, still had a Resident Physician, Frau Doctor Seidemann, who had been there during its contagious-disease days. She still made the rounds in our ward but had not taken over the bandaging.

One day I had a private talk with my little mountaineer. I asked him whether the bandaging really hurt so terribly. Well, no, it really was not all that bad. All right, then he ought to clench his teeth and not scream. Almost all those around him were Poles and Czechs, and the doctor himself was Polish. He ought to show them that a German soldier was capable of putting up with something. Was that so? Were they really all Poles and Czechs? He had not noticed that at all, he said. Good, he would be brave.

Before the next change of bandages was due, I asked once more: "How about the doctor's visit today?"

"Not a peep!" was the firm reply, and he kept his word.

This Polish doctor who never associated with his colleagues from our lazaretto and who knew nothing about me was the only one ever to make undesirable overtures to me. In the surgery, while I was holding a patient's arm rigid to enable him to splint it, the doctor caught hold of my hand. I could not let go of the wounded man without causing him excruciating pain. Nor could I say anything for fear of attracting everyone's attention. The small room was full of patients awaiting care. So a look was my only weapon; it did succeed in getting me released. To my great annoyance the obtrusive fellow later whispered to me in the presence of the patients: "Don't be mad at me!"

I made no comment but simply left the room as soon as my duties there were finished. But the matter had not ended there for me. I wanted to be certain there would be no repetition of the incident. I went to Sister Marie Luise for advice. She was very edified; her experience with aides had been otherwise, she said. Her praise affronted me. I gave her to understand that, on the following day and in the [privacy of the] office, I certainly would be emphatic when giving the doctor a piece of my mind. Sister agreed that would be all right.

The tall, black-haired man in the white coat was visibly uncomfortable when I entered. I began: I had not wished to cause any commotion in the presence of the patients the day before, but now I wanted it clearly understood, once and for all, that I was not going to tolerate such behavior. He muttered churlishly that he had already apologized. But I did not allow myself to be diverted. I took the opportunity to tell him it was improper for him to address me as "Fräulein." On duty he was to call me "Sister"; and when not on duty he was either to speak to me as he would to a lady or he was not to speak to me at all. After this "speech,"[165] I left the room—half satisfied that I had not minced words with the fellow and half mortified because of the embarrassing scene. In any case it did the trick. From then on he was faultlessly polite and dared not speak a superfluous word to me. Some time later when I was absent one day, Sister Marie Luise reported he had inquired at once whether I would be coming back.

Apart from this incident my assignment to help with the bandaging was the occupation I preferred to all others. In the wards there were fewer sick persons who needed our care than well ones who had to be watched as though we were policemen. That did not suit me at all. The majority were people with minor foot or hand injuries. They were ambulatory and, during the day, could go walking in the park. One had only to make sure they kept the schedule, made their beds, etc.

The kitchen maids were my staunchest helpers. As they, too, suffered because of Sister Marie Luise's excitable nature, they soon took a great liking to me and helped me all they could. For example, on one occasion, Sister ordered all the beds from one of the wards to be carried into the other. It was a formidable task, and there was absolutely no reason for the move. But I did not want to irritate her by a refusal; I set a time for the job and was the first to put my hand to it. At once, one of the girls, a lively, cheerful, young thing, joined me; then a patient who was a good friend of hers followed suit. Others emulated him; finally, even the orderlies whose job it should have been, actually, put a hand to it. Our joint forces completed the project in a relatively short time.

I remember two of the patients particularly. One, a tall young Czech or Slovak with scabies, whom I had to anoint from head to foot with salve every evening, was a good-hearted, friendly fellow who endured everything with patience and good humor. The other was a jolly gypsy who often played beautifully on the violin he kept hanging over his bed. Unfortunately he also liked to play cards and managed to let himself get caught by the Director while playing for money with some of his buddies in the park. As that was strictly forbidden, he was sentenced to the guardhouse. So he was no longer on our ward at that time; but as he was still assigned to us, we had to provide him with meals. When I filled out the daily requisition for the kitchen, I continued to order a Formula IV for him as I knew how he detested the rougher V. He was discharged for transport direct from the guardhouse. Dressed in his battle uniform, he made a final appearance on the ward; in his broken German he delivered to me an emotional address of gratitude; and in knightly fashion, like a true Magyar, he kissed my hand.

Of itself, dishing out the meals would have been a very pleasant task for me as the soldiers had very healthy appetites. When I doled out from the huge kettles, they lined up expectantly with their bowls held in readiness. But Sister Marie Luise had thought out the most complicated ritual imaginable for meals, too. To prevent any unjust distribution of left-overs to those who were still hungry, Sister directed that the kettles be lugged several times from one ward to the other, and she herself flew back and forth supervising every spoonful.

There was a lot more of unpleasantness for me to gulp down daily. Things were at their worst when Erna came to visit me in those July weeks. She had her vacation; spending it with me held more attraction for her than any other alternative. After all, Weisskirchen was situated in a beautiful region, a resort ideally suited for relaxation or vacationing. The first problem was to find lodging for her. I found it difficult to get away to look for a place, but several times I went on search during the free-time allotted me. It was all in vain. If I spoke German while inquiring about a room at the boarding houses, I received no answer at all. Matron heard of my problem and sent word that, of course, Erna was to take her meals with me in the lazaretto. Sleeping quarters could also be made available for her if we found them acceptable. Alwine had suggested this to Matron. Our housing arrangements had recently undergone some changes. When Sister Alwine was on leave, Suse Mugdan was invited to be a "vacation replacement in the small community" for Alwine. Next Sister Klara and Lotte also went off for a fortnight which left us two neophytes behind on our own. Finally, the room was needed for patients. Sister Susi, with whom Suse worked, took the two of us into her own quarters. She had a large bedroom on her ward in which there were three of the high beds intended for officers. We hardly noticed her presence and were as undisturbed together as earlier.

Sister Alwine was given a most unusual little realm all her own. A railway station was put up for the lazaretto as was a bath directly adjacent to it; both were hastily-erected wooden structures. As "mistress of the bath," Alwine was provided with a room in this little building. Now she proposed to prepare another room that was still unoccupied there for Erna and myself. Posthaste, she had obtained beds, a table, and chairs. Covers made from a few colorful peasant kerchiefs obtained for very little money at a booth at the market, together with some wild flowers she herself had picked, made the room very pleasant. Of course, we were very grateful for this solution.

Erna made no demands on my time while I was on duty. I rose very early in the morning and prepared coffee for both of us. We had bought a nice coffee pot complete with a Karlsbad filter and two little cups. In late morning and afternoon, my guest went to the park to read or to stroll. Sometimes Suse or Alwine found time to go with her. Friendly Frau Doctor Seidemann had heard about my visitor. She asked me to introduce my sister, and then she took her along to the doctors' mess. Erna was given a tour of the lazaretto; and occasionally she helped with the bandaging. For meals, she would call for me at the barracks; the two of us then went to the mess hall. If I had not finished serving the men by the time she arrived, she helped me in her kind, friendly manner. Neither of us gave the least indication of impatience at such times. Despite that, Sister Marie Luise took offense. She declared to me that she was embarrassed even to see Erna come in; she felt that was a hint to her to let me leave at once.

Shortly before Erna was to go home, Matron once more got wind, probably through Alwine, of my martyrdom. Matron sent me a brief order: I was to take an entire day off to go for an outing with Erna. With gorgeous weather for it, we went on a long hike to the *Helfenstein*, happy to have escaped from my tormentor and to be able for once to talk together without interference. As usual, Erna had a great deal on her mind; and, until now, any really intimate talk had been possible only in the evenings.

When I returned to the barracks the next morning, the kitchen maids looking out of the window caught sight of me. The liveliest of them greeted me jubilantly with: "Our Sister is here again!"

They had supposed I had disappeared forever.

As a matter of fact, as soon as Erna left I was transferred again; this time it was to that First Surgical Ward where I had once helped out. Here the most serious cases were kept close at hand for the doctors' attention.

Sister Margarete, the Ward Nurse, was quiet and undemanding. She neither made a show of authority nor, on the other hand, did she give one any semblance of firm support. She was responsible for an entire floor: one room for officers and three for the troops. Of the latter three I was given charge of the two smaller ones. The large one was entrusted to a second aide, Emmi.

Emmi was pretty as a picture, quiet, and reserved. Because she kept aloof from the others, they called her conceited, adding that she had no reason at all for being so since she was no more than a seamstress by profession; they presumed she was proud of being from Bohemia. Almost from the start, we got along exceedingly well. Without exchanging many words, we helped one another wherever and whenever possible.

Sister Elsa had night duty. She was that Viennese sculptress whom I mentioned earlier, the one who took only night duty. The Chief was that same "Pan Primarius" whom I already knew from the small operating room. The ward doctor was a young Czech, good to the soldiers and not exactly unfriendly toward us; but he had a disconcerting habit of speaking in Czech with the people while failing to translate his directions into German for us.

4

The month of August 1915, spent on this ward, was probably the hardest of all my nursing service. The difficulty was of an entirely different nature than the one I had experienced when working in Barracks Six. Now I *was* caring for people, doing what I liked to do. In the larger room there were nine beds; almost all the occupants had compound fractures of the femur and were in traction. While they were in the large operating room having their bandages changed I had to make their beds quickly, and most carefully, in fact, since they lay there so rigid and heavy. Upon their return the weights attached to their traction apparatus had to be adjusted exactly so as to position the leg in the least painful way. Every change of position necessitated a change in the weights also.

In the evening, I went from bed to bed to give an alcohol rub and to powder the areas where the heavy pressure might cause bedsores. A German sergeant, whose dissatisfaction and complaining gave us plenty of trouble at other times, said, "Sister has more work with us than a mother with nine children."

In that room I was most anxious about Terhart, a Westphalian farmer, whose stiffly splinted leg continually suppurated. He was the color of wax and had absolutely no desire to eat. I fed him as though he were an infant and coaxed him over and over to take yet another spoonful. At the same time I was always a little irritated with him because he was so completely listless and made absolutely no effort toward recovery. Later he grieved over my departure more than any of the others; and for a long time after my nursing stint was over, he wrote me from his Westphalian home.

The second room of which I had charge was a good distance away from the first. There were no more than four people in it, but they required very special care. One of them had a stiff arm and needed daily massaging. But he was able, at least, to be up and about and could perform small services for the others. Three were completely immobile. Andreikowicz, a wealthy wine-grower from Slovakia, had had a leg amputated and the stump had not healed well.

Mikesha, a young painter from Brünn, had a wound in his leg which continually caused abscesses to form. He was a handsome, jolly fellow, very dear, and patient. But just the same, when the thermometer showed an elevation every evening, he became somewhat depressed.

The most pitiable picture was Pöhl, a Tyrolean farmer. When he showed me a photo taken of him in his healthy days, I was terribly shocked. Then he had been a husky recruit, big, broad-shouldered, with a full face. Now he had changed beyond recognition. He had been shot in the back and had developed empyema of the lungs. He was unable to lie down at all. He sat up, leaning against an artfully arranged mound of pillows. Despite our use of rubber and cotton rings in an effort to help him, he already had a number of raw bedsores. Every movement caused him excruciating pain. The most intense agony was caused by the daily change of bandages: being lifted out of bed; transported to the operating room; the bandaging; the trouble until he was back in bed in a position that was at least bearable. Without informing me, they often came for him for the bandaging while I was away in the other room, and they called me only when he was being returned. This always upset me greatly for, in his absence, I wanted to fix his bed so it would provide as much comfort as possible.

On the other hand, the people in the larger room often sent for me while I was in the small one. Since they had no way of knowing for whom I was caring besides them, I got the impression they were feeling neglected. Terhart needed to be fed, but that was even more essential for Pöhl. He was far too weak to take the bowl from the night table or to lift a spoon to his mouth. The nursing aides had always just put his food there and then taken it away again without checking whether he had even touched it. I now arranged to be there at mealtimes, and I spooned as much as possible into him. Often, too, I came early before I had to be on duty to give him his breakfast. Sister Elsa, who had known him for a much longer time, soon informed me that she found him noticeably improved. She took special care of him during the night and was happy to know that now, during the day, he also had someone who really looked after him. Among other things, she had learned that he had a liking for Karlsbad wafers. Now we took turns getting him fresh supplies from town. Despite all the care, though, I had serious doubts that he could get much better. One hardly ever heard anything from him except, "*Weh! Weh!*" ("It hurts! It hurts!")

Usually I got these four men ready for the night first. Then I went on to the larger room. Having taken my leave there, I looked in once more on the four severely ill patients and bade them a good-night. One night when I did so, Pöhl asked suddenly whether I would be back the following morning.

With a laugh, Mikesha said, "Of course, Sister will be here again tomorrow."

The question delighted me immensely; it was the first sign I had that the man of sorrows found my care a blessing.

After Erna's departure, Suse and I went back to sleeping in what previously had been an officers' room in the high school building. I got up very early and prepared coffee for both of us in a small adjoining room so as to spare us the long way to the mess hall. When Suse took two weeks of leave, principally to be with her twin brother who was home on furlough from the front, it was not worthwhile to fix all that just for myself. I went to the ward without taking anything and worked on without breakfast until lunch-time, sometimes until half-past one.

Emmi and I alternated in taking a longer rest period during the lunch hours while the other one took full charge of the whole ward. Then work was resumed until between seven and eight at night.

Since I was on my feet practically the whole day, I was scarcely able to stand up by the day's end. Sometimes I went directly to our room; and Alwine, or some other compassionate soul, brought my supper to my room for me so I would not need to get up again. It was a blessing when I could slip into bed and give some rest to my weary feet; to my feet at least since very soon I was unable to fall asleep at all. I sat up wide awake in the high bed and looked out the huge window at the Beczwa and at the *Helfenstein* on the crest of the hill. It was a lovely picture in the moonlight. But I thought of my patients, and I was glad when morning arrived and I could convince myself that they lacked nothing.

On one occasion the arrival of a fresh transport kept us busy until late in the evening getting the new arrivals properly adjusted in traction. The officers' room which so far had housed only two occupants was now filled to capacity. Going down the corridor very late, I encountered a most remarkable transport: a gigantic figure lay stark naked on the gurney; a rimless pince-nez perched on the sharply aquiline nose; the head was resting on a red silk pillow. A Polish cavalry-captain was being transferred from the operating room to the officers' room. He had refused to allow them to put a hospital gown on him but had positively insisted that he retain those two items.

Very late that evening I was seated at supper in our room, more exhausted than usual, when someone knocked at the door. I was informed that the cavalry-captain required private nursing throughout the night. Emmi was to spend the first half of the night with him; and I then took the second. I stayed in the small prescription room on the ward and went into the officers' room only when this seriously wounded patient, who had been shot in the back, wanted anything. As it proved, that was very frequently the case. He was wide-awake and gave orders in ringing tones which prevented the other officers from sleeping. They were half amused, half despairing. Once he wanted tea and cookies. Luckily the Staff Nurse on night duty had just come and offered me some of both, so I was able to fulfill his request. It was the first time I had seen this nurse. She belonged to the Red Cross. The rumor was going around that she had been serving at the front and had made herself objectionable on moral grounds there. Here, now, she was always assigned to night duty so that she had no association with any of the others. She went from ward to ward to see whether anyone was in mortal danger and in need of her help. How much, if anything, of the rumors was true I do not know. In any case she seemed glad to find an unprejudiced person with whom she could exchange a few words.

Repeatedly, my patient asked me to cool his hands and arms with water. Since I had no one else to care for during the night, I was able to perform for him any service he fancied. To be sure, when the other nurses arrived in the morning, I was free to leave to freshen up a bit. When I returned, I found everyone from the Chief down to the kitchen-maids in an uproar. The badly wounded officer was a nobleman, the nephew of one of the government's Ministers who had already inquired about his condition. One could not satisfy the patient. He made one impossible demand after another and filled everyone who approached him with mortal dread. It was time for one of the girls to bring him his breakfast. Not daring to do so, she asked me to take it for her. While she provided for the other officers, I went over to the fearsome one.

"Good morning, little Sister," he called out to me.

Evidently what he recalled of my services during the night was pleasant.

After we had left the room, the maid said to me in respectful awe: "He likes you, Sister. He called you 'little Sister.'"

When I went back into the officers' room, a captain summoned me to his bedside. He had also come in only the night before.

"Little Sister," he begged, "see to it that this fellow gets moved into another room. One hasn't got a moment's rest."

In the meantime, the highest authorities of the lazaretto had realized this also. In consequence, I was to relinquish my four dear patients in the small room to other wards and was to be given the cavalry-captain in their stead. The order had to be carried out immediately. I stole one minute to reassure myself that poor Pöhl had been safely transferred to another large ward on the floor above. Then the noble lord made his entrance into an entirely transformed room; and from that moment on his bell rang impatiently every few minutes. His condition deteriorated almost hourly. He had been shot in the spinal cord. Soon his legs and lower body were entirely paralyzed; all functions ceased; and his mind was becoming confused. The more disturbed it was, the more stubbornly he opposed any doctor's orders. He refused both food and medication. We were not even to come in to him any more; his orderly was with him, and the patient placed such great reliance on him that he declared the boy would nurse him back to health.

As if he were a trusty dog, Iwan lay rolled in a heap at the foot end of the bed; and he carried out every command without delay or demur. At the same time, his master's hopeless condition seemed not to distress him at all. When he was sent out on some errand, he chatted merrily with the girls.

A few days later the wounded man's brother and sister came to see him. For hours, the brother sat in the room, unable to say much.

For days I was uncertain just what my patient's condition really was. The doctors felt no need to give us any information. I saw his strength fail rapidly; and my despair increased at my inability to prevent that in any way. I kept trying to get him to take some nourishment or some of the prescribed medication. Once when I returned to his bedside with drops, he knocked them out of my hand, yelling: "Get away from me, you bitch!"

When I left the room, his brother followed me, making apologies. Of course, I replied that one could in no way be offended by a person as critically ill as that. All the same, the disturbance attendant on caring for him was the last straw for my already overstrained nerves. I became convinced that it was high time to allow myself that relaxation which two months earlier I had turned down as coming too soon. But the decision to go away was formed only after fighting severe inner battles. Something in addition to my nervous exhaustion demanded consideration. Repeatedly I was plagued by the thought: was it wise, after all, to interrupt my intellectual work so long when, actually, there now was an abundance of personnel available for the kind of work I was doing?

On the other hand, I suspected I might be having an egotistical reaction. I suffered the more because precisely at that time Suse Mugdan was away on leave. I could have discussed my doubts with her.

One day I was in my room at noon. The room was directly above the entrance to the building. I heard a coach arrive and, from the window, saw Suse alighting. I flew down the stairs and was already at the door by the time she had paid the coachman. I was so happy to have her back again! Now everything progressed more smoothly. I asked Matron to let me go home on the first of September. She was at once willing to allow me the furlough and even wanted me to have more than the customary two weeks, leaving it to me if and when I wanted to return. I asked her to recall me if she felt my help was necessary.

The final event of my nursing stint was the cavalry-captain's death. A magnificent wreath came from his brothers and sisters. Then he was taken away. I put the room in order. Thereafter it was time to say farewell. I was able to make lavish gifts of cigarettes to all my people as Suse had brought them back for me from home. The Hungarians and Slavs gratefully kissed my hand. The maids, also, threw kisses and wept a few tears. Sister Margarete and Emmi promised me written reports on our patients.

The surgeon's cousin, Frau Doctor Scharf, who had been working with us for a while, gave me a hearty handshake, saying: "Farewell, colleague 'from the other faculty.'"

The two aides with whom I had arrived were also going on leave with me. (I believe this was their second time.) The night before our departure, there was a notice on the bulletin board in the mess hall: "Tomorrow some Sisters are going to Germany. If someone has letters to go, they can be left here."

Each of us received a thick pack. I carelessly stuck them in my purse and forgot about them. In Oderberg we had to go through customs. While the officials were busy with our luggage, a German soldier passed by and asked: "Have you any love letters with you?"

I handed him my purse and he took the whole pack and confiscated them. The same thing happened to the other two aides.

I was totally unperturbed. My fatigue was so great I just could not get excited over the matter. Nor did I say anything about it when I got home. But a few weeks later I was informed I had been accused before the military court of circumventing censorship. This was punishable by imprisonment. The entire family was thrown into an uproar. A first hearing took place in the Breslau civil court. The second was to be before a military court in Ratibor. I wanted to go there and make a frank deposition that the regulation was not something I had been ignorant of but that rather I had given the whole matter no thought since it was the customary way of getting mail back and forth. No matter what the cost might be, I refused to say I was ignorant of the prohibition; I would rather face a prison term than lie about it.

It occurred to someone that I should write to our old acquaintance from Grunwald, Burgomaster Westram[166] in Ratibor, to ask for his help. He sent a cordial reply: he had spoken to the military judge who had to handle the matter. This man intended to postpone the case until the Reichstag would have passed a law which, it was foreseen, would impose a fine for such cases. Simultaneously, the Red Cross in Breslau put in an appeal for an acquittal for me and my companions. Another official letter arrived one day with the welcome news that the case had been dismissed. The family breathed easily again. And with that this sequel to my nursing stint also came to an end.

5

In no way had I expected my farewell to Weisskirchen to be a final one, but rather, in all honesty, awaited a recall. At first, I used my leave to take the auxiliary nurses' examination for which a six-month practical experience as an aide was a requisite. Next I began to work under full steam at my Greek in order finally to pass [the examination in that subject] the *Graecum*.

Suse had sincerely urged me to allow her brothers and sisters to help me. Her brother-in-law, Julius Stenzel, taught classical languages at the *Johanneum*, a humanistic *Gymnasium*. At the same time, he was diligently pursuing private research in Plato; in this research, his wife Bertha was his faithful and competent collaborator. I went to see them one Sunday morning. At that very time the couple was busy reading Plato's *Republic*. Bertha listened as I explained my situation and declared herself ready to work with me several times a week. She had me translate a few lines of Plato then and there, as a test, and since she found I did not do too badly, she invited me to participate in her Sunday readings. So, for some weeks, I gave my undivided attention to Plato and Homer; twice a week, if I remember correctly, I went to Frau Stenzel. She was already the mother of three children; later she had her fourth. Little Jochen, the youngest of the three, then but a few months old, usually slept in his carriage in the room in which we were working.[167]

Sometimes the man of the house was enlisted to help with the most difficult passages. On his advice, I designated Plato as my area of specialization when I renewed my registration for the *Graecum*; and I requested that I be assigned to the *Johanneum Gymnasium*.

Councillor Thalheim, my old friend with the good heart and

the stern tone, explained to me that the district board of education had no obligation to take such requests into consideration. However I received notification just the same that I was to report to the *Johanneum* for my examination.

The date was set for October. I was following my usual custom of getting such matters over with as soon as possible. Having been informed by Dr. Stenzel, I knew there was no prospect of my having him as examiner. His chief would take care of that business himself; but I *was* given a thorough briefing on his idiosyncracies. For example, one had to know the titles of the individual Homeric songs. And when the elderly gentleman came to speak about Plato, he used to inquire about the *Phaedo* [one of the *Dialogues*] and then ask why Socrates had to wait such a long while before the death sentence was executed. (At the beginning of the *Dialogue* there is an explanation that the return of the ship which had been sent from Athens to Delos was being awaited. This voyage to Delos was part of the state's liturgical rites and executions were prohibited while it lasted.) This was a question posed typically by a philologist; a philosopher would never have hit upon it.

Of course, it was most agreeable to be in a position to prepare myself in this fashion. For the rest, Councillor Laudien was a model *Gymnasium*-principal of the good old days: very dignified yet kind at the same time, evoking respect by virtue of his stately height and his long snow-white beard which was carefully parted in the center. He had me take the written portion in his office. I was a bit anxious about that. I had worked orally for the most part and was unaccustomed to writing Greek from dictation. I feared most of all I would make many mistakes placing the accents. I was reassured when I immediately understood the text being dictated (not Plato but rather from a famous speech of Lysias); there was then no danger of the translation's creating difficulties for me. And then I had a most welcome surprise: Councillor Laudien gave me his paper so I could make a comparison whether I had missed any of the dictation. Happily I took it and checked out all my accents. The oral examination was a bit more solemn since Councillor Thalheim was also present. At a long green table in a very large room I sat all alone opposite the two elderly gentlemen. Again, Plato was not laid before me, rather Isocrates.[168] At the particular wish of Wilhelm II,[47†] the curriculum of the *Gymnasium* provided that the famous orators be carefully studied; and this was done at the expense of the philosophers. But the question from *Phaedo* turned up as did the one about the Homeric songs. If I remember correctly, I also had to read and translate a bit of the *Iliad*. With that, I had gotten through an examination once again. An entry was made in my departure certificate that by successfully passing the supplementary examination in Greek I had earned the equivalent of graduation from a humanistic *Gymnasium*. The two gentlemen inquired further why I had taken the examination. It was seldom given in Breslau because there one was admitted for doctoral studies in all the faculties with no more than an *Abitur* from a *Realgymnasium*.[4‡] I told them about the divergent requirement in Göttingen. Then they wanted to know which subject I had chosen for my doctoral work. When I spoke of the problem of empathy[169] they had no further questions. The following morning Councillor Laudien asked Dr. Stenzel to explain what "empathy" might be.

I had received no summons to return to Weisskirchen. Instead of that, probably still during October, Suse Mugdan showed up with the news that the lazaretto had been closed. Since Galicia had been liberated from the Russians, Weisskirchen was no longer in the military zone; and the cadet academy was to be put to its former use. Suse and I reported again to the Red Cross that we were available for any assignment; but we were never again called up.

Chapter IX

Of Encounters and Decisions of Conscience
1915–1916

1

Now I was free, and I began without further delay on my doctoral thesis after having taken the *Graecum* "as recreation after my nursing assignment" (that, to tease me, is how Husserl termed it). Though I was studying, I remained in Breslau; I would be ready to comply immediately were I to be called for service again. At the same time, I found it most pleasant to work all by myself, without outside influence, and without any interruption for the sake of rendering bothersome accounts to the Master. Our relationship had not suffered from my absence; on the contrary, it had become warmer and more cordial. Having had to let his two young sons enter the Göttingen regiment of volunteers, he fully understood my decision to serve as a nurse. He followed my activities with the liveliest interest; he wrote me long letters in his beautiful, fine, and precise script; and he derived the greatest pleasure from my reportage. He was also moved by the fact that I was serving in Moravia, his homeland.[170] He inquired immediately whether from Weisskirchen I could see the *Altvater* which was so familiar to him from his birthplace, Prossnitz.

Of course, it was always a feast for me to receive a letter from the Master. Once when I realized that one of them had gotten lost, I was miserable! Some time after he had sent it, he was kind enough to inquire solicitously whether all was well with me since he had received no reply to his last letter. I also kept up my correspondence with my friends at the front. How happy I was when Reinach wrote: "Dear Sister Edith! Now we are comrades in arms . . ."

Kaufmann's[171] letters were the longest. He found serving in the military more difficult than any of the others. Despite the fact that he surely carried out all his duties most conscientiously, he never made it beyond Corporal while Reinach was rather quickly promoted from simple Cannoneer to Lieutenant. Besides, when he was outside an intellectual milieu, Kaufmann felt uprooted. And precisely because he himself was still so insecure as a philosopher and particularly as a phenomenologist, he feared he would lose everything through a long interruption of his studies. His contact with me therefore gave him a sense of stability for which he was very grateful. I took careful notes when I attended Husserl's major course on Logic during the first winter of the war. As this material was unfamiliar to Kaufmann, I then had it typed for him from my course notebook. My sister Frieda was always ready to perform such services. This gift made Kaufmann so happy that not only did he thank me himself but so did his only sister Marta who obviously loved her elder brother very much.

She kept on writing to me for years; we never did meet one another; and after she married, the letter-writing gradually diminished, also.

Hans Lipps was the exact opposite of Kaufmann. The routine of civilian life was for him a straight-jacket which he joyfully discarded. The unpredictability of military life suited him so well that once, during a furlough, he said: "What on earth will I do when peace 'breaks out' some day?"

His relationship to philosophy was something so organic that no surroundings nor any unrelated occupation could interrupt it. In the past he had managed to study the natural sciences and medicine, at times even maintaining a medical practice, without deterring his development as a philosopher. Just so, now he could work as ably in a bunker as he had formerly to the accompaniment of music in a café or dance hall in Göttingen or Dresden.

For the most part, his letter contained but a few sentences; his large script, undecipherable to all but the initiate, made an ornament out of every character; and so he managed to fill the page all the same. Husserl said there was no content to Lipps' letters. True, one learned nothing from them concerning the state of the war. But his few words meant a great deal to me: they always gave me a true picture of his condition. Now he might tell of sharing his pralines with a cricket that lived close to his bunker; then again, of an owlet he had caught for himself in a church. He named it Rebecca and kept it with him for a long while. It was a substitute for the owl named Caruso which he had left with his mother back home in Dresden. As she had been directed, Frau Lipps fed Caruso with canaries until, with a heavy heart when she could get no more, she decided to set him free. By taxi, she took Caruso to the Dresden heath and left him there, though later she sometimes visited him.

One could make Lipps very happy with a field post-package. He wrote once: "You have an uncanny knack for finding just what I need."

These were very diverse things: sometimes a Japanese woodcut; sometimes a few essays on the theory of relativity; more often good pralines or other sweets.

In Breslau, as well, there was no dearth of social life. Rose and Metis had by this time also passed their state board examinations, and both began teaching at once. At that time, to acquire the necessary experience in infant care, Erna moved for a while from the Women's Hospital to work as an intern at the Municipal Home for Infants.

I cannot recall exactly what Lilli was doing then: whether she was still in the Women's Hospital or had already gone to the Jewish Hospital. She worked in the latter for many years, finally even becoming the Chief Resident in the Department of Gynecology. Her assistant there later became her husband. Her ability and her sincere kindness won her great respect in the wealthy Jewish circles, and on this excellent foundation, later, she was able to establish her private practice in the southern part of the city.

Often, too, as I said earlier, I found myself going to the Asylum on Einbaumstrasse where Dr. Moskiewicz was Chief Resident. During the first years of the war, things went pretty well; but gradually as his condition worsened, associating with me became more and more painful for him. He wanted us to get together so he could learn from me; but at the same time he dreaded it because it made him more and more conscious of his own shortcomings. The longer his medical duties prevented his working in philosophy or psychology, the less hope he had of ever finding his way back to them. The agitating contact with the mentally ill played a role in the progressive breakdown of his own nervous system. However, I felt that his relationship with Rose [Guttmann] contributed toward it as well. He loved her but still did not dare to propose marriage to her. His unhappiness and her own inner confusion and insecurity caused her to suffer, as well. She believed she loved him but had not the courage on her own initiative to put an end to hesitation and irresolution. Besides that, a very close friendship she had formed with a young mathematician in recent years affected her deeply.

We had a very sad experience with our friend Toni Meyer. She decided to go to Munich in the winter of 1914-15 as, during Reinach's absence, she could not expect to achieve much in Göttingen. Reinach's lectures had been far easier for her to follow than Husserl's. Now she hoped the guidance of the Munich phenomenologists Pfänder and Geiger[172] would help her to advance significantly. Both of them attracted her because of their concern with psychological problems. She had thoroughly studied their articles in the [Theodor] Lipps-*Festschrift* and in Husserl's *Yearbook*, and she had understood them well. She was not disappointed in her expectations, but a recurrence of her former illness in mid-semester forced her to return home. When she made a second attempt to resume her studies, an attack came after an even shorter interval. Now I learned more details about her illness. The doctors treated it as manic-depressive insanity. So far, I had never had occasion to observe Toni in the manic stages but had definitely seen the depressive stage which usually followed. Then, ordinarily, she stayed in bed, feeling incapable of walking or studying at all; and although at other times she had such a lively interest and knew no greater joy than to be informed down to the last detail about my affairs, her thoughts now, during such attacks, revolved exclusively around her own self. Once she had passed the nadir, she could describe her illness with remarkable precision; in fact, using Pfänder's psychological categories, she wrote an analysis of her depression which he considered very worthwhile. She had unboundesd confidence in me, and she kept asking for me during her illness, while she had no desire to see her relatives at such times. In this way, gradually, I became familiar with the entire history of her illness.

Reports from her mother complemented and corroborated her own. The first incident had happened when she was sixteen. She was attending dancing school at the time and came to like one of the participants very much. According to her, he was a quiet, shy person who returned her affection but who did not dare to express his feelings. She believed that once, through some offensive words, she had hurt him and that thereby she had forfeited every chance of personal happiness. She returned in a very upset state from paying a visit to relatives in Gleiwitz, and since then the attacks had recurred at greater or lesser intervals.

The young man had gone on to study law and, at the time I heard the story, was a judge in a lower court in Silesia and was still unmarried though twenty years had passed since the incident in question. Toni believed he was remaining faithful to his first love. However, sometime later he was transferred to Breslau where he married.

When she was well, Toni never spoke about him. Her mother came to recognize the mention of his name as a symptom of an approaching attack. It seems that every time she suffered one, the old memory revived; and at the same time her hope rekindled that the happiness once forfeited might yet be hers.

The elderly Frau Meyer had shouldered the sorrowful burden of her beloved child's dreadful illness for years. She had tried everything that promised possible relief. Toni had been in various sanatoria; in some she was allowed visitors, in others, not. Her mother had also attempted to care for her at home, but that had proved to be impossible. Now, at the first indication of a recurrence, she placed her under competent supervision.

Another symptom the old lady had come to recognize was Toni's "becoming pious," times when she would begin going regularly to the synagogue. Living with her even during the "good times" was not easy. So that Toni should have all the conveniences, Frau Meyer employed two maids. But she could not prevent the maids from becoming irritated that a person who, judging from all appearances, was evidently well should do nothing at all. The mother herself constantly tried to interest her daughter in some occupation or other. But Toni was convinced that the old lady had been too healthy herself all her life to have any understanding whatsoever for those who were ill. Therefore, Toni was continually amazed by the loving way my mother, even though she had no personal experience of illness, made allowances for Toni's little peculiarities. In fact, Toni felt particularly well when she was in our house. The simple lifestyle, the natural and unaffected tone, the growing children, all this attracted and clearly revitalized her. Therefore her mother was very happy about our friendship; and despite her advanced age, at times she came along to our house. Frau Meyer was overjoyed to have my mother occasionally return these visits. These intelligent women, seasoned by life, had much to tell one another.

Toni's mistrust of persons was greatly increased by the relationship with the servants in her own home, and she became paranoid when she was ill. There was always trouble, too, with the extended family. Though she loved her only brother and his children very much, she could not get along with her sister-in-law whose faulty methods of child-rearing distressed Toni so much that she always felt herself obliged to take a hand. Toni believed, probably with some justification, that, as much as possible, she was kept beyond reach and that her influence was seen as a threat. She was not only very shrewd; she also had a keen insight into personalities plus an emphatically persuasive way of speaking; all of which made it difficult for me to discern how much of what she recounted was fact and how much was the fabrication of an unhealthily heightened imagination. This was the case also when later I visited her in sanatoria or in institutions for the mentally ill. On such occasions she gave me her versions concerning her surroundings, the doctors, the nurses, and the patients. Almost every time, she wanted me to speak to her doctor to influence him in her favor, usually in order to effect her discharge.

As soon as the worst of the attack had passed, she rallied with remarkable energy, took a lively interest in everyone near and dear to her, and also resumed her studies. But in the course of the years, the periods of illness grew constantly longer and the attacks ever more and more severe. After her mother's death, her brother and sisters put her into a nursing home run by Franciscan nuns at Scheibe near Glatz. They kept up her apartment in Breslau for her for years until finally they had to abandon all hope of her return.

She must have had one of her better periods at the time I was working on my doctoral thesis. At that time she was regularly reading aloud to Wilhelm Steinberg who, though blind, was studying philosophy. Under my supervision, she also managed to form a small study group in phenomenology. In the group with her and the blind man were Rose Guttmann and Dr. Grete Henschel. (I shall have more to tell later about this new acquaintance.)

Another piece of news awaited me upon my return from Weisskirchen. This, perhaps, affected me even more painfully at that moment than did the suffering of the close friends which I have just described. I had been home for but a few days when Nelli Courant picked me up to go for a walk. It turned out to be a very long one as she had much to tell me.

Leading up to it, she asked whether I had any idea what she had on her mind. That would make the telling so much easier. Unfortunately I had no inkling. I was thunderstruck when she told me she was in the process of separating from Richard.

Next followed a long account of their life together. There had been many a conflict even in the years of friendship which preceded their marriage, especially during the semester when both were students in Zürich. According to her, Richard had been a very inconsiderate husband. He had continued to associate with his friends as though he were still a bachelor. Some of these friends had little appeal for her, and, similarly, her husband failed to enjoy the kind of persons she liked to be with. Nor had he been pleased that she invited me so often to their parties. He had said they ought to associate with elegant and amusing people and that I was neither one nor the other. Of course, to have his wife dress in the new fashion favored by feminists did not suit him either. In order to annoy her, he had sometimes used the Jewish jargon which she could not abide. He had caused her the greatest anxiety by no longer doing serious research. Gradually she had become convinced that he no longer had any confidence in his career as a mathematician. But worst of all had been his friendship with one of his young math students. Frequently he had brought her home to study with him; and apparently the relationship had become very intimate. I knew Luise Lange well by sight. She was a very pretty little thing, lively, and very talented. Chairing the association of women students gave her some prominence in the student body.

This last point in Nelli's long account was the only one I could consider important. I found it inconceivable that any of the others could possibly lead to the dissolution of a marriage. And while I was hurt by the knowledge that during the very time Richard had so often sought my advice on his affairs so trustingly, he could have spoken so disparagingly about me to others, I could still put forth many a point in his defense.

I could easily understand his need for a period of relaxation and indulgence in a bit of youthful joie de vivre after his joyless youth and years of uninterrupted work. And much of what she alleged seemed to me to be merely the naughtiness of an exuberant youth. After all, he had been but twenty-four years old when he had married; and the excessive work he had been doing probably caused his emotional development to lag behind his intellectual growth. Nelli cited incriminating remarks Richard had made about himself. I shook my head.

"You can't take everything literally!" I protested. "What people say about themselves is hardly ever conclusive — especially so in his case!"

"It's precisely this insincerity that repels me."

An impregnable wall confronted me.

But although I could not follow her peculiar train of thought, I was intensely sorry for Nelli. She had said nothing to her father so far. For his sake she had been writing to Richard while he was at the front. Yes, when he was wounded and was brought to the military hospital in Essen, she had visited him there. But precisely at that time she had become convinced she could not bear to resume their life together. Now she would have to inform her father that the marriage for which he had so long refused his consent had collapsed. She would have given anything to spare him this suffering, but now it could no longer be kept a secret.

I saw Judge Neumann soon thereafter when he had heard all about it. He took it very hard; and his anger at the man who had made his beloved only child so unhappy was obvious. He took the matter in hand at once and began proceedings for the divorce. But in the process, he demonstrated how kind and dignified he was by nature. Before sending his letters to my cousin, he showed them to me to make certain there was nothing hurtful in them. During those months I often met him and Nelli. She continued her visits to us as one of our relatives and told her story to my mother and to our beloved Aunt Mika—the two persons in the family whom Richard esteemed most of all. Her account prejudiced all of us a little against him, even though at heart a still voice continued to plead his cause.

2

During this time in which so many human problems pressed upon me, touching me to the quick, I still used every bit of energy to push ahead in the work which had burdened my soul so heavily for more than two years. In Weisskirchen I used to get anxious indeed when I leafed through the pack of abstracts and outlines. And the winter, that dreadful winter of 1913–14, was not yet forgotten. Now I resolutely put aside everything derived from other sources and began, entirely at rock bottom, to make an objective examination of the problem of empathy according to phenomenological methods. Oh, what a difference compared to my former efforts! Of course, each morning I seated myself at my desk with some trepidation. I was like a tiny dot in limitless space. Would anything come to me out of this great expanse — anything which I could grasp? I lay as far back as I could in my chair and strenuously focused my mind on what at the moment I deemed the most vital question. After a while, it seemed as though light began to dawn. Then I was able, at least, to formulate a question and to find ways to attack it. And as soon as one point became clear, new questions arose in various directions (Husserl used to call these "new horizons"). Next to the fine sheets upon which the running text was set down, I always kept a piece of paper on which to make notes of the related questions which occurred to me in this manner. After all, they would have to be treated in their proper place. Nevertheless, page after page was filled. The writing would bring a rosy glow to my face, and an unfamiliar feeling of happiness surged through me. When I was called to dinner I returned, as it were, from some distant world. Exhausted yet exhilarated I went downstairs. I was amazed at all the knowledge I now had about things of which I had been totally unaware a few hours earlier. I was delighted to have so many attached threads which I would be able to pick up later.

However, every day I felt that the ability to continue my work was like a new gift. And continue I did — for nearly three months at one stretch. Then I had the sensation that something had detached itself from me and formed an existence of its own. I was still able to double-check, to correct some details or to enlarge upon them; above all I had to research a lot of literature and critically evaluate it in the light of what I myself had produced. But all this was only polishing a creation which now stood before me a complete whole. But that is as far as I had progressed, probably by the end of January, 1916. At Christmas [1915], I had not written down even half of it. However, I had a good deal completed which I would have liked very much to discuss with Husserl so as to get a preliminary verdict.

Shortly before Christmas I received a letter from Pauline Reinach. Her brother was coming on furlough for the holiday; they would all be very happy if I, too, would join them in Göttingen. Furlough! That possibility had never even occurred to me. So far "seeing Reinach again" had been synonymous, always with "peace at war's end." It was almost too good to be true. I asked my mother's opinion about Pauline's suggestion. After all, it was also a matter of expenses. In our family one did not lightly plan such a long journey, unless there was a very urgent reason for the trip. But on this occasion my mother immediately urged me to go. She was happy at the thought of the joy the reunion would bring me. Besides, it occurred to her that it would also provide an excellent opportunity for a discussion with Husserl.

Pauline Reinach was thoroughly amazed when I told her in Göttingen about what had happened. After she had mailed her letter, her invitation had seemed to her to be an imposition on me. And she herself would in no way have found her own family in Mainz as understanding as mine had been.

So I was back in Göttingen after being away for nearly a year. As in former times, Liane Weigelt sat opposite me at the dinner table.

"You haven't changed a bit, Fräulein Stein," she remarked.

Frau Gronerweg declared, "I don't agree. One can tell just by looking at her that Fräulein Stein has experienced the serious side of life."

Pauline was still living with the Gronerwegs for the time being. But before long she was to move to the Steinsgraben since Frau Reinach, rather than leave again, intended to keep her home in Göttingen even after Reinach's departure.

Reinach's birthday was the twenty-third of December. I had arrived the day before. They expected me in the Steinsgraben some time in the morning. I bought a birthday present, a good timely book, and set out on my way, full of happy anticipation. Even as I climbed the familiar two flights of stairs I saw through the glass door that everyone had congregated near the coatrack. They were saying good-bye to a guest. Someone opened the door; I stepped in and came face to face with my cousin, Richard Courant. We were both equally surprised.

"What! You're here?" he exclaimed. "Come along right now. I have to talk to you!"

I looked at Reinach for assistance. I would have found it intolerable to make an about-face right on the threshold. But once Richard had his mind set on something, he did not readily let go of it. He, too, invoked the host as the highest authority.

"Reinach, do tell her she should come with me."

"It's her decision."

That was probably the equivalent of saying I ought to resign myself to my fate. But then help arrived from another quarter. Frau Reinach intervened.

"Why don't you both come for tea this afternoon? The Husserls will be here also. So will Putti Klein. Then you can slip away to one of the other rooms and talk for as long as you wish without fear of being interrupted."

That was so excellent a suggestion that Richard found himself at a loss for words. He left; we were greatly relieved and could at last greet one another properly.

Reinach had grown broad and strong; military service agreed with him. It was on this occasion that I truly got to know Frau Reinach. Formerly my visits to their home had been mostly on a student-to-teacher basis. But now I belonged to the most intimate circle, to the "mourners of the first rank" as Reinach once facetiously put it when he imagined how things might go should he be killed.[173] That status he awarded to none but his wife, his sister, and to Erika Gothe, and myself. And, in fact, Erika was also expected for a few days. She wished to—had to really—celebrate Christmas at home. But she wanted to come for several days between Christmas and New Year's; and for that reason she made the journey between Göttingen and Schwerin twice.

Of course, for Frau Reinach it was a sacrifice not to have her husband to herself during the all too short days of his leave. But she made it gladly, knowing how happy he was to see us again. After Erika arrived, she and I were taking a walk when we met the two couples, the Husserls and the Reinachs, who were also out walking together. A little ceremony of mutual greetings took place. I had already visited Husserl on several earlier occasions. Erika, however, did not consider it necessary to call on him during her brief stay this time since, after all, she was in Göttingen throughout the semester.

To tease me, Husserl said, "Fräulein Stein has come only because of Herr Reinach." (Husserl was convinced I had come because of my work, however to me it seemed his teasing remark just about hit the nail on the head.)

"Fräulein Gothe, too, has come only because of Herr Reinach," Frau Malvine now seconded.

Over to the good Master again: "Well! What does Herr Reinach have to say to that?"

"I am thoroughly embarrassed," came the modest answer.

Now, the peak of effrontery: "What does *Frau* Reinach have to say to it?" asked Frau Husserl.

We all stood stock still in dismay.

Then in the most delightful Swabian dialect came the reply: "Well, yes, of course. *I* can understand that better than anyone else."

The spell was broken. We took our leave. Rather downcast after those tasteless jests, Erika and I made our way home. Soon we perceived hurried steps behind us. Frau Reinach had come after us and, nearly breathless, she now called out: "Fräulein Gothe, Fräulein Stein!"

We turned around.

"Both of you will come to us this evening, won't you?"

We agreed, joyfully. Our delight in her instinctive kindliness and in the unerring sensitivity which made her a match for every situation dispelled all our distress.

But now to get back to the birthday celebration [on December 23]. The guests were initially received in the gray parlor. Here I got to see Husserl for the first time since my return. This occasion was also the first opportunity I had to get to know Putti Klein personally. Her friends all continued to call her by her childhood nickname. Her father alone called her "Elisabeth" at all times. But to me, of course, she was introduced as "Frau Staiger."

I do not know whether it was immediately after her wartime wedding or only after her husband had died that she returned to live with her parents. She helped her father with his work. Though very ill, he had himself taken in his wheelchair to the university where he taught mathematics.

Putti was tall and slim, of regal stature, undaunted by her

harsh fate. She was too vital to allow herself to be drowned by sorrow.

I believe Courant was the last to arrive. Of course, there was a lot of talk in Göttingen about his divorce. He had arranged his transfer from Essen to the hospital in Göttingen. His household had been dismantled; Nelli wanted none of her furniture to remain in his hands. Upon his discharge from the hospital, the Runge family took him in. So it came about that he was now living in the hospitable house on the Wilhelm-Weberstrasse in which, before him, Bell had found refuge.

Only a handful of people, certainly, were aware of the personal conflicts which led to the separation; among those present on this occasion, only Pauline Reinach and myself. We had already discussed the matter the evening before. During the past semester Luise Lange had lived at Gronerwegs' together with Pauline and had confided in her. Pauline was full of sympathy for Luise and for Courant as well; the account she had received portrayed all of them in a light that differed greatly from the picture I had been given. Luise Lange had heard a great deal about me also and would have liked to get to know me; on the other hand, she shied away from a meeting with me because she knew I had heard Nelli's story. For my part, I was just as glad it never materialized. I was staying with the Gronerwegs during this visit; and if my memory serves me right, she came to the house at least once while I was there, but we did not meet.

When all the guests had arrived at Reinach's, we went to the coffee table. Reinach and I sat opposite one another at the narrow ends of the table. On one of the long sides Husserl sat between Frau Staiger and Frau Reinach; on the other, Courant, between Frau Husserl and Pauline.

Richard dominated the conversation. He told one joke after another. When he made a derogatory remark about the Iron Cross, Reinach and I exchanged a look across the length of the table.

Reinach then said, softly but very definitely: "It meant a great deal to me."

Thereupon Richard became silent. Besides, obviously nervous, he kept watching the clock while he was talking. Pauline and I knew that on this very afternoon his case was coming up in court.

Suddenly he motioned to me, saying: "I have to go, now."

I got up immediately. Taking leave of the others, we went outside. Once we reached the street, he told me he expected his divorce would go through that day; he wanted to talk to his lawyer as soon as possible after the proceedings ended. We passed the courthouse, but we were too early. Consequently, he decided to go in town to buy Christmas presents for all the members of the Runge family—and I was to help him choose them.

We went along Wendenstrasse, going into one book store after another; and as we walked, we talked about his affairs. I found it inconceivable that the divorce should be granted that day. The divorce laws were, after all, more stringent then than they are now; and, actually, there were no valid grounds for the divorce. Richard was somewhat disconcerted when I said so. Although he would never in the least have thought of getting a divorce himself, and had been totally taken by surprise by the suit, he was now eager for its conclusion. What he minded most of all was that Luise Lange's name should have been brought out in the testimony. To avoid as much as possible any mention of his connection with her and to protect her reputation, he himself had provided other grounds which incriminated him. I had not the least doubt that it was a deliberately contrived matter and that there was no actual guilt involved.

This "chess move" had been successful, however, and the case was actually concluded that day. I was completely worn out by the time we said good-bye. We arranged to get together for a long walk on which to continue our discussion. Richard called for me precisely on time. I do not remember now whether it was as soon as the very next day.

On the deserted lanes through parks and woods it was easier to talk than it had been while Christmas shopping in the crowded streets. But even so it was most painful. Obviously Richard minded deeply that Nelli had influenced us against him by the accounts she had given to my mother, to Aunt Mika, and to me. He was anxious to present the facts; clearly, he was also embarrassed at having to justify himself so to me. And, for me, it was no less

Runge Family of Göttingen

(l.r.) Aimée Louise, Wilhelm, Prof. Carl Runge, Frau Aimée Runge, Ella, Nina (married Richard Courant)

Edith, ca. 1916

embarrassing to have to listen to his self-vindication and to respond to it. But he wanted to discuss something else besides.

"Tell me," he asked, "had you actually believed this marriage
was one that could last?"

Apparently, he had not yet come to terms with the whole
matter within himself and was trying to sort it out. I had to admit to him that never on any of the occasions when I had called
on them in their home had I gotten the impression that their
marriage was unhappy. However, from Nelli's account it seemed
to me that by her constant retrospective brooding and dissecting
she had exaggerated trifles so that they had become insurmountable obstacles. Richard's assessment had been similar at first.
But a more fundamental question now arose. Was Nelli actually a person who could live with anyone else?

She was definitely impossible as a housewife. Once, on a cold
winter's day when he had brought a guest along from the university, and had asked for some hot tea, she had inquired pleasantly, "Do you really need it this minute? I'm so involved in my
work just now."

Everything she did was prefaced by complex deliberations;
and, in the process of seeking the good and then the better, the
right moment for action slipped away.

"Actually," said Richard, "I have only witnessed one reaction
in her that was completely spontaneous: her outbursts of rage at
her grandmother."

I found this assertion to be going a bit too far.

"Surely, her love for her father was spontaneous, too."

That he could not dispute. What was more, Richard was
deeply concerned about Nelli. How were things going for her?
He was truly sorry that the whole matter had been so painful for
"Father Neumann." Without fail, whenever we met subsequently,
he would inquire in detail about Nelli while she, for her part,
never again mentioned his name.

When he himself referred to Luise Lange, I discreetly inquired
into the nature of their relationship.

"It was something that may not have been quite consistent
with an ideal marriage," he said.

After that walk, we did not see one another again since Richard left soon thereafter for Berlin. He had been wounded three times — though never seriously. However, he was not sent back into active service again. While at the front he had "invented" something of importance: a means of establishing wireless communications between trenches since, of course, wires were so often destroyed. He had been given permission to test his scheme at the sector of the front where he had been a lieutenant. Now he was being sent to Berlin to establish wireless communication systems at all combat areas. He kept that post until the war ended.

I mulled over our conversations for a very long time. And as was usual with me, subsequently, I felt bound to write and tell him many of the things I had been unable to speak about. I told him quite frankly what I had also told Nelli: in my opinion he had behaved like an "immature youngster" in his marriage. But I could not believe he was seriously guilty of anything which could justify a divorce. I received no reply to that letter. But, thereafter, a trusting relationship existed between us which was never again disturbed.

I never let him know that Nelli had told me about the malicious remarks he had made to her and to others about me. They seemed insignificant to me when compared to the confidence he had shown me in our conversations.

Soon after my arrival in Göttingen, of course, I had made my way up the Hohen Weg, manuscript in hand. The Master had me read long portions to him. He was very satisfied and gave me suggestions for a number of small elaborations. To the Reinachs I had to give detailed reports about my visits, and my accounts surprised them since it was not at all Husserl's custom to listen to anyone for long. Each time I was asked, "Are you still enjoying your meetings with Husserl?"

On Christmas Eve, Pauline alone went to the Reinachs. I completely understood their wanting to have a quiet evening by themselves. I was invited to Liane Weigelt's together with an older student, a friend of hers at that time. She had put up attractive decorations in her cozy little room, doing her best to make everything very Christmaslike for us three birds-without-a-nest. She and I would probably have felt even more at home had we been by ourselves. I detected in Herr Schäfer an impervious shell which resisted her careful efforts. True to form, he caused her deep disappointment not long thereafter.

Liane proposed we go to the midnight Mass in the Catholic church. She had probably done that often in Munich. I was not at all familiar with it but gladly agreed to the suggestion. So we went to the Kurze Strasse that dark winter night. But there was not a soul in sight anywhere, and when we arrived at the church we found the door securely locked. Apparently the Mass of Christmas was to be celebrated only in the morning. Disappointed, we had to go home.

On the second day of Christmas, I was invited to go for supper at Husserls' together with the Reinachs. This was a most friendly gesture on the part of Frau Malvine; and I joyfully looked forward to the evening, although, of course, it would differ greatly from an evening at Reinachs'.

Three other guests were invited besides: Professor Jensen (a medical doctor), his wife, and a student, a young woman from Switzerland. The Jensens, close friends of the Husserls, were total strangers to me. There was a good deal of talk on politics in a manner which did not appeal to us; obviously, the Swiss young lady found it painful, too.

At table the question arose about the origin of the custom of a Christmas tree. Professor Jensen went to get Volume W of the encyclopedia from which he read aloud the article on "*Weinachtsbaum*".

In all seriousness, Frau Husserl challenged us to tell which tasted better: the gingerbread cookies she had baked herself or the genuine "Basle" ones from Fräulein Stählin.[174] On our way home, Reinach suddenly stood still on the street and demanded, "All right! Now tell me honestly, which ones did you prefer: the fake "*Basler Leckerli*" or the genuine ones? I found the genuine ones better by far. But I was very careful not to tell Frau Husserl so!" With that, he laughed as impishly as a mischievous little boy; all of us were freed of the uneasiness we had carried away with us.

I no longer recall when Reinach left Göttingen nor when I did so myself. The conversations with Husserl regarding my thesis had been very encouraging and, consequently, [back in Breslau] my work proceeded smoothly. But it had not yet been completed by the time the amazing news arrived that Husserl had received and accepted a call to Freiburg-im-Breisgau[175] as successor to Heinrich Rickert.

Rickert was going to Heidelberg to replace the deceased Wilhelm Windelband. As heads of the "School of Baden"[176] these two had carried out a joint and therefore very effective activity. To win ground there for phenomenology would be no easy task. But Husserl answered the call without a moment's hesitation.

Doing so freed him from the embarrassing position he had been in for so many years on the philosophical faculty at Göttingen and enabled him to occupy one of the most respected chairs in philosophy in all of Germany.

Without a doubt, Frau Malvine was probably even happier than he was. But this joy was to be short-lived. In the midst of the preparations for the move to Freiburg, news of the death of her beloved Wolfgang arrived. Having made his *Abitur* shortly before the war broke out, he had made definite plans to study languages, induced to do so by his pronounced talent in that field. He had joined the Göttingen regiment of volunteers when only seventeen years old.

The death of this son, youngest of his children, deeply affected the father also. "One has to bear up," he wrote to me.

3

[Husserl's] sudden transfer to Freiburg cancelled out all my plans at one stroke. I had taken it for granted that my oral examination would be administered by the same gentlemen who had conducted my state board examination. That being so, I had felt a brief review would suffice since, after all, during these examinations for a doctorate, much less was demanded in one's minor subjects than was asked for the major—the *facultas docendi*.

Now I had to take into account that I would have as my examiners professors who were total strangers. At the time news of Husserl's transfer broke, I had written to him at once asking whether I might possibly conclude my work immediately and come to Göttingen to get my doctorate. But he replied that this was no longer possible. I was to take my time bringing the *opus eximium*[177] to its conclusion and then come to Freiburg. His arrival there [he wrote] was anticipated with great joy and, he had no doubt, his new colleagues would show every consideration to his doctoral candidates.

Soon my work was endangered from another source: one morning the mailman brought a letter from the Acting Principal of the *Viktoriaschule*. Our old Principal Roehl had died during the war. Probably because so many teachers were in military service, the naming of a new principal for the school was being postponed until after the war. Currently, the administrative duties were being carried out by Herr Professor Lengert, our good old teacher of modern languages.[178]

His characteristic integrity and his great kindness inspired one with hope that he would be able to cope with the problematic human relations attending this position with more success than any one else could have had. It was impossible to imagine a milder or less demanding superior. But it was a tremendous burden for him. Now, without giving any reason, he sent me a few lines asking me to pay him a visit.

With some suspense, I set out on my familiar old way to school at the appointed time, during morning classes. I entered the principal's house which faced the street — one had to go through a large courtyard to reach the school building — and knocked at the office door. I was received with cordial friendliness.

Now, his important request: Professor Olbrich, our former Latin teacher, was in Poland serving as a Captain of the Reserves; so far, the secondary school teacher, Herr Kretschmar, had been instructing the three upper classes of the *Realgymnasium*. He was a young man who had been hired to teach while I was still attending that school; I knew him by sight but had never been in any of his classes. Now, he had become ill and urgently needed recuperation in the mountains. Of course, other men were available who were qualified to teach at the intermediate level; but there was no one at hand who would dare take over the higher grades. So it had occurred to them to ask me to substitute for him.

Actually, I had no certificate for teaching classical languages; but I was still well remembered as an excellent student in Latin. And, after all, during wartime anything goes. Two women, students who had made their *Abitur* a year after me, and who had yet to take the state board examination, were already helping out in mathematics and in natural sciences.

I was shattered by the suggestion. What was to become of my doctoral work? Professor Lengert promised to devise a schedule for me which would leave plenty of time for research.

"Herr Professor, I have never stood in front of a class."

Hand over his heart, he assured me, "O my dear Fräulein, you have always been capable of anything; you will know how to do this also."

As I still hesitated, he asked me to go with him to the school building to speak personally to his ailing colleague. A huge schedule of all the classes of the institution hung in the Principal's office. It was made up of movable colored wooden plaques. A different color represented each member of the faculty. A quick glance showed us in which class Herr Kretschmar was to be found at the moment. We went over and called him out into the corridor.

He repeated the list of things I would have to undertake. Of primary importance was the Latin instruction for the three upper grades; in addition, I would have a few periods each of German, history, and geography.

"If you yourself are absolutely unable to come, won't you find us some other qualified former student? But I would like most of all to have you come yourself."

Laying both hands on his chest, he continued, "I am ill with tuberculosis and need to get complete bed rest."[179]

When I heard that and saw at the same time the look in his feverish eyes, I had no further need for deliberation. Therefore, in early February I began my first teaching assignment scarcely five years after having left this same school upon graduation.

I had only twelve periods a week until Easter since the *Abitur* was over and the *Ober Prima* had been dismissed. After Easter, six periods of Latin and history in the *Ober Prima* were added.

Three girls in this class had not passed the examinations and would have to take them again in autumn. I had to take into account that by then I would also belong to the commission of examiners who gave the Latin tests.

Totally unhampered by any prior training in pedagogy, I set out on my task with very little trepidation. Professor Olbrich's excellent teaching methods, of which I had preserved a lively memory, served me as a guideline.

The Latin classes of my first semester in Breslau provided some new stimuli. My own appreciation of the ancient authors enabled me to awaken an interest in them among my pupils as well. Then, too, I chose to use reading matter which promised to stimulate plenty of response. For instance, with the *Prima* I read much more Tacitus than had been entrusted to us when I was in school. There were very gifted girls in the upper classes; they accepted most gratefully everything which exceeded the hitherto customary subject matter of the school. An introduction to Greek philosophy which I gave them as a preparation for Cicero's philosophical writings was enthusiastically received.

Principal Lengert allowed me complete freedom. The *Ober Secunda* which I took over was very deficient in Latin since they had been subjected to a change of teachers repeatedly. Most of the students in this class failed on one occasion when I gave a translation into Latin as a test. They demanded to be allowed a make-up test, basing their claim on a recent Ministerial regulation that, if more than a third of the class received a mark lower than "3" in a test, it was not to be counted. But I replied: "Oh no! The result shows the true state of affairs. When someone new takes over the class, he will notice immediately that more than half the class achieve less than the expected standard."

Just the same, I did go to Professor Lengert to inquire whether I had a right to ignore the regulation.

"I leave it entirely up to you, dear Fräulein," was his friendly reply. "Do whatever you think best."

Though I may have appeared strict on such occasions, I still had a very good relationship with my students. The girls had voluntarily formed a hiking group and chosen a young gymnastics teacher to lead them. On one occasion when the girls asked me to go with them in Fräulein Walter's place, I agreed immediately and spent the whole of Sunday with them on a real *wandervogel*[180] hike with guitars and mess kits.

On the banks of a millstream, we had a cookout; and one of the girls in the group knew the people at the mill. They gave her a huge kettle of milk out of which the main course was then prepared: chocolate pudding! I was not required to do any cooking, but the pots were brought to me to prove that they were really boiling.

Sitting in the faculty room with my former teachers and taking part in the conferences was for me a most peculiar experience. How often, when we were children, had we wished we could sit, like tiny mice, in some out of the way corner and eavesdrop? Now, it seemed to me, my wish was granted. And remarkably, the proceedings were pretty much as, in those days, we had imagined them to be! There were actually persons who got dreadfully upset over childish mistakes and found in them cause for moral indignation. But, of course, there were also younger teachers who had a comradely relationship with the children and who took their part.

There had been this type of good relationship between the secondary teacher, Herr Kretschmar, and the classes which I had taken over. Throughout, I considered myself merely a substitute for him, and I was careful to do my work as I felt he would have wanted it done. I often wrote to him to report on the state of things and sent him the texts which I had chosen for the oral and written tests before the finals were given. (We were allowed to propose three test questions for each subject; the district board of education then designated one of them.) Herr Kretschmar once came to Breslau from Schreiberhau for a few days; and while we were discussing things thoroughly, I became aware that, thanks to the letters he received from the children, he was informed down to the last detail of all that went on in school. The treatment he got at that time enabled him to resume his teaching once more. But he died a few years later.

The other gentlemen, those at any rate who had not gone into military service, were all of the older generation. Presumably so that they might smoke without being disturbed, they congregated during recess and free periods in a room of their own next to that of the women teachers. The men came over to our room only for the conferences. The Substitute Principal's right-hand man was Professor Köhler from whom I had received my first chemistry instruction. In those days he had been known by the nickname: *"Mariechen-schon's-Chlor!"* ("Marie-go-easy-on-the-chloride!") His classes in natural science were not bad; but he was such a poor teacher of mathematics that most of the girls subsequently needed tutoring. In earlier years, that had been a principal source of income for my cousin Richard [Courant]. Erna, too, had been a victim of this deficient instruction; but later, the math classes—at least in the higher grades—were entrusted to other hands.

Professor Gnerich was among the other "stay-at-homes" on the faculty. In my time as a pupil, when he came to the school as a young teacher, he had been much idolized by the students. It was obvious that this pleased him. But the girls in the *Gymnasium's* higher classes rejected him completely. On one school outing I overheard the question, murmured with a sigh, "Oh, when will he finally be called into the army?"

In the conferences, Professor Gnerich constantly complained about the lack of respect; precisely those pupils who were most gifted and diligent were at swords' points with him. Understandably, then, he was very irritated when Fräulein Zucker and I declared that the girls' behavior toward us was faultless.

Fräulein Zucker was a very intelligent and capable German language teacher; she and I knew one another from our university [of Breslau] days though she was a few semesters ahead of me. She, too, had been called upon to help out during the war. Because of our Jewish descent and because the *Viktoriaschule,* as Professor Lengert once mentioned at one of the conferences, "had always been considered as Protestant," neither of us would have had any prospects of employment in the institution years before.

The two student teachers, Käthe Friedenthal and Lotte Stern, pretty, lively, and talented girls, were very popular. Several times during every recess, there was a knock at the door of the teachers' room and, usually, one or the other of them was called out. The children, it seems, had thought of a question which could not possibly wait. The older teachers would then exchange very eloquent glances.

I was seated between Fräulein Sonke, a capable older woman who taught languages, and Fräulein Heisler, who taught physical education and needlecraft. She, too, had been in school service for decades. Her somewhat hysterically-exaggerated liveliness and cheerfulness were hard to take at times. For her part, she objected that I spent the entire recess period in correcting papers and made little conversation. Otherwise, we enjoyed one another's company.

Professor Lengert had kept his word and arranged my schedule so as not to contain a single free period. After Easter, when Professor Köhler drew up the new schedule for the entire school, I fared less well.[181] Then I used the free time between classes, as well as the recesses, for correcting papers and to prepare my classes; I did that even during the conferences, as long as they were talking about other people's classes. As a result, I had no need of taking any notebooks home.

Soon after I began teaching in school, I had to go for a personal interview with the District Board of Education. I appeared before the Board at the same time as Rose Guttmann, who was then beginning to teach in the *Augustaschule.*

District School Superintendent Jantzen, who had been a young teacher of ours in the *Viktoriaschule* had now been Head of Administration for the *Höheren Mädchenschulen*[4] for some time. From our school he had been sent as Principal to Königsberg but was recalled to serve in the administrative branch of his home province. No longer youthfully slim, he had become broad and hefty; his face, too, was fuller than formerly but was still pale. Unchanged were his light blond hair and his red beard. When we were children, after hearing him tell of the gods of the Germanic tribes, we had called him "Donar" [the thunder god].

Now, at our interview, he continued to hold our visiting cards in his hand after receiving us. I asked whether he still remembered us.

"Of course I still remember you," he replied. "Edith Stein—you were in my Fourth Class."

He had taught us in the Fifth and Third Classes as well but had been our homeroom teacher in the Fourth, and I had particularly fond memories of that year. When he heard that I had passed my state board examination more than a year ago and, so far, had not even begun to get any training in practical pedagogy, he urged me to register for a year's course in education, starting at Easter. I hesitated for a while since I wanted to go to Freiburg as soon as my doctoral thesis was finished. I asked whether I might not take courses in education, there. He strongly advised against my doing so; in a federal state other than my own I would have hardly any prospects of employment. I followed his advice and officially registered for public school service at Easter. At first the district physician who gave me the required medical examination thought I looked a bit delicate but then found, with satisfaction, that I was "completely healthy and fit for permanent appointment to public office."

Our training consisted of a lecture once a week by District Superintendent Jantzen in the District Board of Education Building, and, in addition, of our submitting to him an occasional lesson plan. Sometimes he also visited our classes. He came only once to one of my Latin classes. I wrote out my sample lesson after having given it to the class. I just could not bring myself to do it beforehand as was prescribed. I said that would seem to me like composing a declaration of love in advance! The training conferences were much less appealing to me than his lessons as a young teacher had been in the past. I had a viewpoint that differed entirely from Dr. Jantzen's in many areas. There was a nationalism apparent in some of his statements which I could not share even though I was very patriotically minded. I could only shake my head at his occasional critical comments about the Old Testament. I was not bashful about expressing my dissenting opinion freely. Dr. Jantzen was not at all offended when I did so, and our relationship continued undisturbed.

Most of my companions in this seminar course were familiar to me from our school days. I was probably the youngest of all both in age and in the number of semesters. Rose began her course the same time I did; so did Nelli, who had gotten her doctorate and passed the state board examination before her marriage. Because she was already engaged, she had decided to forego the practice teaching at that time. Now, however, she intended to follow her teaching profession.

Her father had just managed to bring the divorce proceedings to a successful conclusion. Shortly thereafter he died of a heart ailment which he had always concealed from his only child. After his death, Nelli complained bitterly that he had not prepared her for it at all. Had she known, she would have spent the last years of their life together in an entirely different manner. Now, suddenly, she was completely alone. She broke up the households in Göttingen and in Breslau one soon after the other. At my request, my mother opened the doors of our home to her. Gratefully, she moved in, together with all her worldly possessions.[182]

My embarking on a teaching career probably made my mother very happy. She hardly spoke about it, but her happiness was very apparent. Initially, she was not very keen about the teaching profession for she considered it to be a lot of drudgery. But after the peculiar zigzag of my life during the past few years, she now had the impression that I had landed in a safe harbor. Even though my activity at the *Viktoriaschule* was, for the time being, merely a temporary substitution, it might easily lead to a permanent life employment in the respectable position of a senior teacher. (The imposing title of "*Studienrätin*" [Assistant School Mistress] was introduced only after the Revolution of 1918.) For years, my sister Else had tried in vain to get a position as a teacher. As a Jewess, she was unable to find anything in Prussia and was happy when, finally, she was permitted to teach in a private school in Hamburg. But now, it seemed to my mother, luck had dropped into my lap. After our prolonged separation, she could hope to have me at home permanently. In addition, I was in such familiar circumstances — in the very school where I had grown up. Besides, it was an employment which others could understand, one which you could discuss at the family table, whereas my studies had removed me into an inaccessible world. I was back in the circle of my former girl friends.

Frau Stein, ca. 1925

Edith, ca. 1925

I often spent the afternoon with Erna at the Infants' Home, working on the pleasant balcony of her quarters, where it was airier than in the Michaelisstrasse. I believe it was at Lilli Platau's instigation that we started to do the Mensendieck gymnastic-exercises "in order not to get rusty." Lilli and the four of us Stein sisters with Rose and Hede Guttmann met together with a qualified teacher of the Mensendieck program. Suse Mugdan, Nelli, and Grete Henschel also joined us. This last name I have already mentioned in another connection: Grete Henschel also belonged to the circle which did some studies in phenomenology with me. She had made her *Abitur* with Nelli and was thus several years older than I. She had gotten her degree with a thesis in philosophy under Kühnemann. In conversation with her, one got the impression that she possessed a brilliant mind. She also always had ideas for great projects, but they did not materialize. The two of us were as unlike as one could imagine. Her appearance was typically Jewish: dark-haired, more than normally heavy, loud and lively, with an effervescent wit, and sharp repartee. My quiet, serious ways seemed to attract her very much; she often came to me. When our philosophical-evening was held at her home — even though she normally took things easy — she would walk me home around midnight although it took us about an hour. She took a great liking to my mother as well. Also, when she went to the Silesian Commercial Bank of which her brother-in-law was Director and my brother Paul a lowly employee, she never failed to ask for Paul in order to talk with him for a while since she recognized the hidden worth behind his all too modest manner. She soon confided her secret problems to me: she was unable to work according to plan and schedule, a weakness which rendered her talent fruitless. Also, she was incapable of reaching a decision in the matter of forming a lifelong bond. Since her student days she had been a close friend of the philosopher Julius Guttmann. He was the eldest son of Rabbi Jakob Guttmann, himself a well-known scholar. Julius was at the time a privatdocent in Breslau; I had not heard any of his lectures but had met him once at Moskiewicz's and had discussed phenomenology with him for hours since as a Kantian he was opposed to it on principle. In every way he was as totally the opposite of Grete Henschel as I was. Short, unprepossessing in appearance, and modest in his bearing, he was a fine but reticent scholar and a thoroughly kind person. For years, Grete had hesitated to accept his proposal. At the time she spoke to me she was still doing violent battle with herself and thought that, probably, it was already too late. Some years later, however, they married after all.

My mother was rather proud of the fact that as young as I was, I had already achieved a certain prestige among the intellectual and even the financial circles in the city (the two were very closely linked in Breslau). If anything could sadden her in those days it was the enormous workload I was carrying. Upon coming home from school, I put all my school matters aside and took up my doctoral work. The family got to see me at the evening meal; but as soon as it was over, I withdrew again. Only at about ten at night would I begin preparing the following day's classes. If, while doing so, I became so fatigued that I could no longer grasp anything, I would read a bit of Shakespeare. That so renewed my vitality that I was able to begin again. Before going to bed, my mother would come in to me; when she offered me her arm to take me with her, I would ward her off with a smile; and she would leave after a good-night kiss. But she always saw to it that I had some refreshment for this nocturnal labor. If the family had some fruit, then a small plateful of bite-size pieces was prepared and set before me on the desk. Besides that, Rosa had a supply of cookies and chocolate in some hidden place; and she brought me some of it every night. Gradually, despite all this, the results of the continued pressure became noticeable.

First of all, in the summer of 1916, there was a long period during which I totally lost all appetite, and this recurred nearly every year thereafter. I lost about twenty pounds in a very short time. This led me to the realization that in the long run a combination of teaching with simultaneous, serious research was impossible. I saw clearly that, even though I really enjoyed it, I would abandon my teaching career without a moment's hesitation if I had the assurance that I was capable of producing a worthwhile scholarly work. For this reason Husserl's verdict on my dissertation was decisive for me in determining my life's direction.

Chapter X

The Rigorosum[183]
In Freiburg
-1916-

1

During the Easter vacation I dictated my thesis. My cousins, Adelheid Burchard and Grete Pick, both excellent stenographer-typists, put themselves at my disposal and came alternately when they were not working. All Sundays and holidays were spent at it. As the dissertation had swelled to enormous volume, it was a formidable job. In the first section, based on some indications from Husserl's lectures, I had examined the act of "empathy" as a particular act of cognition. After that, however, I went on to something which was personally close to my heart and which continually occupied me anew in all later works: the constitution of the human person.[184] In connection with my original work, research along this line was necessary to show how the comprehension of mental associations differs from the simple perception of psychic conditions. Max Scheler's lectures and writings, as well as the works of Wilhelm Dilthey, were of the utmost importance to me in connection with these questions. Following up on the voluminous literature on empathy which I had to work through, I added several chapters on empathy in the social, ethical, and aesthetic areas. Later, I decided against having these sections printed along with the dissertation.[185]

Typed on strong white bond paper, the manuscript was so bulky that I could not have it bound into a single volume. It would have made a book too unwieldy for the Master to use. So I divided the whole into three sections. Each of these was bound in a soft blue cover; finally, all three were enclosed in a firm case made to order for that purpose. Shortly after Easter, the *opus*, thus constructed, was on its way to Freiburg by parcel post. I asked Husserl to examine it in the course of the summer. In July, during the long vacation, I would come there myself in order to take the orals for the doctorate.

The Master expressed delight upon reception of the imposing thesis, but warned me immediately that he would not readily find time to look through it. It was his first semester in Freiburg. He had an introductory course in philosophy which, with the greatest care, he now prepared afresh so as to unlock for his new students an understanding of the phenomenological methods. This demanded the full application of all his powers.

I was not going to allow all that to intimidate me. Whatever time I had free from school duties I now spent preparing for the oral examination. There were other ways, besides, in which I made preparations for the big trip. Since I had begun to teach, I had realized the necessity of choosing my clothes with greater care. Aware of the intense scrutiny one receives standing at the teacher's desk in front of young girls, I wanted to avoid being conspicuous either through neglect or through being over-dressed. Several new things had to be purchased for the trip. For the occasion of my examination, my mother gave me my first silk dress. (In those days, silk dresses were worn only for solemn occasions. My sisters had received their first ones as part of their wedding trousseaus. Only when wool was no longer available during the last years of the war was silk used for everyday wear.) Together, we chose a heavy but soft silk material, a matte plum-red in color.

I anticipated this trip with joy. For the first time I would cross to the south of the River Main. I had no knowledge at all of southern Germany as yet and had long wished to go there. The sojourn in Freiburg was to be my vacation as well.

Suse Mugdan had studied there for one semester, and she

now gave me various pointers. Above all, I was to stay not in the inner town but rather out in Günterstal for there I would find myself directly in the Black Forest. School closed at the beginning of July. I left immediatedly. I cannot express how deep was my relief as I put the school behind me. I discovered that vacation time is far, far, more enjoyable for the teacher than for the children. (My friend, Erika Gothe, stated later: "Vacationing to relax from school is nice; but vacation without school is even nicer.")

To begin with, a very joyous experience awaited me in Dresden. Hans Lipps was there, visiting his mother. As the first day of my vacation coincided with the last of his furlough, it was just possible for us to meet in Dresden to ride together as far as Leipzig. He was waiting for me at the railway station. He, too, had gotten heavier during the war and looked splendid in his field-gray uniform with the brown leather leggings. There was not enough time for me to pay a visit to his mother, so we awaited the departure of our train in a café near the station. We exchanged news about the others in our circle.

In the course of this exchange, he asked me: "Do you also belong to this 'club' in Munich that goes to Mass every day?"

I could not help but laugh at his amusing way of expressing it, although at the same time, I keenly minded his lack of respect. He meant Dietrich von Hildebrand[186] and Siegfried Hamburger who had become converts and were now proving to be very zealous.

No, I was not one of them. Very nearly I added, "Unfortunately."

"Actually, Fräulein Stein, what's it all about? I don't understand any of it."

I understood a little but was unable to say much about it.

Then, alone for most of the time, we sat opposite one another in a second-class compartment. Lipps had visited the Master in Freiburg on the way home for his furlough.

"Have you any idea whether he has read any of my thesis?"

"Oh, he hasn't read a word! He *did* show it to me. Once in a while he unties the case, takes out the volumes, hefts them in his hand and says, with great complacency 'Take a look at the huge

thesis Fräulein Stein has sent me!' Then, replacing them neatly
in the case, he ties it up again."

Laughing, I said, "Well, that's encouraging!"

I told him how things were going at school and about my giving lessons in Latin. Suddenly, Lipps interrupted me.

"Oh, Fräulein Stein, you have no idea how inferior I find myself compared to you!"

I shook my head. "How can that possibly be so when you consider this kind of a pursuit to be a totally inferior one?"

"The pursuit, yes, but...."

It was evident, the impression was there. Furthermore, the
feeling was entirely mutual. In times past, I had encountered
such a depth of insight in his brief comments that, in comparison, all *my* work had seemed to be mere dabbling. And here,
opposite him in the train, I still felt the same.

2

Echt, January 7, 1939[187]

Introductory Comment

In May, 1935, shortly after my First Profession of Vows [in the
Carmel of Cologne, Germany], I had to interrupt these notes
since my superiors directed me to complete a major philosophical
work.[188] Today, finally, after many wondrous developments, it is
possible for me to resume them once more.

The last event I recounted was my trip from Breslau to Freiburg in July of 1916. After taking leave of Hans Lipps in Leipzig, I rode on all night, going as far as Heidelberg. During all
my years in the *Gymnasium*, I had dreamt of studying in Heidelberg. That had never materialized. Now, at least, I wanted
to get acquainted with the place; so, for a day, I interrupted my
journey. However, I am no longer really certain whether it was
on this particular journey that I did so, or whether it was the
next time I went to Freiburg, several months later. Nor am I

certain any more on which of the two trips I met Pauline Reinach in Frankfurt. We had a great deal to tell one another while we strolled through the old section of the city, so familiar to me because of Goethe's *Gedanken und Erinnerungen* [sic].[189] [Goethe's *Fiction and Truth*]

But the deepest impressions were made on me by things other than the Römerweg and the Hirschgraben. We stopped in at the cathedral for a few minutes; and, while we looked around in respectful silence, a woman carrying a market basket came in and knelt down in one of the pews to pray briefly. This was something entirely new to me. To the synagogues or to the Protestant churches which I had visited, one went only for services. But here was someone interrupting her everyday shopping errands to come into this church, although no other person was in it, as though she were here for an intimate conversation. I could never forget that.

Later, Pauline led me along the River Main to the Liebig Institute where Myrion's *Athene*[190] stands. But before we reached that statue we passed through a room where a sculptured group taken from a Flemish grave of the sixteenth century was displayed: the Mother of God, and John, in the center; Magdalen and Nicodemus on either side. There was no longer an image of Christ in the group. These figures had such an overpowering effect on us that, for a long while, we were unable to tear ourselves away. And as we went on from there to see the *Athene*, I found her very attractive but she left me cold. Only when I paid another visit there many years later was I able to appreciate her.

I also had an excellent guide in Heidelberg—Elisabeth Staiger, daughter of the Göttingen mathematician, Felix Klein. I have probably already mentioned her as I got to know her at Reinach's at Christmastime, 1915.[191] After her husband's death, she resumed teaching and was now employed here in a boys' school. She thoroughly enjoyed exchanging accounts with me of our experiences as teachers. I saw the Castle of Heidelberg, the Neckar, and, in the university library, the minnesingers' beautiful manuscripts. And, again, something other than any of these wonders of the world made a deeper impression on me: a "simultaneous" church, with a separating wall down its center. The church was used for services on one side by the Protestants and on the other by the Catholics.

3

I arrived in Freiburg at noon the following day. My friend, Suse Mugdan, had emphatically urged me to live in the Günterstal so that I should have a little vacation while I was there. A friendly gentleman guided me from the railway station to the stop where I could catch a streetcar for Günterstal. The village is in the southern sector of the city, in which it is incorporated, and extends from the plain to the mountains of the Black Forest. At the edge of the forest, on a slight elevation before you enter the village, there is a large house built in a pure Italian style. This unfamiliar sight immediately catches the eye. The streetcar conductors would tell you that was the Wohlgemut Villa. As often as one passed that way, one longed to be permitted to enter that locked paradise just once. Later, when it had been taken over by the Lioba Sisters[192] it was to become dear and familiar to me.

This time I rode past it, on through the small old gate as far as the terminal of the streetcar line. Close by, I found a nice little room on the ground floor of a neat farmhouse run by a friendly young woman. Her husband was serving at the front; her elderly in-laws were living with her. Diagonally opposite the farmhouse, the country inn *Zum Kybfelsen* provided inexpensive and generous meals. When the weather was good, these were served in the inn's large garden.

As soon as I had my lodgings, I set out for Husserl's. They lived on Lorettostrasse at the foot of the Loretto mountain, halfway between Günterstal and the center of the city. They did not own a house as they had in Göttingen but rented a roomy apartment. As soon as I was admitted to the vestibule, I caught sight through a large glass door of my dear Master seated at his desk in his study. I was sorry about that. In Göttingen he had been able to work upstairs, completely separated from the world. At times when he had been working under particularly heavy pressure, he had not come down even for the evening meal. And here he was, now, seated as it were in a glass house. I was taken to him at once.

He rose to meet me and called out, jokingly: "Execution is at hand!"

No, he had not yet been able to look at my work. His first semester in a new university — he was giving an entirely new structure to his course and needed all his time for that. Incidentally, this course would intrigue me: modern philosophy seen from our standpoint, so that through it the listener would conjointly be introduced to phenomenology. Under circumstances like this it would hardly be feasible for me to take my examinations at this time. Frau Husserl was appalled.

"Fräulein Stein has made the long journey from Breslau to Freiburg especially for that purpose, and now it is all to be in vain!"

The Master remained imperturbable.

"Fräulein Stein is happy to get to know Freiburg and to see how I am settling in here. She will also gain a great deal from my course. She can get her doctorate next time."

I was not totally robbed of my composure but rather thought, without saying anything, that, probably, this was not the final word on this matter. Obviously, I would have to take the course (four times a week, from five to six in the afternoon, with only Wednesday and Saturday free). Frau Husserl also attended regularly. After the lecture, we would wait in front of the university until the Master came from the faculty room. Then, on foot, we made our way to Lorettostrasse. At the first lecture, I saw an old acquaintance from Göttingen again: Roman Ingarden, one of the Polish students who had already taken courses with Husserl before the war. He was in service with the Polish Legion at the beginning of the war but, soon thereafter, he was discharged because of a heart defect. Thereupon he had returned to Göttingen. He was the only one of the old Göttingen circle to accompany Husserl to Freiburg. Rudolf Meyer, a young Protestant theologian, had come along as well. A newcomer joined them as a follower, a Russian woman, Frau Pluicke. Husserl told me that the latter two were "dying" to make my acquaintance. So, shortly thereafter, we were all invited to meet at Husserl's. Frau Pluicke was enthusiastic about phenomenology but even more about Rudolf Steiner.[193] Influenced by her, "little Meyer" also turned to anthroposophy. After a while both of them left Freiburg. I do not know what became of them.

One day as I was returning to Günterstal from Lorettostrasse, the Husserls accompanied me. As we strolled along, he said, "Fräulein Stein, my wife gives me no peace! I am to take the time to read your work. So far, I have never accepted anyone's thesis before I was thoroughly familiar with it. But I will do so this time. Go to the Dean to make an appointment for the *Rigorosum*. But make the date as late as possible so that I can go over your thesis by that time."

Of course, I took care of all the necessary arrangements at once. The case containing the three volumes now had to be taken away from Husserl so that I could hand in the work at the faculty office. I was able to leave a carbon copy with him so he would not have to lose time until the original was returned to him officially. Usually, doctoral students went first to the university's Beadle[194] to slip him a tip so he might help them obtain the board of examiners they would like to have. I spurned using this backdoor approach. I went directly to the Dean of the Department of Philosophy. This was, at that time, Professor Körte, professor of classic languages. While the war lasted, he was a Captain of the Reserves and drilled recruits in Freiburg; in his free time, he discharged his duties as Dean. That is why he was wearing his field gray uniform when he received me.

He was a very kindly gentleman, and there was no need of an intermediary in order to come to an agreement with him. Husserl alone could evaluate the thesis. Therefore he had to be named Examiner. I gave modern history and modern literature as my minor subjects. For these Professor Rachfahl and Professor Witkop could be considered as examiners. I asked to have the third of August set for the examination. School would begin again in Breslau on the sixth; therefore I had to be home by the evening of the fifth. As I wished to stop over in Göttingen for a day, I would have to leave Freiburg no later than the morning of the fourth. Professor Körte told me that I, myself, would have to ask the Professors who were to give the examinations whether they would remain in Freiburg that long. Because of the great heat, the lectures ordinarily terminated by the end of July, and as soon as possible thereafter everyone headed for cooler locations for the summer. With this reservation, the time for the *examen rigorosum* was set for six o'clock in the evening of the third of August.

Thereupon I visited the two gentlemen to introduce myself. After all, it was unusual to be examined by total strangers; and I had to find out, at least, what their leanings were. I had read Rachfahl's books. He was known to me principally through the theory he proposed about Friedrich Wilhelm IV and the Revolution of 1848, a theory which was decidedly rejected by those who had taught me modern history (Georg Kaufmann in Breslau and Max Lehmann in Göttingen) and by most others as well. The March Revolution[195] belonged to the period I specialized in; my thesis for the state board examination in history had dealt with it. So I had to use foresight to avoid a confrontation.

As far as I could tell from the interview, Professor Witkop was not as interested in numbers and dates as he was in ideas. He inquired whether I had read Eugen Kühnemann's books. [196] This told me a great deal. I was as yet unfamiliar with the Herder publication [Kühnemann's latest work] and immediately got it at the library.

Both gentlemen agreed to the date for the examination.

To get acquainted with their thought process, I also attended several of their lectures. I believe I did so no more than two or three times. With that I felt I was sufficiently in the picture. After all, I had to keep in mind that this was my vacation as well; and I needed to fortify myself for another term. So, usually early in the morning, I carried my books from Günterstal to one of the surrounding mountains to stretch out there in some meadow to study for the examination.

4

On one of these days, my friend Erika Gothe arrived from Göttingen. This was supposed to be her vacation, too; but she wanted to be with me so that I should not be entirely on my own on the day of the examination.

I met her at the station. Later, as we sat together in my little room, I took out my map of the Black Forest and pointed.

"There is the Feldberg. We've got to go there one of these days. And, sometime, too, to Lake Constance."

Beaming with joy, Erika embraced me. The Reinachs had tried to dissuade her from coming to me. Surely, since I would be concentrating exclusively on the examination, I would have time for no other activities. Now her faithful friendship was to have its reward.

However, we had to exercise a bit of cunning when planning our excursions. No cutting of any of Husserl's classes. The time between lectures would have to do for the Feldberg visit. We walked the entire way there from Günterstal via the Schauinsland,[197] staying overnight en route; and when the afternoon lecture was over, we could proudly relate that we had been on the Feldberg that morning, gazing at the Alps while having our breakfast.

We postponed going to Lake Constance until the final days before the examination. That excursion required more time so we chose Saturday and Sunday for it. We decided to say nothing about it at Husserl's for the time being since the Master might be upset to learn that I was indulging in such a treat so near to the examination date.

As we stood awaiting the train for the Höllental in the Wiehrer railway station, we noticed the whole Husserl family was also on the platform. They got into a coach near ours and traveled part of the way on the same train, I believe as far as Hinterzarten. We got the impression that they were as reluctant to have us see them as we were to be seen by them. Gerhart was with them; he was home for only a few days of leave; and we assumed the parents preferred to be alone with their son. We rode the whole way through the Höllental as far as Donaueschingen. There we took a train down to Singen. A short while before that, when from the Feldberg we had seen the Hegauer mountains rising to the east like crests of foam, I had decided we would visit the [castle] Hohentwiel. We stayed overnight in Singen. It was wonderful to climb the mountain in the evening, to wander about in the ancient castle, to think of Ekkehart[198] and of Schiller's youth, here where many a captive once languished in the fortress.

In the morning we were off to the lake. To the sound of church bells, an old woman ferried us in a rowboat from Radolfzell to the island of Reichenau.[199] The monastery made little impression on me on that occasion. Vineyards under a deep blue sky, the shimmering sunlight, and the lake's green waves lapping the shores — those are my most vivid recollections of that day.

But we came away with more than memories of happy outings, for impressions of a more serious nature were made, also [in Freiburg]. The first or second night after Erika's arrival there, we were awakened by an air raid. I was accustomed to that by this time and made little of it. Erika slept in another room; her bed was against the wall adjoining the room occupied by the landlady's elderly in-laws. During that night, suddenly, the man knocked at my door and told me in his Baden dialect that my companion was weeping. I dressed immediately and went over to her. She was, indeed, shedding tears but not for herself. She had been told that from Freiburg one could hear the artillery fire from the Vosges Mountains and her brother Hans, a lieutenant, was stationed there.

Now she heard shells exploding and said, "If it sounds so terrible here, what a hell it must be there!"

I knelt beside her bed and comforted her. What we were hearing were the antiaircraft guns from the *Schlossberg* which protected the entire city. All one could hear from the Vosges Mountains was a very dull rumbling. Thereupon the tears stopped at once. Erika was completely comforted. She even noticed the dress I had thrown on so rapidly.

"You have found the style that suits you," she said.

Since becoming a teacher I had taken great care to dress impeccably. After all, I stood at the desk in front of grown girls from the best families; and I knew how closely they scrutinized one's appearance. I wanted to avoid giving offense either by neglect or by an exaggerated elegance, and wished to be as inconspicuous as I could be so as to deflect as little attention as possible from the instructions to myself.

Of course I had to continue preparing for the oral examination despite Erika's vacation. Now we had even more things to carry up the mountain slopes in the morning. While I was occupied with my books, Erika studied my thesis. She also accompanied me faithfully to Husserl's lecture each afternoon; therefore, there were now three of us awaiting him afterwards.

Once, as he came out, he said to me, "It's a good thing you weren't in the faculty room just now or you might get conceited! I was telling the other gentlemen about you, and I also mentioned your valuable service as a nurse during the war."

It was of particular importance to him that I should pass the examination with good marks since none of his students had as yet come up for examination in Freiburg. As the first one, then, it was up to me to make a good impression.

He had been a co-examiner for several examinations since philosophy was often chosen as a minor. Once when we were spending the evening at his home, he recounted some of his experiences. The requirements were very high, he said. *Cum laude* was considered a very good mark; he added that *magna cum laude* was rarely given; *summa cum laude* was reserved for those who were candidates for habilitation.

"Well, then I'll be prepared to get a *cum laude*," I said, teasingly.

"Just be glad if you pass!" was the rejoinder.

This put a slight damper on my high spirits. Besides that, the Master continually moaned about the pressure of having to study my thesis carefully.

Fräulein Ortmann came on a visit from Strassburg one Sunday. That afternoon we went to Husserl's with her. The Master appeared on the veranda for coffee but left again shortly there after.

"I can't spend any time with you at all today," he said to Fräulein Ortmann. "You can thank Fräulein Stein for that. I need all my time for her thesis."

He bade me come to his study; I was to explain something to him that he did not quite understand. Then we spent a few minutes cursorily discussing the thesis as a whole.

"After all, it's no more than a student's paper," I said.

"No, definitely not just that!" he replied, decisively. "I find you to be very independent."

That was the first time I heard him express any verdict, and it had a very promising sound.

Once we were invited to join a somewhat larger circle at Husserl's. If I am not mistaken, it was on this evening that I became acquainted with Martin Heidegger.[200] He had gotten his habilitation while Rickert was still there, and Husserl had taken him over [as assistant in academic duties] from his predecessor. Heidegger held his inaugural lecture only after Husserl was in Freiburg. It contained unmistakable digs at phenomenology.

The future Frau Heidegger, then still Fräulein Petri, was in Husserl's seminar, and she used to put up some lively opposition.

Husserl himself had told us about it, remarking: "When a woman is that obstinate, there's sure to be a man in the background somewhere."

I liked Heidegger very much that evening. As long as there was no mention of philosophy, he was quiet and unassuming; but as soon as a philosophical question popped up he was very animated.

We discussed the evening as we lay in our beds back in Günterstal. (On nights when we came home late, we would find that our youthful landlady had retired in my small room which faced the street, leaving her large bedroom with its two beds for us.)

Erika had held a long conversation alone with the Master. He had complained about being unable to make any headway with his work. He had made an outline of the second part of his *Ideen zu einer reinen Phänomenologie und phänomenologischen Philosophie* [*Ideas*[201]] at the time he wrote the first part in 1912. After that first part had appeared in 1913, he had been pressed to give priority to getting out a new edition of the *Logische Untersuchungen* since the old edition was out of print. Then had come the outbreak of the war, the death of his son Wolfgang, and the move to Freiburg. All of this had torn him from concentration on his work, and he had trouble finding his way back. He was unable to decipher the outline he had then written in pencil and in tiny shorthand; his vision was no longer good enough. He had been complaining for a long while about the weakness of his eyes, and he would have liked to have an operation for cataracts; but the condition would not ripen enough for surgery. Now there was but one resort left; he would have to have an assistant.

We lay there in bed racking our brains: where were we to go to find an assistant for the Master since all his former students were in military service? The one probably best fitted for the task would have been Fritz Frankfurter. But he had been one of the first casualties of the war.

"If I thought I could be of any use to him," I said, finally, "I would come [to stay in Freiburg]."

Erika was thoroughly astounded. "Is that possible? I would not be able to do it. I have to start teaching now, to earn something."

Neither had I any financial resources from which to support myself. But I never bothered with arithmetic. I would just simply do it. But what still seemed inconceivable to me was that he would even consider me. I was such a little thing, and Husserl was the first in rank of all the living philosophers. In fact, I was convinced he was one of those real giants who transcend their own time and who determine history. (An aside: I am writing this on April 27, 1939. One year ago today, the beloved Master entered eternity.[202]) But there was a solution to the problem. "I'll ask him personally. But I can wait until the examination is over. When he has finished reading the dissertation, he will be in a better position to judge."

With that we ended our discussion and said good-night.

5

At six o'clock the following evening, as we were waiting with Frau Husserl at the portal of the university when Husserl came down the stairs, he said to his wife: "Go on ahead with Fräulein Gothe. I have something I want to talk about with Fräulein Stein."

So, two by two, we set out on our way. I waited in suspense for what might follow. Just a few days earlier, the Master had joked: "Your thesis pleases me more and more. I have to be careful that my satisfaction with it doesn't get too exalted."

Now he began to speak in much the same vein. "I have now gotten pretty far into your thesis. You really are a very gifted little girl."

Then he became somewhat more serious.

"I'm only deliberating whether it will be possible to put this work in the *Yearbook* along with *Ideas*. I have an impression that in your work you forestall some material that is in my second part of *Ideas*."

His words gave me a jolt! Surely this was the moment to ask him. Seize the opportunity by the scruff of the neck!

"If that is really so, Professor, then there's a question I have been meaning to put to you. Fräulein Gothe told me of your need for an assistant. Do you think I might be able to help you?"

At that point we were just crossing over the Dreisam. The Master stood stock still in the middle of the *Friedrichsbrücke* and exclaimed in delighted surprise: "You want to help me? Yes! With you, I would enjoy working!"

I do not know which one of us was more elated. We were like a young couple at the moment of their betrothal. In the Lorettostrasse, Frau Husserl and Erika stood watching us.

Husserl said to his wife: "Think of it! Fräulein Stein wants to come to be my assistant."

Erika looked at me. We needed no exchange of words to reach an understanding. Her deep-set, dark eyes were alight with intense joy. That night when we went to bed she said, "Good night, Lady Assistant!"

Now whenever we met the Husserls again, plans for the future were eagerly forged. I had to return to school in Breslau for two months. After all, there was no replacement there for me at the moment; and that autumn I would have to give the Latin examinations for those making their *Abitur*. But I was determined by the first of October I could make myself available. The Husserls themselves were amazed that I was ready, without a moment's hesitation, to put my teaching career on the shelf. Frau Husserl concluded from this that I must be very wealthy. At least, some years later I learned that this was what she had told others about me. There was serious discussion about the matter of a salary. Husserl said he could give me a hundred Marks a month. Naturally, I could never manage with that, alone, but it would still be a help; my relatives would more likely give their consent. I agreed to everything. Such matters were embarrassing for me; I wanted to get them over with as quickly as possible.

Now the examination was no longer in the limelight. Husserl said, laughing: "We can talk about anything you wish. Even about empathy. (That was the topic of my dissertation.) Only we have to avoid using the word itself."

I put a bug in his ear: "Just don't ask as many questions about the history of philosophy as you did in the state board examination."

He remarked that probably was proof that such questions were precisely necessary.

The great day, August 3, 1916, finally arrived. The evening before, in bed, Erika had asked how I was feeling.

I answered: "Well, in any case, it will all be over in twenty-four hours."

She was amazed at such a fatalistic attitude. Of course, she accompanied me to the battlefield. En route we stopped for reinforcements at Birlinger's Coffeehouse.

I liked the place especially because they had several small rooms with Biedermeier furnishings. We even found an empty table in my favorite room, one with a decor all in green and black. I ordered iced coffee and torte which I consumed with such unusual dispatch that Erika almost feared it would make me sick. The day was dreadfully hot.

The Dean had designated the meeting room of the Department for Political Science for the examination because it was coolest there. He had Husserl and me take our seats at the conference table in comfortable leather armchairs. He himself sat at the desk with his back to us, as though he had nothing to do with the matter at all. Naturally, he listened very attentively but he wanted to disturb me as little as possible. So, as far as I was concerned, I was having a very intimate exchange of opinions with the Master. In order to create the best impression, he would preface his questions as follows: "As a matter of fact, it is asking a great deal during an examination to demonstrate one's ability to do some original thinking, especially when it is this hot! But perhaps you could tell me. . .? etc."

I feel sure that the friendly assessor saw through the pious ruse. But he gave no sign of it. The prescribed hour went by very quickly. At the end of it, the Dean jumped up, saying: "But now we have to see that Fräulein Stein gets a glass of water."

He himself hurried through the building in order to bring me something although I felt neither weak nor in need of refreshment.

The other two minor subjects followed; for each, a half-hour was allotted. Professor Witkop asked such artful questions that I was embarrassed in front of Husserl. But I gave the expected answers, and the examiner later paid Husserl a compliment by saying that the philosophical training had been very evident. As a matter of fact he tested me for forty minutes, so that the Dean finally interrupted, saying, "After all, my good colleague, we do not want to torture Fräulein Stein more than is necessary."

After that, the history examination was a mere "appendix." Once, when a name would not come to me, Husserl prompted. I was allowed to leave at eight o'clock. The gentlemen remained to confer over the result. In the great hall downstairs, Erika and Ingarden were waiting for me.

Now the Beadle, whom so far I had not even glimpsed, also appeared on the scene. He congratulated me: "It will hardly have come to less than a *summa*. After what Husserl wrote on your dissertation, that is surely the only verdict possible."

He received his tip although he had done nothing for me.

That evening we were invited to the Husserls'. Since we knew that there we would get nothing but something sweet, we had decided to go for supper somewhere first. As it happened, Ingarden proposed skipping that; but when we would not agree to do so, he took us to a restaurant in the neighborhood. Here he wanted to take leave of us. It developed that he had no money. His monthly check had not yet arrived and there was nothing left from the previous month.

"But," I said, "It's to be taken for granted that you are my guest today!"

When we had finished eating I quietly pushed my wallet over to him and let him pay for us all.

It was already very late by this time. At Husserl's, everyone was awaiting us. Frau Husserl and Elli [her daughter] had wound ivy and daisies into a gorgeous wreath. This was set on my head in place of a laurel wreath.

"Just like a queen," exclaimed little Meyer, all enthused, beside me.

Husserl was beaming with joy. The Dean himself had proposed I be given the mark *summa cum laude.*

By the time we took our leave it was probably past midnight. No streetcars were running any more. We had to walk home in pitch darkness; there was a total blackout because of the danger of an air raid.

Ingarden accompanied us to our little house. He had heard that I would be returning on the first of October and was delighted to know he would no longer be alone in Freiburg.

At the house, the young landlady awoke when we entered. I was still wearing the wreath. "One ought to take your picture like that," she said, "while the glow of happiness is still there. Otherwise, you've always got such a serious look on your face."

The next morning I sent a telegram home informing them of the results and of the time of my arrival [in Breslau]. Then we set out on the return trip. I cannot recall any longer why Erika was unable to go with me to Göttingen. I only remember that I arrived there alone. Frau Reinach awaited me; but I took a room for the night at Gebhard's Hotel next to the station since I had to leave very early the next morning. Then we went by taxi to Steinsgraben.

> [*Here the manuscript ends abruptly.*
> *This Chapter was never completed*
> *by Sister Teresa Benedicta.*]

Chronology 1916-1942

"Your picture should be taken while the glow of happiness is still there . . ." On what kind of a day did Edith Stein — now Sister Teresa Benedicta of the Cross, Carmelite nun — write these memoirs? Was she transported from the small room in the Dutch monastery at Echt to the bridge over the Dreisam to hear once more the joy in Edmund Husserl's voice as he announced she would be his assistant? If she likened the euphoria of that moment to that known by a newly-engaged couple, did these two live happily ever after?

A quarter of a century had passed over time's bridge and one fact became indisputably clear. Measured in purely human terms, the happiness she had just alluded to in her memoirs faded as quickly as did the wreath of flowers. The pictures taken of Edith Stein were again "so serious, always." But then, these were serious years. They led to:

WAR AND WORDS (1916-1921)

Life knows its peaceful plateaus but is struck by tidal waves as well. Edith's family had its foundations swept away, in 1893, when Siegfried Stein failed to return home from a business trip. The impact of that disaster was immediate for his forty-four year old widow. Her tireless work and acumen, in a field few women had entered, restored her family to security.

By 1916, because of World War I, Edith was already venturing into areas which would have given her mother pause. Just as Frau Stein had been catapulted into business by an unexpected event, so did Edith find herself led in an unforeseen way despite her academic prowess.

At the universities in Göttingen and Freiburg, the aftermath to

Sarajevo was also immediate. Student life was "blown to bits," as Edith described it. The male students and many of the professors entered military service. We have seen that, despite her mother's disapproval, Edith joined the Red Cross to nurse the wounded. The prolongation of the war brought her in the summer of 1916 to a position for which she volunteered because her peers were unavailable. Indeed, Fritz Frankfurter, the one she considered most competent among them, had been one of the war's first casualties.

Although it is fruitless to speculate whether under normal circumstances Edith would have been employed by Husserl, one cannot even be certain that she would have considered herself for the position. Edith's admission makes it clear[203] that she thought of volunteering her services after she and Erika Gothe had reviewed the availability of all other possible assistants.

August, 1916, found Edith studying Gabelsberger shorthand, in which system's squiggles Edmund Husserl captured his thoughts on odd sizes of paper scraps. These papers were packed into haphazard bundles and were collected over the years with an expectation of their being put in order eventually. The accumulation of so many bundles, some dated as early as 1903, made the services of an assistant imperative; and Husserl was relieved at the thought of Edith's working with him.

While Fritz Kaufmann was embroiled in the Eastern conflict of the struggle for Rumania, and other former fellow students suffered in the "hell" of Verdun, Edith began working with Husserl. She finished her teaching duties in Breslau and was released from her post as teacher of Latin, history, and geography by the Royal Board of Education in Breslau, September 29, 1916.

The dissertation, about which she wrote in the final pages of her unfinished biography, and her academic achievements were acknowledged in her diploma, which in free translation from the Latin and German, states:

Albert-Ludwig University[204]

[Under its] Eminent Rector Frederick II [of Baden] and under the Prorector Georg von Bülow, by the authority of the Academic Senate and by Decree of the Faculty of Philosophy, I, Alfred Koerte, lawful conferrer [of degrees] bestow on the most

learned woman Edith Stein, resident of Breslau, after her presenting a dissertation "On the Problem of Empathy," and after her passing an examination *summa cum laude*
the **DEGREE OF DOCTOR OF PHILOSOPHY**.
This diploma is official testimony of this conferral.

Witness: (signed)   Freiburg-im-Breisgau
Georg von Bülow   March 30, 1917

That same spring of 1917, Edith had Chapters II, III and IV of this doctoral dissertation, entitled in German *Zum Problem der Einfühlung*, published in Halle, Germany.[205]
While Edith continued to sort and decipher Husserl's notes and lectures, her own work was stirring up response from readers of her dissertation. Some of this critical appraisal was favorable while some of it took the form of argument. Since she had expressed a different opinion on the psyche than one held by Max Scheler, she hoped for a response from him.[206] Her contemporary, Winthrop Bell from Canada,[207] read her dissertation but was forced to confine his comments to a few words on a postcard since he was in detention as an enemy alien.

Edith sent many reports on her work with Husserl to Roman Ingarden who had returned to Göttingen after discharge from military service for medical reasons. To him, Edith admitted her growing dissatisfaction because the Master found no time to review the work he had produced in his earlier years, which Edith had so painstakingly put in order. Edith's flagging courage was revived at times when she came upon important notes such as those on *time-consciousness*,[208] which she recognized as having particular significance for those making comparisons with the thought of Bergson[209] and Natorp.[210]

Disappointment in her assistant's position—Husserl, either stimulated or distracted, consistently set off on new developments of thought whenever Edith persuaded him to read over his former work—was overshadowed by the war's events. Her friends' destinies affected her deeply: Adolf Reinach was killed in action early in 1917, and Edith helped his widow to put his literary legacy in order; Ingarden was in Warsaw seeking a teaching position in Poland's national school system. Hans Lipps was furloughed to recuperate after being wounded slightly, and Fritz Kaufmann was serving in Rumania.

Edmund Husserl's practice remained unchanged; at times, he would even suggest burning his earlier writings as he considered them outdated. Frustration was Edith's daily bread; she resigned at the beginning of 1918. The Master gave her a sincere letter of recommendation as she now sought for a professorship, beginning the search in Göttingen where she was so well known. By November, 1919, Edith ruefully writes to Kaufmann that he is a poor prophet. He had predicted early acceptance for habilitation for Edith; instead, her application was ignored by the faculty. Her thesis went unexamined,[211] and the record makes it clear that there was more than rejection of a woman behind the move.

Unsuccessful in Göttingen, Edith contacted a friend, Heinrich Scholz,[212] at the University of Kiel. He was determined to be so exacting and to find so much fault with any other applicants that she might be given a position there. The ploy was unsuccessful. William Stern,[213] in Hamburg, remained Edith's staunch champion even after she had seemingly deserted his camp to join Husserl. All of these vain endeavors serve to show the unique qualifications Husserl had acknowledged in Edith when he accepted her offer to assist him. Presumably he would have been pleased to have her with him indefinitely had she been satisfied with the Master's working methods.

While her personal friends and family may have felt neglected Edith was interested and aware of all their concerns. Her correspondence shows how willing she was to help her friends. In a letter to Kaufmann, in Freiburg during the winter of 1919–20, Edith expresses her satisfaction at his liking that university while she describes her distress that Hans Lipps, their mutual friend,[214] ignored her advice to complete his dissertation before paying a visit to the Husserls in Freiburg. How well she knew that the critical sparring Lipps met, especially from Frau Husserl, would prove more than he could handle and would complicate his search for a professorship. Evidently, it was not merely a case of having to be male in order to achieve a university post. What was denied Lipps in Freiburg, he found as professor of philosophy in the University of Frankfurt-am-Main.

During the search for a professorial appointment, Edith taught in Breslau, giving private instruction to college and university level students. She wrote articles and essays, and began a lecturing career that escalated during the next decade.

Edith earned the international reputation she had in Germany, Switzerland, and Austria by her careful attention to contemporary topics of her own day which were forerunners of our own vital issues. Her lectures on women's roles—professionals, responsible co-workers in the Church, homemakers, teachers, and mothers—incorporated all the facets of her remarkable erudition. True, Edith went "beyond sociology, psychology, and philosophy" in her treatment of the problems of our time, but she did so not by ignoring these disciplines but by placing them within the faith dimension in which she presented her suggested solutions. She shared the fruits of both, her years of association with important thinkers, and her wide human experience; and she did this sharing in a heartfelt simple manner as of one who had deep empathy for her hearers and their challenging situations. She awoke the conscience of teachers and parents, but did not leave them without the means for waging their own contest.

When Edith first served as Husserl's assistant, she inaugurated what she called a "Philosophical Kindergarten" to acquaint neophytes with phenomenology's founder and his methods. Now, in a similar fashion, Edith gave classes by her lectures and articles in a greater science—that of the Wisdom whose table is set, whose wines are poured, and whose fountains invite all classes and all ages of guests to feast and share. Edith's involvement in current issues provides us with a living model for contributing to our world not merely "what we have but all we *are*."

To enable others to lead and teach is an inestimable talent, and this was one of Edith Stein's great gifts. Her suggestions will stimulate others for years to come; her methodology can be applied to the ever changing situations which teachers must face.

Edith's personal spiritual journey preoccupied her for nearly three difficult years. When, in 1918, she assisted Frau Anna Reinach in putting order to Adolf Reinach's literary legacy, Edith came face to face with the power of Christ's Cross at work in those who believed in Him. Edith expected her mentor's widow would be devastated by her loss. Instead, as the Reinachs had become Christians not long before Adolf's death, Anna displayed such courage and acceptance in her bereavement that Edith acknowledged the source of this strength.

Although a seed of faith was planted, its flowering required time. At fifteen, Edith had decided she did not believe in God; at twenty-four, when she gave herself to phenomenology, the first flicker of faith began to dart into view. Most of her peers at Göttingen were Christian. So, too, were Husserl and Max Scheler. In 1918, faith's spark was so strong that Edith had to live by it, despite her realization that it might cost her the love and understanding of her family and friends. Faithful to her commitment in her search for the fullness of truth, by 1920, Edith was discerning whether to follow Christ in the Catholic or the Evangelical (Lutheran) Church.

On a visit to her friend Hedwig Conrad-Martius in Bergzabern, in the summer of 1921, an unexpected experience settled the matter for Edith. Frau Conrad-Martius was herself a member of the Evangelical Church, and it might have been a natural consequence of their friendship had Edith become Lutheran. Her friends made no attempt to influence her decision but indirectly supplied her with the compass that led her to her goal. During that stay with the Conrads, Edith chose, at random, *The Book of Her Life* by St. Teresa of Jesus, from among the many books in her friends' library. It was Edith's opportunity to learn from the sixteenth-century-Spanish mystic and great woman of Avila. In Teresa's response to Christ's love, Edith found the answer she had sought. She would follow Christ's invitation by entering the Catholic Church. From that moment on, Edith was strongly aware that an attraction to live out her baptismal commitment as a member of the Discalced Carmelite Order, and so as a daughter of Teresa of Jesus, was inseparable from her resolve to enter the Church.

Edith took steps at once which led to her reception of Baptism on New Year's Day, 1922; but she soon learned that becoming a Carmelite was not her immediate destiny. Her choice of vocation was made at that time, however, and she resolved to wait upon God's provident action, fully confident that someday Carmel's doors would be open to her.

Lectern, Pen and Repercussions (1922-1932)

Edith's reception of the Sacrament of Baptism in the Church of St. Martin, Bergzabern, on January 1, 1922, marked the beginning of a distinctly different mode of life for her and the changing of her relationship with her family and friends.

On the Feast of the Presentation, February 2, 1922, Bishop Ludwig Sebastian administered the Sacrament of Confirmation to Edith in his private chapel in Speyer. Soon thereafter, Edith took as her spiritual guide Monsignor Joseph Schwind, Vicar General of the Diocese of Speyer. In obedience to his direction, she postponed the thought of entering religious life until it would become unmistakably evident that this was God's will for her. At her director's suggestion, Edith accepted a position at St. Magdalena's, a Dominican Sisters' training institute for women teachers, located at Speyer.

At St. Magdalena's, Edith was able to live with the Sisters rather than among the students. She taught German and literature at the College for eight years. New friends, among the teachers and the Dominican Sisters, enriched her life; but she suffered at the same time because her entrance into the Catholic Church had caused some of her former acquaintances to withdraw their support and friendship. Edith did not directly complain about the pain this caused her, although she refers to it in Chapter Six. During her own struggle for light, she asked Eduard Metis, one of her most faithful friends of former days, whether he believed in a personal God. His blunt reply caused her deep disappointment, although she might have expected a lack of understanding from that source. Far more surprising, and painful, was the alienation of Fritz Kaufmann. Their correspondence, formerly so regular, was suspended for nearly five years. An illness of his mother's in 1925 enabled Edith to reestablish her relationship with Kaufmann to whom she explained that it was integral to her nature that, having befriended anyone "whom life has put in touch with me," she remained that person's faithful friend for life, regardless of further personal contact.

Edith's correspondence during the decade after her Baptism attests to the truth of this assurance. One can follow the destiny of her family and friends through a reading of her letters. In September, 1927, writing from Speyer to Fritz Kaufmann in Freiburg, she congratulates him upon his marriage.[215] Letters to women religious in these years, and those to Kaufmann, give an insight of her spiritual development. Edith often refers to others who in the course of the years discussed with her their doubts, hesitation, and hopes; they were confident that in her journey she had become acquainted with valid paths, had been warned of dead-end passages, or had been shown that some roads lead to dangerous terrain.

During Edith's assistantship with Husserl in Freiburg, she had taught newcomers to his courses in phenomenology in what she termed her "Philosophical Kindergarten." Among her students was Amelia Jaegerschmid, who later entered the Benedictine Order. By 1930, Amelia, now Sister Adelgundis, was a member of the community in St. Lioba's convent in Günterstal (Cf. P. 402.) From their correspondence and Edith's with Roman Ingarden, we learn that cordial contact with Edmund Husserl was essential to Edith. Four years after her Baptism, she visited Husserl in Freiburg. Both his reception of Edith and their conversation that day were marked with a depth and beauty that she never forgot. It occasioned, however, reflection on her part about the attitude to be taken toward others who do not share one's beliefs. Edith wrote to Sr. Adelgundis, O.S.B., in February, 1930, advising her to exercise care when discussing matters of religion, including the last things, with the ailing Husserl.[216] The risk of impulsive zeal, Edith pointed out, is that it raises the responsibility of both parties concerned, and the instrument of God's grace must not presume upon its own efficacy, rather all of us are to depend on God's mercy.

In this letter to Sr. Adelgundis, Edith writes that whenever an encounter with another person sharpens her awareness, in her own words, "of our powerlessness to exert a direct influence, I have a deeper sense of the urgency of my own *holocaustum.*" The remembrance of Nazi infamy will always be associated with the name "Holocaust;" but for Edith, twelve years before she died during that reign of terror, the word was a challenge to be generous in her everyday life, not only at some moment of extraordinary heroism. That does not lessen the awe we feel at her use of the word, as though she had some chilling premonition of her destiny.

The final two years of Edith Stein's professional career — 1931 and 1932 — were marked with constant activity. So many calls were made on her services as lecturer and writer that she gave up her teaching position at St. Magdalena's in the spring of 1931. Philosophical seminars took her to France. Her speaking engagements continued to take her to Switzerland and Austria to share the podium with prominent lay leaders of Church groups. These, like von Hildebrand,[217] testified in their own memoirs to her effectiveness in the Church.

As yet, her writings have not appeared in a complete collection in German; translations into French, Dutch, Italian, Spanish, and English, are even more limited. Nevertheless, those that are available show that her expertise enveloped all the concerns which are at present of current interest in the Church, in education, and in the areas of social justice and personal responsibility. Her correspondence with old and young friends, with religious and with professional confreres, makes a significant contribution to Catholic thought. No matter how many insights future students will gain from her writings, Edith's assurance that she has but one message in all she wrote and lectured will remain valid. She called it her *ceterum censeo*:[218] *how one may go about living at the hand of the Lord*, that is, being completely dependent on Him. She had no desire to teach any other lesson; like another great teacher before her time, St. John the Evangelist, she repeated her theme over and over in whatever she wrote or said.

Edith was no longer teaching at St. Magdalena's; in January, 1931, she made a renewed effort to obtain a professorship, this time in Freiburg. She prepared the necessary thesis — her doctoral dissertation could not be used in applying for habilitation — and she discussed her wishes with the Freiburg faculty. Martin Honecker,[219] (one of whose students was Karl Rahner) and Martin Heidegger, whom Husserl had engaged as a faculty assistant, both accorded Edith a cordial reception; but that was the extent of their involvement. Edith returned to Breslau.

Hans Biberstein, Edith's brother-in-law, met frequently with colleagues on the faculty of the University of Breslau. One of them, the theologian Josef Koch[220] would have liked Edith to teach at the university. Surprisingly enough, Frau Stein would have accepted Edith's teaching publicly as a Catholic in Breslau where the family was well-known, if that meant her daughter could live at home. But Breslau was not ready to award a professorship to a woman.

The constant traveling made necessary by lecturing engagements in places as varied as Munich, Vienna, Prague, Juvisy-near-Paris, and Zurich, brought Edith into contact with many people. She was invited as guest lecturer to many public events and celebrations. Among these was the Goethe Centenary in 1932.[221] Edith had, by this time, joined the faculty at the Pedagogic Institute in Münster. As in Speyer, Edith lived with the Sisters at the Marianum College, and was happy to be again in a religious house. A new form of apostolate for Edith began in 1932; she delivered radio addresses on the *Bayrische Rundfunk*, the Bavarian Radio Network.

Edith's spiritual life was rarely a topic of discussion in her letters except for references to her retreats or her visits to the Benedictine Archabbey in Beuron. Monsignor Schwind, her director for five years, had died in 1927; he was succeeded by the Archabbot of Beuron, Dom Raphael Walzer. When Edith was told to postpone her entrance into a religious community, she took private vows and, in consequence, considered Archabbot Walzer as her religious superior. Aware of Edith's gifts as a philosopher, the Benedictine archabbot encouraged her participation in international symposia along with other well-known Catholics, among them her old acquaintance, Alexandre Koyré,[222] who was teaching in Paris.

The closing months of 1932 brought Edith back to Breslau for a vacation with her family. Her mother continued in rather good health, although some effects of advancing age were apparent. Rosa Stein, as Edith implies at the close of Chapter III (Cf. Page 114), had found Edith's example more than just attractive; she longed to join Edith. In consideration for their aging mother, however, Rosa remained at home. All too soon, Edith would once more have distressing news for her family.

GARDEN ENCLOSED AND EXIT TO AUSCHWITZ (1933-1942)

February, 1933, found Edith engaged with the other lecturers at the Catholic Pedagogical Institute of Münster in developing an outline for Catholic education. Edith had never intended to teach; her career as a philosopher never became an actuality and, therefore, teaching perforce took its place. A review of the comments and reflections Edith Stein made about teachers and about their profession enables one to express them metaphorically. For her, teaching was not a routine dishing out of successive portions of a textbook prepared by someone else. Rather, having assessed the students' needs and their capability to absorb solid nourishment, a good teacher provides, besides the packaged textbook material, the appetizers of experience and of challenge. Judicious dashes of seasoning are added to stimulate the students' curiosity, encouraging them to individual research and study. Most important in Edith's judgment is the teacher's responsibility to be aware, throughout the process, of the risks and advantages which must be brought to young people's attention. In this method of teaching, the student's initiative is to be respected and encouraged. Edith had exercised great freedom in her own years as a student; the great care she took to provide the best in information and incentive proved that these had been the means she most appreciated.

Her own training in pedagogy was very limited and she was aware of the gaps in her professional preparation. She was happy during the short time she was at Münster that her associates welcomed her searching questions and her challenge to make innovations when these were demanded by the students' welfare.

Scarcely had she immersed herself in the work at Münster than she, along with all other teachers, writers, and professional people who were even partially of Jewish descent, felt the heavy hand of Hitler's National Socialism. Even at Münster where she was never in the limelight, her services were terminated, as she was informed on April 19, 1933. She understood that if employment in Münster was denied her then her academic career in Germany had come to an end. If classroom doors were barred to her by the Nazis, might it mean that the door to religious life was now opened for her by Divine Providence?

She asked Archabbot Walzer's permission to seek admission to the Carmelite Order. He granted her request in mid-May, 1933. At Edith's request, her friend, Dr. Elisabeth Cosack, arranged an appointment for her with the Discalced Carmelite Nuns in Cologne, since Edith had no previous contact with the nuns. Dr. Cosack took Edith's request to the Carmel. On May 20, Edith received an invitation to come to that monastery to discuss the question of her vocation in person; she went to Cologne that same day. On June 19, 1933, Edith received word from the nuns that she had been accepted for admission.

During a month, July 16 to August 15, spent in the extern guest quarters at the Carmel of Cologne-Lindenthal, Edith became better acquainted with the Sisters; and there she prepared herself for those last weeks to be spent at home with her family.

Frau Stein met Edith's latest decision with incomprehension and with tears. But when the time came for Edith to leave home, Frau Stein gave her youngest daughter a warm and loving embrace. The farewell took place after breakfast on the day following Edith's forty-second birthday.

Edith entered the monastery in Cologne on October 14, 1933. For six months, as a postulant, she was acquainted with the "horarium," the daily schedule followed by the nuns. Edith learned, by doing, the contemplative lifestyle introduced into the Church by St. Teresa of Jesus and St. John of the Cross. On April 15, 1934, Edith Stein was admitted into the Novitiate. This made her a member of the Carmelite Order, and her acceptance was symbolized by her reception of the familiar clothing, the Discalced Carmelite *habit*, and she assumed a religious name, signing it from that day on as Sister Teresa Benedicta of the Cross.

A change of name and a new mode of dressing did not mean Edith Stein ceased to exist. Her friends were able to visit her, to attend the ceremonies which marked the stages of her initiation in the community and in the Order. Edith continued to correspond with Fritz Kaufmann; when he passed through Cologne enroute to England, he stopped to see Edith. The Kaufmanns found refuge in England, and later in the United States; Edith continued to hear from them. She kept in touch with Hedwig Conrad-Martius, and, through the latter's intermediacy, with Erika Gothe, Hering, [223] and others. With these former colleagues, Edith shared information on her resumption of philosophical study and original writing.

The Stein family's situation in Breslau was cause for concern. Edith's mother never wrote personally in the first year Edith spent in Carmel. Letters went very regularly from Cologne-Lindenthal to Erna Biberstein, who had two teen-aged children by this time. The rest of the family were beginning to disperse; unfortunately, they did not all succeed in escaping the Nazi persecution.

Breslau had an additional attraction for the Carmelite Nuns at this time. They were hoping to establish a monastery in that city. [224] Rosa Stein informed Edith of an unusual incident involving their mother and the Sisters who were making the foundation. One day in autumn of 1935, without informing any of the daughters at home with her in Breslau, Frau Augusta, eighty-five years old at the time, paid a visit to the construction site of the proposed Carmelite monastery. Shortly after that incident, Frau Stein began to write a few lines to Edith, and to the Superior in Cologne, at the conclusion of Rosa's letters. This was the greatest consolation for Edith, for whom her mother's sadness had been a constant source of sorrow.

By the summer of 1936, Frau Stein was failing. With every report of her mother's decline, Edith heard also that, although Frau Stein minded the departure of grandsons who were going to the "far-off corners" of the world, she brooded far more over the absence of her youngest daughter; this was painful for Edith to hear. Early in the morning of September 14, 1936, the Feast of the Exaltation of the Cross, the Nuns in Cologne observed the ceremonial renewal of their vows, [225] as was the custom at that time. Sister Teresa Benedicta had a strong sense of her mother's presence at her side during the ceremony; a telegram from Breslau later in the day confirmed her intuition. The time of Frau Stein's death coincided with that of the Carmelite ceremony.

Arno Stein sold the family business, intending to join his wife and two of their children in the United States. [226] Rosa, living with Frieda in the family home in Breslau, longed for the day when, like Edith, she could become a Catholic.

During this difficult time, Edith was once more engaged in philosophical work at her Prioress' request. She had brought with her to Carmel her thesis, *Akt und Potenz*, which she had presented to the faculty at the University of Göttingen. Edith revised the work; then, no publisher would accept it because of the Nazi strictures. This scholarly attempt to build bridges between phenomenology and Catholic tradition was Edith's most serious philosophical work. Its present published form is *Endliches und Ewiges Sein*, or *Finite and Eternal Being*. Edith's friend, Hedwig Conrad-Martius, supplied Edith with current literature on philosophical topics; from her, Edith requested specific material such as a book on the soul by Alexander Pfänder,[227] and, remarkably, the latest presentation of that time on atomic theory.

When Edith completed the three years of temporary profession—she had taken vows of poverty, chastity, and obedience upon completion of her year in the Novitiate—as Sister Teresa Benedicta, she made her final profession on April 21, 1938.[228] To signify that she had made a permanent commitment as a Carmelite nun, she was now able to exchange the white veil worn since her days as a novice for the black veil of a Discalced Carmelite nun. She received this sign of her new "profession" as a religious from Auxiliary Bishop Wilhelm Stockums, of Cologne, on May 1. During these festive days at Carmel, she received notification that Edmund Husserl, the "Master" at Göttingen and Freiburg, had died on April 27.[229]

The Nazi repression of the Jews had not slackened during Edith's years in Carmel; Edith was aware that her presence in the Community at Cologne-Lindenthal[230] was certain to bring reprisal on her beloved Sisters. There seemed no alternative but to seek refuge elsewhere. Her superiors felt that the Carmel of Echt in Holland might offer safety; that Dutch Carmel had come into existence in 1875 when the Bismarck government had given Germany's religious communities of men and women an option: exile or secularization. German Carmelites had found refuge in the Netherlands then; they hoped Edith would be safe in Echt now. So it was that late at night on December 31, 1938, Edith, Sister Teresa Benedicta of the Cross, crossed the border into Holland, and began the New Year among her Sisters in Echt.

A week after her arrival in the new community, Edith wrote to Cologne-Lindenthal to inquire whether there was any possibility of having the manuscript of her autobiography brought to Holland. Perhaps she hoped that her sister, Rosa, now also a Catholic, might be able to join her in Holland, and Rosa might bring the manuscript. But Rosa had far more difficulty getting the necessary papers to join her sister in Echt; they were not reunited until Rosa came by way of Belgium, in the summer of 1940.

There were adjustments to make that were difficult for Edith, and, in many ways, for the Echt community as well. In time, her new Prioress asked Edith to resume her writing. In summer, 1941, Edith finished an article on the *Symbolic Theology of Pseudo-Dionysius*, which she wrote purposely for a philosophical journal[231] in the United States.

In Germany, the nuns in Cologne kept informed about Edith's relatives and friends, forwarding news to Echt when this was possible. Even after Edith's departure, the Sisters had to fear some action from the Gestapo. More than one Carmelite monastery had already been requisitioned by the SS, on less than two hours notice in some cases. The Carmel in Luxembourg was the first to be taken over, those of Pützchen, Aachen, and Düren were next. For fear that Cologne Carmel might also be commandeered, the Prioress there had all incriminating correspondence destroyed. Many of Edith's letters were lost because of this necessary precaution for the safety of her German community. Letters to her were sent at risk; often she received them months later. One of these informed her of the death of her friend of Göttingen days, Hans Lipps. She asked her sisters to remember him and the two daughters "for whom he had been both father and mother following his wife's early death."[232]

For Edith and Rosa, the occupation of Holland by the Nazis meant all their search for a refuge would have to begin again. They had to appear before Occupation Force magistrates in Maastricht and in Amsterdam. Notice was given that all non-

Aryan Germans resident in Holland were stateless; they were to report by December 15 for deportation from the country. The Carmelite Nuns wrote to the French-speaking Carmel of Le Pâquier in Switzerland;[233] one of the novices there knew Edith from those long-ago days when she had lectured in Switzerland. A haven was sought for Rosa with a religious congregation not far from Le Pâquier. But such correspondence was very slow moving; and the official papers that had to be obtained in Holland, in Switzerland, and from Rome, since Edith was a professed religious, were so numerous and so reluctantly granted that the whole effort failed.

Meanwhile, it was more and more evident that in Holland as in Germany, the Nazis were determined to eliminate the Jews. On Sunday, July 26, 1942, the Catholic Church made a formal protest against the genocide. By order of the Episcopate of Holland, a pastoral letter was read to the faithful at every Mass. The Bishops informed the Dutch citizens that together with nine other denominational churches in Holland, they had sent a telegram to Arthur Seyss-Inquart, Commander of the Nazi Occupation in Holland, demanding the cessation of measures being taken against the Jews. Since the telegram had been ignored by the Nazis, the Churches were apprising their people through this pastoral letter that the Nazis' tactics were reprehensible. The pastoral letter moved the hearers deeply. The Nazi authorities were enraged.[234]

At this time, news reached Edith and Rosa that their eldest brother, Paul, his wife Trude, and their sister, Frieda Tworoger, had all been sent to the concentration camp at Theresienstadt in Germany. Frieda died there in 1942; Paul and Trude, in 1943.

Listing the events of that week, diary fashion, presents a stark picture of this "Holy Week without an Easter Sunday." The sequence of protest and retaliation requires no further comment:

>   a) July 26: pastoral read in all Catholic churches and in many others in Holland
>
>   b) July 27: "Because the Bishops interfered," *Reichskommissar* Seyss-Inquart orders all Catholic Jews to be deported before the week's end.

c) July 30: official correspondence lists the number of Jews registered as Catholics to be 722 throughout Holland.

d) July 31: official memorandum advises that, to date, six thousand Jews in all have been deported from Holland without interference.

e) July 31: the same memorandum notes that four thousand Jews who registered as Christians have been gathered in one camp, possibly as a step toward bribing the churches to stop protesting general deportation.

f) Aug. 2: at the Carmelite Monastery in Echt, the evening hour of mental prayer began, as usual, at 5 P.M. Sister Teresa Benedicta read the point of meditation, as was also usual. A few minutes of silence followed. Then, heavy pounding at the door resounded through the nuns' Choir. The S.S. men had come; almost before the nuns realized what was going on, Sister Benedicta and Rosa Stein had been taken away.

From Echt, the journey to the East began. The brief stop at Amersfoort prison camp brought together many who had been arrested that Sunday. Within two days, the internees were transported to the concentration camp in Drente-Westerbork, Holland. From Westerbork, Edith sent a final note to her community in Echt; she reported meeting several acquaintances among the prisoners, and assured her Sisters that at the camp the group was calm and cheerful.

The brief postscript requested the nuns not to mention that they had received the note, should they contact Edith by letter.

Silence then shrouded the days and weeks which followed.

In 1948, the Prioress of the Carmel of Cologne published the first biography of Edith Stein. In it, Mother Teresa Renata of the Holy Spirit tells the reader that in Schifferstadt,[235] there was a report of a message given by a "lady in dark clothes"—a message to the Schwind family, and indirectly, to the Carmelites. Valentin Fouquet, the stationmaster, heard himself addressed. He realized someone was calling to him from the transport that was momentarily stopped in that railway station. The "lady in dark clothes" said her name was Stein; she asked Fouquet to tell her friends that she sent greetings and that she was on the way to Poland.

The nuns in Cologne and Echt continued their search for traces of official records. Finally, the Netherlands Red Cross wrote the last sentence of the story of Edith Stein in the following document:

BUREAU OF INFORMATION OF THE NETHERLANDS RED CROSS
9 JAN EVERTS STREET, 's-GRAVENHAGE

's-GRAVENHAGE, 2 JUNE, 1958

SETTLEMENT BUREAU FOR JEWISH AFFAIRS
DOSSIER NO. 108796
YOUR LETTER OF May 16, 1958

CERTIFICATION

THE UNDERSIGNED, CHIEF OF THE SETTLEMENT BUREAU FOR JEWISH AFFAIRS OF THE NETHERLANDS RED CROSS BUREAU OF INFORMATION CONFIRMS HEREBY THAT ACCORDING TO THE PAPERS KEPT IN OUR ARCHIVES

Edith Teresa Hedwig STEIN

BORN ON: October 12, 1891   IN: Breslau
LAST RESIDENCE: Monastery of the Carmelite Nuns,
                        Bovenstestraat 48, Echt (Holland)
FOR REASONS OF RACE, AND SPECIFICALLY BECAUSE OF JEWISH DESCENT
ON 2 August, 1942, ARRESTED IN Echt, VIA K.L. [CONCENTRATION CAMP]
                                        AMERSFOORT (HOLLAND)
ON 5 August, 1942, HANDED OVER IN K.L. WESTERBORK AND
ON 7 August, 1942, DEPORTED FROM K.L. WESTERBORK TO K.L. AUSCHWITZ.
THE ABOVE NAMED PERSON IS TO BE CONSIDERED AS HAVING DIED ON 9 August, 1942* IN AUSCHWITZ.

NOTICE TO THIS EFFECT IS GIVEN ON 15 FEBRUARY, 1950 IN ECHT
. . . [conditions are given regarding legal procedures] . . .

(Signed, official seal applied by Chief of the Bureau)

* For official purposes this date of death was established as deduced from various available facts. Individual statements regarding the exact time of death are not available.

Sr. Teresa Benedicta of the Cross (1938)

On the Fortieth Anniversary of Edith's death, August 9, 1982, a story in the "*Kölner Rundschau,*" a Cologne newspaper, adds a poignant postscript. This account cannot be verified, but there are so many details that make it creditable that one finds it difficult to dismiss. What a distressing thought — Edith's route to the East may well have taken her by way of the very places most dear to her.

The trip from Holland must have been by the rail line south, past Cologne, since we have Fouquet's testimony for the stop at Schifferstadt which is but a few miles from Speyer where she taught. Then Johannes Wieners' story provided a final vignette.

A postal employee in the Cologne branch of the federal postal system, Wieners had been inducted with seventeen other men, three of them officers, to form a mobile postal unit. He was required to report June 15, 1942, for six weeks of military training. They were being sent to the eastern war zone where the Sixth German Army was fighting the Russians. He was assigned a large truck as a mobile postoffice; they were being transported east by train.

On the 7th of August, 1942, he and the others in his unit were standing in the switching area of the railroad depot in Breslau since their engine had been uncoupled for servicing.

A freight train pulled into the station on the track next to theirs. A minute or so later, a guard opened a sliding door on one of the cars. With dismay, Wieners noticed it was packed with people who were jammed together, cowering on the floor. The stench coming from the car almost overpowered the men standing outside.

Then a woman in nun's clothing stepped into the opening. Wieners looked at her with such commiseration that she spoke to him: "It's awful. We have nothing by way of containers for sanitation needs."

Looking into the distance and then across the town, she said, "This is my beloved hometown. I will never see it again."

When he looked at her, questioningly, she added, very hesitantly: "We are riding to our death."

He was profoundly shocked and asked, in all seriousness: "Do your companion prisoners believe that also?"

Her answer came even more hesitantly, "It's better that they do not know it."

Wieners' companions were irritated that he spoke to a Jewess and berated him for it. But one of them who had overheard the conversation joined him; the two men discussed quietly in the face of their angry comrades the possibility of doing anything for the people.

Edith had overheard the objections; when they asked her whether they could get her and her companions anything to eat or drink, she replied, "No, thank you, we accept nothing."

The markings on the car made it plain that it had come from Holland. By this time, the boiler on their engine had been re-filled, and the locomotive recoupled. The men had boarded their train which then left Breslau station.

Johannes Wieners served for a time and then was taken a prisoner of war. When, much later, he was back in Germany, he saw a picture of Edith Stein, accompanying an article about her. He was sure she was the nun he had seen on August 7, 1942. It may be in God's plan that we continue to learn more about her throughout the years. This will bring her story to its last page.

The Carmelite nuns in Cologne have, in their archives, a number of unpublished writings of Edith Stein. Sometimes, these are jottings of her meditations, and it seems fitting to close this chronology with a thought with which Edith sums up all that we have learned about her courage and her spirituality:

> Do you want to be totally united to the Crucified? If you are serious about this, you will be present, by the power of His Cross, at every front, at every place of sorrow, bringing to those who suffer comfort, healing, and salvation.

Translator's Afterword

I

"The translator must be like a window which allows all of the light to enter but which, itself, is invisible."

Such was the criterion Edith Stein set for herself when she translated John Henry Newman's letters and diaries from the English and Saint Thomas Aquinas' *"Quaestiones"* from the Latin. Her words, the standard she set by them, and her example create the obligation to do the same for anyone who translates her writings.

The effort invested in becoming such a window may handicap a translator when the time comes to function effectively as a door. However, a door merely provides access to persons who desire to become acquainted. The decisive introductory comments are those exchanged between host and caller. The door, no matter how sturdy or decorative, disappears as conscionably as does the window.

Therefore, this afterword is designed to furnish a richly variegated background for Edith Stein, for Sister Teresa Benedicta of the Cross, for the child, the woman, the philosopher, and the Carmelite.

For Edith's story, her clear and often witty word-portraits of relatives and friends, her perceptive evaluation of persons and events, and the characteristics she displays while recounting happenings or admitting attitudes will remain the indispensable element.

II

EDITH STEIN — A BOOK WITH SEVEN SEALS

Edith as a child was so reserved, so reluctant to disclose her thoughts, that her sisters called her "a book sealed with seven seals." Their choice of a predicate evokes at once an image of the scroll with seven seals which only the Lamb was able to open. It may also show how readily one comes to the use of biblical imagery when speaking of Edith Stein.

The reticence characteristic of her in childhood was still to be noticed during her teaching and lecturing career. The openness with which she tells the story of *Life in a Jewish Family* is therefore remarkable. She is as frank about herself as she is about her relatives, friends and acquaintances. Evidently, by the time she had become Sister Teresa Benedicta of the Cross the seals of the book had been loosened. The book reveals what her given name Edith also indicates, viz., rich gift:

> the beloved daughter of a Jewish family,
> a staunch German patriot,
> a young woman, confident in the academic world,
> a philosopher whose depth of empathy helped her
> to establish and maintain warm relationships.
> As a Carmelite, she came to see with clarity
> what awaited her, her people, Germany, and the world.

Under these seven aspects, we find that Edith has given us all the elements necessary for a biography. When she wrote the book, it had a purpose of its own: to acquaint the reader with Jewish men, women, and children in a family setting. That it has now become Edith's autobiography "lay not in her plans, but in God's."

God's plan for his own is often unravelled in an individual's life so that it becomes visible only in retrospect. At other times He makes it known by direct command as He once did to Moses:

> The fire that consumes the holocaust on the altar must
> not be allowed to go out. Every morning the priest must
> make it up with wood. He is to arrange the holocaust

on it and burn the fat from the communion sacrifices.
An undying fire is always to burn on the altar; it must
not go out.   (Lev. 6:5, 6)

In Edith Stein—the book sealed seven times—the story of
God's sacred fire may be reread. The Stein-Courant family inherited a religion which for them did not call for orthodox observance. As Jews, they accepted the possession of a doctrinal
treasure which concerned not only mankind and that world and
universe in which they lived but, primarily, God—the one true
God. In obedience to this God, Jewish law regulates a great part
of life; some customs and rites are traditionally passed from generation to generation, as are ceremonies prescribed of old. Sacred
Scripture contains instructions imparted to the Jews by their God,
and God is worshiped by his people in fidelity to that law. We
touch upon this one aspect in the story of Judaism since it is in
accord with the Biblical imagery used to unify the elements of
this book, compiled from various of Edith's writings.

A Daughter of a Jewish Family

From the days of Moses to those of Solomon when the altar of
sacrifice found a worthy enshrinement in the Temple, the Jewish
people kept the fire of sacrifice alive, in fidelity to the command
of God. At the same time, the word of God was preserved by those
who came after Moses. The Jews had left an ineradicable mark
on the Egyptian people; they affected the lives of their captors
from Assyria, then those from Babylon, as well as of the Persians
who freed the Jews and allowed them to return to Palestine five
centuries before Christ's birth.

For two of those five centuries the prescribed sacrifices were
offered to God. The temple was restored, and the fire which had
been hidden at the time of the exile was returned to the altar of
sacrifice. This was the era during which the Scriptures were
translated into Greek. From then on the influence of the Sacred
Writings marked the life of Western civilization even when it
has been unrecognized, or ignored, yes, even repudiated. Every
reaction or response to the Word of God results in a development

within the nation or individual who either accords or denies it the rightful place it commands. God constituted it as a catalyst: "My Word shall not return to Me void" (Isaiah 55:11).

In what does its power rest? In the simple truth that it is God, the Creator, who speaks; His word is honored in the Sacred Scriptures — Torah or Bible — the written Word of God. Since the Creator speaks and has given his human creature ears to hear, the one created to God's image is obliged to listen to the message preserved in the Scriptures. Whether this listening is prompted by the conscious desire for God, or, conversely, whether denial of dependence on God or of relationship with Him expresses itself in a disdain of this Word, the result is the same. Through being loved or hated, even through being sought with insatiable longing when still unknown, God rightly becomes the dominant *Other* in every individual life.

This property of the Word of God became operative in history. The process of Hellenization in the third century, B.C., began almost without notice. Greek manners, customs, and above all, language were assimilated gradually; and imperceptibly again, mores and ethics were affected. We know the development and the denouement: the war of the Maccabees ended in triumph for the Jews who recaptured Jerusalem, purged the Temple, and restored the worship of the one true God.

The history of Judaism as it touches that of Christianity is familiar to most of us, aware as we are of events that occurred well into the second half of the first century, A.D. When the Romans under Titus Flavius Sabinus Vespasianus burned the Temple in the year 70, nearly a thousand years after Solomon first built it, the vindictive enemy assumed this would end the worship paid to the God of the Jews. But He is the God whom no one can mock. Fidelity, expressed for so long in keeping a physical fire alive upon an altar now found new expression under God's inspiration: devotion to the burning Word of God housed not in a temple of stone but on the altar of man's own loyal heart.

The same Vespasian — in those final days of Jerusalem's struggle for survival — was a tool in the hand of the Almighty as the Lord carved out for Himself a new shrine in the Jewish nation, a new Temple. Not made of stone, it was a means whereby God could remain ever present with his people. By an intrepid move of a great rabbi, Johanan ben Zaccai, Vespasian was approached in his own camp and was led to give permission for the opening, within years, of a small academy of Jewish studies. Vespasian could not know that by establishing this school the far-seeing Rabbi ben Zaccai was safeguarding the spirit of Jewish worship of the one God.

The academy was opened in Jabneh. As the Rabbi had foreseen, its head, the "Patriarch," came to be recognized by Jewry all over the civilized world as their spiritual leader. The light that had dimmed over Jerusalem burned brightly in Jabneh. Even after the Jews rebelled twice more against the Romans, in 116 A.D. against Trajan, and in 132 against Hadrian, their spirit was strong. Hadrian could forbid the Jews to enter the ruins of Jerusalem; he could call the colony Palestine, no longer Judaea. He could and did, put to death the rabbis who led the people; but they became heroic figures whose fidelity is commemorated annually in the liturgy of the Day of Atonement, the holiest day of the Jewish year.

Hadrian made the Jewish survivors realize that they must take steps to preserve the Oral Torah. The oral tradition had grown steadily since the school at Jabneh was opened. Near the middle of the second century, A.D., the Academy was rebuilt in Upper Galilee. Since the succeeding persecutions had more than decimated those who had preserved the tradition, the leaders realized that one more such effort at the extermination of the Jewish nation might mean the death of all who kept his Word alive in the community.

Under Judah the Prince, therefore, the code of laws known as the *Mishna* was written down and edited. He used clear, brief sentences in simple Hebrew so that the code would be accessible to all Jews. The task was completed around the year 200.

For two more centuries while the growth of civilization, the fortunes of world history, and politics led — or, under hostile circumstances, drove — the Jews into all parts of the globe, the Academy continued its role.

When conditions in Palestine threatened to remain unsettled, a new center for the study of the Torah was established in Babylon. There, through discussion and debate at its biannual assemblies, the Jewish community produced the Babylonian Talmud. By 500 A.D., it had been written and could be studied. But, most important, it could be taken wherever Jews were to go. In every community the synagogue became the center of the group's religious life. Once the Temple had drawn the Jewish people together for sacrifice and worship. But sacrifice, besides being impracticable in the small synagogues, was often beyond the means of the impoverished Jews; they had come to know, however, that prayer rather than sacrifice satisfied the deepest needs of the human heart. Resistance to Roman and Greek influence and fidelity to the one God were spiritual matters.

Prayer was accompanied by the observance of the traditional festivals and holy days. The most universally known, the *Sabbath*, has remained a day for worshipping God and for rejoicing and rejuvenating those who keep it.

The festivals of *Rosh Hashanah, Sukkoth, Hanukkah* and *Purim* or, respectively, New Year, Tabernacles, the Festival of Lights, and the Day of Lots are not as readily recognized by non-Jews. They have become known through literature and, with the Passover and Pentecost, have ecumenical significance in our own day.

In the personal life story of Edith Stein, two other festivals of the Jewish liturgical year are important: *Yom Kippur* and *Tish'a B'Ab*. *Yom Kippur*, the Day of Atonement, is an opportunity offered as it recurs each year to begin life anew, to return to God and to renew fidelity to Him. In 1891, Edith was born on the Day of Atonement, and Frau Stein saw this as a blessing for her child. Edith's mother was devout; her faith in God was unshakable. She did what she could to instruct her family in her religion but she did not exact strict observance. One can see from Edith's own account that while they had no doubt about their mother's deep faith, the young Stein brothers and sisters seemed to take their Jewish religion rather more for granted than as a serious personal commitment. Edith never forgot she had been born on the day of Atonement.

We, in turn, will not forget that the day of her death is also very reminiscent of a holy day her mother would have kept. The month of Ab approximates the height of summer in the Jewish calendar; in the Gregorian one, its counterpart would be the weeks ending July and beginning August. *Tish'a B'Ab*, the Ninth day of the Month of Ab, is an annual day of black fast in mourning memory of the destruction of the first and the second Temples in Jerusalem. The ninth day of August in the year of 1942 saw the destruction of Edith and Rosa Stein, with countless other temples of the Spirit in the infamy of Auschwitz.

Death in Hitler's persecution did not mean oblivion for Edith and her companions — nor was Hadrian's persecution the end for the Jewish people. The three wars against Rome had cost the lives of many thousands of soldiers and of even more women and children. Seeking to escape further threats of annihilation, the survivors began to follow wherever the trade routes led. A so-called Golden Age, another thousand years of comparative glory having passed, the center of the Jewish life was no longer in the Eastern world. Many Jews had gone to the West, some coming as far as England with William the Conqueror. Others settled at intermediate colonies in Spain or France; from all these centers they moved on into neighboring countries.

As a result of continued fidelity to their own religious laws and their determination to hand these on to their posterity, the Jews, wherever they might put down roots, came to have the highest educational standards in Europe. These standards were applied by single families when, as was frequently the case, there were no colonies of Jews at one location. Settling in the various countries of Europe was one matter, however, while owning the property they lived on was a far different and, usually, an impossible situation.

The forebears of the Stein and Courant families might well have arrived in Germany by way of Spain or France. The Jewish settlers were an important segment of European life, but they would not have shared the experience of "belonging" that would have been the lot of the ancestors of Thérèse Martin-Guerin of Lisieux, or of Elizabeth Catez-Rolland of Dijon, France.

Not more than twenty years separated Edith Stein, in Silesia, from these older, French sisters of hers in the Discalced Carmelite Order. Culturally, however, there were significant differences in their daily lives. Only in the intimate family interrelations does one find, in all three cases, parallel instances of parental love and care, of sibling loyalty, of the extended family's influence and demands. These similarities set into more striking relief the contrasts in social milieu, in civic and political circumstances found in the lives of these young ladies from France when they are compared to Edith's life in Breslau.

German literature and the history of that literature itself provide insights essential for an understanding of the subtleties of situations and relationships facing Jews in Germany in the tumultuous times beginning with the mid-eighteenth century. The transition from life under feudal lords in sometimes miniscule principalities which often depended for survival on the advice of the ruler's advisor known everywhere as *Hofjude*, the Court Jew, to the experience of shared civic rights and responsibilities for all citizens was difficult. The persons around whom the history of those years is constructed were in many instances Jewish — the role of catalyst was often theirs.

Abstracting from literature to gain a glimpse of reality promotes an understanding and appreciation of the contribution that the Jews made in the history of Europe, as well as the suffering they endured, and, it must be admitted, at times caused. In Germany, Jewish families who had lived there for generations were deeply patriotic, and with pride and passion they put all their personal resources at the service of the state.

When discrimination, type-casting of classes, and the toleration of psychological factors which foster prejudice or bias are allowed to grow unchecked, they exercise a strong influence on ethnic and social conditions; when, however, these unfortunate practices find expression in popular as well as classic literature, the uneducated mistrust already rooted in the imagination of the ordinary reader is strengthened; often it is impervious to change.

In a development of history to which these brief remarks can refer only in passing, emancipation for the Jews in Germany followed the upheavals of the Revolutions — 1792–1799 in France, and both 1848 and 1918 in Germany — as the situation of the Jews in Germany seemed to improve.

In Breslau, as in other European cities during the industrial revolution, the acquisition of property and the management of factories—usually at the cost of hard, even incessant labor—meant that many Jews became financially independent; there are several references to the nouveau-riche among some of the Jewish acquaintances in Edith's story. Business success more often than not earned them animosity; history shows how briefly the Jews were able to exercise full civic rights in Germany.

This background must be kept in view when considering the attitude Edith and her contemporaries had toward their country.

Edith's Loyal Love for Germany

When Germany plunged into World War I, Edith interrupted her studies at the University of Göttingen. Her feeling for Germany crystalized in her spontaneous reflection on the situation the day war was declared. In Chapter VII, she writes:

> . . . feverishly tense, I faced the future with great clarity and determination.
> 'I have no private life anymore,' I told myself. 'All my energy must be devoted to this great happening. Only when the war is over, if I'm alive then, will I be permitted to think of my private affairs once more.'

That kind of loyalty to one's country can result only from a day to day living out of a conviction that "this land is my land." Belonging to Germany—*being* German—was so integral an attitude in the Stein-Courant families for generations that again from Edith's recounting we learn of her aunts' relinquishing their beloved family homestead rather than become expatriates in the portion of Silesia ceded to Poland after a plebiscite.

Her relatives, friends, and fellow students enlisted in World War I out of their deep conviction that it was a patriotic duty. Many deplored the political situation that brought the necessity upon them. Many, too, had distressingly close bonds to England since there was much to unite the countries not only socially and culturally but in personal connections. Richard Courant recounts that one soldier in his acquaintance found his first cousin's husband among the British prisoners-of-war entrusted to his custody.

World War II found the countries further apart, but there were at that time instances every bit as poignant which served to illustrate the inborn and even passionate attachment to Germany which was to be found in German Jews. This made the crimes against them deeper for the element of betrayal of a national bond that should have existed and surmounted the rift caused by ideological differences. Edith tells us that her mother herself found unfathomable the notion that she was *not* German. A well-known contemporary of Edith's who succeeded in getting to Switzerland early, Ernst Ginsberg, the actor and poet, recounts with equal affection and horror how his seventy-year-old father felt toward *Germany*, not toward its Nazi government. Only at the cost of forfeiting all his possessions, ailing after a serious operation for intestinal cancer, humiliated by those who prolonged the process and divested him of everything down to the gold case of his pocket watch, an emaciated Dr. Ginsberg was allowed to leave Berlin to go to Zürich. There he read of the Germans' march into Paris, and to his son's consternation commented in all seriousness, in all unawareness of the irony of his remark, "See, *we* are invincible." (How many like him were simply incapable of evaluating and crediting what was going on around them, and *to* them?)

Edith was not blind to the course of events; nor was she a passive bystander. Her understanding went deep; she would have shared Ernst Ginsberg's sadness that the patriotic love of so many millions of Germans could be betrayed and punished by death in concentration camps.

Back in 1914, Edith remarked on the dramatic change in the history of humanity when she reflected that no one who had not lived before World War I could ever imagine the tranquility and order which had reigned. This was before humanity learned it was within mankind's deranged power to destroy the world.

Even to get a small glimpse of that tranquility will help us to appreciate Edith Stein, her family, and her story. Customs and usages, social and business practices were so expressive of the values of those days that to become familiar with them is to experience some of the orderliness and placid flow of the first decade of the twentieth century.

Any account of family life, to be authentic, must inevitably contain constant references to meals. Eating habits and rituals acquired in the family are significant and important; indeed, departures from custom will reflect on a person's character. But external circumstances will also dictate some customs regarding meals; climate accounts for many of the variations found in European countries.

The cohesive and self-contained unit — the family — also was recognized in the manner of keeping vital statistics. Upon their marriage, a couple was issued a *Familien Büchlein*, literally, The Family's Little Book, a register in which the marriage was recorded by the civil clerk; entries were made in it at each birth or death within that family. It is a silent commentary on the culture of those times: a book from which this description is taken, printed in 1916, has lined pages providing space for the vital statistics of a husband and wife, and fifteen children. Mute testimony to the experience of many European families is given in the same Little Book which matter-of-factly provides a space to record the widower's second marriage.

The convenience of having a permanent record in the home was carried over into school and into the working place.

A student received a small book when school attendance began. Not only report marks, but test results, and demerits followed one from year to year, thereby perpetuating plaudits earned, or, for the less fortunate, the stigma.

Edith mentions her mother keeping a laborer's "book" — and the man's ingenious use of it to make known his desire for a wage increase! How far removed from such methods and influence is our life today. It requires a conscious effort to backtrack into those days even if only two or three generations have separated us from such customs. When the contemporaries of Frau Stein emigrated to the New World, they brought their little books with them, but as homesteads in America were usually set up where villages and civic officials would be needed only decades later, the books were quickly supplanted by other ways of keeping statistics, shifting the emphasis from the small unit of the family to the larger one of the community. In schools, also, the books were replaced by report cards; transient friends or foes as they are, they are neither as formidable nor as affirming as the "little books."

These may seem minor examples of the variations in daily life, but they underline the need to project oneself into Edith's milieu when reading her book. Fortunately, she has a gift for adding new dimensions to our knowledge of the Germany of her day. Films and documentaries on both wars and on the Holocaust have acquainted us with the dreadful sights and some of the pitiable sounds that had been part of those events; we must add to this knowledge the warmer, happier, and blessedly humorous sensory data found in Edith's lively account which enables us in our imagination to share in her experiences.

Breslau, Edith's birthplace, is equidistant from the borders which, in her time, marked Poland and Bohemia. The Jews of this area were in large part descended from the merchant Jews of the early Middle Ages who joined migrants from Central Europe and took refuge in Bohemia and Poland during the years of the Crusades.

The new communities formed showed the cultural superiority of the Western Jews who spoke the language of their adopted country. Their skills and creative talents contributed to the welfare of their newly adopted land. This usually won them the appreciation of the indigenous peoples, but, in too many cases, resentment and envy as well.

Breslau, by the Middle Ages, ranked among the large cities of the German empire; it was, even then, a center of trade and had as many as 15,000 inhabitants. The River Oder, so important to the city's development, figures often in Edith's story. Today that river separates the vital regions, East Europe and West. Breslau is now called Wroclaw and belongs to Poland; its roots in history are not ossified, however, and only an omniscient God can know what its future will hold. For us, Breslau's importance lies in its being the place where on October 12, 1891, on that Day of Atonement, Edith, the last of the eleven children of Siegfried and Auguste Stein-Courant was born.

EDITH STEIN—STUDENT, TEACHER, AND LECTURER

The academic journey which began for her in the *Viktoriaschule* of Breslau and led her to that city's university, then to Göttingen and Freiburg, rightly commands the greatest atten-

tion from Edith in her story. Always, her own appraisal puts it
best; she surmises that she was even happier in school than at
home. It was her element; but one does not see her as a bookish
young girl. Her vivacity, her readiness to engage any of her
teachers in dialogue, her admission of coaching her classmates,
and the vexation she confesses to have aroused at times all indicate that learning was an adventure for her—at least, once she
escaped from the despicably humiliating kindergarten!

Identifying the motivation behind her progress from the serious study of psychology to a concentration on philosophy will demand investigation of numerous circumstances. Such inquiry
will produce interesting correlative information; until it is conducted, one can only surmise that Edith Stein had a unique
combination of teachers and fellow-students. The brief allusions to the role played in the history of philosophy by the men
and women with whom she studied are recorded in the notes,
but these are intended to spur further investigation; and only a
thorough study will do justice to Edith Stein. That she will be
seen as a contributor and a collaborator rather than a mere carbon copy of the brilliant thinkers with whom she associated will
be reward enough for the work involved.

One example of all that would have to be covered to do justice
to such a commentary on the minor field of her interest will illustrate the range of unexplored data that is available. During
her student years in Göttingen, Edith describes her participation
in a young psychologist's experiments; she was the guinea pig,
she says. Edith was furnished with no information, but she
intuitively sensed what the experiment was intended to explore.
One wonders whether in those student years she was already as
observant and as competent in describing and analyzing the
psychological factors involved in the relationships she describes
in such detail. But her insights are not presented in clinical
language, nor does she recount events in the family as though
she were writing up case histories. Still, her reason for writing
the story might be seen to be scientific rather than sentimental.

When Edith recounts what happened in her family, the manner of her telling enables the reader to identify the incident with
a similar experience in many another family. Relationships be-

tween parent and child, between siblings, and the demands for and supply of assistance in the extended family are familiar. They are basic relationships, the foundation for an understanding of one another that wipes out all barriers of race, country, and time. External circumstances may be different, but Edith's account of the feelings, emotions, hopes and sufferings of warm, sincere, gifted yet flawed human beings evokes in the reader a conviction of knowing someone just like the person Edith describes.

Another circumstance makes the story of *Life in a Jewish Family* significant. With the destruction of so many Jewish compatriots, the Germans reaching adulthood in the twenty-first century will have an even more limited understanding of an authentic Jewish family life than their twentieth-century counterparts have had. In accord with journalistic custom, depiction of such life now is presented almost exclusively in strict orthodox settings. That many Jewish families, without being fully assimilated into the culture of the countries in which they had settled, were *not* totally different from their Christian neighbors and fellow-workers must be asserted or the events of the thirties and forties will be misrepresented at the cost of justice to Jews and Christians alike.

Edith writes, precisely, of Jews who were German to the very marrow of their bones; for instance, the historic setting is the one when a bright resplendent tapestry seemed at last to be woven for the Jewish community in Breslau. Many were becoming accustomed to owning property; a majority were self-employed; those in professional life were free from "patronage"; and highly talented thinkers were making prodigious contributions to science and education. She shows us this in describing circumstances, not in any superior, pedantic language; in her quiet appraisal of a situation or a person, she manages to show the new position with which some of her companions were not yet at ease. Often, without morbid reference, Edith shows the presence of indicators that this tapestry of the good life was beginning to unravel for the Jewish community before it had been completed.

One has a feeling of her collecting a whole stage full of stars, playing supporting rather than leading roles, to be sure; at the conclusion of Chapter X of this book we have one climactic second, Edith herself wearing a wreath of flowers symbolizing the crowning achievement of her years of study. Many years later she said that, in response to the demands of her decision to devote her talents to the study of philosophy, her style of life had always resembled that of a nun. At the moment when her story stops, Edith appears on that stage as the scholar wed to her science. In the chronological account, we can trace the gradual exit of the supporting stars. Only a very few remain to take curtain calls in the final pages of her story.

This first English volume of her Collected Works sets a new stage for Edith Stein. That its dramatic possibilities are appreciated can be attested to in the telling fact: there are many persons engaged in studying Edith. Two new plays, one opera, two documentary films for television, biographies for adults and for children, illustrated books for meditation, courses for the study of her writings in colleges and universities are in preparation.

That these persons asked for information, sometimes in very general terms or in very specific areas, has had a decisive consequence on the choice of material in the notes.

Edith's manuscript contains only a minimum of footnotes which have been retained as she gave them. These few notes have a distinct quality. They are leads toward an investigation of the background to her story. If Edith's description of a translator's task (mentioned above) created an obligation to live up to it, then, in exact measure, the style of her notes affected the present translator.

When surveying the scene presented to the reader in the translation process, an interesting phenomenon began to recur. The text itself made demands on the translator. Some references made, some skillfully ambiguous statements Edith tucked in about persons or circumstances, some unmistakable tones audible in the remarks began to create disturbances as real as though some of the characters in tableau on stage refused to remain docilely in place.

Edith herself provides an image of what happened. She relates that as an eager student in her early years in school, she was so importunate that she would hop to the front of the room with raised finger, waving to claim the teacher's attention.

Just so, in the translation process, questions began to press for answers: Why would Edith prefer Grillparzer to, say, Platen or Immerman? Why might the Goethe/Faust theme recur at such oddly disparate locations: her family living room in her childhood, the ward of the Red-Cross hospital in World War I, a Christmas party during her university days, and, years later, at the podium on a lecture circuit? What significance is there in her admission that after twenty years she can still *hear* Hermsen sing? How interesting that the verses he sang were sung by Margaret, Faust's victim, while she awaited death in prison; the verses which the Grimm Brothers later recorded in their version of the folktale about the juniper tree? Had Edith made that association, too? What became of the pioneers in psychology and philosophy who taught her in Breslau? Which of her fellow students died during the World Wars, which were to be found in concentration camps, which in professional careers in England or America?

Each time the answer had to be found if only to make any alteration in the phrasing of one of Edith's statements should investigation cast more light on her words. Happily, this seldom happened. In minute ways, however, it became increasingly evident that in learning some of the same things Edith had known, in collecting bits of information that had interested her that also lay at the root of some of her recorded observations, this tasting of the fountain which had slaked some of her thirst for knowledge sharpened one's perception of Edith, the person. By feeding the imagination and confirming the intuition, these assorted items were causing a more personal, more alive Edith Stein to emerge from the text which as a consequence took on a more vital and dynamic spirit. Edith no longer spoke as if from a vacuum. One could assess now the possible reasons for her expressing a sentiment discernible in her writing, which we are expected to understand.

What had long been a conviction took on new meaning. As happens during any genocidal incident, at any time or in any place, many crimes were compounded during the Holocaust. Of these crimes, one of the most heinous was the intent to obliterate the *individual* identity of the victims. A mass grave or mass cremation is not principally an expedient to facilitate disposal or concealment of human remains. It is a final insult to the person who must be deprived not only of life but of even the minutest tangible or recognizable individual trace which could be cherished by posterity.

The photographs of sons which are held up to public view by South American mothers, pictures of MIA soldiers likewise displayed by their children, and names etched in public memorials are all relics sacred to those who love and mourn one whom an enemy has sought to relegate to total oblivion.

Where Edith Stein is concerned, the fortunes of war joined forces with those who decreed the manner of her death. They destroyed places where she had lived, making irretrievable most of the artifacts she had used, putting out of reach the small, intimate articles of personal property that would have given her dear ones some sense of her nearness.

Now, by reconstructing, even partially, some of the rich content of her intellect, friendship and devotedness allow her to live for us in a way the Nazis could not destroy. This naturally gifted, highly intelligent woman who grew to maturity during one of history's most cataclysmic times was eminently learned. Trained in several disciplines, Edith was alive to an association of ideas garnered from the wealth of information she had. She cultivated an awareness of varied worldviews; she marked the interpretations of human questions and values given by her teachers or expressed by her associates in study or in teaching. The positions she espoused and the convictions she held as a result of her careful consideration of a situation with all its ramifications were not always shared by her contemporaries. Examination of their academic achievements made their divergent views accessible to us, and always it was as though Edith personally directed the research. The notes in this volume are presented, therefore, more in tribute to Edith's erudition than for their intrinsic usefulness.

EDITH STEIN — VOCATION AND DESTINY

When an autobiography contains too many instances of anticipation, when one is promised a more detailed account, or an explanation at some future time, the reader tires of the method.

But when one thinks of the unresolved questions we have about Edith Stein, it is natural to wish she had more frequently included comments of later developments in the story. One brief reference to her sister Rosa's close association with Edith in later years, and the sole instance of completing the account of her sister Erna's courtship and marriage are the most patent examples of anticipation in the narrative. Some hints are given, but other developments are not indicated. That her cousin, Richard Courant, for instance, would marry Nerina, one of the daughters of the Runge family of Göttingen is not even remotely suggested. Nor, in her own case, does she include any indication of attitudes which she eventually changed.

The most serious of these questions concern her choice of a profession, and, later, the vocation which was for long years a seemingly unattainable dream.

The omission of specific references, however, does not leave us without aids to discern the stages by which Edith was transformed from child to woman, from a public lecturer to a cloistered contemplative nun. The only risk is that we arrive at a conclusion before we study all the related aspects. Roman Ingarden gives us his unqualified assertion: "Edith Stein would never have written or said anything which she would not have replicated in her actions." She helped the young people whom she taught in their own discernment of vocation, for instance. Whatever she tells them must be consistent with her own approach, and her own actions and intentions with her life's vocation in mind.

This first volume of her works in English as has already been mentioned, concerns itself principally with her childhood and early adulthood. We do not find in it an account of her personal search or decision about the choice to marry, to devote herself to teaching and lecturing, or to follow a call to the religious life.

The brief reference to her attitude toward marriage, and the admission that "at times" she had found among her acquaintances a young man whom she considered a life partner have sufficed to make many readers certain that she would have accepted a proposal of marriage. That she gives no identification of the man is no deterrent since a later episode, again told in an ambiguous account, is taken to be a sequel. This is all a mysterious process for one good reason: it *is* a mystery. Edith tells her readers that she found Hans Lipps most attractive among her fellow students at Göttingen; she writes of a severe crisis which she weathered without support in 1920, at the time of Erna's marriage. Then, within ten years or so, she has told a friend that Lipps, now left a widower with two small daughters, asked her to join them. Her answer has been given the gamut of interpretations, from an exact, and so, ambiguous, statement: "I told him it was too late" to a dramatized version of those words which drips with regret. That regret could not have been *Edith's* if all the evidence of her writings and of her life is considered with Roman Ingarden's assurance in mind.

The incident however brings our attention to the deep and lasting friendships Edith formed. If any one of these relationships was broken off, that had to be at the decision of the other person. Edith tells Fritz Kaufmann categorically that once she has admitted anyone into her friendship it is a lifelong commitment for her. This she proves when one sees how clearly she has noted a person's frailties and, in a few cases, even undesirable qualities; still she shows herself a faithful and true friend. She points out, to the person not merely to her readers, what she finds unacceptable; then, whether there is a change for better, or not, she knows how to take the friend with or without faults, and is always at ease.

When reconstructing her life at home, the customs and habits common in her family and among her friends, there are found many references to a choice of profession, or of a marriage partner, made by someone in her immediate circle. She tells of the affection her cousin Franz had for her; she terms the separation resulting from her decision to return to school as something Franz viewed as "losing me;" and she makes one more statement, relating it almost as a consequence, neither Franz nor his twin brother ever married.

Edith recounts that in the marriage of her second oldest sister Elfriede, the services of a marriage broker—she does not give the Jewish title of the functionary, *shadchan*—were involved. In her sister's case, the marriage proved unhappy; but often that manner of arranging marriages, especially when Jewish families lived where few other Jews were to be found, was responsible for many good matches.

For many years, from her first days at the University of Breslau, until his death when Edith was in Freiburg, an orthodox friend, Eduard Metis quietly enjoyed Edith's loyal friendship. He made it clear soon after their becoming acquainted that his intentions were anticipating hers; Edith told him to expect no more than friendship for the time being. He was important enough to her, one notes, that she put to him the same questions her sister Erna posed to *her* fiancé, Hans Biberstein, on his attitudes on sex. Had either of the young men held unacceptable views, their friendship would have ceased; what is intriguing is that this kind of interrogation was not imposed on any of the young men in Göttingen. In her vacations from Göttingen, Edith mentions spending many hours in study in the company of Metis; and he sent her a weekly letter to Göttingen.

One more circumstance that would have had important bearing on the question of marriage for Edith has hardly been mentioned in the popular biographical accounts that have appeared since she has caught the attention of the world. Even in 1920, it was not a simple matter for a Jewish young man or woman to marry a Christian—or in any case, a non-Jew. Hans Lipps, for instance, was not Jewish, although so many of his best and most faithful friends at Göttingen were Jewish. His service in the German army in World War II gives mute testimony to his non-Jewish descent; instead of serving at the Russian front where a head-wound proved fatal, he would have had to emigrate as so many other professors did. That marriage between a Jew and non-Jew was generally unacceptable, we learn—not in Edith's writings—in the experience of her cousin, Richard Courant. However, difficult though the matter would have been, it was not impossible.

That Edith did not marry was the consequence of only one event: her decision against it. Although she does not refer to this in her book, there are very clear indications in her letters that it was her free choice. At Erna's wedding, the spiritual crisis she suffered involved her decision to become a Christian. She was painfully aware that her becoming a Catholic might possibly estrange her from her own dearly loved family. Edith was also certain that her closest friends, among them Lipps, Kaufmann, and Metis, would find her move alienating. Happily, her mother's deep love surmounted the blow, and her sisters and brothers remained loyal to Edith; Kaufmann broke off contact with her for nearly five years; and Metis, too, was very much in the background — a discreet reference to his grieving family's incomprehension for her changed religious allegiance is all that Edith permits herself to make.

She had already told her readers what Lipps' attitude toward Catholics led him to do: he referred to Dietrich von Hildebrand and Siegfried Hamburger as "members of that 'club' that goes to Mass every day." When he asked Edith whether she also belonged to the club, she admits nearly adding "unfortunately" to her quiet "no." These two friends, Edith and Hans Lipps, were both so gifted and so dedicated to pursuing their studies, and at the same time, had so overpowering a sense of inferiority in one another's company that, no matter how strong the personal attraction, the feeling of not coming up to the other's expectations would have been cause of great unhappiness for one or both of them. If, later, when his first wife died, be it while she was with him and their little girls, or as has been suggested, after she left him, Hans Lipps could have asked with added incentive. He alone might not feel good enough for Edith, but he knew how much she loved children, and the little girls were specifically mentioned in the reported invitation. Her reply, "it is too late" would also have been given with relief; not only was it true but it was not a wounding reply. Edith had no need to say that she saw little chance of a successful marriage with one whose personality she knew so well. She refers to him in a letter to Fritz Kaufmann, their mutual friend.

That such a long examination has been made of this hypothetical matter may seem exaggerated; it belongs, however, with this autobiographical account of Edith. It simply completes the evidence that must be taken into consideration; the reader will decide personally on which side of the scale, pro or con, the balance tips. Perhaps more information will come to light if more letters are found which refer to Lipps. He wrote to Edith in 1923, and she used the back of his letter to continue writing her manuscript for her study on Thomas Aquinas!

One thing is unequivocally stated in her own writings. When, in summer of 1921, she read *The Book of Her Life* by Saint Teresa of Jesus, Edith received a confirmation of her choice of the Catholic Church—it became an interior certainty for her. At the same time she was convinced that she was given a vocation to become a Carmelite daughter of Teresa. That means that from that time on, consideration of marriage with anyone was out of the question for her. It was "too late" simply because she was so certain that she had received a call to become a contemplative nun. That obedience to those to whom she entrusted her spiritual formation as a Catholic should demand postponing the fulfillment of that desire, the joyous answer to that call, had nothing to do with weakening it. She told a young friend that anyone who had a call to the religious life, and, despite that, kept company with young men even though without serious intentions was not strictly fair, and risked losing the religious vocation. That was an implicit admission that, for Edith, the call to Carmel was already a commitment; every word we read after January 1, 1922, when Edith was baptized in the Catholic church in Bergzabern, bears out her fidelity to that call.

EDITH ON THE WAY OF PERFECTION

When her letters are published, the steps along the path to Carmel will be clearly seen. In concluding this afterword, only references to her comments in *Life in a Jewish Family*, or reflections on situations connected with her life in the Stein-Courant family will be made.

Edith Stein, Sister Teresa Benedicta of the Cross, has a singularly interesting qualification for joining the four best known Discalced Carmelites: Teresa of Jesus, John of the Cross, Thérèse of the Child Jesus, and Elizabeth of the Trinity. Each of the five, as a child, lost one parent; in each of the five families, the surviving parent was both loving and influential.

Teresa de Ahumada was thirteen-years old and Thérèse Martin was four when they lost the loving care of a mother; for both of them, the experience of a father's solicitous care, and a surrogate mothering by an older sister offset the suffering that usually attends a mother's early death.

Juan de Yepes was an infant when his father died; Captain Catez, father of Elizabeth, died when she was about seven; Edith, a toddler not quite two-years old, called her father back for an affectionate farewell embrace the day he succumbed to a heat stroke.

It is not with an intention to draw any lightning conclusions that this remarkable coincidence is pointed out. Again, it is mentioned in order to prod interest: did their childhood experience make these five more attentive to a call from God? They each had a strong surviving parent to guide them; it was not that unhappiness in childhood led them to seek a haven in religious life. Was there a quality to the relationship with the living parent that predisposed these women, and the young man, for Carmel? Without exception they were talented persons who found in the uncharted expanse of the spiritual life the one enterprise to offer them a challenge worthy of their total dedication. The doctrine of Spiritual Childhood taught by Saint Thérèse is universally known; Edith Stein found herself in harmony with her older "Little Sister" from France and, paradoxically, that draws our attention to one disparity between the two. For Thérèse, the devoted care and tender solicitude of her father, Louis Martin, seemed to provide a particularly apt image of the provident care of God, Thérèse's Heavenly Father. Edith had a lifelong experience of the provident care of her devoted mother for whom her children's needs, their education, their happiness, and opportunities had become a mission in life. Frau Auguste Stein found it incomprehensible that Edith should come to believe in the Trinity in whom Catholics profess their faith. Edith accepted her mother's grief, understood it, and wished with all her heart she could ease it.

Sometimes, in the telling of Edith's story, a great deal has been made of Frau Stein's tears and remonstrances. But Frau Stein wept, too, when her oldest son left home to marry; and then she helped to set up the young couple in a home of their own. When Edith determined to serve in the Red Cross hospital, her mother forbade it; when Edith persisted, Frau Stein provided all the clothes and equipment the young nurse had to take with her. And, when one reflects upon the documented instances when *Catholic* parents have repudiated a son or daughter for life, in retaliation for the following of a religious vocation, then Frau Stein's tears entitle her to receive warm understanding and respect from us.

Edith Stein's Writings — This Book and Its History

The monasteries of Echt and Herkenbosch in Holland were both damaged in World War II. Fortunately, the thousands of pages of handwritten manuscript which represented most of Edith Stein's legacy escaped destruction. At the instance of Fr. Herman L. Van Breda, a Belgian Franciscan who had rescued Edmund Husserl's library and writings in 1938, the Dutch Provincial of the Discalced Carmelites had Edith's writings brought to the Husserl Archive in Louvain. Fr. Romaeus Leuven, O.C.D., was assigned the task of preparing the manuscripts for publication.

Dr. Lucy Gelber, already on the staff of the Husserl Archive was named collaborator; since her meeting Fr. Romaeus in 1947, the *Archivum Carmelitanum Edith Stein* has published ten volumes of *Edith Steins Werke* [The Works of Edith Stein]. That such a monumental achievement by these two scholars can be described in one sentence does not minimize their contribution to the Discalced Carmelite Order and to the history of philosophy. Nor does it lessen our deep appreciation; our gratitude and admiration for the work of Fr. Romaeus, O.C.D., and Dr. Gelber comes from the heart. Our one regret is that Fr. Romaeus died before this first volume in English was completed for publication. His warm and encouraging messages, even during his final illness, were a great help; it is consoling to know he was aware of our indebtedness to him. He accepted thanks with a kindly reciprocation that only increased the translator's appreciation for his contribution in making Edith Stein's writings available to the world.

In 1980, Romaeus Leuven, O.C.D., and Dr. Gelber published Father Romaeus' *Portret* in Dutch, *Edith Stein: Mijn Weg Naar De Waarheid*, to tell the rest of Edith's story. This book, translated into German, was published by the *Archivum* as *Heil im Unheil* in 1983, the year Father Romaeus died. He included copious quotations from Edith Stein's writings; and his commentary sheds light on both her philosophical and spiritual development. The title given to the book in German differs from that given to Father's Dutch version *My Way to the Truth*, but it is most expressive of Edith's mature life. There is no English equivalent for *Heil im Unheil* to express as succinctly the meaning Fr. Romaeus finds in her writings and in her ecclesial mission. St. Paul's assurance that "where sin is, there grace *abounds*" gives the sense of the title better than any other phrase.

In appreciation for her tireless dedication to the interests of Edith Stein, besides expressing once more sincere gratitude for her work, it is hoped that this present volume in English will bring to Dr. Lucy Gelber some of the joy and satisfaction that the German volumes produced.

For English readers, a listing of those volumes will give the full scope of Edith's contribution to the Carmelite Order's literary treasure. Rather than arranging the writings by volume number, they are described in as close a chronological order as Edith wrote them.

Two volumes of letters have appeared; the first, Vol. VIII, contains letters from 1916 to 1934. More than 160 letters were written before her entrance into Carmel in Cologne.

Not included among the volumes published by the *Archivum* but published in 1917, her doctoral dissertation *Zum Problem Der Einfühlung* was printed in Halle, Germany. In English, it has been published as *On the Problem of Empathy*. (Cf. Note 169.)

Die Frau [*Woman*] which was published as Vol. V, in 1959, presents a collection of articles, and lectures by Edith Stein on the professions of women and on related topics which are still live issues, amazing though that seems, years after she wrote them. I.C.S. will publish a translation of these texts as Vol. II of its Collected Works of Edith Stein.

Welt und Person [*World and Person*], another collection of articles and lectures which Edith delivered between 1930 and 1937 was published by the *Archivum* in 1962, as Vol. VI. This volume presents studies in philosophy. One of them, begun in 1929 and reworked several times, was incorporated in her largest philosophical work; two others in this volume were prepared as appendices for that same major work.

Edith made a German translation of St. Thomas Aquinas' *Quaestiones Disputatae* in 1932. As these two volumes were completed before the ban on publications by authors of Jewish descent, Edith had the satisfaction of seeing them in print. The *Archivum* published them as Vols. III and IV of the *Werken* in 1952.

In September of 1933, Edith wrote the first chapters of *Aus dem Leben einer Jüdischen Familie* while she prepared to enter the Carmelite Order. More will have to be said about this manuscript, and the form in which it reaches readers in English. An abridged edition was published in German, as Vol. VII, in 1965. The complete German edition came out in 1985; this I.C.S. translation presents the complete work.

In 1936, Edith Stein's major philosophical work *Endliches und Ewiges Sein [Finite and Eternal Being]* was written at the request of her superiors in the Carmel of Cologne. A publisher had been found, but the Nazi ban on publication prevented this work from appearing during Edith's lifetime. It was published as Vol. II of her works in 1950 and in a second edition in 1962.

The study which Edith Stein made of St. John of the Cross was written to mark the Fourth Centenary of the saint's birth, 1942, but it did not appear in print until 1950 as the first volume of her works. As *Science of the Cross*, in a translation made by Hilda Graef, it was the first of the *Archivum's* books to be issued in English.

More letters of Edith Stein—Nos. 171 to 342 in Vol. IX—give a wide coverage of Edith's activities from 1934 to 1942. One can glean from them many insights into her spirituality; one can follow events in her family. This comment returns us to Volume VII—*Aus dem Leben einer Jüdischen Familie*—Life in a Jewish Family. Perhaps it is simply appropriate that a manuscript that tells such an engrossing story should itself have had an existence that includes vividly stirring episodes.

Edith began to write these reminiscences at her mother's home in Breslau. In October, 1933, she took the manuscript along to Cologne when she entered that Carmel. Five years later, about to leave for Holland, she not only destroyed the last will and testament she had made—it would be too dangerous to have it among her things—she also left behind the manuscript about her family. But within that very week, the first of January, 1939, in which she began to live a new chapter in Carmel, she began to write another one in the story of her family. Could she have thought to complete a second section which she could take back to Germany when peace returned? She gives no clue of this herself; and we learn what happened at this time from Mother Teresa Renata's biography.

We are told by the nun who was Prioress in Cologne at that time that fear of having her belongings searched at the border kept Sr. Benedicta from taking the manuscript along. But, when she began writing again in Echt, Edith probably realized, although Mother Renata does not mention this, that to produce a true sequel she needed the first part.

Mother Renata recounts that in February, 1939, Sr. Benedicta inquired whether there might be anyone among her friends in Cologne with courage enough to bring her this manuscript. (It would be less risky for a non-Jew to have among other papers, one now conjectures.) There was indeed one intrepid friend, a young Marianhill missionary, Father Rhabanus, C.M.M., who declared himself prepared for such an adventure. His car was stopped at the Dutch border for a search. The official noted the manuscript, hefted the bulky pack, turned to a few random pages with a quick glance, and then returned it to the priest with the verdict: "Looks like your doctoral dissertation, eh!" Not a word to correct this opinion, of course, and thus the precious manuscript made its entry into Holland.

Why, then, were no more than a dozen printed pages written in Echt? The story leaves one with so many questions. The taxi bearing Edith and Frau Reinach from the train station seems to carry them beyond reach. Could one package of manuscript pages have been lost after all? That possibility has never been suggested. It is more probable that Edith found no time for that type of writing. Before long, she was made portress since her facility with the Dutch language was equal to that engrossing task. Then, early in 1940, the unexpected happened again—

the Nazis took over Holland. Edith had firsthand experience what this entailed. She had to register, and she could not doubt that her situation was once more as precarious as it had been in Cologne.

The testimonial volume *Als Een Brandende Toorts* once more comes to our aid with an ususual eyewitness account from one of the Echt Community. It readily allows us to join Edith in her anxious evaluation of the situation. Were the SS to stage an unexpected search of the monastery, the manuscript about life in a Jewish family would not only be destroyed but the community would suffer for "harboring" the Sister who wrote it.

Sister Pia's account mentions only that one day she helped Sister Teresa Benedicta to bury the entire manuscript in the ground "very near to the cemetery" within the monastery enclosure. There it remained for three months. However, Sister Benedicta feared that the manuscript would be damaged or even destroyed in the moist ground, and she dug it up again. Sister Pia reports that, taking pity on Sister Benedicta's helplessness, she took it upon herself to locate a safe hiding place for the manuscript in the monastery.

The building was in danger; it was situated too near the Allied antiaircraft artillery position. Fragments from bursting shells rained on the neighborhood like burning coals. When the community had to evacuate the building, many of the valuable articles of sacristy and library were stored in a basement room which was then walled up. The manuscript was not with these articles, nor with Sister Benedicta's other writings which were taken to the monastery of Herkenbosch for storage in an attic. *Aus dem Leben* remained in Sister Pia's hiding place until the spring of 1945 when rumor reached her that the building was going to be used as quarantine quarters for some two hundred persons who were being repatriated in Holland after performing forced labor in Germany. From a neighboring town where she was caring for one of the sisters who had been wounded by a grenade, Sister Pia went to Echt to retrieve the manuscript which she then entrusted to Father Avertanus, Provincial of the Dutch Carmelites, for safekeeping. Through him, eventually, the two packages reached the Husserl-Archive.

Father Romaeus Leuven, O.C.D., and Dr. Lucy Gelber arranged Edith's thousand pages of manuscript and published the work initially as Volume VII, in abridged form, in 1965.

When Sister Benedicta was forced to leave Germany, she destroyed the last will and testament she had made, according to the Carmelite custom, before her profession. In a new testamentary document drawn up in Echt, she asked that the story of her family remain unpublished during the lifetime of her siblings. Although she had begun the work at the suggestion of a priest advisor, it had not been definite that it was meant for publication in the form in which she wrote it. In her testament, Edith leaves the decision about the publication to the Order.

When World War II ended and the Sisters in the Carmels of Echt and Cologne returned to pick up the pieces, to rebuild or to move into other quarters as the fortunes of war demanded, inquiries were begun regarding the fate of the Stein sisters. Nothing had been heard about them—now all manner of accounts were reported. These had to be followed up. In 1948, Sister Teresia Renata de Spiritu Sancto (Posselt), Prioress of the Carmel of Cologne, published a biography entitled *Edith Stein.*

In 1952, a copy of this biography—then in its sixth edition—was sent to American Carmels by the Cologne community. It served to acquaint the translator with Edith Stein. After that meeting the hope of introducing the Carmelite philosopher to an English-speaking public persisted. It has been more than satisfied in translating Edith's own autobiographical account.

III

Acknowledgments

When Sister Teresa Benedicta wrote *Finite and Eternal Being* she experienced a dilemma which was resolved for her when Professor Alexander Koyré read the first chapter and assured her she must continue the work. In a letter to a mutual friend she mentions this verdict inspired her with courage to continue her work:

> That was very necessary indeed since this kind of project
> is not easy to fit into the frame of our life and demands

many a sacrifice, not only from me but also from my
dear Sisters in the Community. And that is something
you don't want to demand if it won't pay.

The interest that has persisted in Edith's writings demonstrates
that the contribution made by the communities in Cologne and
in Echt has paid rich dividends. This English translation of
Edith's autobiographical work likewise owes its existence to a
community investment, and every one of the Sisters in Elysburg
Carmel has been part of this work.

The lifework of Father Romaeus Leuven, O.C.D.
(1904-1983) and the decades of collaboration by Dr.
Lucy Gelber in establishing the Archivum Carmelitanum Edith Stein are gratefully acknowledged, and
the translator hopes this book may serve as a fitting
tribute to the memory of Father Romaeus, and as a
heartfelt expression of indebtedness to Dr. Gelber.

Sr. Amata Neyer, O.C.D., of the Cologne Carmel has been
tirelessly generous with help, corroborating the notes, furnishing photographs, suggesting additional avenues of research
and, in general, supporting an effort that seemed at times beyond one's capacity.

Father Adrian J. Cooney, O.C.D., has been mentor, editor,
enabler, and consultant at every stage of the translation. His
support will be remembered with a warm gratitude that matches
completely that expressed by Edith for her friend, Koyré.

All of the following have made important contributions to
this work: the Discalced Carmelite Nuns in Tübingen, Germany,
especially Sister Teresia (Waltraud) Herbstrith, O.C.D.; the
communities in Echt, Holland; Le Pâquier, Switzerland; Mariazell and Bärnbach, Austria; and Ben Juffermans, secretary to
the Provincial of the Discalced Carmelite Fathers in Holland.

Once the religious "families" of all concerned have been
thanked, then the natural family of Edith Stein earns our sin-
cerest appreciation. The years of research have meant living with
Edith's family and friends in greater intimacy at times than I
have known with my own dear ones. Not many relatives see infor-

mation about the private history of their loved ones revealed to the extent that this book shares the biography of Edith Stein's extended family. To the descendants of the Stein, Biberstein, and Courant families an acknowledgement of gratitude is accompanied by admiration and recognition; you, your parents, aunts and uncles, and grandparents have enabled us to learn how similar *Life in a Jewish Family* can be to life in our own families. Details may vary, but in each of our lives the experience of joy and sorrow has been very like that described by Edith.

When evaluating the indispensable assistance that has produced this translation it is impossible to equal the contribution made by Edith's beloved sister, Dr. Erna Biberstein, and by Susanne Batzdorff, Erna's daughter.

A note from Dr. Biberstein, dated November 12, 1974, expressed her interest in the work being initiated then, and her readiness to be of assistance. Three talks were all that we could have; in 1978, a letter from Mrs. Alfred Batzdorff informed us of the death of her mother.

That was at the same time an introduction to Susanne and Alfred Batzdorff whose collaboration with this translation has contributed immeasurably to its fidelity to Edith's text. Perhaps the greatest gift was the warm rapport which developed, and, in the name of the Order, it gives me joy to thank the Batzdorffs for the countless ways they have helped to make Edith Stein's message known to an English-speaking public. To them, I am indebted for the stimulus of their suggestions, for the challenge of arriving at a consensus in the few instances of differing interpretation, but most of all for the experience of that family charism that is almost palpable when one reads about Auguste Stein and her Courant relatives, then of Edith and Erna—these wonderful and winning traits are found perpetuated in the younger generation.

Another relative, Nina Courant-Runge, widow of Richard Courant, made an invaluable contribution in presenting to the Edith Stein Center in Elysburg a hitherto unknown picture of Edith Stein. As familiar as Edith's own stories are about the rapport between herself and her very young relatives, a new understanding of her and of this gift with children is inevitable when one studies her, pictured with one of the Courant children, in

Göttingen. A letter accompanied the photograph; in it, Mrs. Courant refers to Edith and gives us a word-picture of her which is the more valuable since it comes from the oldest living member of the extended family which meant so much to Edith. Mrs. Courant wrote (in German):

> Richard and Edith were good friends; they were very fond of one another. I cannot deny myself this opportunity of comparing the cousins. Of course, they do belong to two entirely different worlds — the Catholic Religious one, and the mathematician's scientific one; still, they have something in common, not only that they both attained great fame in these widely disparate fields, but they both possessed extraordinary intelligence, an untiring energy and ability to work, great human goodness, and a selfless surrender to something which I perceive as "the holy Spirit."

A remarkable phenomenon has occurred in the ten years that initiated the complex process of translation. Many persons have been involved in varying roles, but that is true of every effort in education, in evangelization, even in business. Although the help received from each one has been unique, it is not possible to list here all of these contributors. May they recognize their own handiwork in its final form and accept my gratitude. Much of the research had to be done in Europe, or at least, in books from Germany or Switzerland; and a temporary stay in the Carmel of Cologne was part of the project. Funding for that research and for the books was provided by another group of relatives. To them all, especially to Rösli and Henri Joray-Köppel of Zurich, and Otto Frei, a journalist-historian from Berne, Switzerland, *vielen Dank für die unentbehrliche Hilfe. Vergelt's Gott!*

Sr. Josephine Koeppel, O.C.D.
Carmelite Monastery
Elysburg, Pennsylvania

December 19, 1985

Notes

Edith Stein's own notes, and those of the *Archivum* editors, given in the German volume are found at the bottom of pages in the text, as has been mentioned on page 24.

The contextual notes which follow here are provided by the I.C.S. translation since, frequently, the information is found only in German-language sources unavailable to the general English-language readership. This is especially true regarding matters of German customs, history, and geography.

Every person mentioned by Edith Stein has been accorded equal importance because of her awareness of them. Consequently, biographical data is included in the notes or the index for as many of them as possible whether they have international renown or are important merely in a local or transitory sense. This policy was adopted because of the determination to have the book accomplish Edith's purpose in writing it: to share

> what I, a child of a Jewish family, had learned about the Jewish people since such knowledge is so rarely found in outsiders.

1. The women mentioned by Edith wrote their accounts of life in Jewish homes nearly two centuries apart. Glückel von Hameln lived from 1646 to 1724; an English translation of her work by Marvin Lowenthal, 1932, is cited in the *Standard Jewish Encyclopedia*, ed. Cecil Roth.

Pauline W. Wengeroff's dates are 1833–1916. Her work is entitled *Memoirs of a Grandmother, Pictures out of the Cultural History of Russia*.

Like countless other books by Jewish authors, these works are available in very limited numbers since millions of Jewish books were destroyed in a book-burning orgy by Nazis in May, 1933.

2. According to Constance Reid's *Courant in Göttingen and New York, the Story of an Improbable Mathematician* (New York, 1976), this original comment by Edith was amplified by Richard Courant's friend, K.O. Friedrichs, a professor at NYU's Courant Institute of Mathematical Sciences, who suggests that, the coin being a *Thaler*, the surname could have been taken from the term *Thaler courant*, an expression used in money exchanges to indicate the current market value of the *Thaler*.

3. World War, whenever mentioned in Edith's text, is always World War I. She began to write the narrative in Breslau, in September, 1933. She took it along to Carmel in Cologne and, subsequently, to Holland where she resumed writing the story at the Carmel of Echt, in January, 1939. There are indications in the text that she intended to continue the narration, but the final episode she was able to recount in Chapter X took place in 1916.

In Chapter VI, Edith makes an exception; she departs from writing a chronological account of family events by narrating happenings which occurred as late as 1921.

With the beginning of Chapter VII, she returns to 1913. In Part IV of this Chapter, Edith mentions the assassination at Sarajevo which catapulted the world into war. From then on, to the last page of Chapter X which brings to a close her uncompleted manuscript, everything recounted happened during the first World War.

4. So much of Edith's story revolves around her life as a a student that a table ‡ showing the correlation between a student's age and the class attended may be of interest. Although Edith often refers to technical, vocational schools or to apprenticeships when she speaks of her brothers or male cousins, none of these is indicated. The table lists only the educational options available to girls in Edith's time.

After 1906, university study followed upon the *Oberprima* when a student was about nineteen years old. In the British educational system, the *Oberprima* would be designated the upper sixth form. In America, a student's twelfth school year is usually the senior year of high school.

Methods for marking of grades varied. Edith mentions the system that uses 1-2-3-4 as equivalents for a-b-c-d, with 1 as a designation for "very good."

Students had to attend the school in their residential district. Some of the institutions were administered by a religious denomination, for example, by Lutherans or Catholics, while other schools were non-denominational. However, all were public schools, i.e., part of the

‡ (4) Educational system in Germany in Edith's time

School Year	Student Age	SCHOOLS FOR GIRLS	
		Type of School	*Title* of Class
	pre-6	*Kindergarten*	
		Grundschule	
1	6	[elementary]	1st year
2	7		2nd year
3	8		3rd year
4	9		4th year

After the fourth year in school, the student chose to leave school, or to continue in one of the three alternatives below. Only those intending to go on to university study would choose the *Selecta* before 1906, or the *Realgymnasium* which replaced the *Selecta*, as Edith recounts.

THREE TYPES OF SCHOOLS

Year	Age	Titles of Classes		Titles of Classes
		Volksschule [public school]	*Höhere Mädchenschule* [girls high school]	*Gymnasium* [Latin title] [secondary schools]
5	10	5th year	5th class	Sexta [the sixth]
6	11	6th year	4th class	Quinta [the fifth]
7	12	7th year	3rd class	Quarta [the fourth]
8	13	8th year	2nd class	Untertertia [lower third]
				Realgymnasium
9	14	(none)	1st class	Obertertia [upper third]
10	15		Selecta (to 1906)	Untersecunda [lower second]
11	16		(none)	Obersecunda [upper second]
12	17			Unterprima [lower first]
13	18			Oberprima [upper first] (As seen from Edith's text, adults could also enroll in the *Realgymnasium*.)

educational system of the German state by which they were funded. They were not parochial schools such as are found in the U.S., even though religious education was provided in a class situation. Jewish students, as Edith will point out, were excused from religious instruction unless a special teacher was available. The small school she here mentions was a private school begun under the auspices of Salomon Courant, her grandfather.

Instead of assigning new note numbers in the many instances where clarification regarding the educational system may be useful, Note (4) ‡ will simply be indicated as the proper reference.

5. Rosa's comment is not correct, obviously, with regard to his age.

6. Its closest American equivalent is probably a town square like those in New England.

7. Here, Frieda, Rosa and Erna were born. Edith was the only child born in the apartment on Kohlenstrasse in Breslau, in a house which was torn down long before Edith began writing her memoirs.

8. The couple had a son and two daughters; unfortunately, they also were experiencing misunderstandings, as Edith recounts in Chapter IV, section III.

9. This line — "Tumult and cry like thunder's roll" — is the first line of the song, "The Watch on the Rhine" (words by Max Schneckenburger, music by C. Wilhelm), written about 1840, when the French under Louis Adolphe Thiers challenged the boundary of the Rhine. Symbolic of a new wave of German patriotism and enthusiasm, it was one of several songs which became popular during the decade in which Auguste Courant was born.

10. In the absence of conclusive evidence that the page was deliberately removed, there are alternative explanations possible:

1) In the havoc of war, this and the other missing pages in the manuscript may have been lost. (Cf. Page 461)

2) Relatives suggest that, at the request of Rosa, Edith herself may have removed this page, and other missing ones, intending to rewrite them before returning them to the manuscript. According to Edith's family, this would have been characteristic of her if Rosa had given some explanation of her behavior which had not occurred to Edith. It must be remembered that circumstances robbed Edith of the opportunity to edit this book before its publication.

11. Keeping vital statistics, employment, and health records in our American culture differs greatly from the customs in Germany and other European countries.

In Edith's time, upon beginning employment, a job holder was issued a "book" in which entries concerning employment, wages, etc., were kept current by the employer. If the employee changed jobs, the book was returned to him to be presented to the next employer.

12. Cf. Chapter VIII.

13. Cf. Note 4. *Mädchen* is German for "girls."

14. Throughout the book there are references to five regular times for meals, a custom established in several European countries, especially the colder, northern countries.

The meals consisted of 1) an early breakfast; 2) a mid-morning snack sometimes called second breakfast, or, in England, elevenses; 3) the noon meal, either a lunch or the main meal of the day; 4) a mid-afternoon snack, usually of a beverage with sandwiches or cake, similar to English tea; and, 5) supper, which may be a light meal or dinner.

15. Edith mentioned her father's death earlier, but *not* this incident.

16. Friedrich von Schiller's historical tragedy published in 1800. Cf. Note 33, 35.

17. In a marginal note, Dr. Erna Biberstein, Edith's sister, corrected the name of this great-aunt to read Johanna Radlauer. Ernestine was Johanna's mother, and so, Edith's maternal great-grandmother, wife of Joseph Burchard.

18. From what is left of Edith's sentence, one can deduce it refers to her Uncle Jakob Courant's preference for monopolizing his wife's company. Cf. Page 85.

19. On her copy of the manuscript, Edith's sister Erna wrote: "It was Alexander who killed himself; the youngest brother's name was Leo." Leo Walter Stein is mentioned on Page 38.

20. Cf. Page 80.

21. The German language includes many *Fremdwörter*, i.e., words adopted from other languages. The educational system in particular had made many Latin words part of everyday usage. Those most frequently appearing in Edith's text are:

Abitur: the literal meaning is a school-*leaving* examination, with oral and written portions, which is to demonstrate that the student may be advanced to higher study. It is the final examination before one begins university study.

Facultas docendi: permit to teach; qualification for admission to the faculty of a university; needed to teach in any of the buildings belonging to the university.

Graecum: the Latin name given to the examination in Greek. In Edith's case, she was required to take it to attend the University of Göttingen's advanced courses.

Gymnasium: a secondary school with classical studies. The Latin word is defined as a *place for philosophical discussion*. Those intending to go on to University Studies had to earn an *Abitur* from a *Gymnasium*.

Mulus: (a mule, a hybrid animal) the term applied to a student who was no longer attending a *Gymnasium* but had not yet begun studies at a university.

Opus eximium: the doctoral dissertation, a distinguished work.

Rigorosum: a rigorous examination, again with oral and written portions, which had to be passed to qualify for a doctorate.

Other terms are given in Note (4)‡

22. A.E.G. is the abbreviation for *Allgemeine Elektrizitäts-Gesellschaft* which translates to General Electric Company. The company is well known in Europe by its initials as AEG.

23. In 1900, Berlin was the capital of Prussia as well as of the German Empire (*Deutsches Reich*). Hamburg, the Reich's largest port was the second largest city. Because of a steady influx of foreign visitors Hamburg was less provincial than Berlin and offered more opportunities in employment.

24. In her German original, Edith uses "shopping," in English, to emphasize an American custom. Later in the book she uses "speech" to show that the comments she made in protest to someone's behavior were very different from her ordinary conversation. She was proficient enough in English to teach an adult eduation class during her student years at the university. Still later, while teaching, she translated into German the *Letters and Diaries Until His Conversion* of John Henry Newman.

25. *Riesengebirge*: a mountain range about 56 miles southwest of Breslau; part of the Sudeten Mountains, west of the Carpathians, lying between Landeshuter Pforte and Schreiberhauer Pass. Cf. Map.

Hiking trails enabled vacationers to go throughout the region rich in forests and waterworks, those systems of reservoirs, pumping and purifying stations, channels and mains distributing a water supply to the area; lumbering was an important trade.

Riesen translates into *giants*; and according to guide books the range may have gotten its name for any of several reasons: 1) folklore has it that formidable creatures inhabit these mountains. The most renowned of them is named *Rübezahl*; 2) these mountain peaks are the highest in Silesia; 3) finally, many of the lumbermen working in these mountains were Tyrolean. When they had piled felled trees into huge heaps, they sent these down the slope by timber chutes which the men called *Riesen*.

26. *Goyim,* plural for *goy,* Hebrew word for nation. When it is used to refer to Gentiles, it is not a polite term. It is somewhat pejorative, with some condescension in it.

27. The sentence indicates Edith's expectation of completing the story to include her own entrance into Carmel and her sister Rosa's subsequent acceptance into the Catholic Church. Rosa was arrested in Holland with Edith; it is assumed both died on the same day in Auschwitz. Therefore, this reference of Edith's was to prove true in a way she could hardly have foreseen in 1933.

28. *Sie* is the formal, singular, personal pronoun: you. Persons on intimate terms substitute *Du* for *Sie.* When friends, by mutual decision, change from saying *Sie* to *Du* to one another, custom in some circles has preserved a brief convivial ritual to inaugurate this stage of increased intimacy.

29. Edith uses quotation marks with the German word *Picknick* which, like our more familiar picnic, is derived from the French: *pique-nique.*

30. Edith's text often refers to *Bierzeitung* which, literally translated, would be "beer-newspaper." Family and school celebrations occasioned the writing of such programs which not only listed the numbers to be presented as entertainment on the occasion, but also presented, in newssheet format, items in comic fact or fiction mentioning persons attending the event. The papers were intended to add merriment to the party. Hereafter, *Bierzeitung* usually will be translated as "comic program."

31. *Altvatergebirge* literally translates as Old-Father-Mountains. It is another sector of the Sudeten Mountains. Mountains often have been given names suggested by their outlines viewed against the sky. Cf. Map.

32. Arnold Böcklin, Swiss painter, (1827–1901); mythological figures; landscapes and portraits, strong idealism.

The picture: towering trees in the center give an impression of vibrant but somber life as contrast to the unexpected light on the cliff face which seems to instill hope into an otherwise dismal scene. A skiff transporting a garlanded stone coffin to the *Island of the Dead* is, with its rower, more naturally lighted than the brilliantly lit main figure standing immobile, facing the coffin and the island.

It may seem a remarkable choice for a thirteen-year-old student to make; however, Böcklin's works were on display in the Silesian Museum in Breslau, and there was an Academy of Art, as well.

Edith's appreciation of art is demonstrated by her frequent allusions to the works of famous artists, reproductions of which grace the homes of her teachers and friends. In Chapter VII, Edith finds an opportunity to liken scenery encountered on a hike with the setting of "The Bridal Procession", an idyll painted by the Romantic artist, Ludwig Richter (1803–1884). Cf. Page 244.

33. The celebration on Nov. 10, 1909 for Schiller (Cf. No. 35) was of the 150th anniversary of his birth; therefore, Kaethe Kleemann and Erna Stein were nearly twenty years old, and Edith, eighteen, at that time when Frau Kleemann referred to them all as the little ones, or youngsters.

34. Helgoland is one of the Frisian Islands off the northwest coast of Germany. Tours to the Island from Hamburg went north on the river Elbe and into the North Sea at Cuxhaven. Cf. Map.

35. Grillparzer and Hebbel. Cf. No. 51.

Henrik Ibsen, Norway's nineteenth-century poet and dramatist, had a marked influence on German literature as did Shakespeare. Ibsen's lyricism and symbolism, balanced as they are by his naturalism, and his use of literature as a weapon in the fight for human rights found counterparts in Germany where his plays were given a wide audience.

Edith mentions her predilection for Shakespeare; and even a cursory review of the Bard's masterful impact on German writers is impressive. Traveling English actors had appeared at German courts, such as the one of the Duke of Braunschweig even before 1600. But in the pseudo-classic era there was a vigorous effort to cleanse German drama of the excesses of the early English Comedians and to teach a procedure by which great "classical" literature should result. It seems to have been an instance of pedantic bigotry and was soon refuted by the forerunners of the so-called second Golden Age of German literature. As royalty of the House of Hannover was served both in Germany and in England by the music of Georg Friedrich Händel in the eighteenth century, so, by an interchange of performances in these courts, a mutual appreciation of dramas in German or English was developed. We confine our interest to Shakespeare whose *Midsummer Night's Dream*, for instance, had indirectly influenced the German dramatist Gryphius as early as the mid-seventeenth century, little more than four decades after the Bard's death.

The German writers of the next generation were outspoken in their appreciation of Shakespeare: Gotthold Ephraim Lessing (1729–1782) was a true enthusiast; Goethe (1749–1832) made his hero Wilhelm Meister an actor and a Shakespeare devotee; Goethe himself delivered an address for a Shakespeare anniversary in which he praises the

Bard's artistic will; Schiller (1759-1805), whom Edith mentions repeatedly, began to write drama under the influence of Shakespeare whose *Macbeth* he translated into German classical form.

At the very beginning of the nineteenth century, Shakespeare's dramas were translated by August Wilhelm Schlegel, and the Tiecks, father Ludwig and daughter Dorothea; his themes were immortalized by the music of Felix Mendelssohn-Bartholdy. Otto Ludwig (Cf. No. 51) was fascinated by Shakespeare whose dramatic skill he despaired of matching.

The Shakespearean dramas were prominent in the classic repertoire in Germany, and they still retain that prominence. When Edith mentions reading Shakespeare for relaxation, she was able to read him in English as well as in translation. Closest to her own time, Shakespeare's Sonnets were translated by Stefan George (1868-1933) and became popular.

36. Arthur Schopenhauer's important work which appeared in the midst of the Romantic period, 1819. By the time Edith intended to read his work, the philosopher's pessimistic ideas had influenced writers in Germany, many of whom had led tragic lives. This may account for her sisters' fears and their censorship of the sixteen-year-old's reading matter. (Cf. Page 294)

37. Werner P. Friederich's *Outline History of German Literature* in the Barnes and Noble "College Outline Series" (New York: Harper and Row, 1948, 1970 rev. ed.) provides a comprehensive review of developments in the German literature with which Edith was so familiar.

Johann Wolfgang von Goethe (1749-1832) in his mature years was friend and adviser of the young Duke Karl August of Saxe-Weimar. In the poem here mentioned, Goethe eulogized Johann Martin Mieding, Cabinetmaker to the Duke and Theater-Master of the Duke's private theater, whom he had honored by personal mention in his *Faust*, Scene XXII of Part I. The introductory verses of the eulogy to which Edith refers describe the noisy activity and the sentiments of the persons engaged on January 27, 1782, in preparing the setting and costumes of a presentation to be staged at Weimar in celebration of Duchess Louise's birthday on January 30. The ebullience ends abruptly when news is brought of Mieding's death.

Goethe himself valued this poem so much that he suggested it be used as a eulogy at his own funeral.

38. The balance of this chapter contains many references in which classes and schools may be named for the first time. However, the table given in Note 4 will enable them to be identified. No further directions to that table will be given in this chapter.

39. Literally translated, "Gnädiges Fräulein" is the very proper "Gracious Miss." As explained later in this chapter, teachers in the *Gymnasium* addressed their girl students less formally but still not too familiarly as "Fräulein," i.e., as "Miss."

40. An English-speaking companion with, probably, many of a governess' duties. As can be seen later in this same paragraph, the English word Miss was used as a title, a synonym for governess or companion, without adding the surname.

41. This Catholic classmate was Margrete Glatzel whose father was professor of natural sciences at the University of Breslau. She was born a month after Edith, Nov. 15, 1891. In 1924, Margrete entered the Benedictine Abbey of St. Gabriel in Steiermark, Austria, where as Abbess Augustina, o.s.b., she died on August 19, 1963. None of the correspondence mentioned has come to the fore.

42. Reports were not given out on cards. Each student had a *Zensurbuch*, a small book in which marks were entered at the close of every semester, providing a permanent record. Demerits were recorded in the so-called *Klassenbuch*, a large ledger which was also used for keeping records of lesson plans, and the students' grading on class work and on oral and written quizzes. It is most likely that demerits were noted in the individual's *Zensurbuch* also. (Cf. Page 446)

43. Cf. No. 28.

44. Professor Scholz was that predecessor of Professor Olbrich mentioned on Page 162.

45. Cf. No. 39.

46. In this class they covered the history of Prussia from the time of the Thirty Years' War (1618–1648) until the new German Reich was founded in 1871 by Otto von Bismarck who was its first Chancellor.

47. Edith's intention of showing how much of Germany's history had been integrated into her family's history will be best served by an overview of the history of Prussia as she was taught it. Later references in her account will have more meaning against this background.

Besides giving the facts pertinent to each of the *three* rulers, whose names are given in italics in the table 47†, listing the succession of monarchs of the kingdom known as Prussia will provide a capsule history of the political background from which Edith's family came.

Friedrich I was the first monarch to assume the title of King, and at the direction of Emperor Leopold I, that title was to be expressed as King *in* Prussia.

Friedrich III was married to Victoria, the daughter of England's Queen Victoria. He succeeded his father, Wilhelm I, in 1888, bringing hope to the Liberals; however he died after only 99 days and was succeeded by his son who was inclined toward autocracy.

† (47) Monarchs of the House of Hohenzollern

BORN	MONARCH	TITLE	REIGNED	WAS SUCCEEDED BY
1620	*Friedrich Wilhelm, the Great Elector*		1640–1688	his son
1657	Friedrich I who was Elector of Brandenburg from and became	King in Prussia	1688–1701 1701–1713	his son
1688	Friedrich Wilhelm I	King in Prussia	1713–1740	his son
1712	*Friedrich (II) the Great*	King in Prussia	1740–1786	his nephew
1744	Friedrich Wilhelm II	King in Prussia	1786–1797	his son
1770	Friedrich Wilhelm III	King in Prussia	1797–1840	his son
1795	Friedrich Wilhelm IV	King in Prussia	1840–1858 died–1861	his younger brother
1797	*Wilhelm I* and became	King in Prussia Emperor of Germany	1861–1871 1871–1888	his son
1831	Friedrich III	King in Prussia and Emperor of Germany	1888–1888	his son
1859	Wilhelm II	King in Prussia and Emperor of Germany	1888–abdicated	

He was the *Kaiser* (Emperor) [when Edith was born] and he and his son, Crown Prince Friedrich Wilhelm both abdicated as a result of the revolution which came at the conclusion of World War I, November, 1918. They fled to Holland.

479

48. Wilhelm II was only 29 years old when he succeeded his father as King in Prussia and as Emperor of the German Reich. Described by some historians as ambitious, impulsive, easily influenced, and inclined to be autocratic, he had difficulty with Bismarck, Chancellor of the Reich. In 1890, Wilhelm II summarily dismissed Bismarck, then 75 years old, from the office of Chancellor. That was one year before Edith Stein was born.

The political situation was in turmoil for most of her life. From 1888 when Wilhelm II succeeded to the throne there were seven Chancellors of the Reich in the years preceeding and during the First World War. One gains new understanding of English-German bonds, and therefore, of the tragedy of World War I by reflecting that George V of England and Wilhelm II were cousins. Many German families had relatives living in England, and the war was the more dreadful for that.

49. In the war between France and Germany, on September 1, 1870, the French army under Comte de MacMahon, and with the Emperor Napoleon himself, capitulated at Sedan, a city northeast of Reims on the river Meuse. Napoleon III was taken prisoner and deposed as Emperor of France. After a brief internment, he and his wife Eugenie went to England.

50. With an altitude of 5,260 ft., this is the highest peak of the *Riesengebirge*. Cf. No. 25.

51. Franz Grillparzer (1791–1872), foremost Austrian dramatist. His own inner struggle was mirrored in his works, as is the influence on him of the Viennese theatre, especially of the popular plays. Grillparzer was eventually so frustrated by censorship imposed under Metternich that he gave up publishing his writings.

The Jewess of Toledo, one of Grillparzer's best known dramas, tells the story of a Spanish King's neglect of his duties of state and family because of his admiration of the beautiful Rahel. The girl's murder, ordered by the queen and the royal council, shocks the King into accepting his responsibilities, strengthened in his character at Rahel's cost. This play was based on one by the renowned Spanish dramatist Lope de Vega Carpio who was born in Madrid in 1562, the year in which Teresa of Jesus began her Reform.

Although Lope de Vega's first play was written six years before Teresa's death, she may not have known about him. However, as he was in the service of the Duke of Alba for several years, before and after serving in the Spanish Navy and participating in the Armada's expedition against England, de Vega was almost certain to have heard about Teresa.

For both Teresa of Jesus and Edith Stein, the reading habits they formed in adolescence influenced them personally and developed their understanding of womanhood. Both, in their own personal situations, contributed toward encouraging women to live out of a greater appreciation of their own dignity and rights. Lope de Vega, whatever his personal shortcomings, is credited by Fitzmaurice-Kelly with "placing woman in her true setting as an ideal, as the mainspring of dramatic motive and of chivalrous conduct."

Grillparzer, in dealing with psychological problems heightened by political situations, excelled in portraying the stages of a woman's maturing through the experience of duty, passion, and grief. Edith's interest in psychology at the time she studied the Austrian's plays created the disposition which made her call him an intimate friend.

Friedrich Hebbel (1813–1863), German dramatist, wrote tragedies, many of which were pervaded by a pessimism influenced by Hegel. Two of Hebbel's works are about Jewish heroines: *Judith*, and *Herod and Mariamne*. He was particularly skilled in endowing his heroines with qualities delicately delineating feminine psychology to show strong characters facing life situations that demanded the limit of courage. (Cf. No. 52)

Otto Ludwig (1813–1865), in his effort to establish a theory of drama, analyzed Shakespeare so exhaustively as to despair of writing worthwhile dramas, himself. His prose work was good but melancholic. One of his departures from the usual rustic settings of villages, peopled by roofers, foresters, game wardens, and gossiping neighbors, was *The Maccabees*, based on the Biblical history of the Jews.

52. This tragedy by Hebbel tells of a beautiful woman, a courageous commoner who, daring to marry a young Duke of Bavaria in the fifteenth century, was assassinated at his father's orders for reasons of state.

Edith does not go into detail about the difference of opinion with her teacher; one might assume, however, it concerned Agnes, the woman, rather than Hebbel, the author.

53. Cf. No. (4) ‡. Marking of papers was by number, 1 equalling A, 2 a B, and 3 a C; alternatively, *very good* was an equivalent of the 1.

54. Ludwig van Beethoven (1770–1827) wrote some of his most noble music for his only opera, *Fidelio*. One example: the deeply stirring prisoners' chorus immortalizes their feelings as they emerge to freedom from the hopelessness of their cells, owing to the indomitable courage of Leonore. In her disguise as Fidelio, she was Beethoven's symbol of the love that brings about the liberation of the oppressed people of the world.

Edith and her fellow prisoners at Auschwitz were not to have personal experience of such a rescue before the curtain on the last act fell to hide them forever.

55. Ernst Haeckel (1834–1919), a professor of zoology at Jena, which is now in East Germany. In 1899, his *The Riddle of the Universe* propounded a monistic philosophy based on Darwin's evolutionary hypothesis. Cf. No. 75.

56. Cf. Page 116.

57. Thirty Years' War (1618–1648). It began as a rebellion of the Bohemian states against Emperor Ferdinand II, and it was a war of religion which ended as an armed struggle for power among the European nations. Aggression between Catholic and Protestant states, between cities and feudal lords, between the cities of the realm and the Emperor of Germany, between the Hapsburg dynasty and France—these erupted until Sweden and Denmark were involved; and these as well as Spain and France all fought on German soil. The destruction of property and the despoliation of the land defy description; about 35 percent of the population of that time perished, largely due to plagues brought on and spread by the devastation wrought in this war.

58. David Courant, a pharmacist, lived in Chemnitz. In 1953, the name of the city was changed to Karl-Marx-Stadt. For more on this relative, see Pages 64 and 230.

59. Cf. Page 65.

60. This line of Ibsen's is probably from his *Brand*. Edith repeatedly numbers Ibsen among her favorite dramatists; and Professor Olbrich's choice was certain to strike a sympathetic chord in her.

61. A student who had successfully completed the *Abitur* was known as a "*mulus*" in the interim between the examinations and the beginning of university studies. *Mulus* is the Latin for mule, the hybrid offspring that is neither donkey nor mare.

Class trips are usual in many countries. The *mulus* trip was taken individually, not by an entire class.

62. Galicia (*Galizien* in German) was part of Poland in 1809; having come into the possession of the Austrian crown in 1815, it remained such until by the Treaty of Saint-Germaine of 1919 when it reverted to Polish rule. In 1945, its eastern portion was ceded to Ukraine. (This Galicia is not to be confused with that of northwest Spain.)

63. Cf. Page 80.

64. Cf. Page 85.

65. This Latin phrase is also given frequently as "Audi alteram partem." "Hear the other side!" serves as translation for either.

66. Chemnitz (Karl-Marx-Stadt) is the largest industrial city of Lower Saxony. Products manufactured include machines, motors, motorcycles, and textiles.

67. This was the University of Breslau in Edith's hometown. She attended it for two years.

68. Core courses were not demanded by the universities. Students selected the courses they preferred and then contracted with the university, or, if the course was taught by a *privatdozent*, with the teacher, personally. More on this is given in Note 71.

69. William Stern (1871–1938), a German philosopher, better known as pioneer in child and adolescent psychology. He developed testing by cloud-pictures, and his formula for measuring the I.Q. is still used as he developed it in 1911.

Edith visited him in Hamburg in 1919. Stern is one of the many brilliant Germans who found refuge in England or America when Hitler's regime ended their careers in the universities where they had made such tremendous contributions to the sciences. William Stern died in America in 1938.

70. Richard Hönigswald (1875–1947). His writings on philosophy and philosophers, on the theory of knowledge, on Ernst Haeckel, on Kant, on psychology and languages are listed in The National Union Catalog of Pre-1956 Imprints. His Archive is located in the Philosophy Seminar of the University of Bonn, West Germany.

71. *Privatdozent*, now listed by Webster as privatdocent, designates a lecturer admitted to teaching after passing a special examination which included the presentation of a scientific thesis beyond the doctoral dissertation. Although authorized to teach at a university, he did not receive a salary from the university. The students arranged with the lecturer to attend the classes, and they paid the fees directly to the teacher. Several of Edith's courses in Breslau, and later in Göttingen, were taught by a privatdocent.

72. Cf. No. 68.

73. Tatian the Assyrian, of the second Century, wrote this *Diatessaron*. Like Tertullian, Tatian was a Christian apologist whose later writings were classed heretical.

74. "Ulfilas" is the Greek spelling for Wulfila (311–383). This missionary Bishop of the Visigoths invented the Gothic script and made a Gothic transcription of the Bible which is still extant. Known as the Codex *Argenteus*, it is kept in Uppsala, Sweden.

75. Darwinistic nationalism would propose that a true nation can be formed only of people who share a like descent and race, a premise based on the theories of Charles R. Darwin (1809–1882), the British naturalist. Darwin's ideas were popular in Germany; though they were championed by Haeckel, acknowledged by David Strauss, they were not universally accepted. The Darwin-inspired theory that a nation

must strive to achieve and maintain superiority over other nations through culture was opposed by Nietzsche who proposed that the emergence of superior individuals was of prime importance.

Edith could not accept the notion of the Darwinistic theories of selection and survival of the fittest as being formative for nations, although she recognized that certain distinctive characteristics establish the identity of a nation.

Edith and her classmates were in their late teens at this time. Any of her contemporaries who misconstrued that notion of superiority of race which was being offered to them, in what was practically a laboratory situation, could understandably have nurtured the seed for the next quarter of a century. It could then produce the lethal fruit of that Aryan cult for whom it seems that survival of the fittest (*their* self-evaluation) came to mean annihilating all the others.

76. Friedrich W. Foerster (1869-1966) is a German educator of worldwide influence. His theory of education stresses the discipline of the will. A pacifist, he was a bitter opponent of German militarism and nationalism.

George Kerschensteiner (1854-1932) in following the theories of John Dewey (1859-1952), the American philosopher and educator, advocated the latter's principle, "productive work in groups," be applied in education.

Gaudig and Wyneken's influence was more localized.

77. This connection of Edith with Castle Obernigk acquaints us with the admirable work of the Evangelical Deaconesses founded by Mother Eva, the Countess Tiele-Winckler (1866-1930). She converted the castle at Miechowitz, in which she had been born, into the first of her "homes for the homeless" some time around 1885.

In 1910, the Kisslings, a married couple from Breslau, gave Mother Eva Castle Obernigk in what is now the Polish town of Oberniki (in Silesia). The orphanage which Edith often visited was therefore a very recent foundation.

This Protestant community of Sisters whose motherhouse is now in Düsseldorf, Germany, had two members of Jewish descent at the time of the Hitler regime. One of them, like Edith, was killed at Auschwitz.

78. *Wandervögel* is a youth group founded in 1901, therefore one of the earliest of such associations in Germany. The literal translation — migratory birds — indicates the orientation of the group to nature studies and hiking activities.

79. Wartenburg (not to be confused with the *Warteberg*) is located about 30 miles to the northeast of Breslau. Peter, one of the children in

this noble family, would have been about nine years old when Hermsen went there. Later as Count Peter Yorck von Wartenburg (1904-1944), he was with Count Helmut James von Moltke co-founder of the *Kreisauer Kreis*, a small group within the German Resistance movement. With Count Moltke, he was executed after the unsuccessful attempt to assassinate Hitler on July 20, 1944. The *Kreis* had another member who has become well known for his non-violent opposition to Hitler: Alfred Delp, s.j., who was executed in 1945.

80. The young man to be educated was in all probability the son of Prince William of Wied (1876-1945). The Prince and his family returned to Neuwied, Germany, shortly after World War I began. For a few months, after the August, 1913, Treaty of Bucharest, Prince William had ruled the newly independent principality of Albania.

Hermsen's stay with the family was also brief since he served in the first World War from which he did not return.

81. Neuwied is situated on the Rhine north of Koblenz.

82. In 1779, Gotthold Ephraim Lessing (1729-1781) wrote the dramatic poem *Nathan the Wise* using as model for the hero his friend Moses Mendelssohn, leader in the Jewish emancipation in Germany and grandfather of the great musician Felix Mendelssohn-Bartholdy.

83. William Stern is best known for his intellectualistic conception of speech development in the child. His concept of "convergence" holds that when a child is nearly two years old, a moment comes when it realizes that speech is thought made vocal. His theory, although contested by some who consider it an over-simplification, still serves as a stimulant in the study of language and thought many years after Edith was in his classes. Cf. No. 69.

84. This revolution was triggered on October 29, 1918, by the mutiny of the German Fleet at Kiel when orders were given for going to sea to fight the British. Revolutionary activity followed in Munich on November 7, and in Berlin on the 9th. The Armistice was signed that November 11. Edith also mentions this revolution in Chapter VI.

85. Hermann Ebbinghaus (1850-1909) conducted experiments on learning and memory functions. He was instrumental in the publication of a new journal *Zeitschrift für Psychologie* at a time when psychology was still studied under philosophy. His was pioneer work in "association" in the learning process. In 1897 he advocated and promoted intelligence tests in schools.

86. Habilitation is the result of qualifying as a lecturer in a university under the patronage of a professor for whom a special thesis, beyond the doctoral dissertation, was prepared; at root, the word refers to ability.

87. The Würzburg Method, represented principally by Oswald Külpe (1862-1915), A. Messer, and K. Buehler, studied the psychology of thought and thinking. Their experiments in observation of associations showed that while associations have the tendency to "go all over the place," thought has a "determining tendency" which keeps it goal directed. These experiments would have been going on in Edith's time. Cf. No. 101.

88. The four members were Lilli Platau, Rose Guttmann, Edith, and her sister Erna. The clover-leaf is mentioned originally on page 122.

89. Speusippos, nephew of Plato, headed the Athenian Academy after Plato's death. This costume ball, late in 1911, occurred shortly before Eugen Kühnemann went to America to be the first Carl Schurz memorial professor at the University of Wisconsin. The efforts of Kühnemann, after World War I, to reconcile Germany and the U.S. are also documented. Edith's reference to the conflict between Turkey and Italy, involving the Dodecanese Islands, reminds us that territorial strife was building up for years before W.W. I.

90. This society was named for Baron Karl Wilhelm von Humboldt (1767-1835), a Prussian statesman, who was Minister of Education for Prussia in 1809-10. He founded the new humanistic *Gymnasium* and the University of Berlin. He was a pioneer in the comparative study of language; and his insights have proven, eventually, to be more helpful than he realized at the time. Humboldt observed that poetry and music are inseparable while prose is dependent entirely on language and is dominated by thought.

91. Mortification of the eyes, alternatively referred to as custody of or modesty of the eyes, is an ascetical practice with which Edith would become acquainted upon her entrance into the religious life. The ascetical practice consists in not looking fixedly at persons, and not glancing around just to observe one's surroundings, or to look at things out of curiosity; at times, it also meant denying a good but not strictly necessary observation of people or other visual attractions.

92. Cf. No. 47.

93. Emperor Leopold I (1640-1705) was of the Hapsburg dynasty. The University of Frankfurt-on-the-Oder was founded in 1506. At the beginning of the sixteenth century, Philipp Melanchthon remarked on the erudition of the inhabitants of Breslau, pointing out that "in no other city within the kingdom are there as many men of the common people occupied in the study of the sciences." This is the intellectual heritage handed on to Edith and the other students of the University of Breslau.

94. Breslau is situated on the Oder River which at present serves to demarcate eastern Europe from western Europe. Three islands dot the river; on the middle one, the first Bishop of Breslau built his Cathedral church, which in turn gave its name of *Dom*, or cathedral, to the street, the bridge, and the island. Because of its location on Sand Island, another of Breslau's landmarks is called the Sand Church. The parish church named for the Holy Cross is on the same island as the cathedral. Much of the beauty of Breslau was destroyed during World War II. It is now part of Poland and known as Wroclaw.

95. This was in April, 1911. Cf. Page 185.

96. The German mark's value fluctuates with an average evaluation of between 1/4 to 2/5 of the American dollar.

97. Cf. No. 74.

98. Karl Gutzkow (1811–1878), whose social novels placed emphasis on his characters' milieu rather than on the plot, was among the first to use his writing as a plea for the emancipation of women from unjust treatment in the home. At the same time, he advocated freedom from censorship and argued forcefully for religious tolerance.

99. Despite the marked effect this novel had on Edith, no record of it appears in general studies of German literature of her time.

100. During the centenary celebrations of 1911, there may not have been sufficient opportunity to display to maximum effect the organ built specifically for the *Jahrhunderthalle* [Centennial Hall]. A Bach Festival in 1912 would do justice to this organ, which, with its sixteen thousand pipes and more than two hundred registers, is still one of the largest of the world.

101. Already mentioned in No. 87, the psychologists of the Würzburg Method [Külpe-Messer-Buehler (who identified the "Aha-experience" in 1907)] dissented from the new ideas presented in *Logische Untersuchungen* possibly misunderstanding the author's theory of categorical intuition. That was Husserl's own evaluation of their disagreement. These dissenting remarks acquainted Edith with the man who was so great an influence in her intellectual life. Information on Husserl is given in No. 113.

102. Edith introduces here the couple who were to become such close personal friends. In the library of their home in Bergzabern, Edith found *The Book of Her Life* by Teresa of Jesus which introduced her to the mystic of Spain whose daughter she was to be as a Discalced Carmelite.

103. This cousin, Richard Courant, formed close ties with his aunt,

Edith's mother, in his childhood. (Cf. Page 84) He was brilliant as a student; as an excellent mathematician, he frequently tutored those attending classes he had not yet reached.

Richard appears in Edith's story at nearly every stage of her academic journey; there was a strong bond of affection between these cousins. Despite the divergences in their life story, many family traits and characteristics, especially excellence in their academic careers, whether in research or in teaching, are found in equal measure in Edith Stein and Richard Courant.

Like the majority of the Göttingen mathematicians and physicists, he emigrated to the United States with his family, in the 1930s. Constance Reid's book about him, *"Courant in Göttingen and New York—The Story of an Improbable Mathematician,"* was published by the Springer-Verlag (New York, N.Y., 1976).

104. Cf. No. 86.

105. Cf. No. 84.

106. This cousin's story was told in the preceding pages where she was not identified.

107. The picture was a reproduction of a work by the Florentine painter Cimabue (1240 to about 1302). He was the teacher of Giotto, who is famous for his *Legend of Francis* told in frescoes.

108. "Göttingen's Seven" were professors dismissed from that university in 1837 for their protest and refusal to take an oath prescribed by King Ernst August of Hannover. Among them were: Jacob Grimm (1785-1863) and his brother Wilhelm (1786-1859), who are better known for their compilation of fairy-and folktales; Wilhelm Eduard Weber (1804-1891), pioneer in telegraphy; Friedrich Christoph Dahlmann (1785-1866), a liberal historian and politician; and the historian, Georg Gottfried Gervinus (1805-1871).

109. Kassel and this region are shown on the Map.

110. Danziger is also mentioned on pages 224, 297.

111. Adolf Reinach (1883-1917) has been called the phenomenologist *par excellence*, and he was valued as teacher by the earliest students of Husserl. Reinach's version of early phenomenology was simpler and clearer in form and more concrete and suggestive in content than that of the "Master." Husserl himself saw in the clear-headed, warmhearted, and widely read Reinach a philosopher who had thoroughly understood and assimilated the phenomenological method in the sense of the *Logische Untersuchungen*. Reinach's death in action in 1917 cut short not only his promise but that of the Göttingen Phenomenological Society.

Hans Theodor Conrad (1881-1969) was one of the earliest Göttingen students of Husserl. He married Hedwig Martius (1881-1966), another of Husserl's students. Both taught philosophy in Munich and influenced the generation of phenomenologists who followed them, including Edith Stein. It was at their home in Bergzabern that Edith read *The Book of Her Life* by Teresa of Jesus and was led to become a Catholic. Hedwig Conrad-Martius was her godmother. The close friendship which existed between the Conrads and Edith is attested to by her many letters to them, and by her addressing them, familiarly, as *Autos* for Hans Theodor and *Hatti* for Hedwig.

Moritz Geiger (1880-1937) was first of the early phenomenologists to come into direct contact with American philosophy. He met James and Royce in 1907 when he studied at Harvard for a year. He was a guest professor at Stanford University in 1926. Because of his Jewish ancestry, he was deprived of his chair at the University of Göttingen in 1933; he subsequently became chairman of the Department of Philosophy at Vassar College.

112. Theodor Lipps (1851-1914) was both psychologist and philosopher. His students formed a club as early as 1901, and this led to their introduction to Husserl's work. By 1905 a steady stream of students from Munich went to Göttingen, and vice versa. Edith did not study under Lipps but as her doctoral dissertation was on empathy, she had to review his teaching on it, at Husserl's direction.

113. Cf. Page 220. Edmund Husserl was born April 8, 1859, in Prossnitz (now Prostějov), Moravia, of Jewish parents. He received his Ph. D. as a mathematician in 1882, then continued his study with the philosopher and psychologist, Franz Brentano, in Vienna in 1883. Three years later, Husserl became an Evangelical Lutheran. In 1887 he married Malvine Steinschneider; and three children were born to them: Elisabeth, who married Jacob Rosenberg, and eventually lived in Boston where she died in 1982; Gerhart, who became a lawyer; Wolfgang, whose great gift as a mathematician was evident before he enlisted at seventeen in the First World War from which he did not return.

In 1887, Husserl also achieved habilitation at the University of Halle, Germany, where he delivered an inaugural lecture on metaphysics. In 1900-1 he wrote the *Logische Untersuchungen* [Logical Investigations] which introduced phenomenology — a method of analysis which was revolutionary for philosophy.

Husserl then spent fifteen years teaching at the University of Göttingen, being called there as an "extraordinary" professor — the position was created for him, and he never had an ordinary professorship at Göttingen. His intention as a teacher — and his students all called him "Master" — was to present to his classes the problems of philosophy and to equip them to use the method he had evolved in working out these problems in the years ahead. He never thought of transmitting finished results.

Every master craftsman has an individual method of working. Husserl developed his thoughts by writing them, and this he did in short-hand—the Gabelsberger method—which Edith had to learn in order to be able to transcribe his notes when she became his assistant. An estimate may be formed of the prodigious work he achieved in his life-time, and a measure of the patience and skill demanded of his assistants, when one learns he wrote more than 40,000 pages in steno-graphic script.

Edith studied under Husserl in his final years in Göttingen, and she gives details of his being called to Freiburg-im-Breisgau. As his new position as ordinary professor of philosophy enabled him to develop his theories, he taught that philosophy's task is to renew life; and he continued to clarify the relationship between logic and consciousness, analyzed phenomenologically and psychologically.

He was the first German scholar to be recognized by the British after World War I; he lectured in London in 1922. He retired in 1928, but he continued his work; his exclusion from the university as a result of Nazi repression in 1933 led him to concentrate on the function of phenomenology as support for the freedom of the mind. In the spring of 1935, he was invited to address the Cultural Society in Vienna, and he gave a memorable talk on "Philosophy in the Crisis of European Mankind"—so impressed were the hearers that he had to repeat the talk, lasting almost three hours, two days later. Despite the shadow of Hitler's reprisal, he again spoke in the name of free philosophy in the fall of 1935 at the German and Czechoslovakian University in Prague where his listeners were overwhelmed at the sovereign and absolute sureness of his thought while all about him there was the confusion of the time. He continued to work until, in the summer of 1937, illness made it impossible. From that time on, he concentrated on preparing for death which came to him on April 27, 1938.

Frau Malvine, who was always actively interested in her husband's work throughout their life together, saw to the preservation of her husband's writings. Although already eighty years old, she managed in 1940 to transfer all his manuscripts and books, indeed, his entire scientific legacy, to Belgium. Frau Husserl found refuge in a Belgian convent where she remained in hiding until, in 1945, she could be conducted in safety to her son's home in New York. Five years later, then back in Freiburg, Germany, she died at the age of ninety. During her years in Belgium, she became a Catholic.

114. The translation of Husserl's work is given the English title *Logical Investigations*. The first volume was published in Germany (Halle, 1900) and was revised in 1913. Volume II appeared first in 1901 and was revised in 1922. The revised Halle editions were published in a translation by J.N. Findlay in 1970 (New York: Humanities Press). Husserl's own introduction to the *Logical Investigations* was translated by Philip J. Bossert and Curtis H. Peters in 1975. W.R. Boyce Gibson and others of Husserl's translators refer to the work as *Logical Studies*.

115. *Ideas: General Introduction to Pure Phenomenology* is the full title in English of Husserl's *Ideen zu einer reinen Phänomenologie und phänomenologischen Philosophie*. As Edith here mentions, it appeared in 1913 in the *Yearbook*, that is, *Jahrbuch für Philosophie und Phänomenologische Forschung*. Husserl wrote an "Author's Preface to the English Edition" of *Ideas* which was published in 1931 in a translation by W.R. Boyce Gibson (London: Collier Macmillan Publishers. New York: Collier Books).

116. Hans Lipps (1889-1941) was born in Pirna, an industrial city south of Dresden, Germany; he died of a headwound received while serving with the German Army in Russia in World War II. As professor of philosophy in Frankfurt-am-Main, he published phenomenology of a highly personal type, as, for instance, two volumes on *Phenomenologie der Erkenntnis* (Phenomenology of Knowledge) leading in the direction of "hermeneutic" anthropology; they appeared in 1927-28. Hans Lipps also occupied himself with the phenomenology of language. Cf. No. 232.

117. Adolf Reinach (Cf. No. 111) was among these founders; so were Hans Teodor and Hedwig Conrad-Martius. How interesting it is that in this paragraph Edith mentions the husband by his surname alone and gives the wife's maiden name! (Cf. Nos. 102, 111)

The others she mentions are: 1) Dietrich von Hildebrand, born October 12, 1889, two years to the day before Edith. He, too, studied in Göttingen; then he taught philosophy at the University of Munich until the advent of the Nazis forced him like so many others to leave Germany. He became a professor of philosophy at the Graduate School of Fordham University in 1940 and remained there for life.

D. von Hildebrand died in New Rochelle, N.Y., on January 26, 1977. He was one of the earliest of several of the phenomenologists whose study led to their profession of faith as Catholics. (Husserl is reported to have said, in gentle jest, that he should someday be canonized since so many of his students had become Catholics; he was an Evangelical Lutheran.)

2) Alexandre Koyré (1892-1964), born in Russia, was educated in

Paris, and from there he went to Göttingen. Edith knew him as one of the older students; his opinions served her as guidelines. In her letters, she mentions a visit the Koyrés paid her in Germany and tells of her plans to see them when she goes to Paris. He was teaching philosophy there at the École des Hautes-Études. He died in Paris.

3) Johannes Hering (1891–1966), an Alsatian philosopher and theologian, is better known under his name in its French form, Jean Hering. His work in early phenomenological ontology was considered provocative. When, later, Alsace was reunited to France, he became one of the ablest interpreters of phenomenology to the French scientific community.

118. Fritz Frankfurter was among the promising young phenomenologists who did not survive World War I. Edith tells the rest of his story in Chapter VII, page 307.

119. Georg Simmel (1858–1918) was a pioneer in formal sociology.

120. Fritz Kaufmann (1891–1958) was born in Leipzig little more than three months before Edith's birth in Breslau. They first met as fellow students in Göttingen when they formed one of the strongest and deepest friendships of her life.

The significant dates of Kaufmann's life are quickly told: during World War I, he served in the German army in Rumania and in the occupied parts of Russia. After the war he completed his studies in Freiburg, where he then began his teaching career. In 1927, he married Alice Dorothee Lieberg.

In 1933, he was allowed to continue teaching when others were ousted from their prestigious positions; he carried on in that profession until 1936 by which time he was at the Academy for the Study of Judaism in Berlin. But then the "most vicious and humiliating anti-Jewish legislation and anti-semitism" forced him to leave. Having received a grant for a year's research in London, he went there in 1936.

He paid the second visit to Edith in the Carmel of Cologne that year on his way to England. It was possibly during this visit about which she wrote to a mutual friend in October, 1936, that Edith, as Kaufmann related, "exhorted me, urgently, to forget cleverness and to become like a child in order to enter the kingdom of Heaven."

In 1938, Kaufmann left England for the United States, where, at Northwestern University, he taught a wide range of subjects during the next eight years: History of Philosophy, Ethics, the Great Philosophical Poets, and the Philosophy of Religion. He also lectured at the Chicago College of Jewish Studies, giving an Introduction to Jewish Philosophy.

When his wife and their two children were leaving Germany to join

Dr. Kaufmann in the United States, they experienced the same humiliation, frustration, and anxiety that was the portion of the families of prominent intellectuals who had managed to flee Germany. As it was, they made it, as they said, "by the skin of their teeth"; but the courageous and determined Mrs. Kaufmann also succeeded in bringing to the United States all of the five thousand volumes in her husband's private library, along with other valuable personal property.

In 1946, Dr. Kaufmann joined the faculty of the University of Buffalo. The head of the philosophy department there was Dr. Marvin Farber who had met Dr. Kaufmann when they were both studying in Göttingen. Dr. Farber is credited with beginning, in 1940, the quarterly journal on phenomenology for which Edith intended an article (Cf. Page 429).

Although the Kaufmann family had found a new home in the United States, the hardships they had known in Europe were followed by illness and difficulties. The first Mrs. Kaufmann died in 1953; Gustav, the only son, had very poor health and died, at the age of 22, in 1956; and that same year, Dr. Kaufmann retired from his teaching position.

Of Edith Stein's letters, published in two volumes by the *Archivum*, the number of those addressed to Fritz Kaufmann is second only to the number which Mother Petra Brüning, o.s.u., collected. She received hers during the ten years in the convent of Dorsten, so keeping them was both natural and easy for her. The first six letters Kaufmann kept had reached him while he was at the Rumanian front in 1916, in World War I. Most of the two dozen additional letters were sent to Kaufmann in Freiburg, and he must have taken all of them with him to the United States. When he returned to Europe after his retirement from the University of Buffalo, he apparently carried them back to Switzerland, for his widow, Frau Luise Kaufmann, received public thanks from the *Archivum Carmelitanum Edith Stein* for the letters she made available to the Archive after Prof. Kaufmann died in Zürich in 1958. Cf. No. 149.

121. Paul Natorp (1854-1924) is the German philosopher and composer who specialized in social pedagogy and who was a cofounder of the neo-Kantian Marburg movement with Hermann Cohen (1842-1918).

122. Winthrop Pickard Bell (1884-1965) was born in Halifax, Canada. Edith tells more of his story in Chapter VII. (Cf. Page 301). As a Canadian national, he was interned at Ruhleben-Döberitz until 1918. Bell studied under Husserl between 1911-1914. He had done graduate work at Harvard under Josiah Royce, and Husserl had Bell write a highly critical thesis on Royce's theory of knowledge. This thesis was

printed in Göttingen University's *Yearbook* in 1922. Winthrop Bell died in Chester, Nova Scotia, in 1965.

123. Moritz Schlick (1882–1936) is a German philosopher who, with R. Carnap and O. Neurath, founded the Vienna Circle (1922–1936), the school of neo-positivism influenced by Ernst Mach and Ludwig Wittgenstein.

124. Max Scheler (1874–1928), philosopher and sociologist, conceived phenomenology as the concerted effort to go from symbols back to the things themselves; he advocated giving attention to the "what" (the *essentia*) while suspending the question of the "that" (the *existentia*); he held that attention was to be given to the a priori, i.e., to the essential connections which exist between these "whats."

During World War I, Scheler served semi-officially on diplomatic missions for Germany to Switzerland and to the Netherlands. After the war, Scheler returned to the academic life; he held a special chair for philosophy and sociology at the University of Cologne, and he taught there from 1919 until his death in 1928.

125. Cf. No. 103.

126. Ludwig Börne, whose real name was Löb Baruch (1786–1837), and Heinrich Heine (1797–1856), through their poetry and journalism exercised a tremendous influence in favor of liberal, democratic action; with Karl Gutzkow, they formed a radical literary group known as *Junges Deutschland* [Young Germany].

127. Leonard Nelson (1882–1927) is known principally as the founder of the so called Neo-Friesian School. Jakob Friedrich Fries (1773–1843) was a philosopher who taught at Jena, Germany. He wrote on psychological and religio-philosophical themes; he was influenced by Kant and Jacobi.

Fries regarded the development of idealism by Fichte, Schelling, and Hegel as a great mistake. Fries psychologized the Kantian critique; he was defended for so doing by his disciple, E.F. Apelt (1812–1859). Jakob Fries influenced Rudolf Otto (1869–1937), the celebrated philosopher of religion.

128. Georg Elias Müller (1850–1934) made a traditional application of the psychology of associations; he produced a monumental work on the role of associations in the learning process; and he made a study regarding raising the sensitivity of parts of the brain to stimuli. Müller developed and taught theories regarding perception of color; he formulated five well known "psycho-physical axioms for empirical psychology."

129. David Katz was born in Kassel, Germany, in 1884; he died in Stockholm, Sweden, in 1953. For a time he studied under Theodor Lipps; but Katz did not find the lectures to his taste. For several months

he was at Külpe's Institute at Würzburg. After 1907, he became Georg Elias Müller's assistant at Göttingen; he was also a privatdocent beginning in 1911.

Katz wrote an account of his academic career for *A History of Psychology in Autobiography*, Volume IV, published by the Clark University Press (Worcester, Mass., 1952). The article informs us, indirectly, that Edmund Husserl in no way discriminated against Edith Stein in the matter of her assistantship — even though others at the university refused to consider a woman for habilitation. Edith mentions the salary she received as an assistant; it was the same amount which the Prussian government paid to other assistants at the university — one hundred marks a month.

David Katz verifies the amount when he tells of having to forfeit his salary for the duration of the war because of a patriotic impulse on Müller's part. The professor wished to save the Prussian government money during the costly war and arranged that his assistant's salary be suspended. Edith's assistantship was served in these same years.

Katz married Rosa Heine in 1919; like all other Jewish professionals, his career in Germany ended in 1933. Despite harassment, he succeeded in getting to England; from there, he and his family came to the United States. The hardships of their situation help us to understand Edith's worry that some of her relatives who were trying to leave Germany might suffer more in the long run.

Edith again brings David Katz into her story on page 315.

130. Baron Heinrich Friedrich Karl vom und zum Stein (1757-1831), Prussian statesman, dismissed and proscribed in 1808 by Napoleon, organized the East Prussian rebellion in 1813. In 1819, he founded a society for the preservation of German historical material and the collection of artifacts relating to the years 500 to 1500 that is known as the *Monumenta Germaniae Historica*.

131. Leopold von Ranke (1795-1886), historian, held a professorship in Berlin for nearly half a century, 1825-1871; he advocated source criticism in history. He wrote extensively, treating among other subjects the Roman Papacy in the 16th and 17th centuries; German history during the time of the Reformation; the history of France, and that of England.

132. Gerhart Hauptmann (1862-1946), the playwright, is considered one of Germany's great literary figures. His compassion for the poor and downtrodden was vigorous and sensitive. In his earliest works he was a representative of Naturalism; his plays often showed the influence of Ibsen and Zola.

133. This organ in the *Jahrhunderthalle* is already described in No. 100.

134. M. Wertheimer, A. Gelb, and especially W. Köhler made contributions to the developments of Gestalt psychology.

135. It is interesting to note how Edith here passes from references to Reinach to an explanation of Husserl's choice for philosophy. Her use of the masculine pronouns is balanced by the reference to mathematics: Husserl began as a mathematician, Reinach's earlier field was law. Again, Reinach was a privatdocent in Göttingen; only Husserl "had been called" to the university.

136. In 1803, the secularization which was mandated by the German Diet, responding to pressure from France and Russia, and supported by Napoleon, changed the map of Germany. By taking almost a hundred ecclesiastically owned properties from the archbishops, bishops, and abbots who administered them and giving the properties to secular rulers, compensation was said to have been made to the temporal princes of Germany who had lost all or part of their territory as a result of the Treaty of February 9, 1801.

137. Felix Dahn (1834–1912) is best known for this thrilling historical novel *The Struggle for Rome* written in 1876. It told of the last desperate battles of the East Goths in Italy in the sixth century. Frau Reinach's comment was a play on the words: *Krieg*, a noun, meaning "war" or "struggle," and *kriegen*, a verb, meaning "to get."

138. Edith later makes clear that Max Lehmann was the third member on her commission of examiners.

139. Cf. Page 267.

140. Cf. Page 269.

141. Cf. Page 224.

142. Pauline Reinach, Adolf's sister, formed a lasting friendship with Edith. Independently, both of them were admitted to the Catholic Church; and both became religious. Pauline entered the Benedictine Order in Ermeton, Belgium, and received the name, Sr. Augustina. She died in September, 1969, at the Abbey in Ermeton. (Reinach's widow, Anna, also became a Catholic some years after his death.)

143. The German edition gives this ship's name as *Empress of India*. An entry on steamship disasters in reference books makes it clear that the Canadian vessel did carry the name "Empress of Ireland." Edith's comment, "Now that ship had sunk," and the fact that it was 1914 at once conjures up the thought of submarine warfare. However, this disaster, in which 1,023 lives were lost within twenty minutes, was the result of a collision in dense fog— not on the high seas, but in the Gulf of St. Lawrence. A Norwegian coal barge rammed the steamer, tearing it in half so that there was no chance of saving any of the

passengers or crew. The date was May 29, 1914, one month before the conflagration of World War I.

144. The German text says *serbischen Königsmordes* which could be translated literally as "Serbian murder of the King"—but it was, of course, the assassination of two royal personages, Crown Prince Franz Ferdinand, successor to the throne of Austria-Hungary, and his wife, at Sarajevo, on June 28, 1914, by the Bosnian student, Princip.

145. That was Sunday, August 2, 1914. It could literally be called, as Edith puts it, "the Sunday of the Declaration of War" since the day before, August 1, Germany had declared war on Russia, and followed it on August 3 by a similar declaration against France. There were fifty-three declarations of war made throughout the world for that massive conflict between July, 1914 and July, 1918.

146. Felix Klein (1849-1925), a mathematician, specialized in research in geometry and the interrelation between mathematics and the natural sciences.

147. The camp is designated in the volume of Edith's letters as Döberitz. Edith refers to Bell in two of her letters to Roman Ingarden, in April and September, 1917; evidently, at Bell's request some philosophical theses were sent to him while he was interned. He was at Ruhleben-Döberitz until 1918; after that he was German correspondent for a British newspaper. Later, he returned to Canada and to his profession as a philosopher. Cf. No. 122.

148. Cf. Page 244.

149. Roman Ingarden was born in Kraków, Poland, in 1893, and died there in 1970. He was a faithful friend and confidant of Edith Stein. He received, according to an article of his which appeared in the quarterly journal, *Philosophy and Phenomenological Research*, Vol. XXIII, No. 2, December, 1962, over 150 letters from her which he intended to publish someday, at least in part. Seventeen of them appear in the volumes of letters published by the *Archivum Carmelitanum Edith Stein*. Ingarden and Kaufmann were Edith's fellow students; Ingarden, as a Catholic, was able to understand her journey of faith which, on the contrary, caused a temporary estrangement with Kaufmann. Roman Ingarden came to Edith's defense when her method of working with and for Husserl was challenged; and the article mentioned above is of primary importance when reconstructing her situation as Husserl's assistant. In a letter to a mutual friend, Edith mentions Ingarden's four sons; hopefully, his heirs will someday publish, or make available to the Discalced Carmelites, this important correspondence between these significant Catholic phenomenologists.

Roman Ingarden can be credited with bringing phenomenology to his native Poland, where the next generation of philosophers is distinguished by having among them Karol Wojtyla, now Pope John Paul II.

150. Helmut Plessner evidently persevered in his studies since he published a testimony on Husserl's attitude toward German idealism. He wrote it in 1959, the centenary of Edmund Husserl's birth.

151. Heinrich von Kleist (1777–1811) is a tragic figure of a man who lived in hopelessness, so depressed by his failure to achieve literary greatness with his first work that he never recovered; becoming more and more despairing of success and embittered by the political situation of Germany, he chose to end his life. He was not a person to interest Edith.

152. Wernher der Gartenaere (Werner the Gardener) was an Austrian poet of the mid-High-German era, whose novel in verse, *Meier Helmbrecht* was written about 1270.

153. Cf. No. 129.

154. Mährisch-Weisskirchen is now Hranice. See Map.

155. Lazaretto, the English equivalent of *Seuchenlazarett*, has the same meaning: a hospital for infectious disease, an isolation hospital. The translator chose to keep lazaretto in preference to calling it a military hospital since this hospital was set up, equipped, administered and staffed by the German Red Cross, not by military personnel or funds.

From Edith's own account, we learn the hospital was in the Moravian sector of the Carpathian theatre of World War I; soldiers who had contracted cholera, typhoid or other virulent fevers, dysentery, or other contagious diseases were brought to Märisch-Weisskirchen.

Many of the men had been wounded as well. During Edith's final days of service, the character of the hospital changed noticeably. This denotes that at the beginning of her tour its principal use was that of an isolation hospital.

156. The title *Geheimrat* literally means secret advisor, or, more familiarly, Privy Councillor. Usually, this was an official appointed to serve in a private advisory capacity to an executive. In the present instance, the *Geheimrat* was in school administration. Herr Thalheim is mentioned again at the close of this chapter. Cf. Page 365.

157. Matron is the translator's choice for the German *Schwester Oberin* which is translated, literally, Sister Superior. (Cf. No. 158) Edith and the rest of the nursing personnel at the hospital addressed their chief administrative official as Matron, and spoke of her by that title without adding to it any definitive article, just as Edith used "Mother" when speaking of her own mother.

Although "Head Nurse" might be an equally acceptable translation it is not used because it does not imply necessarily that she is the administrator of the entire operation of the hospital as was Edith's Matron, Sister Margarete.

158. *Schwester*, i.e., Sister, is the title used for trained, professional nurses in German speaking countries, and in most countries in the British Commonwealth. It does not indicate affiliation with any religious congregation. Sister Kenny is perhaps the best known person to have familiarized us with this designation for a nurse.

There is an additional word in German, and Edith used it for some of those serving at the lazaretto: *Krankenpflegerin*, i.e., one who cares for the sick. These included the aides, those not formally trained, and they were often addressed as "Nurse." Under an emergency program sponsored by the Red Cross Organization in Germany, Edith completed a brief but intense training course, and this entitled her to be addressed as *Schwester* at Märisch-Weisskirchen. When later as a postulant in Carmel, she was again called *Schwester Edith*, it must have recalled for her many experiences and associations.

Edith was awarded a medal for bravery for her nursing stint.

159. Calling the residence the "Faust House" was an allusion to the fact that Faust's ill-used love in Goethe's tragedy was named Margarete.

By her reference to Skoda as the "Austrian Krupp," Edith tells us that a munitions firm founded in Pilsen, Austria, by the cavalier Emil von Skoda (1839-1900) is the counterpart of the munitions firm in Essen, Germany, founded by Peter Friedrich Krupp in 1810. Edith, prompted by her deep national feeling, had considered working in a munitions factory if she were to be unsuccessful in getting into nursing; her closest friends from the university were serving their country, and she wished to be as actively involved as they.

160. Cf. No. 62. The German army's winter offensive in the Carpathian mountains sought to drive back the Russians who were advancing on Hungary.

161. Cf. No. 28.

Strictly speaking, Edith and Suse Mugdan were using a formal address with one another; but, psychologically, they were expressing both mutual respect *and* an inner personal bond.

The Mugdan family continued to figure significantly in Edith's life. Suse's sister and brother-in-law helped Edith when she resumed her studies. Cf. No. 167.

Readers, reflecting that Edith's mother died in 1936, are gratefully relieved that she was spared the horror of arrest by the Nazis. Surviving octogenarians were not spared; this thought is inexpressibly painful.

Frau Käthe Mugdan, Suse's mother, then in her eighties, committed suicide rather than permit herself to be sent to a concentration camp. She lived in Breslau; and it was from that city that Edith's brother Paul, his wife, and their sister Frieda, were sent to a concentration camp in 1942.

162. This familiar manner of address is a combination of the Czech or Polish *Pan*: man, and the Latin *primarius*: in the first rank; the Chief was designated "Number One Man."

163. In May, 1915, the battle of Tarnów and Gorlice signalled the move of the opposing armies away from the Carpathian theatre toward Warsaw.

164. The *Johanniter* (Johannine) Order was founded in 1812 by Prussian Protestant nobility; it was devoted to the care of the sick in 1852, and hospitals in which nurses were trained were supported by the benevolent Order. In 1949, state support for this group was restored. Not identical with the Order of Malta, also engaged in care of the sick, the *Johanniter* communities can be found functioning in Hungary, France, Finland, and Switzerland according to current information.

165. Edith's own appraisal of this incident can be surmised from the use, in her German text, of the *English* word "speech" to describe the lecture she delivered on this occasion.

166. Edith and her friends met Burgomaster Westram on a hiking tour at Grunwald. Cf. Page 132.

167. Dr. Julius Stenzel is well known for his writings on Plato which are cited by Frederick Copleston,s.j., in his *History of Philosophy*. When Hitler assumed power in 1933, Dr. Stenzel, although not Jewish, was deprived of his position as professor of philosophy at the University of Kiel because he had disciplined pro-Nazi students years earlier when he was rector of the university. His daughter Anna was assisted by Edith's cousin, Richard Courant, with funds to enable her to emigrate after her father's death in 1935. Courant, already teaching in the United States, was courageous enough to visit Germany in summer of 1936 at the risk of being detained.

168. Isocrates (436–338 B.C.) is the Greek rhetorician and philosopher.

169. Edith's doctoral dissertation was entitled *Zum Problem der Einfühlung*, printed in Halle, Germany, in 1917.

An English translation, *On the Problem of Empathy*, made by Waltraud Stein (Edith's grand-niece), was published in the Netherlands under a 1964 copyright by Martinus Nijhoff, The Hague.

170. Cf. No. 113.

171. Cf. Nos. 120 and 203.

172. Elisabeth "Putti" Staiger, nee Klein, who, as Edith tells us mar-

ried Robert Staiger against her father's wishes just before he began his military service. She was widowed within months when he was killed in action.

Putti Staiger was three years older than Edith. In the course of her teaching career, she became director of a *Gymnasium* for girls in Hildesheim, Germany. Although she was not Jewish, she was removed from her position by the Nazis because she had been consistently loyal to her numerous Jewish friends despite the risks incurred in her position. She died in 1968.

173. This comment, though made in semi-jest, turned out to be prophetic; the event of his death in action in late 1917 brought Edith to Frau Reinach's side. She assisted the widow in putting in order Reinach's important philosophical writings. Mutual friends of Reinach and Edith were convinced that Adolf Reinach personified all the qualities she would have sought for in a life-partner. Both Reinachs impressed Edith and confirmed her in the search for truth which began at the time she met them in Göttingen. If Scheler introduced her to Christian thought, then the Reinachs lived what Scheler taught.

174. The Fräulein Stählin mentioned without further identification is the Swiss student who came to this party in the company of the Jensens. It is equally obvious that she brought the "Leckerli", the famous Christmas gingerbread cookies made in Basle, Switzerland, as a Christmas gift to her hosts, the Husserls. No wonder the other guests were embarrassed by the hostess' request that they pronounce her homemade cookies the "better of the two"!

175. Freiburg-im-Breisgau, cf. Map. The university in the main city of the lower Black Forest region of Germany was founded in 1457. The city is designated "im-Breisgau" to distinguish it from the other university town, Freiburg, alternatively Fribourg, in Switzerland.

Freiburg-im-Breisgau itself was founded in 1120; it was in the possession of the French for a time late in the seventeenth century; since 1805, it has belonged to the Baden-Württemberg region, now the third largest section of West Germany.

176. The philosophers of the "School of Baden" placed great emphasis on the cultural sciences, and they developed a philosophy of value.

Wihelm Windelband (1848-1915), Heinrich Rickert (1863-1936), and, to a certain extent, Hugo Münsterberg (1863-1916) are the philosophers associated with the formation of the school.

177. *Opus eximium* is the name given the dissertation written to earn a doctorate; because of the high quality demanded of the work (*opus*), it was designated as distinguished or extraordinary (*eximium*).

178. Professor Lengert was a very influential friend and teacher of Edith's. Her first acquaintance with him is mentioned on Page 167.

179. The italicized sentence, probably an afterthought, was written in the margin of her manuscript by Edith. It seems best to incorporate it within the text itself.

180. Cf. No. 78.

181. The new schedule no longer allowed her to go to her home after having taught all her classes early in the day. Now she had to remain at school with free periods interspersed between the classes she taught.

182. Nelli resumed her maiden name and her career. In the 1930s, Doctor Neumann began teaching mathematics in Essen, north of Cologne. Later, she was presumed to have been among the victims at Auschwitz. According to information received in 1982, a neighbor of Nelli's in Essen remembers clearly that, in 1942, Dr. Neumann was ordered to leave Essen on a labor-transport to the east where the Germans were advancing in the war with Russia. Nelli told her neighbor it would mean her death since the Nazis "have no need for mathematicians and I have no practical abilities." In 1943, a soldier returning home to Essen informed the same neighbor that he knew with certainty that Dr. Neumann had been killed in Minsk, in 1942. That Byelorussian capital city is not far from Katyn where, in 1943, grim testimony was found that shooting was the customary method used by the Nazis in that area. A mass grave was discovered to contain the bodies of some 4,000 Polish army officers shot at the site.

The information about Nelli's fate was received in March, 1982, by Constance Reid from an acquaintance in Essen who had read the Reid book on Richard Courant. Cf. No. 103.

183. *Rigorosum* was the designation given the very difficult, i.e., rigorous, examination which was given in written and oral sections; and it had to be passed in order to qualify for a doctorate.

184. Under "constitution of the human person," Edith examined among other topics, for instance, the "pure I," the stream of consciousness, the psycho-physical aspects of the individual, and personality.

185. As the doctoral dissertation was printed, at Edith's cost, after she had begun her work as assistant to Husserl, she did not undertake any revision of the dissertation. Husserl himself had noticed that in the portion of his *Ideas* which they were working on, he had treated the same subject matter; Edith did not want to incorporate any new thinking of hers which was due to the work with Husserl.

She had only Parts II to IV printed: these treated of the essence of acts of empathy, the constitution of the Psycho-Physical Individual and empathy as the comprehension of mental persons.

Whether Part I, an historical approach to the problem of empathy, and the additional material she mentions as excluded, i.e., the social, ethical, and aesthetic aspects, will turn up somewhere someday is one of the unresolved questions which the future may answer.

186. Dietrich von Hildebrand and Siegfried Johannes Hamburger both emigrated to the United States. Hamburger's literary remains are preserved in the Karol Wojtyla/John-Paul II Library of the International Academy of Philosophy, Irving, Texas, which hopes to receive eventually von Hildebrand's literary legacy also. Cf. No. 117.

187. Here Edith refers to her leaving the Carmel of Cologne to go to Holland on December 31, 1938. More information on this move will be found on Page 429.

That Edith should resume writing the history of her family within one week of her arrival in Holland, when it had lain untouched for four years, is a mute testimony to at least two probabilities:

1) As a newcomer in the monastery, she had few community tasks assigned to her until she was well settled in; rather than be idle, she took to hand something she had earlier been given to do and which, through circumstances, she had been unable to complete.

2) Having had to leave her homeland, she was farther removed than ever from her family. Writing the story would have been a healing, strengthening exercise of love, bringing close to her the persons she had known and loved during her years in Germany.

Edith quickly learned the language spoken in the Netherlands, succeeding so well that here, too, she was entrusted with the office of portress or turn sister, which meant she spoke to persons who came to the monastery on business or to request the sisters' prayers.

188. This was her *Endliches und Ewiges Sein* (*Finite and Eternal Being*) in which she strove to construct a synthesis between St. Thomas Aquinas' theology and phenomenology. She completed it in Cologne in 1936. A publisher had accepted it; it was already typeset, but the ban on the publication of any writings by a Jewish author prevented its being printed. In 1950, after extensive comparison of the original manuscript, the galleys from the 1936 unpublished version, and their own reconstructed manuscript, the *Archivum Carmelitanum Edith Stein* presented it as Volume II in their collection of her works.

189. The *sic* is inserted here since Edith was correct in recalling that Goethe wrote about Frankfurt but was not correct in identifying the book as *Gedanken und Erinnerungen* (*Thoughts and Recollections*). That title belongs to the autobiography of Bismarck whose *Kulturkampf* led to the founding of the Carmel of Echt, Holland, as a refuge for the Carmelite nuns in exile from Cologne, Germany.

Goethe's description of Frankfurt is found in his autobiography *Dichtung und Wahrheit (Fiction and Truth)*.

190. Myrion, or Myron, Greek sculptor of the 5th century, B.C., was the first to portray the human body in the moment of motion. *Athene* or Athena is the Greek goddess of wisdom.

191. Cf. No. 172.

192. The first Benedictine nuns in Germany came from England in the eighth century to assist St. Boniface in the evangelization of Germany. One of these pioneering women was a cousin of Boniface, St. Lioba.

From the name of their illustrious ancestress in the Order, the teaching Benedictine Sisters derived the name by which they were familiarly identified, the Lioba Sisters.

193. Rudolf Steiner (1861–1925), born at the Austria-Hungary border, devotee of Goethe, known for his research on and enthusiasm for that writer's views, for a time espoused theosophy which he abandoned however for his own anthroposophy, a religious system which centers on man rather than on God and which has a strong pantheistic aspect.

Born into a Catholic family, Steiner was baptized but not confirmed as his father would not permit it. Among other tenets, Steiner's anthroposophy holds that the individual undergoes a type of evolution in which, during periods lasting seven years each, his "bodies" develop, first the physical, then in succession, the ethereal, the astral and the spiritual bodies. Reincarnation is also among its tenets.

His theories are upheld since his death; in the mid-1980s these are taught in schools numbering some two hundred and fifty; they are to be found in twelve European countries, in the United States, Canada, South America, South Africa, Australia, and New Zealand.

Rudolf-Steiner-schools, modelled on his first one which he named the "Goetheanum," differ from other educational institutions in more than their pedagogic systems. The teachers wholeheartedly, personally, espouse anthroposophy, although the students receive religious training from the churches to which they belong. The Steiner theories are taught intensively; the "epochs" are presented to the students not as a religion but, perhaps, as a worldview. Eurythmics has a prominent emphasis in the curriculum. In order to provide the students with a valuable experience of continuity and security, the same teacher stays with a class from the first to the eighth grade, thus becoming a most significant person in their lives; that they accept this teacher's views readily is a desirable side-effect of this method of education.

When one takes into consideration Edith's awareness of the philosophy or even religion offered to the young in such schools, it is easier to understand her cautious approach to Goethe's ideology, as she presented it in her lecture to educators.

194. The university's *Pedell* (Beadle) was a minor official, usually a clerk in one of the administrative offices, who functioned in some of the public ceremonies, for instance, carrying the mace in processions, and served in other auxiliary positions. The designation for the assistants of officials was first used in Germany in the fourteenth century; derived from the Latin *pedellus*, it is akin in meaning to "footman, one who runs errands."

195. This March (1848) Revolution in Austria and Prussia was an aftermath of the French Revolution of that February. Students in Vienna rebelled on March 13; March 18 found the citizens of Berlin in revolt.

196. This was, most probably, Kühnemann's revised edition on Johann Gottfried von Herder, published in 1912. Like many of the other philosophers and psychologists under whom, or with whom, Edith studied, Eugen Kühnemann (1868–1946) is known in many universities in the United States. The improvement of relations between Germany and the United States was of prime importance to him, and lectures on that subject are included in the material mentioned in 67 listings in Volume 308, *The National Union Catalog of Pre-1956 Imprints*, along with his writings on Socrates, Plato, Schiller, Kant, Nietzche, Herder, and Goethe's *Faust*.

197. Schauinsland (its descriptive name literally means "a view of the land") is a mountain, alt. 4,211 ft., in the Black Forest region near Freiburg.

The excursion Edith mentions making to Lake Constance would have been by train through the gorge Höllental (the Valley of Hell) to the towns of Donaueschingen and Singen.

198. This is not Meister Eckhart the well known Dominican theologian and philosopher of the thirteenth century even though his name can be spelled in this alternative way.

The monk to whom Edith refers is Ekkehart II (Palatinus, "the Courtier") one of five monks named Ekkehart who were associated with the Benedictine Abbey of St. Gall, Switzerland. Ekkehart II was sent from the Abbey to this Castle of Hohentwiel in the year 973 to serve as Latin tutor to the Castle's ruler, the Duchess Hadwig of Swabia. Ekkehart continued to serve the Abbey through intervention when differences arose between his abbey and that of Reichenau; he was also prominent in the court of Emperor Otto I. He died in Mainz in 990.

These castle ruins also reminded Edith of "Solitude," the more recently built castle near Stuttgart which served as the military acad-

emy where Schiller spent seven miserable years in training for a career
he abandoned soon after attaining majority.

199. Reichenau is an island in the Lake of Constance, about one
mile wide and three and three-quarters miles long. In the seventh century, a Benedictine Abbey was built there; and the island was under
the jurisdiction of the abbot. The abbey is credited with having a prodigious civilizing influence in Europe, especially during the important
centuries, the ninth to the thirteenth.

200. Martin Heidegger was born two years before Edith. He first met
Husserl in Freiburg, and an intense philosophical and personal relationship and friendship developed between them. Heidegger was
Husserl's assistant in his academic duties. His years as professor in
philosophy in Freiburg brought him to form his own conception of
phenomenology. His thought places greater demands, because of his
style of thinking and the language in which he expresses his thought,
than most other philosophy, according to some historians of
philosophy.

201. Cf. No. 115.

202. Cf. No. 113.

203. Cf. Page 410.

204. The University of Freiburg was founded in the middle of the fifteenth century by Albrecht VI, one of some 340 independent dukes,
bishops, counts, abbots, barons, and rulers of cities within Germany
who kept that country in the constant upheaval of internal war.

The university's royal patronage ceased at the very start of the twentieth century, again a war-troubled time, when this Frederick II, Grand-
Duke of Baden, mentioned in Edith's diploma as the university's "eminent rector/ruler," along with all the other German heads of states
abdicated together with Emperor Wilhelm II in 1918.

The Prorector, when signing Edith's Decree, used *de Below*, the
Latin form of his German name *von Bülow*.

205. Cf. No. 169, No. 185.

206. Max Scheler's appreciation of her opinion was made public in
1923. In the second edition of his book, *Sympathiegefühle* [*The Nature
of Sympathy*, trans. by Peter Heath (London: Routledge and Kegan
Paul, 1954)], Max Scheler refers three times to Edith Stein's analysis
of his theory.

207. Winthrop Pickard Bell was born in Halifax, Canada, in 1884;
he died in Nova Scotia, 1965. Cf. No. 122.

208. These pages became the material for Husserl's lecture course
on inner time consciousness which was prepared for publication by
Edith Stein, although Heidegger signed as editor. This information

comes from Herbert Spiegelberg, Professor Emeritus of the Department of Philosophy, Washington University, St. Louis. His monumental historical introduction *The Phenomenological Movement* [Third Edition published by Martinus Nijhoff (The Hague, 1982)] gives a wealth of essential background for Edith's years with Husserl.

209. Henri Bergson (1859-1941), French philosopher, won the Nobel Prize for Literature in 1928.

210. Cf. 121.

211. A thesis other than the one used as dissertation had to be written to qualify for habilitation.

Careful reading of the correspondence of this time leads to the conclusion that there was more to the non-consideration of Edith's thesis than objection to the habilitation of women. In her letter Edith tells Kaufmann that Georg Elias Müller, then Professor of Philosophy and Psychology at Göttingen, had stated that her thesis would "completely unseat psychology as it is taught here." His comment literally said she "would lift psychology right out of the saddle" which Edith called "slightly in error."

Müller's reference to its consequences in the department of psychology, and Edith's further correspondence with Kaufmann at this point in 1919 discussing the contents of "my thesis" justify identification of the "ignored work" as the material published three years later in the *Jahrbuch* as an article on "The Philosophical Foundation of Psychology and of the *Geisteswissenschaften* [Sciences of the Spirit]." Meant here are the social sciences and humanities, as opposed to the natural sciences.

212. Heinrich Scholz (1884-1956) professor of philosophy in Kiel, was no phenomenologist but is renowned as a logician and also as a philosopher of religion. Later he taught in Münster, but he was not one of Edith's teachers. Her reference to him, however, accentuates the remarkable consistency with which the best known pioneers in philosophy and psychology turn up in Edith's scholarly history, either as her teachers or fellow students. When she wrote about her associations with them, Edith could not have known of the many contributions they would collectively make to interdisciplinary scholarship. A comprehensive study of the numerous philosophical and psychological developments with which she was associated, and the degrees of her involvement, will prove rewarding as she becomes better known.

213. Cf. No. 69.

214. This is Hans Lipps who is familiar to us from Edith's many references in *Aus dem Leben*. Edith comments that, although Lipps'

friends are aware of what he lacks, they are unable to help him, even when "one is terribly eager" to do just that.
Cf. No. 116, 232.

215. His bride was Alice Dorothee Lieberg. Cf. No. 120.

216. Edith refers here to the Catholic teaching regarding death and the afterlife. The four so-designated "last things" are death, judgment, heaven, and hell.

217. Dietrich von Hildebrand. Cf. Nos. 117 and 186.

218. *Ceterum censeo*: moreover, in my opinion; or, "however, as I see it." Cato concluded each of his speeches to the Roman Senate with a statement beginning with the "Ceterum censeo." Used in Edith's sense, it signifies a "stubbornly reiterated challenge," as the German encyclopedic "*Duden*" records.

219. Martin Honecker (1888–1941) was professor of philosophy and a neo-Thomist. He taught at Freiburg.

Martin Heidegger's work interested Edith greatly and her scholarly writings will include analyses of his work. As they are important, defying one to make as brief a synopsis as lies within the scope of these notes, this reference to Heidegger (1889–1976) is intended merely to document his encouragement of her attempt to gain habilitation in the University of Freiburg-im-Breisgau, and to show that even his influence was ineffectual in removing all obstacles from her path as she sought academic status as a full professor. Cf. No. 200.

This time, in 1931, the thesis Edith intended to submit in order to qualify for habilitation was written after her entry into the Catholic Church; and it reflects her study of St. Thomas Aquinas. At that time, Edith entitled the work *Potenz und Akt*. In Carmel, she expanded it, calling it, finally, *Endliches und Ewiges Sein*. Cf. No. 188.

220. Josef Koch (born in Münstereifel, 1885 — died in Cologne, 1967) was Professor of Catholic Theology in Breslau, then in Cologne.

221. This lecture on "The Natural and the Supernatural in Goethe's *Faust*" was delivered in St. Dominicus-Ludwigshafen, Germany, on June 26, 1932, to an audience of teachers. Speaking not so much about Goethe, the man, or his literary talent, Edith, as an educator and guide of students, spoke, rather, to fellow teachers about the responsibilities they shared.

222. Cf. No. 117.

223. Cf. Johannes, or Jean, Hering. Cf. No. 117.

224. Two Carmelite Nuns from the Carmel of Cologne were in Breslau, and they were engaged in the establishment of this foundation, even while Edith was still at home. One of them, Sister Marianne, paid several visits to Frau Stein; she was cordially received each time.

The monastery was being built; it was not a matter of adapting an existing structure. Edith herself visited the site and the two Carmelites. Understandably in those turbulent times when Hitler's power was increasingly felt in Germany, the building project ran into serious difficulties; its completion was delayed, and unfortunately, although they did establish themselves there for a time, the Discalced Carmelite nuns did not live in the building very long.

225. The Discalced Carmelite nun makes three vows. First, there is a solemn promise to lead a life of consecrated chastity, in preparation for the contemplation of divine things, by renouncing, for love of God, the married state, and by dedicating herself totally to the service of God. Second, the solemn promise is made to be poor both in fact and in spirit, to hold all things in common, and in the use and disposition of goods to abide by the decisions of superiors. Third, intending to offer God the complete dedication of will, the nun makes a solemn promise to observe the evangelical counsel of obedience.

These vows are made for the first time when a canonical period of novitiate has been concluded; they must be made for a temporary period totalling three years before they can be made for life. During the time of temporary profession, it is possible for the nun to obtain dispensation and leave the religious life. The community, for its part, has the responsibility to accept the perpetual profession only if there is reasonable certainty that the person making it has the capability to follow the *Rule* and ordinances of the Discalced Carmelite Order.

Under the *Constitutions* which were in effect during Edith's years in Carmel, a liturgical ceremony of "renovation" took place twice a year: on Epiphany, January 6, and on the Feast of the Exaltation of the Cross, September 14. This ceremony was a devotional act. It provided the nuns with the opportunity to reconfirm their commitment and to instill renewed vigor into their dedication to God. Most of all, it enabled the nuns to make a shared and public avowal of their freely chosen way of life as a group, since most had made their profession individually, on separate days. Such a communal rededication can strengthen the bonds which unite a community by giving visible testimony to the purpose which they hold in common.

226. From Edith's correspondence we learn that several of her nephews had already gone to "far-off corners" of the world. Arno was reunited with his family, but only after an arduous process. The Gordons joined their son in South America; the Bibersteins, as well as Richard Courant and his family, and Paul's son settled in the United States.

227. Alexander Pfänder (1870–1941) was in Husserl's opinion "our

Edith Stein

most substantial worker" in the evolving phenomenology of the 1920s. Edith refers here to his *Die Seele des Menschen* [*The Human Soul*] which has not been translated from the German. Edith's reference to the work is an indication of her appreciation of this phenomenologist who is often overlooked because of his unassuming scholarship; Jacques Maritain, however, recognized Pfänder's contribution as essential to the understanding of the development of phenomenology.

Edith's reference to her reading of reviews on philosophical offerings and to this book by Pfänder, published in 1933, shows that in Carmel she was able to follow up on the writings of her contemporaries in philosophy.

228. In 1938, solemn vows for religious women were considered to be, if such a thing were possible, more binding than simple perpetual vows. Expressed in non-canonical terms the difference was that, while dispensation from simple perpetual vows might be granted for very serious reasons and only in rare cases, dispensation from solemn vows was entirely out of the question.

Communities did not automatically have the privilege of making solemn vows, and the Cologne community applied to the Holy See only years later. The Carmel of Echt had solemn vows; upon making a permanent transfer to that community, Edith would have been able to make her solemn profession. As things turned out, that transfer was not finalized by the time of her arrest.

229. Edith said there was no truth in rumors that Edmund Husserl had become a Catholic. Jewish by birth, Husserl had been baptized an Evangelical Lutheran in Vienna at the age of 27. His Protestant commitment was relative in that he professed respect for all authentic religious belief and espoused a concept of the self-responsibility and freedom of man in his immediate relationship to God. He wished, he said, to die as a philosopher; but as the end of his life approached, he seemed to be occupied with the supernatural life.

Professor Ludwig M. Landgrebe, Husserl's research assistant from 1923 to 1930, provides an excellent account of him in an article that appears in Encyclopaedia Britannica, *Macropaedia*, Vol. IX, Chicago, Ill., 1974. (Landgrebe's article gives April 21 as the date of Husserl's death; the correct date for this is April 27, 1938.)

230. The monastery in the Lindenthal sector of Cologne where Edith lived was not the site of the original foundation in that city. The original monastery, located on Schnurgasse, had been confiscated during Bismarck's *Kulturkampf*, and the chapel had become a parish church. It had remained under the patronage of Mary, Queen of Peace. Edith

visited this church after leaving Lindenthal on Dec. 31, 1938, on her way to Echt.

Both the Lindenthal and the Schnurgasse properties sustained heavy damage during the bombings of Cologne in World War II. Of the two, Lindenthal was in much worse condition. The Cardinal Bishop of Cologne decided it would be the right moment for the Discalced Carmelites to return to the site of their origin in the Schnurgasse. The Church of the Queen of Peace was the first to be restored enough to hold public worship in that sector of Cologne; the entire interior was destroyed by fire, but the walls and roof were sound. A monastery, attached to the church, was rebuilt; and the Sisters had a "homecoming" to the location where in 1643 Carmelite Nuns but one generation removed from St. Teresa had begun Carmel's history in Germany.

When the historic sites of Cologne are listed, Schnurgasse is still used to designate the monastery's location. The postal address however for the Carmelite Monastery is Vor den Siebenburgen 6, 5 Cologne 1, West Germany.

231. The journal is the one founded at the University of New York at Buffalo to continue the work of Husserl's *Jahrbuch*. It is the *Journal of Philosophy and Phenomenological Research*, a quarterly first published in 1940 by the University of Buffalo with Dr. Marvin Farber, one of Husserl's students at Freiburg, as editor. In 1923, Dr. Farber had met Fritz Kaufmann, another graduate student at the time, and the friendship was renewed in Buffalo in 1946 when Kaufmann joined the faculty there under Farber.

Edith sent the article intended for the *Journal* to a friend in Switzerland, a Dr. Siebe who was probably the former family physician of the Conrad-Martius couple. He succeeded in forwarding the article. Dr. Farber released it to Dr. Rudolf Allers in Washington, D.C., in the fall of 1941, for translation and publication. In Dr. Allers' translation the article appeared in No. 3 of Volume IX of *The Thomist*, a quarterly published by the Dominican Fathers in Washington, D.C. With the permission of *The Thomist*, their copyrighted article was reproduced and published in booklet form by the Edith Stein Guild, Inc., Our Lady of Victory, 60 William Street, New York, N.Y. 10005, in 1981. Since she wrote it with an American readership in mind, it seems to be a parting gift intended to bring a message to the land which she had given as an *eventual* destination when she filed a petition with the Nazis to go to Switzerland. Negotiations with the U.S. were impossible during the war.

232. From this reference, it seems that Edith had not been informed by mutual friends of Hans Lipps' second marriage shortly before

World War II began since she mentions only his daughters as survivors. She did know that his first wife had died; some biographical accounts of her life have implied that the first Lipps marriage ended in divorce, which is not necessarily correct since Edith never referred to it in correspondence that has so far been collected. The widow corresponded with the Archivist at the Cologne Carmel and sent some photos among other items for the archives. She said her husband frequently spoke of Edith. No mention of a bond deeper than of friendship appears to have been implied by Lipps; the friendship however, according to her, had meant much to Hans.

233. Le Pâquier Carmel was founded in the Swiss Canton of Fribourg, (the "other" Freiburg) in 1922 from the Carmel of Narbonne, France. At the time Edith sought to go there, it was the sole Carmelite monastery in Switzerland. Since then two more were founded: Locarno, founded in 1946 by Nuns from Rome; and Develier, in the Jura Canton, which came there from Montelimar, France, by way of Middes, Canton of Fribourg, in 1969. The new monastery in Develier was built and occupied within a decade.

234. A volume of documentary information was published in Echt, in 1967, by "friends of Dr. Edith Stein." This book, *Als Een Brandende Toorts* (As a Burning Torch), contains testimony from personal acquaintances of Edith Stein, and provides copies of official papers that have bearing on her story. The details of the last week Edith spent in Holland have been taken from this valuable source.

235. Schifferstadt — see Map.

Photo Credits

Edith Stein's relatives, her religious family, and her friends treasured photographs of her. The publishers and the translator of this book express deep gratitude for the permission granted us to include some which have not been published elsewhere.

The following provided photos:

Mr. and Mrs. Alfred Batzdorff (Edith's niece)— nos. 2, 3a, 4, 5, 8, 11, 12

Archive of Theodor Conrad (husband of Edith's close friend, Hedwig Conrad-Martius), directed by Dr. E. Ave-Lallemant, Munich and preserved at the Bayerische Staatsbibliothek, Munich— nos. 6, 10

Sr. Amata Neyer, O.C.D. (Prioress of Cologne Carmel and Edith Stein Archivist of the monastery)—nos. 7, 13

Mrs. Nina Courant, nee Runge (widow of Edith's first cousin, Richard Courant)—1 (Frontispiece), 3b, 9

In order of appearance, the photos contain:

1. (Frontispiece) *Edith Stein with a Young Relative, 1921*: never before seen in print, this photo of Edith with one of the Courants' sons was given by Mrs. Nina Courant to the Edith Stein Center, Elysburg, PA.

2. *Edith's Family in 1895*—portrait of the Siegfried Stein family.

3a. *Stein House—Michaelisstrasse, 38*—the family home in Breslau

3b. *Richard Courant as a Student*—reproduced with the permission of Springer-Verlag of New York, in whose publication *Courant in Göttingen and New York: The Story of an Improbable Mathematician* by Constance Reid, this photo first appeared.

4. *Frau Platau, Frau Dorothea Biberstein, et al*—a group photo including Frau Auguste Stein and four of her daughters, one granddaughter, and six friends.

5. *Sophie Mark, Frau Guttmann, et al*—Edith, Erna and Hans Biberstein, and friends, on vacation in the mountains.

6. *Göttingen Philosophical Society*

7. *Edmund Husserl, 'The Master'*

8. *Nurses' Free Time Activities at the Lazaretto*—Edith and some of the nurses and aides at a party in Mährisch-Weisskirchen.

9. *Runge Family of Göttingen*—the family portrait showing Nina Runge Courant's father, Professor Carl T. Runge of Göttingen, with his wife, son and daughters. A second son's death in Flanders was the occasion for this photo.

10. *Edith, ca. 1916*—taken, perhaps, in Bergzabern at the Conrad home. This and photo no. 6 from the Conrad Archive carry the signature: Ana 378, C, II, 2.

11. *Frau Stein, ca. 1925*—at home in Breslau.

12. *Edith, ca. 1925*—at home in Breslau.

13. *Sr. Teresa Benedicta of the Cross (1938)*—probably the most familiar picture of Edith as a Carmelite nun.

INDEX

This index lists all persons and places. When they figure constantly in Edith's everyday life, although her mention of them is intermittent, this is indicated by adding the indicator, passim, to the initial reference and the closing one for the particular period.

Relatives and friends, when listed as families, are named in alphabetical order. The list begins with the person with the closest tie to Edith Stein. In Edith's immediate family, the listing is by birth order.

The work's biographical genre warrants an index which is not exhaustive nor entirely selective, but, at times, merely representative. It is meant to serve as a guide and an incentive to use the work as Edith Stein intended.

Aachen 429

Absolutism and Englightenment, Age of 266, 290

academic: achievement, 18; citizenship, 191; freedom, 187, 188; journey, 447. Academic societies. *See* societies

Academy of Arts, Munich, 163; Athens, 486

Achenbach, local artist 253

acrostic 166

actor 38, 445

actresses 50

Adersbach-Weckelsdorf 132, Map

adult education 52, 202; Breslau Institute for, 199

AEG 88, 474

Agnes Bernauer 170, 481

Ahumada, Teresa de. *See* SAINTS

air: pollution, 183; —raid, 407

Albania 485

Aldor, an M.D.* 329

Allers, Prof. Rudolf 511

Allied antiaircraft artillery 463

Alpine Hunters Regiment 196

Alps, the 406

Alsace 492

Als Een Brandende Toorts 463, 512

Alster, river, pavilion and port 92

Altheide. *See* Bad

Althoff, Minister of Culture 251

Altvater (gebirge) 133, 134, 368, 475, Map

America(n) 46, 47, 85, 95, 107, 147, 182, 183, 446, 451, 470, 472; emigration to, 18; —students, 108, 243, 256, 257, 281

Amersfoort, Holland 431, Map

Amsterdam, Holland 429, Map

Anabasis 189, 290, 314

Andersmann, an M.D. 338, 350

Andreikowicz, patient 358

angel, image used by non-believer 284

Angelus, the 240

anger 37, 45. *See also* EDITH STEIN: emotions

anthropology 491

anthroposophy 404, 504

anti-German. *See* GERMAN(Y)

anti-Semitism 88, 343

Antwerp, Netherlands 293

apprenticeship 43, 45, 156

Aquinas, Thomas. *See* SAINTS

Arch: abbey. *See* Beuron; abbot. *See* Walzer; —bishop, Prince, of Breslau, 205

Archivum Carmelitanum Edith Stein viii, 4, 7, 459, 460, 461, 465, 493, 503

Arctic Ocean 257, 258

*The unusual qualifier is used to denote a *medical* doctor since many other doctors are in list, and M.D. might look like initials for his first name which Edith does not mention.

Armistice 485
army surgeons 225. *See also* soldiers, war
ART(ISTS) 52, 165
—Böcklin, Arnold (*Toteninsel*) 145, 475
—Buonarroti, Michelangelo (Creation of Man) 248
—Cimabue, Giovanni (Saint Francis) 238, teacher of Giotto, 488
—Flemish sculpture (Calvary) 401
—Myrion, alt. Myron (Athene) 401, 504
—Richter, Ludwig (The Bridal Procession) 244, 476
—Schaper (Goose Girl Fountain) 241
—van Rijn, Rembrandt, attributed to (Man with Golden Helmet) 304
Aryan(s) 127, 484; non-, 85
assassination, attempts at 271, 485; of royal couple at Sarajevo, 293, 470, 497; in literature, 480, 481
associations. *See* societies
Assyria 438
Athens, Greece 366
atomic theory, Edith's interest in 428
attachment to "flames" 50
Auditorienhaus, Göttingen 241, 242
Aula, the 205
Aupa 131. *See also* Gross-Aupa
Aus dem Leben einer Jüdischen Familie 461, 462, 463
Auschwitz 433, 442, 475, 481, 502, Map
austerity measures in WW I 299
Austria(n) 161, 249, 318, 328, 335, 348, 423, 465, 478, 480, 482, 499; Austria-Hungary, 333, 497
autobiography 1, 437, 452, 465
Ave-Lallemant, Dr. Eberhard 513
Avila, Teresa of. *See* SAINTS
Awkford, American student 281

Babylon 438; —ian Talmud, 441
bacteriologist 229
Bad Altheide 132, 133, Map
Baden 407, Map; School of, 386, 501
Bad Nauheim 293
Bad Reinerz 132, 133, Map
Bad Salzbrunn 32, Map
Baerthold, Lotte (m. Neumann) 131; description of, 130
Baligaud, Herr von, student 292

bank employees 43, 151, 156, 395
barracks 321, 323, 358
Basel (Fr. Basle), Switzerland 385, Map
Bauer, Grete 319, 326, 329, 335, 336, 343, photo 8
Bavaria(n) 339; —Radio Network, 424; *Bayerische Staatsbibliothek*, 513
beadle 204
Beczwa Stream 336, 360, Map
"being German" 35, 47, 444, 445
Belgium 429, 459, 490
Bell, Winthrop Pickard 257, 292, 293, 301, 302, 303, 381, 417, 493, 506
belles lettres 171
belonging 442, 444
Benedictines. *See* RELIGIOUS
Berg, Municipal Architect 271
Berg, Paul 127. *See also* Platau, Lilli (m. Berg). Photo 4
Bergius, Grete 164
Bergzabern 253, 420, 421, 457, 487, 489
Berlin 24, 35, 45, 83, 84, 88, 90, 94, 100, 110, 131, 141, 147, 179, 180, 182, 183, 226, 228, 230, 240, 258, 263, 271, 384, 445, 474, 492, 495; —'s fashionable West End, 147, 181
Berne, Switzerland 467
Bertran de Born 47
Beskids, mountains 336
Beuron, Benedictine Archabbey 424, Map. *See also* RELIGIOUS
Beuthen 32
BIBERSTEIN
—Erna (1890-1978, b. Stein, Edith's sister) born in Lublinitz, 40; 41, 45, 53-56; 115-238, passim; 285, 289, 321, 355-57, 360, 370, 395, 427, 453, 454, 455, 466, 472, 473, 486; personal reminiscences of Edith, 14-18; death in U.S., 1978, 466; photos, 2, 4, 5
—Hans (1889-1965, husband of Erna) 16, 17; 117-238, passim; 289, 455; editor's acknowledgment, 14; Edith's description of him, 117, 118; photo 5
—Ernst Ludwig (1922, Erna's son), 17, 18, 427
—Susanne (1921, Erna's daughter, m. Batzdorff) 17, 18, 427, 466, 513;

her husband, Alfred Batzdorff, 466, 513

—Frau Dorothea (1855-1934, b. Ledermann, Erna's mother-in-law) 118-238, passim; 297, photo 4

—Dorothea's husband, 118; D.'s stepson, Fritz, 118, 229; her stepdaughter, Rudolfine (m. Böhm) 119

Biberstein, Lene (b. Koppel, Edith's friend) 163, 165

Martin, Dr. (Lene's husband, cousin of Hans B.) 163

Bier-drama, zeitung (comic play or program) 129, 175, 178, 475

birthplace, Edith's. See Breslau, 40, 447

Bismarck, Otto von 243, 266, 478, 480, 503, 510

—Tower, 243, 247, 256

Black Forest 196, 228, 399, 402

blind, education of the 193

Blücher Street 176

boarding: house 208; —school, 246. See also Scheel's

Bohemia 129, 321, 334, 447

Bolshevist unrest 230

Bonn Map

Book of Her Life, The (Teresa of Jesus) 420, 457

bookkeeping 34, 43, 48, 139

books: as awards, 66; brother-in-law's library unsuited, 148; daily bread during teen years, 150; and reviewer, 211; for school borrowed from relatives, 53; vacation fare, 131

Boral, Councillor 323

border inspection 18, 364, 462

Böse, Herr inventive landlord 54, 55

Brandenburg 168

Braunschweig, North Germany 193, 476

Breslau 7-238 passim; 240, 242, 246, 254, 256, 261, 268, 270, 271, 276, 286, 290, 295, 296, 307, 312, 315, 316, 318, 319, 326, 352, 364, 368-78, 386-98, passim; 416, 417, 419, 423, 424, 427, 433, 434, 435, 443, 447, 449, 451, 461; description of—'s *Dominsel* (Cathedral Island), 205

Brockau 189

broken homes, children from 193

Brünn 358, Map

Brussels, Belgium 5

Budapest, Hungary 232

Buffalo, N.Y., U.S.A. 511

builders 43

Bülow, Georg von (alt. de Below, Latin) 416, 417

Bundes für Schulreform (Leagues for School Reform) 192

BURCHARD

—Joseph (ca. 1785-1874, Edith's maternal great-grandfather) 27

—Ernestine (1798-1891, b. Prager, Edith's great-grandmother) 27, 29; named, but inaccurately, on 75, 473

—Adelheid (1824-83, m. Courant, Edith's grandmother and mother of Cilla below). See COURANT

—Emanuel, Edith's grand-uncle, 28

—Jakob (d. 1914, Edith's grand-uncle and husband of Edith's aunt) 43, 139-45

—[Cilla (d. 1906, b. Courant, Edith's maternal aunt and wife of Jakob, above) 43, 139-53; their three children: Adelheid 139, 143, 397; Fritz 139, 141; Martha 139, 140, 232]

—Johanna, eldest daughter (b. ca. 1818) 28, 473

Bursfeld-an-der-Weser 276

Burgomaster, deputy 176. See also Westram

businessmen 28, 60, 110. See also Customs

cabinetmakers 43

calendar, Jewish or Gregorian 68

Canada 257, 293, 301, 497; Chester, N.S., 494; Halifax, N.S., 258, 506

Canons, Breslau 205

cantor 27, 30

capital investment 30. See also money

career opportunities. See WOMAN

CARMELITE(S) (Discalced friars, nuns, monasteries, vocation) vii, viii, 3, 4, 7, 8, 400, 420, 426, 430, 436, 437, 457, 458, 475, 480, 487, 489, 497, 499, 509, *History and Spirit of Carmel*, 8; in:

—America, 465; Elysburg, Pa., 465; Washington, D.C., viii;
—Austria, Bärnbach and Mariazell, 465;
—France, Dijon and Lisieux, 442; Montelimar and Narbonne, 512;
—Germany, Aachen and Düren, 429; Köln (Cologne)-Lindenthal, 5, 426, 427, 428, 429, 462, 470, 492, 508; Köln-Schnurgasse, 431, 432, 435, 460, 461, 464, 465, 510, 511, 512; Tübingen, 465; Pützchen, 429;
—Italy, Rome, 512;
—Luxembourg, 429;
—Netherlands, the Dutch Province, 459, 460, 463, 465; Echt, 18, 428, 429, 432, 433, 461, 462, 463, 464, 465, 510; Herkenbosch, 459, 463;
—Spain. See SAINTS John of the Cross, Teresa of Jesus
—Switzerland, Develier, 512; Le Pâquier, 430, 465, 512; Locarno, 512, Middes, 512
— See also RELIGIOUS: for individual listings of friars and nuns
Carpathian Mts. 196, 319, 474
castles 193, 244, 406, 505
Catez-Rolland, Elizabeth (Elizabeth of the Trinity) 442, 457; and her father, Captain Catez, 458
CATHOLIC(S) vii, 17, 456, 457, 458, 475, 482, 504;
—Church: dispossessed by Germans, 496; past history of St. Alban's, 240; visit to a, 401
—education: pedagogy, 425; —school, 30; —student, 160. See Glatzel
—ideals: 260, —of marriage, 227; —thought, 423
—priests educated by Jew, 118
—youth groups, 23
cavalry, academy 321, 367
celebrations 270, 327; birthday, 28, 33, 66, 146, 215; class, 175; political, 168
cemetery 29, 34, 463; the Our Father prayed in Jewish cemetery, 183
centennial and hall 270
chaplain, military 335
character traits. See FEMININE; Jewish; MALE; EDITH STEIN

chauvinism, display of 168
chemist(ry) 30, 164, 165; —Institute, 246
Chemnitz (Karl-Marx-Stadt) 64, 65, 177, 182, 183, 208, 482, Map
Child Speech 197
CHILD(REN) 27-35, 37-42, 44-45, 456, 457, 458; abused, 57; adults good with infants, incompatible with older, 51, 97; attached to Edith, 218; and broken homes, 193; condescension alienates, 79; coping with illness, 86, 95, 96; correcting, 56; difficult maternal relationship with, 38, 57, 84, 97; ideal, 58; family tension harms, 83, 97; five-year-old wants *not* to grow up, 98; generosity to, 28, 32, 33, 83; good influence sought for, 146; handicapped, 103; helpless father of, 57; homes for, 193; —appalled by story of expulsion from Paradise, 106; public assistance to, 52, 53, 57, 193; reacts to teasing, 140; resents affected compliments, 142; tale-bearing corrected, 56; thought process of, 221; tutor: accepted, 153; deeply attached to, 194; objections to, 154; unloved at home, blossoms elsewhere, 98; war's effect on, 193; "what are you—Jewish?", 252
Chinese puppet 169
choreographer 76
Christ. See God
Christian vii, 68, 343, 420, 431, 449, 455; —celebrations, 385; devotions in school, 65; —widow at Jewish funeral, 183
Christmas specialities in Jewish home, 73, 94, 377; gifts made without celebrating, 52, 56, 309, 310; Midnight Mass, 385
church(es) 205, 401, 402. See also CATHOLIC; SAINTS
cities, size of 242, 447, 474, 482, 501
civic: rights and situation of Jews 443, 444
civilization 439, 440
Clemens, Rudolf 253, 258; photo 6; death reported, 307
clothing 42, 90, 109

clover-leaf of friends 122
Coesfeld Map
coffee 29; —shops. *See* inns
cognition act of, 398; theory of, 198
coins, currency. *See* money
Collected Works of Edith Stein viii
Cologne 8. *See also* Köln; monastery of, *See* CARMELITES
Colombia, South America 509
colonial administration (German) 28
colonies, Jewish in France and Spain 442
comic programs. *See Bierzeitung*
Commandments, the 31
commitment at time of Baptism 457
community contribution to individual's work 465
companionship 66. *See also* EDITH STEIN: friendships
concentration camp(s) (KZ) 445, 451. *See also* Amersfoort; Auschwitz; Theresienstadt; Westerbork
confidence in others 32
Conrad-Martius, Hans and Hedwig. *See* PHILOSOPHERS
conservative views on state 191
construction of homes 235
contemplation vii
contractors 43
convent school 180; —of Good Shepherd, 235
Cosack, Dr. Elisabeth 465
COURANT FAMILY 27–35, 37, 442, 443; the brothers, 85; birth order of the fifteen children, 37;
—Salomon (1815–96, Edith's grandfather) 27, 32, 33, 472
—Adelheid (1824–83, b. Burchard, married to Salomon 1842) 27, 29, 31, 34, 40
—their fifteen children:
—Alfred (13th in birth order), family hardware business, 33; food distribution, 35; moved to Oppeln, 35; wife, Else, 50
—Auguste (4th, m. STEIN), Edith's mother. *See* STEIN FAMILY
—Berthold (7th, known as B.C.), 37, 180, 181; his four children: Adelheid, 180, 181; Helmut, 181; Martha, 180, 181, look-alike of

Edith Stein, 150;   Sigurd, 181
—Bianca (1st). *See married name* Schlesinger
—Cilla (2nd, married her maternal uncle). *See* BURCHARD
—Clara (14th, unmarried), 35, 36, 37, 50
—David (9th), 37, 76, 177; pharmacist in Chemnitz, 64; wife and two sons, Erich and Walter, 182; Walter's Christian widow and two small children, 183
—Emil (12th, unmarried), 35, 37, 100, 226
—Emma (15th). *See married name* Pick
—Eugen (1861–1934, 11th), 37, 179, 180, 181, 182; mediates for nephew, Arno, 110; wife and three sons, 179; son, Fritz, demonstrates family charism, 179–81
—Friederika (1859–1926, 10th, unmarried, known as Mika), 34, 35, 36, 37, 51, 377, 382; forced to pay rent to her own tenant, 36
—Jakob (3rd, eldest son), 37, 80, 83, 84, 181, 473
—Mälchen (8th, full name Amalia). *See married name* Pick
—Selma (5th). *See married name* Horowitz
—Siege (6th, full name Sigmund), 37, 83, 84; wife, Martha (b. Freund), and three sons: Ernst (youngest) 56, 81; Fritz, 85, and Richard (eldest), *see* MATHEMATICIANS-Courant
courtship 131
criticism 43
Critique of Pure Reason 122
Crusades 447
culture 122, 442, 446, 472. *See also* CUSTOMS
customers 60
CUSTOMS: address, forms of, 121, 155, 163, 178, 343, 354, 475, 477; baking, 70, 129; birthday, 28, 33, 38, 66, 75, 76, 179; Carmelite, 464; carnival time, 238; collecting and sewing for poor, 29; engaged to be married, 229; excursions-en-famille, 129; eyes, mortification of, 486;

funeral, 81, 144, *see also* cemetery; labor, 472; meals, 55, 177, 446, *see also* food; New Year's Eve, 128;
— religious: Sabbath, beginning of, 47; lights, 29; Seder night, 69, 70; retiring time, 456;
— school: 65, 168, 170, 173; never dispensed from, 53; prompting, 161; taxed for good grades, 171;
— university, 241; ignored by Husserl and Nelson, 243;
— wedding, 45, 47, 90, 235, 237, 238
Cuxhaven 149, Map
Czechoslovakia(ns) 333, 334, 339, 357; were anti-German, 322
daily life 447
dancing 38, 117, 182, 209, 237, 243, ballet, 76; "Thank God, we don't live for—alone.", 201
Danish psychologist 265
Danube River (Donau) Map
Danziger, Dr. Erich 224, 246, 273, 288, 289, 297, 488
Darwin. *See* NATURALISTS
dating young men 457
Day: of Atonement, 68, 71, 441, 447; of Lots, 441
Deaconesses of Mother Eva Tiele-Winckler 193, Sister Friede, 193
deaf, education of 193
death Edith's brush with, 216; certification of her, 433; coincidence of date with Tish'a B'Ab, 442; of E.'s family members: father, 41; mother, 427; siblings, 39, 430, 466; other relatives, 28, 29, 33, 37, 39, 40, 58, 80, 82, 84, 86, 139, 145, 150, 231; of friends, 70, 196, 208, 213, 300, 303, 307, 337, 386, 387; Hermsen, missing in action, 196; Husserl, 428; Metis, 213; Reinach, 417; Msgr. Schwind, 424; witnessed by Edith for first time, 338
debts 41, 42, 43
Delos, Greece 366
demerit in school 53
democratic party, Germany 229
Denmark 265, 482
dermatolog(ist,y) 89, 90, 229
desire 2
devils 216, 217

devotions in school 65
Diamant 170
Diatessaron 483
different, "they are altogether—from us" 46
Dijon, France 442
diploma 416, 417
Discalced Carmelites. *See* CARMELITES; RELIGIOUS
discrimination 443
disgraced by: becoming an actor, 38; failing in exam, 223
dishonest employees 39, 57
dissertation (doctoral thesis) 221, 222, 269, 368, 376, 377, 397-414, passim; 416, 417, 460, 500, 502
divorce 49, 113, 375, 381, 394
Döberitz. *See* Ruhleben
doctorate 224, 268, 269, 270, 386, 404, 417, 460, 485. *See also* dissertation
documentaries 447, 450
Dodecanes Islands 486
Donaueschingen 406, Map
Dorsten 493, Map
"double standard" 68
Drachenschlucht 244
Dreisam, Freiburg 411, 415
Dresden 254, 369, 370, 399, 491, Map
Dresdener Bank 208
drink, Edith's abstention from 74
Düren 429
Düsseldorff 253
Dutch border 18, 462

East: the, 442; East vs. West, 447
East Africa 28
Echt, Holland 7. *See also* CARMELITES; Netherlands
ecumenism 441
EDITH STEIN, the person. *See* STEIN FAMILY, EDITH
Edith Stein, (title) Center 19, 466, 513; Guild, 511; Mother Teresa Renata Posselt biography, 464
Edith Steins Werke (Archivum) viii; 459-64, passim
Edith Stein's World, a map viii, Map
education: 30, 43, 44, 53, 442, 458, 467, 470, 483; adult, 52, 202, 203, 207; appreciation of, 191; deficien-

cies in teacher training, 192; Edith's views on, 425; mass versus tutorial system, 194; school system of, 138; special, 193

EDUCATORS

—Foerster, Friedrich W., 192, 484

—Gaudig, Herr, 192, 484

—Humboldt, Baron Karl Wilhelm von, 202, 486

—Kerschensteiner, George, 192, 484

—Steiner, Rudolf, 404, 504

—Wyneken, Karl, 192, 484; as gloomy, fanatical debater, 272

efficacy of prayer 193

Egypt 69, 160, 438

Eichenberg 296, Map

Eisenach 244, Map

Ekkehard 406, 505

Elbe River 149, 476

Elbingstrasse 58

electricity 215

Elizabeth I of England 74

emancipation of Jews 443

emigration 182, 427, 430, 500

emotion 1

empathy 269, 367, 376, 397, 417, 460

employment 24, 472. *See also*
   CUSTOMS

"Empress of India" 293; "—of Ireland", 496

enclosure 463

Encyclopedia, Standard Jewish 469

Endliches und Ewiges Sein 7, 428, 461, 503, 508

England 110, 258, 480; actors from, 476; comedians from, 476; liberalism in, 266; —opposes militarism, 315; students from, 243, 257, 301

English: constitutional history, 185; —language course taught by Edith, 202

epidemics 39

Episcopate (R.C.) of Holland protests 430

Ermeton, Belgium 496

Essen 381, 499, 502, Map

Essence of Thomism (Wesen des Thomismus) 12

estrangement due to Edith's convictions 213, 420, 456

ethics 195; Spinoza's book on, 132;

"exalted" idealism in, 195

ethnic conditions 443

Europe 442, 443, 467; central, 447; east versus west, 447

Evangelical (Lutheran) Church, 420, 489, 491; Deaconesses, 484

examinations 159, 173, 174, 217, 269, 276; for doctorate, 412; exemption from oral, 176; preparation for, 284; procedures in, 176, 268, 285; requirements, 187, 270, 275, 284, 285

exercise, physical 395

Exhibition and Exposition, Centenary 271

Exodus 69

expense of studying 208

experience(s) 1, 24, 37; depressing war, 299; a doctor's nasty human, 226; family's, 446. Others are to be found under specific headings

Experimental Psychology 122

factories 27

faith in God 441. *See also* God; **STEIN FAMILY-EDITH**

family vii, 437–46, 449, 457, 465; charism, 179, 180, 466; estrangement from—possible, 455; extended, 443; interrelations in, 442; outings, 89, 129; —prayer, 31; sketches of, 124; —spirit, 46; —traits, 32, 85, 466, 467; withdrawal from family hurts them, 215

Farber, Dr. Marvin 493, 511

farewell party at *Abitur* 175

farmers 32, 34, 37, 41, 42

fasting, rules for 72

faults in friends 454

Faust theme 182, 310, 313, 318, 499

Feldarzt, Ober-, Unter- 224

Feldberg 406, Map

Fellman, Herr 203

FEMININE, the, as Edith Stein sees it:

—Attitudes and Attributes: attractive, 164; capable, 36; courageous, 42; decisive, 42; diligent, 36; the "elephant chick", 164; generous, 40, 41; gracious, 34, 124, 130; grateful, 36; high-spirited,

34; maidenly purity, 34; mourning, 41; precocious, romantic student, 207; quiet, even-tempered, 160, serious, 34; sharing confidences, 137; skilled in sewing, 48; weaknesses, 46
— Family relations:
aunt: doting, 64, 140; fussy, 51; daughter, helpful, 29, 30, 124; in-laws, placated, 46; mother, deep insight in son, 252; siblings, loved, 40, 44, 68, 91
— Role models:
adviser, 31, 34; businesswoman, 30, 34, 36, 39, 42, 48, 61, 112; career woman, 123; confidante, 34; dictator, 48; employer, 39, 57, 123; friend, 31, 34. *See also* **friendship**; governess, 44, 89; homemaker, 36, 48, 108, 124; peacemaker, 85; student, 189
— Traits exhibited:
affectionate at last, 36; anxious over unmarried daughters, 233; caring for younger siblings, 44; dismisses son in disgrace, 38; excessive in bestowing admiration, 50; feeling inferior, 52, 126; gardening a release, 39; hardworking even as a child, 37; harassed or jeopardized: by landlady/lord, 41, 55; by male teacher, 160, 203; by own tenant, 36, 235; homemaker even in illness, 232; hysterically-exaggerated lively teacher, 392; ignoring pain, 38; loyal to parents, 36, 45, 48; preserved faith when family did not, 34; rejects "public assistance", 53; richest girl in town, 160; social work for benefit of children, 52; teacher at swords' points, 174; victim of employee's deceit, 39, 57; widow supports children in home-business, 123; wife lovingly deflects innuendo, 380; wrote and acted in plays, 35
festivals 441
feudal lords 443
fidelity to God 438, 440, 441, 442
field trips 192
figurative speech. *See* **Nicknames**
films 450; — portray orthodox Jews almost exclusively, 447, 449

Findlay, J.N. 491
Finite and Eternal Being 7. *See* **Endliches und Ewiges Sein**
Finland 500
Flanders 252, 300
Flusser, Dr. (M.D.) 344, 345
folktales 451
food 32, 33, 35, 39, 41, 42, 51, 69, 89, 141, 176, 193, 234, 241, 473; berry picking, 132; class parties, 174, 175; at exams, 177, 412; garden produce, 40, 58; gov't distribution of, 35; on holy days, 69; at hospital, 360; at inn, 242; kosher, 127; late snack, 396; monthly bill for, 295; picking mushrooms, 133; nurses', 337; at orphanages, 193; packages for soldiers, 307; patients', 330, 344; picnics, 129, 390; in *Ratskeller*, 92; students', 214, 243, 244, 272, 305; treats, 51, 56, 78; at Women's Student Union, 200
forced labor 463
Formalism in Ethics and Non-Formal Ethics of Values 258
Fouquet, Valentin 431
France 27, 76, 168, 423, 424, 442, 443, 458, 472, 480, 482, 496, 500, Map; war with, 299
Franciscan. *See* **RELIGIOUS**
Frankfurt-am-Main 274, 401, 491, 503, 504, Map; National Assembly of, 267
Frankfurt-an-der-Oder 204, Map. *See also* **UNIVERSITIES**
Frankfurter, Fritz 254, 307, 308, 410, 416, 492; Frau F., his mother, and Magda Frankfurter Frei, his sister, 307
Franz Edith's cousin, a twin. *See* **Horowitz,** Selma (b. Courant)
fraternities drinking in, 216; uniforms of, 204
Frau, Die 460
Frauenplan 245
Frauenwaldau 41
freethinkers 193
Frei, Otto 467
Freiburg-im-Breisgau 17, 196, 208, 213, 226, 228, 251, 386, 387; 397–414, passim; 455, 490, 501, 506, Map

Freier, Prof. Dr. 53; his antics, 54
Freyhan, Frl. 163
Fribourg, Switzerland 501
Friede, Sister. *See* Deaconesses
Friedenthal, Käthe 391
Friederich, Werner P. 477
Friedrichs, K.O. 470
FRIEND(SHIP, S) advice sought from, 31; attitude on criticism from, 195, 454; brought none of her—home, 215; —not dependent on correspondence, 454; —dispel depression, 216; estranged from, 213, 456; fidelity to, 454; giving or lending to, 29, 32; prompting—in class, 162; prospective life-partner, 227; social life with, 214.
—Significant friends of Edith Stein:
—(female) Baerthold, Lotte, 130; Gothe, Erika, 225; Guttmann, Rose, 121; Hamburger, Toni, 165; Kleeman, Kaethe, 146; Koppel, Lene, 163; Platau, Lilli, 121; Scholz, Käthe, 188;
—(male) Biberstein, Hans, brother-in-law, 117; Courant, Richard, cousin, 262; Hermsen, Hugo, description of, 194; esteemed and loved him, 196; saw him as greatest influence since her childhood, 194; Horowitz, Franz, cousin who felt she was lost to him, 156; Lipps, Hans, 254; distressed at his absence, 280; Metis, Eduard, 209-14; Moskiewicz, Georg, 199; Popp, Hermann, lecture not romance at garden gate, 198.
—*See also* individual listing for more on persons named above;
     PHILOSOPHERS: Kaufmann, Reinach; STEIN, EDITH
Friesian Islands 476
From the Family History-the Two Youngest 7
frugality 33, 42
funeral Catholic, 81; Jewish, 42, 81, 144; attended by Christian widow, 183
Furtwängler, Märit. *See* PHILOSOPHERS, Scheler, Max

Gabelsberger shorthand 416, 490

Galicia(n) 192; —sector, 324, 331, 367, 482
games: alphabet, 164; chess, 164; children's, 209; at costume ball, 201; "forfeits", 67, 166; *zum Kopfstehen*, 219; party, 67; puppets, 182; tennis, 117
garden 39, 40, 112; at children's home, 193; English, 192
Gelber, Dr. Lucy 5, 18, 19, 459, 460, 463, 465
"general culture" 313
genocide 451
geography 33
GERMAN(Y) vii, 23, 24, 28, 33, 46, 47, 107, 181, 235, 244, 258, 293, 318, 355, 386, 472, 478, 480, 484, 486; anti—: Canadian, 301, Czechs, 322; Chancellors of, 480; Constitution of, 266; Democratic Party of, 229; —German Diet of 1803, 496; —Empire, 447; government, 312; heart of, 256; —money, 487; nationalism and militarism, 484; new —Reich (2nd), 478; Reich, Third, 39; —Resistance Movement, 485; repression begins in, 425; ruled by, 479, *See also* RULERS; soldiers of, 333, 334, 335; southern, 398; —ic tribes, 392; —and the United States, 505; provided daughters with— upbringing, 180; West—, 501. *See also* LITERATURE
Germanists 211, 255, 262
Gibson, W.R. Boyce 491
Ginsberg, Ernst, actor 445; his father, Dr. G., 445
Giotto 488
Glatz 83, 374, Map
Glatzel, Margrete, unidentified Catholic student 160, 478
Gl(atzer) Schneeberg 133, 134, Map
Gleichen (Mts) 244, 304; the false, 304
Gleiwitz 39, 40, 82, 119, Map
Gnerich, Prof. 391
GOD (includes references to CHRIST)
—Edith's references to—in *Aus dem Leben:*
—family: observance of religious duties, 68-72; proverbs and views on God's care and existence, 28, 29, 60, 108,

277; nephew dressed like "Christ-child", 87
—prayer: 30, 31, 70. *See also* **devotions in school**
—E. asks her friend to comment on a personal—, 213
—retrospective comments on events in her story: efficacy of submission to—, 82; on her own non-belief, 316; on the Lord and his disciples, 69; on the Lord's institution of the Blessed Sacrament, 69; on the Sacraments, 335; [her reception of these, 421]; on statue of Mother of God, 401
—"Thank—" used colloquially, 201, 344; by others and quoted by E., 116, 274;
—spirit, at death, *said* to return to—, 81

Edith's references to—in her other writings quoted:
—*ceterum censeo*: how to live at hand of—, 423
—*Eternal Being. See* **Endliches und Ewiges Sein**
—'s grace and mercy, 422
—'s plan, 1, 435
—Others write about—: the Almighty, 3; call from, 458; the Jews and, 438-42; —'s providence, 4, 425; E.'s surrender: to Christ, 420, to the Cross's power, 435, "to the Holy Spirit", 467; on the Trinity, 458; —the Father, 458

Goethe. *See* **LITERATURE**
"golden mean" 197
Golgotha 242
Goose Girl, Fountain of 241
GORDON Else (1876-1956, b. Stein, Edith's eldest sister), 15, 42-102, passim; 148, 198, 233, 286, 288, 289, 316, 394, 509; Max, her husband, 89-102, passim; 233, 239, 509; their three children: Anni (1908-), 97, 98, 509; Ilse (1904-), 93, 95, 509; Werner (1906-), 95-99, 509
Gorlice 500
Goschütz 41
Goslar 244, Map
Gothe, Erika 255, 303-17, passim; 379, 380, 399; 405-14, passim;

and her family: Frau, her mother, 307; Georg, stepbrother, and Lene, sister, 307; Hans, stepbrother, 307, 309, 407
Gothic architecture 205, 241
Gothic German. *See* **LANGUAGE**
Goths, the ancient 229
Göttingen 85, 99, 154, 172; 195-224, passim; 239-317, passim; 368, 369, 371; 377-87, passim; 394, 395-98; description of town's center, 240, 241; coffeehouses, 242; forest, 243, 247; fortification, 242; "In—, one philosophizes day and night", 218; population, 242; the —"Seven" [best known of them: Dahlmann, Friedrich Christoph; Gervinus, George Gott-fried; the Grimm brothers, Jacob and Wilhelm; Weber, Wilhelm E.], 242, 488; its streets, 242; townsfolk, 244; —, a university town, 242. *See also* **UNIVERSITIES**
governess 44, 88, 89; known as a "Miss", 160
"goyim", the 110, 475
Graef, Hilda 461
Gräfenberg 133, 137, Map
Gray, Dorian 259
Greece (Greek). *See* **Athens, Delos LANGUAGES**
Gregorian calendar 68
grocery store 30
Gronerweg, Frau and Herr 305-8; 313, 315, 316, 378, 381
Gross-Aupa 129, 131, Map
Gr(osse) Wartenburg 484, Map
Gr(osser) Inselberg 244, Map
Grossman, Dr. 154, 155
Grünberg Dr. and Frau, and daughter, Mariechen 146, 157
Gründell, General von 292, 296
Grunwald 132, 136, 137, 210, 364, Map
Guild, the Edith Stein 511
Gulf of St. Lawrence 496
Günterstal 399; 402-14, passim
Guttmann, Julius 395; his father, Rabbi Jakob, 396; married to Grete Henschel, 396
Guttmann Rose (m. Bluhm, Edith's friend) 16, 17; 111-38, passim; 270, 272; photo, 4, 5; Herr and Frau—,

her parents, 124, 129, 130, 132; photo, 5; siblings: Hede, 124, 219, 395, photo, 4; Karl, 124; the enfant terrible, 128

Gymnasium 30, 43, 49, 52, 67, 68, 84, 85, 115, 138, 145, 146, 148, 149, 152, 156, 171, 172, 181, 185, 217, 275, 285, 290, 313, 320, 367, 400, 501; the *Johanneum*, 365, 366; *Realgymnasium*, 153, 387; tutoring while at, 206

gynecology 100

habilitation 200, 227, 247, 485; Edith's pursuit of, 418, 423, 507, 508; — of women, 507

habits of behavior, 446, 454; of simplicity and thrift, 42

Hadrian 440, 442

Hague, The 500, 507

Halifax, N.S.. *See* **Canada**

Hallah (*challah*) 70, 306

Halle 251, 259, 417, 491, Map

Hamburg 18, 46; 89-102, passim; 115, 139, 147-51, 187, 197, 221, 239, 240, 256, 286, 300, 316, 476, 483, Map; Edith's ten months in, 96

Hamburger, Dr. Hermann 206

Hamburger, Siegfried. *See* **PHILOSOPHERS**

Hamburger, Toni 164, 165, 177, 298

hand-crafted furniture 235

Hanna (Moravian) 336. Map

Hannibal 314, 315

Hannover 285, 303; House of, 476, 488; Hannoverisch-München, 224

Hanukkah 441

happiness 458; — in school, 448

Hapsburg dynasty 333, 482, 486

Hartung, Frau 304, 305, 312

Harz Mountains 16, 224, 244, Map

hatred of Jews, Hitler's 23

Havelsee 221

health insurance 91, 228

Heath, Peter 506

Heaven, blessed by 60

Hebrew. *See* **LANGUAGES**

Hector (Homer) 294

Hegauer Mountains 406

Heidelberg 217, 386, Map; library at, 267

Heil im Unheil 2, 460

Heimann, Julia 160, 161, 164, 176, 177, 205

Heine, Heinrich. *See* **LITERATURE**

Heine, Rosa. *See* **Katz, David**

Heisler, Frl. 392

Heister, Herr and Frau von 252

Helfenstein 336, 345, 356, 360, Map

Helgoland 149, 476, Map

Hellenization 439

Helmut Harringa 216, 487

Henschel, Dr. Grete 374, 395; married Julius Guttmann, 396

Henschel, Lotte 163

Hering, Johannes (Jean). *See* **PHILOSOPHERS**

Herkenbosh, Holland. *See* **CARMELITE** — Netherlands

Hermann, the workman 56, 57

Hermsen, Hugo 193-95, 199, 451, 485; esteemed and loved, 196

Herzogenhorn 228

Hess, Else 201

Hesse 263

Heymann, Betty 256, 259

High Holy Days 27, 69, 73; and Christian liturgy, 71

hiking 133, 134. *See also* vacations

Hildebrand, Dietrich von. *See* **PHILOSOPHERS**

Hildesheim 224, 288, 501, Map

Hinterzarten 406, Map

Hirschberg 289

HISTOR(IANS,-Y) 78, 157, 165, 168, 172, 176, 190, 211, 275, 445; — Lehmann, Max, 249, 265, 268, 281, 285, 289, 290, 314, 315, 317, 405, 496; an anglophile, 312; description of, 266, 267; — Livy, Titus (Livius), 312, 314 — Mommsen, Theodor, 312 — Ranke, Leopold von, 266, 290, 495 — Stein, Baron Heinrich Friedrich vom und zum, 265, 495 — Tacitus, Cornelius, 389 — Thucydides, 276 — Xenophon, 290; *Anabasis* of, 189, 290, 314

Hitler, Adolf 18, 23, 425, 442, 483, 485, 490

Hofjude (court Jew) 443

Hohe Sonne 244, Map
Hohen Mense 132, Map
Hohen Weg 250
Hohentwiel Castle 406, 505
Hohenzollern 271, 478, 479
Holland 4, 428-35; 462-64; 479, Map; Jewish oppression in, 429-31
Höllental 406, 505, Map
Holocaust, the 422, 447, 451
home(s) 33,34,45; apartment as, 54; description of R. Courant's, 261, 304; E. Husserl's, 250, 251; A. Reinach's, 248; "going-", 94, 97; joy in the, 38; of landowner who was irrelevant as a philosopher, 253; well-ordered, 46
Horowitz, Selma (b. Courant, Edith's maternal aunt) 37; twin sons: Franz, 68, 142, 144, 147-51; distressed over Edith, 156; Hans, 142, 149
HOSPITALS 16; *Allerheiligen*, Breslau, 165; training at, 298; Gynecological (Women's), Breslau, 225, 226, 228, 285, 298, 321, 370; Jewish Hospital, Breslau, 370; lazaretto, 318-64, passim; 498, 499; Municipal Home for Infants, Breslau, 226, 370, 395; Municipal Institute for the Insane, Breslau, 300, 371; Rudolf Virchow, Berlin, 226. See also RED CROSS; UNIVERSITIES
hospitality 32
hostel 205
hotel at Mittelwalde 135
housekeeping 30, 48, 51, 52, 94, 112; far removed from mathematics, 262
housing crowded, 59; difficulty and injustice in obtaining, 36, 235; simplicity of, 53; held application #23,000, 235
human person constitution of, 397; questions on, 452; rights of, 452
Humanities 252, 507; and philosophy, 275
humiliation of the Jews 445
humor 32, 151, 447
Hundsfeld 27, Map
Hungar(ians, -y) 333, 500
Husserl Archive 459
Husserl, Edmund and family. See PHILOSOPHERS
hymn. See MUSIC

I.C.S. (Institute of Carmelite Studies) vii, viii, 18, 19
Ideas (*Ideen*) 250, 252, 258, 339, 347, 491
ideology 445
illnesses mentioned by Edith Stein: abdominal, 231; asthma, 57, 124, Polish remedy for, 57; bronchitis, 231, 299; cancer, 139; cholera, 321, 498; coma, 36; "consumption", 56, 57, 231, (*see* tuberculosis); *dementia praecox*, 130; dysentery, 498; empyema, 359; epidemics, 39; eye diseases, 107, 232; fever, 105, 325; food upset, 135; gonorrhea, 342; heart ailment, 133; heat stroke, 41; hyperthyroidism, 130; insanity, 371, 372, 373; lung ailment, 56, 57; manic-depressive, 372, 373; mental, 286; migraines, 212; paralysis, 36; paranoia, 29, 373; pleurisy, 325, 344; pneumonia, 105, 213, 325; scarlet fever, 39, after effects of, 39; sprained foot, 134; stroke, 36; stupor, 325; syphilis, 91, treatment of—with salvarsan, 91; typhoid fever, 319, 323, 324, 325, 343, 498, spotted—, 325; tuberculosis, 298, 344, 388, 390, (*see* "consumption")
Ilmenau 245, Map
imagery maiden in tower, 205; shepherdess and flock, 203; of war, 300. See also Nicknames
Immerman, Karl L. 451
Imperial Austrian Railroad 135
income 60, 208. See also money
inflation 209
Ingarden, Roman. See PHILOSOPHERS
inns 130, 134, 135; for vegetarians, 243; Birlinger's, 412; Gebhard's, 414; Illgen's Coffeeshop, 51; Kehr's, 244; *Kron und Lanz*, 241, 315; *Landhaus Martha*, 128; *Mütze, Die*, 302; Rohns, 244, 250; Thuringian, 245; *Zum Kybfelsen*, 402
Institute for Applied Psychology Berlin, 221, 222; of Göttingen, 241
Institute of Carmelite Studies. See I.C.S.
intelligence testing 197

intermarriage of Jews and Christians 60, 183, 455

international efforts of socialists 191

International Academy of Philosophy 503

internment of enemy aliens in WW I, 301; of Napoleon, 504

interrogation, experimental 200

intuition, the categorical 487

Investigations of Truth 8

Iron Cross, the 381

Irving, Texas, US 503

Israel people of, 69; historical resumé of, 438-44. *See also* **JEW(ISH)**

Italy 179, 182, 201; architecture of, 402; soldiers from, 333

Iwan, the orderly 362

Jabneh, Palestine 440

Jägerstrasse 54, 55, 59

Jakobi, the medical student 127

janitor 58, 206

Jantzen, Dr. (Prof.) 392, 393

Jena 241, 246, 249, 482, Map

Jensen, Prof. and Frau 385

Jerusalem 439, 440

Jesuits. *See* **RELIGIOUS**

JEW(ISH)

— Characteristics of — men or women: empathetic, 24; good-hearted, 24; helpful, 24; humorous, 35; proud to acknowledge — descent, 252, 343; understanding, 24. These and more are to be discerned in all the following situations.

— Ethnic situations: assimilated Jews, 127; Eastern, 31; German, 23, 24; Polish, 43

— Family attitudes: anxiety over offspring, 233; assistance in family crises, 83, 85; genuine Jewish mother, 236; uncles willing to educate nephew only for profitable career, 173

— Religious observance of: 34, 68-72; close friend who is orthodox, reserved, 209-13; funeral rites, 42, 81, 144; future life not an article of belief, 82; instruction, 30, 36, 160, 177; Jews who became Protestant, 252, 343, 491; kosher home, 127; orthodox in observance, 127;

prayer: cantor, 27, 31; kaddish, 3; — at wedding, 238

— Social attitudes and situations: academic advancement denied, 186; bourgeois circles, 68; double standard accepted, 68; employment denied, 89; hospitality proffered, 38; plays performed for Third Reich, 39; political right inimical to Jews, 229; proneness to suicide, 82; treated as pariahs, 24; wealth of girl student, 160; wealthy quarter in city, 228

— Vignettes, personal portraits: able to suffer much, 82; lively and witty, 206; self-made success in business, 147; shrewd sale of home at cost to buyer, 183, 184; type of Eastern Jew, 200; type of Jewish personality, 197

Johanan Ben Zaccai, "the Patriarch" 440

Johannesbad 129, Map

Johanniterin 352, 500

Joray-Köppel, Rösli and Henri 467

journalism 449, frivolous tone in, 212

Judaea name changed to Palestine, 440

Judah, the Prince 440

Judaism 24, 71, 439; study of, 492. *See also* **JEW(ISH)**

Juffermans, Ben (†) 465

Juniper Tree, The 194

Jura, Swiss canton 512

Juvisy, France 424, Map

kaddish 3

Kaiser. *See* **RULERS**

Kaiserstrasse, Freiburg 196

Kaiser Wilhelm Park 247

Kaminski, Frau 167

Kamm, Dr. family physician and cousin, 146

Kantorowicz, Ruth 12

Karlsbad coffeemaker, 356; wafers, 359

Karlsbrunn 135, Map

Kassel 224, 244, 296, 494, 512, Map

Katowice (Kattowitz) 118, Map

Katyn, Byelorussia 502

Katz, David 265, 315, 494; Rosa, his wife (b. Heine) 264, 265; career, 495

Kaufmann, Fritz. *See* PHILOSOPHERS
Kaufmann, Georg 405
Kaufmann, Privy Councillor 190
Kenny, Sister 499
Kickelhahn 245, Map
Kiel 418, 500; mutiny of German fleet at, 485
King's Ballerina, The 39
Kirch-hof 240; —*weg*, 247
Kissling, Herr and Frau 484
Kleemann, Kaethe (Edith's friend), 146, 147; Frau—, her mother, 146; her siblings: Emil, pharmacist, and Emma, married to rabbi, 146, 147
Klein-Glieneke 221
Koch, Prof. Josef Catholic theologian, 424, 508
Kohlenstrasse 40, 54
Köhler, Prof. 391, 392
Köln (Cologne) 426-32, 461, 464, Map. *See also* CARMELITES: Germany
Königsberg 145, 392
Kopf, Hedi 164, 165, 166
Koppel family home, 165; Leni. *See* Biberstein, Dr. Martin
Körte, archaeologist at Göttingen 276
Körte, Alfred, Dean of Philosophy, Freiburg 404, 412-16
kosher home, 127; meal at party from —restaurant, 178; pastry, "what I can't define", 213
Koyré, Alexander (Fr. Alexandre). *See* PHILOSOPHERS
Kraków, Poland 497
Kretschmar, Herr, teacher 387, 388, 390
Kreuzberg 40, Map
Kreuzkirche 205
Krupp, Peter Friedrich, munitions mfg. 328, 499
Küttner, Privy Councillor 225
Kuznitzky, Trude 235

laborer's "book" 57, 446
Lake Constance 406, 505, 506, Map
land (lady, lord) 272, 273, 304, 402, 409, 414; embattled, but inventive, 54; formidable, 278; meals from, 243, 272; quarrelsome, 41; rejected Germans, 355; women as tenants, 240
Landgrebe, Prof. Ludwig M. 510
landowners 31, 43, 190, 253
Lange, Luise 375, 381, 382, 383
Lange Geismarstrasse, Göttingen 240
LANGUAGES 30, 127, 165, 172, 202, 312, 473; comparative study of, 486; compositions, 162, 174; modern, 155
Edith's familiarity with:
—Dutch (Holland), 503
—English, vii, 116, 157, 159, 178; taught course in beginner's—, 202; used—words for emphasis, 474
—French, 116, 157, 159, 162, 178, 510
—German: 78; Gothic, 190, 211; High, 256; Indo-Germanic, 185; Low, 194; Middle High, 263, 311, 313; Old High, 189, 263; drama, 185; grammar, 185; Psalms in, 31
—Greek: 164, 185, 187, 189, 190, 275, 276, 290, 312, 314, 318, 325, 366, 367; taught—philosophy, 389; *Graecum*, 365, 368
—Hebrew, 31
—Hungarian, 333
—Italian, 160, 340
—Latin, 149, 153, 155-62, 172, 174, 187, 189, 332, 482, 500; class titles, *see* Table 4‡, page 471; *cum laude, magna—, summa—*, 408; *mulus*, 179, 473. For additional terms, *see* 473; *Physikum*, 223; quotations, 181, 423, 482, 508; *Rigorosum*, 397, 474
—other languages at hospital, 333
last things, the four 422, 508
Laudien, Councillor 366, 367
laughter in the home 30
laundry day 38
Laurahütte 118, Map
law, code of 440
lawyer 28, 151
layperson vii
Leagues for School Reform 192
lectures given by Edith 419
Lehmann, Max. *See* HISTORIANS
Lehnel, Capt. 229

Leine Mountains (*Leineberge*) 224, 242

Leipzig 256, 399, 400, Map; — Medical Association, 90

Lena, a Polish student 207, 208

Lengert, Prof. 167, 168, 387-92, 502; embarrassed at party, 178

Leopoldina 241

Letters and Diary of John Henry Newman vii

Letters of Edith Stein 460, 461

liberal party, 478; politics, 168, 178, 190, 191

Lichtwitz, Prof. and Frau 295

Liebig Institute, Frankfurt 401

Life in a Jewish Family/vii, 5, 12, 13, 449, 461. See also *Aus dem Leben einer Jüdischen Familie*

Lights, Festival of 441

Lindt chocolates 137, 344

Lioba. See **RELIGIOUS; SAINTS**

Lipps, Hans and Theodor *See* **PHILOSOPHERS**

Liselotte von der Pfalz 39

Lisieux 442

LITERATURE 52, 78, 121, 172, 275, 285; classic poets, 170;
— Individual authors, orators, playwrights, poets: Börne, Ludwig, 262, 494; Caesar, Gaius Julius, 153; Carpio, Lope de Vega, 480, 481; Cicero, Marcus Tullius, 175, 389; Dahn, Felix, 281, 496; George, Stefan, 477; Goethe, Johann Wolfgang, 14, 137, 151, 245, 424, 451, 476, 477, 503, 504, 505, 508; Grillparzer, Franz, 150, 170, 451, 480, 481; Grimm Brothers (Jacob and Wilhelm), 194, 242, 292, 451, 488; Gryphius, Andreas, 476; Gutzkow, Karl, 211, 487, 494; Hameln, Glückel von, 24, 469; Hauptmann, Gerhart, 270, 495; Hebbel, Friedrich, 150, 170, 481; Heine, Heinrich, 242, 262, 494; Herder, Johann Gottfried von, 186, 505; Homer, 189, 294, 308, 339, 345, 365, 367; Horace, Quintus Flaccus, odes of, 175; Ibsen, Henrik, 150, 179, 476, 482, 495; Isocrates, 367, 500; Körner,

Christian Gottfried, 164; Lessing, Gotthold Ephraim, 311, 476, 485, — 's *Faust*, 313; Lowenthal, Marvin, 469; Ludwig, Otto, 170, 477, 481; Lysias, 366; Mieding, Johann Martin, 477; Newman, John Henry, vii; Nietzsche, see **PHILOSOPHERS**; Ovid, Publius (Ovidius) Naso, 153, 161; Roth, Cecil, 469; Rousseau, Jean Jacques, 290; Schiller, Friedrich von, 14, 47, 74, 147, 164, 170, 186, 245, 406, 476, 505, 506; Schlegel, August Wilhelm, 477, 505; Shakespeare, William, 150, 476, 477, 481; Stein, Leo Walter, 38, 39, see also **STEIN FAMILY**; Stein, von, Frau, 175; Tatian, the Assyrian, 189, 483; Tieck, Ludwig and Dorothea, 477; Uhland, Ludwig, 47; Ulfilas (Wulfila), 189, 211, 483; Voltaire, François, 290; Wengeroff, Pauline, 24, 469; Wernher der Gartenaere, 312, 313, 498; Xenophon, 189; Zola, Émile, 495

liturgy consoling, 81; of the Church, vii, 70, 71

logic 314

Logos 2

Logische Untersuchungen (Logical Studies) 217-58, passim; 487-91

Lombards (stocks) 96

Louvain, Belgium 459

love for country 444, 445

loyalty to country 35, 444; to family, 37

Lublinitz 27, 32, 33, 35, 39, 40, 66, 73, 94, 102, 146, 147, Map

Ludwig, Herr and family 41

Ludwigshafen 508, Map

lumber yard 40, 42, 54, 58, 66, 109, 112, 215; senior Frau Stein's, 38

Luther, Martin 216

Lutheran (Evangelical) Church 420, 470

Luxembourg 429

Maass, Frau 278

Maastricht 429, Map

Maccabees 439; a play, 481

Machandelboom, Der 194

McMahon, Comte de 480

Mädchenschule, Höhere 471. *See also*
    Note 4‡
Madrid, Spain 480
Mährisch-Weisskirchen, Austria 16;
    318-67, passim; 368, 374, 376, 498,
    499, Map
maids 38, 51, 286, 287; resentful
    through misunderstanding illness,
    373
Maier, Prof. Heinrich 306
Main River 398, 401
Mainz 248, 283, 300, 378, 505
**MALE CHARACTERISTICS cited by
    Edith Stein:**
— Attitudes and Attributes:
    brusque, 124; cheerful, 31, 34;
    good-humored, 31; hard-working,
    167; inconsiderate, 199; mule-
    headed, 85; obsequious, 127; obsti-
    nate, 85; pampered, 124, 134, 136,
    210; quiet, 127; responsible, 35;
    serious, 127; silly, 199; stately, 124;
    taciturn, 124; teasing, 141; tender,
    80; touchy, 85
— Family Stance:
    brothers, ready to help widow, 42;
    brother-in-law, delighted at visit,
    94; father: affectionate, 97, con-
    cerned, 207, "second", 81, taciturn,
    unable to earn enough, 124; filial
    loyalty, 47, 85, 121; grandfather,
    devoted, 28, 31; husband: good-
    humored, 94, grateful for wife's
    thrift, 102, living comfortably on
    credit, 49, misjudged by wife and
    daughters, 139, 140, mortified by
    show of affection, but an ideal—,
    280, tender, always, until paranoid
    in old age, 291; uncles' jealousy
    causes family crises, 85, 181, kind-
    ness, 34, 80; widower raising
    daughter(s), 261 456
— Personality Sketches:
    antifeminist's "conversion", 263;
    aristocratic German, 261; avuncular
    advisor, 64; brilliant mathematician,
    84; business tyro, 127; comic spec-
    tacle, 162; comic tragedian, 85;
    dancing enthusiast, 201; friend not
    to be forgotten, 194; professors,
    260, 266; teachers: moral menace,

160, 202, an original type, 165;
    tutors: annoying, 154, correct, 153,
    ideal, 194; valiant little tailor type,
    292
— Traits displayed:
    conciliatory friend becomes "cham-
    bermaid", 127; delicacy of feeling
    shown consistently, 212; delighting
    in philosophizing, 254; Don Quixote
    appearance, 196; strict as father
    and teacher, 27; most deeply
    impressive man, 254; most deeply
    influential man, 194; observant in
    prayer, 31; scolded frequently but
    never struck, 27; sensitive, upright
    youth, 210; trustworthy in business,
    32
Malsburg, Dr. von 328
manager dishonest, 39
Manebach 245, Map
Mann, Alfred 199
manufacture of chemicals, 164;
    machine embroidery, 123; soap, 27;
    surgical cotton, 27; uniforms, 286
manuscript 461-64, 470, 472, 473,
    474, 503
map 245, 246, Map
Marburg movement 256, 493
Marek, Herr Dr., tutor 153, 154, 158,
    159
Margaret, in *Faust* 451
Margarete, Matron. *See* Sisters
    (Nursing)
Maria Sprung 243
Maria Stuart 14, 74, 75
Mark, Sophie photo 5
Mark (German). *See* money
marketplace (*Marktplatz*) 240, 241,
    321
marks, scholastic 166, 171, 470, 481
Marne, first battle of the 299
marriage 45, 47, 131, 165, 218;
    — broker, 49, 454; career versus,
    123; difficulties not mentioned, 41
Martin-Guerin, Thérèse 442, 457;
    Louis, her father, 458
Martius, Hedwig. *See*
    PHILOSOPHERS-Conrad-Martius
Mass, the 399, 456
"Master", the 251. *See also*
    PHILOSOPHERS-Husserl, Edmund

MATHEMATIC(IAN, -S) 122, 128, 152,
159, 218, 243; mental exercise, 155;
—Courant, Richard, (1888-1972 in
U.S., Edith's first cousin), 84, 148,
152, 158, 172, 218; 239-305, passim;
320, 342, 374-84, passim; 444, 453,
470, 488, 500; Edith came to appreciate—fully, 153; family charism,
85, 466, 467; hospital stay, 381;
humor, wit, 85, 246; —and the
Institute of Mathematics at NYU,
470, 488; outstanding intellect of,
85; photo 3b
   -Nelli (1886-1942, shot by Nazis
   in Minsk) Richard's first wife
   and friend of Stein family, 239,
   309-20, passim; 374-84, passim;
   394, 395, 502
   -Nerina (1891, b. Runge, known
   as Nina) Richard's second wife,
   381, 453, 466, 467, 513; photo 9,
   of the Runge family
—Hilbert, David, 85; his son, Franz,
on being Jewish, 252
—Klein, Felix, 85, 300, 380, 401, 497.
See **Staiger, Putti** (Klein)
—Landau, Edmund, 315
—Pythagoras, 154
maturity needed to write
autobiography, 1
Mauser work on St. Thomas, 12
Max, an orderly 346, 347, 349
meals 214, 446. *See also* **CUSTOMS,**
food
Mecklenburg 255
medical profession advertising, 90;
doctors, 225, 247; ethics, 90;
jealousy in, 91; licensed without
internship, 225; polyclinic care,
226; practice, 228, 230, 232; trans-
port train, 225; 318-63, passim
Meier Helmbrecht 311, 313, 498
Meissner, Herr wife abuses child, 57
Melanchthon, Philipp 486
Memoirs of a Grandmother 469
Mendelssohn, Moses 485
Mense, Dr. 281
Mense. *See* **Hohe Mense**
mental health 151, 193, 287
Mensendieck fitness exercises Edith
with nine others takes, 395

merchants 30, 34, 447
Merk, Frl. 295
merriment 38
Mervins, Trude 157, 159
mesalliance 183
Metis, Eduard (Edith's close friend)
203, 209-13, 370, 455, 456; com-
panion in studies, 213; degree of
estrangement, 213; question about
personal God, 213
Metternich censorship 480
Meuse River 480
Meyer, Rudolf 403, 404, 413
Meyer, Toni 224, 286-96, passim; 307,
371-74; description of friend in
health and in sickness, 287; Frau—,
Toni's mother, 286, 287, 372, 373
M I A remembrance 452
Michaelisstrasse 38 228; moved in, 102
Miechowitz 193, 484, Map
Middes, Switzerland 512
Middle Ages 447
Mieding's Death, On 151
Mighty Fortress, A the hymn, 216
migrants 447
Mijn Weg Naar de Waarheid (My
Way to Truth) 459
Mikesha, a patient 358, 360
militarism 315
military service 190; soldiers bring
home captain's body, 229
Miller, Herr 313
millers 41
minnesinger manuscripts 401
Minsk, Russia 502
Mishna 440
"Miss, the" 160
Mittelwalde 133, 135, Map
Moltke, Count Helmut James von
485
monarchist loyalty 229
money 43, 51, 56, 208; "are you rich,
Mama?" 220; good grades cost—,
171; hiked sales price, 183; Mark
value, 487; one-hundred-Marks per
month, salary, 495; Pfennige and
Pukade, 30, 60; savings, 208; three-
penny cookies, 56; travel funds, 295
Montelimar, France 512
Monumenta Germaniae Historica 495
moral aberrations 216

532 *Edith Stein*

Moravia(n) 249, 321
Morgenroth, Prof. Julius bacteriologist in Berlin, 230
mortification of the eyes 202, 486
Moses 437, 438
Moskiewicz, Dr. Georg (familiar name, Mos, friend of Edith) 199, 217, 218, 220, 221, 246, 248, 252, 254; thirteen years older than Edith; two, older than Reinach, 247
motion, problems of Reinach's, 275
mountains 129, 134; Edith's first glimpse of, 132. *See also* Carpathian; Leine; Vosges
mourning with black fast 442
Mugdan, Susanne (Edith's friend and co-worker in Red Cross hospital, known as Suse) 320-67, passim; 395, 398, 402, 499, 500; has twin brother, Albrecht, 320, 360. *See also* Stenzel, Bertha; Frau Käthe—, Suse's mother, 320, 343, 499, 500
Municipal Home. *See* Hospitals
Müller, Günther 255, 309
mulus trip 179
Munich 187, 241, 247, 253, 258, 371, 385, 424, 485, 489, 513, Map
Münster 7, 18, 424, 425, 507
Mütze, Die 241
MUSIC
— Composers, Classical:
   Bach, Johann Sebastian, 216, 271, 487; predilection for, 172; Beethoven, Ludwig van, 68, 418; Gregorian chant, completely at home with, 172; Händel, Georg Friedrich, 476; Mendelssohn-Bartholdy, Felix, 477, 485; Strauss, Johann, 38; Wagner, Richard, repudiated music of, 172
— Composers, Popular:
   Wilhelm, C., with lyricist, Max Schneckenburger, 472
— Operas: bought piano scores to memorize, 172; Carmen, young Polish girl's ambition to be real-life—, 207; Fidelio, always remained Edith's favorite, 172; Magic Flute, The, first—Edith ever heard, 172; Meistersinger, Die, only Wagner —she could tolerate, 172; student

songs of Heidelberg—attract her to that university, 217
— Piano and singing: 38, 67, 68; four-hand piano, 124, 126; festival with chamber, orchestral, vocal—, 216; lute to singing, 126; organ, 271; special song for wedding, 47; teaching—, 46, 126
Mussman, Frau, landlady 272, 289
My Mother Remembers 7
mystical teaching vii
Nathan, the Wise 197, 485
national health insurance: Erna's patients from, 228; physician's antagonism to, 91
national liberal politics 190
National Union Catalog of Pre-1956 Imprints 483, 505
nationalism 190
nationalistic outrage at Bell's cost, 301; plays, 39
nationalities of soldier-patients: Austrian, 333, 358, 359, man of sorrows, 362; Czech, 333, 334, 339, 346; German (Bavarian), 331, 333, 334, 337, 339, 358; gypsy, 337, 354; Hungarian, 333, 334, 339; Italian, 333, from Trieste, 324-40, passim; Polish, 333, 350, nobleman-eccentric, 361; Slovak, 333, 354, 358; Slovene, 333, Rumanian, Russian, Ruthenian, Turkish, 333
nations, necessity for and significance of individual,190
Natural Sciences 122; approach to psychophysics, 265; Husserl on, 252; mathematics and, 275; —versus social sciences and humanities, 507
NATURALISTS Darwin, Charles R., 190, 482, 483; Haeckel, Ernst. *See* PHILOSOPHERS
Nature and Spirit 252
Nature of Sympathy, The 506
Nauheim. *See* Bad Nauheim
National Socialist German Workers Party (NAZI) 3, 7, 18, 23, 422, 425, 427, 428, 442, 445, 451, 452, 463; offical party records, 430, 431; reprisal on non-Jews, 500, 501; requisition Nuns' monasteries through SS, 429

Neckar River 401

neo-Kantianism 250, 256

Netherlands 490-500. *See also* **CARMELITES**, Holland

Neumann, Councillor 261, 295, 296, 376, 383; Nelli, daughter. (*see* **MATHEMATICIANS**, Courant, Richard).

Neumann, Friedrich Germanist enriched by phenomenology, 255

Neumeister, Lotte 336

Neuwied 195, 196, 485

New England, U.S. town squares in, 472

Newman, John Henry Cardinal vii, 436, 474

new scholasticism 250

newspapers Edith read—regularly, 167; but only liberal, 168; *Berlin Zeitung am Mittag*, 294; *Breslauer Zeitung*, 211; British—has German correspondent, 497; *Frankfurter Zeitung*, studied it thoroughly daily, 310; *Schlesischen Zeitung*, conservative paper protested against Bell, 301

New World, the 446

New Year. *See* **CUSTOMS**

NICKNAMES and other imagery; common in Edith's milieu: "Abbot's wife, the", 276; Bi-Ba-Bo, 169; big wigs, 300; book sealed with seven seals (Edith), 63; Bridge of Calumny, 149; Bummel, 241; "Cavalry-ettes", 346; chick (Edith), 132; clear water, 63; cloverleaf, 132, 137, 200, separated, 138; cow's tail (Edith), 60; crow (Erna), 62; Donar, 392; Dragon (Napoleon), 169; elephant chick, 164; expert, the (Edith), 219; Fidelitas, 206; "flames", 50; frog (Frieda), 47; go-getter (Edith), 141; Great O, the, 170; Idiots, the, 191; Julius and Raphael, 164; "kitten", 424; lambs, 203; *Lämmchen*, 168; lion (Rosa), 50; "little Meyer", 404; lock-up, the, 302; Lotte, 165; Mariechen-schon's-Chlor, 390; Magnificence, His, 206; old boys, the, 205; Pan Primarius, 347; Philistines, the, 198; pussycat (Edith), 62; Rex, 65; Göttingen Seven, the, 242; small

blue stone (Edith), 220; smart(y) (Edith), 141; strayed chick under wing, 49; stray lamb, 203; strong character, the (Edith), 162; Super-Margarete, 350; tot, the (Edith), 62; Snow-White, 62; Walls of Salamanca, the 243; zoo, the, 62

Nikolaistadtgraben 203

Nikolausberg (erweg) 241, 242

nobility: 31;

—Barons: Humboldt, Karl Wilhelm von, 202, 486; Stein, Heinrich Friedrich Karl vom und zum, 265, 495;

—Counts: Gleichen, 244; Moltke, 485; Rothschild, 194; Yorck von Wartenburg, 194

—Duchess Hadwig of Swabia, 505; Duke and Duchess of Weimar, 477;

—Polish noblemen, 326, 361;

—Prince of Wied, 194, 485. *See also* **RULERS**.

non-believers, utter 90, 128, 148

non-Jews 455, 462; penalized for Jewish sympathy, 430, 500, 501

North Sea 476

Norway 475; Norwegian coal barge, 496

novellas 211

nurses 318-65, passim. *See* **Sisters** for individual names

Nurses, Professional Organization of German (B.O.) 326

nursing-in-home 29, 36, 39, 44, 52, 58, 83, 86, 93, 103, 104, 105, 106, 107; for Red Cross, 318-65, passim; mother's appearance better than, 73

obedience 55; deliberate decision, —to mother and sister, 75; to spiritual guides, 457

Obernigk 193, Map

oblivion not for Edith 442

occupation forces in Holland 429

Oderberg 319; customs at, 364

Oder River 116, 168, 204, 447, 487

offensive talk 37, 74; —and action, 353

office work, repugnant 43

Ohlau 89

Ohlbrich, Prof. 151-79, passim; 387, 389, 478, 482

Olmütz (Olomouc) 345, Map
Olschowka, Herr and Frau Viktor 55
Operas. *See* MUSIC
Oppeln 40, Map; uncle moves to—
  from Lublinitz, 35
orphanage 193, 484
Ortmann, Grete 255, 278, 292, 408
outdoors 243; meals, 122. *See also*
  Scheitniger Park, vacations

Pabst, Herr and Frau 304
pacifist Edith is not a, 168
Palestine 440
Pan Primarius 347, 357
Paris 131, 209, 253, 299, 424, 445,
  492, Map
Parmenides 214
parties 129; games at, 219; verse for
  215, 219, 220
partisanship, pro-German 35
Passover, the (*Pesah*) 68
pastoral letter of Netherlands'
  Bishops 430
patients at Märisch-Weisskirchen. *See*
  nationalities
patriotic chauvinism 168
patriotism of German Jews, 35, 47,
  445; war loans demonstrating, 209
patronage 443
peace before WW I, seemingly
  indestructible, 293; Lipps not eager
  for, 369
pedagogical group in Breslau 193–200,
  213
Pedagogical Institute of Münster,
  Catholic 425
pedagogy Edith's lack of training in,
  425
Peiskretcham 27, Map
Pentecost 207, 244, 345
people of God 3
peoples 190
perception seen once more as
  reception 250
persecution 440, 442
Persians 438
Person und Sache (Person and Thing)
  197
Peters, Curtis H. 491
Petri, Frl. *See* PHILOSOPHERS,
  Heidegger

Pfennig. See money
Phaedo 366
phenomena 218
phenomenological method 249; and
  philosophy journal. *See* Philosophy
Phenomenological Movement, The 507
phenomenologists 220, 247–317, passim
phenomenology 217, 222; Edith's study
  of, 247–317, passim; 345–435,
  passim; Hönigswald against, 219
Phenomenology of the Spirit 283
*Phenomenology and Theory of the
  Feelings of Sympathy* 260
philology 64, 201, 211, 253, 276, 285,
  291; question in—would never occur
  to a philosopher, 366
PHILOSOPHERS
  Apelt, E.F., 494
  Bergson, Henri, 417, 507
  Brentano, Franz, 489
  Carnap, R., 494
  Cohen, Hermann, 493
  Conrad, Hans Theodor (familiar
    name, Autos), 218, 247, 253,
    420, 488, 491, 513, 514; photo 6
  Conrad-Martius, Hedwig (Edith's
    friend, familiar name Hattie,
    wife of Hans Theodor Conrad),
    218, 253, 275, 420, 427, 428,
    489, 491, 511, 513; photo 6
  Dewey, John, 484
  Dilthey, Wilhelm, 397
  Fichte, Johann G. 494
  Fries, Jakob Friedrich, 263, 494
  Geiger, Moritz, 247, 371, 489
  Haeckel, Ernst, 173, 482, 483
  Hamburger, Siegfried, 399, 456,
    503; photo 6
  Hegel, Georg W.F., 283, 481, 494
  Heidegger, Martin, 409, 423, 506,
    508; his wife, (b. Petri), 409
  Hering, Johannes (Fr. Jean), 253,
    278, 280, 292, 307, 308, 508;
    career, 492; photo 6
  Hildebrand, Dietrich von, 253, 399,
    423, 456, 503, 508; career, 491
  Honecker, Martin, 423, 508
  Hönigswald, Richard, 185, 187, 483;
    his dialectic, 186; on Husserl,
    219; follows critical philosophy
    of Kant, 186, 483; on Stern and

PHILOSOPHERS (*continued*)
the school psychologist, 197
Hume, David, 314
Husserl, Edmund, 17, 217, 218, 220,
243, 247, 249-317, passim; 368-
71; 377-86; 397-414, passim;
415-18; 420, 422, 423, 489, 490,
491, 498, 502, 506, 509, 510,
511; career, 490; Edith *sees*, 249;
becomes his assistant, 411; called
the "Master", 251; his death, 428;
— family: wife, Malvine (b. Steinschneider), 249-317, passim;
418, 489, 490, 501; daughter,
Elisabeth (m. Rosenberg), 251,
489; sons, Gerhart and
Wolfgang, 252, 489
Ingarden, Roman, 309, 403-14,
passim; 453, 493; career, 498;
letters from Edith, 497
Jacobi, Friedrich H., 494
James, William, 489
Kant, Emmanuel, 122, 186, 254,
505; Kantian schools, 250
Katz, David. *See* **Katz**
Kaufmann, Fritz, (Edith's close
friend), 256-309, passim; 369,
416, 421, 422, 429, 454, 456,
497, 508, 511; career in U.S.,
492, 493; correspondence with
Edith, 493; her description of,
257; final visit with Edith, 426
— his family: first wife, Alice, 492,
508; Dr. Luise, second wife, 493;
sister, Marta, 369; son, Gustav,
493; daughter, 492
Koyré, Alexandre, 253, 492; career,
491; photo 6
Kühnemann, Eugen, 201, 486, 505;
on Schiller, 186
Lipps, Hans, (Edith's classmate),
253-307, passim; 369-99, passim;
455, 456, 507, 511; career, 491;
his criticism shatters Edith, 279;
her description of him, 254, 279,
418; mutual feeling of inferiority,
400; his pet owl, 370; studies
sleep, 279; wound fatal in
W.W. II, 429; photo 6
— his family: Frau L., his mother,
370, 399; first wife and children,

456, 512; second wife, 511
Lipps, Theodor, 247, 269, 277, 285,
489, 494
Lotze, Rudolf Hermann, 292
Mach, Ernst, 494
Maritain, Jacques, 510
Martius, Hedwig. *See* **Conrad**
Montesquieu, Charles, Baron, 290
Münsterberg, Hugo, 501; School of
Baden, 386
Natorp, Paul, 256, 417, 493
Nelson, Leonard, 243, 263;
description of, 264
Neurath, O., 494
Nietzsche, Friedrich Wilhelm, 131,
484, 505
Otto, Rudolf, 494
Pfänder, Alexander, 371, 509, 510
Plato, 201, 214, 486, 505
Plessner, Helmut, 309, 498
Reinach, Adolf, 247-300, passim;
371, 377-85, passim; 419, 488,
501; description of, 248; age,
247; manner of lecturing, 274;
death, 417; photo 6
— his wife, Anna, 248, 419, 462,
501; delicacy of feeling, 380
— his brother, Heinrich, 291
— his sister, Pauline, 305, 315, 377;
becomes Sr. Augustina, 496
Rickert, Heinrich, 409, 501; School
of Baden, 386
Royce, Josiah, 258, 489, 493
Scheler, Max, 258, 260, 279, 420,
501, 506; career, 494; description
of, 259; photo 6; wife, Märit
(b. Furtwängler), 258
Schelling, Friedrich Wilhelm von, 494
Schlick, Moritz, 258, 494; co-founder
of Vienna Circle, 494
Scholz, Heinrich, 418, 507
Schopenhauer, Arthur, 150
Socrates, 505
Speusippos, 201, 486
Spinoza, Baruch, 132
Stern, William. *See*
PSYCHOLOGISTS
Strauss, David, 483
Windelband, Wilhelm, 501; School
of Baden, 386
Wittgenstein, Ludwig, 494

"Philosophical Foundation of
Psychology and of the *Geisteswissenschaften* (Sciences of the
Spirit)" 507
Philosophical Society (*also* Circle)
248-307, passim; founders of the,
253, 256, 292, 488, 489; society's
promise ends, 488
philosophy 122, 172, 173, 191, 219,
448, 451; —and history versus
mathematics and natural sciences,
275; —instead of courting, 198;
introduction to, 187, 422;
psychology and, 192; —Seminar
rooms, 241
Philosophy, History of 500
*Philosophy and Phenomenological
Research, Journal of* 429, 493, 497;
continues the work of Husserl's
Jahrbuch, 511
photography a possible career for
Edith, 152; hobby, 96; memorial,
196
PHYSICISTS Gauss, Carl Friedrich,
242; Weber, Wilhelm Eduard, 242
physiology familiar because of
psychology, 223. *See* Mensendieck
Pick, Amalia (b. Courant, known as
Mälchen, Edith's aunt), had family
of five daughters and two sons, the
youngest, 66; daughters: Adelheid
(Heidel), 151; Grete, 151, 232, 397;
Leni, Edith's classmate, 66, 142,
143, 148, 149, 151, 158
Pick, Dr. (M.D.) 326-44, passim
Pick, Emma (b. Courant, Edith's
youngest aunt), with husband and
three children, none named, 94
"Picknick" 128, 475
Pilsen, Austria 499
Pirna 491, Map
Platau, Lilli (m. Berg. *See* Berg,
Paul), 121-237, passim; 370, 395,
486; photos, 4, 5
—Frau, Lilli's mother, 123-27;
photo, 4
—Hans, Lilli's brother, 127
Platen, August Graf von 451
plebiscite 35
Pluicke, Frau 403, 404
poesy 217

poetry 28, 194, 215; parlor—, 129;
school—, 47, 166, 175, 178
Pöhl, patient 359, 360, 362
Poland (Polish) 35, 57; —doctor, 326,
353; —Jews, 43; —landlady, 55;
—Legion, 403; nobleman, 326, 328,
329; —officer-patient, 361;
—soldiers, 333, 350, 351; —student
tutored by Edith, 207; —women in
army, 324
political situation after WW I, 229,
443, 444; disagreement with, 168
polyclinic medical care, free 226
poor, giving to 29, 40; medical students
attend—to get practice, 226
Pope John Paul II (Karol Wojtyla)
library at International Academy of
Philosophy, 503; studied
phenomenology, 498
Popp, Dr. Hermann 196-201, 211
Posen (Poznan) 27, 235, 261, Map
possessions, divesting emigrees of 445
posterity, legacy to 442
poverty, lived in great 29
Prager. *See* Burchard
Prague, Czechoslovakia 424, 490, Map
prayer 2, 29, 31; answer to, 193; deliberate and conscious decision of Edith
to give up—, 148; —in family, 27;
—found on dead soldier, 338; —in
Latin, 156; —satisfies human need
more than sacrifice does, 441. *See
also* JEW(ISH), Religious observance
prejudice fostered 443
Princip, assassin 497
principal (school) 65, 78, 138, 143,
159, 169, 178, 206, 207
prisoners-of-war, relative among
enemy 444
"private life" forfeited for country
444
private school, family supported 30
privatdocent (Ger.: *privatdozent*) 186,
218, 247, 251, 483
Prochere, Madame 76
professional ethics in medical practice
90
programs for celebrations or parties
129, 134, 178, 215
prompted in school 175, 223. *See also*
CUSTOMS

property nouveau-riche owning, 444;
forbidden to Jews, 442; Edith's
mother finally able to afford —, 58
Prossnitz (Prostéjov) 368, 489, Map
protest of Church in defense of Jews
430, 431
Protestant(s) 128, 130, 190, 252, 276,
291, 308; churches, 316, 401;
engaged to marry Jewish lawyer, 291;
— nobility found nursing order, 500;
sermons mix politics with religion,
316; "simultaneous", 402; — states
war with Catholic states, 482;
theologians, 276, 403
Providence reflected in parent 458
Prussia(n) 89, 132, 270, 315; allegiance
(Edith's), 266; anti — teacher, 266;
— character, 266; conservative, 168,
190; history of, 185, 478; militarism
and —, 505; myopically —, 190;
rulers of, 478, 479; — statesman,
486, 495
**Prussian Society for Women's Right
to Vote** 191
Psychological Institute, the 265
psychologism 249
PSYCHOLOGISTS
Bühler (alt. Buehler), Karl, 200,
217, 487; Würzburg method, 486
Ebbinghaus, Hermann, 200, 485
Gelb, Adhemar, 274, 496
Hönigswald, Richard. *See*
PHILOSOPHERS
Katz, David, 265. *See under* **Katz**
Köhler, W., 274, 496
Külpe, Oswald, 200, 217, 487, 495;
Würzburg method, 486
Lipmann, Dr. Otto, 221, 222;
family, 221
Messer, A., 200, 217, 487; Würzburg
method, 486
Meumann, E., 122
Müller, George Elias, 265, 494, 495;
— on Edith, 507
Stern, William (alt. Wilhelm),
Edith's teacher, 185, 186, 187,
192, 194, 195, 199, 217, 287,
418, 485; career, 483; on prob-
lem of association, 197; on
separation of philosophy and
psychology, 197

— his wife, Frau Stern, diaries used
as basis for book, 287
Wertheimer, Max, 274, 496
psychology 122, 185; dissertation
planned in —, but abandoned, 221;
interest in, 186; — and philosophy,
191, 192, 241; procedures in, 265;
state of, 221; — of thought, 217,
219; thought-process in children,
221
Psychology of Early Childhood 197
*Psychology, A History of, in
Autobiography* 495
psycho-physical individual 502
Psychophysics of Visual Perception
265
public assistance 53
Publishers:
*Archivum Carmelitanum Edith
Stein. See* **Archivum**
Barnes and Noble, Inc., 477
Clark University Press, 495
Collier Books; Collier-Macmillan,
491
Edith Stein Guild, 511
Encyclopaedia Brittanica, 510
Encyclopedia, Standard Jewish, 469
Harper and Row, Inc., 477
Humanities Press, 491
ICS Publications, vii, 460
Jüdischer Verlag, 24
Martinus Nijhoff, 500, 507
Poppelaner Verlag, 24
Routledge and Kegan Paul, 506
Springer Verlag, 470, 488
Vandenhoeck and Rupprecht, 264
— of magazines:
University of New York at Buffalo:
*Journal of Philosophical and
Phenomenological Research*, 511;
Dominican Fathers of Washington,
D.C.: *The Thomist* magazine, 511
Pukade 60
**puppets banned from portraying
royalty** 271
Purim 441
Pützchen 429

qualms of conscience 222
Quaestiones Disputatae 461
Quixote, Don 196

rabbi(s) 81, 238, 440
Rachfahl, Prof. 404
racial hatred, youth raised in 24
radical thinker 198
radio addresses 424
Radlauer, Johanna (b. Burchard,
    Edith's grand-aunt), 28; has eightieth
    birthday, 75, 473; two sons, Ernst
    and Jakob, 28
Radolfzell 407, Map
Rahel 480
railway 35, 129, 406; — stations, 134,
    209, 414
Ramsau 134, Map
Rathaus, Göttingen 241
Ratibor 132, 364, Map
Ratskeller, Hamburg 92
reading 59; her "daily bread", 150;
    influence of, 480. *See also* **books**
realists, young phenomenologists are
    confirmed 250
Red Cross hospitals, 16; Netherlands,
    433; nursing training, 58, 296, 298,
    318, 367, 416; of Silesia, 321, 345
Reich the "new" (2nd), 168, 190; the
    Third, 39
Reichenau 407, 506, Map
Reichstag 364
Reid, Constance 470, 488
Reinach, Adolf and wife, Anna. *See*
    PHILOSOPHERS
Reinach, Pauline 291-317, passim;
    377-85, passim; 401, 496; Edith
    describes—, 291; becomes
    Benedictine nun, 496
Reinerz 136, Map. *See* Bad Reinerz
relativism 249
Religious Congregations and Orders
    provide refuge for Frau Husserl,
    490;
    Augustinian chapterhouse, 205
    Benedictine Abbeys: Beuron, 424;
        Bursfeld, 276; Ermeton, 496;
        Reichenau, 506; St. Gabriel,
        161, 478; St. Gall, 505; St.
        Lioba's, 402, 422, 504
    Carmelite, founded in Germany in
        1643, 511. *See also*
        CARMELITE(S)
    Dominican: St. Magdalena's, Speyer,
        421; Washington, D.C., 511

Franciscan, 374, 459
Good Shepherd, 235
Jesuits, 204, 500
Marianist, 462
Protestant Deaconesses (Mother
    Eva's), 193; one died in the
    Holocaust, 484
Ursulines, 65, 493
RELIGIOUS
—Sisters: Adelgundis Jaegerschmidt, OSB,
    422; Amata Neyer, OCD, 465;
    Augustina Glatzel, OSB (Abbess), 160,
    478; Augustina Reinach, OSB, 496;
    Friede, Deaconess, 193; Marianne
    (Countess Praschma), OCD, 508;
    Petra Brüning, OSU, 493; Pia, OCD,
    463; Teresia Herbstrith, OCD, 465;
    Teresia Renata Posselt, OCD, 464
—Priests: Adrian Cooney, OCD, 465;
    Alfred Delp, SJ, 485; Avertanus, OCD,
    Provincial, 463; Ekkehart II
    (Palatinus), OSB, 505; Frederick
    Copleston, SJ, 500; Herman Van
    Breda, OFM, 459; John Sullivan, OCD,
    viii; Karl Rahner, SJ, 423; Raphael
    Walzer, Dom (Archabbot), OSB, 424;
    Rhabanus, Father, CMM, 462;
    Romaeus Leuven, OCD, 465
remedial lessons given by Edith 207.
    See also tutoring
Rennpfad 244
repatriation, quarantine before 463
republican party, German 229
resistance movement in Germany
    Kreisauer Kreis, 485
Revolutions (French and German) 199,
    290, 405, 443, 485, 505; control of
    military during, 228, 229
Rhine River (alt. Rhein) 472, Map
Rhineland 323
Riddle of the Universe, The 482
Riesengebirge 52, 102, 128, 129, 208,
    231, 238, 474, 480, Map
Rigorosum 397, 404, 405
Ritterplatz 65, 116, 160
Roehl, Prof. 143, 157, 168, 178
Roethe, Prof. 263
Rohns. *See* inns
Roman(s) 312, 439, 440, 441; — Papacy,
    495
Rome 84, 430, 442

Romanticism 313
Rosenstrasse 54, 55, 58
Rosenthal, Felix, M.D. 224
Rosh Hashanah 441
Rosinenstriezel 128
Roth, Cecil 469
Rothschild, Count, student 194
royalty 190; patronage by, 506;. *See also* nobility, RULERS
Rübezahl 474
Rubin 170
Ruhleben-Döberitz 303, 497
RULERS
  Alba, Duke of, 480; Albrecht VI, 506; Ernst August, King of Hannover, ignored by Göttingen Seven, 488; Ferdinand II, Emperor, 482; Franz Ferdinand, Crown Prince of Austria-Hungary, and wife assassinated, 497; Frederick II, Grand-Duke of Baden, 416, 506; Friedrich I, King in Prussia, 478, 479; Friedrich the Great (II), 168, 479; Friedrich III, King, 478, 479, English wife, Victoria, 478; Friedrich Wilhelm, Crown Prince, abdicated, 479; Friedrich Wilhelm, the Great Elector, 168, 479; Friedrich Wilhelm I, King, 479; Friedrich Wilhelm II, King, 479; Friedrich Wilhelm III, King, 479; Friedrich Wilhelm IV and the Revolution, 405; 479; George V, King of England, cousin of Wilhelm II, 480; Karl August, Duke of Saxe-Weimar, 477; King of Saxony, the, 271; Leopold I, Emperor, 478; Napoleon I, 496; Napoleon III, and wife, Eugenie, 480; Otto I, Emperor, 505; Victoria, Queen, 478; related by marriage to Friedrich III, 478; Wilhelm I, Emperor, 168; Wilhelm II, Emperor, ruled Germany in Edith's time, 479, 480; William the Conqueror, 442
Rumania 81, 416, 421, 493; cousins from, 180; folk costumes of, 180, 181
Runge, Prof. Carl T., and family 303, 381; Bernhard and Wilhelm, sons, 303; Nerina, daughter. (*see* MATHEMATICIANS, Courant).

Russia(n) 110, 455, 496; border with— within hours of Breslau, 295; invasion possible, 299; professor, 292; soldiers, 297, 333, advancing on Hungary, 499; "we'll take a broomstick to the—", 297
Ruthenian soldier-patients 333

Sabbath 29, 47, 441
Sacraments Baptism, Edith's, 420, 421, godmother for, 489; Confirmation, Edith's, 421; Holy Eucharist, institution of, 69, to patients, 335; Last Anointing (Sacrament of the Sick), to patients, 335
sacrifice 441
Sagan 130, 131, Map
SAINTS and Blessed(s)
—patrons and patterns: in artistic representation:
  Crucifixion scene with sculptures of the Blessed Mother, John, Magdalen, and Nicodemus, 401; St. Francis, portrait, 238, 488; *Legend of*, 488; John, statue, 34; Mary, 401, 424; Queen of Peace, 510, 511;
  in religious families:
  Benedictine: Boniface, 504; Lioba, 402, 422, 504
  Carmelite: (Bl.) Elizabeth of the Trinity (Catez-Rolland), 442, 457; John of the Cross (Juan de Yepes), vii, 7, 426, 457; Teresa of Jesus (de Ahumada), 420, 426, 457, 480, 487, 489, 511; Thérèse of the Child Jesus (Martin-Guerin), 442, 457, 458
  Dominican theologian, Thomas Aquinas, 436, 508
—as patron of churches, schools or shrines: Alban, 240; Anthony, 335; the Holy Cross, 205, 427, 487; James, 241; John, 241; Magdalena, 421, 423; Martin, of church where Edith was baptized, 421; Matthias, 205
—quoted: John (Epistles), 423; Paul (Romans), 460. *See* SCRIPTURE
Salamanca, walls of 243
salary of Husserl's assistant 495
Salzbrunn. *See* Bad

Salzburg Edith's Austrian tour included, 423, Map
sanitarium 56
Sarajevo 416
sawmill and jolly miller's family 41
Saxony Lipps has accent from, 256; Red Cross aides from, 321
Schäfer, Herr, student 385
Schaffgotsch-garten 168; —palace, 65
Scharf, Dr. (M.D.) 348; Frau Dr.—, his cousin, 364
Scharf, Käthe 289, 290, 295, 308; Frau—, her mother, 290; accompanied at university, 291
Schauinsland 406, 505, Map
Scheel boarding house 208
Scheibe 374
Scheitniger Park 192, 210
Schiesswerderstrasse 54
Schifferstadt 431, Map
Schindler, Bianka sufferer from hyperthyroidism, 130
Schlesinger, Bianca (b. Courant, Edith's eldest aunt), 232; estranged over engagement, reconciled upon marriage, 233
—Jenny, her eldest daughter, married widower with three daughters; son and second daughter in Berlin, 232; youngest daughter, Selma, illness and death, 231, 232
Schmiedebrücke 192
Schnee -*berg,* 134; -*koppe,* 169, 170
Schnurgasse 510, 511
scholasticism, Husserl's "new" 250
Scholz, Kaethe 188, 190, 191, 209
Scholz, Prof. 162, 164, 165, 478
SCHOOL(S) 40, 63, 65, 471; Catholic, 180; celebration: best marks pay for, 171, 175, at year's end, 173; children, ten thousand singing, 271; dedication to study in, 63; devotions in girls'—, 65, 143, and demerit for talking during, 144; ethics on copying, 161, and on prompting, 146; jargon, 159; League for—Reform, 192; learn that which earns, 172, 173; morale, 162; novel about, 216; promotion in, 66; —psychologists, 197; records, 66, 162; scolding in, 27; system, 138, 173, 470, 471;

—trips, 179. *See also* **vacations**
Schreiberhau 138
Schröder, Eduard 262, 310
Schulz, Hermann philologist, 276
Schurz, Carl German-born American General, 486
Schwerin 255, 307, 379
Schwester. See **Sister** (Nursing)
Schwind, Monsignor (Ger.: *Prälat*) Joseph 421, 424
science, scholar wed to 450
SCRIPTURE, HOLY Oral Torah, 440; Torah, 440; Word of God, 438; study of, 31, 71, 437–42, passim; without sacred meaning for student, 190; transcribed Bible into Codex *Argenteus,* 483; Bible, 189, bible stories, 106
—books of, alphabetical order: Daniel: (sealed book—Dan 12:4), 63; Exodus 12:3–27, 69; Genesis: Paradise expulsion shocks child (Gen 3:23, 24), 106; Jacob's twelve sons (Gen 35:23,24,25), 36; Isaiah 55:11, 439; Leviticus 6:5,6, 437, 438; 16:21,22, 71; Maccabees, 439; Psalms, in German, 31, 71; New Testament: Gospels, 189, 190, 211; Golgotha, John 19:18, 242; Epistles: 1 John 4:7, and 2 John v.5, 423; Paul, Romans 5:20, 460; Rev. 5:5, 63
—plays with biblical story lines: Herod and Mariamne, Judith, The Maccabees, 481
Sebastian, Bishop Ludwig 421
secularization alternative to exile under Bismarck, 503, 510; mandated in 1803, 496
security of living before 1914 293
Sedanfeier (Sedan Day) 168, 169, 177
Seele des Menschen, Die (The Human Soul) 510
Seidel workman, 57; Frau—, nimble tongued, 58
Seidemann, Frau Dr. (M.D.) 352, 356
self-employed many Jews in Edith's time, 449
Serbia 144, 497
servants 51, 252, 323, 373

sewing Edith learns at age five, 140; convent-made trousseau, 235

sex, attitude to and information about 68, 93, 100, 148, 212

Seyss-Inquart, Arthur 430

schadchan 454

shopping 95

Sieben, Dr. 511

Silesia 27, 36, 57, 89, 128, 190, 228

simplicity and thrift 42

Singen 406, 505, Map

singing 28, 47, 77, 92, 126, 172; — lessons, 53

Sisters (*Schwestern*) the nursing staff at Märisch-Weisskirchen: Alwine, Edith's closest friend, 343; Anna, Ward sister, 323; Anni, platinum blond, 346; Elsa, sculptress from Vienna, 357; Elsbeth, pretty brunette, 328; Emma, passionate, 323; Emmi, quiet, reserved, 357; Helene, ward maid, 349; Klara, capable, lively-humored, 336; Loni, warm-hearted, 323; Lotte (Neumeister), jealous, 336; Marga, eighteen years old, 326; Margareta (von Skoda), 328; Margarete, on surgical ward, 350; Matron Margarete, the "Super", 322; Marie Luise, difficult, a St. John's girl, 351; Sophie, Ward sister (B.O.), 326; Steffi, fragile, melancholy, 324; Susi, "High School" ward sister, 342. *See also* **Grete Bauer; Susanne Mugdan; Polishwomen in army; Note 158, 499**

— description of social evening shown on photo 8, 336;

— Edith horrified at notion of celebration, 327, later has identical reaction, 349

Sisters (Religious). *See* **RELIGIOUS**

Skoda, Cavalier Emil von, Austria 328, 499

Skupin, medical student 127

sleep Frau Stein prizes, 59; Lipps experiments with, 279

Slovak(ia). *See* **nationalities of patients**

social conscience, 190; democracy, a topic to distract teacher, 168; — life, 214; — responsibilities, 191; snubbed architect becomes a — democrat, 271

socialistic concepts never influenced Edith 191

SOCIETIES to which Edith belonged: Academic Branch of the Humboldt Society for Adult Education (abbr. Humboldt Society), 202-9; Leagues for School Reform, 192; Pedagogical Group (Breslau), 192-200, passim; Philosophical Society (Göttingen), 248-58, passim; Prussian Society for Women's Right to Vote, 191; Society for Women's Education and Women's Studies, 309; Women's Student Union, 200-14, passim

sociological homes 193

Sociologist: Simmel, George 492

Socrates. *See* **PHILOSOPHERS**

soldier(s) 318-67, passim; declared "missing", 196; encounter in cemetery, 310; knitting for, 308; seventeen-year-old — die in Flanders, 252, 303

"Solitude", the 505

Sommerfest, **summer fun** 129, 209

Sonke, Frl. 392

South Africa and South America Steiner schools in, 504

spa. *See* **Bad**

Spain 482, 487; Armada, 480

spelling, adult education Edith taught, 202

Speyer 421, 423, 424, 434, Map

Spiegelberg, Prof. Herbert 507

Spohr, Elisabeth 178

sports tennis, 117; tobogganning, 438

Stadttheater 76

stage director 39

Stählin, Frl. 385

Staiger, Putti (b. Elisabeth Klein) 300, 380, 381, 500, 501

— Robert, her husband, 300, 501

state, the 190; Edith's gratitude to, 191

State Board examinations 16, 172, 194, 198, 213, 217, 269; Edith's, 268, 269, 270, 275, 290, 299, 310, 386

steamship 149, 168; Empress of India/ Ireland, 293, 496

STEIN FAMILY portrait, photo 2

Stein, Siegfried, (1843-93), Edith's father: met Auguste when he was fifteen, 38; married in 1871, 38; early death, 41; Edith's last embrace, 73
— his mother, Johanna (b. Cohn), 38; legacy to her grandchildren, 208
— his brother Alexander (died c. 1903), 82; A's twin daughters move in at Stein home, 83
— his brother Leo Walter, playwright, 38, 39, 473
Stein, Auguste (1849-1936, b. Courant, known as Gustel) Edith's mother, 14, 17, 18, 29–238, passim; 368-96, passim; delayed honeymoon, 133; difficulty supporting family, 41; encouraged Edith to make own choices, 152, 173, 187; on God's help, 60, 108; on sleep, 59; photo: at age 46, 2; at 63, 4; at 76, 11
STEIN CHILDREN in birth order:
—**Paul** (1872-1943), born in Gleiwitz, 39; 40-114, passim; effect of childhood illness, 39; twenty-one when father died, 43; marriage, 45 and silver anniversary, 114; victim of German Holocaust at Theresienstadt, 1943, 430
— Gertrude (1872-1943, b. Werther, Paul's wife, Trude), 46; their two sons: Gerhard (1902), 86– 109, passim, [G's daughter, Waltraut, 500]; Harald (1905-7), 86, 150
—**Selma** (1873-74), born and died in Gleiwitz, 39
—**Else** (1876-1956, m. Gordon), born in Gleiwitz, 40; engaged to a Catholic, 61; professional training, 64; engaged to Max Gordon, 89; photo 4. *See* **GORDON** for continuation
—**Hedwig** (c.1877-80), born and died in Gleiwitz, 39
—**Arno** (1879-1948 in U.S.), born in Gleiwitz, 40; 45-111, passim; 147; taught Edith to dance, 76; sold business to emigrate to U.S., 427
— Martha (1879-1947 in U.S., b. Kaminsky), his wife, 47-111, passim

— their four children: Wolfgang (b. 1912), his mother expected twins, 103; Eva (1915-43 in concentration camp), birth, 103; Helmut (b. 1916), blond, blue-eyed, 103, engaged to twenty-nine year old Edith when he was four years old, 105, his critical illness, 106, emigrated to U.S., 427; Lotte (b. 1917, full name Charlotte), birth, 103, emigrated to U.S., 427
—**Ernst** (1880-82), born in Gleiwitz, died in Lublinitz, 39
—**Frieda** (1881-1942, full name Elfriede), born in Lublinitz, 40; her mother's faithful helper, 47; 49-238, passim; married by "arrangement", 49; photo 4. *See* **TWOROGER** for continuation
—**Rosa Adelheid** (1883-1942), born in Lublinitz, 40; 18, 33, 37, 39; 49-238, passim; 424, 427; now a Catholic, intends to join Edith in Holland, 429; arrest and death with Edith, 430, 431; photo 4
—**Richard** (c. 1884), born and died in Lublinitz, 39
—**Erna** (1890-1978 in U.S.), born in Lublinitz, 40; 14-18; 33, 41-238, passim; description by Edith, 63; studied medicine, 64; married, 238. *See* **BIBERSTEIN** for continuation
—**EDITH** (1891-1942), born in Breslau, 73; died in Auschwitz, 433
— About herself, she records: personal physical data: appearance, 62, 76, 78; dress, 63, 201, 413; illness: childhood, 73, 75, later, sprained foot, 134, poor health due to stress, 237; physical development, 139, 150; results of severe personal crisis: appetite is lost, 214, health declines sharply, pain is severe, 237, sleep becomes a lost art, 277; unusual experience of near-death from asphyxiation, 216
— Development, or significant transformations she mentions: wilful child, 54, 74, 140; at age of seven, stops petulant, stubborn behavior, decid-

STEIN—EDITH (*continued*)
ing mother and sister know best, 75;
at age fourteen, deliberately cuts
free, becomes independent, 138,
having "lost" her faith, 138, and
deliberately and consciously gives up
praying, 148
— Emotional and social development:
reticent in inviting friendship, 164;
understands more than age might
warrant, 76; rejects double-standard,
68; forms clear views on sexuality,
212; relational experiences and intimate confidences, 93, 96, 100;
hears and reads more than is good
for her, 148; dreams of great love
and ideal marriage although appearing cool and unapproachable, 227;
aware of being courted, 209, 210;
resents being chaperoned, 179; in
combat for peace with self at great
psychic and physical cost, 237;
achieves new, deep tolerance of
others, 234; adopts as guiding principle, giving in whenever not morally
bound to do otherwise, 236
— Fidelity to herself meant Edith could
and would:
be advocate for her mother and
sisters in family crisis, 110; be en-
chatingly malicious, 196; be Jewish
comfortably, 343; be shamed by her
mother's working clothes and work-
worn hands, 215; delight in "putting
one over on people" for sister's
benefit, 224; direct play she wrote,
67; effectively check unwanted attention, 353; enjoy exceptional rapport
with children, 104–7; like friends
very much, yet give no indication of
it, 67; love theater and opera
passionately, 171; play piano reluctantly, 77; point out friend's
weakness ruthlessly without offending
her, 126; read books avidly and
newspapers thoroughly, 75, 78, 167,
310; refuse alcohol always, 74, but
be accustomed to smoking, 241, 336;
waltz-to-the-left, 182, and whistle for
joy, 155; write with pleasure and
readiness, 78, 79, 170

— Interior attitudes in her own evaluation: accepted reproach from a
friend, 196; was angered by flattery,
142; appreciated solitude, 132; was
deeply disturbed at sight of drunk or
mention of murder, 74; disliked
domestic chores, 68; disliked fuss
made over her, 79, 142, 153; was
grateful to the state for her education, 191; liked and appreciated solitude, 132; loved to make discoveries,
240; rejected flattery about "being a
Hit", 201; was unaccustomed to being criticized, 195; was brought to
verge of despair over studies, 278;
won awards but never took it for
granted, 66
— Manner of displaying attributes:
ambition, 141; anger and imperti-
nence, 75; audacity in Philosophical
Society, 252; care in discerning, 152
fatalism about exams, 412; fidelity
to friends, 308; indefatigability in
study, 155; imperviousness to blame,
77; independence, 65, 138; intracta-
bility and stubbornness, 73, 75; naive
conviction of own perfection, 195;
obedience to mother and older sister,
75; punctuality, 154; severe criticism
of others, 195; surprise at her excellence in school, 66; timidity in
Reinach's group, 275; unreal
estimate of world at times, 150;
unrestrained zeal as a student, 78
Stein, Gertrud (no relation), Red Cross
director, 321
Steinberg, Judge and Frau 309
Steinberg, Wilhelm, blind student
374
Steiner, Rudolf. *See* **EDUCATORS**
Steinsgraben 247
Stenzel, Dr. Julius philologist, 320,
365; not Jewish, but penalized by
Nazis, 500; Bertha, his wife (b.
Mugdan), 320, 365; Anna, daughter,
emigrated with assistance of R.
Courant, 500; Jochen, infant son,
365
Stern, the landmark, 245
Stern, Lotte 391
Stern, William. *See* **PSYCHOLOGISTS**

stock market 96

Stockums, Bishop Wilhelm Auxiliary of Cologne diocese, 428

Strassburg 253

Strietzel, Willy 128

strikes 230

STUDENT(S) 24, 63, 78; activities, 213; apathetic, 191; excursion, 169; jargon, 159; —life portrayed in disturbing novel, 216; marks, 170; reports, 161; songs, 130, 170; struggle to learn, 47; wartime—life, 416. *See also* school

Stuttgart 284, 505

Sudeten Mts. 474, 475

suffering caused and endured, 443; redemptive, 459; vicarious, 460

suicide 81, 82, 500

Sukkoth 441

Sumpf, Prof. 165, 176; mortified Edith, 166

Swabia 280, 380, 505

Sweden 482, 483, 494

Switzerland 385, 424, 430, 465, 467, 493, 494, 501, 505, 512

sympathy 208

synagogue(s) 29, 34, 71

systematic philosophers 269

Tabernacles, Feast of 441

tachistoscope Edith in experiment with, 265

Talmud 31; —ic sophistry, 213

Tarnow 500

Tarnowski, Dr. lawyer, 206

tax on good grades in school 171

teach(ing) 50, 53, 78, 79; sole opportunity for higher education for women, 44; popular teacher, 45; unfair, 54

techniques in teaching 161, 165, 170, 171, 266, 274

temper tantrums 45, 54, 73, 75

Temple, the 439; of the Spirit, 442

tenant extorts rent from landlady, 36; proves tenacious, 235; relating to her, 74

Terhart, patient kept up contact by correspondence long after discharge, 358

territorial strife 486

testament Edith's last will and—destroyed, 464

Texas, U.S. 503

Thalheim, Councillor 320, 328, 365, 366

theater 171; indifferent to operettas, light comedies, 180

THEOLOGIANS Meister Eckhart, 505; Protestant, 276; Pseudo-Dionysius, 429; Thomas Aquinas, St., 436, 508; —symbolic—, 429

Theresienstadt concentration camp 430

Thiers, Louis Adolphe 472

Thirty Years' War. *See* WAR(S)

Thomist, The 511

thrift 53; becomes habitual, 42

Thuringia(n Forest) 141, 244, 245, Map

Tiefurt 245, 246, Map

Tiele-Winckler, Countess (Mother) Eva 193. *See* RELIGIOUS Congregations

time-consciousness 506

Tish'a B'Ab 441, 442

town life 34, 35

transcendental idealism 250

Treaties: of Bucharest, 485; February 9, 1801, 496; of St. Germaine, 482

Trieste, Italy (at one time in Austria), 324, 340

troops transports, 35, 295; war-dead brought back by, 229

Turkey 201, 486; soldier from, 333

tutoring 206, 209, 220

TWINS Horowitz, Franz and Hans, Edith's cousins. *See* Horowitz; Mugdan, Albrecht and Suse, friends. *See* Mugdan; Stein, daughters of Alexander (Edith's cousins). *See* STEIN

—Edith and Erna treated as, 62

—expectant mother convinced she will have, 103

—from broken home, 193

TWOROGER, Elfriede (1881-1942, b. Stein, known as Frieda), (*see* Stein family for position in family); married, divorced, 49; sent to labor group by Nazi, later to Theresien-

TWOROGER, Elfriede (continued)
stadt concentration camp; death
there in 1942, 430
—Erika, daughter, 49, 103; both are
on photo 4
Tworoger, Hanna 163, 165 (no
relation)
Tyrol 359

Ukraine 482
United States of America. *See* **America**
UNIVERSITIES and Colleges
associated with Edith, her class-
mates, or their mentors:
—American: 204; Clark, 495; Fordham,
491; Harvard, 493; NYU at Buffalo,
493; NYU in New York, Courant
Institute of Mathematical Sciences,
470, 488; Northwestern, 492; Stanford, 489; Washington U. at St.
Louis, 507; Wisconsin, 486; and
colleges: Chicago College of Jewish
Studies, 492; Vassar, 489
—Czechoslovakian: German and Czech
Univ., Prague, 332; Husserl at, 490
—German: Albert-Ludwig (*see* Freiburg), 416; Berlin, 205; Bonn, 483;
Breslau (Silesian Friedrich-Wilhelm),
129, 185-222, passim, Breslau popu-
lace most represented in science in
German kingdom, 486, centenary
celebration, 204, 205, 206, Gynecology Department, 224, of Univ. Hospital, 204, 231, professor of Catholic
Theology, 508; Cologne (Köln), 494,
508; Frankfurt-am-Main, 418; Frankfurt-an-der-Oder, 204, 486; Freiburg-
im-Breisgau, 217, 418, 490, 501, 506,
508; Göttingen, 239-317, passim,
purging at, 85, is a university town,
242; 489, 494, 507; Halle, 489;
Heidelberg, 217; Kiel, 418, 500, 507;
Leopoldiner, 204; Munich, 489, 491;
and colleges: Jesuit, of Breslau, 204;
Marianum, 424; St. Magdalena's, 421
university: alumni, 206, choice of
courses, 187, 188; concessions and
benefits to students, 191; president,
206; student indifference in politics
and current events, 191; study, 43,
132; Usages or practices. *See*
CUSTOMS

Upper Galilee 440
Upper Silesia 27, 32, 34, 35, 39, 60,
67, 129, 144, 157, 158, 193, 235
vacations 42, 64, 92, 97, 128, 239;
Christmas, 128; at sea with Paul,
149; Black Forest, 406; summer
hikes, 244, 245, 246, 474; photo 5,
129, 130; teacher's—excels that of
students, 399; train through Höllental to Lake Constance, 505, Map
Verdun 307, 416
Vespasian(us), Titus Flavius Sabinus
439, 440
Victoria School (Viktoriaschule) 14,
48, 78, 159, 180, 188
Vienna 249; "Circle", neo-positivist,
494; Cultural Society, 490;
sculptress from, 341
"Villa", the Stein home in Lublinitz,
39
Virchow Hospital (Rudolf Virchow
of Berlin). *See* **Hospitals**
vocation career above any, 123; received
at Baptism, 457; to share suffering,
435
Volkschule 196
vom Stein, Baron. *See* **nobility**
von Kleist, Heinrich 498
von Stein, Frau (Charlotte) 175
vows of religious vii, 509, 510

Walter, Frl. 390
Walzer, Archabbot Raphael, OSB. *See*
RELIGIOUS, Priests
Wandervögel 194, 390, 484
WARS covered in Edith's study of
history, or in her life:
500-479 B.C., Persian, 312;
Hannibal in, 314;
264-241/218-201 B.C., Punic,-s, 312
6th Century, Goths, involved in
"Struggle for Rome", 281, 496
1618-48, Thirty Years' War, 176,
478, 482
1803-after Treaty of Feb. 9, 1801,
secularization and divestiture,
276, 496
1813, Under vom Stein, East Prussian rebellion, 265, 495
1840, French/German controversy
on border of the Rhine, 47, 472

WAR (*continued*)
  1848, Revolutions: France in
    February and Austria and Ger-
    many in March, 405, 505
  1870, Germany vs France, latter's
    capitulation at Sedan, 168, 480
  1911, Turkey vs Italy, involving
    Dodecanese Islands, 201, 486
  1913, Treaty of Bucharest, Prince
    of Wied ruled in Albania, 194,
    485
  1914, assassination June 28 causes
    World War I, 293-414, passim;
    497; flash-backs, 28, 84, 145,
    165, 193, 194; end of, 228
  1918-Oct. 29, Revolution begun
    by mutiny of sailors at Kiel, 485
  1918-November, Armistice signed,
    479, 485
  1919, Treaty of St. Germain,
    Galicia to Poland, 482
  1933, NSDAP under Hitler takes
    control of Germany, 425
  1942, World War II, 491; Edith's
    death during, 433;
- black plague destroys 35% of popula-
  tion, 482; finances during, 209;
  missing-in-action, 196; refugees
  after, 235; war loans, 209
Warsaw, Poland 193
Wartburg 244, Map
Warteberg, the 193, 195, 484
Wartenburg 194, 484. *See* Yorck
Washington, D.C., U.S.A. viii, 511
Waspik, Holland 4
weaknesses ridiculed 195
Webster's dictionary 483
Weckelsdorf 132, Map
Weender (gate, *-strasse*) 241
Weigelt, Liane 306, 307, 316, 378,
  384, 385
Weimar 151, 245, 246, 477, Map
Weiss, student 121
Weissenfels, Richard 262
Weisskirchen. *See* Mährisch
welfare: of country, 447; —institutions,
  193; living on, 53
Wengeroff, Pauline 24, 469
Weser(land) 224, 244, Map
Westerbork, Holland 431, 433, Map
Westphalia 358

Westram, Burgomaster 132, 137, 364,
  500
wheelwrights 43
"Wichs" 204
Wickersdorf 245, 246, 272, Map
Wied, Prince of 194, 485
Wiehrer station 406
Wieners, Johannes 434
Wilhelm, Emperor. *See* RULERS
will, last Edith's, 464
"Wine, Women, and Song" 38
Winkler, Lotte 291
Witkop, Prof. 404, 405, 413
Wohlgemut, Villa 402
Wojtila, Karol. *See* Pope
Wolf, Artur Wilhelm 202
Wölfelsgrund 133, Map
WOMAN
—career opportunities taken by: chem-
  ist, 165; doctor, 225, 226; lecturer,
  32; mathematician, 124; music
  teacher, 124; phys. ed. teacher,
  169; psychologist, 264; —rows ferry
  boat to island, 407
—'s rights, 123, 191; —suffrage, 191;
  some—make unwise choices regard-
  ing education, 188. *See also* The
  FEMININE
woodcarvers 43
work 29, eight-hour day, 58; —records,
  57
Works of Edith Stein (*Edith Steins
  Werken*) 459, 460, 461
World as Will and Idea, The 150
Wroclaw. *See* Breslau
Württemberg 501
Würzburg method in psychology 486

**Yearbook for Philosophy and Phe-
  nomenological Research**
  (*Jahrbuch*) 250, 507; supplied for
  by Journal for Philosophy and
  Phenomenological Research, in the
  U.S., 491, 493, 511
Yom Kippur. *See* Day of Atonement
Yorck von Wartenburg, Count 194,
  195; Count Peter, 485
Young Germany, literary group 494

Zarathustra 131
Zeitschrift für Psychologie 485

Ziekursch, Prof. 190
zoology 223, 482
Zucker, Frl., teacher 390
Zum Problem der Einfühlung Edith's
    dissertation, 417
Zürich (alt. Zurich), Switzerland
    152, 467

List of Places

The **bold** print used for eleven places indicates that Edith lived there for a time. The SMALL CAPITALS mark five stations on her way of the Cross from Echt to Auschwitz.

Adersbach-Weckelsdorf G-9
Altvater(gebirge) H-10
AMERSFOORT A-1
AMSTERDAM A-1
Auschwitz E-13

Bad Altheide H-9
Baden I-5
Bad Reinerz E-10
Bad Salzbrunn D-10
Basel J-2
Beczwa G-12
Bergzabern G-3
Berlin A-8
Beuron I-3
Beuthen E-13
Bonn D-2
Breslau C-11
Brünn G-11

Chemnitz (Karl-Marx-Stadt) . . . D-7
Coesfeld B-2
Cuxhaven A-4

Danube (Donau) River I-9
Donaueschingen H-6
Dorsten B-2
Dresden D-8

Echt C-1
Eichenberg C-5
Eisenach D-5
Essen C-2

Feldberg J-2
Frankfurt-am-Main E-3
Frankfurt-an-der-Oder A-8
Freiburg-im-Breisgau I-2

Glatz E-11
Gl(atzer) Schneeberg H-10
Gleiwitz E-13
Goslar B-5
Göttingen C-4
Gräfenberg H-9
Gross-Aupa G-8
Gr(osse) Wartenburg C-12
Gr(osse) Inselsberg F-5
Grunwald H-9
Günerstal H-5

Halle C-6
Hamburg A-5
Hanna (Moravian) H-11
Hannover A-4
Harz Mountains B-5
Heidelberg G-3
Helfenstein G-12
Helgoland A-3
Hildesheim B-4
Hinterzarten H-5
Hohe Mense H-9
Hohe Sonne F-5
Höllental H-5
Hundsfeld C-11

Ilmenau D-5

Jena D-6
Johannesbad G-8
Juvisy G-1

Karlsbrunn E-11
Kassel C-4
Kattowitz (Katowice) E-13
Kickelhahn F-5
Köln (Cologne) D-2
Kreuzberg D-12

Lake Constance J-4
Laurahütte E-13
Leipzig C-7
Lublinitz D-13
Ludwigshafen G-3

MAASTRICHT D-1
Märisch-Weisskirchen F-12
Manebach F-5
Miećhowitz E-13
Mittelwalde E-11
Mödling I-11
Münden C-4
Munich I-6
Münster B-2

Obernigk C-11
Oberschreiberhau F-8
Oder River A-9
Olmütz (Olomouc) F-11
Oppeln D-12

Paris G-1
Peiskretcham E-13
Pirna D-8
Posen (Poznan) A-11
Prague F-9
Prossnitz G-11

Radolfzell H-6
Ramsau H-10
Ratibor E-12
Reichenau I-6
Rhine River E-2
Riesengebirge D-10

Sagan C-9
Salzburg J-7
Schauinsland H-5
SCHIFFERSTADT G-3
Schneekoppe G-8
Schreiberhau G-8
Singen H-6
Speyer G-3

Thüringer Wald F-5
Tiefurt E-6

Vienna I-11

Wartburg D-5
Weckelsdorf G-9
Weimar D-6
Weserland B-4
WESTERBORK A-2
Wickersdorf G-6
Wölfelsgrund H-9

Zürich J-3

Map and list courtesy of © Edith Stein Center, Elysburg, Pa. 17824

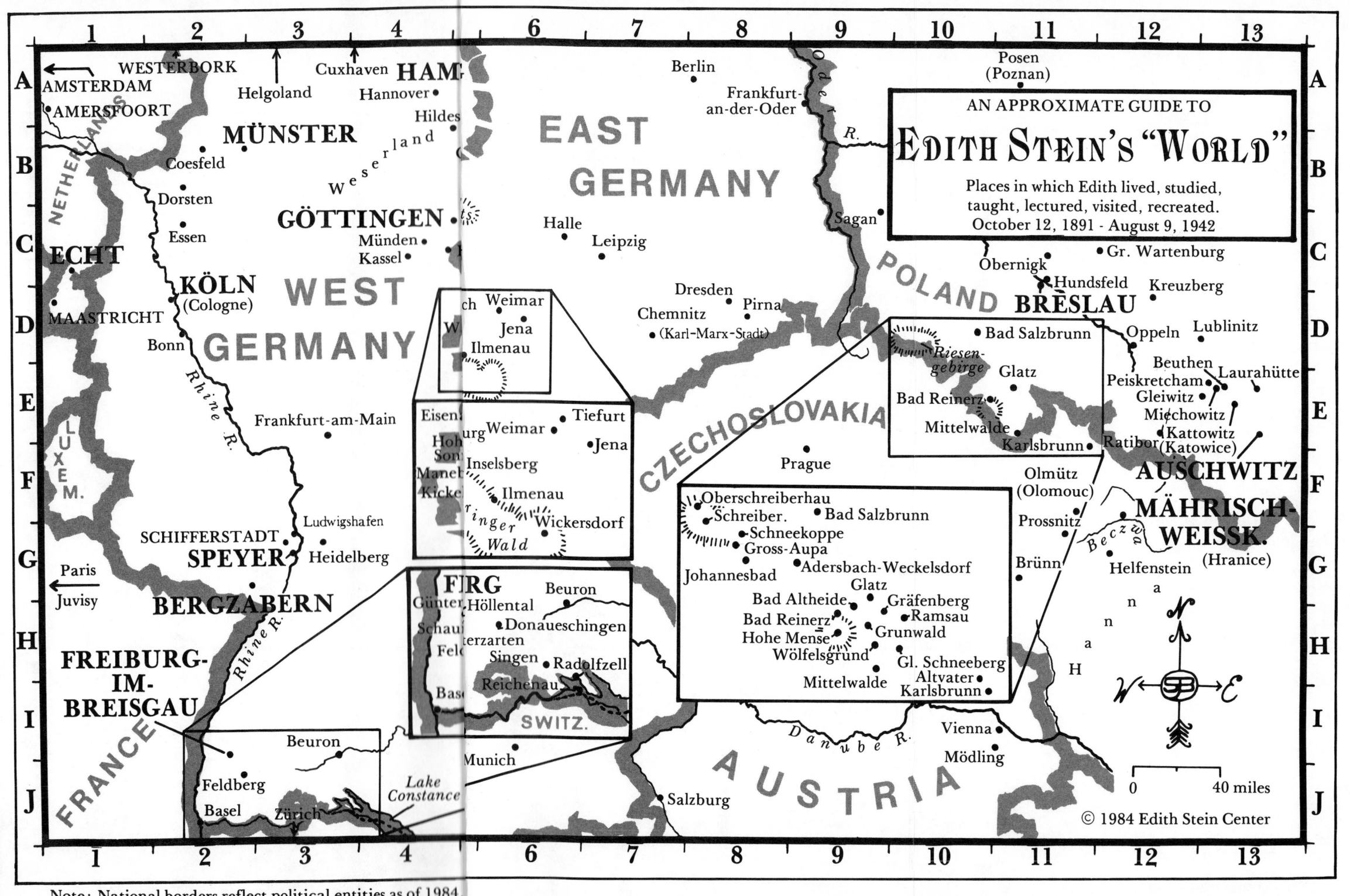

An Approximate Guide to

EDITH STEIN'S "WORLD"

Places in which Edith lived, studied,
taught, lectured, visited, recreated.
October 12, 1891 - August 9, 1942

© 1984 Edith Stein Center

Note: National borders reflect political entities as of 1984.